The History of Polish Literature

The History of Polish Literature

CZESŁAW MIŁOSZ

SECOND EDITION

UNIVERSITY OF CALIFORNIA PRESS
Berkeley   Los Angeles   London

University of California Press
Berkeley and Los Angeles, California
University of California Press, Ltd.
London, England

Copyright © 1969, 1983 by Czesław Miłosz
First Printing
The Macmillan Company
Collier-Macmillan Canada Ltd., Toronto, Ontario
Printed in the United States of America

4   5   6   7   8   9

First California edition published 1983

Library of Congress Cataloging in Publication Data
Miłosz, Czesław.
    The history of Polish literature.
    Bibliography: p.
    Includes index.
    1. Polish literature—History and criticism.
I. Title.
PG7012.M48   1983   891.8′5′09   82–20227
ISBN 0–520–04477–0

Acknowledgments

Opinions of Claude Backvis on Polish drama are quoted after his essay: "Teatr Wyspiańskiego jako urzeczywistnienie polskiej koncepcji dramatu," Warsaw, "Pamiętnik Teatralny," VI, 1957, 3–4.

Fragments of a secret memorandum written by Prince Metternich for Czar Alexander I are taken from: Charles and Barbara Jelavich, *Habsburg Monarchy: Toward a Multinational Empire or National States?* New York, Rinehart and Co., 1959.

Acknowledgments are made to the Noonday Press for Adam Mickiewicz's "The Romantic," from: *Adam Mickiewicz: Selected Poems*, Clark Mills, ed., translated by W. H. Auden, New York, 1956. To *Botteghe Oscure* for Cyprian Norwid's poems, translated by Christine Brooke-Rose, and Norwid's letters, translated by Jerzy Pietrkiewicz, both published in the issue of 1958. To Doubleday, Inc., for the following poems which appeared in *Postwar Polish Poetry, an Anthology*, Czesław Miłosz, ed. and trans., New York, 1965: "The Bridge," by Leopold Staff; "Hamletism" (translated jointly with P. D. Scott), "To the Germans," by Antoni Słonimski; "A Word to Orphists," by Kazimierz Wierzyński; "Sketch for a Memoir," by Adam Ważyk; "A Poor Christian Looks at the Ghetto," by Czesław Miłosz; "In the Middle of Life," "The Deposition of the Burden," by Tadeusz Różewicz; "Apollo and Marsyas," "The Stone," "Elegy of Fortinbras," by Zbigniew Herbert; "Before Breughel the Elder," by Aleksander Wat; "The Pencil's Dream," by Tymoteusz Karpowicz; "A Green Lowland of Pianos," by Jerzy Harasymowicz; "Clean Men," "The Breasts of the Queen Are Turned Out of Wood," by Stanisław Grochowiak; "I Am Too Near," by Wisława Szymborska; "Revolt in Verse," by Bogdan Czaykowski. To the University of California Press for Jan Kochanowski's *Poems*, translated by Dorothea Prall Radin, Berkeley, 1928. To St. Martin's Press for Stanisław Jerzy Lec's *Unkempt Thoughts*, translated by Jacek Galazka, introduction by Clifton Fadiman, illustrated by Barbara Carr, New York, 1962. To Little, Brown and Co. for *Unkempt Thoughts* from *The Modern Poish Mind*, an anthology edited by Maria Kuncewicz, 1962.

Contents

Preface
TO THE SECOND EDITION

This edition reproduces the original hardcover edition published by The Macmillan Company and Collier-Macmillan Ltd., London, in 1969. The book was completed a couple of years earlier, so the material it covered did not extend beyond the middle 1960s. In order to give the reader some idea of later developments in contemporary Polish literature, a brief epilogue has been added to this edition. The bibliography has also been considerably updated.

C.M.
Berkeley, 1982

Introduction

My intention while writing, or rather dictating, this book was purely utilitarian. I wanted no more than to provide university students with as much information as possible within a limited number of pages and, at the same time, to avoid the scholarly dryness which, more often than not, comes from the author's lack of emotional involvement with his subject. At no moment during my work did I feel boredom; indeed, I was playing more than toiling, and several passages preserve, I hope, a trace of my smile. Since every reader is able to sense the mood in which given sentences were conceived, my hope is that I will not bore either students or the general public.

Since Polish literature has always been oriented more toward poetry and the theater than toward fiction, it has remained little known in English-speaking countries and has been often victimized by clichés. Romanticism, both as a literary trend and as a political attitude, has been considered the very core of Polish letters, and Roman Catholicism an inseparable ingredient. But, in fact, these commonplaces are of relatively recent origin, and the story of their elaboration is one of the themes of my book. Let us keep in mind that of all the modern Slavic languages, Czech and Polish were the first to reach maturity as instruments of literary expression. In the kingdom of Bohemia, this happened during the Middle Ages; in the kingdom of Poland it occurred during the Renaissance. Consequently, the "Golden Age" of the six-teenth-seventeenth centuries has given a durable shape to Polish litera-ture, and nearly half of my work is dedicated to literary phenomena previous to the emergence of Romanticism on the European scene. As for Roman Catholicism, the truth is that the vernacular, stifled for a long time by Latin, the language of the Church, won its ascendancy in Poland primarily thanks to religious controversies engendered first by the ideas of Jan Hus, then by Luther's and Calvin's. Poland of the "Golden Age" was largely a Protestant country, a "paradise for heretics." And despite the subsequent victories of the Counter Reformation, the heritage of intellectual rebelliousness has never been lost; it was transmitted through the publicists of the Enlightenment and the democrats of the nineteenth century to the liberal intelligentsia of our time. A curious dichotomy may be observed as a more or less permanent trait of Polish letters; namely, an emotional moralism obviously nourished by a strong residue of Christian ethics has coexisted with anticlericalism and an utter skepticism as to any dogmas (religious or political).

As I said, my ambition did not reach further than putting together a decent textbook to fill the obvious gap, for the only other possible source of information, *A Survey of Polish Literature and Culture* by the late Manfred Kridl (once my professor in Poland; later on, a professor at Columbia University), is out of print; besides, it does not cover the decades that separate us from 1939 and that are, in many respects, of capital importance, if only because they answer the question as to what influence historical cataclysms of extraordinary violence may have upon writers.

Although an author of a textbook should be as objective as possible, this does not mean he has to become an impersonal machine computing data. He brings into his enterprise his own personal frame of reference, visible in the very selection of his material and in the stress he puts upon certain personalities and trends. Let me say, therefore, a few words about my personal slant.

Brought up in Poland, I am imbued, for better or for worse, with the historicism typical of many European intellectuals. For the reader who is expecting an eager search for purely aesthetic values, this will not be a good credential. Literature, to me, appears as a series of moments in the life of the species, coagulated into language and, thus, made accessible for reflection by posterity. While severe discrimination is a necessary quality for anyone who wants to explore the jungle of time, the human voice we hear in that jungle deserves respect even if it is awkward and faltering. Because I feel this way, I have given much space to those developments which are not directly responsible for any masterpieces but which are very characteristic of a given period. I have not scorned the crazy, the funny, or the bizarre. Moreover, since literature in Poland has always strongly reacted to historical situations and one cannot always assume the reader's knowledge of facts, I have introduced every chapter with a brief sketch of the international and domestic political scene. The tendency in these prefatory remarks is toward a history of institutions and ideas.

To me, the history of Poland and of its literature seems extravagant and full of incongruities: a Slavic nation whose writers, up to the Renaissance, used only Latin; a huge state which, for centuries, stood up to the Teutons, Turkey, and Muscovy but owing to the abuse of its parliamentary system literally fell apart while its once weaker neighbors partitioned it and erased it from the map of Europe for some one hundred and twenty years; an astonishingly vital people who sink easily into moronic apathy and who show their virtues only in circumstances which would crush and destroy any other human group; a refinement of taste, which produced lyrical poetry comparable to that of Elizabethan England, combined with irony and brilliance but always threatened by drunken torpor and parochial mumblings; habits of religious and political tolerance, acquired in the multidenominational and multinational *Respublica* headed by an elected king, which gave way, as a result of collective misfortunes, to a wounded, morbid nationalism; a country whose loyalties in this second half of the century are courted by two equally matched powers, the Communist Party and the Roman Catholic Church. This chaos of elements seemingly so disparate, yet interrelated by a logic of their own, may contain some lessons of universal portent.

Due to the fusion of two political organisms—the kingdom of Poland and the Grand Duchy of Lithuania—the area with which I have had to deal was, for several centuries, much vaster than Poland proper. It also included Lithuania, Byelorussia, and the Ukraine. I tried, therefore, as far as possible, not to bypass the role of languages other than Polish, especially of that Eastern Slavic (neither Polish nor Russian) dialect which was called "Ruthenian" before it evolved into Byelorussian in the north and into Ukrainian in the south. I also felt it necessary to dispel misunderstandings about the word "Lithuania": once it was used to denote both the small Baltic peninsula inhabited by people speaking a non-Slavic language and a much larger territory, watered by the Dnieper river system, whose inhabitants, for a long time, were called "Lithuanians" just because they had fallen under the rule of the Lithuanian dukes. I am aware, however, that the linguistic imbroglios in this area are beyond the scope of any brief exposition.

For the sake of ordering the material, textbooks usually employ a system of periodic divisions. A certain amount of arbitrariness must be reckoned with, as the flux of history rarely lends itself to imprisonment in neat compartments. Scholars like fine-sounding words such as the "Renaissance" or the "Baroque," but one should be aware of how relative and imprecise a meaning is communicated through these words. Any phase in the life of a given civilization witnesses coexisting and crisscrossing currents; the new and the old contaminate each other, and it is far from certain whether everything new in thought or sensibility always plays a leading role just because it is "in advance." Furthermore, the vagueness of such terms that we take for granted discourages me from taking up the hopeless task of capturing their "essence" through a definition. As Paul Valéry justly said: "It is impossible to think—seriously—with words like Classicism, Romanticism, Humanism, Realism. . . . One does not get drunk nor does one quench one's thirst with bottle labels." For an author of a textbook, labels are indispensable; he does not, however, have to employ them necessarily in dead earnest. I confess that, contrary to those who see in literature a protracted interplay of, say, the "classical spirit" and the "Romantic spirit," I do not go beyond treating notions and literary devices prevalent in a given period as something that in its specific variety occurs but once, at a definite point of time.

All the problems confronting me became more acute as I started work on the last part of the book, dealing with contemporary literature up to 1966. A reader, presented with a picture of religious strife in the sixteenth century, takes it with a considerable dose of detachment. It becomes less easy when we move toward the present day and have to use emotionally loaded words such as Marxism, revolution, Communism. A history of literature is not a proper vehicle for conveying one's perhaps too-complex views on issues which provoke so much heat. My effort, therefore, was aimed at remaining as factual and unbiased as possible, although such reticence may well irk those who would prefer an arrangement of facts more favorable to their respective causes. Another difficulty I had to cope with in approaching our day was my double perspective: as a creative writer who has been engaged in Polish literary life for several years and as a self-appointed chronicler. One has an uneasy feeling, wearing a judge's wig, when it is necessary to pass sentence on the merits or failures of one's colleagues, the more so since the names omitted outnumber those I could include; otherwise the chapters on contemporary literature would resemble a gossip column on the Writers' Union. I have assumed the risk of being attacked for my choice, and the only consolation I can offer the maltreated is both the lack of space and the unavoidable errors of judgment. I expose myself to possible sarcastic remarks by saying a word about Czesław Miłosz as one of the Polish contemporary poets. But I would have been a pharisee had I pretended to be much more severe toward that person than are Polish literary critics.

Any discussion of literature not accompanied by a sampling of styles is of a doubtful use. The scarcity of valid versions in English compelled me to look for improvised remedies. I started from the premise that a literal translation of a poem is more relevant than an inadequate artistic transposition. Wherever poets have used syllabic or "syllabotonic" verse with rhymes, I relinquished in advance any pretense at rendering the sound of their lines in English. In some cases the original is followed line by line; in others (where the poet's ideas are of main concern), the translation is transcribed as prose. Occasionally, I have had recourse to translations other than my own. A respect for certain high achievements in poetry, which would look pale when stripped of their sound and their sensuous connotations, inclined me to refrain from quoting them in English. Contemporary Polish verse, however, being more translatable than the poetry of the preceding centuries, owing to the widespread abandonment of meter and rhyme, is represented by several poems that, I hope, can stand in English on their own.

I wish to express my deep gratitude to the following persons: Professor Francis J. Whitfield, who suggested that I choose the form of "old-fashioned" textbooks as a most practical model and who was the first reader of the manuscript; Miss Catherine S. Leach, my student and assistant, who gave proof of rare patience, discernment, and capacity for hard work when writing the whole text under my dictation and whose contribution in giving it a definite shape cannot be overrated; Professor Arthur Mandel, who supplied me with data for the chapter on religious movements among the Polish Jews in the eighteenth century; the students who participated in my seminars on poetry translation and whose pertinent remarks often served to improve my versions of modern Polish poems.

I also feel honored by the assistance I received from the Center for Slavic and East European Studies of the University of California at Berkeley.

C.M.

The History of Polish Literature

CHAPTER I

The Middle Ages

BACKGROUND INFORMATION

THE WESTERN SLAVS in prehistoric times inhabited the plains *The Western* area watered by the river systems of the Vistula and the Oder. *Slavs* From that territory they expanded their settlements between the fifth and ninth centuries southwest to the valleys of Bohemia, and west, along the shores of the Baltic. With the development of archaeology and from recent excavations made in Poland, much data has been acquired concerning the life of these tribes. Although marshes and virgin forests covered most of the territory, the Slavs, clearing and cultivating the land, brought agriculture to a rather high level, thus providing a basis for the gradual transformation from agrarian tribal settlements into states. Tribal agglomerations preceded the division of Western Slavs into larger ethnic units, but only some of those units survived, namely, the Poles, the Czechs, the Slovaks, and a small group of Lusatian Sorbs. The Western Slavic tribes situated further to the west were conquered by the Germans in the early Middle Ages and disappeared.

Archaeological research has not confirmed theories, maintained by *The Formation* some nineteenth-century scholars, about a presumed conquest by the *of the Polish* Norsemen. The Polish state formed slowly under the leadership of *State* native chiefs who succeeded in uniting the separate tribes which inhabited the territory between the Vistula and the Oder. In all probability, this formative period lasted from 880 to 960 A.D. As early as the tenth century, the German chronicler Thietmar used the name "Polonia" to designate the area of what is roughly present-day Poland. Excavations made in our time have revealed remnants of primitive but functional fortresses built of wood and earth. (Incredibly enough, huge wooden beams survived.) These fortresses protected the country from the west: first, from other Western Slavs; later, from Germanic invaders. With the appearance of the ruler, Mieszko I, whose deeds were mentioned in early chronicles, Poland entered history. He was preceded by a certain Piast, whose existence remains in the realm of the half-legendary. His name, however, was attached to the whole dynasty ruling throughout the greater part of the Middle Ages.

A major event determining the future fate of the country took place in 966. After the marriage of Mieszko I to a Czech princess, Dobrava, Poland accepted Christianity in its Western form. In this way, the country became part of the cultural, political, and social organism known in history as Medieval Western Christendom. From that moment on Poland was subject to the changing currents which went into the making of Europe. The consequences of this integration were unfavorable, at first, for native society. Thanks to archaeology, we can make reasonable guesses about the pagan culture of this region: jewelry, tools, arms, Roman coins and musical instruments give evidence not only of a fairly rich life but of the existence of native songs, legends, and beliefs connected with the pagan Slavic religion, which bears traces of Iranian influence. The newly established Roman Church could not look with favor on pagan survivals, and thus the only learned men of the time, the clergy, did not see fit to write down any testimonies of that heritage which was doomed to extinction. Further, only Latin, the language of the Church, was used in writing, and for a few centuries Latin was also the language of Polish literature. The first sentence in Polish, written down by chance, was found in a monastery's book of inventory dating from the thirteenth century. It is moving in its awkward cordiality. A peasant, obviously addressing his wife, says: "Give me, and I will grind; you take a rest" (*"Day at ya pobrusa, a ty pocivay"*).

The Temporal and the Spiritual Medieval Christendom formed a peculiar, many-leveled structure. Its spiritual center was located in Rome, but political power resided north of the Alps with the Germanic states. The Germanic Holy Roman Emperor considered himself ruler and protector of all Western Christians. In accordance with the universally recognized doctrine of the primacy of papal over lay power, the emperor was customarily crowned by the Pope. However, attempts of the Holy Roman Emperors to reverse the procedure by influencing the nomination of the Pope were carried on regularly and often successfully. Several centuries were filled by this conflict between the spiritual and the temporal. These tensions offered Polish rulers the possibility of playing the Vatican against the Empire and of winning complete autonomy for themselves. In addition, Poland paid high tribute in kind to the Church and, thus, was looked upon by the Church as a valuable ally.

The Polish prince Bolesław the Brave (*Bolesław Chrobry*, reigned 992–1025) opposed German pressure in a series of victorious battles, made peace with the Emperor Otto, and was crowned by him as a king. He ruled over a huge state whose western borders extended beyond the Oder. In the east he intervened in the quarrels between the Kievan princes, once even occupying Kiev. An involved relationship between the temporal and the spiritual power within Poland itself led to an event which corresponds to the murder of Thomas à Becket in the time of Henry II: King Bolesław the Bold (*Bolesław Śmiały*, reigned 1058–1079) ordered the assassination of Stanisław, Bishop of Kraków. The event is mentioned here because the figure of Bishop Stanisław (later on canonized by the Church) makes frequent appearances in literature. Historians, however, do not uphold the legend of an evil king versus a good bishop and interpret the tragedy as the result of a clash between the centralizing policy of the king and opposition to it on the part of lords, both lay and clerical.

Medieval Poland was composed of provinces, some of which have preserved their names till today. The nucleus of the state was Greater Poland, situated between the Vistula and the Warta, tributary to the Oder. One of its towns, Gniezno, was the first capital of the country and the seat of the archbishop. Later on, kings moved the capital south, to Kraków, the main town of Lesser Poland. Silesia bordered those two provinces in the west, Mazovia extended toward the northeast, and Pomerania along the Baltic coast. *Feudal Divisions*

In the Middle Ages the country went through phases which can be defined as centrifugal and centripetal. The unity of a single state was preserved by the first kings; later on, however, owing to the practice whereby the king bestowed a province on every son, several small principalities emerged, bound loosely to each other. This resulted in the temporary estrangement of some regions like Silesia and Pomerania, which gravitated toward the Germanic orbit. Only the last Piast kings succeeded in gathering again the majority of provinces into their hands—King Władysław the Short, literally Forearm's Length (*Władysław Łokietek*, reigned 1306–1333), and Casimir the Great (*Kazimierz Wielki*, reigned 1333–1370). Yet one of the most vital assets of the Polish crown, Silesia, was lost in the fourteenth century. The same century marks the beginning of the Polish expansion toward the Eastern Slavic principalities of "Ruś."

At the time of feudal divisions, Polish princes were confronted in the northeast by the pagan tribes of Prussia. The Prussians were not Slavs, nor did they possess anything in common with the Germans. Their language belonged to the same family as Lithuanian and Latvian. This Baltic linguistic group is considered to have preserved the greatest similarity to the original Indo-European lingual pattern. *The Teutonic Knights*

Eager to oppose the heathen, one of the Polish princes, Konrad of Mazovia, invited in 1226 the Order of the Teutonic Knights to settle on the northern borders of his possessions. The Order had been created and financed during the Crusades by German towns along the Baltic coast to care for the sick and wounded Christian knights in the Holy Land. Due to friction with the leadership of the Crusades, the Teutonic Knights migrated from the Holy Land to Hungary, where their political ambitions brought them nothing but expulsion from that country. Once on the border of Prussia, they soon conquered the whole territory, converted the heathen, and turned them into serfs. Conducting continuous raids against still-pagan Lithuania, they pushed farther and farther eastward. Their methods of conquest created an image (one might call it an archetype) in the consciousness of the surrounding population that has survived up to modern times and that today has come to be identified with the methods of the Nazis.

A similar order, the Knights of the Sword (which later merged with the Teutonic Knights), took possession of Estonia and Latvia, even invading the domains of the Russian princes, but it was defeated by Prince Alexander Nevsky in 1242 at a famous battle on the frozen Lake Peipus in Estonia. The Teutonic Knights also threatened their former Polish protectors and even cut them off from the Baltic. This fact explains why Poland and Lithuania, pressured by a common danger, entered into a close alliance with each other.

The Union between Poland and Lithuania   The Grand Duchy of Lithuania was a paradox, one of the curiosities of the Middle Ages. Starting with the thirteenth century, a small Baltic tribe, shunning Christianity, extended its possessions far to the south and to the east. This policy was greatly facilitated by the Tartar (Mongol) invasion of "Ruś" principalities, which left their territory devastated and their internal structure weakened. Kiev and other centers of power turned to the Lithuanian rulers, preferring to accept their sovereignty rather than be prey to the Tartars. Lithuanian successes can also be explained by the fact that the native Lithuanian territory on the Baltic peninsula was much more densely populated than the vast areas inhabited by the Eastern Slavs. By the fourteenth century the Grand Duchy of Lithuania, harassed by the Teutonic Knights from the west, had grown into a large body extending from the Baltic coast to the shores of the Black Sea. The pagan creators of this state did not attempt to impose their religion upon their new subjects, who were Eastern Orthodox Christians. Orthodox Christianity, however, penetrated to the court of the Lithuanian Grand Dukes —the result of marriages with Eastern Slavic princesses. But Lithuania was looking for an ally in the west, and the acceptance of Western Christianity seemed to constitute the best move to paralyze the Teutonic Knights, who justified their encroachments with a religious motive. For Poland, a powerful Lithuanian dukedom also offered great possibilities, especially since the common border between Poland and Lithuania had been extended farther east after Casimir the Great conquered the Eastern Slavic principalities of Volhynia and Halich (Galicia). Due to an agreement between Polish and Lithuanian lords, a personal union between Poland and Lithuania was finally effected: that is, the hand of the Polish Queen Jadwiga (daughter of Louis d'Anjou, King of Hungary, who ruled in Poland after the Piasts died out) was offered in marriage to the Duke of Lithuania, Władysław Jagiełło (*Jogaila*, in Lithuanian), along with an invitation to ascend the Polish throne. This union led to the baptism of Lithuania in 1386. A few decades later, the combined forces of the Polish and Lithuanian armies defeated the Teutonic Knights in one of the largest battles of medieval Europe, the Battle of Grunwald and Tannenberg in East Prussia in 1410.

Merchants in the Middle Ages carried on trade over land routes. *Commercial* Two such important arteries connected Western and Central Europe *Routes* with the shores of the Black Sea and the countries of the Levant. One of them extended south of the Carpathian Mountains through Hungary; another, north of the Carpathians through southern Poland. In spite of Tartar raids which periodically disrupted trade, these routes remained in use, contributing to the prosperity of towns for a long time, until they were cut off by the rise of a new power: the Ottoman Empire. The trade routes were responsible for the growth of a prosperous burgher class, both in Poland and in Hungary. It should be kept in mind that the later breakdown of land trade with the East will partly explain why these countries had to maintain a purely agrarian economy.

Germanic encroachment upon the Western Slavs was not limited *The German* to occasional military expeditions. It was also a question of population *Colonization* pressure, a frequent occurrence when densely populated areas border on those which are more sparsely settled. In the thirteenth century, the Tartars, having conquered large areas of Russia, conducted raids against Poland, which, even though they usually ended in the immediate withdrawal of the invaders, nevertheless devastated the countryside. For obvious economic reasons then, the Polish rulers hastened to invite settlers from the west, granting them special charters and privileges. In the thirteenth century a new phenomenon made its appearance: towns whose ethnic composition had been Polish, such as Wrocław, Kraków, Gdańsk, soon swelled with burghers whose native tongue was German. This led to many conflicts which can hardly be defined as nationalistic, but should rather be termed class conflicts. The situation may be defined as such: the richest segment of the town population was of German extraction, while the poor artisans and merchants were Polish. The latter increased the friction, which began to arouse some awareness of national differences, by rioting against the patricians and elders of the guilds. The Middle Ages also saw an influx of German Jews fleeing persecution. They brought with them the German dialect known as Yiddish. As early as the eleventh century, Jews had been living in Poland, and their number gradually increased as economic reasons motivated rulers to look on them with favor.

The Feudal Structure Medieval Poland possessed a feudal structure somewhat similar to those of other states in Western Christendom. To the modern mind this structure presents a rather obscure picture. It did not result from programs of ideologists, but grew organically, and it requires some effort to grasp the attendant mentality of that age. How Poland's feudal structure differed from those of other countries, such as France, where it existed in its most highly elaborated form, is a question which still interests historians and serves as a vast field of research. Without entering into details, it can be said that the land was considered the property of a prince. To those who pledged arms in his service, he granted new areas of virgin forest. In their turn, these knights settled the areas, at first mainly with prisoners of war. Since there was, at the time, a shortage of manpower, a system of charters for towns and villages was gradually established in order to attract settlers. This charter system was patterned after the one worked out in the German town of Magdeburg, the so-called "Magdeburg Law." Recent conceptions should not be projected into the past, such as the cliché of Poland's having been inhabited by proud nobles and miserable peasants. This commonplace can hardly be applied to the country in the Middle Ages, when class divisions were not so sharply marked. Since a money economy hardly existed, the peasant did not work for his lord directly. The knight, who was changing gradually into a landowner, received taxes in kind from his peasants, but beyond this basic demand he allowed them to live as they pleased. His own farm was small and supplied only his immediate needs. Besides, the distance between knight and peasant appears to have been much less great than it was later on. Opportunity for advancement through distinction in military engagements was offered to the peasant, whose participation was obligatory. Even though the situation of the peasants worsened in the fourteenth century, there were rulers who took up their defense. The last king of the Piast dynasty, Casimir the Great, was labeled "King of Peasants." He was also, in a way, a king of the Jews, perhaps because of his tie with a Jewish beauty, Esther. The names of some Jewish localities, like the district of Kazimierz in Kraków, for instance, still preserve the memory of this king's protection and favor.

From its establishment in the tenth century, the new Christian cul- ture in Poland, fostered by the monastic orders and the secular clergy, began to manifest strong ties with the countries situated west of the Rhine, i.e., present-day France and Belgium. Monasteries did not confine their activities to the religious field, but contributed to economic and artistic life as well. Relations were maintained with their mother houses in Western Europe, thus permitting a mutual exchange of people and ideas. Every monastery, for example, used to send its most gifted young monks to study abroad.

That early Polish architecture followed the Romanesque style of construction is demonstrated by a few buildings still in existence and by quite recent studies of historians of art who have discovered original walls and columns under the several layers of subsequently erected church edifices. The bronze gate of the cathedral in the first capital of the Polish state, Gniezno, is a fine specimen of sculpture in the Meuse style (after the river Meuse), elaborated during the twelfth century in the northeast of France. It is unknown whether the artists were Western-educated natives or foreigners. In any case, the figures and the events represented on the gate are strictly native.

Literature was, as a rule, identified with the Church, since education and the art of writing were monopolized by the orders and the clergy.

LITERATURE IN LATIN

The earliest written works were preserved in monasteries and con- sist of brief accounts, called annals, of the most important events occurring at a given date. They should be distinguished from chronicles, which can already be classified as literature. Chronicles were usually written by monks or clergymen; attached to the court of a king or prince, they were striving, therefore, to gain his favor. The earliest chronicle was written, as the related events incline scholars to believe, in the years 1112–1113. Its author is known only as Gallus Anonymous. He was a monk of foreign extraction, but whether he came from France or not has never been ascertained. That he was not a German is shown by his strong bias against that people.

In his chronicle he evinces a surprising knowledge of the history of Hungary, so there is no doubt that before he wandered to Poland, he had lived a long time in Hungary. His style surprises the scholars because it possesses the vanguard features of the epoch. Medieval Latin was undergoing many changes, and exactly at the time Gallus's *Chronicle* was written, a strongly rhymed prose was considered the latest fashion in Rome. The author uses precisely this fashionable Latin; therefore, he was probably a man well acquainted with current novelties. Factual descriptions of events, battles, and personalities of the monarchs do not constitute the only interest of the *Chronicle*. Personal difficulties of the chronicler himself are revealed in his dedication and in certain passages where he enters into polemics with his enemies. In all probability his undertaking to write the chronicle provoked much envy and intrigue on the part of other clergymen. He emphasizes that he does not want to usurp anyone's position, that he merely wishes to obtain a recompense (there are constant more or less discreet allusions to the greatest virtue of a prince, his liberality) and to return, on completion of his work, to his monastery abroad.

Anonymous drew his materials from conversations with, as he says, "wise men." By this he understands the high clergy, to whose circles he had free access. He also made use of some documents, probably because he worked in a prince's chancery. His chronicle opens with a geographical description of the "country of the Slavs," which according to him extended to the south, including Dalmatia, Croatia, and Istria, as far as the Italian border. His subsequent account of the beginning of the Piast dynasty was responsible for the introduction of legendary motifs taken over later by many writers. Perhaps the most striking is that of the peasant-king. According to Gallus, a peasant named Piast and his wife Rzepka invited some strangers to participate in a pagan celebration of their son's seventh birthday. In return for this hospitality, the mysterious strangers repaid the couple by miraculously multiplying the food and drink at the feast, somewhat along the lines of the biblical miracle at Cana. Later, the son of these peasants became ruler of the country.

Anonymous also mentions a previous ruler named Popiel, who, dethroned by the people because of his cruelty, was forced to seek asylum on an island in the middle of a large lake. There, he was sorely persecuted by mice and rats until finally these vile and merciless creatures devoured him in his tower. These fables, which scholars treated lightly until recently, contain nevertheless, under a layer of fantastic adornment, some elements of truth. Today it is more or less an accepted fact that Piast, the founder of the dynasty, was a man of lower social origins, perhaps a tutor to the previous ruler's children. Nor is the name of Popiel an author's invention. In any case, the legend of the peasant-king is related to early Polish patriarchal patterns.

When dealing with less legendary material, that is, while commenting on events, Anonymous evinces courage and independence of mind. For instance, the quarrel between King Bolesław the Bold and Bishop Stanisław, which ended in the latter's assassination, is presented objectively, without a condemnation of either side. As a whole, Anonymous' chronicle is a literary work of some value.

Still another chronicle gained great popularity in the Middle Ages. Written some one hundred years later, around 1200, it is known as the *Chronicle of Master Vincent*, who was a bishop by the name of Kadłubek. It is mainly a display of medieval rhetoric, containing a number of allegories and paradoxes probably learned during the author's studies in the West. To give a few examples of his figures of speech: "Nothing is more perfect in man than his imperfection"; or a story which leads to the conclusion that "the most fierce animal, more fierce than the lion, the tiger, and the dragon is the most gentle – woman."

Master Vincent's aim was panegyric and didactic. He invented absurd facts to flatter the national pride of his readers, omitting no opportunity to introduce edifying stories corresponding to his scale of values. He was a staunch partisan of absolute dependence of lay power upon the power of the Church; consequently, only those rulers were virtuous who obeyed the clergy in all matters and provided for the welfare of religious orders. The historical reliability, therefore, of Master Vincent's chronicle is slight, and it deserves mention rather as an indication of the tastes of the public able to read Latin.

The so-called *Chronicle from Greater Poland*, written in all probability by Baszko, a clergyman at the end of the thirteenth century, and covering the events up to 1272, also is of a half-historical, half-literary character and tempted many writers as a source of chivalrous romances. Its authorship has been sometimes ascribed to Janko of Czarnków, an astute politician, vice-chancellor of King Casimir the Great, and author of memoirs in Latin, which abound in details from the life of the court.

In the Christian West sermons were preached to the secular clergy *Sermons* and monks in Latin; to the laity, in the vernacular. For a long time the sermon was not regarded as an art, i.e., subject to certain rules. In the beginning it was usually quite short. The sermon developed gradually, becoming a strictly codified genre only in the thirteenth century. Its development paralleled that of Scholastic philosophy and reached its high point first of all in Paris. There, a professor of theology, in addition to his academic duties, was obliged to preach a certain number of sermons. Since elaborate, often highly renowned, sermons were written in the universal language of Latin, they circulated all over Europe and were copied in the monasteries. The sources of some sermons found in Polish monasteries have been traced to France, Germany, and Italy, while some sermons originating in Poland have been discovered in those countries. The clergy, when addressing the people, often translated on the spot from Latin texts into the vernacular and only noted over the less translatable Latin words their approximate vernacular equivalent.

Other Genres A detailed treatment of medieval literature would be of interest to specialists only. A certain number of religious songs have been preserved. They repeat motifs common to all Western Christendom. There also exist several lives of native saints—in particular, of Bishop Stanisław and of the pious women Saints Kinga and Salomea. The history of the Polish theater can be traced back to the liturgical drama which was performed within the church building and consisted of dramatized dialogues taken from the Gospels. In the later Middle Ages the dramatic spectacle left the interior of the church building and began to be enacted in the vernacular outside, often on the steps.

LITERATURE IN POLISH

The most ancient literary monuments in Polish are the *Sermons of the Holy Cross*, named after the Holy Cross monastery in central Poland. They were accidentally discovered in the nineteenth century when the binding of a Latin manuscript was found to be made of scraps of these Polish sermons. They were probably written down at the end of the fourteenth century, but the archaic quality of the language points to a more remote past. They deserve mention because they provide linguists with valuable material for the study of ancient Polish.

Bogurodzica The first poem composed in Polish was the *Bogurodzica*. This is a religious hymn which, as we know from the chronicles, used to be sung by soldiers before battle. It dates, most likely, from the thirteenth century. Several versions of it, together with musical notations, have been preserved, and, as a matter of fact, the song became, for a few centuries, a kind of national anthem. The hymn has been a puzzle for scholars because Polish religious songs were usually translations from Latin; and for the *Bogurodzica*, no Latin source has been discovered. Owing to the absence of a Latin equivalent, some scholars, like Professor Roman Jakobson, have advanced the thesis that the song came from a Church Slavic original via a Czech translation. An equivalent does exist, but only in medieval iconography. The motif of the so-called *deësis*—Christ with the Virgin Mary appearing on one side and John the Baptist on the other—occurs not only in Byzantine but also in Romanesque painting, and precisely in Poland, a Romanesque polychrome painting with that motif was discovered. The name of the hymn, *Bogurodzica* (she who gave birth to God), derives from Old Church Slavic, and was actually a translation from the Greek *Theotokos*. The first two stanzas, which are the oldest, address, respectively, the Mother of God, begging her intercession with her Son, and then Christ, asking him to grant, for the sake of John the Baptist, a good life on earth and a sojourn in paradise after death. The curious rhythmical pattern of the hymn continues to fascinate literary historians.

What has survived of literature in Polish from this period possesses a fragmentary character. Writings in the vernacular become more abundant in the late Middle Ages and will be discussed separately. The Polish language, it should be noted, underwent a period of strong Czech influence at the end of the thirteenth and in the fourteenth centuries. For a while Czech kings even ruled over a part of Poland, but the cultural impact should be explained first of all by the fact that Czech literature and language had developed earlier and were thus richer in notions which, at that time, scarcely existed in Polish.

CHAPTER II

The Fifteenth Century:
The Late Middle Ages

BACKGROUND INFORMATION

Breakup of the Teutonic Order

THE MAJOR EVENT of the period was the victory of the united kingdoms of Poland and Lithuania over the Teutonic Knights in 1410. In spite of the attempts at a recovery on the part of the Teutonic Order (as the Knights were also known), which led to wars lasting for several decades, the resistance of the Order was eventually broken completely. Poland regained access to the ports on the Baltic Sea, which had been for a certain time separated from her by the Order's possessions. This opened up a new commercial trade route from the south to the north and over the Baltic Sea. To the east, Poland and the Grand Duchy of Lithuania found no enemies powerful enough to resist them. To the southeast, however, the Turkish empire was growing. Fidelity to the Vatican and the traditional alliances with Hungary led to military involvements with Turkey. This is the period when Poland and Lithuania were ruled by the dynasty of the Jagiellons (after King Jagiełło). One of the kings, Władysław, who was also king of Hungary, perished while still a young man on a battlefield near Varna in Bulgaria while fighting the Turks in 1444. The lost battle of Varna gave to the Turks a greater freedom of maneuver against Byzantium, which fell in 1453.

Political and Social Transformations

Towns were small in size but strong and rich. Already a tendency was visible on the part of the nobility to limit the power of the king and to transfer financial burdens to the towns and the peasants. The date used to mark the beginning of this effort is that of the so-called "Privilege of Košice" in 1374. After the end of the Piast dynasty, a

Hungarian king, Louis d'Anjou, ruled Poland for a while, and since he wished to secure the throne for his daughter, Jadwiga, he was compelled, in exchange, to grant certain privileges to the Polish nobility. According to the Privilege of Košice, the nobility was exempt from all taxes except those strictly defined in the agreement; the nobles were obliged in case of war to render military service within the borders of the state, while for any service performed beyond its borders, they were to receive remuneration from the king. A constant struggle between the Crown, interested in new taxes for military purposes, and the nobility, who resisted those demands, resulted in the emergence of provincial "dietines," that is, representative bodies of the nobility that met in cases of urgent need to vote an agreement to exceptional taxation. Gradually, the dietines began to send their deputies to a general, representative assembly, a diet. From 1493 on, diets convened periodically as a permanent institution. The nobles protected their freedom of dissent also by a privilege received from the king in 1425, the so-called *Neminem Captivabimus*, according to which no settled knight could be punished without trial.

The first university in Poland was founded in Kraków in 1364. *University* This makes it the second oldest university north of the Alps: the *of Kraków* University of Prague was founded in 1347; the University of Vienna, in 1365; and the University of Heidelberg, the oldest in Germany, in 1385. Since educational institutions possessed an essentially ecclesiastic character, authorization was required from the Pope for their establishment. Because of controversial issues in Scholastic philosophy, the Pope, desiring to maintain papal ascendency in these matters, was not eager to grant the new universities permission to open a faculty of theology, which assured full-fledged status to a school. But after some delay the University of Kraków as well as the University of Vienna received authorization. The Krakovian school was reconstructed as a full-fledged academy in 1400, and, because Queen Jadwiga (the wife of King Jagiełło) donated her jewels for this cause, the school has been known up to the present day as the Jagiellonian University. It embraced all faculties common to medieval higher institutions: liberal arts, theology, medicine, and law. Undoubtedly, a factor which contributed to the opening of that center of learning was the need for lawyers who could be employed in diplomatic affairs. In this century, Poland was involved in protracted feuds with the Teutonic Order, which were not only resolved on the battlefield, but debated at international forums. The Teutonic Order made skillful use of propaganda, presenting itself as a victim of Lithuanian heathens and Polish Christians of doubtful orthodoxy. At the Council of Constance (1414–1418), the Polish delegation took an honorable stand in counteracting the accusations of the Order by invoking the primacy of international law. The Polish delegation, in addition, defended the principle of the Council's superiority over the Pope.

The Jagiellonian University was known at the end of the fifteenth century as an important center of astrology and astronomy. Professor Wojciech (Adalbert) of Brudzew had at least one very gifted pupil, Nicolaus Copernicus. Let us add that professors were mostly of plebeian origin and often quite radical in their defense of the lower classes.

Hussitism   The country found itself in the orbit of a pre-Reformation movement known to us as Hussitism. Originated by Jan Hus in neighboring Bohemia, it was, in a way, a continuation of that plebeian religious ferment in Europe which throughout the Middle Ages periodically surged to the surface, marked by the names of such groups as the Waldenses in France and the Lollards in England. Jan Hus and his followers were strongly influenced by the writings of the English clergyman, John Wycliffe. The tenets of Hus's teaching were aimed less at dogma than at the organization of the Church. His protest was chiefly directed against the corruption of the clergy, especially of the higher clergy, and against the hierarchical structure of the Church headed by the Pope. A national conflict also played its role, as the higher clergy in Bohemia was mostly of German origin. The movement reached Poland thanks to cultural ties between Prague and Kraków, with the result that the Jagiellonian University became one of the centers of ideological contagion. As to the ties between the two countries, let us add that Jan Žižka, before he became a famous military commander of the radical Hussites, known as the Taborites, had commanded Czech units at the Battle of Grunwald against the Teutonic Order. At the Council of Constance, to which Jan Hus was summoned and where, despite an imperial guarantee of safe conduct, he was arrested and burned at the stake, only the Polish delegation made efforts to negotiate a compromise rather than back the condemnation. Even this was risky, as the Poles were under pressure from the propaganda of the Teutonic Order, which labeled Poland heretical. For example, a Latin poem circulated by the Order reads:

> If someone advances a schism, the Poles ally themselves with him.
> If anyone scorns the Christians, look and see if he's not a Pole;
> And when priests are slain, see if Poles are not in it again.
> If someone insults the Pope, he is sure to be a Pole.
> If someone insults the Holy Virgin and Saints
> Or tramples upon the body of Christ
> Or refuses the Sacrament and destroys the holy vessels,
> See if his companion is not a Pole.

In such an atmosphere, the Polish delegation had to tread carefully. In any case, Poland did not take part in the crusade proclaimed against the Hussites. Hussitism had many sympathizers in Poland, but their attempt to impose their religious views by an armed revolt was crushed with royal troops. In spite of its suppression, Hussitism was a considerable factor contributing to the development of literature in the vernacular. Because its followers addressed the lower strata of the population, to whom Latin was unfamiliar, recourse was made to the native tongue. However, since the Church spared no efforts to destroy heretical literature, only a few remnants of these writings have survived.

The Renaissance, or the rebirth of art and literature based upon *Beginnings* models taken from Greek and Latin antiquity, was already flourishing *of Humanism* in Italy in the fifteenth century, known in the history of arts and letters as the Quattrocento. Poland, though still medieval, was by the end of that century touched by the humanistic ferment as a result of her lively relations with Italy. As Italy was considered the most important center of learning, many scholars who began their studies in Kraków completed them at the universities of Padua, Bologna, and Ferrara. In Poland, there was a turning toward the study of classical authors, especially Virgil. Some bishops whose courts attracted scholars and poets—like the Bishop of Lwów, Gregory of Sanok—can already be called Renaissance figures. A very active propagator of that renewed interest in man as a measure of all things, which received the name of Humanism, was a figure from Italy, Philippo Buonacorsi from San Gimignano. He signed his Latin poems with a Greek name, Callimachus. In Rome he had belonged to the famous academia of Pomponius Laetus, whose members went so far in their love for antiquity that they dressed in Roman togas. Endangered by enemies in Italy, Buonacorsi fled to Poland, where he found powerful protectors, mostly among bishops who were no less fond of old Latin authors than himself. The first circles of humanist learning, such as *Sodalitas Vistulana*, were created at this time in Kraków, but the trend comes to fruition only in the next century.

A lively exchange maintained by the burghers of German extraction *Arts and* with towns in Germany contributed to the creation of some works of *the First* art in a style bearing resemblances to that prevailing at the time in *Shops* southern Germany. Veit Stoss (called also Wit Stwosz), a sculptor from Nuremberg who spent thirty-six years in Poland, completed in 1489 his famous altarpiece in painted wood for St. Mary's Church in Kraków. A great richness of detail drawn from the life of towns in Poland lends a realistic quality to the work, which is justly famous for its vivid portrayal of human types seen through the particularity of their dress, their occupations, and their social behavior.

Profiting from the invention of the Gutenberg press, the burghers in Kraków began to invest money in printing shops. The first books

produced in Kraków, however, were not Polish. Since they served
religious purposes, they were either in Latin or in Old Church Slavic.
Because Kraków was the seat of the royal court, which included many
lords from the Grand Duchy of Lithuania who professed the Eastern
Rite, there was a demand for books acceptable to their denomination.
One, however, of such books in Old Church Slavic, published in 1491,
bore an imprint in a vernacular, in "Ruthenian." That Eastern Slavic
dialect, called also Old Byelorussian or Old Ukrainian, is rather difficult to classify in terms of modern Eastern Slavic languages. Employed in writing instead of Lithuanian, which was not understandable
to the Slavic subjects of the Grand Duchy of Lithuania, it continued
to be used there through the fifteenth and sixteenth centuries as an
official language in legal codices and in diplomacy.

LITERATURE IN LATIN—PROSE

Jan Długosz
(1415–1480)
Jan Długosz is regarded as the most important Polish historical
writer up to the end of the eighteenth century. His chronicle gives
detailed descriptions of events of his own as well as of former times.
He was well prepared for his task by his career, rather typical for an
educated clergyman. His father, a knight, distinguished himself at
the Battle of Grunwald; and his uncle, serving as chaplain of the
forces, celebrated the mass before the same battle. Since the family
was not rich and numbered many children, Jan Długosz was destined
for learning, in other words, to become a clergyman. He studied
liberal arts at the University of Kraków, but instead of continuing in
the department of theology he, being rather rather bored by Scholasticism, entered the court of the bishop of Kraków and soon became
his right-hand assistant. The bishop, Zbigniew Oleśnicki, possessed
a strong personality and practiced his own policy in domestic and
foreign affairs; in effect, he competed with the royal court. At certain
periods he acted as virtual ruler of the country. It was his policy
which successfully counteracted attempts at an alliance with Hussite
Bohemia. The Bishop, active in international politics, defended the
position of the Vatican and the higher clergy in international politics,
the crucial issue of which concerned the defense of Western Christendom against the Turks. Let us remember that these were times which
were to see the seizure of Constantinople by the Turks and the end
of Byzantium in 1453. The efforts of the Bishop were directed toward
alliance with Hungary in a common struggle against the Turks.
Bishop Oleśnicki's involvement in big diplomacy necessitated much
foreign travel on the part of his delegates, and Jan Długosz proved
to have a talent in this field. He made three journeys to Italy, where,

among other things, he succeeded in obtaining a cardinal's hat for his protector. In Italy he became acquainted with Renaissance culture, but he remained really a medieval man, though he modeled his Latin on Cicero and chose Titus Livius as his ideal in historiography. An active participation in politics and diplomacy together with a scholarly mind prepared him to write his life's work, known under several titles and called today *Annales Poloniae*. Długosz grasped the importance of his enterprise. For his time, he was an exception in that he knew how to use sources, drawing his material from annals and chronicles in a critical way. Moreover, he did not limit himself to Poland. He realized that the understanding of interdependences requires a knowledge of the history of neighboring countries; therefore he employed Czech and German chronicles. In order to read the latter, he mastered the language. He also learned the Cyrillic alphabet to have access to the Eastern Slavic *Letopisi*. Although he endeavored to be unbiased, his objectivity is doubtful. Yet it is precisely his arguments in defense of certain theses which add to the lively character of his work. Besides being descriptive, it is also a historical interpretation and a polemic with his adversaries. As could be expected, the policy of his patron, Oleśnicki, colors the work. Długosz, a faithful son of the Roman Catholic Church, was convinced that Providence would only look upon Poland with favor if she placed herself in the position of a servant to the Vatican, for lay power should be subjected in all things to the spiritual power. In the assassination of St. Stanisław he saw a crime which had been punished by the extinction of the Piast dynasty and by the subsequent ascendancy of a foreign dynasty. He reproached the Jagiellons for having more concern for the welfare of Lithuania than for Poland.

In his *Annales* Długosz gave vent to certain animosities. He despised the Czechs because the majority were heretics, and accused them of servility toward German emperors in the past. The defeat of the Teutonic Order he considered a just punishment for its crimes, cruelty and vainglory. He scorned the Lithuanians, whom he called half heathen, and, of course, he was hostile toward the Eastern schismatics. In accordance with Oleśnicki's policy, he saw Poland's mission in an alliance with Hungary and a common struggle against the infidel. Nevertheless, in spite of its tendentiousness, his work cannot be called panegyrical. His concern for truth led him to reveal a great number of unflattering facts about particular eminent figures. The nearer he approached the period of his own lifetime, the more he was inclined to base his account on the direct testimony of actual participants in the events. The relation of certain facts prevented for a long time the printing of his work in its totality, as it was accused of divulging "the secrets of the kingdom." Długosz's chronicle was a constant source for compilations, but its publication, begun in 1614, was interrupted by the king's order. It was published in its totality for the first time at the beginning of the eighteenth century in Germany by a Russian diplomat, Heinrich Huyssen.

Długosz, like all his contemporaries, took no account of the time factor in history. He imagined, for example, the political structure and class divisions of the tenth century exactly as if they had been no different from the fifteenth century. But apart from serving as a rich mine of information, his work, through the vivacity of its narrative, through the author's attention to causes and effects, through his relatively critical use of sources, merits a place of considerable importance in Polish letters. Written in a well-balanced, serious, functional language which is an improvement over the medieval Latin, it may be classified stylistically as standing on the border line between the Middle Ages and the Renaissance.

Jan Ostroróg   Jan Ostroróg may be called Poland's first lay political writer. Un-
(1436–1501) like Długosz, who was attached to a bishop's court, Ostroróg was a man of the royal court, and his writings reveal the impact of Hussite ideas upon that milieu. His political treatise, the *Monumentum pro Reipublicae Ordinatione* (*On the Organization of the State*), opens up a rich literature in this genre in Poland.

Ostroróg, generally speaking, favored a strengthening of the royal power at the expense of the great lords and the clergy. A crucial problem for the country was created by the enfeeblement of kingly power, which resulted from the granting of extensive privileges to the nobles. Exploring opportunities to reassert his authority, the king attempted to play one social group against another. This game, played by the royal court throughout the fifteenth and sixteenth centuries, consisted in seeking alliances with those forces which opposed both great lords and Church prelates, namely, the gentry and the towns. In exchange, the gentry demanded greater and greater privileges and, having acquired them, exerted strong pressure on the towns and the peasants. The parliamentary system and, later on, the "free election" of kings had their roots in those frictions.

Ostroróg looked with disfavor on the power of the towns and the autonomy of the great lords. He defended above all the interests of the state, represented by the power of the king, and, implicit in this, the independence of the king from the clergy. His proposals consisted of the following: (a) Poland should reject the claims of the Vatican and cease to be a Roman fief. (b) All payments (tithes) to Rome should be suspended. (c) In case of necessity, the king should be empowered to seize the treasure of the Church. (d) The number of monasteries should be limited. (e) The clergy should not be allowed to accept money for marriages, funerals, and baptisms.

Ostroróg advocated a unified jurisdiction. He rejected, for instance, the separation of town and state jurisdictions. Perhaps the influence of Hussitism may be seen in his theory that the army should be composed not only of the nobles but also of burghers and peasants. The political program of this aristocrat, whose family members were represented in the circles of the royal court, proved to be slightly chimerical in that he endorsed an alliance between the king and the gentry—a policy which, in effect, was to lead to an even greater weakening of the throne, since the gentry had no wish to see a strong central authority.

LITERATURE IN POLISH

Literature in the vernacular made considerable progress. But Polish still belonged to the realm of "low-brow" culture, while the language of "high-brow" culture remained Latin. Yet the Bible, collections of prayers, and juridical books were already being translated into Polish, often at the queens' commands, who, since women were excluded from education, represented culture on a popular level. These translations, circulated as manuscripts, later on were supplanted by new versions, as their language seemed too archaic. The literary language was only just beginning to take shape under constant efforts to adapt a Latin syntax based on dependent clauses and tense sequence to a Slavic idiom. This struggle with Latin grammatical forms determined to a large extent the character of the Polish language as a very pliable instrument.

Poetry

How strongly Poland was still medieval is shown by a poem in the form of a dialogue entitled *Conversation of a Master with Death* and subtitled *De Morte Prologus*. It is written in "imperfectly syllabic" verse with a rhyme scheme of *aabbcc*. (See Appendix for a discussion of the rules of Polish verse.) *The Dance of Death*

The poem tells the story of a learned man, "a magister," who has asked God to show him the shape of Death. Once, while he is alone in a church, Death appears to him, and (the following is a prose transcription):

he saw a naked being of female sex whose form was girded with white linen. She was lean and pale and her yellow face shone like a wash basin. The end of her nose had dropped off; bloody dew was seeping from her eyes. Her head was wrapped with a kerchief as a savage would do. There were no lips at her mouth. When she opened her mouth she was gnashing her teeth. Her eyes shot round in all directions. In her hand she carried a rattling scythe.

(Let us keep in mind that the word "death" in Polish is a feminine noun.) The master swoons, but seeing that Death had come with peaceful intentions and was waiting to answer his questions, he soon recovers his senses. The master asks about her origin and her parents. Death answers that she was begotten in Paradise when Eve picked the apple: "Adam tasted me in the apple." Angry and ironic, Death then unfolds the image of her power over everything alive—animals and man alike. She enumerates her victims in a kind of catalogue of all medieval estates and professions. Thus, provided with an opportunity for moral satire, the author criticizes the pleasure-loving clergy, light-minded women, and corrupt judges. The master now timidly inquires about the purpose of having physicians. Death enlightens him by replying that they are all charlatans. He may hide himself behind walls, behind guards, or bury himself in the earth; Death will reach him everywhere. His only hope is to meditate on life beyond the grave, to imitate good monks and pure, pious women.

A surviving "Ruthenian" translation of this poem is more complete, as it possesses an ending lacking in the Polish text. Although the Polish poem is itself an adaptation of a Latin prose version, *Colloquium inter Mortem et Magistrum Polycarpum*, it is more picturesque than its Latin model, containing many more details related to local customs and much macabre humor. For this reason, the work is considered as one of the more interesting specimens of Polish medieval poetry.

The personification of death was a standard motif in medieval literature and painting. It did not appear, however, in the early Middle Ages. Likewise, antiquity did not know an allegorical identification of a skeleton or corpse with death. This appeared only gradually around the thirteenth century. At first, Death was represented as a kind of mummified corpse of dried-up skin and bones. In the Renaissance and Baroque eras it was symbolized by the skeleton. In our poem, Death is depicted as a decaying corpse; thus, an element of horror is added, but this was not an exception for the time. The basic concept of the poem corresponds to the so-called *danse-macabre* or *Totentanz* popular in the Middle Ages as a subject for painters and for spectacles in the marketplaces. Death was portrayed leading a dance in which people of various ages and estates take part. The most frequent participants included a Pope, an emperor, an empress, a cardinal, a king, a bishop, a prince, an abbot, a knight, a monk, a mayor, a canon, a nobleman, a usurer, a chaplain, a bailiff, a sacristan, a merchant, a hermit, a peasant, a young man, a young girl, a child.

The *Lament of a Dying Man* was a song so popular that it passed into folklore. It is an account of a man's life related at the moment of his last agony. The dying man expresses regret for his sins and for his preoccupation with worldly affairs which had caused him to neglect his soul. No friend is able to˙help him now. God is his only hope. Evil spirits have surrounded his deathbed, and they now lie in wait for him. Rather heavily didactic, the poem concludes with the following advice: he should leave his land to his family, donate his savings to the Church, and bestow considerable gifts on his friends. The song is probably an adaptation of a Czech work called *On the Separation of the Soul from the Body*. Lament of a Dying Man

From abundant Hussite religious literature in the vernacular not very much has survived, and the only existing example of poetry is the *Song on Wycliffe*. It was written by Jędrzej (Andrew) Gałka of Dobczyn, who was a professor at Kraków University. We know that he was a fervent Hussite and that not only did he lose his university chair because of his views, but also he endangered his very life because of them. Forced to escape from Kraków, he joined his brethren in Bohemia. Song on Wycliffe

The subject of the song is significant, as the name of Wycliffe, who first dared to step forward against the Church hierarchy in England, was a rallying cry for all Hussites. The author addresses "Poles, Germans, all languages." (Let us take notice that, although there was no conception of nationality then, the notion of the "lingua," or language, was deeply implanted.) The song already contains a motif which will be repeated later on in the Protestant literature of Western Europe, namely, the Pope represented as Antichrist: "Imperial Popes are Antichrists. Their power comes not from Christ but from Antichrist, from the emperor's letter." Yet the song does not call for an armed revolt; it pleads for the use not of an "iron sword but the word of Christ."

Anthologies of Polish poetry usually start out with a poem entitled *The Lament of the Mother of God at the Foot of the Cross* because it is the first really moving piece of poetry in the vernacular. This *planctus*, or lament, probably formed part of a mystery play on the Passion which is now lost to us. It, thus, also belongs to the history of the theater. The chief value of the poem lies in its spontaneity. This is a true lament of a mother who, while she sees her Son being tortured, is forbidden to help him: The Lament of Holy Mary

My Son, if I had you down here, I could have helped you. Your head hangs askew; I could have propped it. You are covered with blood; I could have wiped it away. You thirst; I could have given you water. But I cannot reach your Holy Body.

O Angel Gabriel, where is your joy of which you promised me so much? I am full of sadness and sorrow. My flesh and all my bones are rotten.

Other Works   There are a considerable number of religious songs and versified legends, of which the best preserved is the *Legend of Saint Alexis*. We see also the beginning of secular poetry manifesting a satirical tendency. These works deal with subjects such as behavior at the table or class animosities. Plebeian songs, directed against higher social classes, were probably censored out of existence, because those which have survived represent only the attitude of the nobility, for instance, *A Satire on Lazy Peasants* or *A Song on the Assassination of Tęczyński*. The latter concerns a knight who ordered a suit of armor for himself in Kraków and, when it was not ready on time, slapped the armorer in the face, the injustice of which provoked a riot and resulted in the death of the knight at the hands of the angry burghers.

Prose

Religious Prose   Of religious prose extant, there is an abundance. We possess not only translations from the Old and New Testaments but also "spiritual romances" of some originality. A large work, *The Life of the Holy Family*, for example, is an attempt to collect picturesque details from the four Gospels and from the Apocrypha.

Secular Prose   Legal books and a certain number of love letters form a modest contribution to the sphere of lay literary activity. Written in a rhymed prose which we could consider today as free verse, the following love letter of a Kraków university student is a charming example:

In the steadfastness and firmness of my heart I reveal this to nobody but you, my Beloved! My consolation and I add my greetings, and a bow as well, of which there are a great deal in good manners; and so, for the second time, my greetings and a bow on both knees to the very ground.

The student then tries to depict his sadness and love: "Had all the doctors used their arguments, they would not have described my sorrow. . . . Had all the birds gathered around, they would have been surprised by such love." He ends his letter with: "and if I am dear to you, I should like this letter to look at you always. The words of the letter will not wear out as long as you are in my heart. Amen."

CHAPTER III

Humanism and Reformation: The Sixteenth Century and the Beginning of the Seventeenth Century

BACKGROUND INFORMATION

D EEP SOCIAL AND ECONOMIC transformations occurred which *The* were to prove decisive for the future of the country. The *Parliamentary* knightly class plainly changed into a landowning class, that is, into *System* a gentry attached to the land. This gentry was still under the obligation (proper to a knight) to perform military service in wartime, but thanks to its representation in the Diet, it now actually exercised the supreme power in the country. The Diet tended toward an even greater limiting of royal power until, finally, a political system emerged which was unique for Europe of that time. It may be called a system of one-class democracy. The king's hands had been tied by the Diet, particularly since it passed in 1505 the law called *Nihil Novi* (nothing new unless approved by the Diet and the Senate). He could neither impose new taxes nor wage war without its agreement. Moreover, after the dynasty of the Jagiellons had died out, it became the practice to elect the king at a general gathering held in the meadows outside of Warsaw open to all who possessed a title of nobility. The first king to receive the throne in such a "free election," Henri Valois (later to be king of France, known as Henri III), was forced in 1572 to sign the so-called *Henrician Articles* and *Pacta Conventa*, both amount-

[25]

ing to a constitution. He not only promised to rule in strict accordance
with that charter but agreed that in case of a breach of law on his part
his subjects would be released automatically from their duty of obedience. Although the king was elected for life, his authority was no greater
than that of modern presidents.

This, perhaps, explains why there were no cases of regicide in
Poland. The king was viewed as a symbol, and in political literature
he was compared to the queen bee. His real power provoked no envy.

After the Union of Lublin in 1569 between Poland and Lithuania,
the omnipotent Diet represented both countries. This marked a step
toward a fusion of the two organisms. The process was accelerated
by the fact that Lithuanian boyars coveted for themselves the same
privileges that the Polish gentry had won. Still, the Grand Duchy of
Lithuania preserved many of its own institutions, for example, its
own laws (the "Lithuanian Statutes"). The local nobility spoke its
own idioms, but it was already beginning to adopt the Polish language.
The *Respublica*, as the Polish-Lithuanian state was called, covered
a vast expanse. Its wars in the east, especially with Ivan the Terrible,
were, for the most part, successful and did not diminish its territory.

But the gentry took advantage of this peculiar political system to
secure economic benefits for themselves. The transformation occurring
in Western Europe, the growth of towns and of manufactures, created
enormous markets for agricultural products, and those products were
exported from Poland. They were brought by barges down the rivers
to the Baltic coast, then by ship from the port of Gdańsk (Danzig)
to the West. To maintain a constant supply of products, it was not
enough to rely solely upon the taxes-in-kind paid by the peasants. To
meet increasing demands, the landowners organized a plantation-type
agriculture. It was now necessary to force the peasants to work on the
manor fields. At first, the peasants were required to work one day
a week for their lord, then two, then three, and so on, until their lot
was reduced to a state of enslavement. Serfdom, not only a Polish
phenomenon, took root throughout all of Eastern Europe, and predetermined a different rhythm of development in the two parts of
Europe: Eastern Europe exported wheat in exchange for the manu-
factured goods imported from the West. The Diet, utilized as an
instrument to enslave the peasants, voted successive laws inhibiting
their freedom. The peasant thus became tied to the land and was
forbidden to leave his village. Jurisdiction over him passed from the
state into the hands of the master, or serf-owner.

The gentry waged war not only against the peasants, but also
against the towns. Obviously, the precarious situation of the peasants
had an adverse effect on urban life. Serfdom and the resulting impoverishment of the village hindered the flow of labor and money into

the towns. Moreover, the gentry persistently strove to lower the prices of town-made products. This tendency explains, for instance, a law forbidding domestic merchants to export their goods abroad. The ominous consequences of such a state of affairs were to be felt later. If we are to take a balanced view, however, we should not underestimate certain advantages of the system. The gentry, protected by *Neminem Captivabimus* since 1425, feared no authority. This explains the large degree of religious tolerance in Poland, not met anywhere else in Europe at the time. Every law against tolerance was considered as an attempt to limit the rights of those "who are equal to kings because they elect kings." Finally, this situation favored the penetration of new and sometimes very radical religious ideas.

The marriage of King Sigismund I to an Italian princess, Bona *Italian* Sforza of Milan, in 1518 gave decisive impetus to the spread of *Influence* Italian influence in Poland, which had been in progress already for several decades. The result was a genuine invasion of Italian courtiers, clergymen, architects, and artists. Kraków, the capital of the state, which until that time had been a predominantly Gothic town, changed its character. The royal seat, Wawel Castle, rebuilt in Renaissance style, remains to this day a testimony of that new impact. For a long time Italy was to form one of the prime components of Polish culture. This is still apparent today in some aspects of the language, in architecture, and even in cuisine. Vegetables and culinary dishes were imported from Bologna and Padua together with their names. Particularly active in transplanting the Italian style of church building was the Jesuit Order, brought to Poland in 1564 to combat Protestantism. (The Jesuit Order reached its zenith during the Baroque era, and Baroque churches as far east as Polotsk and Vitebsk bear testimony to the extent of "Italianization.") The good manners of higher society were modeled on those universally observed south of the Alps. A Polish gentleman was not considered accomplished unless he had traveled abroad for study; such young gentlemen usually attended northern Italian universities, although interest in Protestantism directed many of them to Wittenberg, Zürich, and Basel. Of course, literary models and theories imported from the same source shaped Polish literature.

Erasmus of Rotterdam was regarded throughout Europe of the *Erasmus of* sixteenth century as the fountainhead of all wisdom. In Polish intel- *Rotterdam* lectual circles his name was surrounded by genuine veneration. Accessible to every educated man, his Latin works were avidly read, and his faithful readers, not confining themselves to letters of gratitude to the author, would send him golden rings, goblets, knives and forks of pure gold, etc. The Polish king, Sigismund I, when writing to Erasmus, used to treat him as a kind of monarch. Polish humanists addressed him as "the only adornment of our age," "the prince of humanities and of ancient, purest theology." One of them says in his letter, "Oh would that I could kiss not only that hand, but also that head which has contrived so much, that heart which has conceived works that have spread your glory all over the earth and over this Poland, our dear country." Coxe, an English humanist who had settled in Kraków, described in a letter to Erasmus how he and his friends used to get up, eat their breakfast, walk, and eat dinner, talking all the while only of Erasmus. Erasmus received considerable sums of money from Poland from the parents of pupils who studied with him in Switzerland. And he knew how to show gratitude—several of his works were dedicated to his Polish admirers. In order to help Erasmus, one of his pupils bought his library while granting him its use for life. The pupil, Jan Łaski, was later to become an eminent figure in the Polish as well as the German and English Protestant movements. (He was known in England as Johannes à Lasco.) To say that Erasmianism in Poland paved the way for the Reformation would not be an exaggeration. This does not mean that the writings of Erasmus, especially his exegesis of the Scriptures, led necessarily to the acceptance of the teachings of Luther or Calvin. Among fervent Erasmians, we find both future Protestants and staunch Roman Catholics, for instance, Cardinal Hosius, the most eminent leader of the Counter Reformation in Poland and one of the pillars of the Council of Trent. Erasmus himself rejected the overtures of Martin Luther, and tried to steer a middle course between the fighting denominations. Several people in Poland, loyal to his spirit, attempted to follow his example.

The Reformation   The growth of Protestantism in Poland was rapid, broad in scope, but relatively short-lived. If we were to imagine a man born in 1500, he would have been seventeen at the moment when Martin Luther came out with his famous theses. In Poland and Lithuania, our man would have witnessed a prompt response to new religious ideas coming from Germany—a response which soon changed into enthusiastic attention to the teachings of Calvin. Between his forty-ninth and sixty-fourth year, he would have seen a virtual triumph of Calvinism, indicated by a Protestant majority in the Diet. But if our man reached the age of seventy or eighty, he would have noticed signs of an imminent breakdown of Protestantism. His sixty-fourth year would have already been marked by a bitter feud within the Protestant camp. At that time the Reformed Church split into two branches—Calvinist and Anti-Trinitarian (Unitarian). A bitter struggle ensued in 1564, while their common enemy, the Jesuit Order, proceeded to implant itself in the country.

In Poland, the influx of new doctrines followed upon a local ferment against the clergy which harked back to the time of Hussitism. An early nineteenth-century Protestant historian, Valerian Krasiński, described the situation:

Many Polish students attended the school of Goldenberg in Silesia, run by the Bohemian Brethren, which openly taught doctrines condemned by Rome. A strong feeling against the ecclesiastical body was manifested at the Diets of 1501 and 1505 by attempts to curtail the competence of ecclesiastical jurisdiction, but no legislation in this direction was enacted. Public opinion so opposed the influence of the clergy that the decrees of the ecclesiastical courts fell into general contempt. The secular magistrates assumed superiority over the ecclesiastical tribunals, and investigated the competency of their jurisdiction as well as of the justice of their decrees which were generally left unexecuted. Excommunication, since it did not imply loss of political rights, produced no effect whatsoever.

The Catholic hierarchy, becoming alarmed, recommended the re-establishment of the tribunal of the Holy Inquisition to fight the Hussites and the Lutherans. The Church compelled the king to issue an order prohibiting Polish students from attending heretical universities. As the above-mentioned V. Krasiński explained:

This ordinance could not, however, produce any effect as it carried no force of law, not having been confirmed by the Diet, and consequently was not binding, particularly for the nobles. The latter, sheltered by their constitutional privileges from every arbitrary restriction, continued to frequent the forbidden universities, particularly that of Wittenberg, the cradle of the Reformation and the seat of Lutheranism. The ordinances passed in 1535 against the Anabaptists in Kraków and the Lutherans in Wilno, as well as that of 1541, whereby the king threatened with the loss of nobility all those who might have heretical priests in their homes, remained likewise a dead letter.

The Diet in 1543 formally granted the freedom to study at any university abroad. The Church also demanded restrictive measures against those printers who issued heretical books, but the hierarchy was unable to obtain secular assistance for the confiscation of that material, while the king declared in his decree of 1539 that the press was free to issue whatever it pleased.

The personalities of the kings Sigismund I and his son, Sigismund August (Sigismund II), were of no small importance. Both showed prudence in aligning themselves with the clergy and at the same time, without being Protestants, followed the advice of their Protestant counselors, thereby avoiding those tensions which in Western Europe, particularly in France, led to bloody persecutions and wars. For these reasons, Poland of the sixteenth century was called *Paradisus Hereticorum* (a paradise for heretics).

The Rise of the Reformed Church

During the reign of Sigismund I, except for the German-speaking cities in the north which promptly embraced Lutheranism, the Reformation in Poland existed as a state of mind rather than an organizational entity. Many bishops shared this mental disposition, and now and then, a nobleman substituted a Protestant minister on his lands for a Catholic priest. But, in general, it was hoped that the Vatican would soon settle the controversies and introduce a reform of its own. Most, therefore, preferred to wait. Great expectations were connected with the Council of Trent (1545–1563), and it was only when the Council evinced a rigid attitude toward the new trends that partisans of the new ideas determined to organize.

The efforts of Stanisław Hosius, Bishop of Warmia and the leading fighter for the Roman Church, who sought (at the time of the Council) to impose upon the king an edict requiring that the holding of all public offices be dependent upon the signing of a "creed of orthodoxy," proved to be vain. The creed ran as follows:

Tu credis, aquam benedictam, invocationem sanctorum et consecrationem herbarum esse efficacem? Credis purgatorium, Papam, missam, jejuniam, votam, atque celibatum?
(Do you believe in the efficacy of holy water, the invocation of the saints, and the consecration of herbs? Do you believe in purgatory, the Pope, the mass, fasting, votive offerings, and celibacy?)

Conversion to a new denomination became more and more widespread among the gentry. But their ready acceptance stemmed mainly from economic and political motives. This turbidity of intention constituted the basic weakness of Polish Protestantism, which was abandoned as soon as the gentry found new ways of securing their interests. For the time being, the dream of a national church was taking the peculiar shape of a church governed by the gentry—just as the state was governed—through the election of deputies who would regulate the activity of the Church. The gentry aimed to liberate themselves from the Catholic clergy, whose dominion was political as well as spiritual; to seize Church property for themselves or for the state; to free themselves from the burden of paying annual taxes to Rome; to substitute Polish for Latin as the language of the liturgy.

The same political ambitions resulted in preference for Calvinism over Lutheranism: Calvin had established in Geneva a republic, ruled by *elected* elders. In contradiction to Calvinism, Lutheranism was more authoritarian, as it favored, from the start, the strong ruling power of a prince, and, as a matter of fact, needed his protection.

The embracing of Protestantism by a Polish noble presented a constantly recurring pattern. He announced his intentions by expelling the Catholic priest; then he confiscated Church buildings, disposed of images and statues, invited in a Protestant minister of his liking, and defied all authority, lay or spiritual. If a whole town was subject to him, he often financed Protestant schools, printing shops, etc. Such was the case of Pińczów near Kraków and Nieśwież in Lithuania.

The clergy was attracted by Protestantism, as it provided a means to legalize relationships with women. For the clergy, the widespread custom of concubinage had created a problem of a numerous but illegitimate posterity. Many priests, however, who became Protestant ministers were animated by a passionate interest in theology, but they soon discovered that dependence on their new lay masters was no more comfortable than their previous submission to the discipline of the Church. Already in the formative period of Polish Protestantism a conflict between gentry and ministers was present, as the latter were mostly people of humble origin and, moreover, intellectuals.

The establishment of a Reformed (Calvinist) Church in Poland was the work of Jan Łaski, who after a long exile in Germany and England, returned to his homeland in 1556. The Polish king at that time, Sigismund August, was urged constantly in letters from Calvin himself to undertake a national reformation. But since the ruler was not inclined to listen to these requests, Calvin had to rely upon Jan Łaski, in whom he placed his full confidence. After his return to Poland Łaski exercised uncontested authority as head of the Reformed Church, the centers of which were located chiefly in Lesser Poland and Lithuania. He strove for a union of all the reformed confessions, namely, of Calvinists, Czech Brethren, and Lutherans. He was also interested in contacts with sympathizers in Muscovy. Refugees from the East, Orthodox monks, had informed him that several groups of Protestants were either imprisoned (around seventy boyars) or were in hiding (around five hundred "brethren") in Muscovy. A close alliance between Calvinists, Czech Brethren, and Lutherans became a reality, however, only after Łaski's death in 1560.

A conflict between some ministers, inflamed with a passionate yearn- *Arianism* ing for true Christianity (conceived as a return to the simplicity of the first Christians), and the gentry who dominated the Calvinist Church lay at the origin of a ferment within Polish Protestantism which resulted in one of the most fascinating movements in European history, namely, Arianism. Its adherents in Poland and Transylvania, the so-called Arians, were the predecessors of the Unitarian Church.

Arianism is best understood if regarded as an amalgam of three elements. One is the concept of separation of Church and State. The Polish Reformed Church did not attempt to introduce a rigid, theocentric rule as Calvin did in his Genevan republic; had it wished to do so, it would have been impossible, as the forces of Catholicism and Protestantism were equal at that time. The Reformed Church's constitution reflected the parliamentary spirit of the gentry, and, in fact, a real separation of the Church from the State was accomplished. Arianism was created mostly by those ministers who, dissatisfied with their lay masters, raised the complete autonomy of the Church to the dignity of a principle. Absolute religious tolerance was likewise considered a cornerstone of Christianity. That this conviction makes it difficult to reduce the tenets of the sect to a few uniform affirmations is indicated by one of the most common reproaches leveled at the Arians, namely, that cobblers, tailors, and women each interpreted the gospel in his own way.

The second element in Arianism is an anti-Trinitarian intellectual trend. Renaissance man was boldly proclaiming the power of human reason; therefore, he felt obliged to explain religious dogma in purely intellectual terms. A few minds began to rebel against the dogma of the Holy Trinity. This trend marked the resurgence of an old controversy which had raged, at the beginning of Christianity, around the mutual relations between God the Father, God the Son, and God the Holy Spirit. At that time, it resulted from the residue of Greek philosophy in the early Christian mind. Arius proclaimed that Christ was "homo*i*ousian" (of like substance, from the Greek: ὅμοιος = like, similar + οὐσία = substance) but not "homoousian" (of the same substance, from: ὁμός = same + οὐσία = substance) with the Father. In 325 the Council of Nicea condemned the heresy of Arius. The renewal of this heresy, which took definite shape in Poland, was transmitted from northern Italy, where certain intellectuals were involved in theological disputes and threatened by the Holy Inquisition (re-established in 1542), were forced to escape. Many took refuge in Poland. Among them were such eminent minds as Stancari; Blandrata; later on, Fausto Sozzini (Faustus Socinus); as well as a famous figure of the Reformation in Europe, a prior of the Capuchin Order, Bernardino Ochino, whose defection was considered by Rome as a major blow to its cause.

A sensational event provoked violent animosity toward Calvin among many Polish Protestants. A Spanish theologian, Michael Servetus, living in France as a refugee, by training a physician, had come to the conclusion that the dogma of the Holy Trinity was contrary to reason. Since his religious opinions incurred persecution in France, he fled to Geneva, naïvely believing he would find there a safe haven. Condemned by Calvin, he was sentenced to death and burned at the stake in 1553. The news of Servetus' death created a deep impression in Poland.

The Anabaptist plebeian trend constituted the third element of Arianism. The dream of a pure, communistic, primitive Christianity abolishing all social hierarchy persisted throughout the Middle Ages among the lower strata of the population and was combined with the expectation of a millennium. At the beginning of the Reformation in

Germany and Holland, it took the form of the Anabaptist movement, which penetrated to Poland and fused with the aforementioned intellectual trends. The Arians were known for their social radicalism, their negation of the existing social order, and their attempts at communal living. They attracted poor Protestant ministers, scribes, and blacksmiths, but there were also.many nobles who sold their estates in order to share with others a simple life. This trend was basically anti-intellectual and intuitionist, stressing not theological concepts but the reading of the gospel.

In the history of Arianism it is possible to distinguish two periods: one of growth, the other of maturity. The first may be reckoned from the moment when Piotr of Goniądz (Petrus Gonesius) attacked the dogma of the Holy Trinity in 1556. The Arians broke away from the Calvinist "Major" Church in 1563 to found a so-called "Minor" Church. The Anabaptist or anti-intellectual trend dominated throughout this formative period, which was characterized by acute religious controversy among the Protestants. Theology evidenced leanings toward Ditheism (i.e., the theory that God the Father and God the Son are not of the same substance) or Tritheism. But the principal questions under discussion at innumerable synods regarded ethics and the organization of society:

a) *Integral Pacifism.* A Christian cannot use the sword. Since the State uses the sword as an ultimate sanction, a Christian should neither accept public office nor take part in war. The chief proponent of this view was a brilliant polemist, Marcin Czechowic, a burgher from Lublin. Adoption of such a program would have, in effect, completely severed the Polish Brethren (Arians) from society. It was combatted by realists like Szymon Budny from Lithuania, who invoked the Old Testament to back his arguments.

b) *Serfdom.* Since all men are brothers, a Christian cannot own serfs nor profit from their labor, but should live by the work of his own hands. Not all the Polish Brethren were ready to accept such precepts. But some, particularly in Raków, a famous center of the movement, went so far as to attempt communal living. These dedicated men even sent a delegation to the communes of the Hutterites, a radical German Anabaptist sect that, after fleeing Germany, had settled in Moravia. It was in the report of that delegation in 1569 that the word "communist" was used for the first time in the Polish language. The rigid discipline enforced on the collectively owned farms of the Hutterites, the privileges enjoyed by the elders, and the system of surveillance organized by the latter over the simple workers did not satisfy the Polish delegates. They wrote in their report: "These are not communists, but economists" ["*To nie kommunistowie są, ale ekonomistowie*"].

Since their appearance, the Arian Polish Brethren had been violently attacked by other Protestants, and Hosius, then already a cardinal and the mainspring of the Counter Reformation in Poland, rubbed his hands with satisfaction, since: "war among the heretics means peace for the Church." The anger of the other Protestants increased as the Polish Brethren tended to adopt more and more radical theological views. Some rejected the belief in the immortality of the soul (which did not imply the rejection of religion, since they put their trust in Christ, who had promised the resurrection of the body). Some recognized only the human nature of Christ, solving in that manner the problem of the Trinity. Others, particularly in Kraków, Lublin, and Wilno, were fascinated by Judaism and carried on discussions with Jewish rabbis. "Judaizers" were especially strong in Lithuania, where they had a dynamic leader in the person of Szymon Budny.

The second period of Arianism was marked by the victory of a rationalistic approach which set in at the very end of the sixteenth century and lasted until the moment when the Arians were accused of collaboration with enemy Sweden and banished from Poland. This second phase of Arianism is referred to as Socinianism, after its leading theologian, Faustus Socinus (Sozzini), an Italian whose powerful mind left its imprint upon the whole thinking of his coreligionists.

The following constitute the main points of Socinian teaching:

1) There is no separate, conscious life of the soul after the death of the body. But man possesses a divine spark which distinguishes him from animals, and which returns to God after death.

2) Before sinning, Adam and Eve were not immortal. Through their sin they realized only their wretchedness and acquired a longing for immortality. Socinus rejected both the Catholic and Protestant versions of the doctrine of original sin as radically affecting the nature of man.

3) God did not create the world out of nothing, but out of matter which exists eternally. He is not omnipresent nor omnipotent because He cannot alter the laws of nature, but He is infinitely good and, applying to mankind a divine pedagogy, leads man by degrees through history. At first, He was concerned only with the subsistence of the species; then He gave man a guide to earthly happiness, the Old Testament; and at last, He sent Christ.

4) Christ was born of a virgin through God's intervention. He was only man. But his perfect obedience to the will of God enabled him to rise from the dead and to sit at the right hand of God, who gave Christ the power to judge mankind. Judgment will occur at the end of the world, when Christ will give back his kingdom to God.

5) The resurrection of Christ was the first victory over death and opens the era of man's immortality. Yet only those who have been

obedient to Christ will rise on the Day of Judgment. There is neither hell nor purgatory.

6) Stressing free will and reason, Socinus rejected the need for grace. He recognized that certain things in the Holy Writ could be above reason, but if they were contrary to reason, they must be rejected. Except for holy communion, which was the fulfillment of a direct order from Christ, all liturgical rites were considered unnecessary and even harmful. This applied also to baptism.

7) The earlier social radicalism of the Polish Brethren was mitigated by Socinus. He did not oppose the possession of serfs, but advised Christians to treat them well. He also counseled his followers not to take part in a war, or, if this was impossible, to refrain from the act of killing.

Although the doctrine of Socinus dominated the thinking of the Polish Brethren from about 1600, it was not imposed as an obligatory credo of the Minor Church. The principle of complete tolerance was observed in respect to the views of its members. Socinus himself stressed the relative insignificance of theology and the importance of moral life. The Socinian doctrine was elaborated in southern Poland, in Raków, the intellectual center of the Polish Brethren, who established an excellent academy there which gained international renown and attracted students from many European countries. Basically, it was an interdenominational school, though, as one might easily imagine, Roman Catholics were absent. The Rakovian school was active throughout the first decades of the seventeenth century, and its printing presses issued works of philosophy and theology.

The counteroffensive of the Roman Church was led by eminent *The Counter* clergymen, one of whom, a man of great learning and of iron will, *Reformation* Stanisław Hosius, we have already mentioned. In 1564 he brought the Jesuit Order to Poland. The Jesuits began their mission by founding schools to compete with Protestant institutions and placed their hopes in the young generation. Conscious of the victorious emergence of the vernacular, they realized that, to reach the public, only Polish could serve effectively and that in their school theaters they disposed of a powerful instrument of propaganda.

At the end of the sixteenth century, Protestants began to return gradually to Roman Catholicism; after 1600 the movement gathered speed. The Jesuits regarded the whole *Respublica* as a territory for their activity and established colleges even in the eastern parts of the state, largely inhabited by a population professing Eastern Orthodoxy. As faithful servants of the Vatican, the Jesuits steadily sought to bring Eastern Christians into the Roman fold. Famous for their adaptability to local conditions, they accomplished a union between the Roman and Orthodox Churches, the so-called Union of Brześć, in

1596. The Union was facilitated by the internal decay of the Orthodox Church and the related fact that the nobility of Lithuania and the Ukraine had switched in great numbers to Protestantism. The Greek Catholic Church, created by the Union, preserved the liturgy in Church Slavic as well as the freedom of priests to marry, but recognized the Pope as its head. The new Uniate Church was opposed by the plebeian segment of the Orthodox faithful. It has already been noted above that the higher classes had, for the most part, abandoned Eastern Orthodoxy. The Uniate denomination made great strides in Byelorussia and in the western parts of the Ukraine.

The role of the Jesuit Order cannot be reduced to a few epithets, as its policy underwent several phases. Its members made a considerable contribution to Polish literature, though, in general, the victory of the Counter Reformation marks the end of the "Golden Age."

Cultural Centers   Kraków continued to be the cultural center of Poland. Not only the capital, the seat of the royal court (until 1596), it was also the site of a university which attracted students from all over Poland as well as from the neighboring countries of Hungary, Germany, and even from Switzerland. Its role, however, diminished after the first half of the sixteenth century owing to the conservatism of the curriculum and to the competition of other schools.

A rich burgher class had arisen in southern Poland, not only in Kraków but also in other towns. If that class, mostly German in origin, had maintained its native tongue over several generations, now it thoroughly assimilated Polish. The burghers established many enterprises, such as mines, forges, paper mills, and, in Kraków, printing shops. The first books in Polish (also in Hungarian) were printed at the beginning of the sixteenth century. Another center of printing, Wilno, the capital of the Grand Duchy of Lithuania, catered to the needs of those who read the Eastern Slavic idiom. The gradual growth of the number of printing shops throughout the country as a whole was due mostly to the multidenominational character of the state, as each denomination issued its own polemical literature.

The Victory of the Vernacular   If the "Golden Age" of Polish literature has been so designated, it is because literature in the vernacular produced artistically valid works. The Polish language, previously scorned, now became a pliable instrument of serious literary expression and rapidly attained maturity. This did not mean the abandonment of Latin, which, in fact, dominated the early part of the period and later competed with Polish. Some authors used only Polish, some were bilingual, some clung to Latin, which they considered more dignified and more fitting for serious subjects. The transition from a largely medieval Polish to an elegant expression modeled on Latin classics occurred very swiftly. In some authors we find a mixture of many elements. Since the impact of the Baroque style was already felt at the end of the sixteenth century, medieval and Baroque sensibilities often converged in the works of that time.

Printed translations of the Bible, the outgrowth of rivalry between the denominations, made a significant contribution to the enrichment of the literary language. The first printed Bible, however, was not in Polish, but in Old Byelorussian. It was translated by Franciszek Skoryna from Polotsk, who had studied at the University of Kraków, where he received the degrees of Doctor of Liberal Arts and Doctor of Medicine. As a Roman Catholic, he was fiercely attacked both by Eastern Orthodox Churches and by Protestants. But he enjoyed special favor with the king, who protected him from his enemies. His Bible was printed between 1517 and 1525—first in Prague, then in Wilno. (Let us remember that the Bible of Martin Luther, an event in the history of German literature, appeared in 1522.) The first complete Bible in Polish was edited by a scholar and a Roman Catholic priest, Jan Leopolita, in 1561. The Calvinists translated and printed the so-called Bible of Brześć in 1563. Next came the Bible of the Arians, published in Nieśwież in 1572. The Eastern Orthodox Church was also busy providing its coreligionists with a Bible, not in the vernacular, but in Church Slavic, the liturgical language. This Bible was printed in 1589 thanks to the efforts of Prince Ostrogski in Ostróg (Volhynia). A new Catholic Bible in Polish, the work of a Jesuit, Jakub Wujek, was published in 1599 and has been used ever since by Roman Catholics as the standard version.

The vernacular was fostered not only by religious dispute. Since the political life in Poland was dominated by heated parliamentary debates, polemical literature, both in prose and in verse, flourished.

LITERATURE IN LATIN

Prose

Though Nicolaus Copernicus is far more than a literary figure, it is difficult not to mention him here. He belongs to a discussion of literature if only for the reason that he provoked innumerable controversies after his death.

Nicolaus Copernicus (Kopernik) (1473–1543)

Many words have been wasted on the absurd question of his ancestry—absurd because it results from the projection into the past of quite recent notions of nationality. Whether he was a Pole or a German is immaterial. The epoch in which Copernicus lived knew loyalties only toward the territory one inhabited. Though he came from a German-speaking burgher family, the language of his studies and written works was Latin. His forebears were settlers in Silesia—plebeians—

traders, mostly in copper ore. Some moved from Silesia to Kraków, and one of them, after he had amassed some money there, moved to Toruń on the borderland of East Prussia. The city of Toruń (Toronia, Thorn) was founded by the Teutonic Order, but nearly always sided with the king of Poland against the Order. Nicolaus' mother came from a noble family, Watzenrode, originally of Silesia, that had settled in Toruń. The influence of his uncle, a Watzenrode, bishop of Warmia, determined Nicolaus' career. Watzenrode maintained contacts with the leading intellectual figures in Poland and was a friend of Philippo Buonacorsi. He sent Nicolaus to study at the University of Kraków, and courses in astronomy taken there proved to be decisive for the future interests of the student. But having made Nicolaus a priest and then a canon in his diocese, Bishop Watzenrode planned a thorough education for his nephew. Thus, Nicolaus studied canon law in Bologna for many years, obtaining his doctor's degree in Ferrara (where the fees for final examinations were lower). Again, submitting to the wishes of his superiors, he studied medicine in Padua for several years. After his return to his native land Copernicus led a solitary life devoted to a multitude of occupations: he was an administrator and a lawyer; he practiced medicine, wrote treatises on money and trigonometry, and studied new methods of building fortifications. Simultaneously, he conducted astronomical and astrological observations in preparation for his life's work, *De Revolutionibus Orbium Coelestium*, which he was not eager to publish, as he feared to provoke a scandal. It appeared the year of his death, in 1543.

Some of his close friends turned Protestant, but Copernicus had evidenced no tendencies in that direction. The first attacks on him came from the Protestant side. Wilhelm Gnaphaeus, a Dutch refugee settled in Elbląg (Elbing), composed a comedy in Latin, entitled *Morosophus (A Stupid Sage)*, and staged it in the Protestant school theater in Elbląg. All understood that the funny character of an *astrologastrus* was a caricature of Copernicus. He was presented as a haughty, cold, and aloof man who not only dabbled in astrology and considered himself inspired by God, but was rumored to have written a large work which was rotting in a coffer. Elsewhere, Protestants were the first to react to the news about Copernicus' theory. Melanchthon wrote:

> Some people believe that it is excellent and correct to work out a thing as absurd as did that Sarmatian astronomer who moves the earth and stops the sun. Indeed, wise rulers should have curbed such light-mindedness.

And Martin Luther wrote:

> There is talk of a new astrologer who wanted to prove that the earth moves and revolves and not the firmament or the sky, not the sun and the moon. . . .

Such are today human follies: whoever considers himself wise has to conceive something of his own. And that he does is supposedly the best. That fool wants to overthrow all the art of Astronomy! But as the Holy Writ shows Joshua ordered the sun to stop and not the earth.

Up to our day Polish libertarian and democratic movements have invoked the name of Andrzej Frycz Modrzewski as that of their patron. Among the humanists following the inspiration of Erasmian thought, he was the most eminent figure, and his writings, so striking in the breadth of their horizons, were quite exceptional for his time. *Andrzej Frycz Modrzewski (1503–1572)*

By origin he was a poor nobleman. His father held a hereditary headship in a small town of southern Poland, Wolborz. Modrzewski attended the University of Kraków and, after completing his studies, entered the service of Bishop Łaski as a young cleric, where in the chancery of the diocese he gained valuable experience sitting in on diets, synods, and observing all layers of society in the tribunals. His contacts with the powerful Łaski family of ecclesiastics and diplomats determined his subsequent fate and enabled him to travel and study abroad. The Bishop's nephew, Jan Łaski (Johannes à Lasco), also a priest, became Frycz's protector. They were bound by their common interest in new religious trends. Łaski sent Frycz to study in Wittenberg. There he lived at the house of Melanchthon, one of the luminaries of German Protestantism, and, in fact, acted as an emissary between Melanchthon and Łaski, sending to the latter information in ciphered letters. Since Łaski had bought the library of Erasmus, leaving its usage to the scholar, he directed his employee, Frycz, to Basel after Erasmus' death in 1536, ordering him to pack and send the library to Poland. A few years later, Jan Łaski broke publicly with Roman Catholicism and went abroad, organizing Reformed Churches in Germany and England, suffering persecutions at the hands of Lutherans as well as Catholics, and only returning to Poland at an advanced age. Frycz did not follow his friend and benefactor along this path, and never officially changed his faith, although he interpreted dogma very freely and in theology went even further than did some of the Calvinists. True to the spirit of Erasmus, he was a persistent mediator. He deplored the rift within the Church and constantly hoped that the Vatican would retreat from its intransigence. In this he shared the illusions of many Renaissance thinkers who had lost their touch with medieval philosophy and therefore underestimated the seriousness and depth of theological disputes. Not only were his attempts to mediate between Protestants and Catholics in vain. During his last years his views closely approached those of the Arians, and at that time he endeavored, without success, to prevent a rupture between the Arians and Calvinists.

For several years Frycz served as secretary in the royal chancery and took part in diplomatic missions to Augsburg, the Netherlands, and Prague. Throughout his life he was an intellectual committed to the defense of many causes, which were for him a matter of moral principles. He combatted, for example, the incongruity between punishments and crimes in Poland: a murder, if committed by a nobleman, was less severely punished than if committed by a burgher or peasant. The first treatise published by Frycz was devoted to that question. Also a partisan of complete religious tolerance, he wrote: "Confession of faith enforced by violence is not in accordance with truth nor is it pleasing to God, nor can one consider such a work good which was accomplished against a man's will." Living through the period of religious strife as through a tragedy, he tried to prove that the quarreling camps merely used different words to say the same thing. He saw all those who believed in Christ as belonging to one universal Church and in some of his writings even went so far as to acknowledge a certain moral superiority of the Eastern Church over the Roman Church. His disinterested search for truth and his tenacity in the face of violent attacks from every side were the cause of his many personal misfortunes. He escaped imprisonment and death thanks only to the personal protection of King Sigismund August.

His most important work, *De Republica Emendanda* (*On the Reform of the State*), is considered as the first treatise in Europe to discuss problems of the State as a whole. The first three books ("On Mores," "On Laws," and "On War") appeared in Kraków in 1551. The opposition of the Polish clergy prevented publication of the entire work, which included books on the Church and on schools. It appeared in a complete and unabridged edition in Basel, Switzerland, in 1554. Having provoked vivid interest in humanist circles both in Poland and abroad, it was soon translated into Spanish, German, and French, becoming a target for attacks especially from French Catholic political writers.

De Republica Emendanda is a sort of codification of those democratic ideas which found their radical expression in the social teachings of the Arians. It is a thorough investigation of the essence of the Christian State, its ideal structure, and the rights and duties of its citizens. The main theses can be summarized as follows:

a) "Kings are established for the people and not the people for the kings."

b) Laws should be the same for all estates. (Frycz did not question, of course, the division of society into gentry, burghers, and peasants.) Laws should be ratified by a representation of all citizens, and not by the gentry alone. All estates should be equal before the law, since all are useful to the State, each in its own way. The State should treat the burgher and the peasant as free citizens. The privileged position of the gentry is a usurpation.

c) A good judiciary system implies three parties: the judge, the plaintiff, and the accused; therefore, a nobleman cannot be a judge of his peasant. A State tribunal is the proper place, notwithstanding the social status of the people involved.

d) Nobody should avoid public service. Offices should be held not only by noblemen but also by burghers and peasants, and personal qualifications should constitute the only criterion. Offices cannot be hereditary. Special supervisors appointed by the king should exert control over the local administration.

e) All the citizens should work: "In any case it was made a holy thing by the Divine Word that everybody should eat his bread in toil and in the sweat of his brow, and whoever does not work let him not eat." Appointed "keepers of the poor" should assist those who are unable to work or who, for one reason or another, cannot earn their living.

f) The peasant should hold the land he toils. He should pay rent to his lord in an amount strictly defined by law.

g) Education is a great blessing and the mainstay of the Christian State. Schools should be controlled by the State and instruction given not in Latin but in the native tongue. (It is obvious that by stressing these points, Frycz is speaking out against the clergy and its hold over education.)

h) The Church should be national and independent of Rome. It should be ruled by a synod composed of bishops elected by the population. Celibacy of the clergy should be abolished.

i) Instead of calling the gentry to arms in the event of war, the State should possess a standing army recruited not only from the gentry but also from among burghers and peasants. Relations between States should be based on international law. As the only sure means of preventing war, international treaties should be binding.

It is clear that, for Frycz, the State should be the guardian of Christian ethics. His ideal State is a utopia reflecting the temper of the Renaissance man. (Let us remember that the *Utopia* of Sir Thomas More appeared in 1516.) Frycz, however, did not treat his proposals as impossible to realize, even if they did collide with the interests of the ruling gentry. He seemed to be an addict of intellectual optimism. Unshakable in his belief that an appeal to reason was sufficient, he was a true humanist in that he identified a well-conducted argument with its embodiment in reality.

Of the number of authors using both Latin and Polish one figure

¶ A notable example of Gods vengeance, vppon a murdering king. Written in Latine by Martine Cromer the writer of the hiſtorie of Polonia, and is to be founde in the xxxvii. page of the ſayde hiſtorie as it was printed at Baſile by Oporine in the yeare of oure Lorde 1555. wyth Charles the Emperours priuilege. Truely tranſlated according to the Latine.

⟫ Ʃmprinted at London by Iohn Daye ouer Alderſgate.

¶ And are to be ſolde ready ſtitched for a penny.

The title page of a story in English translation ("The Legend of King Popiel") taken from Marcin Kromer's history of Poland (sixteenth century).

Marcin Kromer (1512–1589) should be mentioned here, that is, Marcin Kromer. A burgher by origin, from the sub-Carpathian region, and a man of high humanist culture, well-trained in Latin and Greek, he was a clergyman, a staunch enemy of the Reformation and a formidable anti-Protestant polemist. He is the author of *Conversations of a Courtier and a Monk*, in Polish. His history of Poland (1555), a sort of textbook, based mostly on Długosz, as well as a much-read description of Poland (1577), dealing with its geography, its institutions, and its customs, were written in Latin.

Wawrzyniec Goślicki (1530–1607) A nobleman educated in Italy, Wawrzyniec Goślicki, during his stay in Padua, wrote (in Latin) a book based upon his meditations on the Polish political system, *De Optimo Senatore*, published in

Venice in 1568. Later on, he followed an ecclesiastical and diplomatic career, becoming bishop of Poznań and the holder of many honors at the royal court. His work is another example of the Renaissance faith in the strength of argument. He draws a picture of the ideal statesman, thus making an appeal to reason as the dominating quality of man's soul. Perhaps this explains the response his book found in rationalistic England of the seventeenth and eighteenth centuries. A complete English translation appeared in 1733 during the era of Sir Robert Walpole as *The Accomplished Senator: in two books written originally in Latin, by Lawrence Grimald Gozliski, Senator and Chancellor of Poland and Bishop of Posna or Posen.* The translator, Mr. Oldisworth, in his delication to the Dukes of Beaufort and Argyll, the Earl of Oxford, and Sir Robert Walpole, explains his reasons for translating the book, traces similarities between the Polish and British parliamentary systems, and praises Goślicki for presenting a perfect equilibrium between power and liberty, between "the prerogatives of the crown and the interests of the people." In his introduction, where he shows an excellent knowledge of Polish historical works written in Latin, he says, among other things:

The POLISH Nation had a Full and Free SENATE long before our PARLIAMENTS were possessed of all Those Rights and Privileges in which their Liberty and Authority are at present happily Established. Thus much we learn from older Best and more Approved Historians. And on this Account it fell much sooner in their Way than in ours, to make themselves acquainted with the Nature, Dignity and Extent of the SENATORIAL OFFICE. Of this they set us a very Early Precedent. But many years had not passed, before GOZLISKI'S Book, in which LOYALTY and LIBERTY are so well Tempered and Reconciled, and the WHOLE DUTY of the Senator is so fully and so clearly explained, was happily brought over and imported into ENGLAND where we never yet had any Particular Tract or Essay written upon this Important Subject by any of our own Countrymen: For the *METHODUS TENENDI PARLIAMENTUM*, and some few Books to the same purpose, do by no means enter into the SENATORIAL CHARACTER, in the Manner GOZLISKI has done; who seems entirely to have exhausted this Important Subject. In the REIGN of Queen ELIZABETH, when the Prerogative ran high; and soon after the Decease of CROMWELL, when the Pretensions to Liberty ran altogether as high, and were flying out into Anarchy and Confusion, some few EXTRACTS of This Work were printed in the ENGLISH Language, but so miserably Maimed and Incorrect, that they Died away insensibly, and were soon Lost, as containing only some few Popular Scraps and Fragments, altogether in Favour of the REPUBLICAN SCHEME; whilst all that was said of the LEGAL POWERS AND PREROGATIVES of the CROWN was willfully concealed and Suppressed.

The translator, being a Protestant, feels a little uneasy about his author's Roman Catholicism, but he finds a way out of the dilemma:

The Truth is the CHURCH of ROME always had a much better Interest in POLAND, than the Court of Rome. The State took Care to maintain its Rights in a much better Manner, than was done in many other POPISH Countries; and such has been the Spirit of Liberty in POLAND, that the Protestant Religion hath met with much better Treatment There, than in any Nation whatsoever which hath all along been in Communion with the SEE of ROME. It is true, that GOZLISKI has openly declared for the EXTIRPATION of Heresy: But then by HERESY he means an avowed Revolt from the ESTABLISHED CHURCH whereby the Public Peace may be Threatened and Invaded: As to DISSENSION, he does not so much as mention it; and we are at Liberty to imagine, that He, who allows of Differences in Lesser Matters relating to Policy, was of the same Opinion in Matters of Religion. That this is no wild Conjecture of my own Invention, the following Historical Fact is of very material Evidence. During the Reign of SIGISMUND the Second, when GOZLISKI was in Full Truth and Power, the NOBLES and GENTRY of Poland were permitted to send their Children to the PROTESTANT SCHOOLS and UNIVERSITIES of GERMANY: by which means they brought the REFORMATION into their own Country, where it spread itself far and near, and might possibly have prevailed in a more extraordinary manner, had not ARIANISM, and its Twin monster SOCINIANISM, taken advantage of this Indulgent Grant, and under Colour and Coverty thereof, made their Way into the North, threatening Ruin and Desolation to the Common Faith of CHRISTIANITY. The POLONI FRATRES have dressed out These two HERESIES with all the artificial GLOSS that Good Language and Fallacious Way of Reasoning possibly let them; whilst they carefully concealed the Monstrous ERRORS, Absurdities, and Blasphemies of their Fellow-Sectaries, who had written upon the same Subject, and of which there is a very Full and Authentick Collection to be met with in the Works of BROCKMAN, a very Learned Professor of the UNIVERSITY OF COPENHAGEN. Upon the breaking out of these Heresies, some Restraints were thought to be Wholesome and Seasonable, if not absolutely Necessary; and the Papists made their advantage of the Critical Juncture.

Poetry

Andrzej Krzycki (1482–1537) At the end of the fifteenth century, poets imbued with the spirit of Humanism began producing a secular poetry in Latin. Of the few who were to enjoy considerable popularity the most celebrated was Andrzej Krzycki. He came from a noble family, studied in Bologna, and, advancing rapidly in his ecclesiastical career—first as a canon of Poznań, later bishop, then archbishop—he combined his clerical duties, for a time, with those of a diplomat and a secretary to King

Sigismund I and Queen Bona Sforza. He wrote occasional poetry on marriages of monarchs, on military victories, on the life of the court, but was at his best in short epigrammatic poems, usually on love and often quite frivolous—an attitude not uncommon for a Renaissance dignitary of the Church. To give an example of his love lyrics, he says, addressing a certain Lydia:

> You struck me, maiden, with a white snowball,
> Yet the snow was not cold, it preserved so much fire!
> That fire inflames me, a strangely pleasant fire,
> As the snowball was rolled by your hands.
> How could I succeed in escaping love if fire is
>   engendered in me by a snowball?
> And your red lips entice me—
> I shall not escape; I shall be on fire.

Krzycki, of course, modeled his poems on Horace, Catullus, and Martial, and they are interesting mostly as examples of dexterity in handling conventions. From his epigrams on political subjects, let us quote one on the Teutonic Order:

> It is known there are three crosses of different colors.
> Every human condition wears a different cross.
> There is a red cross justly called by Christ's name
> Since the blood of Christ gave to it its red color.
> There is a white cross which befell to the good thief
> Whose sins were washed away by a few words
> And there is a black cross of the thief on the left side;
> Not without reason, the Prussian monk wears it on his cloak.

Jan Dantyszek (1485–1548)

The pen name of Jan Dantyszek (Dantiscus), another poet quite well known in humanistic circles, indicates his birthplace. A burgher from Danzig (Gdańsk) whose family name was von Höffen, he studied at Kraków University, served for many years as a royal secretary and diplomat, traveled extensively in Europe, and was at the end of his life the bishop of Warmia. He was said to have been the most widely educated among the Latin humanist poets. His voluminous literary output reveals a strong Virgilian influence. A large number of those many poems were devoted to patriotic and religious themes.

Klemens Janicki (1516–1543)

In spite of a very small literary output, Klemens Janicki (Janicius) succeeded in creating his own legend, which persists in Polish letters. Son of a peasant from the neighborhood of Gniezno in Greater Poland, he finished a local school, and, being very gifted, he found protectors who sent him to a college in Poznań, then to the University of Padua, where he received a doctor's degree in philosophy and won the title of Poet Laureate. After he returned to Poland, he received a parish, but an incurable illness took his life at an early age. His poetry, modeled upon Ovid, Propertius, and Tibullus and written in exceptionally pure Latin, is nonetheless not imitative. On the contrary, it is very moving in its personal tone and autobiographical detail. It is an elegiac, melancholy poetry of a man aware that his dreams of literary fame were coming to nothing because of approaching death. In his elegy "On Myself for Posterity" he addresses the future reader:

> If anybody when I am in my grave
> Will desire to learn something about me,
> Let him read this page
> Which upon myself I wrote in the time of my sorrow.
> Beyond the swamps of Żnin there is a village
> Called by the name of Januszek
> By the road which the Polish kings used to take when going
> from Gniezno to Prussia.
> There my father, a villager,
> Labored honestly the soil of our grandfathers
> And there, when the plague
> Destroying our region took his children,
> He found a solace
> In seeing me born into God's world.

He describes his father's anxiety to give him an education and how after attending an elementary school he found himself at a college:

> There I heard the name of Virgil
> And the name of my master Ovidius Naso.
> There I admired the poets so much that I worshipped them
> like gods.

He relates his first triumphs as a poet, his pecuniary troubles interfering with his work, his finding a protector in the person of Krzycki and, following his benefactor's death, in another, who sent him to Italy. He describes himself as a man of good stature but weakened by illness, his face gay, blushing easily—a man inclined to outbursts of anger and enthusiasm, with many enemies and few devoted friends, of a tender disposition, moved easily by human miseries, and despising war: "Many considered me, unjustly, as a man too preoccupied with women, either because I have always liked music, songs, and jokes or because since my early youth I have been writing love poems." Until his twentieth year he drank nothing stronger than water, and to this he ascribes his illness (dropsy). He says farewell to his friends and thanks especially his Polish physician, Dr. Antoninus (a well-known personality to whom Erasmus of Rotterdam had dedicated one of his books). He regards the poems of his youth as childish and deplores the lack of time to write what he feels he should write. He asks his friends to put the following words on his tomb:

> Alien to hope, fear, and sorrow
> Here I repose under the coffin lid.
> Here only, I live a true life
> And God be with you, my earthly existence.

His poems written in Italy were also highly personal; for instance, in a letter in verse, a form very popular among the humanists, he starts with political news from Italy but soon passes to the real subject: the joy of being in Italy. The poem is a hymn of rapture to the beauty of Italian nature, art, and poetry. Perhaps an anxiety lest his stipend be withdrawn and he be recalled to Poland too quickly dictated the declaration of attachment to his own country which follows:

> Not that I am sad because I am a child of Sarmatia.
> No, I am proud of my Sarmatian birth.
> This world is large and filled with beauty
> But there is no land above my native land.
> I wonder at Italy, I admire Poland sincerely;
> Here I live by wonder, there by my love.
> I belong legitimately to Poland,
> Here, I have my quarter; there, are my gods.

Because poetry was considered a proper instrument to deal with any subject, even with one which later rightfully came to belong to the domain of prose, we have some curious examples of descriptive poems in Latin. Mikołaj Hussowski from Lithuania, possibly a son of one of the royal Masters of the Hunt, being a priest and a protégé of a high dignitary, found himself in Rome when his patron was appointed ambassador to the Vatican. The Pope, Leo X, was a passionate hunter and took an interest in the stories which Poles and Lithuanians related about hunting in their countries. Hussowski, a skillful versifier, was ordered by his superior to write a poem for the Pope on the most exotic of game animals, namely, Lithuanian bison. A curious treatise in verse thus came into being, in which Hussowski displays a thorough knowledge of Lithuanian forests, habits of bison, methods of hunting it, etc. This was the first work of natural science to deal with the subject, since the European bison had long been extinct in other parts of Europe.

A Poem on Bison

Most of the poets of this time were bilingual, and they produced works both in Latin and in Polish. We will deal with them when discussing particular authors in the chapters devoted to poetry in the vernacular. If the Golden Age of Polish literature saw a rapid growth of works in Polish, the victory of the Counter Reformation soon brought about a comeback for Latin, the language beloved by the powerful Jesuit Order. The last poet to use Latin exclusively was a Jesuit, Maciej Kazimierz Sarbiewski (1595–1640), known all over Europe under the name of Casimire.

LITERATURE IN POLISH

The New Book Market

With the invention of print and the appearance of publishing enterprises, the broadest possible base of potential readers was sought (for obvious commercial reasons). To reach the average public, unschooled in Latin, it became desirable to publish books in the vernacular which were interesting, amusing, and familiar both in their outlook and in their literary motifs. The Middle Ages possessed a great number of works circulating as manuscripts. These were mostly fantastic stories, chivalrous romances, or collections of anecdotes and extraordinary happenings centered around half-legendary figures such as Alexander the Great or the Holy Prince, Josaphat, and his wise mentor, Barlaam (both of whom became saints of the Roman Catholic Church, though "Josaphat" was none other than Buddha). These legendary stories, like *Barlaam and Josaphat*, often originated in the Orient but were transmitted from one culture to another altered and embellished. Drawing on this rich heritage, enterprising printers in Poland commissioned translations and adaptations of medieval romances. From the very beginning of the sixteenth century such books were extremely popular in Poland. They constantly reappeared in new editions, sometimes ending their career only in the twentieth century as pulp literature sought after at country fairs.

Works borrowed from the West migrated from Poland to the domains of the Eastern Slavs, including Muscovy, where they often encountered other versions of the same stories transmitted through Byzantium. The wandering of plots and literary devices, sometimes traceable as far back as several thousands of years, forms a fascinating subject for scholars. In Poland, clerks, primarily of plebeian origin, were the translators and adapters of these romances. Since, in addition, a large number of the buyers were found in the towns, these books can be ranged with bourgeois literature.

Biernat of Lublin (c. 1465– after 1529) Biernat of Lublin was the first Polish author to write solely in the vernacular. He was a burgher by origin, and, as a priest, he spent his life in the service of various noble families. Scant information is available as to his biography, perhaps because his principal work was placed on the Index of Forbidden Books by the Catholic Church. He was looked upon with suspicion as a "protestant" writer—before Martin Luther was even heard of. His writings stemmed from the Hussite tradition. His native town, Lublin, was, at the end of the fifteenth century, the scene of numerous trials of heretics who were accused of upholding Hus's doctrines, namely, a return to communion given in two forms (bread and wine) and the belief that transubstantiation could not take place if the priest celebrating the mass was in the state of sin. It is also possible, as some scholars maintain, that Biernat fell under the influence of German Anabaptists. He was quite radical in his fight against the death penalty: "Since God gives life to man, so only God can take it, not the State." His theological views show that he was following the path taken a little later by Luther. In a letter written by him in 1515 we read: "It seems to me that judgments of the Lord are a great abyss, and beyond the Gospels we should recognize no rules, because they are vain and unsure and change with the passage of years. . . . And even if simple faith could easily preserve us from those troubles, suppose we believe in what those who inherit the seat of Moses teach us, yet human reason cannot be stopped in its search for truth and in its striving to embrace truth as its proper object." These sentences seem very far from a medieval outlook, yet when read in the context of Biernat's creative work, the quotations regain their just proportions.

Biernat was the author of one of the first books printed in Polish, *Paradise of the Soul* (*Raj Duszny*, 1513), a prayer book adapted from Latin and reprinted later in many editions. His main work was written in verse: *The Life of Aesop the Frygian, a Virtuous Sage, Together with His Proverbs* (*Żywot Ezopa Fryga, mędrca obyczajnego, z przypowieściami jego*). So immense was its popularity that the first edition was literally read out of existence, and we can only speculate about its date (probably 1522). Aesop, as a Greek author of fables from the sixth century B.C., was probably a mythical figure, and his fables, actually folklore (i.e., the product of a collective authorship), were still alive throughout the Europe of the Middle Ages. Animals used as allegorical figures to exemplify human behavior belonged to an old tradition of literary devices and were extensively used, for instance, in the French *fabliaux*. The very term "Aesopian language," suggesting unpleasant truths about the powerful but clothed in an innocent disguise, testifies to the strength of the tradition. The legend of Aesop himself, the slave who, thanks to his wit, liberated himself from his less intelligent master, was revitalized in the Renaissance owing to a translation of a Greek story into Latin by an Italian humanist, Ranuccio D'Arezzo, that was published in Milan in 1471. The work belongs to the order of those fantastic romances already mentioned. It is a kind of humorous fable originating in the Near East.

published in Milan in 1471. The work belongs to the order of those fantastic romances already mentioned. It is a kind of humorous fable originating in the Near East.

Although Biernat's poem is an adaptation from D'Arezzo's Latin version, the addition of the Polish writer's own views lends a new combativeness. Aesop, in his poem, is a hunchbacked dwarf, and the relish with which Biernat describes his ugliness can be explained as a reaction to medieval idealization—a tendency noticeable both in art and in hagiographic literature. The reader cannot avoid thinking of the dwarfs and giants appearing some years later in France under the pen of Rabelais. Aesop the Slave's ugliness seems to bring into sharper relief those other qualities which make him superior to his master, Xantus. He displays an earthy, practical wisdom and a great deal of wit. The conclusion is obvious: a good mind is worth more than noble birth or good looks. In the encounter between slave (plebeian) and master (nobleman, prelate), the latter makes a fool of himself. The poem is, therefore, a kind of manifesto confirming what we know from elsewhere of Biernat's views. It is composed of little scenes contrived to show different approaches to the same events on the parts of Aesop and Xantus. For instance, when both are confronted with the problem of why wild plants are more luxurious, Xantus ascribes this to the will of God, while Aesop challenges him: "Every shepherd would know how to answer in such a way. Whoever throws everything on God does not explain any cause." Thus, observation, the foreshadowing of empirical science, is praised. Attacks on Scholasticism are not lacking either. Aesop symbolizes the simplicity of folk wisdom: "Since with simple words we understand truth more quickly." Altogether, the *Life of Aesop* is the story of a man of lower origin who makes good and, thus, provides the reader with the sly satisfaction of seeing the powerful of this world turned to ridicule. The *Life of Aesop* owed its popularity, of course, to its coarse, not too fastidious—in fact, quite medieval—humor, which appealed to the tastes of the average public. Standard devices for obtaining humorous effects were used, such as words relating to physiological functions and attacks on women. As we all know, antifeminism has been, for centuries, a basis for popular jokes.

The second part of the poem consists of fables presumably invented by Aesop. These fables form the common property of many nations, but their literary interest resides in the large number of Polish proverbs introduced by Biernat. Thus, the second part of the poem is the first collection of Polish proverbs in existence.

Another poem of Biernat's, *The Dialogue of Palinurus with Charon* (*Dialog Palinura z Charonem*), is also an adaptation from a prose dialogue written in Latin. Palinurus, who in his lifetime had been a helmsman on Aeneas' boat, carries on a conversation in Hades with the ferryman on the river Styx. Curiously enough, Charon passes on to him all that one need know about the wickedness of the rich and the powerful who scorn and oppress ordinary people.

Biernat of Lublin, so widely read in his lifetime, was, after his death, forgotten and for a long while only mentioned by some Protestants historians as a representative of the pre-Protestant movement. Perhaps this fate of his can be explained by his medieval language. Within a few decades of the sixteenth century, Polish made such strides that there was no use for Biernat's style, even though it had vigor, especially in his fables. Today, Biernat is recognized as an important link in the development of Polish verse. He was still using the "imperfectly syllabic" form of verse, i.e., the eight-syllable line is interspersed with lines of nine and even eleven syllables. Biernat is a transitional figure; he belongs both to the history of "pulp literature" and to the history of poetry.

Another figure somewhat similar to Aesop made his appearance at the same time. In European literature he was called "Marchlandus" or "Morolph" or "Markol" or "Marchult" and he comes in all probability from Jewish legends about King Solomon. Marchult was represented sometimes as a helper, sometimes as an antagonist, of King Solomon. Through the Apocrypha he entered medieval manuscripts and became the hero of a Latin work which received its final form in Germany. Marchult, like Aesop, is ugly, vulgar, and

Marchołt

Illustration from *Conversations which Wise King Solomon had with the Coarse and Bawdy Marchołt*, 1535 edition.

obese, and always outwits King Solomon in this collection of fantastic anecdotes written in prose full of obscene puns and boorish humor. A Polish translation (by Jan from Koszyczki) appeared in 1521 as *Conversations which Wise King Solomon had with the Coarse and Bawdy Marchołt* (*Rozmowy, które miał Salomon mądry z Marchołtem grubym a sprośnym*). Marchołt (Marchult acquired a new name) became so widely known in Poland that the name has survived up to our time as a synonym for a jolly, clever man of low origin, a glutton, a lusty drunkard, and a wit, even reappearing in the works of some twentieth-century poets (Kasprowicz, Tuwim). A strong element of parody runs throughout the work, as for example in the genealogy of Marchołt, who comes from twelve generations of strangely named country fools and twelve generations of harlots. As is proper to this literary genre, jokes on the subject of women, sometimes very indecent, are plentiful. Marchołt always finds a way to extricate himself from even the most difficult of situations. For instance, as he is about to be hanged, he asks as a last favor that he may be allowed to choose the tree on which to hang. Since no tree suits his taste he escapes death. (Both Aesop and Marchołt foreshadow the "good soldier Schweik.")

Sowiźrzał   A later addition to this company of popular heroes was Eulenspiegel. A literary character of Flemish and German origin, he was a wandering artisan, a scapegrace, who journeyed from town to town playing tricks on rich burghers, tradesmen, princes, etc. The knaveries of Till Eulenspiegel (known in English as Owlglass, and in French as Espiègle) were published in book form in Germany in 1510. The first translation was made into Polish around 1530. The work has a hero called Sowiźrzał whose adventures were treated by many writers in Poland. More and more pranks were ascribed to Sowiźrzał, and in this way a large body of anonymous literature arose known as *literatura sowiźrzalska*, which was closely allied with that of the *żaki* of Kraków and its environs. (*Żak* was a name, derived from *Diak, Diaconus*, given to the students of Kraków University.) Sowiźrzał reached Russia from Poland quite late, at the end of the eighteenth century, and his name underwent there an amusing modification: the adventures of Sowiźrzał became the adventures of Sovjest'dral, which can be roughly translated as "damned be conscience." (*"Pokhozhdeniya ozhivshogo novogo uveselitelnogo shuta i velikogo v djelach lyubovnykh pluta Sovjest-drala bolshogo nosa, perevod z polskogo i drugich yazykov."*) There were four editions of *Sovjest'dral* in the eighteenth century.

In Poland, humorous stories, anecdotes, and jokes were drawn from many sources, not only from *Eulenspiegel* but from the Latin works of humanists and from the *Decameron* of Boccaccio. Collections of such varied stories were called *facezie* in Italy, whence the Polish word of the same meaning. The most popular collection of this sort, *Facecje Polskie*, was compiled at the end of the sixteenth century and appeared in many editions throughout the next century.

Polish versions of pseudohistorical romances dealt, for instance, with the fantastic adventures of Alexander the Great, which were well known also to the Eastern Slavs, to whom they penetrated from Byzantium. *A Story on the Destruction of the City of Troy* (1563), which is a compilation from various Latin sources, recounts events not to be found in Homer: beginning with the expedition of the Argonauts at the time of the Greek abduction of Medea, it passes on to the abduction of Helen, the arrival of Greek messengers to Troy demanding her delivery, the war of Troy, and the subsequent wanderings of Ulysses and Aeneas. The work, as befitted a popular romance, is tinged with strong antifeminism: all misfortunes are due to women.

Attila, another half-legendary figure, appears in a translation of a heroic tale written in Latin by a Hungarian bishop: *A Story of the Affairs of Attila, King of Hungary.*

The heroine of a chivalrous romance, Melusine, attracted quite a following among Polish readers. The romance, born in medieval France, was translated and adapted in many languages. The figure of Melusine was derived, perhaps, from "Mère Lusine," presumably ancestress of the aristocratic family, de Lusignan. Like the heroines of many fairy tales, she was a half-human, half-animal creature. Once a week (on Saturday) this beautiful maiden was transformed into a mermaid and would spend the whole day in a spring. When she married, she gave birth to many children but forbade her husband to see her on Saturdays. Unfortunately, informed by malicious gossipers that she was betraying him, he was induced to spy on her. His decision led to many misfortunes. The romance is lavish in its descriptions of duels with giants and dragons, etc. It reappeared in many editions and could still be found in our century on bookstands at country fairs. From Poland, the romance wandered to Russia.

The name "Melusine" came to denote a chandelier of a special kind, secured to the ceiling by an ornament in the form of a mermaid. Beautiful, not overly strict girls were also called "melusines" in Polish.

Among the abundant fiction of a religious character, mostly embroidering upon lives of biblical figures or the saints, the story of Adam and Eve after their exile from Paradise is an interesting example. Even rather touching is the account of the difficulties encountered by our first parents in their struggle against new tempta-

A Story of Troy

A Story of Attila

Melusine

Adventures of Adam and Eve

tions of the devil. As a penance assigned by Adam (to Eve and to himself), they remained hungry for many days. In fact, for thirty days, Eve was supposed to stand on a stone in the Tigris in water up to her neck, while Adam followed suit in the river Jordan for a little longer (forty days). But the devil, in the shape of an angel, told Eve that God had already forgiven them, so there was no reason to persist. Particularly moving are the last moments: Adam and Eve die surrounded by fifteen thousand descendants (not counting female descendants). Theologically, one chapter is quite enigmatic; in it, Satan, asked by Adam and Eve why he persecutes them, tells the circumstances of his fall. He had been one of the sons of God, but when man was created, in the image and likeness of God, and he was asked to pay homage to this inferior creature, he rebelled, insisting on his own priority. Punished for his refusal, he has, since that moment, been tempting man. Thus, according to the story, Satan's fall and the impetus for his subsequent activity came about through a jealous rivalry with man, an interpretation advanced in the first centuries of Christianity by St. Ireneus, Tertullian, and St. Cyprian but subsequently abandoned by the Church.

Encyclopedias and Picturesque Reports

Marcin Bielski
(1495-1575)
Marcin Bielski (1495-1575), a nobleman by birth, who enjoyed a long career as a courtier and as a soldier, was always a passionate bibliophile. In his mature years he dedicated himself to literature. To maintain close touch with the intellectual trends of his time he settled in Kraków and became a burgher in his habits. There, in his library, he led a laborious life as a writer. When he later settled on his landed estate, he was more concerned with books than with agriculture. His voracity as a reader was not accompanied by a creative talent, but he did possess a great gift for gathering and compiling information. From innumerable books in Latin and Czech, from manuscripts in Church Slavic and "Ruthenian," he drew data for his voluminous work in Polish, *A Chronicle of the Whole World* (*Kronika wszystkiego świata*), which is a kind of encyclopedia dealing with geography and history, including that of India, Egypt, Greece, and Rome. Certainly, Bielski was not a scholar in the modern sense. His encyclopedia can be placed on the border line between the popular imaginings we have seen in the "pulp literature" of the time and scholarly investigation. Let us say in his defense that the European mind of the sixteenth century did not distinguish clearly between myth and historical truth, especially when it turned toward exotic regions. In any case, Bielski's *Chronicle*, published in 1551, became the first Polish work on universal history. A considerable part of it is dedicated to the geography

and history of neighboring countries, like Bohemia, Hungary, the domains of the Eastern Slavs, and Turkey. Here, of course, Bielski writes as a historian and not as a collector of legends. In a separate section, he deals with the history of Poland. Thus, he also became the first to write a history of Poland in the vernacular, since up to that time, all books on that subject had been written in Latin. These, of course, he used as sources for his descriptions of past events. Bielski's capacity for work and his intellectual curiosity are astonishing, and his apirations betoken the scope of a Renaissance mind. Although a Roman Catholic, he bore pronounced sympathies for the Reformation and was often ranged with Protestant writers. In some of his works, elements can be found which recall the popular literature of medieval origin with which we dealt in the previous section. Before he wrote the *Chronicle,* he had published *Lives of Philosophers* (1535), an adaptation of a Czech work, itself an adaptation from Latin. In that book, because of his colloquial language, he resembles Biernat of Lublin or the translator of Marchołt.

Bielski was a moralist and imparted this quality not only to the *Chronicle* but also to his other writings. These include a morality play and some verse satires in which he ridiculed the vices of public life: cupidity, oppression of the peasants, and dishonest judges. Not drawn with great sympathy, his realistic pictures of burgher life in Kraków reflect his loyalty to his own class, the gentry.

The Union of Lublin in 1569, which joined Lithuania and Poland, drew public attention toward regions still little known to the Poles. Matys Stryjkowski, a native of Mazovia, was fascinated by Lithuania, which still preserved traces of paganism in folk rituals and customs. He wrote a work to which he gave the traditional title of "chronicle": *A Chronicle of Poland, Lithuania, Samogitia, and of all Rus',* 1582 (Samogitia was a northern province of Lithuania). Not only a history, it is a picturesque, firsthand report on local deities, rituals, and folk customs in Lithuania. The author obviously was fond of that country of primeval forests, lakes, and marshes as well as sensitive to the memory of its medieval battles with the Teutonic Knights. This explains why, later on, Romantic writers like the poets Mickiewicz and Słowacki, together with their novelist contemporary, Kraszewski, often exploited motifs taken from Stryjkowski's *Chronicle.*

Matys Stryjkowski (1547-1582)

Łukasz Górnicki
(1527-1603)

Perhaps Łukasz Górnicki occupies such a high place in Polish literature less because of the intrinsic value of his literary achievements than because of his significance for literary history. He was the first to publish a work in an elegant, sophisticated Polish prose, thus distinguishing himself from those who wrote to satisfy a larger public.

A burgher by origin, he received a thorough humanist education in Italy, translated Seneca, and acquired renown through his verse writing. His literary connections and his service at the royal court won him a title of nobility and a fortune. Engaged in serious pursuit of the Renaissance ideal, he spent many years on a work through which he desired to effect a grafting of Italian manners onto Polish cultural and intellectual life. Great effort was poured into his adaptation of the famous Renaissance work by Baldassare Castiglione, *Il Corteggiano*. Górnicki's work, entitled *The Polish Courtier* (*Dworzanin polski*), appeared in 1566. The original, written in the form of conversations between learned gentlemen and ladies gathered at the court of the Prince of Urbino, is imbued with Neoplatonism, and the notion of the identity between the good and the beautiful is conveyed by the example of the ideal gentleman. Górnicki transferred the action to the court of Bishop Maciejowski in Prądnik near Kraków, introduced native characters modeled upon his acquaintances, eliminated women (who in Poland participated neither in too frivolous nor in too solemn conversations), and supplanted many jokes and anecdotes with those taken from Polish court life. His prose, which closely follows the rich and elegant modulations of the Italian original, is the most valuable aspect of his experiment. It set the pace for many later writers, although the appearance of the *Courtier* met with little recognition. It was destined, obviously, for a narrow elite. Some fragments of the *Courtier* which contain original anecdotes and stories are not far removed from the popular humor of a Marchołt or an Eulenspiegel, but the phrasing sets them on a much higher level. Górnicki's balanced prose and excellent sentence structure contrast strikingly with the exuberant prose of Mikołaj Rej, whose most important book, *The Mirror*, appeared two years after the *Courtier*, in 1568.

Mikołaj Rej
(1505–1569)

Called the father of Polish literature and very popular in his lifetime, Mikołaj Rej remains for his countrymen a symbol of "merry old Poland." Whether he can be called little more than a glutton, a drunkard, a lecher, a gossiper, a man of obscene language, or a blasphemer is doubtful. Jesuit writers, indeed, succeeded in spreading just such an image of him at the time of the Counter Reformation because Rej was a Protestant. He was certainly a man of many contradictions; the medieval man in him struggled with the Renaissance man, and his affirmation of life, of earthly pleasures, of conviviality did not quite fit his didactic Protestant zeal.

He was born into a gentry family which had migrated to Ruthenia from the neighborhood of Kraków. His father, though a nobleman, was illiterate, and Rej himself spent his childhood and adolescence hunting and fishing, like a young savage. Sent to the court of a lord to learn some civility of manners, he gradually acquired a fondness for books as well as a somewhat chaotic but extensive knowledge. He even learned some Latin—though not to the extent of being able to write in it. For this reason, he used only the vernacular. Through efficient administration of his estates, a profitable marriage, the successful outcome of innumerable lawsuits, he amassed considerable wealth. Though constantly busy, gregarious, beloved by his drinking and hunting companions, he found time to write, usually at night, and left behind him an enormous literary *oeuvre*, at least in terms of the number of pages. His writing grew out of the light verse and little jokes which he was fond of composing to amuse his friends. A typical squire, he attended diets and a few times was a deputy himself, but he avoided struggles of factions. He devoted himself, instead, to serious religious and moralistic pursuits. He handled verse and prose with equal facility and, let us say, with equal garrulousness, borrowing freely from other authors (an accepted practice at that time). As to his religion, he followed the way of many of his contemporaries. From an anti-clerical attitude in his youth he moved toward an open and fervent Protestantism.

His poetry can be placed between that of Biernat of Lublin and the fully developed poetry of the later Renaissance Polish poets. It follows a syllabic, regular pattern but sometimes hesitates between "imperfect" and classical rhymes.

Too wordy and rambling for the modern reader, his prose shows its virtues when read aloud. It reproduces everyday talk in a way curiously reminiscent of the French writer, Rabelais. Innumerable expressions of joviality reveal the visible pleasure the author took in releasing a stream of words. An excellent twentieth-century translator of Rabelais into Polish, Tadeusz Boy-Żeleński, modeled his translation on Rej.

In his verse Rej often used the form of the dialogue. It is this device that he employs in his *Short Conversation between a Squire, a Bailiff, and a Parson* (*Krótka rozprawa między trzema osobami Panem, Wójtem a Plebanem*, 1543), which is, in fact, a very lengthy conversation between the three estates. Though Rej was a nobleman, his sharp satire spares no class. The Peasant joins forces with the Parson against the Squire; the Squire with the Parson against the Peasant; and so on. Familiar accusations, the standard anticlerical barbs, point out the avarice of the clergy. And it is the clergy and the nobility who bear the brunt of the blame.

Another dialogue in verse, the *Life of Joseph of a Jewish Tribe* (*Żywot Józefa z pokolenia żydowskiego*, 1545), has a plot drawn from the Bible and from some Latin humanist works. It is actually a verse play and, as such, has been staged by avant-garde producers in our time. Even if Joseph is very boring in his Puritan virtue, one cannot say that the siren who tries to seduce him, the wife of the Egyptian lord Potiphar, does not make a lively figure of a woman possessed by her passion.

The Merchant (*Kupiec*, 1549) is also a play in verse, a free and colorful adaptation from a much drier anti-Catholic morality play, *Mercator*, written in Latin by the German, Naogeorgus. As befits a morality play the sinner, in this case a merchant, is judged after his death, together with many powerful people, i.e., princes, bishops, abbots. The latter throw onto the scales of justice all the churches and monasteries founded by them, all their good deeds, and even papal letters of indulgence, but the scales remain motionless. The merchant has no good deeds to bring with him. He was a swindler and a scoundrel in life, but his faith saves him. The play thus advances the thesis of justification by faith alone.

His religious zeal led Rej to write a huge work in prose, an exposition of true, i.e., Protestant, faith. *Postilla* (1557) is a somewhat naïve treatise of homespun religious wisdom. In spite of its bulk, it became a great success with the public, was reprinted many times and translated into Lithuanian. Rej, also, prompted by the pious hope of supplanting Latin versions of the "Psalms of David," made his own prose adaptation from a Latin text and published his psalms as *David's Psalter* (*Psałterz Dawidów*, 1546).

Throughout his creative life Rej wrote short, jocular poems to please his friends and companions, and up today his name is associated above all with humorous occasional verse. Instead of a fable, so common in the Middle Ages, an anecdote or a joke provided the subject. Rej's style is earthy, ribald, often obscene. Details of everyday life play a considerable part. These trifles, which Rej called *figliki* (*figiel* = prank), are, like much in the general atmosphere of his work, quite Chaucerian.

But Rej can be credited with another very extended work in verse called *A Faithful Image of an Honest Man* (*Wizerunk własny żywota człowieka poczciwego*), published in 1558 and reprinted in 1560 and 1585. Although he took the idea from an Italian author very popular at the time (Palingenius), he modified considerably whatever he borrowed from the original. He introduced the figure of a young nobleman who wanders from philosopher to philosopher asking how man should behave in order to live wisely, virtuously, and happily. This explains why certain chapters have such titles as "Aristotle," "Diogenes," or "Epicurus." The poem is full of ethical and metaphysical digressions. Although its aim is didactic, there are some fine pictures of nature, and various details of behavior are given a vivid description. The young man at last finds happiness after choosing a good wife and settling on his quiet country estate.

The same search for the rules of a good life that is found in many Renaissance writers, for instance, Montaigne in France, led Rej to write a work, partly in verse and partly in prose, which secured his position with his contemporaries. *The Mirror* (*Zwierciadło*, 1568) is a free-flowing meditation filled with innumerable quotations from the Bible and from classical literature. Its first part, written in prose, is titled, much like his long poem mentioned before, the "Life of an Honest Man" and is a particularly vivid reflection of the mentality and behavior of the Polish gentry of that century. For Rej, man is subject to external forces which are stronger than his will; for example, his birth depends on the conjunction of planets. But even within himself, man, according to Rej, is determined by his temperament (true to his medieval heritage he distinguished four temperaments: choleric, sanguine, melancholic, and phlegmatic); reason, nevertheless, can prevail. In this, Rej is not very far from the idea of sublimation. For instance, in one of his stories, a choleric young man with a penchant for killing becomes a butcher at the behest of his parents. Rej's ideal of education seems like a foretaste of Rousseau's *Emile*. A young man should be capable of some reading and writing, but he should avoid grammar and logic like the plague. He should learn how to ride a horse, throw a javelin, and shoot a musket. Learning will come through experience. A long voyage is recommended. But great attention should be given to the most important act in one's life, the choice of a good wife. Finally, he should settle on his country estate and refuse to be tempted by the life of the court. Rej openly praises sybaritism (but also advises measure in everything), a squire's ease in his own home, the joys of nature, of hunting, and of good cuisine. Pious Christian behavior can be achieved without asceticism by keeping to the middle of the road through the control of one's ambitions and one's overexuberant passions. The holding of public office should be avoided because being humane cannot be reconciled, for instance, with being a tax collector! Any public office menaces its holder with nepotism, a terrible scourge—yet how can one escape one's relatives? The only duties which cannot be eschewed are those of a soldier in case of

war and those of a deputy to the Diet. A deputy should participate
in the affairs of state as seriously as if he were administering sacra-
ments.

Rej is a curious blend of disparate tendencies. Through his exaltation of reason as the dominating force in man, he is undoubtedly in
the mainstream of his time. Yet a chaotic richness of his sensual
nature goes against any restraint in style, which differs him from
his contemporary humanists, such as Górnicki. Love of his native
tongue he justifies with the saying: "Let the neighboring nations
know that Poles are not geese, but have their own language." His
achievement is, first of all, in the realm of language, which he
handled with a feeling for realistic and humorous detail. He could
say, for instance, "his eyes shine like those of a rat when it gets
out of flour." His torrents of epithets and fondness for diminutives,
however, make him untranslatable.

Jan Kochanowski
(1530–1584)

Until the beginning of the nineteenth century, the most eminent
Slavic poet was undoubtedly Jan Kochanowski. He was a contemporary of the French poet Ronsard, who was six years his elder.
The year that Kochanowski left Poland as a twenty-two-year-old
youth to continue his studies in Padua Torquato Tasso was a child
of eight. In England, at about that time, Edmund Spenser (1552?)
and Sir Philip Sidney (1554) were born. Kochanowski set the pace
for the whole subsequent development of Polish poetry. In his work,
the language reached maturity, and today he is considered a classic
of Polish syllabic verse. It is rather difficult, though, to present a
precisely drawn portrait of Kochanowski. In his poetic work he was
discreet to the point of secretiveness about his personal adventures,
and it is that work which remains today our only biographical
source. The very character of his poetry adds to the difficulty. At
first glance there is nothing striking or extraordinary about it;
classical, limpid, it is simply an act of perfect ordering of the language. It flows naturally, so to speak, without any apparent effort;
one might call it a pure "breathing" of Polish, and in this respect
analogies can be found between Kochanowski and the French poets
of *La Pléiade*. Also, both drew from the same Latin and Italian
sources.

Kochanowski's father was a nobleman of only average means, but
he possessed the same spirit of industriousness, the same businesslike
approach, which we saw in the biography of Mikołaj Rej and which
was typical of the ascending middle stratum of the gentry class.

He had eleven children, and they proved to be of literary disposition. Among Jan Kochanowski's brothers two were writers: one translated the *Aeneid* of Virgil; the other, Plutarch. The son of the latter (the nephew of Jan Kochanowski) is known in Polish literature for his excellent translation of Torquato Tasso's *Jerusalem Delivered*. Piotr Kochanowski's translation influenced several generations of Polish poets, including Adam Mickiewicz.

Nothing is known of Jan's first education. One may surmise that, growing up in the country, he was well acquainted with local folk songs, but he also received a classical training in Latin and the humanities. At fourteen, he became a student at Kraków University, and the next fifteen years he spent in study and travel. In other words, he was a perfect young gentleman, free from financial responsibilities, supported by his family or by benevolent lords, patrons of young humanists. Scanty biographical data indicate that he lived three years in Kraków, and a year in Königsberg at the court of Prince Albert of East Prussia, a Lutheran ruler, with whom he maintained lasting cordial relations. Moving on to Italy, most probably in 1552, he studied classical philology at Padua, where he acquired not only an excellent knowledge of Latin poetry, but also a working knowledge of Greek, and thus was able to read Homer, Theocritus, and Pindar in the original. For family reasons Kochanowski returned twice to Poland, for a while studied again in Königsberg, then went back to Italy, where he remained, with interruptions, for several years. In his poems, an unidentified Italian lady appears under the name of Lidia, and his travels on horseback throughout the whole European continent are sometimes referred to. Finally, from Italy, Kochanowski went to Marseille, crossed France, stayed in Paris (where he probably met Ronsard), and returned in 1559 through Germany to Poland. He was then approaching thirty. One period of his life had come to an end—that as an itinerant scholar—and another began—that as a courtier. Kochanowski served at the courts of both lay and ecclesiastical magnates and, for a while, was secretary of King Sigismund August. He was offered lucrative parishes and even toyed with the idea of becoming a clergyman. But he preferred to retire from the turmoil of society and, after passing forty, married and settled on his hereditary estate, Czarnolas (near Lublin), where he devoted all his time to writing. Since his mature and best works were written there, the name "Czarnolas," which means "Blackwood," has unique legendary connotations for Polish poets. Kochanowski died suddenly at the age of fifty-four.

Kochanowski's poetry ripened slowly, as a result of his extensive studies and life experience. There was nothing in him of a precocious genius. Perfectly bilingual, he composed his first poems in Latin during his stay in Italy. But in Paris he was already writing in Polish. From that city he sent his famous song of gratitude to God: "What Do You Wish, O Lord, In Return For Your Bounteous Gifts?" Later on, he employed both languages. His literary models were Latin and Greek poets, above all, Horace.

Though Kochanowski lived in a period of violent religious disputes, he attacked neither Protestants nor Catholics unless it was to aim ironic remarks at the corruption of the clergy or the proliferation of Protestant sects. He maintained ties of friendship with eminent personalities both Protestant and Catholic. Notwithstanding his deeply religious attitude, he was skeptical of the value of theological distinctions and remained primarily a humanist who observed the golden mean. If one can say that Montaigne avoided entanglement in France's Catholic-Protestant quarrels through his philosophical skepticism, the same was true of Kochanowski. Even more, the pagan element of Stoicism in the latter's poetry, far from contradicting his deep piety, rendered his religious verse ecumenical, that is, acceptable to both Protestants and Catholics.

Longer poems of humorous, satirical, or simply didactic nature do not occupy a prominent place among Kochanowski's works, though as his tribute paid to these genres, so popular at that time, they are interesting. *The Game of Chess* (*Szachy*, published around 1564) was the first attempt in Polish to write a humorous epic, or heroi-comic, poem. It was written under the obvious influence of a Latin poem by an Italian humanist, Vida. Kochanowski, unlike his model, places the action not on Olympus, but (and the detail is amusing) at the royal court of Denmark. A kind of novelette in verse about a battle on a chessboard and two young men who compete for the hand of a beautiful princess, it is presented with a considerable amount of true humor.

Poems like *Harmony* (*Zgoda*, 1564), *The Satyr, or The Wild Man* (*Satyr albo Dziki Mąż*, 1564), *The Banner, or Homage from Prussia* (*Proporzec albo Hołd Pruski*, 1569) can be defined as journalism in verse which rather faithfully expresses contemporary political concerns, formulated along the lines of official court views. In the first of the poems mentioned, a personified Harmony addresses the Poles, advising them to end their quarrels, especially those between religious denominations. The Satyr in the poem of that title serves a similar admonitory purpose; in particular, he, as an inhabitant of Poland (and a baptized one, we may presume), complains of the devastation of nature provoked by the economic boom: as a consequence of the intense cultivation of land and the high volume of exports required to buy foreign luxuries, forests are being destroyed. The Satyr reproves the citizens who are losing their chivalrous virtues and who believe that gold will protect them from their enemies, and this at a time when the country's outlying provinces are being devastated by the Tartars, and the Muscovite despot has not only taken Polotsk but claims that Halich (Galicia) belongs to him by "natural law." The Satyr adds: "I would rather uphold your side because the Muscovite despot has never paid much heed to constitutions." Nor are concerns of education alien to the Satyr. Though Kochanowski himself spent many years in Italy, his Satyr considers studies abroad too expensive, advising instead substantial endowment of Kraków University as the necessary first step toward creating a Polish institution which could rival the Sorbonne.

The Banner is a tableau representing the ceremony of homage paid by the prince of East Prussia in 1525 to the king of Poland in recognition of the latter's sovereignty over that province. A banner held at that ceremony provides the point of departure for the poem. One side of the standard depicts the history of Polish-Lithuanian relations with the Teutonic Order. The reverse side pictures, we learn, the entire history of the Slavs, beginning with the Amazons who landed in Scythia, then migrated toward the north over the river Don and founded two Sarmatias (Poland and Russia). The poem ends with an appeal to the king to continue the policy which had produced the union of Poland and Lithuania and a common victory over the Teutonic Order. The tableau posseses a certain hieratical grandeur.

Kochanowski's journalistic works were addressed mainly to voters and members of the Diet. They are written in thirteen-syllable verse with a caesura occurring after the seventh syllable—the so-called Polish Alexandrine. Kochanowski also displayed his civic interests in Latin poems, such as the one he composed in answer to a violent satire on the Poles written by a French poet, Desportes, who had come to Poland with Henri Valois, the Polish king-elect. Kochanowski's poem was entitled *Gallo crocitanti* (translatable as either *To a Crowing Gaul* or *To a Crowing Cock*).

Some of his public political pronouncements are also significant. After Henri Valois abandoned his foreign (Polish) throne in 1574, Kochanowski favored the nomination of either a Hapsburg or a son of Ivan the Terrible, justifying the latter proposal by the hope that the young Russian prince would learn to obey the Senate. These considerations did not stand in the way, however, of his immediate endorsement, later on, of the firm anti-Muscovy policy of the king who was finally elected in 1576: Stefan Batory.

Kochanowski's first published collection of poems was an adaptation in verse of the Psalms, entitled *David's Psalter* (*Psałterz Dawidów*, 1578). As models he had used Latin poems by a Scottish humanist, Buchanan, written in the Horatian manner on subjects drawn from the Psalms. That many of Kochanowski's psalms were put to music and became practically part of folklore, surviving up to our time, may be a measure of his success. In his course on Slavic literatures given in the 1840s at the Collège de France in Paris, Adam Mickiewicz gave high praise to Kochanowski, who is "in his translation of the Psalms, inspired, [and who] has a noble, clear, and lucid style, a bold flow, free and magnificent phrases, and everywhere the same venerable gravity and priestly solemnity."

A short occasional poem was called in Kochanowski's time in Italy a *frasca* (literally, "little twig"); thus a collection of his short poems in this genre, published in 1584, received the name *Fraszki*. All of them are distinguished by conciseness of form and concentration of material, but their character varies from anecdotes, humorous epitaphs, and obscenities to pure lyricism. Combined, they form a sort of very personal diary, but one where the personality of the author never appears in the foreground, as if the poet took pleasure in confounding his future biographers. In his *fraszka* "To the Muses," Kochanowski says:

> Maidens, who inhabit the immense Parnassus
> And wash your hair in Hippocrenian dew,
> As I have comported myself well toward you
>   while alive,
> I do not ever want to separate from you.
> As I do not envy kings their pearls or their gold
> And I prefer virtue to money,
> As I do not want you to flatter anybody
> Or to beg for me among ungrateful people,
> I ask you, let my rhymes not perish with me,
> But let them be famous when I am dead.

> Panny, które na wielkim Parnazie mieszkacie,
> A ippokreńską rosą włosy swe maczacie,
> Jeslim się wam zachował jako żyw statecznie,
> Ani mam wolej z wami rozłączyć się wiecznie;
> Jesli królom nie zajźrzę pereł ani złota,
> A milsza mi daleko niż pieniądze cnota;
> Jesli nie chcę, żebyście komu pochlebiały
> Albo na mię u ludzi niewdzięcznych żebrały:
> Proszę, niech ze mną za raz me rymy nie giną,
> Ale kiedy ja umrę, ony niechaj słyną!

Recurrent motifs are transience and *beatus ille*, appearing, for example, in the *fraszka* "On Human Life":

> Everything that we think is trifles,
> Everything that we do is trifles,

There is no certain thing in the world,
In vain men take so much care.
Virtue, beauty, power, money, fame
Will pass like the grasses of the fields.
We and our order will be laughed at
And into a sack we will be cast like puppets
    after a show.

Fraszki to wszytko, cokolwiek myślimy,
Fraszki to wszytko, cokolwiek czynimy;
Nie masz na świecie żadnej pewnej rzeczy,
Próżno tu człowiek ma co mieć na pieczy.
Zacność, uroda, moc, pieniądze, sława,
Wszytko to minie jako polna trawa;
Naśmiawszy się nam i naszym porządkom,
Wemkną nas w mieszek, jako czynią łątkom.

Or in "On the Linden Tree":

My guest, seat yourself beneath my leaves and take a rest!
The sun will not reach you here, I promise,
Even if it is high, and straight rays
Make the short shadows run back under the trees.
Here cool breezes always blow from the fields,
Here nightingales and starlings comfortably complain.
From my fragrant flowers hard-working bees
Draw honey which ennobles the tables of lords.
While I know how to murmur so softly
That one falls easily and sweetly asleep.
I do not bear apples it is true but my master praises me
As if I were the best tree in the garden of Hesperides.

Gościu, siądź pod mym liściem, a odpoczni sobie!
Nie dojdzie cię tu słońce, przyrzekam ja tobie,
Choć się nawysszej wzbije, a proste promienie
Ściągną pod swoje drzewa rozstrzelane cienie.
Tu zawżdy chłodne wiatry z pola zawiewają,
Tu słowicy, tu szpacy wdzięcznie narzekają.
Z mego wonnego kwiatu pracowite pszczoły
Biorą miód, który potym szlachci pańskie stoły.
A ja swym cichym szeptem sprawić umiem snadnie,
Że człowiekowi łacno słodki sen przypadnie.
Jabłek wprawdzie nie rodzę, lecz mię pan tak kładzie,
Jako szczep napłodniejszy w hesperyskim sadzie.

Throughout his mature years Kochanowski wrote songs. It was only in 1586, however, shortly after his death, that they were collected and published in book form. They reflect his attachment to antiquity, his devotion to Horace—sometimes they are just adaptations of

Horace—and his interest in Italian lyricism. Some resemble his versions of the Psalms. They are very diverse, both in their topics— religious, philosophical, erotic—and in their use of various syllabic meters. A long "Song of St. John's Eve" is composed of twelve choruses or poems, each sung by a different country maiden. The maidens are celebrating the midsummer night according to the ancient pagan custom preserved in Poland, but "christened" through its connection with the religious feast of St. John. In the poem, young people have gathered to light bonfires, to leap over the flames, and to sing. The maidens praise love, the delights of country life, of peaceful nature, of joyous landscapes. A certain philosophy is clearly traceable throughout all of Kochanowski's songs, namely, an affirmation of the Renaissance principle of the individual as an autonomous subject meditating upon the human condition and establishing his own relationship with the universe. A Christian attitude is fused with the Horatian *carpe diem* so popular among the poets of the Renaissance. If Kochanowski consciously competed with Horace, he succeeded not only in completely "Polonizing" the motifs which he drew from the ancient poet, but in preserving the sensuous quality of his native language, rooted as it was in the physical world and very far from any classical dryness. Conscious that he was creating a Slavic poetry which could rival works in Latin, the poet presumes:

> About me Moscow will know and the Tartars
> And Englishmen, inhabitants of diverse worlds.
> The German and the valiant Spaniard will be acquainted
>   with me
> And those who drink from the deep Tiber stream.

> O mnie Moskwa i będą wiedzieć Tatarowie,
> I różnego mieszkańcy świata Anglikowie;
> Mnie Niemiec i waleczny Hiszpan, mnie poznają,
> Którzy głęboki strumień Tybrowy pijają.

The main value of the songs lies in their tone of serenity, their quiet affirmation of existence—a bucolic tone so typical, for a long time, of Polish poetry. Mythological deities, if they appear, have Slavic faces, and satyrs inhabit, undoubtedly, Polish forests. Some songs are related to events of the moment, and there is no lack of political topics. For instance, one such song refers to the current preoccupation with the election of a king:

> Don't worry, Nicholas, about who will be our king.
> A ready decree is before God
> Not written with a pen but carved in a hard diamond.
> Let us not await our master from the south
> Or from the north, from the east or from the west.

Whoever is nominated by God, that man will be king.
God will bend human hearts with ease.
He turned to derision our vain councils
And in spite of better-known neighbors, brought a king
    from a distant land,
Though soon the throne was taken by another.
Where are those mountains of gold?
Where are the Gascons and the arrayed troops?
What were our cannons for and our tournaments?
Hopes filled with wind burst asunder.
Fortune rules the ships at sea,
Fortune gives victory in battles,
Gatherings and diets listen to her decrees
And human deliberations are turned to nothing.
Out eloquent speakers! Out arguments! And let us hang a
    golden crown somewhere in the field.
If it doesn't befall a wiser man
May chance at least give it to the more skillful.

    Nie frasuj sobie, Mikołaju, głowy,
    Kto ma być królem; już dekret gotowy
    Przed Bogiem leży; nie piórem pisany,
    Lecz w dyjamencie twardym wykowany.

    Nie z pół lub nocy, lub dnia, nie ze wschodu
    Ani czekajmy pana od zachodu;
    Ten królem będzie, kogo Bóg mianuje,
    Łatwie On ludzkie serca spraktykuje.

    Tenże nam mimo znajomsze sąsiady,
    W śmiech obróciwszy nasze płone rady,
    Przywiódł był króla z dalekiej krainy.
    Po którym wrychle miał usieść kto iny.

    Gdzie ony złote góry nieprzebrane?
    Gdzie Gaszkonowie i wojska ubrane?
    W co poszły działa i nasze turnieje?
    Wiatrem nadziane puknęły nadzieje.

    Fortuna nawy na morzu sprawuje,
    Fortuna w bitwach zwycięstwem szafuje;
    Onej rakosze i sejmy słuchają;
    A ludzkie rady wspak się obracają.

    Precz, krasomowce! Wywody na stronę!
    A my gdzie w polu na słupie koronę
    Zawieśmy złotą; jesli nie mędrszemu,
    Niech ją da szczęście przynamniej rętszemu.

Kochanowski's songs reveal him as a man who sought an equilibrium between his quiet country life, on the one hand, and a preoccupation with public affairs, on the other. A recurring image is that of evening, glowing logs in a fireplace, a jug of wine. The changing seasons provide a background for the poet, whose moods harmonize with those of nature. The *Songs* includes his earliest and his latest poems, and one of them has already been mentioned—"What Do You Wish, O Lord, In Return For Your Bounteous Gifts?"

The Dismissal of the Grecian Envoys is the finest specimen of Polish humanist drama. The short play was commissioned by Lord Jan Zamoyski, Vice-Chancellor of Poland, later Chancellor and Royal Hetman, and performed in the presence of the king in 1578 at a feast celebrating the wedding of the former in Jazdów near Warsaw. Published in the same year, it bore a dedication to Zamoyski, part of which follows:

As late as yesterday I received two letters which Your Excellency had written to me on the subject of this tragedy. And until then I knew nothing of those letters; I supposed that due to the delays of our time my tragedy was also due to be delayed or rather that it was destined to remain with me, to feed the moths, or to serve as wrapping paper in our pharmacy. When I read the letter from Your Excellency there was no time for corrections as I had to *insumere* [use] all my time for copying. *Quicquid id est* [however it is], and, I wager, it is a trifle, and Your Excellency will probably say the same, I sent it to you, the more boldly as there is nothing to send, as I told you before; it is not *ad amusim* [regular, according to all the rules], since the master is too weak for that. There are other things which do not suit our ears. *Inter caetera* there are three choruses, and the third seems to imitate Greek choruses, as they have a peculiar *characterem* of their own. How it will sound in the Polish language I do not know. But let Your Excellency pronounce his *arbitrium* on this or rather on everything.

Kochanowski wrote the tragedy at the peak of his artistic maturity —a few years before the death of his daughter, when he produced his best poetry in the *Laments*. It seems that only after some hesitation he finally settled on a subject suitable for a wedding feast. The work could not be a bloody tragedy. He had intended to translate Euripides' *Alcestis* but dropped the idea almost as soon as he started. The war of Troy had been popular in medieval Europe as a literary motif, and its popularity lasted into the Renaissance. Horace had advised dramatic poets to choose themes from the *Iliad*, and Kochanowski knew Horace well. The arrival of some Greek messengers to Troy, preceding the outbreak of hostilities, is mentioned in the *Iliad*. In addition, Erasmus of Rotterdam, so popular in Poland, had translated into Latin the work of a Greek rhetorician of the fourth century A.D., Libanius, *The Envoy's Speech Pronounced by Menelaus to the Trojans on the Subject of Helen.* Kochanowski was also familiar with a romance on the Trojan War in Polish. In any case, he finally chose an episode preceding the war, as some authors continued to do after him, even as late as the twentieth century— for instance, Jean Giraudoux in *Tiger at the Gates.* A preoccupation with wise statesmanship directed his interest toward the mechanisms of political decision-making rather than toward individual heroes. *The Dismissal* is neither a tragedy of passions nor a tragedy of a revealed fate. We can hardly say that his characters are heroes. They are necessary initiators of action, while the true hero is a collective one: the Trojan state. The messengers arrive with offers of peace on condition that Helen be restored to her husband. A group of wise statesmen led by Antenor is for fulfilling the Greeks' demand, but a faction led by Alexander (Paris), Helen's abductor, wins the majority through skillful demagoguery at a council presided over by King Priam (and in its deliberations similar to the Polish Diet). Our feeling of impending doom is enhanced by a reference to the traditional story of Troy, which the viewer knows in advance, and by Cassandra's vision, which confirms our knowledge. Yet the fatal outcome is due not to an inexorable fatality but merely to stupidity and demagoguery. The tragedy centers about those characters who understand what is at stake but who cannot reverse the trend. Thus, one can say that it is the very futility of human passions which provokes horror and pity. Perhaps the most pitiable are those who are unaware, like Alexander, Helen, and Priam (a weak man and a constitutional monarch like the Polish kings).

For its construction the play follows the rule of Renaissance poetics based on Horace and codified by the French theoretician of Italian origin, Scaliger. Thence, the division into five "epeisodia" or acts. The plot proceeds from the exposition to the announcement of the catastrophe and finally to the catastrophe itself. The action which takes place beyond the stage is related in dialogue: a messenger, for instance, reports on the deliberations of the council; the future is shown through a vision of Cassandra; and the first step of fulfillment is announced by an officer who brings the news of the Greek attack. A chorus of Trojan maidens, like a detached voice of judgment, delivers three long speeches: the first is on the folly of youth; the second, on the responsibility of rulers; the third and most interesting is an apostrophe to the boat used by Alexander (Paris) on his trip to Greece.

Kochanowski uses blank verse of thirteen or eleven syllables, and in this we see the trace of his years in Italy. The first Italian tragedy modeled after Greek tragedy was written in the first half of the sixteenth century by a patrician from Vicenza, Trissino. In his theoretical writings Trissino advocated the use of *verso sciolto* (unrhymed verse) as more "natural" in tragedy. *Verso sciolto* wandered from Italy to England in the same century, where, adapted to the rhythmical needs of English, it became known as "blank verse." And this is what Kochanowski adapted to Polish in *The Dismissal*. Following the natural tendency of the language, his verse, both in dialogue and in choruses, is syllabic. The third chorus, however, mentioned above, is somewhat of an exception. In it he attempted to mold his native tongue into a form duplicating the qualities of Greek verse. (The first line is a translation from Euripides.) Greek versification, of course, is based upon entirely different principles, but thanks to the poet's struggle, what we receive is a daring and beautiful poem. Together with Cassandra's lament, it is the highlight of the play. Kochanowski, by basing the pattern of versification on the count of syllables combined with dactylic and trochaic feet, produces in that chorus a syllabotonic verse.

The Dismissal, so majestic in its clarity, equilibrium, and economy, nevertheless remained an exception in old Polish literature. Humanist tragedy, which had reached such perfection in Kochanowski, was not destined to develop further either quantitatively or qualitatively. The question arises as to why this is so. Professor Claude Backvis, an eminent Belgian specialist in old Polish literature, is probably right in affirming that the cause should be looked for in the nature of the hero of *The Dismissal*, which is Troy.

Whatever were the differences between the French, English, and Spanish theaters, the history of these theaters has one common feature: they all developed in the town and at the court of the monarch. Their peculiar features were shaped by the closed and dangerous milieu of the court. Dangerous because between the courtiers, few in number and well known to each other, there was a constant set of relations—very lively and astonishingly unstable. Competition at the court was as ruthless as it was carefully disguised: with politeness, hypocrisy, self-mastery. The courtier, under the threat of ruining his career and often of losing his life, had to learn: to distinguish the psychological truth from deceiving appearances; to show confidence and reticence when it was necessary; to judge immediately the mood of his adversary or his superior; to excel in the art of allusions clear enough to be harmful and disguised enough to avoid consequences. . . . Quite different was the situation in the "Parliamentarian" *Respublica* of the gentry. The towns were losing power; as a result, their importance disappears in politics as well as in culture. The role of the royal court weakened, too; besides it was but a secondary force. Here [Poland] the surest way to get a dignity or a grant was certainly not to conduct meticulous psychological studies of the ruler. It was sufficient to exert pressure on him in the Chamber of Deputies or in the Senate, or to swim with the current of indignation over some insult dealt to a darling of public opinion.

In contrast to Western Europe, Polish authors and readers belonged predominantly to one class: gentlemen farmers. Their life was patriarchal and static. "Therefore," says Professor Backvis, "not a fearful observation of the individual nor a combination of weak will and passion were everyday fare but a meditation on general problems, on practical morality and politics. And, first of all, an immense reservoir of experiences connected with nature, with family, with everything which is praised as the glory of the manor." The gentry collectivity was one big family. Mutual relations were marked by inexhaustible hospitality. Meetings were numerous, protracted and culminated in such gatherings as religious synods, dietines, and diets:

A session [of the parliament] was announced—and, immediately, authors hastened to incite printers to publish new editions, as they wanted to send a considerable number of copies there. A session was announced— it meant that all the celebrities would meet in the lobbies even if they were not deputies. In Poland, the parliament took on itself the role of social catalyst, played in the rest of Europe by the court and the town. There, and only there, a lively competition of talents and individualities developed. But even in ideological discussions—and in their best period, adversaries used to exhaust all resources of oratorical art—a feeling of community was present. Traditionally, the debates were closed by a manifestation of unity and universal fraternity. A ceremony rather emotional than intellectual: the parliamentary constitution was read or, at a religious synod, hymns were sung. . . . Let us not be surprised, then, that in such a society what caught on immediately belonged to literary genres most in harmony with the way of life: lyric poetry, political literature, and—in periods of great danger, of cultural conformism—the epos, which was infinitely different here from the paper lucubrations fabricated in the West. . . . To the contrary, drama emerged slowly and with difficulty. Already, from what has been said, it is easy to guess that drama could develop from but one phenomenon of old Polish life in which human relations were antagonistic: from the ideological quarrels in the assemblies.

However, according to Professor Backvis, the principles of unanimity, of harmony destroyed dramatic power.

Only upon the background of such a stituation of drama in Poland can we appreciate the value and the modern spirit of Kochanowski's *Dismissal*. Kochanowski lacked, it is true, dramatic dispositions, but I do not hesitate to affirm that in a historical situation of a Trissino or a Robert Garnier he could have done for the theatrical culture of his country what they did for Italian-French culture. Western writers of drama who were under the spell of the tradition of antiquity groped toward the solutions of the seventeenth-century tragedy. Kochanowski, too, carefully preserved the antique form, or strove to.

Yet, Kochanowski, according to Professor Backvis, filled that form with new content not centering on conflicts of human will and destiny.

Even less are we concerned with psychological characteristics—with the feelings of Helen, of Paris, of Antenor, or Priam, or of Menelaus—which would have made for the charm of a similar French tragedy and, even more so, of an Elizabethan tragedy. We are concerned and moved by the fate of the Trojan nation. We are concerned and moved by the sight of a happy nation deciding to unleash a war for such a trifle.

In *The Dismissal* we have a prediction full of pathos: many-faceted, lyrical, symbolic (Cassandra's). Kochanowski created a historical drama, a drama of a collectivity, and overcame the narrow frames of his theater in space as well as in time. He produced on the stage a crowd of the Trojan people and the entire ten years of its subsequent fate. At the end of a Greek tragedy the victim of Fate makes an act of sublime acceptance. Its corresponding moment in *The Dismissal* is a curiously informative scene. Without a doubt tension is less [here] than in Cassandra's outburst, the philippic of Ulysses, or the curse of Menelaus. But it is a nucleus and a sample of the events yet to happen. Thus, we receive a new kind of drama ending with a tragedy of the future. The author constructed this spectacle in such a manner that the public has to leave the theater with painful thoughts and apprehensions. It is not a myth which determines events, as in *Oedipus Rex*. On the contrary, the causes of the fall of Troy, far from being left in the dark, are shown in full view "as a social phenomenon." We are made acquainted with the mechanism of causes and effects which proceed according to sociological laws. It does not matter how we judge that "sociology" today. It is enough to say that observations result from a combination of reasoning and experience. Once we are aware of that, we are convinced of the approaching doom not by a probability but by a feeling similar to anxiety, to a panic which arises in a besieged city or an invaded state.

Professor Backvis sees in Kochanowski's *Dismissal* a prototype of the future Polish theater and thus, in connection with its subsequent development, a significant contribution to the history of world theater. He argues as follows:

In its further evolution one should have expected a drama more or less symbolic, since attitudes and events which decide the fate of a collectivity can be dramatized only by incarnating them in dramatis personae. These will be personifications rather than individual characters. We should not have expected an intellectually overpowering dramatic construction acting with the precision of an infernal machine, but rather sublime situations and an emotional atmosphere. Everything seemed to lead toward a poetic drama in Poland. The poetic would perform the function of a compensatory element, that is, it would create sufficient emotional tension to avoid the dangers threatening similar enterprises—the coldness of allegory or boring didacticism. Both elements, the poetic and the symbolic, would assist each other, as such a drama has to appeal to the imagination of the spectator and to invite his cooperation, since the real subject of the tragedy cannot be shown but only suggested.

Professor Backvis traces a specifically Polish theater from Kochanowski's *Dismissal*, but the line of development does not see its continuation in the Baroque seventeenth century nor in the "classical" eighteenth century; the French-influenced drama of the Enlightenment belongs, he claims, to the history of the "Western theater" in Poland. With the advent of the Romantic era the line is resumed and proceeds to the twentieth-century symbolic theater of Wyspiański. Professor Backvis judges the Polish Romantic theater as follows:

I am not going to explain what an enormous step forward in the direction I have described was made by poets of the Great Emigration. Above all, in Słowacki we again have a series of dramas in which the fate of the whole nation hangs in balance. The tragedy consists in the necessity of choice— the future depends upon the choice. The meaning of the "critical moment" is shown in an exceptional individual living through that moment. He embodies the desires and ambitions of the collectivity. Even happenings and figures brought from historical reality to these dramas are carefully purified of any traces of authenticity. Magnified, idealized, endowed with fantastically sharpened features which are strangely pitted against unnatural stage lighting, these characters take the shape of superhistorical myth. Yet they are very real and historically probable. They overcome all criticism and even induce a feeling of fraternity. Sometimes even—in the dramas I like best—they are molded into a baroque jocularity and at the same time are rich in an irrational element which inclines us to accept the role assigned to them by the artist. And everything is submerged in a tincture of the most imposing, purest poetry that merges contradictions, makes improbabilities probable, and blurs contours, raising the temperature of the poetic matter to the boiling point.

It is difficult to agree entirely with Professor Backvis, as he excludes the very Polish comedy of the eighteenth century, which bore fruit all through the nineteenth century. Yet the pattern he establishes is extremely useful, and it explains much that has happened in the Polish theater of our time. The naturalistic, photographic theater has never experienced great success in Poland, while the poetic transformation of reality, akin to mystery and morality plays, has attracted many writers. We shall see later that not the drama of the individual as such will attract the poets, but that of the individual as redeemer of the collectivity.

If the hero of *The Dismissal* has been called a collective one, it was not meant to imply the existence of a clearly defined political tendency. There is no doubt that Kochanowski was voicing deep concern with the proper functioning of the State and that the factional struggle within the drama was modeled upon the familiar Polish parliamentary scenery, but otherwise, it is difficult to find any thesis. When Kochanowski wrote the tragedy, he probably did not imagine it would be staged in a climate of acute political excitement. But, as it happened, Ivan the Terrible decided exactly at that moment to invade Livonia (a tributary duchy recognizing Polish suzerainty), and preparations for war were under way in Poland. The question arises as to how the play could have been interpreted. What, in reality, was Troy? And who were the Greeks? The Poles certainly did not consider Ivan the Terrible a representative of justice. Basically, the play was pacifist, and the spectacle only received a political flavor thanks to a poem in Latin written by Kochanowski and recited after the performance to the accompaniment of a lute. The king, Stefan Batory, who was present at the spectacle, hardly understood Polish, being of Hungarian descent, but he, of course, knew Latin perfectly.

The poem, entitled "Orpheus Sarmaticus," is an address to the Poles opening thus:

> Poles, what hopes and what designs do you nourish in your hearts?
> It is no time for laziness, no time for sleep, believe me; neither for festivities with a lute, a cup, and light dances.

The enemies which threaten the country are enumerated:

> From the east, the rider throws his poisoned arrows, he is as dangerous in attack as in flight.
> He leads his troops from hyperborean fields.
> He is hardened in the Ural snows and frosts of his country.
> And if I am to tell the truth, his glory is due only to your inertia.
> His are allies who, using false talk, enter into alliance with you but in their hearts hide thoughts of war.
> Envy and deceived hopes torture their souls.

Kochanowski probably had Austria in mind here. But a longer passage is devoted to Turkey:

> Why should I mention the conqueror of Asia and the tyrant of Europe?
> Our ancestors feared him even when he sailed through the faraway Ionian Sea on one thousand ships and besieged the Island of Rhodes.

Now that victor on land and on sea dominates the entire Danube
  with his fleet,
And spreading terror, rules over both its banks. Not content, he
  has led his troops to the Dniester and looks with greedy
  eyes at the fields of Podolia.

The list of Poland's enemies is followed by a call to arms:

And you, Sarmatian, when suddenly you have found yourself
  amid so many arms and arrows, you stand petrified as if
  seized by a dose of old age.
Do you believe these are only dreams?

Yet you do not possess towns surrounded by strong walls, or
  inaccessible fortresses on high rocks, or rivers flowing under
  old ramparts,
Or anything serving men to defend their lives. Today the only
  hope is the hand armed with a sword.

The poem ends by praising King Stefan Batory as a man not given
to drinking, dancing, and carousing, but trained for military action.
    Kochanowski's poetic art reached its highest achievements in the
Laments, a series of nineteen poems written after the death of his
small daughter, Ursula. Here artistic perfection takes on an enigmatic
quality. The only example of a direct confession of Kochanowski's
personal feelings, it is, nevertheless, expressed in a strictly conventional form, according to the rules elaborated by the poets of his
epoch. *Epicedium* or *threnos* (lament) possessed a long tradition
reaching back to antiquity, and was based on the fundamental principle that a poet can only weep over the death of some eminent
personality. A contemporary of Kochanowski's, the French-Italian
humanist Scaliger, in his codification of classical rules, preserved this
principle while introducing, in addition, that of a logically organized
sequence of themes: praise of the deceased; the presentation of loss,
its burden, sadness, solace; and, finally, moral conclusions. Kochanowski was bold enough to apply this closely elaborated formula to
a personal misfortune, thus violating the very foundation of the form
and transforming it into something completely different. Because the
Laments sings of a father's despair at the loss of his child (an "insignificant" person), some of his contemporaries were scandalized by his
boldness. It lacked the necessary decorum, but, perhaps, that is the
way masterpieces are created: the convention is at the same time
preserved and broken. Kochanowski wrote something unique in
world literature, because not one poem but a whole cycle is centered
around the main theme. The theme itself is not so much the dead
person as a highly subjective description of what a person who has

lost a child lives through: a history of personal sorrow. The *Laments*, published in 1580, has a complex construction in which we can trace the pattern advised by Scaliger, but which has suddenly recovered a *natural* logic of feeling. In Lament I, the poet calls on the literary tradition itself to aid him in his enterprise: he invokes "the tears of Heraclitus, the complaints of Simonides, and all human regrets and troubles." In Lament II, he comments wistfully that it would be better to use one's pen to write verse for children than to write threnodies: "I did not want to sing for the living; now I must sing for the dead." Laments III, IV, V are addressed either to the little girl or to Persephone, as a journey to her realm seems to hold the only solution for the poet's grief. In Lament VI, the little girl is addressed as "my dear little singer, my Slavic Sappho, heir not only of my estate, but of my lute as well." By its reference to little Ursula's budding talent and by its transposition of snatches of a wedding song, this lament is particularly moving. Touching also is Lament VII, where not physical or spiritual traits of the dead child are remembered but the trifles surrounding her.

> Sad trinkets of my little daughter, dresses
> That touched her like caresses,
> Why do you draw my mournful eyes? To borrow
> A newer weight of sorrow?
> No longer will you clothe her form, to fold her
> Around, and wrap her, hold her.
> A hard unwaking sleep has overpowered
> Her limbs, and now the flowered
> Cool muslin and the ribbon snoods are bootless,
> The gilded girdles fruitless.
> My little girl, 't was to a bed far other
> That one day thy poor mother
> Had thought to lead thee, and this simple dower
> Suits not the bridal hour;
> A tiny shroud and gown of her own sewing
> She gives thee at thy going.
> Thy father brings a clod of earth, a somber
> Pillow for thy last slumber.
> And so a single casket, scant of measure,
> Locks thee and all thy treasure.*

> Nieszczęsne ochędóstwo, żałosne ubiory
>   Mojej namilszej cory!
> Po co me smutne oczy za sobą ciągniecie,
>   Żalu mi przydajecie?
> Już ona członeczków swych wami nie odzieje —
>   Nie masz, nie masz nadzieje!

* Translated by Dorothea Prall Radin.

Ujął ją sen żelazny, twardy, nieprzespany . . .
    Już letniczek pisany
I uploteczki wniwecz, i paski złocone,
    Matczyne dary płone.
Nie do takiej łożnice, moja dziewko droga,
    Miała cię mać uboga
Doprowadzić! Nie takąć dać obiecowała
    Wyprawę, jakąć dała!
Giezłeczkoć tylko dała a lichą tkaneczkę;
    Ojciec ziemie bryłeczkę
W główki włożył. — Niestetyż, i posag, i ona
    W jednej skrzynce zamkniona!

In Lament VIII, a sense of loss is conveyed: "Thou hast made all the house an empty thing." But, starting with Lament IX, the whole cycle assumes a philosophical tone, and the Renaissance fusion of Stoicism and Christianity, temporarily at least, falls apart. Wisdom (the Stoic virtue) is of no use for a suffering man, who sees it as an inaccessible temple:

> I am an unhappy man who has spent his life trying to reach
>   your doors.
> Now I am thrown down from the last steps and counted among
>   the other people,
> One among the many.

The voice of the poet-father rises, in Lament X, in a question: "Where, my charming Ursula, have you gone?" The narrator answers himself in a series of mixed images drawn from Christianity and from ancient mythology: perhaps, lifted above many heavens, she is numbered among little angels? Or has she been taken to the islands of the blessed? Perhaps Charon is ferrying her across "languid lakes" and she drinks from the waters of Lethe, or she has changed into a nightingale or is being purified in purgatory.

> Wherever you are, have pity on my sorrow,
> Comfort me as you can,
> Appear before me as a dream, as a shadow, or as a miserable
>   phantom.

Not only wisdom, but virtue is discovered to be useless, and in Lament XI the narrator reaches complete skepticism, reminding us of some passages of the Book of Job:

> Who was ever helped by his piety?
> Who was ever preserved from evil by his goodness?

or:

> Some unknown foe mixes up human things
> Without heeding whether men are good or wicked.

or:

> My grief! What are you doing to me?
> Must I lose both my solace and my reason?

Death and poetry form the subject of Lament XIV:

> Where are those gates through which a long time ago
> Orpheus descended, seeking his beloved one?
> O, could I but find that path!

The poet will take his lute with him to the kingdom of Pluto: "that god cannot have a heart of stone, insensible to the begging of mortal men." Perhaps Erato, the Muse of lyric poetry, may also be of help to the narrator: in Lament XV, he describes Niobe turned into stone by her grief and identifies himself with her through the force of empathy. Kochanowski introduces conceits which sound quite Baroque, for instance:

> This tomb doesn't hold a dead woman.
> The dead woman has no tomb;
> She's dead and a tomb to herself.

This is, however, a literal translation of a short Greek poem from the Hellenistic period (*Anthologia Graeca*, VII, 311).

Again, in Lament XVI, Stoicism is brought to trial. The narrator asks himself whether all that he is experiencing is a dream or reality. Man is influenced by his situation; he is subject to the power of circumstances. When we are rich, we praise poverty; when we are happy, we care little about sorrow—we are unable to think about our own death. Cicero used to write that all the world was his homeland, but wept when he had to leave Rome. He pretended that he was afraid of one thing only, dishonor, but he mourned the loss of his daughter. He maintained that only a bad man should be afraid of death, but when his life was in danger, he did not want to die: "you persuaded others; you did not persuade yourself." The narrator, who has arrived at complete doubt, now relies on Time, "father of desired forgetfulness," to cure him. But in Lament XVII, the tide turns another way, and the Christian takes precedence over the discarded Stoic wisdom. This lament, which, like many songs of Kochanowski's, is written in stanzas of eight-syllable verse, stands out from the rest of the cycle, which for the most part sustains a thirteen-syllable line. It is a song of Christian humility:

> Mine a life so far from fame,
> Few there were could know my name,
> Evil hap and jealousy
> Had no way of harming me.
>
> But the Lord who doth disdain
> Flimsy safeguards raised by man
> Struck a blow more swift and sure
> In that I was more secure.

Poor philosophy so late
Of its power wont to prate
Showeth its incompetence
Now that joy procedeth hence . . .

Let my tears prolong their flow.
Wisdom I most truly know,
Hath no power to console:
Only God can make me whole.*

Lament XVIII is like a psalm, a prayer addressed to God by one of his unruly children who think of Him rarely when they are happy, and here the narrator beseeches God to show him mercy. The last, Lament XIX, has a subtitle, "The Dream," and is a consolation. The narrator sees his dead mother in a dream; she is holding her little granddaughter in her arms. His mother explains to him that he should not sorrow, as his child is far happier now than if she had lived. She speaks of human life as a chain of unending sorrows. Yet, paradoxically, his mother restores, to a certain extent, the validity of Stoic reasoning. She recalls that her son spent his life pouring over books, little profiting from the pleasures of this world. Since he knew how to bring solace to other people in similar misfortunes, she advises him now: "Master, cure yourself." From the consolation we may infer that a certain precarious balance between Christian faith and antique philosophy has been regained by the author, who thereby remains true to his Renaissance ideals.

In the history of Polish poetry, the author of *Laments* represents a moment of perfect, classical equilibrium—a moment soon cut short by the vigorous wave of the Baroque, releasing the pressure of scarcely subjugated medieval elements. Kochanowski personifies the bucolic longings so persistent in Polish poetry and shares with other Renaissance poets, who also drew from the poetry of Horace, the ideal of peaceful retreat from the turmoil of the world. His estate, Czarnolas, became as legendary as the forest of Arden in *As You Like It* or Prospero's island in *The Tempest*. One may point out even greater similarities, of course, to Ronsard and the group of *La Pléiade* in France, but the use of common Latin and Italian sources accounts for them. The direct influence of *La Pléiade* remains doubtful. A fusion of borrowings from the poetry of antiquity with details drawn from the specifically Polish scene is, in Kochanowski, no less successful, and perhaps even more so, than similar fusions by the poets of *La Pléiade*. The very nature of the Polish language, with its highly nuanced lexical equivalents for sense experience, its reluctance to accept abstractions, renders Kochanowski's poems very

* Translated by Dorothea Prall Radin.

different—not necessarily a disadvantage—from those of his French contemporaries.

Other Lyric Poets

Mikołaj
Sęp-Szarzyński
(1550–1581)
Born into a noble family, Sęp-Szarzyński left Poland as a young boy to study abroad in Wittenberg and Leipzig (an indication of Protestant sympathies) but later, according to some scholars, also visited Italy. After his return to Poland he moved among those Protestants who, precisely at that time, were abandoning their faith for Roman Catholicism. He became a fervent Catholic himself and established lasting ties with the Dominican Order, among whose ranks was one of his brothers. His first poems consisted mostly of patriotic odes strongly influenced by Horace. Later on, a new vein appeared in his poetry. Though indebted, certainly, to Kochanowski, he devised a language of metaphysics not present in his master. He may be considered a kind of "metaphysical poet" of human fear and trembling in the face of decay and death. His literary sources seem to have been Spanish spiritual writers, probably coming through Italian translations. Nor is his work devoid of references to classical mythology. Like Kochanowski he often brings into play symbolic accessories taken from antiquity. His work is known to us thanks to a small collection published by his brother in 1601 (already two decades after his death) entitled *Rhythms* (*Rytmy*). It probably contains only a fraction of what he wrote, but a few sonnets of this collection have secured for Sęp the distinction of being called one of the best Polish poets of all time. The sonnet form employed by Sęp consists of two quatrains rhyming *abba abba*, one quatrain rhyming *cdcd*, and a final couplet rhymed *ee*. The form, of course, derives from that brought from Italy (both to England and to Poland). Earlier, Kochanowski had fitted some of his *fraszki* to that form, but Sęp molded it in his own very peculiar language of purposeful obscurity based on an inverted word order. Even the titles bear the imprint of the style, for instance, "On our War that We Wage against Satan, the World, and our Flesh." In that sonnet he says:

> Peace is happiness but struggle
> Is our existence under heaven. That hetman of darkness
> And the luring vanity of the world
> Strive hard to spoil us.

> Pokój — szczęśliwość, ale bojowanie
> Byt nasz podniebny. On srogi ciemności
> Hetman i świata łakome marności
> O nasze pilno czynią zepsowanie.

The next lines of the sonnet define what was, perhaps, his permanent attitude toward life:

> What can I do in such a terrible battle,
> Weak, unheeding, divided within myself?

> Cóż będę czynił w tak straszliwym boju,
> Wątły, niebaczny, rozdwojony w sobie?

Or if we take another sonnet—"On the Nondurable Love of the Things of this World"—its first line is nothing less than a translation from the Greek epigrammatic poet, Anacreon, but utilized for a distinctly different purpose.

> It is hard not to love, but no solace is in love.
> When our thoughts, seduced by desire, sweeten
> Those things which must change and decay.

> I nie miłować ciężko, i miłować.
> Nędzna pociecha, gdy żądzą zwiedzione
> Myśli cukrują nazbyt rzeczy one,
> Które i mienić, i muszą się psować.

In the concluding lines Sęp returns to St. Augustine's motif of spiritual nostalgia caused by unsatisfied love, as long as the soul does not see the Eternal Beauty, the aim of its love. One can say that in Sęp another, darker side of the Renaissance is glimpsed, the same which is felt in the paintings of Dürer. Stylistically, he is already on the verge of the Baroque. Some of his poems abound in conceits proper to that style. Let us also notice that he has a predilection for enjambment, consisting of a suspension of the voice at the end of a line while the sentence is not yet finished—the sentence ends at the beginning of the next line, receiving, thus, in its closing a greater emphasis. This is a device favored later on, particularly by symbolist poets. As a typical Baroque exercise in style, Sęp's "Epitaph to Rome" can be quoted. Its source is a Latin poem by an Italian humanist completely forgotten today, Ianus Vitalis from Palermo.

> You, who want to find Rome in Rome, pilgrim,
> And are unable to find Rome in Rome itself,
> Look at the rings of walls, the theaters, the churches,
> Turned into rubble and broken columns:
> They are Rome. . . . That city in conquering the world
>   conquered itself too,
> As nothing could escape its conquest.
> Today in vanquished Rome, unvanquished Rome
> (Which means a body lying in its shadow) lies buried.
> Everything in it has changed, the Tiber alone

Persists amid the change and runs mixed with sand to the sea.
Look, what tricks Fortune plays. What was immobile
Is in decay, what was in movement endures.

Ty, co Rzym wpośród Rzyma chcąc baczyć, pielgrzymie,
A wżdy baczyć nie możesz w samym Rzyma Rzymie,
Patrzaj na okrąg murów i w rum obrócone
Teatra i kościoły, i słupy stłuczone:
To są Rzym. Widzisz, jako miasta tak możnego
I trup szczęścia poważność wypuszcza pierwszego.
To miasto świat zwalczywszy i siebie zwalczyło,
By nic nie zwalczonego od niego nie było.
Dziś w Rzymie zwyciężonym Rzym niezwyciężony
(To jest ciało w swym cieniu) leży pogrzebiony.
Wszytko się w nim zmieniło, sam trwa prócz odmiany
Tyber, z piaskiem do morza, co bieży, zmieszany.
Patrz, co Fortuna broi: to się popsowało,
Co było nieruchome; trwa, co się ruchało.

Metaphysical nostalgia and lament over the human condition will occur frequently in Polish Baroque poetry. Yet Sęp, that tormented man, was not destined to have valid successors in seventeenth-century Poland, contrary to what happened in England of the same period, with her flowering of metaphysical poets.

Sebastian Grabowiecki (1540–1607)   Sebastian Grabowiecki illustrates what happened to the successors of the metaphysical trend in Polish poetry. Dominated by pious Roman Catholics, poetry became devotional, drawing solace from the protection and intercession of the Blessed Virgin. Grabowiecki, a nobleman by birth, studied probably abroad, and for a long time served at the royal court, becoming a priest after the death of his wife and ending his life as an abbot of a Cistercian monastery. His *Spiritual Rhymes* (*Setnik rymów duchownych*, 1590) is a graceful collection of devotional verse modeled upon Italian poetry. Grabowiecki deserves attention as one of the more sophisticated if not somewhat ethereal minor poets:

Heavenly, pure spirits
High above, circles and orbits,
And you, heavenly, transparent crystals,
Which, moderating eternal fires,
Have boundaries at the limits of the universe
And a power whereupon all things
Known in the world were born:
The shining sun, the somersaults of all the elements,
The winds, the thunder, the clouds,
Warm and cold climes, the rains,
The ice, the snows and dews—
Raise your voices to the eternal glory of the Lord!

Duchy niebieskie, czyste,
Zwierzchnie kręgi i biegi,
I wy, niebieskie przejźrzyste kryształy,
Które, ognie wieczyste
Miarkując, w kresiech brzegi
Macie i władze, skąd wszytkie powstały
Rzeczy, co się poznały
W świecie: słońce świecące,
Wszech żywiołów przeskoki,
Wiatry, gromy, obłoki,
Zimny i ciepły czas i dżdże moczące,
Lody, śniegi i rosy,
Ku wiecznej chwale Pańskiej nieście głosy!

A nobleman from Greater Poland, Kasper Miaskowski received *Kasper Miaskowski (1550–1622)* his education in Polish schools, first in his native district, then in Poznań, after which he settled on his estate and spent the rest of his life as a gentleman farmer. His poems, published in 1612, *Collection of Rhythms* (*Zbiór rytmów*), are proof of a high level of sophistication among minor poets of the period. By their purely Baroque quality, they also remind us of the brevity of the classical phase represented by Kochanowski. Miaskowski's imagery is sometimes astonishingly modern as, for instance, in the poem "On a Painted Glass Goblet":

Glass is ash; though they paint it with colors
When working marvels with it at glass works.
Is this not like the sun who, sending down
Foamy horses before it sinks
(If, bidding farewell with eye serene
It glides along a humid cloud),
Adds to the world rainbows of various tints,
As does an artisan who presents glass
In the guise of a new shape adorned by
His green, golden, and sapphire brush.
But what then? A glass before you drink
Your fill easily falls from your hands
And that magnificent crystal turns to dust;
Blue smoke carries off the remains.
Glass is ash; but man is ash too
Even if he were to extend his life as Phoenix does,
For that bird made of sunny rays
Rises from ash, turns into ash.
But why should I recollect Arabic wonders?
A day will come when this white-haired world
Like straw will burn in a huge flame
Before the eternal judge will sit upon his throne.

Popiół śkło, choć je farby malują,
Gdy sztuki w hucie nim wyprawują:
A nie tak, kiedy pieniste konie
Spuszczając z góry słońce, niż tonie —
Jeśli żegnając pogodnym okiem,
Zboczy się z wilgim pozad obłokiem —
Różnych barw tęcze światu wyprawi,
Jako rzemieślnik, gdy śkło postawi,
Zielonym, złotym i szafirowym
Pędzlem i kształtem pozornie nowym.
Ale cóż po tym? Śklanica snadnie,
Niż się napijesz, z rąk ci wypadnie;
A on spaniały kryształ w perzyny
Poszedł, ostatek dym niesie siny.
Popiół śkło, ale i popiół człowiek,
Choćby rozciągnął jak Feniks kto wiek,
Bo i z słonecznych ten ptak promieni
Z popiołu wstaje, w popiół się mieni.
Lecz co arabskie wspominam dziwy?
Przyjdzie dzień, kiedy i świat szedziwy
Walnym płomieniem jak słoma spłonie,
Niż wieczny siędzie Sędzia na tronie.

Szymon Szymonowic (1558–1629)   The border line between the Renaissance and the Baroque must be established rather arbitrarily. Szymonowic is, perhaps, the representative of a still purely Renaissance diction. He was born in Lwów into a burgher family; he studied at Kraków University and, for a few years, abroad. After his return, he dedicated himself to pedagogical and literary work. His poems in Latin, which he signed with the name Simon Simonides, earned him admirers who became his powerful protectors. Among them was Chancellor Jan Zamoyski (the same who commissioned Kochanowski's *Dismissal of the Grecian Envoys*). Zamoyski founded a town on his possessions, Zamość, which today remains one of the purest examples of Renaissance architecture in Poland. His ambition was to establish a college able to compete with the University of Kraków. Szymonowic organized Zamość Academy for his benefactor and established a model printing shop in the town. Because of his literary renown he was ennobled by a decree of the Diet. In his advanced age he retired from his pedagogical functions to his estate, which he had received from Zamoyski.

He is a bucolic poet, remembered in literature thanks to his *Idylls* (*Sielanki*, 1614). In these poems, Szymonowic followed, above all, Virgil's *Eclogues* but was even more dependent upon the poet who had been a model for Virgil, namely, Theocritus. Other Renaissance models can also be detected, for the genre of pastoral poetry was then quite fashionable. Like Kochanowski, Szymonowic blends elements taken from antiquity with observations of Polish nature and native customs. The idylls are written in the form of monologues and dialogues of shepherds and shepherdesses who often bear the names of classical convention: Daphnis, Menalkos, Thyrsis, or, for girls, Phyllis. Some have peasant, even Ukrainian peasant, names. They converse on love, on various everyday topics (for instance, country fairs), while constantly invoking Apollo, Pallas Athena, and Cupid. The proportion of conventional ingredients to realistic details varies, depending on the poem, though all twenty idylls have a limpid and balanced language. Two are still quoted today as masterpieces. They are practically free from mythological references and are quite realistic images of country life.

"Kołacze" derives its title from the name of the round wedding cake, *kołacz*. This idyll consists of an account of the ceremonies connected with the arrival of a bridegroom at a small gentry manor and the wedding feast which follows. The account is recited by a chorus of maidens and a series of ladies who speak in pairs. The chorus of maidens begins its narrative with an address to a magpie (according to common belief, a magpie seen near the house meant visitors):

> A magpie screeches on the fences, new guests will arrive
> A magpie sometimes deludes, sometimes tells the truth.

For a young girl in the house, this is an announcement that the expected guest is near. The chorus then, addressing either the bride or the bridegroom, relates the events, including the wedding, up to the moment everybody sits down to dinner, at which the ceremonial *kołacze* are served. The pairs of ladies speak now to the bride and now to the groom, making humorous references to the impatience of the young couple and the pleasures of marriage. As an idyllic portrait of a social ritual, the work has a rather dynamic movement; and the author acts somewhat like a stage director, composing the richness of details into a harmonious whole.

Quite different is the idyll entitled "The Harvesters" ("Żeńcy"). We are now in a peasant milieu, and the idyll consists of a dialogue between two female serfs working hard at cutting the harvest with their sickles. They are acid-tongued shrews who do not hesitate to use brutal expressions and obscene allusions. They complain of their toil, of the heat, and of the strictness of their supervision. The supervisor (*starosta*), armed with a whip, is the object of their gossip and malicious remarks. Talking of his private life, they say he would be a good man if not for his tie with the manor housekeeper, who is an old hag, and a witch in addition. A presentation of only the content of the poem tends to give a wrong impression of its quality. The brutally realistic report of peasant life on a plantation-type farm contrasts sharply to the harmony of poetic composition. The reader receives a nearly operatic exchange of parts with recurring refrains. One refrain repeated by the two women is addressed to the sun:

> Sun, you pretty eye, eye of the beautiful day,
> You have different manners from our starosta.

Every time the refrain appears, it is followed by various comparisons between the sun and the starosta that are obviously highly unfavorable to the latter:

> You rise when your time comes; this is not enough
> For him, he would like you to rise at midnight.
>
> You run till noon, always on your track; he would
> Like to marry noon and evening.

In another refrain, with an equally mocking intention, the women tease the supervisor:

> Starosta, you will not be a little sun in the sky.

Here is the whole passage in Polish:

> Słoneczko, śliczne oko, dnia oko pięknego!
> Nie jesteś ty zwyczajów starosty naszego.
> Ty wstajesz, kiedy twój czas; jemu się zda mało;
> Chciałby on, żebyś ty od północy wstawało.
> Ty bieżysz do południa zawsze twoim torem,
> A on by chciał ożenić południe z wieczorem.
> Starosto! nie będziesz ty słoneczkiem na niebie.

They achieve their goal, though, and are given permission to rest.

The use of refrains is a normal device of the Classic idyll. Quite unexpectedly, in "The Harvesters" the pastoral genre embraces crude realism and tells an accurate story of the peasant's lot. Szymonowic, and this is his distinctive trait, handles thirteen-syllable verse rhymed in couplets in such a way that he creates the impression of a certain dynamism, a fast pace of action. His clear, logical syntax is closer to Kochanowski's than to the involved sentence structure of Sęp-Szarzyński.

Descriptive and Satirical Poetry

Sebastian Klonowic (1545–1602)   Poetry, as Hussowski's Latin poem *On Bison* illustrates, served various, not to say unusual, purposes. A poet whose verse was typical in this respect was Sebastian Klonowic. A burgher from Greater Poland, he settled as a young man in Lwów, but later moved to the city of Lublin, where he embarked upon a career in local government as a city magistrate. For a while he taught at the Academy in nearby Zamość. Toward the end of his life he became the mayor of Lublin. Like his predecessor, Biernat of Lublin (also of burgher stock), Klonowic appeared to have some Protestant sympathies. Lublin was a strong center of the Arians, and he maintained cordial relations with them. He was once even accused of being the author of a libelous pamphlet against the Jesuit Order. Well-educated, even erudite, Klonowic knew Greek, and he wrote in both Polish and Latin. His most curious work, a long poem in Latin, *Roxolania* (*Ruthenia*), published in 1584, is an ethnogeographical or anthropological treatise in verse. At the poet's bidding, expressed in the invocation, the Muses abandon Parnassus to accompany him in his travels throughout Ruthenia. There follow images of nature, of cities like Lwów, Kiev, and Kamieniec, then a detailed description of various occupations, such as lumbering, cattle raising, hunting, beekeeping, fur trading, etc. Local beliefs in magic and witches, as well as baptismal, wedding, and funeral rites, also find a place in his Latin verses. Today we would consider this the province of ethnography. Klonowic describes, for instance, professional mourners at a funeral, noting what they sing; he observes how an Orthodox priest writes a letter of recommendation to St. Peter, how the letter is put in the coffin together with a coin to aid the dead man in his journey and, in particular, to pay for the ferry across the river Styx(!). As to the last item, we may suspect that the poet in Klonowic outdid the ethnographer. In its mass of interesting details, *Roxolania* is comparable to the largely "ethnographical" Lithuanian *Chronicle* of Stryjkowski.

No less distant from what we may expect of poetry is another poem of Klonowic's, the voluminous *Victoria Deorum* (*Victory of the Gods, c.* 1595), a satirical, pedagogical treatise in Latin where the conquest of the Olympian gods over the Titans symbolizes the triumph of the spirit over the flesh and its passions. Another incongruous mixture, full of allegories, it draws not only upon mythology, but also upon medicine, history, etc., and indicates the persistence of medieval attitudes then converging with the rising wave of the Baroque.

Klonowic's Polish poems are akin, in a way, to his Latin works. *The Raftsman, or the Launching of Boats on the Vistula* (*Flis, to jest, spuszczanie statków Wisłą,* 1595), written in a sapphic stanza, is a sort of guide for bargemen and merchants transporting wheat down the Vistula all the way to its mouth at the port of Gdańsk (Danzig). The Vistula, the main Polish north-south trade route, is described in the poem from a practical point of view, i.e., its deep and its shallow places, its dangerous currents, its landing points, etc. *The Raftsman* also contains a history of sailing, from Noah through the Argonauts up to the discovery of America; also technical data on the construction of ships, on the types of river barges and rafts, on the customs and the language of the boatmen; and, finally, advice on how to deal with the German merchants of Gdańsk. It is full of didactic digressions with a satirical edge directed against the wheat export trade as the source not only of luxury but of oppression: this is the voice of the burgher criticizing the economic basis on which the wealth and power of the gentry rested. That Klonowic wrote a manual for a trade which he condemned is not the only oddity of his poem. At times, in his work, sailing on the Vistula signifies the temporary wandering of a Christian on earth.

Judas' Bag (*Worek Judaszów*, 1600) is a treatise in verse on criminology. Klonowic, having gained wide experience in the municipal courts of Lublin, was able to depict various tricks employed by thieves, bandits, and charlatans. In his treatise, he also describes some misdeeds which, to his regret, can be committed legally but which, nevertheless, are crimes. According to a medieval legend, Judas, who stands as the paragon of scoundrels for all Christians, had a sack made from the skins of four different animals—wolf, fox, bobcat, and lion. The poem follows the same four-part division. It groups the activities which violate the commandment "Thou shalt not steal" into four sections, corresponding to the four skins. In the wolfskin section appear thieves, bribers, mischievous gypsies, slave traders (those who sell people to the Turks), etc. The foxskin is used to symbolize swindlers, impostors, tricksters, and those who would use religion as a means of enriching themselves. The bobcat-skin section is dedicated to those who operate ostensibly under cover of the law: usurers, merchants who use false weights and measures, or who lure people with false advertisements, as well as gamblers who profit in cold blood from others' real passion for the game. The fourth part is barely outlined because, the author confesses, it might be dangerous to describe the open banditry practiced by the rich and powerful. "Those Judases have strong teeth," he says, "and it is advisable not to enter into details."

The value of *Judas' Bag*, as well as that of *The Raftsman*, lies in Klonowic's use of innumerable details pertaining to lower-class life and in his reproduction of the slang spoken by various marginal groups, thieves included.

Walenty Roździeński (c. 1560–1622)   Verse was put to an even more curious use by an ironsmith from the Kraków region, Walenty Brusiek, coming from the village of Roździeń (hence the name Roździeński). He was the owner of an ironworks which he inherited from his father and was the author of a long poem in Polish, based upon his own experiences and observations, in which he describes the work and life of craftsmen like himself. The title is a mixture of Latin and Polish: *Officina Ferraria, or Foundry and Workshop of Ironsmiths Engaged in the Noble Activity of Ironmaking* (*Officina ferraria abo huta i warstat z kuźniami szlachetnego dzieła żelaznego,* 1612). Here again, we have to do with a treatise in verse, but written in honor of a profession of which the author is obviously very proud:

> I don't know why you wonder so much at my person.
> Don't you like the figure I cut?
> It seems that I'm black as a chimney sweeper.
> I am a foundry man—such as you see.

Polemical Prose

In sheer bulk, polemical literature of the sixteenth century surpassed all other genres taken together. With readers intent on aligning themselves in political and religious quarrels, it was no wonder that of all writers the most famous were publicists who reached the public through their pamphlets on current topics. One such writer, in particular, distinguished himself by the violence of his style: Stanisław Orzechowski. He is often mentioned in the same breath with Frycz Modrzewski because his temperament and views constitute a direct antithesis to those of the latter. Besides, as one of Frycz's bitter enemies, Orzechowski played a part in the poisoning of his opponent's life. *Stanisław Orzechowski (1513–1566)*

He came from a noble family which had destined him for the priesthood and had sent him abroad for his studies. In Wittenberg, under the influence of Luther's teaching, he became a Protestant, but later in Rome he re-embraced Catholicism. After some sixteen years abroad, he made his way back to Poland, and, since his parents presented him with a bill for his education, he had little choice but to become a priest. He was a man of adventurous temperament and great literary talent, able to handle both Latin and Polish. Quite adamant in his rejection of celibacy, he performed marriage ceremonies for his clerical colleagues and finally took a wife himself. These initial violations marked the beginning of his innumerable clashes with Church authority, which turned the issue of his behavior into a *cause célèbre* of his time. A master of demagoguery, he knew how to flatter the broad masses of the gentry, by whom he was adored. Instead of becoming a Protestant, as did many similarly motivated Catholic priests, he chose another path. While swearing undying loyalty to the Vatican, he attacked in an unscrupulous manner not only his superiors, but also the Protestants. He was too precious an ally of the Church to be taken lightly. In spite of constant litigations in ecclesiastical courts, he succeeded in never abandoning his wife.

It would be practically impossible to summarize the positions assumed by Orzechowski, as he changed sides with great facility. (Sometimes he attacked what he had only the day before defended.) If Frycz Modrzewski was a noble-minded liberal searching for a utopia, Orzechowski was the incarnation of those features of the gentry which aroused such indignation in his antagonist. Orzechowski maintained a scornful attitude toward the lower classes, while singing paeans to the glorious "golden freedom" of the gentry and accusing the king of scheming against that freedom. In addition, he considered the Poles a God-chosen nation—the proof, in his opinion, was "golden freedom" itself. The clergy, according to Orzechowski, did not sufficiently dominate public life. Theocracy, namely, a complete subservience of the State to the Church, constituted his ideal. In his well-known work written in Polish, though bearing a Latin title: *Quincunx* (*Pyramid*, 1564), he uses the geometrical figure to illustrate his argument. Given: if the pyramid symbolizes the State, the top is the Roman Catholic Church; its sides are faith, the priest, the king, and the altar. Were it not for his brilliant pen, Orzechowski would not have merited a place in literary history. Yet no other writer so fully exemplifies the vices of the gentry, and their inability to distinguish between self-interest and the good of the community. By his chauvinism and his attacks on those alien to his social group (for instance, he dismissed the Lithuanian gentry as culturally inferior), he foreshadows the so-called "Sarmatism" of the next century.

*Piotr
Skarga
(1536–1612)*

An exhaustive list of Protestant, especially Arian, polemists would occupy a good deal of space, but curiously enough, not one of their number equaled in literary stature the exceptional Jesuit, Piotr Skarga. Born the son of a lawyer in Grójec near Warsaw, he went to school in his native town; then he studied at the University of Kraków while working as a tutor for aristocratic youths. Later, after having become a priest, he won renown in Lwów as a dynamic preacher. Then he went to Rome, where he entered the Jesuit Order. On completing his novitiate, he was dispatched to Lithuania, where heresy enjoyed the most powerful protection and the most energetic champions. He became the first rector of Wilno's Jesuit Academy (raised to university status in 1578) and was also the founder of new Jesuit schools in Polotsk, Riga, and Dorpat following the victories of King Stefan Batory over Ivan the Terrible. Although the King acted as protector of the Jesuit Order, his attitude was far from fanatical, and during his reign a certain equilibrium prevailed between the denominations. All this changed after his death, when a Swedish prince was elected king of Poland and Lithuania. Sigismund Vasa (who ruled as Sigismund III) had been supported by the Protestants, but they soon realized their error when (not long after the election) the new king showed his true colors as a Roman Catholic zealot. It was then that Skarga was named royal preacher, a position from which he could influence state policy in the direction of the Counter Reformation. A born fighter, wielding both the spoken and the written word, he differed from the equally bellicose Orzechowski in his predilection for a high-flown style and in the firmness of his convictions. Nonetheless, he established a new, obscurantist pattern of dealing with Protestants, condemning them in advance as "sons of hell": "Whoever blasphemes the name of God let him die"; "Lead the blasphemer before the camp and let the whole populace stone him to death." Expressions such as these must be considered as mere flights of rhetoric, since Skarga himself did not advocate—in practice—violent measures. Young people, however, educated in Jesuit schools, sometimes took that rhetoric literally, translating it into riots directed against the Calvinists and the Arians. The student riots rarely led to loss of human life but often resulted in material destruction and contributed to the creation of a new atmosphere of intolerance. Leaders such as Skarga undoubtedly saved Poland for the Vatican—a fact which proved later to have great importance, as Poland, with the center of its church lying beyond its borders, remained impregnable even when subjugated by foreign powers. Skarga also concerned himself with the question of Christian unity, conceived, of course, as obedience to the Vatican. He was one of those who elaborated a gigantic plan for the unification of the Western and Eastern Churches. The Jesuits succeeded in gaining the support of the higher clergy of the Orthodox Church in the Grand Duchy of Lithuania and in the Ukraine for this idea, thus paving the way for the Union of Brześć (1596). As a result of that agreement, large areas of the *Respublica* witnessed the gradual substitution of Greek Catholicism for Eastern Orthodoxy. One should be careful not to project arguments of much later periods into sixteenth-century religious disputes. The question of the Greek Catholic Church played a central role in the Polish-Russian feud of the nineteenth century. To repair the evil done to Orthodoxy by the vicious Poles, the Czars destroyed the Greek Catholic Church with administrative measures. To the Poles the persecution of the Greek Catholics by czarist authorities meant nothing less than an act of a foreign invader, based on no right whatsoever to claim the allegiance of the population. In the nineteenth century, the religious question was entangled with the national question. Not so in Skarga's time: national consciousness was practically nonexistent in the Grand Duchy of Lithuania. Although its inhabitants were defined as Lithuanians, the variety of languages used at home or in documents does not allow for clear distinctions. The adherents of Eastern Orthodoxy spoke mainly an Eastern Slavic dialect (Old Byelorussian or Old Ukrainian). But where there was a resistance to the Union it had nothing national in it. In some provinces of the Duchy and especially in the Ukraine, a class conflict undoubtedly formed the background of this opposition, since allegiance to Rome was becoming synonymous with submission to the ruling class. The Uniate (Greek Catholic) Church was destined to be primarily a church of the villages. The "Lithuanian" (in fact, Eastern Slavic) gentry changed its faith mostly from Orthodox to Protestant in the first generation, from Protestant to Roman Catholic in second generation; while the Greek Catholic village priest with his wife and children catered to the spiritual good of more modest parishioners. In the Ukraine, the opposition to Catholicism emanating from Poland added to class tensions, but, on the other hand, it is true that the Greek Catholic Church served as a vital cultural factor in the awakening of Ukrainian national consciousness later on.

Skarga's homiletic activity was not limited to the religious sphere. He was deeply concerned with the duties of a citizen toward the State, and many of his sermons are of a political nature. Among these, the most famous are his *Sermons to the Diet* (*Kazania sejmowe*, 1610). Though it is difficult to separate spoken and written word in Skarga, we may assume that he used the sermon as a literary form in which to enclose a political treatise. The excellently constructed work begins with a sermon on wisdom, seen as an indispensable virtue for members of the Diet. Each of the sermons which follow deals with a separate topic: the second, with love of country; the third, with the evil flowing from the internal discord in the *Respublica;* the fourth and fifth, with another threat to the nation, namely, religious heresy; the sixth, with the malady resulting from the increasing weakness of the royal power. The seventh, dealing with unjust laws, contains a strange mixture: bad laws include those which prevent the secular arm from coming to the assistance of the ecclesiastical jurisdiction, those which guarantee *habeas corpus* (*neminem captivabimus*, in Polish law), and those which reduce the peasants to the condition of serfs. The eighth sermon brings to light public transgressions which go unpunished, such as blasphemy, luxury, usury, oppression of the peasants, venality of magistrates, etc. Skarga, as the list of subjects discloses, takes a conservative stand favoring strong, central power (obedient to the Church) and social justice in a theocratic and paternalistic spirit. The *Sermons* also reveals a fanatic patriotism. He addresses the gentry as "the ruling class" in the state, and, hoping to provoke feelings of civic responsibility, he impugns the conviction common among members of that class that Poland stands by virtue of her lack of government ("Nierządem Polska stoi"). Skarga employs a highly rhetorical, explosive style modeled upon the Bible, especially upon the angry harangues of the prophets. Like Bossuet, later on, in France, he treats the history of nations as a series of rewards and punishments dispensed by Divine Providence. Since he observes sin all around him, Skarga seeks to convince his readers that the *Respublica* will fall, and, making use of quotations from Isaiah, Jeremiah, Ezekiel, and Jonas, he unfolds prophetic pictures of the country's doom. The style of his parables often sounds evangelical; for instance, comparing the state to a ship, he writes:

When the ship is sinking and winds overthrow it, only the stupid man cares about his bundles and coffers and does not go to help save the ship. He believes that he loves himself, while he is actually preparing his own undoing. For when the ship is without defense, he, too, with everything he gathers together will be drowned.

If we compare Skarga with such political writers as Frycz Modrzewski, we see that a detailed analysis of evils—for example, the oppression of the peasants or bad laws—is supplanted, in the former, by generalized appeals to cast off sin and return to virtue. The style, though magnificent within the limits of the convention, should not blind us to the relative poverty of content. Skarga's thought is a regression from the fruitful ferments of Humanism and the Reformation. Yet he set the pattern for the homiletics of the following period, which was to bring forth, without being swayed by, a flood of sermonizing. The importance of Skarga's particular blend of religion and politics cannot be overlooked, for, along with his characteristic biblical style, it will reappear in Polish literature under various forms throughout the following centuries. He can be called, too, the herald of messianism in Polish literature, and similarly inspired intellectuals of the nineteenth century recognized their indebtedness to Skarga. Thus, Mickiewicz in 1841, in his course on Slavic literatures at the Collège de France, said of Skarga:

In all history he sees only two peoples who, in his opinion, are fully capable of the high notion of the fatherland (*patrie, patria, ojczyzna*): the Chosen People, i.e., the Hebrews, and the Polish people. He sees the proof of the divine mission in the singular blessing which assured Poland of a long succession of kings without one tyrant among them and which permitted Bolesław the Bold, the only one who committed a crime, to do penance before he died. He sees in Poland's [geographical] position as the farthest situated Christian country in the north another testimony to her mission of preserving and promoting civilization. And lastly, for Skarga, the freedom which Poland enjoys is one more evidence of a Divine "Plan" in calling that state to life. The state works in the same way as does a human organism. The soul, he says, has power over the body, but that power is constitutional, not despotic. It performs exactly the same functions in the body as the king when ruling the Polish *Respublica*. This is why Skarga calls that freedom a "golden freedom"—an expression which should be understood in its hidden meaning: gold, according to medieval notions, often signified, as we know, perfection, excellence; for the alchemists, it was a concentrated light; votaries of hermetic science searched for gold which was to give eternal life and health. It was in this sense that the Bull which spelled out the political organization of the Holy Roman Empire was called the "Golden Bull," and in this sense Skarga and writers after him termed the political freedom of the Polish kingdom a "golden freedom" which not only assured every citizen of the possibility for full development but vested each with the responsibility for his own actions. Thus, Skarga's love of country inspires him to defend Poland as a New Jerusalem in which God has placed great hopes. But Poland, as he conceives it, exists only in his own mind—separated from the people. Those people who betray that country [*patrie*] established by Providence betray their mission. Skarga addressed his words to a generation which he regarded as criminal, as treading a pernicious road leading to great misfortunes.

Although it articulates what Skarga had perhaps hardly defined himself, Mickiewicz's interpretation is worthy of note because it suggests that the pride with which Poles viewed their political institutions formed the source of their belief in a special national destiny. On the other hand, the quotation describes something which resembles a typical Polish attitude up to this day, namely, an attachment to an ideal Poland combined with a bitter denunciation of the reality, a loathing even, of its inhabitants. One more factor contributing to the feeling of exceptional mission should be mentioned: the nearness of Moslem Turkey. Contrary to the Southern Slavs, to most of Hungary and to Walachia, Poland successfully opposed the Turkish power. Likewise the awareness of an emerging stronghold of Eastern Orthodoxy in Muscovite Russia, which paralleled the renewal brought about by the Counter Reformation of Poland's attachment to Roman Catholicism, served to increase the Poles' sensibility to their unique position as a frontier of Western Christendom. Messianism, foreshadowed by Skarga, found proponents as early as the seventeenth century. Later, in the nineteenth century, the messianic myth underwent a strange transformation with the impact of the French Revolution and the cult of Napoleon. The ideal Poland then became the embodiment of democratic ideas as opposed to the autocracies of the Holy Alliance.

With time, Skarga's stature acquired the proportions of greatness, and what should have been regarded as the devices of a splendid style were taken literally as prophecies foretelling the actual ruin of the state. Transformed into a symbol of deep concern with public affairs, the author of *Sermons to the Diet* was exaltedly portrayed by nineteenth-century painters as a fiery preacher with arms outstretched, white mane flowing.

We have stressed the kinship between the spirit of the Middle Ages and that of the Baroque. Skarga himself drew upon medieval hagiography as the author of *Lives of the Saints* (*Żywoty swiętych,* 1579). Its nine editions issued during his lifetime testify to his immense popularity. The work contains stories of martyrs, hermits, and ascetics taken from the annals of Christianity. It also includes figures of the sixteenth century, for instance, those who suffered death for their faith at the hands of Henry VIII. Among the saints whom Skarga popularized was his contemporary, a Polish Jesuit, Stanisław Kostka. Kostka, of aristocratic lineage, fled as an adolescent from his family, who had forbidden him to join the Jesuit Order. From Vienna, where he studied under the supervision of his brother, he traveled on foot and in rags to Rome, where he fulfilled his aim; but not long after his entrance into the Order he died, a very young man, *in odore sanctitatis*, and was canonized a saint. Skarga presented other Polish saints, such as Jacek Odrowąż (1183–1257) and Jan Kanty (1390–1473). *Lives of the Saints* is a specimen of the purest sixteenth-century Polish. Though Skarga is usually quoted as a model of Polish Renaissance prose, his spiritual rootedness in the past makes him a bridge between the pre-Renaissance and the Baroque.

A brand of polemical literature very popular in the last decades of the sixteenth century was pamphlets in prose and verse called *Turcyki*. Directed against Turkey, their contents ranged from well-reasoned arguments on the Ottoman danger to a stream of invective, a vicarious massacre of the infidels. Let us keep in mind that the spread of Turkish power absorbed the attention of the entire European continent at this time.

Turcyki

The Theater

What little is known about theater in Poland before the sixteenth century comes to us from fragments of Latin liturgical dramas performed inside or outside the church buildings and from a few songs or laments which once were part of mystery plays. To say that the history of Polish-language theater began with the Renaissance is not to imply that strictly medieval forms fell into disuse. According to the eminent Belgian scholar, Professor Backvis:

It is true that dramatic work does not belong to the great achievement of sixteenth-century Polish literary culture. Compared with the flourishing genre of lyric poetry, with its perfection of form and content, and with political writings, drama still remains in its childhood. There is nothing extraordinary in this—the belatedness resulted from the very sociocultural structure of Polish society. Yet as I remarked in connection with another type of work giving rise to some dissatisfaction [namely, Kochanowski's *Satyr*]—one can also see the sun in a drop of water; so, too, with Polish Renaissance theater. In it we see clearly rudiments of forces which in the domain of literary creativity—and we limit ourselves here to that realm—led to a blending of imagination, subtlety, and charm—a phenomenon proper to that part of Europe, to one country only, unique in its specific features not to be found anywhere else.

The point of departure is Humanism, Humanism again and again, or rather, the manner in which Humanism was not so much taken over as assimilated in that country, not so much accepted as creatively transformed.

Humanism penetrated all theatrical genres. Around 1500 we see a decline of the liturgical Latin drama and the appearance of a modern Latin dialogue in plays. In the middle of the century Latin is superseded in the theater by Polish.

Mystery Like the Latin liturgical dramas, mystery plays celebrated the
Plays Christian feasts and sought to illustrate their significance in the life of the individual. In Western Europe mystery plays were of a purely medieval stamp, but in Poland they bore traces of a new, more secular outlook, combining many disparate features. Mystery plays remained a popular genre throughout several centuries, though sinking by degrees to the level of folklore. They are connected with such customs (more properly, perhaps, called theatrical performances) as *Szopka* (a puppet show on the Christmas theme, including such standard figures as King Herod, Death, and the Devil), the masquerading of children as the Three Magi on Epiphany, the guarding of the Holy Sepulchre at Easter time by lads in Roman helmets, or the celebration of the eve of the Resurrection by a prolonged salute of muskets and small cannons—a custom still prevalent at the beginning of the nineteenth century. Mystery plays reflected to a considerable extent, as we said before, the public's newly awakening secular interests. Undoubtedly, the best among these plays, and one which has been staged with great success by leading theater directors in our own day, is *A Story of the Most Glorious Resurrection of Our Lord* (*Historia o chwalebnym zmartwychwstaniu Pańskim*), written, or perhaps only edited, around 1580 by Mikołaj of Wilkowiecko, who belonged to the order of Paulinian Brothers in Kraków. Because of its formal perfection it is thought to be the final product of a series of works whose evolution came about through the repeated application of a single model. The construction is excellent; conciseness and realistic vigor add to its freshness, while an eight-syllable verse line links the play with the versification of the past era. The play includes detailed staging instructions and finally begins when the expository figure, Prologus, takes the floor to explain the contents. His speech ends with:

"Be quiet now, folks, and listen attentively. Wishing to rouse you out of the afternoon doze, we will use singing, which will wake you up between the verse lines." Plot is nonexistent: a fragment from the gospel is read, then acted out by the players on a stage. The action begins at the moment when the high priests (called bishops), desiring to avert danger, come to Pontius Pilate (called starosta) and ask him to post guards at the tomb of Christ, who had promised to rise from the dead. The guards are portrayed as typical hirelings from the mob, ruffians of the kind then to be found in every Polish town. When Jesus terrifies them by rising from the dead, one cries out in Ruthenian, another in German, and a third in Hungarian.

A short scene follows with the three women who find the tomb empty; but a scene in hell is enacted with special relish. Jesus, it seems, has driven the devils to despair, for now he would deprive them of their property, i.e., the souls imprisoned there since the beginning of the human race. Jesus is quite rude, even brutal, with the devils. Meeting Adam, the prophets, and St. John the Baptist in hell, he loses no time in liberating them. Next, he asks for a messenger to send to his mother with the news of his resurrection. Adam offers his services, but they are rejected because, wandering around as he was wont to do, picking apples, figs, and lemons, he might forget about the aim of his trip. Abel is also rejected because, having accounts to settle with Cain, he might meet him on the way. Noah is no good because of his drunkenness. St. John the Baptist might scare the mother of Jesus with his outfit of camel skin. The good thief is willing to go, but his legs had been broken by the executioners, so Jesus sends an angel. The play ends with conversations between Jesus and his mother, Mary Magdalen, and the apostles. Lyrical, moving, and comical, the work testifies to the author's (or authors') great theatrical skill and ability to entertain the plebeian audience.

To provide local color, mystery plays often contained comic interludes in the language spoken by the peasants of the eastern areas of the *Respublica*. Thus, the interludes from *The Image of Death of the Most Holy John the Baptist* by Jakub Gawatowic (performed in 1619) are quoted by historians of Ukrainian literature as an example of the first theatrical dialogues in Ukrainian.

Mystery plays were performed in all probability by guilds and amateur actors who used as a setting the so-called "mansions." Singing filled the time during which the actors passed from one "mansion" to another and marked the passage to the next "act." Later on, probably in the beginning of the seventeenth century, the Elizabethan method of staging a play was borrowed from wandering English comedians.

Antique drama in Latin, especially comedy, was introduced in Poland first of all to court and university circles. Transformed sub- *Humanist Drama* sequently by various adaptations and borrowings, it passed on in the vernacular verse to a less fastidious public. The humanist drama, shaped according to ancient models, was relatively short-lived, since the rich middle class of the towns, which was best equipped to receive it, just at that time (i.e., at the turn of the sixteenth century) was losing its importance. Nevertheless, the impact of that genre upon Polish literature was a strong one. A few decades sufficed for the passage from awkward beginnings to well-balanced plays written in a rich language. The first humanist drama printed in Polish, *The Judgment of Paris, Prince of Troy* (1542), an adaptation from the Latin text of an obscure German humanist, Locher, stands on the border line between the medieval and the Renaissance approach. Three goddesses who ask Paris to be a judge of their charms quite unexpectedly appear as allegories of three ways of life: Pallas Athena represents the life of knowledge and contemplation; Juno, the life of power and success; Venus, the life of pleasure and beauty (she is also suggestive of security, as provided by women's money). Paris offers the award to Venus and, in exchange, receives Helen, whom the unclever husband, Menelaus, before setting off for Bohemia (yes!), had left with him. Paris, losing no time, quite unceremoniously asks Helen to sleep with him, since she had been promised to him anyway by Venus. It would have been immoral to show Paris and Helen enjoying each other for ten years, so the play introduces a punishment quite swiftly: Paris, struck by the sword of Menelaus, falls with a shout: "Jesus and Mary, help me, they have cut my flesh on me, I beg you, don't delay, but let me go to confession, O priest, I beg you, come now before my life is over." The very hierarchy of allegorical personification contains a moral lesson: Pallas Athena, the highest; Juno, the second; Venus, the third.

A chasm separates such a play from Kochanowski's drama on the subject of Troy, *The Dismissal of the Grecian Envoys*, which is the most perfect specimen of humanist drama in Poland. The high standard of versification and construction introduced by Kochanowski was, however, maintained by his immediate successors, for instance, Piotr Ciekliński, (1558–1604), who adapted one of Plautus' comedies, *Trinummus*, into Polish (*Potrójny*). Plautus, in his turn, had adapted his plays from Greek originals. Staged at an aristocratic court probably in 1595, and published in 1597, Ciekliński's comedy shows its moralistic intent through his introduction of native scenery and local human types. In the prologue, a poem addressed to Plautus says:

Plautus, you who in vain chafed Rome with your jokes, since Rome, being too happy, caused itself harm—shed your toga, Plautus, and put on our heavy boots, and speak Polish; let our people understand what yours did not want to hear. When they see that Rome lost its freedom and perished though greater [than Poland], perhaps, the Poles will take heed, and you shall gather the fruit of your work.

Following Kochanowski's lead, the author uses blank verse—a thirteen-syllable line with a caesura (seven + six) and a great number of enjambments. His verse is quite vigorous and achieves humorous effects especially in short dialogues.

The plot, that novelty discovered along with the antique theater, centers around a prodigal son figure, Pangracz, who has been squandering his fortune during the absence of his father on a journey to France with his second son, a prospective student at the Sorbonne. The guardian, Dobrochowski, under whose care the father has placed the family affairs, is given a rather hard time by the young rake, whose ambitions prevent his sister's marriage to a decent young man, Szczęsny. Although a brother should provide a dowry for his sister, the rake is penniless; and though Dobrochowski is in possession of a hidden treasure left by the father, he is afraid to reveal its existence. The action takes place in the city of Lwów among the nobility already leading burgherlike lives. Figures of comical servants, of local capitalists, like the Greek, Filoktet (Lwów had a considerable number of Armenians and Greeks), add to the liveliness of the action. The most amusing figure is that of a plebeian, a petty scrivener named Pierczyk, who, at a certain moment, owing to the intricacies of the plot, is mistaken for a messenger from the father in France and who evidences most extraordinary notions of the geography of Europe. But the father returns unexpectedly, the rake is brought back to the path of virtue, and all ends well.

The play is a fine example of humanist concern with the education of youth. Training abroad is praised, though the instruction available in local Jesuit schools is favorably regarded. Discussion also revolves around the ways of advancement open to young people and around the question of military service. At this time, the Poles were preparing an expedition against Muscovy; thus, military service to the state became a topic of greater concern than politics. The latter, based upon words alone, is like "water frozen over" or like "snow heaped by the wind"—"it lasts while the Republic lives through evil days as through a winter, but melts in the spring." The plot taken from Plautus served Ciekliński only as a skeletal structure. He transformed it into a vivid picture of Polish life, which becomes almost tangible in his tirades against luxury, against gossip, that is, against:

those who pretend to know everything—what one is thinking or is going to think, what the king whispered into the ear of the queen, what is happening in Calcutta, in America; who receive news from all countries; who even know what God himself commanded to the archangel Michael.

A play called *The Beggars' Tragedy* (*Tragedia Żebracza*) is not a tragedy at all (the terms "tragedy" and "comedy" were used inter- changeably at that time) but a specimen of plebeian humanist comedy, secular and combative in its observation of life. An original Polish work printed in 1551, it won popularity also in Czech translations.

The title page of *The Beggars' Tragedy*, second edition, 1552.

The action takes place in a tavern among a group of beggars that include persons of both sexes. Far from being a haphazard assemblage, their company is organized with a democratically elected chief at its head and has come together to celebrate the wedding of a certain couple, i.e., a ragged old man and an ugly old hag. They announce that, having slept together many a night, they are duly married, and now since they have decided to stick together, no church is necessary. Music and dances follow but are interrupted by a merchant who stops at the inn. Immediately a conflict arises between him, a repre- sentative of established society, on the one hand, and the beggars, who constitute a society within a society, on the other. The merchant enters into dispute with the beggars and enumerates their evil deeds: to procure money, they deceive people with their sham blindness, illness, lameness. The beggars repay him by characterizing the merchant profession, which, they say, consists in lying and cheating. Finally, one after the other relates how he (or she), too, had once been rich but had lost everything, and now was happy being free. They pronounce an ironic encomium of their profession:

Our estate is famous, known everywhere, ancient. We are surprised that people hate us; they obviously forget how the Holy Writ praises us above all the other estates. If you want proof: Christ himself blessed us with his favor and promised us the heavenly kingdom.

In the course of the hot dispute, the merchant is thrashed by the beggars, and the next day he appears before the chief with a complaint. Just as before we witnessed a travesty of a wedding, now we are spectators at a mock trial. The chief pronounces the following verdict for the offense committed: the one-eyed beggar shall be without one eye; the one-legged beggar, without one leg; and the old hags shall be unable to bear children. The satire is equally distributed between merchant and beggars. If the merchant does not emerge a paragon of virtue, the beggars, too, receive their share of blame. According to the merchant's words, all of them have iron blades in their sticks, terrorize villages, burn down inhospitable houses, act as spies for the Turks, deceive humble folk by pretending they are saints, engage in sorcery, and pay visits to witches' Sabbaths. Altogether the comedy resembles a painting by Pieter Breughel.

The Beggars' Tragedy may be considered as opening up a whole genre known as *komedia rybałtowska*. The Polish word *rybałt* appears to come from the Italian *ribaldo*, designating church employees of a lower order, such as bell ringers, sacristans, etc. These were plebeians with a smattering of education; often they could be met in private houses as hangers-on, acting as teachers or musicians. The literature which they created bears such a resemblance to that of the *żaki*, or students (i.e., *literatura żakowska*), that the border line between them remains a fluid one. The plebeians' comedies of crude realism reflect not only their way of life but their awareness of themselves as a social stratum. Always on the lookout for a few pennies with which to set up a drinking bout, they pestered tavern patrons with their perpetual laments over the wrongs inflicted on them by the world, in particular, by parsons and their women-servants or concubines (presented as terrible shrews). They applied their wit to a little world familiar to them through direct experience. As a rule, they expressed the outlook of the urban mob and were anti-Protestant; Protestants were regarded as high-brows. *Komedia rybałtowska* flourished during the second half of the sixteenth and first half of the seventeenth centuries in that section of the country where towns were the most powerful, i.e., the south. Within the genre we can distinguish several recurrent themes; foremost is that of beggars. (This class already formed part of a common European folklore.) The petty employees of the Church, to whose lot fell the supervision of mendicant activities—the "good" beggars were allowed to solicit near the churches while the "bad" were barred from access to such advantageous locations—profited from their familiarity with beggardom, exploiting the theme for humorous purposes.

In *The Beggars' Peregrination* (*Peregryncja dziadowska*), a sort of dramatized "novella" in verse, we are spectators at a secret council of beggars who have come together on the occasion of a country fair. They appear as experts on the topography and living conditions of Poland, Bohemia, Hungary, even of Italy as far south as Rome, and of the territory of the Eastern Slavs as far north as Moscow. They manifest complete cynicism in respect to things sacred, and regard witchcraft as the only serious pursuit. They coldly exploit peasant naïveté, as is shown, for instance, when one of the beggars recounts how, in Silesia, he pretended to be a werewolf and how this brought him a goodly income from frightened peasant women. They connive with other outlaws, forest and mountain bandits, and serve as spies for the rebellious Cossacks. Rather than work, they prefer to have their limbs broken and their eyes plucked out, because this brings money.

Another theme, that of "marauding soldiers," appears in a cycle of comedies whose central figure, Albertus, is none other than the braggart soldier (*miles gloriosus*) of ancient comedies brought to life again. Albertus is a church employee about to be sent off for military service by the parish priest, who, compelled by law, must supply one soldier to the army. Equipped with what a naïve priest and the stupid clerk were able to buy at secondhand dealers in Kraków, namely, outdated weapons of another century and a half-dying horse, Albertus goes off to war. After two years of service he returns a perfect knave. Following the counsel of his employer, he had carefully avoided battles, but had waged war with chickens and geese on peasants' farms. He had even earned some money by putting his talent as a choirmaster to another use, namely, as a singer of bawdy songs at military camps. In other variations, Albertus bears the name of Matthew and is the son of a Protestant minister. When Matthew and his father go to buy equipment in Kraków, they are sold an old coat which, though full of holes, was supposed to have belonged to a son of Martin Luther, a valuable sword used in battle by the leader of the

Hussites, Jan Žižka, and a dagger with which Lucretia committed suicide and which later found its way into the possession of Queen Elizabeth of England. To the knaveries of Albertus, Matthew adds yet another: he becomes a Roman Catholic for reasons of expediency.

A third theme is directly connected with the life of the "ribalds" themselves. In *A New Ribald Comedy* (*Komedia rybałtowska nowa*) a magister (school teacher), a choirmaster, a bell ringer, and our acquaintance, Albertus, roam the countryside in search of something to eat. They try to convince a peasant to feed them, but receive only an adamant refusal under the pretext that marauding soldiers had already consumed everything there was to eat. Just then, one such soldier enters the hut, and soon is joined by two beggars. A heated political dispute arises which betrays a thorough understanding of the political problems of the day. The soldier, who had to bear rebukes for the troop's pillage of the countryside, invokes the suffering undergone by the Poles when, after having captured Moscow, they were besieged by the Muscovites in the Kremlin. There they were forced to eat cats and dogs, and for some, "a prisoner's leg tasted like the best venison." But the beggars continue to taunt the soldier and reproach him for not hanging on to Moscow while it was in Polish hands and for showing valor only in the plunder of defenseless peasants. In the skirmish which follows, the beggars disarm the soldier, but Albertus recognizes in him his old friend and prevails upon them to release him. The peasant, grateful for the end of the argument, stands treat with some food he had hidden away in a safe place. Dances and songs performed by a pair of beggars fill the interludes. This is one of the most lively of the "ribald comedies" and contains a multitude of details of everyday life. Originating sometime in the beginning of the seventeenth century, it, too, can be compared to realistic Dutch and Flemish paintings of the same period.

In *A Synod of Highland Clerks* (*Synod klechów podgórskich*), "ribalds" from towns and villages south of Kraków and from the highlands at the foot of the Tatra Mountains gather together at a sort of trade-union meeting touched off by the desire to air grievances against the circumstances of their lives: constant underpayment and maltreatment. The play consists of parliamentarylike debates. A clerk gets up, describes in great detail his miserable fate, and casts his vote for such and such a collective decision. Some are for radical solutions, such as refusing to perform their functions or completely changing their profession, learning crafts or enlisting as soldiers. But when one announces that he has decided to become a Protestant with the hope of becoming a minister, they spit on him and chase him from the assemblage. Finally, they vote on a charter summing up the major rights and duties of their profession. Such proceedings were hilariously funny at that time, especially on the parts of bell-ringers, choirmasters, and elementary school teachers.

Disguise, often a Carnival disguise, provides thematic material for a fourth variation of "ribald comedy." A play of this type is usually set in a tavern, where all sorts of drinks, mugs, glasses, bottles are described with great relish. In one such comedy, a company gathered at a tavern is visited by the fantastic characters Bacchus, his court of satyrs, and two devils. To every member of the group, Bacchus, who presides over the Carnival, offers as many tankards of beer as there are letters in the name of the given person. As might be expected, the names read like: Kufo-beczko-baryło-cebr-bokłako-kuflowski (Cask-barrel-tank-tub-bottle-jug-owski). When one of those present falls under the table, the rest play a practical joke on him. They fix cow's horns to his head and paste hair on his face and hands. His adventures when he wakes up and begins to roam the neighborhood occupy a considerable part of the play. This comedy of Carnival time (*Mięsopust*) has a crazily careening movement; one is tempted to say, movielike.

The best-known comedy employing the disguise motif, and one which eventually made its way into the repertoire of the court theater, is *Peasant into King* (*Z chłopa król*) by Piotr Baryka, first staged in 1633. It is built around a prank played by some soldiers on a peasant found in a drunken sleep. They put rich garments and a crown on him and pretend that he is a king. The peasant, though not comprehending his situation, soon drives the pranksters to despair with his enormous capacity for food and drink. The soldiers, since at that time there were many Cossacks in the Polish army, speak not only in Polish but also in Ukrainian. An epilogue on the Carnival closes the play. In it, the author announces that the season is over and that those young men who did not find wives, as well as those girls who did not find husbands, must wait until Easter. Thanks to its concise structure and its pure but realistic language, the play makes excellent reading even today. It is written in thirteen-syllable verse, which the author handles with great facility.

Komedia rybałtowska, as a genre, lasted for some one hundred years, coming to its end in the middle of the seventeenth century, exactly when *Peasant into King* was written.

Morality Plays   Highly appreciated in medieval Europe, the morality play reached its perfection in the fifteenth century in the English version of *Everyman*. Usually, a morality play told the story of a sinner who stands before God's tribunal. As for Poland, we have already mentioned the fifteenth-century fragment, *The Lament of a Dying Man;* later on, Mikołaj Rej, in his *Merchant* (*Kupiec*), transformed the genre into a vehicle for Protestant truths. During the Baroque period, with its fondness for images of hell, the form was revived, and it flourished throughout the seventeenth century, particularly in the Jesuit theaters. An example of a curious transitional variety, printed in 1604, is *A Tragedy of the Polish Scilurus* by a plebeian writer, Jan Jurkowski. The original Scilurus was a legendary king of the Scythians who, in order to show his sons that strength lies in unity, ordered them first to break a bunch of arrows tied together, then to break them singly. In Jurkowski's play, Scilurus on his deathbed summons his three sons, who turn out to be: the Polish Hercules, who is a soldier warring against the Turks (he represents the Active Life); the Polish Paris (brought up in France and Germany, who leads the Life of Pleasure); and the Polish Diogenes (who pursues the Life of Wisdom and Virtue). The father, like his legendary predecessor, imparts the lesson of the arrows to his sons. Soon after, Death enters (wearing a crown), followed closely by the Devil, who has come for the soul of Scilurus. But because two of his sons are good, an angel drives away the Evil One. The interlude at the end of the first act consists of a humorous dialogue between two scoundrels hurrying to a funeral repast. This conversation is held in typical thieves' slang of the period.

In the second act, Hercules (who, according to the stage instructions, "should be girt in lion or leopard skin") is approached by Pleasure ("should be ornately dressed and holding a candle in one hand, a sword or a dagger in the other") and by Virtue ("should be simply and neatly dressed, holding an anchor in one hand, a green wreath in the other"). Hercules chooses to follow Virtue, thus meriting a eulogy pronounced by Glory ("should have white and black wings, many plumes and eyes[!], holding in one hand a green wreath; in the other, a burning wick or two trumpets").

In the third act, Paris ("should be dressed in the Italian or German manner, and carrying a zither") is prepared to give priority to Venus over Juno (served by his brother, Hercules) and Pallas Athena (served by his brother, Diogenes). He also pays homage to a new character, namely, Wielki Chwał—a sort of master of ceremonies of all the vanities of the world. Glory announces that Paris will end shamefully, and the act concludes with a dance of Paris and Helen accompanied by Wielki Chwał, who spreads a carpet for them. Devils with amusing names (Kostruban, Duliban, Mędrela) play dice for his soul. The interlude in this act is closely allied to *komedia rybałtowska* because it concerns a squire's bad treatment of his children's tutor, a student.

In the fourth act, the Polish Diogenes ("should be attired in priestly fashion, carrying books") in vain seeks a man leading a virtuous life.

Curiously enough, Alexander the Great appears and engages him in conversation. The play ends with a speech pronounced by Glory in praise of Diogenes.

Dialogues   The dialogue as a genre grew out of the Middle Ages, but it was given a new direction at the time of vehement interdenominational quarrels. The form itself hovers on the line between printed literature and the theater. For example, Mikołaj Rej's *A Short Dispute Between A Gentleman, A Bailiff, and A Parson* was destined to be read, not played. But dialogues with a point to prove were employed by both Catholics and Protestants in a more theatrical form. For instance, in a *Comedy on Shrovetide*, dating from the middle of the sixteenth century, a Roman Catholic parish priest carries on a long theological dispute with his guest, a Protestant burgher. The latter, finding himself cornered in the discussion, resorts to bodily threats upon his host, whereupon he receives a good thrashing from the servants. In the next act the burgher, who does not know his Bible well enough, returns, bringing with him a student presumably well prepared by his stay in Wittenberg. But the student, to tell the truth, is more interested in the prospect of a good dinner. As soon as he sees that such an event is in the offing, he valiantly leads a discussion on the problems of fasting and the Carnival. In the third act, after the dinner, the student, who has more or less lost the dispute, asks the priest to call in his housekeeper, Maśka, for he wants to dance. She angrily objects: "I am all covered with soot, I smell of smoke; how can I go to the guests if I haven't been to bathe?" But she comes anyway, and Maśka, who had impressed the student with her beauty, proves to be the best theologian. She, together with her employer, defeats the Protestants, who, at the end of the play, offer their apologies.

Jesuit   Up to the second half of the eighteenth century, theater as a
Theater permanent institution was unknown in Poland. Plays were staged by guilds or amateur groups under the sponsorship of a wealthy man, a lord, or a king. As students were ideally suited for acting, various schools also put on performances for a mixed public composed of pupils and local citizens. The Jesuit Order turned these school theaters into effective weapons against the Protestants. The Jesuits, fully aware of the theatrical value of the liturgy (no Protestant service could offer the faithful anything comparable in color, sound, or movement to the Roman Catholic rite), also applied their histrionic talents to the school stage. Jesuit theater in Poland had a history of some two hundreds years, and if we accept the opinion of a specialist in the field, Julian Lewański, it may be divided into four periods: The first, a period of experimentation—lasting from the foundation of the first Jesuit college in 1564 up to the end of the

sixteenth century—was characterized by vacillation between dialogues and morality plays, on the one hand, and dramatic forms midway between the drama and the musical spectacle, on the other; the second, a period of flowering, covered the first half of the seventeenth century, when the Jesuit style distinguished itself by its well-constructed plays with lively interludes and by the achievement of a certain equilibrium between word, sound, music, and stage effect. Both Polish and Latin were used in the writing of the text, and an interesting innovation, the magic lantern, became part of Jesuit stage-craft. (This type of theater is an excellent illustration of Polish Baroque.) The third, a period of decadence, began in the second half of the seventeenth century and reached into the first decades of the eighteenth century. Pantomime, along with lighting and sound effects (especially the magic lantern), took priority over other elements. Texts were awkward and naïve. Latin predominated, and all traces of polemics and discussion vanished. The fourth, a period of slow recovery—from the middle of the eighteenth century up to 1773, when the Jesuit Order was disbanded by the Pope—saw a return to the Polish language, the gradual substitution of prose for verse, and translations of good foreign drama.

The Jesuit theater is interesting for a Slavic scholar because of its role in the migration of many dramatic forms from Western to Eastern Slavdom. In the eastern territories of the Polish-Lithuanian *Respublica* there were some twenty-three Jesuit colleges, reaching as far as Mogilev, Polotsk, Smolensk, and Vitebsk. The Jesuits, with their peculiar facility for adapting themselves to local conditions, sometimes staged plays in Old Byelorussian or Old Ukrainian, and subjects especially dear to Orthodox Christians were not scorned, for instance, the lives of the martyrs Boris and Gleb.

The Protestant schools in the predominantly Lutheran cities of northern Poland devoted much attention to plays in Latin or in German. But the Polish Protestant school theater is primarily indebted to a Czech writer, one of the glories of European literature of the early seventeenth century, Jan Amos Komenský (Comenius). After his native country had been crushed by the Hapsburgs in 1620 and Roman Catholicism established there as the official religion, Komenský emigrated to Poland to join his coreligionists, known as the Czech Brethren, who maintained the traditions of Jan Hus. In Leszno, in Greater Poland, he founded an internationally famous Polish school to propagate what he called *pansophia* (universal knowledge—in this he foreshadowed the Encyclopedists). Komenský saw the theater as an ideal instrument of communication, more effective in teaching than textbooks because better adapted to the needs of the pupils. Of his Polish experiences Komenský wrote:

The Protestant Theater

I was told that such games should be left to the Jesuits; I have supposedly been called to more important things. I answered: those games lead to serious goals. It is true, the Jesuits are sons of the world, very clever at managing their affairs; we are sons of light, not skillful enough. Through the pleasures of their methods they attract gifted minds from all over the world, and with their exercises they prepare them for the tasks of life, while our methods have atrophied. I added: if we had not had such exercises in our schools in Poland, everything would have stopped; only thanks to them can we not only prevent our people from sending their sons to the Jesuits but even expect some to come from the Jesuits to us.

The advantages Komenský saw in the school theater can be summarized as follows: First, no discipline can incite students to such efforts as participation in a theater performance. Since they see pleasure in it, they assimilate knowledge more quickly than by studying books. Second, the actor-students are strongly motivated by hope of praise and fear of failure. Third, teachers work harder, since they must show tangible results on the stage. Fourth, the parents, pleased by the public successes of their sons, do not spare money for education and theater spectacles. Fifth, talented individuals are able to show off their gifts, and the educator is afforded a better chance than in the classroom to observe who should receive a scholarship. Sixth, the pupils receive a training necessary for their future careers; that is, they learn how to move, to speak and to play any social role.

WRITINGS IN OTHER LANGUAGES

As a multinational state, the Polish-Lithuanian *Respublica* fostered literary efforts not only in Polish and Latin. The Reformation and the polemics provoked by it favored other vernaculars besides Polish. In the towns with a predominantly German population such as those on the Baltic coast, German began to compete with Latin so successfully that a rich body of literature came into being. For our purposes, however, it is more interesting to note that the territory of the *Respublica* was the birthplace of three new literatures: Lithuanian, Byelorussian, and Ukrainian. Although the territory which could be called ethnically Lithuanian was situated in the Grand Duchy of Lithuania, a small western piece of it belonged to East Prussia, then a dependent principality of the *Respublica*. The capital of that principality, Königsberg, was an important Protestant printing center, and from there in 1547 issued the first book to reach the Lithuanian people in their native idiom—the *Catechism* of M. Mažvydas. From that moment, the number of printed works published in Lithuanian steadily increased, but until the eighteenth century practically all those works retained the character of religious (Protestant or Catholic) publications, except for the first trilingual dictionary of Polish, Latin, and Lithuanian, printed by K. Širvydas in Wilno (Vilnius) in 1629.

Ever since the Middle Ages, when the borders of the Grand Duchy of Lithuania embraced populations speaking several Eastern Slavic dialects, these dialects, along with the Cyrillic alphabet, had been used in official documents. But also the ruling nobility of Lithuanian stock gradually abandoned the use of their native tongue, switching to Slavic in its Polish or Eastern Slavic variety, and already in the sixteenth century, Lithuanian was considered a language of the peasantry, and so it remained until the end of the nineteenth century. The official language of the Duchy was called Ruthenian, and in the sixteenth century it already showed signs of a division into a northern variant, i.e., Byelorussian, and a southern variant, Ukrainian. But the linguistic situation was extremely fluid, and Ruthenian absorbed many Polish words. Some texts sound practically like Polish texts written in Cyrillic with Eastern Slavic case endings added. Besides it is far from clear as to what relation existed between the written official language and that spoken by the people. In any case, nobody who studies the life and institutions of the Grand Duchy and the history of the Reformation there can bypass such rich material, consisting of edicts, regulations, juridical formulas, and, occasionally, religious polemics. The first Bible in the vernacular (the work of Franciszek Skoryna) to be published within the borders of the *Respublica* was, as we have already mentioned, not in Polish but in Old Byelorussian. A monumental juridical work, the *Lithuanian Statutes*, was published in Old Byelorussian in Wilno in 1529. The native Protestants of the Grand Duchy did not forget their compatriots whose knowledge of Polish was insufficient. Thus, the most vigorous leader of the Arians in Lithuania, Szymon Budny, used to write his polemics in either Polish or Old Byelorussian. Let us add that the two languages stood on an equal footing, and the lords of the Duchy used Old Byelorussian when speaking in public in Warsaw. One instance of this is the speech of the Vice-Chancellor of the Duchy, Lew Sapieha, in 1588. Panegyrical verses honoring local magnates were written by local squires, often in Byelorussian. (The poems of Andrzej Rymsza are one instance.)

But the memoirs of a nobleman (from the neighborhood of Nowogródek) are perhaps the most interesting lay literary work in Old Byelorussian. (They make pleasant reading today.) Teodor Jewłaszewski (1564–1604), a Calvinist, used to send his children to Arian schools, while he himself maintained excellent relations with the Roman Catholic clergy in Wilno. In his memoirs, written at the end of his life, he turns back with nostalgia toward an era of perfect tolerance in both religious and human relations among peoples professing different creeds and speaking different languages in their homes. That era of tolerance was fast drawing to a close under the impact of the victorious Counter Reformation. Jewłaszewski's language abounds in "Polonisms" and illustrates the moment of transition in the history of the Grand Duchy when squires of "Ruthenian" stock such as himself were beginning to abandon their native idiom in favor of Polish, just as they were discarding their Protestant or Orthodox faith for Roman Catholicism.

Old Ukrainian literature has for its first important representatives men connected, in one way or another, with the polemics centering around the question of union with Rome. The side in favor of union possessed a most gifted polemicist in the person of Adam Ipatiï Potij (or Pociej, in Polish), who presented his arguments either in Polish or in Ruthenian (in its Old Ukrainian version). The target of his attacks was Prince Ostrogski and his followers, the center of opposition to the union. That group, located in Ostróg in Volhynia, was responsible for the printing of a Bible in Old Church Slavic, known as the Bible of Ostróg.

A fiery preacher who thundered in writing against any attempts at *rapprochement* between the Eastern and Western Churches was Ivan Vishenski (born in the Ukraine in the middle of the sixteenth century; died around 1620). He spent most of his life as a monk on Mount Athos, but in his missives from the monastery to the *Respublica* he attacked in his flowery and high-flown style Polish and Ruthenian magnates, both lay and clerical, whose behavior he saw as sinful. Curiously enough, there is a noticeable similarity of style and of attitudes between the Jesuit, Piotr Skarga, and his contemporary, the Orthodox monk from Mount Athos, which would indicate that Vishenski, despite his contempt for the Roman faith, did not scorn a certain Western type of rhetoric in the defense of his cause.

It is not our intention to give an outline of the development of Byelorussian and Ukrainian literatures but merely to point out that the "Ruthenian" language was a constant presence on the literary scene and was well understood by the inhabitants of even ethnically Polish areas.

CHAPTER IV

The Seventeenth Century: Counter Reformation and the Baroque

BACKGROUND INFORMATION

B Y THE BEGINNING of the seventeenth century, the equilibrium *Political* of the political and economic structure, which had remained *and* *Economic* quite stable during the previous century, began to show signs of *Structure* imbalance. The Diet enacted many laws obviously intended to curb the privileges of the burghers. Thus, towns, despite a relative prosperity, entered a phase of decline. For a while, they continued to be productive in the realm of learning and literature, but in the middle of the century devastating wars spelled final ruin for Polish urban life. The country returned to a purely rural pattern of existence, just at a time when Western Europe was witnessing the ascent of the bourgeois class to economic power. A system of plantation-type farming gradually became an accomplished fact, bringing with it misery and oppression for the peasants. The gentry's "golden freedom" was understood more and more frequently as a sanction to license and anarchy. Almost every decade saw movements of the gentry, known as "confederacies," organized against the authorities, who were accused of limiting freedom in some respect or another. These confederacies usually ended in compromises which weakened respect for law. The central authority was looked upon with suspicion and even hatred, although, if compared with absolutist-inclined monarchies of other European states of this period, its power was nonexistent. Paradoxically, the gentry, who had emerged as victors from their long struggle with the lords and the bishops and were now the real rulers of the country (through the Diet), proved to have little political sense, allowing themselves to be used as servile tools in the hands of a few magnates. The *szlachta* or average gentry —who made up around 10 per cent of the population—found more and more of their members sinking into poverty. The amassing of large fortunes by the few coincided with the impoverishment of the many, i.e., of the average landowners. (In the middle of the fifteenth century the average gentry owned 44.9 per cent of all the land; in the middle of the seventeenth century, only 16.9 per cent; and in the eighteenth century, only 9.2 per cent.) As a result, every rich nobleman or magnate was surrounded by a multitude of "clients" whose voices he was able to buy easily at the local dietines for the election of deputies to the main Diet. The parliamentary body was thus transformed into a battleground of factions controlled by magnates for the defense of their private interests. Certain magnates carved for themselves immense "latifundia," especially in the Ukraine, where they openly defied the king, and each practiced his own policy of oppressing the local population. The principle of unanimity in the Diet, which had been applied with moderation in the sixteenth century, as everything then was settled in caucuses before the actual voting, now produced the *liberum veto*: a "free protest," expressing individual disagreement and called out by a deputy in the Diet, automatically broke off the session in progress and rendered all laws voted during that session null and void. The *liberum veto* was used for the first time in 1652.

War with Muscovy   Taking advantage of the dynastic disorders in Muscovy, the Poles backed a pretender to the throne ("The False Dmitry"), and in 1609, after capturing Smolensk, defeating the Muscovite army on its way to rescue the besieged town, they marched on Moscow. Their commander in chief, Hetman Stanisław Żółkiewski, was an extraordinary personality—a diplomat and soldier, as well as a writer, who left behind him an interesting account of the Moscow campaign. With the Russian boyars he negotiated an agreement by which the throne of the czars would be offered to Władysław, son of the Polish king, Sigismund Vasa (Sigismund III). But although the Polish troops succeeded in occupying the Kremlin, Żółkiewski received neither the backing of the Diet nor the assurance of King Sigismund, who apparently coveted the Russian throne for himself. In any case, the Polish ruler returned a flat "No" to a proposal from the Russian boyars that the Polish prince adopt the Russian Orthodox faith. Meanwhile, the Russians rallied a resistance force against the invaders and successfully carried out a long siege of the Kremlin. The Polish troops which had occupied it since their entry into the city were forced by the threat of starvation to capitulate in October

1612. (Żółkiewski also commanded Polish troops in a war with Turkey. He was killed in the desperate battle of Cecora in 1620.)

The oppressive rule of Polish magnates in the Ukraine was aggravated by a religious conflict, as the peasants, unlike those in Byelorussia, remained mostly Orthodox and, therefore, sensitive to the appeals of the lower Orthodox clergy. The situation was rendered potentially explosive by the presence of the Cossacks, a peculiar social group for whom no equivalent can be found in any other part of Europe. The Cossacks formed a sort of military order, living in settlements on the river Dnieper and recognizing no master save, with a vague loyalty, the Polish Crown. These free men, who used to make military expeditions for booty as far as the Turkish shores of the Black Sea, acted as the defenders of the *Respublica* on its vast southern steppes, constantly endangered by Moslem (Tartar) assaults. In 1648, the social discontent, combined with some national stirrings, erupted in a rebellion of the Ukraine against Poland. The military know-how was supplied by the Cossacks. The rebellion had the character of a peasant uprising, and it caught on in provinces further west, touching off movements even in a few ethnically Polish districts. In the Ukraine, though, it was transformed by its leader, a Ukrainian nobleman, Bohdan Chmielnicki, into a war for political autonomy. There were, however, more than two camps involved. The king recognized the grievances of the Ukraine and was prepared to give redress, while Chmielnicki (at least in the initial phase) was seeking to enlist royal help against the magnates. The latter, however, pursued only one policy, that of suppression, and the war was waged with unspeakable cruelties on both sides. Chmielnicki, after winning initial successes, was finally cornered and in 1654 forced to conclude with Muscovy the Treaty of Pereyaslav, which placed the country under the protection of the czar. This opened the way to Russia's subsequent annexation of the Ukraine. After the death of Chmielnicki, Poles and Ukrainians made an attempt to find a compromise solution in the Agreement of Hadziacz in 1658, which conceived of the *Respublica* as a federation of three states: Poland, Lithuania, and Ruthenia (the Ukraine). The latter was to recognize the Polish monarch, to send deputies to the Polish Diet, and to commit herself to a common foreign policy. On the other hand, the Ukraine received an autonomous judiciary and broad privileges for the members of the Orthodox faith. The metropolitan of Kiev and Orthodox bishops were given seats in the Senate. Muscovite diplomacy, however, intent on the destruction of the agreement, supported successfully local leaders who were hostile to it. A long war between Poland and Russia, provoked not only by those tensions, was ended

The Ukrainian Question

by the Truce of Andruszów in 1667, which cut the Ukraine in two, along the river Dnieper. The *Respublica* retained the provinces on the western bank of the Dnieper, while Kiev went to Muscovy.

The Swedish War From the moment Poland elected, in 1587, a Swedish king of the Vasa line, dynastic embroilments became the immediate cause of constant wars with Sweden. Clashes took place mostly in Livonia on the Baltic peninsula and on the Baltic Sea. In 1655, Swedish troops led by King Charles Gustav landed in northern Poland and at first encountered minimal resistance. This was due, mainly, to the defection of large numbers of the Polish Protestant nobility, outraged by the victorious Counter Reformation, to the camp of the Protestant Swedish King, though many Catholics ranged themselves in his ranks too. Sweden occupied most of Poland but suffered severe reverses after an unsuccessful siege of the monastery of Częstochowa, regarded by the populace as a national shrine. This event took on a symbolic character and even sparked a guerrilla-type war of fanatic peasants led by Roman Catholic priests against the foreign heretics. The Polish army, which in the meantime had undergone a reorganization, finally overwhelmed the Swedes in a series of battles and drove them out of the country. The effects of that war were particularly disastrous. Towns were completely devastated, and, due to their already advanced financial weakness, they were unable to carry out reconstruction. The depressed condition of urban areas remained a constant factor in determining the direction of Polish cultural history for the next two centuries. The date 1655–1656 marked the end of bourgeois literature. Moreover, that the Protestants could be accused of collaboration with the enemy brought ignominy and ruin to the upholders of Arianism. After the war, Catholics and Calvinists, casting about for a scapegoat in order to exonerate themselves, accused the Arians of complicity with the foe, and in 1658 the Diet passed a law ordering the Arians to accept either Roman Catholicism or banishment from the *Respublica*. It was thus, after a history of nearly one hundred years, that the Minor Church ceased to exist. The most active Arians migrated to Holland, where they published *Bibliotheca Fratrum Polonorum*, a monumental collection of the writings of the movement. Either directly from Holland or via England, Arianism eventually reached America, where it took shape as the Unitarian Church. After 1655–1656, Calvinism and Lutheranism were gradually reduced to the status of insignificant minorities.

Education This was a time of continual decline in the standards of education. Jesuit schools, adapting themselves to the prevalent tastes of the gentry, taught no more than the art of flowery expression in Polish and in Latin. We should distinguish, though, between the first and second halves of the century. Some Jesuit colleges, e.g., the Jesuit

Academy of Wilno, flourished during the first decades of the seventeenth century, when they represented the best of what can be called "the Jesuit tradition." And though the country in general moved toward obscurantism and programmatic anti-intellectualism, some Protestant schools were actually in advance of the intellectual trends in Europe. Among them the Arian (Socinian) College of Raków, an institution of international renown, deserves special note. Socinian books printed there were one of the strangest Polish contributions to European thought. These books, written mostly in Latin, were avidly read in many countries as the most daring reinterpretation of Christian faith in its encounter with rationalism. Socinians were attacked by all Christian denominations for being, in effect, "deists" (a term which came into use only later on). For this reason their books provoked curiosity, though few dared to confess in public that they were acquainted with them. Such philosophers of the seventeenth century as Spinoza and John Locke borrowed many ideas from the Socinians, although Locke, when accused of this in his lifetime, denied it. As H. J. McLachlan says in his work *Socinianism in Seventeenth Century England* (Oxford, 1951): "He always repudiated his debt to the 'Racovians' even to the point of declaring (in the *Second Vindication of the Reasonableness of Christianity*) that he had never read a page of Socinus or Crell." McLachlan goes on to prove that Locke had a rich collection in his library of "Rakovian" books whose margins were covered with notes in his own handwriting. The Raków School prospered between 1602 and 1638. It was closed because of a student prank interpreted by Roman Catholics as a desecration of the Cross. The tribunal of the Diet passed a sentence liquidating the school in spite of strong opposition from many deputies, both Calvinist and Catholic. The Protestant College in Leszno, endowed by the aristocratic family of Leszczyński and directed by the Czech refugee Jan Amos Komenský (Comenius), was another important center of learning. Komenský's works, written in Latin, constituted an important factor in the intellectual movement preparatory to Cromwell's revolution in England. On a visit to London during Cromwell's rule, Komenský found himself surrounded by admirers, and it was then that he was invited to become the president of a college in the New World, in Cambridge, Massachusetts (Harvard). He declined the offer, however, because, after the miserable voyage he had made from Danzig to London, the thought of sea-travel was unbearable. In 1656 the school in Leszno and Komenský's own rich library were reduced to ashes by Catholic troops in pursuit of the retreating Swedes. Komenský himself reached Amsterdam with only the clothes on his back.

Thus, for education, too, the years 1655–1656 were of crucial importance. From that date on, the Jesuits had no reason to exert themselves, since theirs was a monopoly in teaching. The University of Kraków gradually lost its ascendancy, and, in addition, the city itself had ceased to be the capital of the *Respublica* when Sigismund Vasa, in 1596, had moved his court to Warsaw.

Mentality of the Gentry   The stock image of the Polish *szlachta* not only in Polish but also in foreign literature refers, above all, to that phenomenon which took shape during the seventeenth century, "Sarmatism." The gentry's mentality reflected then a rural, parochial life—more parochial than it had been in the preceding period. Travels abroad for educational purposes ceased. They were considered unnecessary, since Poland, enjoying "golden freedom," could boast of the best political system in the world, and thus had nothing to learn from other nations. The gregarious, turbulent, anarchistic, hard-drinking, and litigious provincials imagined themselves, when reading Cicero or Seneca, as Roman statesmen. They were fond of pomposity in both oratory and dress. The displays of luxury at that time, the fascination with glittering fabrics, with jewels, and with richly decorated arms were, in large part, the result of Eastern influences. Constant contact with Turkey, despite open hositilities between the two countries, was responsible for the many oriental details of the gentry's dress, arms, harnessry, introduced along with the corresponding Turkish words. The preceding century's bucolic ideal of the gentleman farmer, which we saw in Rej and Kochanowski, was transformed into an attitude of self-centered complacency deprived of intellectual curiosity. Religious life, divested of those anxieties and torments which characterized, for instance, the poetry of Sęp-Szarzyński, became conventionalized. Since Catholicism of the Counter Reformation made its appeal through the senses, the liturgy acquired a Baroque, operatic character. These tastes and preoccupations found faithful confirmation in the literature of the period.

Wars with Turkey   Proximity to the Ottoman Empire induced, besides many oriental tastes, an acute awareness of Poland's position on the outskirts of the Christian world—a world menaced by Islam. The Turks had, in fact, subjugated the Southern Slavs, Walachia, and the greater part of Hungary, and the Vatican considered the struggle against the Moslem threat the most important task facing Christendom. Because of its loyalty to the Vatican and because of its alliances with Hungary, Poland had been a party to that struggle since the fifteenth century. Its southern borders were sometimes directly, sometimes indirectly, under Turkish control; thus, the area was plagued by intermittent periods of war.

From a cultural standpoint, orientalism, which became fashionable as a literary motif in Western Europe at the end of the eighteenth century and the beginning of the nineteenth, can, in Poland, be traced back to Baroque literature written by men who received a firsthand acquaintance with the world of the Levant, as either diplomats or soldiers or prisoners of war. Alliances with Turkey's traditional enemy, Persia, were also of no small consequence. Whether for this or for other reasons, Polish literature possesses a translation of a masterpiece of Persian poetry, Saadi's *Gulistan*, or *A Rose Garden*, that precedes by some fifteen years the first French adaptation of the work and by some thirty years the German translation. Samuel Otwinowski, a Polish envoy in Istanbul, adapted it around 1620 into prose interspersed with verse. This is also why certain epic works relating to the Crusades, such as the Polish translation of Tasso's *Jerusalem Delivered*, were treated as something quite contemporary by readers and called "campaign stories."

Polish wars against Turkey brought hope to subjugated Southern Slavs, and the Croatian epos *Osman*, by Ivan Gundulić, celebrated a successful opposition to the Turks by the Poles at the Battle of Khotim in 1621. The consciousness of fighting for the defense of all Christendom colored chivalrous writings of the time with the feeling of a special mission of Poland as an *antemurale Christianitatis* (a rampart of Christendom). This should be stressed as one of the components of the much later Romantic historiosophy. That sense of pride in Poland's particular vocation reached its peak during the rule of Jan Sobieski, the last Polish king to be successful on the field of battle. Sobieski defeated the Turks at the southeastern border of the *Respublica* in the Ukraine; he then concluded an alliance with Austria and rushed to the rescue of besieged Vienna, where he routed the Turks completely in 1683. That battle ended the last Ottoman attempt to secure a position in Europe.

It is impossible to fix a definite date for the victory of Baroque elements in Polish literature. In many respects, the end of the sixteenth century and the first half of the seventeenth could be considered together. The Baroque artist strove to take his reader by surprise through a juxtaposition of incongruous details presented in an expressive combination of the humorous, the ugly, and the sublime; hence the fascination with striking metaphors and conceits. These traits of style were epitomized in Western Europe by the Spanish poet Góngora and the Italian poet Marino, both of whom claimed devotees in Poland. But, above all, a change in religious sensibility akin to that of the late Middle Ages determined a new vision of things. In Poland this transformation was closely connected with the victory of the Counter Reformation. Poems on Christ, the saints, and the Blessed Virgin reintroduced motifs which during the Renaissance had been relegated to the province of low-brow litera-

The Baroque Style

ture. A certain ascetic scorn for the world went together with a vulgar sensuality and found its expression in a fascination with the macabre. Let us say that seventeenth-century literature has been not only long ignored by the Polish reading public, but surrounded with contempt for its barbaric grotesquery. Such a perspective was, of course, imposed by classical writers of the Enlightenment, but it was not the sole reason for the underestimation of Baroque artistry. That literature remained literally unexplored until the end of the nineteenth century and the beginning of the twentieth.

The Baroque period was marked by a universal mania for writing. If the standards of educational excellence in Jesuit schools could not be called the highest, their training of masses of gentry youth in the skill of writing occasional verse resulted in a prodigious output of that genre, only a small part of which found its way into print. Owing to the decline of printing presses and to the way writing was regarded (i.e., as merely a desirable ornament of social intercourse), manuscripts circulated from hand to hand and were copied, but the various calamities which visited the country during that epoch brought about the loss, destruction, or theft of much of this material. Some valuable works did survive, however, thanks to the widespread custom of keeping notebooks, called *silvae rerum*, i.e., "forests of things," containing anecdotes and records of important events. There, diary entries neighbored with poems, either of home production or taken from any source which happened to please the taste of the writer.

What also predisposed posterity in a hostile way toward the Baroque was the peculiar mixture of two languages, Polish and Latin, in the so-called "macaronic" style: to inject a Latin sentence for every two Polish sentences was considered a proof of sophistication, not to speak of an odd habit of declining Polish words with Latin endings or Latin words with Polish endings. That the Latin language regained its popularity was due especially to the Jesuits. But this time it was not the language of classical authors but rather the so-called "silver" Latin of the minor writers of the Roman decadence. They were imitated and found many translators, which does not mean that the best Latin authors were neglected. Ovid, for some reason, attracted attention above all others, especially his *Metamorphoses*.

If we exclude that literature of the first half of the seventeenth century where an almost imperceptible passage from the era of Humanism and Reformation takes place, we find in the Polish Baroque two main currents. Sophisticated poets, mostly those attached to the royal court, practiced a poetry of conceits, the equivalent of Gongorism and Marinism; while the multitude of prolific scribblers, the average noblemen, reflecting in their approach to subject matters and technique a rather narrow, parochial outlook, created what we call today the Sarmatian Baroque—a style sometimes graceful but often hair-raising in its combination of the most disparate and contradictory elements. Perhaps the twentieth century has accustomed us to far-reaching freedom in handling literary forms and this tolerance accounts for the not entirely unfavorable reappraisal of the Sarmatian Baroque; in any case, we do not share the indignation of the classicists.

The history of Polish newspapers begins in 1661 with the appearance (initially in Kraków, later in Warsaw) of the *Merkuriusz Polski*, the first paper devoted to current events. It was an extremely well-informed publication, providing its readers with a great number of reports from various countries and analyses of the political embroilments in England, France, Turkey, Sweden, Holland, etc. It paid much attention to economic developments, especially trade routes and prices. In several issues the texts of diplomatic documents, particularly letters between monarchs, were reproduced in full. Politics, especially the internal affairs of Turkey and a war between Portugal and Spain, occupied most of the space, and sensations of another nature, such as tempests, floods, epidemics, or earthquakes, received slight consideration. The selection of news, leaving no doubt as to the sympathies of its editors, was geared to show the benefits of a strong royal power and, by implication, seemed to criticize an anarchic parliamentarism.

The Press

LITERATURE IN LATIN

A native of Mazovia, from a gentry family of average means, Maciej Kazimierz Sarbiewski entered the Jesuit Order while still a young boy. He received his education at the Jesuit Academy of Wilno and, later on, was a professor of poetics there as well as at the Jesuit Academy of Polotsk. He also spent a few years in Rome, where his Latin poetry was awarded high honor by Pope Urban VIII. All his works are in Latin, and his voluminous treatise *De Perfecta Poesi* (*On Perfect Poetry*) is valuable for anyone who desires to acquaint himself with Aristotelian poetics of the period.

Maciej Kazimierz Sarbiewski (Casimire) (1595–1640)

Sarbiewski brought to perfection a long tradition of Latin poetry in Poland, and up to today no Polish poet has earned such fame abroad as did Sarbiewski in his lifetime and in the decades immediately following his death. His *Liricorum Libri* (*Books of Lyrics*), first published in 1625, had some sixty editions in various countries of Europe. Called "the works of a Christian Horace," his poems were translated and imitated particularly by authors in the Netherlands, England, and France. His poems consist mostly of odes where the themes of his avowed master, Horace, are curiously blended with motifs taken from the Bible, especially from the Song of Songs. Many of these odes are not religious but political in character and celebrate events such as the military victories of the Christians, often of the Poles, over the Turks. But his main contribution to world poetry is his religious lyricism. It is this aspect which explains his popularity in England. If, from our perspective, the English metaphysical poets represent one of the high points in the history of poetry in any language, proper credit should be given to Jesuit mysticism, from which they borrowed many attitudes, and Casimire, as Sarbiewski was called abroad, should be recognized as one of their sources. The Norwegian Professor Maren-Sofie Roestvig, who investigated the question, says: "The fine lyric quality of Sarbiewski's poetry and the fact that he often fuses classical and Christian motifs made a critic like Hugo Grotius actually prefer the Divine Casimire to Horace himself, and his popularity among English poets is evidenced by an impressive number of translations." The first book

The title page of Sarbiewski's odes in English translation, 1646.

of English translations, entitled *Odes of Casimire*, appeared in 1646, and Professor Roestvig in her introduction to a new edition (Augustan Reprint Society, No. 44, Los Angeles, William Andrews Clarke Memorial Library, University of California, 1953) gives the following collections where individual poems of his were included: Henry Vaughan's *Olor Iscanus* (1651), Sir Edward Sherburne's *Poems and Translations* (1651), *The Miscellany Poems and Translations* by Oxford Hands (1685), Isaac Watts's *Horae Lyricae* (1706), Thomas Brown's *Works* (1707–1708), and John Hughes's *The Ecstasy* (1720). "In the Romantic period," says Professor Roestvig, "Casimire's fame was again revived. While still a young man, Coleridge planned a complete translation of Casimire's odes but never finished more than the ode, 'Ad Lyram.' It was also Coleridge who said that with the exception of Lucretius and Statius he knew no Latin poet, ancient or modern, who could be said to equal Casimire in boldness of conception, opulence of fancy, or beauty of versification." Quite striking is the parallel which Professor Roestvig draws between certain motifs used by Henry Vaughan and by Casimire. In Casimire's poetry she finds traces of his direct acquaintance with hermetic writings, and comments: "Since Henry Vaughan was familiar with Casimire's poetry it is reasonable to suspect that Vaughan's own treatment of hermetic motifs owed much to this influence. If one compares Vaughan's religious nature lyrics and Casimire's odes, a number of common poetic motifs are easily found, and so we are here again faced with the fact that themes which became popular in England in the mid-seventeenth century were anticipated in the Latin odes of Casimire." "The originality of Casimire consists," according to Professor Roestvig, "in Neoplatonic or hermetic interpretation of the classical landscape of retirement" and "the addition of three new themes: the theme of solitude, the theme of the Earthly Paradise, and the theme of Nature as a divine hieroglyph." By his blending of disparate devices borrowed from the ancients and from the Judaeo-Christian tradition, Sarbiewski follows, of course, the procedures known already to his Polish predecessors such as Kochanowski, but there is a Baroque oddity about his poetry which won the applause of his contemporaries. Sudden passages from biblical imagery to that of Christian devotion, though completely justifiable for a Roman Catholic, surprise, nevertheless, by their unexpectedness. A few poems in G. Hils's translation (1646) will illustrate this quality:

Who Is Thy Beloved? (Out of Cant. 5, Lib. Epig. 37)

Who is that Spouse of thine? that fairest Hee?
  The barb'rous people said, of late, to mee.
A Pen I tooke, and in a Tablet drew
  Whatsoe're, O Christ, in thy blest orbe I view.

> Roses, and Gold I paint, gems, groves, Corne-land,
>   Green gardens, Lakes, and Stars with nimble hand;
> Would you need learne, what might my fairest bee?
>   Look o're this tablet, pray, o such was Hee.

Or in "Out of Solomon's Sacred Marriage Song" (Ode 19, Lib. 2)
he pursues a roe which turns out to be Christ, and again his goal
takes on a sensuous character: that of a being in nature:

> At length give o're thy sad and carefull flight:
>   Thou shalt not scape me, th' evening bright
> With its so watchfull centry, thee'l betray,
>   And th' moone with golden hornes doth stray.
> By th' groves of the neglected shores I'le find
>   Thee; and by th' sighs o' th' Westerne wind;
> Thee the night's watch, the starrs that walke about
>   With lively signes will point thee out.

The modern reader notices in Sarbiewski an obsession with flight.
Various images are used to express it: writing in Wilno, he mounts
a Pegasus and describes rivers, lakes, towns which shrink and disappear while he moves westward to visit his friends, poets in Brussels
or Antwerp; or he grows wings and soars above an earth plagued by
wars, natural calamities, and disturbed by the passing glory of
peoples and kingdoms. In any case, the flight always symbolizes a
contrast between the withering and decay of the terrestrial and the
expanding, growing might of the spiritual. But Sarbiewski is able to
counterbalance the elevated tone with a sober reference to reality in
the best Baroque fashion; for instance, in his "Ode to Albertus Turs-
cius" (Turski), he calms a friend who has reminded him of the fate
of Icarus:

> Yet, *Turscius*, thou hast often told,
>   And warn'd mee, lest then *Icarus* of old
> By a true fall indeed, I make
>   A lowder tale and change the name o' th' Lake.
> In vaine: Remembring Him, I had
>   A care, and counsell, to my folly, add:
> For when I sleep, in bed I lye,
>   And if I write, my secure chaire holds mee.

Sarbiewski is the last Polish poet to use Latin exclusively, though
for a long time there were poets perfectly capable of handling that
language. Even the generation of Romantics in the nineteenth century received a sufficiently thorough classical training in schools to
compose, on occasion, poems in Latin.

*Szymon
Starowolski
(1588–1656)* Among Latin prose writers, first place undoubtedly belongs to
Szymon Starowolski. After completing his studies at the University

of Kraków, he sojourned abroad for long periods at a time, as a tutor for aristocratic families. He became a priest and finally a canon, in his later years. Extremely prolific, he left behind him some seventy works both in Latin and in Polish and merited the name of "poly-historian," bestowed on him by his contemporaries. He became the first bibliographer of Polish literature with his work *Scriptorum Polonicorum Hekatontas* (1625), where he listed one hundred authors, giving their biographies and works. He organized another similar inventory of orators and warriors. But most of his Latin works, printed either in Poland or abroad (in Venice, Florence, Cologne, and Amsterdam), dealt with Poland's political institutions and provided foreign readers with information on that subject. In Polish he wrote as a publicist, advancing practical ideas on political strategy. For instance, he proposed fortifying the Ukraine on the southern side, to protect it from the attacks of the Tartars, and maintaining permanent garrisons there, composed not of nobles, but of burghers and peasants. Some of his views on the necessity of reforms seem to be inspired by writers of the Renaissance. His somewhat lyrical work, the *Lament of the Sorrowful Mother, The Dying Polish Crown, Over Her Wayward Sons* (*Lament utrapionej matki, Korony Polskiej, już konającej, na syny wyrodne*), is a bitter denunciation of public vices, which he saw as leading the state into anarchy. The tone of the *Lament* is not very far from the mournful predictions of Piotr Skarga.

LITERATURE IN POLISH

Lyric Poetry of the First Half of the Seventeenth Century

The development of lyric poetry followed a line of perfect continuity from the previous epoch—a line which was blurred, however, in the middle of the seventeenth century. Up to this point many poets carried on and further elaborated the conventions of their Renaissance predecessors.

Not the works of authors known today, but anonymous love songs and dances made up the common fare of the average public of that period. These verses, composed in great numbers to existing melodies, remain for us today perhaps the most charming part of all old Polish poetry. They were the outcome of a relatively refined taste which had been trained upon the literature of the Renaissance and now found a new application on the more popular level. The somewhat childish tenderness of the songs and dances and the use of diminutives place them on an intermediate level between folklore and more

Lyric Songs and Dances

learned forms. The necessity to follow a musical tune brought about the use of extremely involved metrical patterns which make an interesting contrast to the simplicity of vocabulary. It was not the works of eminent poets but those gay and serene madrigals which spread to the non-Polish-speaking provinces of the *Respublica* and were responsible for the position acquired by the Polish language there—that of a language of civility and elegance. From the Ukraine and Byelorussia, they wandered to Moscow, where their popularity was kept alive until the beginning of the eighteenth century. The evolution of that humble genre lasted some one hundred years, beginning in Kochanowski's time. Authors were often of plebeian origin, and a large number of those lyrics were written in the cities (especially in Lwów and Kraków) by burghers and students. Collections of those poems enjoyed great success with the public, and they appeared regularly from 1614 up to the second half of the century. Those who prepared such editions paid no heed to the rights of the authors and often included, without mention or recognition, the verses of well-known literary figures. Owing to complete license in using works without giving credit to authorship and, as sometimes happened, the signing of poems with names other than those of their authors, it is often difficult to ascribe particular works to any given person. The refinement of that lyricism should modify the standard deprecatory opinion concerning the fate of literature in a country ravaged by wars and undergoing a decline in education.

Deep similarities can be found between Elizabethan love lyrics and their Polish counterparts. Though the specific character of Polish lyrics eludes description, these hallmarks can be noted: a frequent use of diminutives, a recurring half-amorous, half-humorous mood, and obvious references to folk songs (sometimes even Ukrainian folk songs are inserted into the text). If we only reconstruct in our minds the tunes, we are won by the presence of the human voice in those lyrics; for instance, when a girl sings:

> Farewell, my only one, my beloved
> You are to my liking more than any man,
> You took with you all my joys
> And I would allow you to do anything
> Only to be with you,
> My sweetest, my dear.
>
> My heart cares so much about you
> It is hardly alive because of great sorrow,
> Don't act that way to make me sad,
> You will regret
> What you lost
> To become rich with my poignant weeping.

And the boy answers:

> I do not feel at all
> That you, my darling, would have any sorrow
> As you did not want
> To keep in mind my good services,
> Thus, I do not wish
> To keep in mind yours.

> "Bywaj, jedyny, mój kochany.
>   Tyś mi nad wszytkie insze upodobany;
>   Wszytkie uciechy zabrałeś z sobą
>   I ja bym z tobą
>   Tam przyzwoliła,
>   Bym z tobą była,
>   Mój namilszy, drogi.

> "Serce dla ciebie tak troskliwe,
>   Od smutku wielkiego ledwie że jest żywe.
>   Nie czyń mi tego, byś mię frasował,
>   Będziesz żałował,
>   Żeś mię utracił,
>   Abyś się zbogacił
>   Przez mój płacz serdeczny."

> "Nie myślę o tem,
>   Abyś ty kiedy, miła, z kłopotem
> Żałować miała,
>   Gdyżeś nie chciała
>   Służb pomnieć moich.
>   A ja też twoich
>   Nie chcę mieć w pamięci."

Christmas carols (*kolędy*), sung in Poland till today, are closely *Christmas Carols* related to the love songs and dances, and they express a similar sensibility. They were composed over a period of several centuries and thus reflect the changing styles. Mostly, however, they bear the imprint of the Baroque. Some were written by poets whom we can identify by name, but authorship of the great majority cannot be traced. If the rest of the literature of that period has remained the domain of connoisseurs, the Baroque Christmas carols are cherished by the whole nation. Some of them were gathered in modern times into a sort of mystery play by the eminent theater director, Leon Schiller, and they provide a charming spectacle incorporating both songs and dances.

Lyric poets of the time who are known by name made use of the existing tradition, bringing to it greater sophistication and more learned metaphors from mythology. At their best, though, they match in simplicity their anonymous rivals.

Jan Żabczyc (?—after 1629)

The case of Jan Żabczyc only serves to confirm the offhand treatment of authorship. His work was so well plundered that for a long time scholars doubted whether the writer had existed at all. As a courtier attached to a family of magnates, the Mniszeks, he was well initiated into the plots which were to lead Dmitry the Pretender and his Polish wife, Maryna Mniszek, to the czarist throne, and in 1605 he published an epic poem called *The Bloodthirsty Muscovite Mars* (*Mars moskiewski krwawy*) which deserves mention only as a Baroque curiosity. In it, Żabczyc makes use of a single acrostic: the first letters of every couplet when read vertically spell the name of Dmitry Ivanovich together with all his titles. Sometimes Żabczyc can be quite medieval; for instance, in another long poem of his, virtues and vices are grouped into sets of four and presented in quatrains. His most enduring volume of poems, *Angelic Symphonies* (*Symfonie anielskie*, 1630), was published under the name of Jan Karol Dachnowski, which, for a long time, was considered the author's real name. It is a collection of Christmas carols which contain many of the earthy motifs so typical of Polish carols: conversations between the shepherds after hearing the news of the Nativity; their decision to bring gifts to the Child—a crock of butter and a basket of pears; their quarreling with old Joseph, who does not want to let them enter the stable because the Mother and Child are receiving the Three Magi; their efforts to amuse the Child by dancing and playing on flutes and pipes; the ox and the donkey who knelt down when they sensed a child in the manger; etc. One carol especially, entitled "The Shepherds Came to Bethlehem," proved more durable than the whole quarrel over authorship and survived several centuries of turbulent and tragic history, becoming an inseparable part of the celebration of Christmas. Some of his poems, however, include characters and motifs from Greek mythology, while some are written in the "macaronic" style, a mixture of Polish and Latin:

> Let *Deus* bless and increase
> *Domi*, in the grange, in the larder, in the stable;
> For the new year let Him *mittat tibi gaudia*
> *Et prosperet* according to your wishes *omnia*.

> Niechżeć Deus błogosławi a sporze
> Domi, w gumnie, szpiżarni, na oborze,
> Na Nowy Rok mittat tibi gaudia
> Et prosperet według myśli omnia.

Kacper Twardowski (c. 1592– before 1641)

Kacper Twardowski's poetic career began with a volume of frivolous love poems, *Cupid's Lessons* (*Lekcje Kupidynowe*). Here he combines praise for the beauty of many girls with complaints against the obstacles to love: unfortunately maidens, widows, married women, relatives, and nuns are all a forbidden domain. But later, after undergoing a severe illness (which he considered God's punishment), he turned to religious poetry. Paraphrasing his own *Cupid's Lessons* in his *Torch of Divine Love with Five Fiery Arrows* (1628), he changed Venus into the Holy Virgin and Cupid into the Child Jesus. Attacked by diabolical forces personified as maidens, but saved from them by an angel, he goes hunting on a horse—his flesh—accompanied by two dogs—Nature and Bad Habit; while pursuing a cross-bearing deer, he meets a doe—Mary Magdalen—who shows him the way to salvation. Twardowski also wrote an elegy on the calamities which beset the country in the beginning of the century—the Tartar raids and an epidemic of the plague—and Christmas carols which abound in lively details. A typical one describes how the shepherds reach the stable and see little angels who are planing a piece of dry willow wood to make a cradle for Jesus; others are gathering dry twigs or blowing on a bonfire or drying wet swaddling clothes or heating water for a bath, while the moon, smiling down from the sky, begs the favor of Mother and Child in return for its services.

A burgher from Lwów, the son of a mason, Szymon Zimorowic was, for a long time, confused with his brother, Bartłomiej Zimorowic, who enjoyed a long life and held many dignities, among them that of mayor of the city of Lwów. But Szymon, who died at the age of twenty, would, in fact, have remained completely unknown if not for his brother. A good education had acquainted Szymon with both Latin and Polish poets, and he began his literary work doing translations. He remains in Polish literature, however, as the author of only one work, written during his stay in Kraków, where he died soon after. The work was a gauge of his brotherly love: unable to attend his brother's wedding in Lwów, he sent, instead, a bouquet of love lyrics in the style of the love songs and dances so appreciated at that time. In elegant speech Ruthenia was called "Roxolania," and he entitled his collection *Roksolanki* ("Ruthenian girls"). For a long time it remained unpublished, but finally Szymon's brother had it printed in 1654. Bartłomiej, however, was also a poet, though of inferior talent, and desired to publish his poems too; only, owing to his civic rank, he preferred to do so under the name of the dead Szymon—a fact which, for a long time, went undiscovered by scholars. Not just a loose collection of lyrics, *Roksolanki* opens with a speech in verse, pronounced by Hymen, the god of marriage, followed by love poems recited by young girls and boys who step forward one at a time as if participating in a contest. There are two choirs of girls and one chorus of young men. If anonymous love songs and dances of the

Szymon Zimorowic (1608–1629)

time are appealing, Zimorowic's great poetic gifts make these poems modeled upon that genre even more so. A great variety of metrical patterns occur in around seventy, sometimes gay, sometimes melancholy, occasionally even faintly macabre, poems. They can be defined as pastoral madrigals in which all the metaphors relating to love make their appearance: fire, ash, flowers, wreaths, doves. Zimorowic was a poet versed in mythology, and the amount of mythological allusions sometimes exceeds the patience of a modern reader far less familiar with this realm. Sometimes these allusions enable the poet to make multivocal and queer Baroque metaphors; for instance, one of the boys, Serapion, sings:

> When sailing by Cyprus I refused
> To pay due homage to its mistress.
> Her angry child shooting at me
> Broke his bowstring.
>
> At once I understood that it was over
> And that I was free from customs duty,
> That I was safe without being a smuggler.
> I was already boasting of it.
>
> But suddenly behind me emerged from the sea
> A beautiful nymph resembling Maryna.
> Instead of sails she unbound her hair
> Of chestnut braids.
>
> When Cupid caught sight of her
> In one eager leap he was nearby
> He twisted a bowstring out of her braid
> Just to make me sad.
>
> And really in flight the mischievous child
> So pierced my ship with arrows
> That rich merchandise together with my vessel
> Was taken as contraband.
>
> That is why I stay so long on Cyprus,
> Hoping that I may recover my loss;
> Will I succeed, I am not sure, as you well know
> What the law is on smuggling.

> Płynąc mimo Cypr, gdym zwykłej dani
> Wzbraniał się oddać tamecznej pani,
> Strzelając ku mnie jej dziecko gniewliwe
> Zerwało cięciwę.

Jużem rozumiał, że za tym kwitem
Byłem wolnym przed powszechnym mytem,
Żem cało uszedł, żem nic nie przemycił;
    Jużem się tem szczycił.

Ali̇ści za mną z morza wypłynie
Nimfa śliczna, podobna Marynie,
Na miejsce żaglów rozpuściwszy włosy
    Z kasztanowej kosy.

Tę skoro zajźrzał Kupido okiem,
Przyleciał ku niej skwapliwym skokiem
I z jej warkocza cięciwę ukręcił,
    Aby mię zasmęcił.

Jakoż latając tak moję nawę
Ustrzelało dziecko niełaskawe,
Że mi z okrętem towary obfite
    Wzięto za przemyte.

Przetoż tak długo w Cyprze się bawię
Mniemając, że stratę wzad wyprawię;
Wskóramli, nie wiem; wszak jakie na mycie
    Prawo, wszyscy wiecie.

A great many metaphors, of course, are built around the image of
fire. Another boy, Hippolite, sings:

Rozyna, when we danced, gave me an orange
And then she promised to give her maiden's wreath.
But when I helped her in her joyous dance
That orange turned into fire.
That fruit became for me a glowing coal
Burning my miserable soul, it burned my flesh too.
O my fire, Rozyna, I caught you fast.
Quickly the golden apple kindled you in my heart.
Now I know what love is; not gracious Venus
Begot it but a bloodthirsty lioness in the desert,
A tigress without mercy for erring man
Nourished it in the Caucasus with the milk of madness.

Rozyna mi w taneczku pomarańczę dała,
A potym i wianeczek dać przyobiecała,
Ale gdym jej pomagał wesołego tańca,
W ogień się obróciła ona pomarańcza.
Ono jabłko żarzystym węglem mi się stało,
Spaliwszy duszę nędzną, spaliło i ciało.
Ogniu mój, o Rozyno! prędkom cię zachwycił,

Prędko mi cię na sercu złoty owoc wzniecił.
Teraz wiem, co jest miłość; nie Wenus łaskawa
Spłodziła ją, lecz lwica na pustyni krwawa,
Tygrys niemiłosierna nad błędnym człowiekiem,
Na Kaukazie szalonym karmiła ją mlekiem.

Some metaphors refining the madrigal convention are extremely daring; for instance, a girl says that she caught fire from a young man:

> Like a candle which kissing a candle
> Steals a flame.

But not only elegant conceits are applied in *Roxolanki*. Some of the most direct and most moving poems are hardly distinguishable in style from anonymous songs and dances. Zimorowic did not hesitate to inject occasionally the local flavor of Lwów, nor did he scorn colloquial expressions in Ruthenian. Yet the girls and boys, reciters of the poems, only rarely have local names like Serapion, Ostapi, Filoret, Alexy, or Simeon. On the contrary, practically all the girls have fancy literary names, chosen, perhaps, for sheer sound: Pomosia, Coronella, Antonilla, Amorella, Janella, Pavencia. The tone of the work as a whole is predominantly gay, and the setting is usually in an ordered nature such as a flower garden, often a rose garden. But there are also notes of sweet melancholy, even sadness. To quote a description of the land of dreams:

> There is an inaccessible cave where never
> People are awakened by the crested bird,
> Where no sunrays are able to penetrate,
> Only the grayish night sows eternal darkness;
> Out of a silent dungeon leaps a spring
> Of Lethean water which sweetens dreams
> With its pleasant rustling; black-winged night
> Flies everywhere in the hall of longing.
> On a sluggish bed lazy sleep dozes
> And around him the drowsy poppy grows
> On which dumb flocks of black birds
> Build their nests.

> Jest niedostępna jaskinia, gdzie ludzi
>   Śpiewak czubaty nigdy nie przebudzi,
>   Gdzie nie dochodzą promienie słoneczne,
>   Tylko szarawa noc ćmy sieje wieczne;
> Z lochu cichego potok wyskakuje
>   Niepomnej wody, która sny cukruje
>   Szumem miluchnym, noc czarnoskrzydlata
>   Wszędzie po gmachu tesknociemnym lata.

> Na łożu gnuśnym sen drzymie leniwy,
> Wokoło niego mak roście senliwy,
> No którym ptaków czarnych nieme roje
> Budują gniazda i mieszkania swoje.

Biblical references are often used to season songs in honor of love
with the awareness of transience and the thought of death. The last
poem treats of life as the vanity of vanities:

> It is wisdom of wisdoms
> To see a deadly chase after us
> Which without cease or respite
> Throws condemnations onto the world.

> As the wind forces down
> A rock which it has overthrown,
> So our years when their end comes
> Are interrupted. . . .

> As when a ship pushes through the sea
> With great violence,
> But when it passes no trace is left
> Where once was its wake.

> Mądrość jest nad mądrościami,
>   Widzieć śmiertelną za nami
>   Pogonią, która wyroki
>   Miece na świat bez odwłoki.

> Jako z pędem na dół wali
>   Wiatr skałę, którą obali,
>   Tak się nasze przerywają
>   Lata, kiedy koniec mają. . . .

> Właśnie, jako kiedy morze
>   Okręt wielkim gwałtem porze;
>   Skoro ujedzie, by znaku
>   Nieznać jego namniej ślaku.

Bartłomiej Zimorowic was a much less gifted writer than his *Bartłomiej*
brother. Some of his works which bear an intimate relation to the *Zimorowic*
history of Lwów, whose defense against the Turks in 1672 was *(1597–1673)*
undertaken during his mayoralty, illustrate the persistence of the
idyllic style. In his *Idylls* (*Sielanki*) he attempted to follow Szymonowic's example, but failed to achieve either the clarity or the conciseness of that most eminent representative of the genre.

Poets of Baroque Conceits

A refined courtier and diplomat, Jan Andrzej Morsztyn was not only a master of political intrigue (sent by the king as an ambassador to several foreign courts) but also one of the most sophisticated personalities of old Polish literature. Intimately involved with state affairs, he was the head of the so-called "French Party" and was, as a matter of fact, a French agent. After losing at his political game of chess, he emigrated to France, where he died under the assumed name of Comte de Chateauvillain. A neat profit, however, accrued to Polish literature from his French ties, namely, his translation of Corneille's *Le Cid*. First staged in Warsaw at the royal court in 1662, it is an excellent work unsurpassed in vigor of language up to today, though Morsztyn is a purely Baroque and not classical poet. His language is racy, sensuous, sometimes brutal, and his *Cid* bears, perhaps, a greater resemblance to the Spanish original by Guillen de Castro (which served as a model for Corneille) than to the more disciplined French version.

Throughout his life, Morsztyn wrote short poems which he did not intend to print. Destined to amuse his friends, they alluded to a little world of gay bachelors and demimondaines. Gathered into two collections, *Dog Days* (*Kanikuła albo psia gwiazda*, 1647) and *Lute* (*Lutnia*, 1661), they were published for the first time in the nineteenth century and secured Morsztyn his present place in Polish poetry, that as the most skillful user of fancy conceits. Morsztyn was influenced by the Italian poet, Marini (or Marino), who was admired at that time in many countries and whom he also translated. Playing with literary conventions of an Anacreontic type, he seems to treat all his poems on the sufferings of love as mere exercises of craft. He is fully aware of the relative character of language and of its distance from reality. This can be felt especially in his inverted metaphors, as for example, in "Inconstancy":

> The eyes are fire, the brow a mirror;
> The hair is gold, the teeth pearls, the complexion buttermilk.
> The lips are coral, the cheeks are carmine,
> As long as you, my lady, are at peace with me.
> But if we should quarrel: the cheeks will be leprous,
> The lips a cavern, the complexion bleached white;
> The teeth a horse bone, the hair a cobweb,
> The brow a breadboard, the eyes hot ash.

> Oczy są ogień, czoło jest zwierciadłem,
> Włos złotem, perłą ząb, płeć mlekiem zsiadłem,
> Usta koralem, purpurą jagody,

Póki mi, panno, dotrzymujesz zgody.
Jak się zwadzimy, jagody są trądem,
Usta czeluścią, płeć blejwasem bladym,
Ząb szkapią kością, włosy pajęczyną,
Czoło maglownią, a oczy perzyną.

In fact, there is no "sincerity of feeling" in Morsztyn, except a few desperate poems on illness, and his poetry forms a contrast to those lyrical songs and dances which found so vivid a response among his less sophisticated contemporaries.

The following poem may serve as another example of his literary calisthenics:

When laughter dimples your rosy cheeks
My soul has its funeral in the hollows of your beauty;
While when your eyes are locked by tears
I, dead man, am resurrected by that water.
I swear I do not know, I swear it without sinning,
Whether to praise you because of your laughter or your tears.

Kiedyć różane wierci śmiech jagody,
    Dusza ma pogrzeb w dołach twej urody.
Kiedyć zaś łzami oczy się zawarły,
    Tą wodą wstaję wskrzeszony umarły.
Przysięgam, nie wiem, przysięgam bez grzechu,
    Skąd cię pochwalić: czy z płaczu, czy z śmiechu?

The character of Morsztyn's poetry, conceived of as a conscious game of literary fashions, attracted some avant-garde poets of the twentieth century, who, reacting against Romantic autobiographical lyricism, reached for an ironic "distance." But the name Morsztyn is famous in Polish literature not only because of the author of *Lute*. Other members of the family were also skillful poets. Stanisław Morsztyn, the nephew of Jan Andrzej, and by profession a military man, translated Racine's *Andromaque* (1698) and in his poems pushed his uncle's manner of inverted metaphors even further, as, for instance, in this mock erotic poem:

Ladies, if I flatter you one day by saying:
The blue rays from those beautiful eyes
Kindle in my heart a blaze and flames,
And that I will be consumed for certain in that blaze,
And that already I have ashes instead of my heart,
Do not believe me, ladies, I beg you.

Damy, powiemli wam kiedy pochlébnie:
"W pięknych tych oczu niebieskie promienie
W sercu mi niecą pożar i płomienie,"

I że w tym ogniu stleję niepochybnie
I już popioły miasto serca noszę:
Nie wierzcie, damy, nie wierzcie mi, proszę.

The poem proceeds by a series of negations, enumerating what beauty, the heart, the face are not, and punctures the overblown, overused metaphorical image of tears as rivers in which one can drown: rivers do not flow from the eyes but from sources, and disappear not in a handkerchief but in the sea; neither are fish "in tears" but in rivers.

Zbigniew Morsztyn (1624–1698) Another member of the same family represented a different attitude toward poetry. Zbigniew Morsztyn was an Arian, and a serious, melancholy tone is heard in his writings. He saw action as a soldier in the Cossack War and the Swedish War, but, instead of a song of victory, he presents bitter pictures of inhumanity and suffering. Among the collections of religious poetry written by the Arians, his verse occupies an eminent place.

The Story of Princess Banialuka Writers at the end of the sixteenth and in the seventeenth century were inspired by the Italian Renaissance *novella*, which provided themes often put into verse form. A lesser-known poet, Hieronim Morsztyn (died c. 1625), drew heavily upon such themes, and one of his stories in verse contained in his collection, *Matrimonial Appetizers* (*Antypasty małżeńskie*, published posthumously in 1650), was to have a strange career. This fantastic tale, entitled "A Diverting Story about the Virtuous Princess Banialuka from an Eastern Land" ("Historia ucieszna o zacnej królewnie Banialuce ze wschodniej krainy"), became so popular that the word "banialuka" passed into the Polish language and is used today to mean utter nonsense.

Daniel Naborowski (1573–1640) A son of a Kraków apothecary, Naborowski pursued his medical studies abroad and after his return to Poland served various Protestant magnates. A physician and a diplomat, Daniel Naborowski, in his free moments, also wrote poems of rare virtuosity revealing a good knowledge of Western European literature and an admiration for Kochanowski. Some of his obscene "trifles" even passed into folklore. But, above all, Naborowski gave poignant expression to that fascination, so typical of the Baroque, with the ephemerality of all things human, as for instance, in his poem "The Shortness of Life":

An hour incomprehensibly follows an hour,
There was an ancestor, then you, a descendant is born.
A short affair: tomorrow you will not be what you are today,
And because you have lived, you will receive the name of dead
  man.
Sound, shade, smoke, wind, a flash, a voice, a point: glory of
  human life.

The sun once set never rises the same.
Fleeting time escapes like an unbraked wheel
From which many a man, who aimed at old age, has fallen.
When you are thinking, already you are, poor soul, he who was;
Between death and birth our existence hardly can be called
A quarter of an instant; many are those for whom the cradle was
A tomb, many are those for whom the grave is their mother.

Godzina za godziną niepojęcie chodzi:
   Był przodek, byłeś ty sam, potomek się rodzi.
Krótka rozprawa: jutro — coś dziś jest, nie będziesz,
   A żeś był, nieboszczyka imienia nabędziesz;
Dźwięk, cień, dym, wiatr, błysk, głos, punkt — żywot
     ludzki słynie.
Słońce więcej nie wschodzi to, które raz minie,
Kołem niehamowanym lotny czas uchodzi,
   Z którego spadł niejeden, co na starość godzi.
Wtenczas, kiedy ty myślisz, jużeś był, nieboże;
   Między śmiercią, rodzeniem byt nasz ledwie może
Nazwan być czwartą częścią mgnienia; wielom była
   Kolebka grobem, wielom matka ich mogiła.

A friend of Naborowski's, Olbrycht Karmanowski, who translated Ovid as well as several Latin Anacreontic poems, was the author of none too edifying songs which gained considerable popularity. Later, while gravely ill, he wrote a cycle called *Penitential Songs* (*Pieśni pokutne*) which expresses deep religious feeling and reveals a strong impress of Arianism. What was said of Zbigniew Morsztyn applies equally to Karmanowski. Both can be considered as leading Arians in Polish poetry. Karmanowski dedicated several poems to a famous personality of his time: his coreligionist, Krzysztof Arciszewski, a general of the artillery, who, owing to a murder conviction, emigrated abroad, where he led an extraordinary life of adventure, acquiring the rank of admiral of the Dutch fleet that fought the Spaniards off the coast of Brazil.

Olbrycht Karmanowski (first half of the seventeenth century)

Moralistic and Satiric Poetry

The voluminous works of Wacław Potocki in their entirety would occupy many bookshelves today, but during his lifetime they remained in manuscript form and were circulated only in handwritten copies. He was so prolific that not everything he wrote has been printed yet. It is difficult to agree with nineteenth-century scholars who, after he had been discovered, were prepared to name him the major figure of the Polish Baroque. But it is true that an acquaintance with his life and works affords an insight which goes straight to the heart of his age.

Wacław Potocki (1621–1696)

Potocki was born and spent practically all of his life in the upland of southern Poland, a region which was, then, a stronghold of Calvinism and Arianism. He came from a fervent Arian gentry family, received his education in his native region at schools of his faith, and married Catherine Morsztyn (related to the Arian poet, Zbigniew Morsztyn), a woman of firm religious beliefs. During the Swedish invasion, Potocki, like practically all his neighbors, sided at first with the Swedes, to fight against them later. When the law banishing the Arians was passed in 1658, he preferred to embrace Roman Catholicism. His wife, however, remained true to Arianism until her death, and their home became a center of clandestine activity, owing to which Potocki was often accused of shielding his wife's anti-Catholicism. Many calamities touched him during those turbulent years: he lost his two sons, who died while serving in the army, and a daughter.

His Arian upbringing, even if he repudiated all connection with the doctrine, is clearly visible in his poetry. His opposition to the magnates who were steadily concentrating greater wealth and power in their hands provides another key to his work. Potocki idealized the patriarchal way of living with its chivalrous virtues, and in many ways he can be justly considered a representative of the Sarmatian Baroque, but his yearning for social justice and his humane attitude toward the peasants distinguish him from the majority of his contemporaries. He was, strictly speaking, a publicist in verse, thus continuing the line of such poets as Klonowic, who were primarily concerned with a message to be conveyed. Plagiarism, a habit peculiar to his era, finds a perfect illustration in Potocki, who turned a great quantity of his Latin readings into Polish verse without so much as a cursory acknowledgment of the source. He can be read today because of his rich, colloquial language and multifaceted social and political interests. Some of his shorter poems, especially those where anger at injustice is visible, are still good poetry. To write some 300,000 lines of poetry, one must have a great technical facility; therefore, we are a little amused by a poem of Potocki's where he describes how he often spent a whole day unable to write a sentence until inspiration came, finally, in the evening; then he could not stop until morning. His short occasional poems were gathered into two volumes: *A Garden of Trifles* (*Ogród fraszek*) (or, to give the full title, *A Garden, But Not Weeded, A Haystack, But at Every Sheaf a New Kind of Grain, A Stand of Diverse Wares, etc.*), and *Moralia*. They consist of notes on various events, anecdotes, satires, stories borrowed from literature but adapted in such a way that they resemble neighborhood gossip. Today, we prefer Potocki's satirical invective, where he evidences an awareness of his moral duty. In several of his poems, he compares himself to a watchdog who barks alone "while the world, drunk with wine, sleeps." He attacks over-indulgence in luxuries, oppression of the citizenry by the powerful, the disorders resulting from a disregard of law, and the Jesuits as proponents of conversion by force, but he especially takes up the cause of the peasants. Sometimes, for instance in a series of verses he called "tombstones," he introduces inventive images such as the peasant who, buried like wheat, awaits the spring to rouse him, while his plow and horse work the soil above. Extremely loquacious, Potocki yields the reader occasional happy finds amid a sea of lines.

Of his long poems, the best known today is *The War of Khotim* (*Wojna chocimska*), an epic written several decades after the events that took place in 1621 when the Polish and Cossack army successfully resisted the assaults of much more numerous Turkish troops. Its capricious structure reminds one of medieval chivalric chronicles, and confirms what we have said about the persistence of medieval mentality in the Polish Baroque. Factual descriptions based on the diary of a soldier who participated in the battle are interlaced with moralistic and satirical digressions. Here, too, Potocki appears primarily as a publicist criticizing his environment and contrasting it with past heroism. If Potocki's counterpart of the sixteenth century, homespun and garrulous Mikołaj Rej, characterized an ascending movement in old Polish poetry, the author of *A Garden of Trifles* is associated with the decline of that peculiar occupation of largely self-taught men, which consisted in filling volumes with unrestrained verbosity.

Krzysztof Opaliński has been remembered more as a political traitor than as a literary figure: while *wojewoda* (governor) of the Poznań province, he was instrumental in the surrender of the whole of Greater Poland to the Swedes in 1655. The nineteenth century, especially, was sensitive to such an ugly act, even though it belonged to the remote past. But Opaliński's treason, in fact, stemmed from his personal views of the problems besetting the Polish state. He saw in the Swedish king a powerful monarch, perhaps capable of curing many evils in the country. *Krzysztof Opaliński (1609–1655)*

Of aristocratic birth, Opaliński, together with his brother (who also figures in the history of Polish literature), was educated abroad at the University of Louvain, in Orléans, and in Padua. After his return to Poland he was elected deputy to the parliament and received many honors, but during a moment of disillusionment he retired to his estate, where he founded an exemplary school based on the precepts of the famous Comenius (Komenský), who at the time was directing his own school in neighboring Leszno. In 1645, he served in Paris as ambassador for King Władysław IV, who, obtaining the hand of the French princess, Marie Louise, in marriage, had sent him to bring her to Poland. Opaliński's only work, his *Satires* (*Satyry*), the outcome of his years of solitude, was published for the first time in 1650 and found great success with his contemporaries, though his critics soon prevailed and proclaimed it not only crude but slanderous. *Satires* testifies to the intellectual maturity of the author, who took a clear position in the conflicts surrounding him. Contrary to the gentry who looked back toward the patriarchal virtues, Opaliński obviously yearned to reform Polish institutions along the lines of the Western absolute monarchies. Though himself a magnate, he would have preferred to sacrifice oligarchic rule in Poland for the sake of a strong central power capable of developing cities, of organizing a good army, and of bettering the situation of the peasants. Some of his social and economic opinions were very advanced, and some fragments of the *Satires* amount to almost a treatise on sound economics. His civic preoccupations were motivated by a fear of the dangers inherent in oppression of the peasants, a fear of peasant rebellion, which, as the revolt in the Ukraine showed, was fully justified. But the value of his *Satires* cannot be reduced to his political or social views. In old Polish literature there is no other example of such violence of style. He chose Juvenal's satires for his model and in his own work acknowledges the indignation which dictated his verse ("indignatio fecit versum") and caused him to abandon rhyme even though he was capable of writing in it. He writes in unrhymed syllabic verse of thirteen syllables (seven + six), pursuing "unrhymed truth," as he paraphrases a German expression: *ungereimte Wahrheit*. The *Satires* covers a wide range of evils prevalent in both private and public life; for instance, his satire "On the Burdening and Oppression of Peasants in Poland" begins as follows:

In my view God is punishing Poland for nothing more than the cruel oppression of her subjects, [a serfdom] worse than slavery, as if the peasant were not only not our "neighbor" but also not a man. Recalling this slavery more burdensome than the pagan one, the heart is seized by fear, the flesh shivers. Great God! Poles, are you insane? All the goods [of the earth], your well-being, food, harvests you have from your subjects. Their hands nourish you—why do you treat them so cruelly? They talk of the camel who would not bear a load beyond his strength, yet when they encumber him and he feels overburdened, he immediately lies down and doesn't want to get up. Here the reverse is true because the peasant has to bear, beyond natural and divine laws, what his lord and master puts on his shoulders, even if he drops dead.

The author then enumerates the duties imposed on peasants, speaks about the beatings they receive, describes witch hunts in the villages when tortured peasant women, held responsible for the death of oxen or the illness of the master, denounce their neighbors. He even reports *compulsory* (!) drinking:

I'll say it because it's difficult to keep silent. When I was passing through certain villages, I ordered them to bring me some beer from the inn. They brought it.

I asked, "Is your beer always such?"

"A hundred times worse," they answered, "and yet we must drink because the master every week gives the innkeeper a certain number of barrels for which the innkeeper must give him money whether we drink it or not. The innkeeper recovers his loss from us by calculating in advance what quantity falls upon every peasant. If one doesn't come to the inn, his quantity is delivered home. You drink it, even though it's bad, and if you don't want it, you give it to the hogs, but you pay the innkeeper."

And it's the same with barley, flour, salt, and with herring, which are imposed again and again upon the peasants.

He concludes by invoking the memory of the peasant rebellions in the Middle Ages and of the recent shame inflicted upon the nobility by the energetic Ukrainian rebels. By contrast with what he says about peasant life, the denunciation of the laziness, drunkenness, and luxury of the gentry seems the stronger. For instance, in the satire "On Polish Excesses in General" he says:

What other countries, tell me, please, in the sun's orbit can be likened to Poland and her luxuries and prodigality? We never have enough. Only when there is too much—too many servants, too many dishes, too many horses and dogs, too much silver, too many mouths, and too many greedy stomachs.

and in the satire "On Drunkards and Unrestrained Drunkenness":

I affirm that drunkenness has built its nest in Poland. Here it multiplies, and here it raises its nestlings. A kid barely gets his teeth before he is shaking drops out of glasses and looking for something to drink. Sometimes even the cruets used at mass are not safe because after the altar boy pours a bit for the priest (according to the ritual), he drinks the rest behind the altar and thus passes his first test. Poland can be called drunk: bishops and senators drink themselves stiff; prelates, too, as well as soldiers and the gentry; they drink in towns, they drink in manors, they drink in villages.

Opaliński again and again returns to his obsession, namely, the lack of a solid standing army. "On Undefended Walls" gives us a striking comparison:

Poland stands by virtue of its lack of government, somebody said nicely, but another answers that it will perish through a lack of government. God keeps us as fools. And this comes close to the saying that, among people, a Pole is God's plaything. If the Divine Hand of the Almighty did not hold us up, long ago we would not have escaped from our foes and, I will add, from utter destruction. . . . God has grown used to treating us as a lord treats his fool. When a crowd of young boys closes in around a fool—one pinches his bottom, one pokes him where it hurts; the fool defends himself and shouts, once, twice, and the lord listens patiently, while the boys maul the fool without a respite and he begins to yell at the top of his voice, mouth wide open, so that he annoys the lord with it, and finally the lord calls to the boys: "Quiet down! How much more of that?" And the boys dive into the bushes away from the fool and playing. Thus God sometimes waits till our enemies have had their fill of swarming all over our miserable Poland. And only when they annoy her too much and Himself, He calls: "Be quiet Turks! Be quiet, Tartars!" And the Turks take to the bushes together with the other infidels.

Opaliński, true to the license of "macaronism," interlards his verse with Latin expressions, even whole quotations from Latin poets. So brutal and straightforward is his language that some editors saw fit to expurgate the coarser idioms. Reproached in his time for writing nothing more than prose arranged in lines, today he has been largely rehabilitated because of his rare conciseness and clarity as a socially committed writer.

Sarmatian Epic Poetry

The mania for versifying led writers to seize any opportunity to produce poems, a practice which yielded a strange assortment of topics. We have, then, the first topographic urban treatise on Warsaw in verse, a report on a sea trip to Lubeck (Germany), and a long memoir by a woman (*Description of the Whole Life of One Orphan* by Anna Stanisławska). But the most popular subjects were provided by historical events, especially the era of constant warfare beginning with the Polish occupation of Moscow, through the Cossack, Turkish, and Swedish wars, and ending with the rescue of Vienna by the Polish troops in 1683, which marked a decisive victory over Turkey. In these lengthy narratives overloaded with technical descriptions of battles and rather chaotic in composition, we have some of the best examples of the Sarmatian Baroque. A strong panegyrical element runs throughout, as authors usually wished to ingratiate themselves with powerful people or with their family clans.

Samuel Twardowski (1600–1660)   In no way can Samuel Twardowski be called an eminent poet, but his enormous narrative in verse, *A Civil War with the Cossacks, the Tartars, Muscovy, Later On, with the Swedes and Hungarians, Which Has Lasted Twelve Years until Now, Divided into Four Books*, enjoyed great popularity, although it was published only after the author's death, in 1681. Twardowski, an impoverished nobleman, was a hanger-on at various magnates' courts, and while traveling as secretary with one of his patrons to Turkey on a diplomatic mission, he wrote a diary of the journey, of course, in verse. But he practiced poetry for pleasure's sake, too, bringing into it pastoral Baroque motifs, as in his gay and frivolous love story, *Daphne into Laurel Tree* (*Dafnis drzewem bobkowym*, 1638), where (in octaves modeled on Piotr Kochanowski's translation of Tasso) he sings of the quarrels and pursuits of lovers, among them the love of Apollo for a chaste virgin, Daphne, who, escaping his passion, became a laurel tree. Another narrative in verse, *Fair Pasqualina* (*Nadobna Paskwalina*, 1655), probably borrowed from Spanish sources, is so heavily ornamented with mythological images and meticulous descriptions that it is barely readable. There are some passages of good quality, but the reader does not always find it easy to follow the adventures of Pasqualina, who, desperately in love with a gallant cavalier, travels in search of the goddess Juno, meets Apollo, Diana, Cupid, becomes a nun, and founds a convent, to the dismay of Cupid, who hangs himself on a myrtle tree. Twardowski seduced his contemporaries with his sham erudition, and his mixture of often incongruous images apparently failed to discourage them.

The national shrine, the monastery of Jasnogóra (in Częstochowa), *The Siege* which contained (as it still does today) a miraculous image of the *of* Blessed Virgin, was besieged unsuccessfully by a Swedish detachment *Jasnogóra* in 1656. The defeat of the Swedes was presented by the Catholic clergy as a miracle signaling the turning point in the war against the heretics. A long anonymous poem on these events, which is a sort of chronicle written to honor the heroic abbot of the monastery-turned-fortress, attracted popular favor. Miracles abound in the poem: for instance, the Virgin appears not only to the abbot but to the Swedish commander, Miller; artillery bullets are deprived of their destructive force by supernatural intervention; moreover, the author, in the manner of Tasso, introduces completely fictional elements. These are mostly stories of lovers, justified by the fact that among the besieged there was a considerable number of civilians. Nothing is missing in these tales, not even an English girl, Lioba, who, after her fiancé is killed, becomes dangerously ill and in her delirium visits the other world, from where after meeting the young man she brings back his assurance that the monastery soon will see the end of its troubles. Similarly, a young Swedish officer, Horn, has a vision of his fiancée, who foretells his death in the attack.

In the nineteenth century the poem served writers of historical novels, especially Henryk Sienkiewicz in his *Trilogy*, as a source for the reconstruction of that episode of the Swedish War.

Perhaps the most typical representative of the tastes and preoccupations in the second half of the seventeenth century was Wespazjan Kochowski, whose work abounds in farfetched devices, some merely amusing, but some not without appeal for modern poets. As was usual for his time, he received a superficial education, then for ten years served as a soldier fighting the Cossacks and the Swedes. Later on, he settled on a small hereditary estate, where, by his experience, civility, and tact, he won the respect and affection of his neighbors, who showered him with many local dignities. In spite of his many duties he managed to produce a literary yield of huge proportions. He was a deeply religious man but in a way fitting the epoch. His zealous Roman Catholicism was marked by superstition, by a ritualistic approach, and often by fanaticism: writing about a wound he had received during a battle, he explained it as the result of his disbelief, which he had expressed before the engagement in a story of a crucifix which spurted blood; or again, when the Arians were expelled from Poland, he wrote a violent diatribe against "those grandsons of Beelzebub." But one result of his devotion provides us today with some delightful discoveries. This is a poem consisting of several thousand epigrams, each built around a different epithet applied in religious literature to the Blessed Virgin. The title is long: *A Virgin's Garden, Measured by the Chain of Holy Writ, the Doctors of the Church, and Orthodox Preachers, Planted with Flowers, Which Are the Titles of the Mother of God, by the Lowest Slave of That Mother and Virgin* (1681). The Baroque conceits and playing with words are here inspired by such Latin names as Fulgetra Divinitatis, Pluvia Salutis, Aurora Consurgens, Regina Mundi, etc. But the best-known collection of his poems, *Non-idle Idling* (*Niepróżnujące próżnowanie*, 1674), includes both historical and lyric poems of a serious, often religious, nature as well as short *fraszki*. Kochowski, perhaps, felt most at ease in short love lyrics like that on the "game of Green," a youthful amusement the point of which was always to be able to present a green leaf when asked by fellow players. The poet takes his fellow player, a girl, by surprise early one morning when she is still in bed, and because she has left her green leaf in her clothes, she loses the game. Some of his short poems continue the bucolic trend of Jan Kochanowski, and his attachment to the author of *Laments* dictated his poem "Apology for Kochanowski," where he defends him against accusations of having been a heretic in his heart and not a good Roman Catholic. Other songs of that collection, on heroic soldiers who fell in the battles against Cossack and Tartar forces, are moving in their simplicity. As to versification, Kochowski sometimes makes use of the *ottava rima*, which appeared in Polish for the first time with the translation of Torquato Tasso and was to attract many enthusiasts among Polish poets. Short epigrams, traditionally called *fraszki*, follow sixteenth-century models while often reflecting a Baroque fondness for the bizarre. Yet Kochowski considered history, not poetry, his main pursuit. He labored for a long time over a huge, four-volume annal in Latin prose covering the rule of a few seventeenth-century Polish monarchs and divided into what the author calls "climacterics" in accordance with the belief he shared with the ancient Romans that a state undergoes decisive political changes every seven years. Because a subjective appraisal of events dominates his annal, Kochowski has been called a historical memorialist.

His most interesting poetic work was written in old age; *A Polish Psalmody* (*Psalmodia polska*, 1695) is an application of biblical verses to subjects taken from the author's personal life and from the country's recent history, a kind of song of gratitude to God where all events are taken as God's just punishments and rewards. For recognizing in Poland's past and present visible signs of divine protection, the author was remembered later as a precursor of Polish Romantic messianism. After Skarga, whose prose often had the ring of biblical verses, Kochowski was the first to choose the biblical verse as a poetic form. Just as David's Psalms relate the military conflicts of the Hebrews, *A Polish Psalmody* reasserts the effectiveness of that form in singing the triumphs of Polish arms over the Turks. The victory at Vienna won by King Jan Sobieski, whom Kochowski greatly admired, inspired him to raise his voice in particularly elevated tones:

The rising sun saw their haughtiness; and the evening saw them badly smitten.
The moon was ashamed of its crescent and, to hide its shame, desired not to shine for the fleeing.
The false prophet helped them not in that terror; nor did frequent ablutions purify the wicked of their sin.
They lay in the field like fat bulls after slaughter; and the victor, out of pity, ordered their filthy corpses to be covered with earth.
The captured prisoners were kept alive: and the sword, cooled down, was put back into the scabbard.
Thou hast ordered thus, Our Lord, who makest miracles; so that those who attempted at others' health paid with their own.
So that those who snatched bread from the mouths of the innocent might not eat it and that the weaker might take spoil from the stronger.
Three days were not enough to gather booty. Not only were soldiers taking the abandoned riches, but also small children and the common mob.

Those splendid tents from Sidon and those embroidered with gold from Jarbet stood empty like a shelter wherein dwells the watchman of an apple orchard.

Their horses were ridden and their own spears were smashed against their bodies by the more powerful one who let bullets fly at their backs.

Their crimson-vested overlords who would have said: "Let us possess the Christian land," have all perished.

Their vizir died in an unmanly way, strangled with a rope; and Jael soon drove a nail into the temple of that destroyer of the Lord's churches.

And to them happened what happened to the Midianites and to Jabin at the river Kishon.

Thou hast laid them low, O Lord, like a wheel on its side, and like a stalk in the wind the proud came to naught.

Patrzało na hardość ich wschodzące słońce; a toż na odwieczerzu widziało sromotnie rozgromionych.

Wstydził się miesiąc piątna swego, a żeby sromotę zakrył, nie chciał świecić w nocy uciekającym.

Nie pomógł w trwodze fałszywy prorok; ani częste umywanie nie oczyściło wszetecznych z grzechu.

Leżeli w polu, jako bycy tłuści po rzezi; a plugawe ścierwy kazał zwycięzca ziemią nakryć, z politowania.

Jeńcy w zatrzymaniu żywi zostali; a miecz po zwycięstwie ochłodnął w pochwy włożony.

Tyś tak kazał, Panie Boże nasz, cuda czyniący; aby którzy po cudze zdrowie przyszli, swojem nałożyli.

Aby chleb od gęby niewinnym wydzierający, nie pożyli go, a słabszy z mocniejszego zagarnął łupy.

Mało trzy dni było do zbierania korzyści. Brali nietylko żołnierze odbieżane dostatki, ale i dzieci małe z pospolitym gminem.

One pyszne w Sydonie, czy w Dziarbecie złotem tkane namioty, odbieżane, stały jako buda w sadzie, w której jabłek pilnowano.

Konie ich poosiadał mocniejszy, dzidy ich o nichże skruszył, i kulami do grzbietu uciekających strzelał.

Przepadli wszyscy purpuraci ich, którzy mówili: posiądźmy ziemię chrześcijańską.

Zginął wezyr niemęsko, powrozem uduszony; a onemu kościołów pańskich burzycielowi, niedługo w skronie młotem Jachel gwóźdź wbiła.

I stało się im tak jako Madianitom, i jako Jabinowi u rzeki Cisson.

Położyłeś ich, Panie, jako koło na odwrocie, i jako źdźbło przed wiatrem, tak pyszni zniknęli.

With the death of Kochowski at the very beginning of the next century, the Sarmatian Baroque was drawing to a close. The period which followed, known as the "Saxon Night," lacked even those few attributes we found in the literature of the self-taught, soldierly, and pious representatives of Sarmatism. Kochowski was the last, for some time, to extol the idea of a Christian knight as his personal ideal. (The idea of a Christian knight was, however, to be revived by poetry of the "Confederacy of Bar," 1768–1772.)

Prose

Seventeenth-century Polish prose is composed of diaries, journals and memoirs, and of a multitude of political writings which today would rank as journalism. The novel, whose promising beginnings in the adaptations of the sixteenth century had augured so well, failed, however, to develop—probably because of the decline of the bourgeois class. The most interesting example of prose is a memoir which remained in manuscript form until the nineteenth century, when it was printed for the first time. No purer example of a Sarmatian *szlachta* could be imagined than its author, Jan Chryzostom Pasek. He also shared many characteristics of the gentry in his native province of Mazovia, famous for its anti-Protestantism, its turbulence, anarchy, and obscurantism, its bravery, drinking, and also for its poverty. Pasek received some education at a Jesuit school in his native district; namely, he learned to declaim pompous speeches in Latin or in a mixture of Polish and Latin, also how to write extremely bad verse. Such equipment was to suffice for all his life, as there are no traces that he ever read any books. As a young man of nineteen, he enlisted in the army, and took part in the campaign against the Swedes in Poland. Then his division, commanded by the most distinguished general of the time, Hetman Czarniecki, was sent to Denmark to aid the Danes (Poland's allies) in their struggle against Sweden. After a stay in Denmark, Pasek found himself again in the army, this time in combat with Muscovy, and later on with Turkey, not to mention his involvements in periodical skirmishes of a civil-war character. Battles, duels, drunken brawls, boasting and joking in good company were his life for eleven years. But even after his retirement from the army and his marriage (to a rich widow), Pasek could not settle down. Undisguised hatred for his neighbors, lawsuits, acts of scarcely concealed banditry finally caused him to be condemned by a tribunal and sentenced to exile—a penalty handed down rarely and only in cases of grave crimes. The state of anarchy in the country around 1700, however, was such that the sentence was not enforced.

Pasek's famous *Memoirs* was written in his advanced age—perhaps we should not say written but rather noted down, for they are mostly

Jan Chryzostom Pasek (1636–1701)

spoken tales (*gawędy*) which Pasek had probably told innumerable times before putting them on paper. The stories are stitched together with passages where Pasek applies the doubtful stylistic training received at his Jesuit school. But except for these passages, the narrative is amazingly swift, colorful, and racy, endowed with great comic force and free from prescribed devices. On the contrary, Pasek uses everyday language, its diction and its exclamations. Mickiewicz rightly remarked in his lectures at the Collège de France that Pasek's phrases should be punctuated with special signs denoting gestures. The narrator of the tales appears in a more favorable light than does Pasek himself, from what we know of the author's own behavior. He composes a tall tale about himself as a hero who is always resourceful and clever. His standards are those of the average gentry, and measured by ours are surprisingly uninhibited. Thus, the author produces a doubly humorous effect: while contriving to provoke our laughter, he is himself unintentionally amusing. A superstitious man of limited intelligence, scornful of foreigners, a drunkard, and a duelist, he treats what, to us at least, is odd as the most natural thing in the world. For instance, he describes with relish a theatrical performance in Warsaw given by foreign actors at which the audience, composed of the gentry, became so incensed at an evil ruler in the play that it began to send a shower of arrows onto the stage and, ultimately, killed the unfortunate actor playing the king. Pasek does not, however, favor war; he does not even present himself as heroic. On the contrary, he goes to battle with a sort of fatalism and considers it simply obvious that during an engagement one should pick out richly dressed adversaries, riding good-looking horses, since after killing or capturing them one would be recompensed with their possessions. Making no effort to hide his greed, he reports how, as a commissary in Denmark, he drove the Danes to despair by pretending he did not understand anything they said (actually, he could have communicated with them in Latin). This state of affairs lasted until his hosts guessed the reason for his ignorance and brought him a gift, i.e., a bribe; quite suddenly Pasek ceased to be dumb—to the joy of the Danes. Yet in various morally dubious affairs, Pasek always invokes the aid of Divine Providence. We should not overlook, perhaps, one of Pasek's more sympathetic traits, namely, his fondness for animals and the delightful passages devoted to them in his work—for example, the story of his tame otter.

Because Pasek's narrative reads like a novel, Mickiewicz observed that Pasek anticipated the genre of the historical novel, invented by Sir Walter Scott. The *Memoirs*, thanks to its realistic and vivid descriptions, the richness of material—wars, civil wars, dietines, diets, anecdotes, lawsuits, duels, hunting, travel, etc.—set the pace for the future Polish historical novel.

The military conflicts of Pasek's time were not the only events to inspire memorialists. Rich material was also offered by earlier diplomatic and military action, especially Polish intervention in the affair of "Dmitry the Pretender" in Muscovy. Among the diarists of this era, the most serious author was Hetman Stanisław Żółkiewski (1547–1620), the commander of Polish troops who entered Moscow. His *Beginning and Progress of the Muscovite War* (*Początek i progres wojny moskiewskiej*, 1612) is a model of severe, concise prose, the work of a soldier and, by necessity, a diplomat. The whole affair of the Pretender is also described by Stanisław Niemojewski, who, as Polish emissary to the new czar, was imprisoned by the Muscovites after the assassination of Dmitry and later, in a camp of internment in the far north, consoled himself by reading Petrarch in the original and translating Horace. His memoirs, like those of Pasek, could form a colorful novel.

Pasek had another predecessor in the person of Samuel Maskiewicz (*c.* 1580–1640). A soldier of Lithuanian extraction, a man of little education, he treated war as an opportunity for adventure and self-enrichment. Yet his stay in Moscow did not yield any other riches than a memory of funny and extraordinary scandals, duels, and brawls. He was no less typical than Pasek in his dubious mores (which we can glimpse in his short account of a visit: "We drank mead; we broke his sister's leg—not I, but the marshal—and together we all went to Białowicze").

The wars with Turkey also led some participants into quite fabulous situations: for example, Marek Jakimowski, taken prisoner at the Battle of Cecora in 1620 (which cost the life of Hetman Żółkiewski), was sold as a slave to Egypt. While toiling on a galley, he organized a successful mutiny, using the conquered galley to reach Italy—not without booty, since he brought a former slave from the same galley to Poland with him as a wife. The anonymous report in which these events are related is entitled *A Short Description of the Taking Over of a First-Rate Alexandrian Galley* (*Opis krótki zdobycia galery przedniejszej aleksandryjskiej*).

The seventeenth century abounds not only in memoirs but also in correspondence, and a writer of letters who surpassed the memorialists, if not by the vigor of his language, at least by its richness— the result of incomparably higher sophistication—was the last ruler of the century, King Jan Sobieski. His *Letters to Marysieńka* (Mariette, his French-born wife), written every few days, often every day, between the years 1665 and 1683, make up a huge volume. He does not reserve certain subjects for his wife, but he writes

Other Memorialists

Correspondence

to her as to a companion in political intrigues, the conduct of war, court gossip, not to speak of love, which occupies an eminent place. These letters, of course, were not destined for publication. In their sometimes startlingly intimate details they remind us of Samuel Pepy's *Diary*, but more important, they herald a new literary form: the novel in letters. Sobieski was well acquainted with the French novel *L'Astrée*, by Honoré d'Urfé, and borrowed from it many pseudonyms—for instance, Celadon, Sylvander, and Phoenix, for himself, and Astrée, Diana, Clelia, Cassandra, Aurore, and Rose, for his wife.

Sermons   The Jesuit Piotr Skarga had established a tradition of employing a flowery style in sermons geared to political circumstances. He found a successor in Fabian Birkowski (1566–1636), a Dominican who, as a chaplain of troops, specialized in fiery but cordial sermons to the soldiers, extolling the manly virtues. His *Sermons Before a Military Camp* (*Karania obozowe*), published in 1623, shows a fondness for bizarre effects and marks a change from the essentially Renaissance discipline of Skarga's style.

Maxims   Andrzej Maksymilian Fredro (1620–1679), castellan of Lwów, was, like many of his contemporaries, a prolific political writer. But if he is remembered today, it is not for his civic-minded treatises in Latin; Fredro belongs to literary history thanks to a work that he wrote in Polish, his *Proverbs of Common Speech* (*Przysłowia mów potocznych*, 1658). Besides drawing upon old Polish proverbs, he himself invented maxims, which were a sort of exercise in the art of succinctness. A good observer, a skeptic, inclined to paradox, he is, in a way, a counterpart of the poets of conceits, though he does not convey his ideas through images. On the other hand, his maxims could not be further from those of his French contemporary—La Rochefoucauld. Fredro, as a Sarmatian nobleman, constantly imposes his conservative views favoring "golden freedom" and anarchy as the mainstays of the *Respublica*. Aside from perspicacious remarks on human nature, we find in him an isolationist's distrust of everything foreign, and undoubtedly that mentality contributed to the success of his proverbs with the public.

The Theater

Besides the Jesuit and Protestant school traditions and besides *komedia rybałtowska*, which survived only up to the second half of the century, theater appeared in an additional form: for the first time, theater was an established, though short-lived, institution at the royal court. That was the result of a personal whim of the monarch. On a visit to Italy the future King Władysław IV became captivated by Italian music and its then avant-garde form, the opera. After his ascent to the Polish throne, he maintained "talent scouts" in Italy whose duty it was to attract promising artists to Poland by offering them large sums of money. The court opera company thus came into being. It flourished during the years 1637–1646. Its members formed a large troupe, made up not only of composers, singers, and actors for comic roles in the *commedia dell'arte*, but also of Italian architects and painters in charge of set design, construction, etc. Even the King himself took an active part in stage direction. From what we know of that troupe, extremely complicated stage machinery was used, since the Italian opera company was famous for lavish light and color effects (gods appeared, monsters entered the scene, etc.). For instance, in one opera, entitled *Africa*, the young *cantatrice*, dressed as Africa, appeared riding an elephant with a movable trunk. A ballet with girls dressed as Negroes followed her aria. In stage decor, Baroque opera showed a fondness for the effects of perspective—many rooms opening into one another. There were actually two stages: a large one for the effects of perspective and for the opera proper, and a small one for *commedia dell'arte* (often—to believe the report of a papal nuncio in Warsaw—very indecent). The Italian influence, so strong during the Renaissance period, continues throughout the seventeenth century, and the opera company established by King Władysław is not the only example of it. Many devices used in the Jesuit Baroque theater also seem to have been inspired either directly by Italian opera or by the opera at the royal court. The French tragic theater, in spite of the efforts of Andrzej Morsztyn, failed to take root in Poland at this time.

The common fare of the theatergoing public is best exemplified by a spectacle dating from 1663, an anonymous work, which can be called a morality or passion play in opera form. The title is *A Skirmish of the Bloodily Warring God, Lord of Hosts, for the Sins of the Human Species, Presented in Good Friday Scenes for the Eternal Memory and the Education of the Audience* (*Utarczka krwawiewojującego Boga i Pana zastępów za grzechy narodu ludzkiego na nieśmiertelną pamiątkę wielkopiątkowymi scenami i na zbudowanie audytora reprezentowana*). Since medieval personifications and allegories were enjoying a heyday, it is not surprising that Love, "dressed in linen, a wig, a crown, and stockings [as the stage instructions tell us], will sit in a chair, holding a burning heart in one hand, in the other—a cross." Cruelty pierces Love with a sword: Cruelty "should be in armor with a helmet and a sword; on its arms—metal bands." A prologue is recited by twelve persons, "richly dressed." The play follows the gospel at first, telling the story of Herod, the high priests, and the seizure of Jesus in the garden. Thus, it begins as a mystery play, but soon we enter another reality: A Sinner appears, who meets the World "richly dressed, in a wig, golden chains, and stockings, holding in one hand a scepter; on his head will be a crown; in the other hand he will hold a crown and a mitre. He should be the most highly adorned possible." The Sinner pays homage to the World, who promises him all riches and power; then Fortune enters, "dressed in white in the manner of a woman, having wings, turning a wheel in her hands, her eyes covered with a black strip, on her head a wig, on her legs stockings." Fortune leads the Sinner toward Happiness. . . .

In the next scene we see the magnificently attired Sinner sitting in a chair, drinking wine. While an orchestra plays, the Sinner boasts: "I am king, I am lord; there is probably no equal to me in the whole world." And now, as the Sinner sinks deeper and deeper into self-assurance, a film technique is applied, namely, the magic lantern. Thus, two actions develop simultaneously: in the first, the Sinner rejects the warnings of his guardian angel, while behind him the audience sees images (shown *per umbras*, in the seventeenth-century terminology) which are scenes from the Passion of Jesus. At last, Death appears on the stage, and all the Sinner's servants flee. Justice has also entered, and gives the Sinner over to Death. Pity quarrels with her, but Justice rejects Pity's arguments. Here, Time strolls in: "He should have a clock in one hand; in the other, a trumpet; and when he speaks, the hour should be struck behind a curtain. He should be tall, should wear a wig, a long gray beard, should be dressed in linen and have wings. He will sing in a bass voice." Time then sings, half in Polish, half in Latin:

> Vigilate quia nescitis diem necque horam.
> Thus I explain it to you, miserable one,
> Who will perish because you did not heed the last hour.
> Vigilate serio quia nescitis diem necque horam.

And when Death is ready to behead the Sinner, Time addresses the public in Latin:

> Mors ultima ratio rerum, ultima linia dierum,
> Vigilate quia nescitis diem necque horam.

In the next scene, the Sinner has been transformed into the Damned: "Dressed in white, he will sit on a stool at the entrance to Hell; his head should be covered with a kerchief; in his hands he will have a burning bowl, and in the bowl will be vodka and salt. He will, thus, be clearly visible, and should hold the fire in front of his face. Powdery fires will burst from Hell; four masked devils will stand beside the Damned." A song of the devils, *cantus daemonum*, is heard:

O you miserable soul,
Where will you have your peace?
In dark hell,
In the fire eternal,
Unpleasant even to me.
Ugly corners,
All loathsome,
There Darkness and stench are for dinner.
To be in hell,
To live there forever, forever, forever.

The Damned is then seized by the devils and dragged into Hell, wherefrom he exclaims: "Woe, woe, woe in aeternum, woe forever, forever, forever." The stage directions suggest: "Here, everything should be absolutely silent; then the curtains will be drawn and music played."

In the last part of the play, the motif of *planctus* (or lament) common to medieval passion plays is used. The Blessed Mother, anxious to learn what happened to Jesus, converses with St. John. When he tells her that Jesus was crucified, she faints. A new sphere of action is introduced, this time not by using the magic lantern, but by drawing apart a second curtain, behind which is revealed a rock, a cross, and Jesus on the cross. Angels take the body from the cross and give it to the Holy Mother, who pronounces a moving speech:

I say to you farewell, Phoenix, my only Son,
Forgive by your love the executioners for their crimes.
Do not forget me, too, your sad mother,
Recompense lavishly the loss of my solace.

The instruction for the staging of this scene runs as follows: "Here, angels with candles will walk in twos bearing the body on a bier. The band will play and sing 'Weep Today Every Living Soul' until they depose the body in the tomb. Then all will stop; let the silence be complete. Mary will kneel in the tomb with the angels."

Since the scenes were set apart by music and the text was sung, the work constitutes, in effect, a libretto to a religious opera. The play's composition is excellent: Beginning with an introduction (Love and Cruelty), it moves to the scenes preceding the Passion of Jesus. The unfolding of the Sinner's life simultaneously with the Passion of Jesus seems to stress the principle that the Crucifixion did not occur once but repeats itself throughout all time. The play ends with Mary's lament, which coincides with the final moments of the Passion and the death of Jesus on the cross.

The first Polish comedy in prose came from the pen of Stanisław

Herakliusz Lubomirski (1642–1702), who has remained a somewhat controversial personality. He was one of the most powerful magnates of his time and a man of extensive learning, often referred to by his contemporaries as the "Polish Solomon." He tried his hand at pastoral and devotional verse, made adaptations of Ecclesiastes in verse, and wrote prose in Latin as well as in Polish. His writings are marked by a skepticism and a disillusionment with the world which, as is known from his biography, went together with unlimited, and very worldly, personal ambitions. He merits his page in the history of the theater thanks to his maintenance of a private theater on his estate. He amused himself by contributing to it as an author. One of his pieces, the *Comedy of Old Lopez*, in prose, preserved in manuscript form, seems to have enjoyed especial popularity, for it has survived in several versions copied by various hands. The title suggests a Spanish influence, though it is not certain whether Lubomirski looked to Spain directly for models, or whether they reached him through Italy. The humor of that comedy consists in a contrast between old pedants, characters drawn as caricatures, and the quite earthy appetites of young Melisa, married to Lopez, an old man not up to the task of a husband. With the appearance of servants on the stage, the play becomes farcical and quite obscene. It ends in Melisa's marriage to a young pirate, Spiridon, who had been her fiancé before her unconsummated union with Lopez. Lubomirski's attempt to introduce prose into comedy was a daring innovation which paved the way for a new type of theatrical play whose development belongs to the next century.

CHAPTER V

The First Half of the Eighteenth Century — The "Saxon Night"

BACKGROUND INFORMATION

AROUND 1700 THE weakness of a stagnant economic and political system became only too apparent. A rigid class division into masters and serfs was stronger than ever in the nearly ruined country. Wars had devastated towns so completely that some of them had lost up to 90 per cent of their inhabitants. The country as a whole sustained a population decrease of about 30 per cent due not only to wars and epidemics but also to the utter misery of the peasants. The concentration of the only existing capital, land, in the hands of a few lords resulted, as we have already seen, in an unequal division within the nobility itself: on the one side, a small number of powerful magnates; on the other, masses of petty gentry. While the former counted the towns which they possessed in dozens, the villages in thousands, and maintained their own private armies, private courts, even private diplomatic relations with countries abroad, the latter lived on a level scarcely above that of the peasants, retaining, however, a pride in their titles and their right to vote, which enabled them to treat their rich "brethren" as equals. The poorest gentry entered most directly into the service of the "latifundia" as employees on different levels of administration. This structure contributed to the spread of sycophancy, servility, intrigue, and false politeness in social behavior and to a specific culture which we will call the cult of eating and drinking: at the marriage of a magnate, for example, the guests devoured the following items: 80 oxen, 300 calves, 50 sheep, 150 hogs, 21,000 fowl, 12,000 fish, plus a proportionate number of barrels of wine and aquavit.

Declining Social Structure

[153]

Further Lowering of the Educational Standards Although there were some fifty-one Jesuit colleges in operation, the Order, adapting itself more and more to prevalent tastes, had become a mainstay of Sarmatism. The University of Kraków likewise fell into decline. The whole curriculum in Jesuit schools was practically limited to the teaching of Latin. (It was even forbidden to speak Polish on the premises.) But though the pupils of these schools could read and write in Latin, they were frozen in tradition, chauvinistic, isolated from the rest of Europe, and insensible to any new ideas. Wealthy aristocrats did travel abroad, where they acquired a fondness for everything French, but, in general, they imitated only the superficial features of Western civilization. These two calamities—either Sarmatism or a stupid imitation of everything foreign—became the targets at which the Polish representatives of the Enlightenment were to aim their most vigorous attacks.

Devout Obscurantism The situation of Protestants as well as of other denominations worsened gradually. This was a time of religious persecutions when "blasphemy" sometimes was met with a death sentence. Religion actually meant little more than fear of devils and witches. Devotional literature proliferated, but a sampling of titles suggests a rather doubtful profundity: *The Army of Sincere Feelings Newly Recruited*, or *Celestial Cavalry and Infantry*, or *The Terrible Echo of the Last Trumpet*, or *The Golden Key to Heaven*, or *A Four-wheeled Vehicle Carrying You to Heaven*. The prevailing mentality can be illustrated by the great success of a book by a certain Father Benedykt Chmielowski published in 1745 and bearing the title *New Athens, or the Academy Full of All Knowledge, Divided under Many Titles into Classes, Written as a Memorial for the Wise, as a Lesson for Idiots, as a Practical Aid for Politicians, and as Entertainment for the Melancholy*. This was an almanac providing answers to many questions of a practical nature, such as how to prevent sleep: "By putting a swallow's eye in a person's bedsheets, you will take sleep away, a good method for lazy people." For those interested in foreign countries, it supplied the necessary information: "In Italy there is a town which preserves the Blessed Virgin's garments, the stove on which she cooked for Jesus and Joseph, and an earthen dish from which she fed them."

The Military Weakness of the State The balance of power in that part of Europe underwent a radical change. The *Respublica*, until now a rival of Muscovy, had, in spite of its enormous territory, no standing army of any account and, owing to internal disintegration, was already a pawn in the hands of its neighbors, Russia and Prussia. During the so-called Northern War, the ruling king, August II (from a Saxon dynasty), who had been elected under foreign pressure, sided with Peter the Great against Charles XII of Sweden, and the country became a theater of military operations. He and his son, elected king of Poland in a similar way, cared little about the interests of their subjects. For the reasons presented above, their rule is known as the "Saxon Night."

The lowest point in the economy, in education, and in literature was reached around 1750. After that date, new and vigorous forces began to flow through the *Respublica*, preparing the ground for the fruitful, though short, period of the Polish Enlightenment.

POETRY

Rhymesters abounded throughout the "Saxon Night," but their verbosity, the legacy of a decaying Sarmatian Baroque, makes their efforts painfully dull reading. Those who sound most genuine are the writers who took over the previous century's main religious theme, juxtaposing transient human glory and omnipotent death. They embroidered it with images of the uncouth macabre. It is to such a style that the Jesuit Father Józef Baka (1707–1780), owes his niche in the national literary pantheon. His work is quoted as an example of the worst poetry ever written in Polish; it is so bad that it cannot but give pleasure to all seekers after oddities. His *Remarks on Ineluctable Death* (*Uwagi o śmierci niechybnej*, 1766), set in a gay dancelike rhythm, an orgy of inelegant rhyming, was re-edited in the nineteenth century for humorous purposes. In this collection, he issues dire warnings to people of various stations in life. His predictions for women (he describes in detail how their bodies will disintegrate in the grave) obviously provided him with sadistic gratification.

Some merits may be found in a prolific poetess, Elżbieta Drużbacka (c. 1695–1765), who was not scorned even by the literati of the Enlightenment. A better mastery of verse, especially in her descriptions of the seasons or in her poem praising the created world and rebuking the atheist, distinguished her from her contemporaries. As Professor Wacław Borowy, her defender in our century, has justly said, the rich sensuality that bursts forth whenever she speaks of love is her saving grace. In her lifetime, she published *A Collection of Rhythms, Spiritual, Panegyrical, Moral, and Worldly* (*Zbiór rytmów duchowych, panegirycznych, moralnych, światowych*, 1752).

Polish literature is also obliged to Professor Borowy for the rediscovery of Konstancja Benisławska, a forgotten author of religious poems. Unfortunately, her *Songs Sung to Oneself* (*Pieśni sobie śpiewane*, 1776) was published when the burgeoning Enlightenment trends made it appear already old-fashioned. Superior to Drużbacka's, her work seems to stem from Kochanowski's *Psalter* stylistically, while the intensity behind her devotional lines points to the influence of Spanish mystics, like Saint Theresa d'Ávila (copiously translated and published by the Jesuits). Her poems, in fact, deal with paradoxes of love:

> Abolish, O God, Hell, I do not care about Heaven:
> I will love, just as I love, for your sake.

> Znieś, BOŻE, Piekło, nic mi i po niebie:
> Będę kochała, jak kocham, dla Ciebie.

Little is known about Benisławska, except that she was a noblewoman living in a remote province of the *Respublica*, in Livonia, and turned to religious poetry at the "advanced age" of twenty-eight, after having given birth to many children. Her volume suffices to rank her with the good poets of the Baroque, of whom she is a late descendant.

THE PRECURSORS OF CHANGE

Stanisław Konarski (1700–1773)   Against the background of general marasmus, a handful of energetic and intelligent individuals, active in various fields, stands out in brilliant contrast. One of them, Stanisław Konarski, was a Piarist monk. He received what, for his time, was an average education, i.e., training in Latin and pompous Baroque rhetoric; but his innate intellectual vigor and curiosity led him far beyond the narrow sphere of his contemporaries. As a young priest, he studied in Rome for a few years; then, after his return home, he plunged into politics. A man with a curious personality, Konarski was devoured by the need for action, though the politics into which he threw his energies consisted mainly of petty intrigues and factional struggles. In any case, he journeyed constantly between Poland and France, combining, until the age of forty, a program of social commitment with self-education. The failure of his political ambitions directed him to other fields, namely, pedagogy and writing. In Warsaw he founded and directed a school which made the Piarist Order a pioneer in the field of education. Known as the Collegium Nobilium, the school was established to train the sons of the rich nobility (the only group with a relatively high interest in education). New pedagogical methods were introduced, such as cordial relations between teachers and pupils, a group spirit among the students, and a curriculum which embraced the natural sciences, mathematics, physics, geography, and Polish. The school's success soon compelled other orders to imitate it. For Konarski, however, the Collegium Nobilium was a political instrument. His idea was to create a small elite who would be capable of introducing reforms in the country.

Konarski was steeped in the best traditions of the Polish Renaissance, and in his intellectual qualities he resembled the Polish humanists of the sixteenth century, but he was born in unpropitious times. Among foreign writers, he particularly admired Montesquieu, who satisfied his passionate interest in state institutions and laws. In his writings (both in Latin and in Polish) we find the ever-recurring problem which occupied the attention of all thinking citizens of the period, namely, how to remove the legal foundation of anarchy, the *liberum veto*, and how to strengthen the central authority. This, in short, forms the subject of his four-volume work, *On Effective Counsels* (*O skutecznym rad sposobie*, 1760–1763). Like most pioneers, Konarski really could not hope for personal fame in his lifetime. As the progressive movement gathered momentum and rationalist ideas of the French Enlightenment along with the classical style made their way into Poland, he appeared more and more old-fashioned. In his old age, he received a medal from the king, Stanisław August, with the inscription: *sapere auso* (to him who dared to be wise). But he was not highly regarded by the new brilliant writers, though they recognized his *Tragedy of Epaminonda* (*Tragedia Epaminondy*, 1756) as marking the beginning of a new, classical Polish theater.

Konarski's views on state institutions were far more daring than those of Stanisław Leszczyński, who, backed by Sweden, reigned briefly as king of Poland from 1704 to 1710 and again in 1733. After losing the throne a second time, he retired to France, where he wrote a political treatise directed against the *liberum veto* under the sly title of *A Free Voice Assuring Freedom* (*Głos wolny wolność ubezpieczający*, 1749). It is mainly a piece of election propaganda, as the author nourished the hope of being re-elected king. Reforms are timidly proposed, and there is an obvious fear of offending a gentry accustomed to "golden freedom." *Stanisław Leszczyński (1677–1766)*

Education, literature, and the theater came to be looked upon as the main instruments of change by all those who opposed the unbearable state of things. And the man who opens the history of modern theater in Poland happened to be an educator and playwright in one person. If many things can be said against the Jesuit Order in Poland, credit is due at least to its ability for self-renewal. Bohomolec was a Jesuit who left his imprint on the entire final phase of the Jesuit theater. In sharp reaction to the traditional and popular Jesuit spectacles, which were medieval in spirit, he turned to comedy in prose by adapting the plays of Molière and his imitators. Since he wrote for the school theater, love motifs and women's roles were eliminated. The moralistic theater of Bohomolec, which often presented a richness of realistic detail, indicates considerable progress toward a new dramatic concept, but his school comedies constitute only the first part of his long literary career. He was to become one *Franciszek Bohomolec (1720–1784)* of the key figures in the theatrical movement of the Enlightenment.

Similarly, Andrzej Załuski, whose name is still remembered thanks to his passionate interest in books, was a clergyman. As bishop of Kiev, he gathered, at his own expense, a library of some 300,000 volumes and 10,000 manuscripts which he donated to the Polish Government. This library (named after him) was to meet a curious fate. After the partition of Poland, the czarist government somehow found itself justified in removing this valuable material to Russia; thus, the whole collection was transported to St. Petersburg. On the way, the officers and soldiers who carried out the operation lost or damaged many precious items. The library (though not in its totality) was returned to Warsaw after the Russian Revolution by the new Soviet Government. In 1944, the Załuski Library, one of the main centers of research for students of literature, was completely burned down by the Nazis.

Załuski acted also as an editor of Old Polish authors and as a bibliographer. The *Bibliographia Zalusciana*, written at his inspiration by his librarian, Janocki, was the first scholarly attempt in this field. Załuski was also something of a poet, writing satires in the French style and translating Boileau.

CHAPTER VI

The Second Half of the Eighteenth Century—The Enlightenment

BACKGROUND INFORMATION

IF THE RENAISSANCE is called the Golden Age of Polish letters, *The Camp of the Reform* the short but intense period of the Enlightenment is, in many respects, a link between this seemingly lost heritage and the literature of modern times. The cultural revival coincided with the reign of the last king of Poland, Stanisław August Poniatowski, and it is for this reason that we speak of the "Stanislavian" period. In fact, however, the situation of the country was such that men of the Enlightenment with their broad vistas and daring ideas were unable to change the course of events. Yet in both education and literature, conceived by them as instruments of political and social commitment, they left a decisive mark upon the fate of the nation. The influence of France, which, in the beginning of the century, had been no more than a vogue in aristocratic circles, now took on deeper significance as the ideas of such French writers as Diderot, Voltaire, d'Alembert, and Rousseau began to penetrate Polish minds. The current of rationalism in Poland represented by Socinianism had been cut off after the expulsion of the Arians. New rationalist trends were, however, reaching Poland from abroad, and a parallel can be drawn between that phenomenon and the fruitful borrowing from the Humanism of Erasmus in the sixteenth century. The "men of the Enlightenment" were not numerous. They struggled against great odds, owing to the stubborn resistance of the larger mass of the ruling class, the gentry, who, true to "Sarmatism," opposed any novelties. That is why those who belonged to the so-called Camp of the Reform (both

[159]

in the political and in the cultural sense) often resorted to slightly conspiratorial tactics, facilitated by the fact that practically all of them were connected with Freemasonry. In view of the odds, their accomplishment is remarkable. The obstacles they encountered were not only internal. The international position of the country was nearly hopeless because of the military strength of Russia and Prussia. The Russian policy toward the *Respublica* consisted in backing the *status quo*, since the existing system would guarantee the maintenance of inertia in Poland. Russia, therefore, appeared in the guise of defender of the "golden freedom" (which cannot be said to have been her specialty at home). The Camp of the Reform, following French philosophers who advocated the equality of man and the right of the individual to assess institutions by reason, was acutely aware of the consequences brought about by the lack of an absolutist phase in Polish history. Therefore, their concern was not the increase of Sarmatian "golden freedom," but the strengthening of the executive through the establishment of a hereditary constitutional monarchy with a parliament functioning on the basis of majority rule; as a consequence they struggled for the abolition of the *liberum veto*.

Religion and Freemasonry   The "Age of Reason" placed the seat of authority in man himself, not in divine revelation, which since the seventeenth century had been submitted to rational inquiry and accepted only insofar as it confirmed supposedly inborn notions of reasonableness. Deism, that belief in God as a wise clockmaker dispassionately observing the mechanism he invented, contributed to the growth of religious skepticism and contaminated both laity and clergy alike. Without exaggeration, it can be said that the mainstays of the Enlightenment in Poland were elegant, skeptical, often libertine, priests who displayed all the airs of French politeness. On their account a new label entered the vocabulary: *labuś* (from the French *l'abbé*). Many of them, including high dignitaries of the Church, belonged to Freemasonry. The role of Masonic lodges was an eminent one, as they provided a meeting ground for various layers of society. Not only nobles and clergymen were admitted but also well-to-do burghers, including some Jews. The strategy of the Camp of the Reform was prepared at Masonic meetings, and, let us observe, the king himself was a member.

The Personality of the King   Stanisław August Poniatowski (1732–1798) was not of royal blood. He came from a wealthy, aristocratic family, was given an excellent education in Poland and in Paris, spoke several foreign languages, and, undoubtedly, belonged to the intellectual elite of Europe. As a young man, he became a lover of Catherine the Great and later on, in 1764, under strong Russian diplomatic pressure, was elected king of Poland. He has remained a highly controversial figure, accused by some historians of infinite evasions and vacillations in his policy, of pusillanimity in the face of Russia, and of undue concern for collecting mistresses. Yet the King was also the mainspring of the Camp of the Reform, whose plans obviously collided with the interests of Russia; while at the same time, loyal to Catherine and fully realizing the disproportion of power between Poland and Russia, he was sometimes compelled to separate himself from the more ardent reformers—a policy which threw him into unresolvable contradictions. As to his pursuit of pleasure, the eighteenth century was a time of general license, not only in Poland. Perhaps the capital of libertinism was Rome (not to speak of Venice). The laxity of morals was such that young women of the Romantic generation at the beginning of the nineteenth century looked with horror upon the frivolous attitudes of their grandmothers.

"Confederacy" was the name given to any organized movement of the gentry directed against the central authority. International tensions preceding war between Russia and Turkey (1768–1772) caused repercussions in Poland, which had a common border with Turkey: in Bar, a town in Podolia near the Turkish boundary, the gentry took an oath to fight against the Polish king and against Russian troops stationed in some parts of the country. The motives were patriotic in the most traditional sense; the Confederacy of Bar in no way reflected progressive tendencies. Turkey's defeat was paralleled by the quelling of the Confederacy by Russian troops. (One of the leaders of the Confederacy, Kazimierz Pułaski, emigrated to America, where he became a hero of the American Revolutionary War). The Confederacy provided a pretext for the first partition (in 1772) of Poland—a step which had long been anticipated in diplomatic talks between the neighboring powers. Russia took for herself the territories to the east of the rivers Dnieper and Dvina; Pomerania went to Prussia; and southeastern Poland (called Galicia, from the Ukrainian *Halich, Halychyna*), to Austria. The shock endured by the Poles brought home the need for reform and facilitated the endeavors of those who opposed the existing state of affairs.

The Confederacy of Bar and the First Partition

In 1773 the Commission for National Education was founded, and with such broad prerogatives that it has been justly called the first ministry of education in Europe. It completely transformed the patterns which determined the training of young people and created a unified network of schools. That task was made possible, first of all, by the disappearance of the Jesuit Order, dissolved in the same year by the Pope, who yielded to many accusations leveled at the Order from various parts of Europe. The enormous estates of the Order, its school buildings and libraries, were taken over by the Commission for

The Commission for National Education

National Education. The Commission's work extended from universities to elementary schools. The Jesuit Academy in Wilno was reorganized as a university by an astronomer (and clergyman), Marcin Poczobutt; while Hugo Kołłątaj, one of the most radical leaders of the Camp of the Reform (also a clergyman), brought new life to the University of Kraków, introducing modern pedagogical methods and a new curriculum which stressed the natural sciences.

The need for textbooks led the Commission to create a Textbook Society which organized contests to stimulate the writing of manuals. Polish scientific vocabulary was being elaborated at the same time by eminent scientists like Poczobutt (already mentioned), in astronomy; Jundziłł (author of the *Lithuanian Flora*), in botany; and the brothers Śniadecki: Jan, in mathematics, and Jędrzej, in chemistry.

The work of the Commission for National Education had a lasting effect reaching far into the nineteenth century. One may even say that, thanks to it, a new type of writer made his appearance: no longer a self-educated amateur but a man with a good humanistic training obtained in a high school and at the University.

The Press   The first newspaper appeared in Poland in 1661, but the general lowering of standards did not favor the development of the press in the following decades. In the Stanislavian era the situation changed radically. Some ninety titles of periodicals (around sixty in Warsaw itself) can be counted, though many of the publications were short-lived. The most important molder of public opinion was *The Monitor*, modeled upon the *Spectator* of London. The magazine, edited by Franciszek Bohomolec, began to appear in 1765, and continued its activity for some twenty years. It can be defined as a moralistic periodical and the first literary journal in Poland. Not satisfied with the reading matter available in the press, many well-to-do people in the provinces maintained correspondents in Warsaw whose duty consisted in relating by letter all the latest news and gossip to their patrons. Also at this time a new institution instrumental in spreading the knowledge and appraisal of events came into being, namely, the coffeehouse. By the end of the Stanislavian period the Warsaw population not only was well informed and passionately interested in politics but, as a powerful ally of the progressives, including Jacobin sympathizers, constituted a political force of the first magnitude.

The Classical Style   The Polish literary language at this time underwent a true revolution. The ideal of the men of the Enlightenment was a clear, precise style, modeled upon French Classicism and the poetics of antiquity. Boileau, who, reacting against the Baroque, had codified the rules of French versification, was considered a lawgiver in Poland too. Franciszek Ksawery Dmochowski (1762–1808) wrote an adaptation of Boileau's *L'art poétique* "Polonizing" it completely and submitting the writing of his contemporaries to critical discussion (1788). Purity of language was stressed and "macaronic" incrustations combatted. Periodicals and leaflets of the time were filled with fierce polemics centering around the rules of good taste. Baroque "overabundance" in literature and in the theater was rejected as barbarous. It was toward the Polish poets of the Renaissance as models of a limpid and balanced style that attention now directed itself.

It would be unjust to bypass other aspects of the eighteenth *Another* century, as it was not only a century of rationalism. Sentimental litera- *Side of* ture, to which, after all, a large part of the work of Rousseau belongs, *of Reason* enjoyed great popularity. The novels of Richardson and Fielding were translated into Polish. On the other hand, there was also a pronounced inclination toward the pietistic and mystical. Some Poles played a prominent role in the French "mystical" lodges which proliferated during the last decades before the Revolution. Europe was extremely cosmopolitan, owing to the new universal language, French, which replaced Latin; and ideas were transmitted from one country to another with great rapidity. Thus the mysterious, the bizarre, the supernatural fascinated all the European capitals, as the incredible international career of Cagliostro testifies. The demonic also captured imaginations, and the Marquis de Sade was not the only representative of that current. In view of this, the figure of the Polish writer Jan Potocki, author of the *Saragossa Manuscripts* (*Rękopis znaleziony w Saragossie*), is less incomprehensible.

For several centuries the Polish Jews led a life completely separated *The Jews* from that of the surrounding Christians, having judicial, penal, fiscal, religious, and educational institutions of their own. The Federation of Jewish Communities, established in the sixteenth century for the purpose of collecting the Jewish head tax, possessed great autonomy; however, in the next century its semiannual sessions (*Zjazd Żydów koronnych*) presented a picture similar to that of the Polish Diet, with *liberum veto*, jealousies, and factional struggles. What applies to the country as a whole, namely, the devastating effects of the Cossack Rebellion and of the Swedish War, applies even more to the Jews, who, as tax collectors, tenants, and agents of the Polish lords, were massacred by the thousands in the Ukraine, while the general decay of the towns after the war against the Swedes touched them very strongly. This prepared favorable ground for the feverish expectation of a messiah, and, in fact, Poland numbered a great mass of believers in a messiah known by the name of Sabbatai Zevi, who revealed himself in the city of Smyrna. In 1701, some twelve hundred Jewish heretics went on a penitential journey from Poland via Austria and Italy to Palestine. Believers in Sabbatai Zevi, not deterred by the fact that he died a Moslem, were persecuted by the rabbis;

nevertheless, the expectation of a messiah persisted throughout the eighteenth century and contributed to two powerful movements within Polish Jewry: Hasidism and Frankism. Hasidism (from the Hebrew word *hasid*, i.e., "pious") was founded by Israel ben Eliezer, called Baal-Shem (1700–1760), a simple village Jew from the region of the Carpathian Mountains near the southern border of the *Respublica*. The name *baal-shem* in Hebrew means "master of the name" and denotes a messianic prophet. In its beginning, Hasidism bore the imprint of the founder, a dreamer roaming the woods, influenced by Ukrainian folklore and perhaps by the ecstatic (Christian-Orthodox) sect of the Hlysts. In opposition to the rabbinic tradition, Baal-Shem created a joyful, mystical religion of communication with God through songs, dances, drinking, and work, and not through the synagogue and the study of sacred writings. That mystical trend, the spirit of which is sometimes compared to the teaching of St. Francis of Assisi, soon degenerated into a new kind of established confession, by shifting the stress to the person of the "tsaddik" or holy man having superhuman powers at his command, communicating with God for the sake of the community, and in fact, placed above good and evil. The "tsaddiks" amassed enormous wealth, maintained large retinues and luxurious courts. Heretical members of the movement were persecuted to the point of assassination or life imprisonment. Yet Hasidism, especially in its beginning, produced religious thinkers of high quality and became a common heritage of our time, thanks especially to the writings of Martin Buber. It was combatted violently by the rabbis, and, thus, the eighteenth century is filled with struggles between rabbinism and Hasidism, but both joined forces against the common enemy—the first manifestations of "Haskalah" (Enlightenment), which strove to bring the Jews out of their closed communities.

The second offspring of messianic hopes was Frankism—from the name of its founder, Jacob Frank (?–1791). Frank's father had fled Poland to escape persecution as a follower of Sabbatai Zevi, and Jacob Frank himself traveled widely in Romania and Greece, where (in Salonika) he met those believers in Sabbatai who had followed their master into Islam but had remained Jews underneath. Initiated into the secret teachings of the sect, Frank proclaimed himself the messiah (*Santo Señor*, in the Spanish idiom of the Salonika Jews). He had a vision of Poland as the Promised Land, and upon his return there, he was greeted enthusiastically, mostly by poor folk opposing the rabbis, but also by some Jewish notables. Frank, as a new messiah, proclaimed the end of Jewish law and, as a matter of fact, of all law—"I have come to abolish all laws and religions in order to bring life to the world." The ascent to the kingdom of freedom and wealth was to be accomplished by a descent into abomination and perversion. A Manichean tradition, so strong in the Balkans, is clearly perceivable in Frank's teachings. Evil was to be overcome by doing evil, sin by sinning. The Frankists, like the Hasidim, practiced ecstatic dancing and singing accompanied by the clapping of hands, but also held orgiastic rituals whereby men and women undressed "to see truth in its nakedness" and copulated indiscriminately—while only the leader stood apart. Frank reinterpreted the idea of the mystic trinity in the cabala as a union of the Holy Primeval (*Attika kadisha*); the Holy King (*Malka kadisha*), who was the messiah (Frank himself); and the Primeval Mother (*Matronita elyona*), who was none other than Frank's daughter, Eve. The Frankists, because of their rites, provoked horror, and in 1756 they were excluded from the Jewish community by the rabbis—their wives and daughters were declared harlots, their children bastards, and any contact with them anathema. After protracted negotiations with the Roman Catholic hierarchy, a minority of their number chose conversion to Catholicism; they were granted titles of nobility. The majority, however, submitted themselves to the Jewish elders and publicly recognized their errors, though many of them continued to contribute financially to Frank's cause. Frank himself was baptized in Warsaw in 1759 (with the king as his godfather) and imposed upon those who followed him on that road a strictly dual religious life. In harmony with his teaching, baptism was seen as the lowest debasement necessary to bring about a new world. The faithful were advised to get some military training to prepare themselves for the battles of the final upheaval. Perhaps because of that, several brave Polish officers in the Napoleonic army came from the ranks of the Frankists—for instance, Aleksander Matuszewski, general of the artillery. The Catholic clergy soon discovered Frank's double game and imprisoned him in the monastery of Częstochowa, where he spent twelve years. Later on, he migrated to Offenbach in Germany, where, as "Count Frank," he was surrounded by a mounted bodyguard in fanciful uniforms and used to drive in a princely coach. The French Revolution seemed to be an accomplishment of Frank's prophecies, and many Frankists joined the Jacobins (among them, the heir apparent and nephew of Frank, known in Vienna under the name of Frank Thomas Edler von Schönfeldt, and his brother Emanuel), only to be beheaded on the guillotine in 1794 together with Danton. "Frankists" remained a vital part of the Polish scene, and several eminent Polish families renowned for their active part in Freemasonry and the Polish uprisings of 1830 and 1863 were descendants of Frank's followers. At first they preserved their identity and married only among themselves. Gradually, though, they merged completely with the upper classes.

The Four-Year Diet The Four-Year Diet (1788–1792) served as a battleground for the Camp of the Reform, which maneuvered feverishly behind the scenes (a tactic which incurred accusations of dishonesty from conservatives). The progressive bloc was successful in its attempts to strengthen the state by introducing new laws, in particular, those which established a standing army of 100,000 men. (Owing to lack of funds, however, that number was never reached.) Utilizing the press, the theater, and pressures of the Warsaw population, the Camp of the Reform managed to railroad through the Diet a new constitution, known as that of May 3, 1791, which provided for a hereditary throne, abolished the *liberum veto*, and recognized certain rights of burghers and peasants. In the struggles which followed the partitions of Poland, the Constitution of May 3 stood as a landmark indicating the road of a new type of democracy. Catherine's reaction to it was immediate. At Moscow's instigation, a few Polish magnates in 1792 formed the Confederacy of Targowica, turning to Catherine the Great for protection against the "tyranny" of the Diet which threatened Polish "golden freedom." Russian propaganda presented the new constitution as evidence of the ominous spread of the Jacobin plague from France. A Polish-Russian war ensued; Polish troops were routed, and the second partition (1793) took place. Since Russia could not occupy Poland alone without encountering the opposition of the Prussian king, Poland's neighbors carved out enormous stretches of territory for themselves. The provinces occupied by Prussia reached practically to the neighborhood of Warsaw, while Russia took over nearly all of the Ukraine and the larger part of the Byelorussian region north of the Pripet Marshes. (Austria did not figure in the second partition.) In the town of Grodno a new Diet was called into session. Under the shadow of Russian bayonets, it ratified the treaties of the partition and abolished the laws of the Constitution of May 3.

The Insurrection of Kościuszko Progressive opinion roused by the Camp of the Reform responded to the second partition with a call to arms. Let us remember that sympathies with Revolutionary France were already strong and much hope was placed in the consequences of the French upheaval— a hope which, though premature, was not without foundation, as the victories of the Napoleonic armies soon proved. The leadership of the insurrection was given to Tadeusz Kościuszko. The descendant of a family of poor noblemen, Kościuszko was educated at the military academy in Warsaw, then studied artillery, fortification, and naval construction in France for a few years. On his return to Poland, he found that owing to the weakness of the Polish army he could find no employment which would require his skills as an artillerist. Finally, a personal misfortune (a girl whom he had fallen in love with was forbidden to marry him by her aristocratic parents) led him to seek his fortune in America. As an army engineer in the American Revolutionary War, he erected the fortifications of Saratoga and West Point, and by the end of the campaign had acquired the rank of brigadier general. Before returning to Poland, he liberated the Negro slaves he had received along with an estate. In his political views he was a Jeffersonian and sympathetic toward the French Revolution. He fought in the Polish-Russian war of 1792 (commanding at the Battle of Dubienka) and after the defeat was compelled to leave Poland, but in 1794 at the news of the insurrection, he crossed the border and reassumed command. He tried to apply his American experience by organizing the peasants into militia detachments, and he armed them with scythes in view of the lack of firearms. The peasants, attacking Russian cannon, contributed to the first victory of Kościuszko, at Racławice near Kraków. Besides Kraków, Warsaw and Wilno became centers of insurrection. The latter was the scene of the capture of the Russian garrison by Jakub Jasiński, a revolutionary of Jacobin inclination. (In Warsaw a club of Jacobins was founded.) Demonstrating crowds passed, and carried out, death sentences on magnates accused of connivance with the Russians; among the hanged was one bishop. In May of 1794, Kościuszko issued a declaration abolishing the personal serfdom of the peasants and considerably reducing the number of days they were obliged to work on their lords' fields in exchange for the piece of land which they tilled for themselves. But the Polish insurrectionist army could not resist the joint forces of two military powers, Russia and Prussia, indefinitely. Prussian troops occupied Kraków and for some two months unsuccessfully besieged Warsaw, where the mob clearly sided with the most radical Jacobin revolutionaries.

At Maciejowice in a bloody battle between Polish and Russian troops in which both sides lost some 40 per cent of their men, Polish forces were defeated and Kościuszko taken prisoner. The Russian general, Suvorov, after taking the Warsaw suburb of Praga, ordered the massacre of some ten thousand men, women, and children and, thus, terrorized Warsaw's defenders into surrender. Poland's three neighbors did not fail to spread self-justificatory arguments abroad, pretending to have acted to prevent the birth of a new revolutionary center in Europe. The third and last partition of Poland (this time with Austria's participation) took place in 1795, and the *Respublica* disappeared from the map.

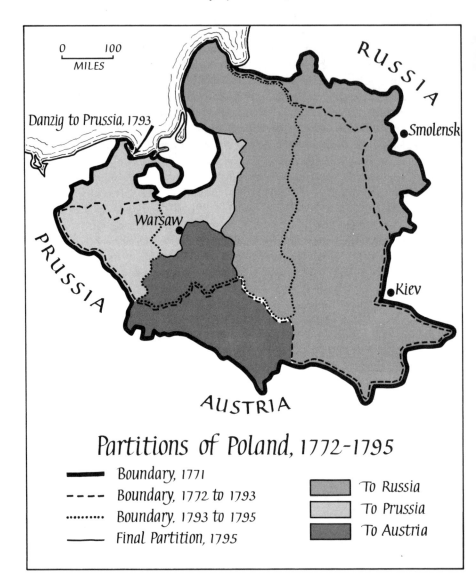

Partitions of Poland.

The Polish Napoleonic Legions Two years had not yet passed after the last partition when a new Polish army was created as part of the French Revolutionary army, commanded by Napoleon Bonaparte. The Polish legion in Italy attracted numerous volunteers and participated in many battles—among others, in the overthrow of the kingdom of the Bourbons in Naples. These troops counted among their number some enlightened officers who organized themselves into lodges and produced literary works which constitute a link between the Enlightenment and the literature of Romanticism. A song written by one of those Napoleonic officers, Józef Wybicki, was later to become the Polish national anthem, "Poland Has Not Yet Perished."

THE THEATER

It seems appropriate to start here with the theater, since it focused newly found energies and constituted the most effective weapon of the Camp of the Reform. The school theaters, both Piarist and Jesuit, brought a French classical repertoire to the audience, but in Poland it was comedy, and not tragedy, which expressed the new spirit. The realistic comedies of Franciszek Bohomolec, modeled upon Molière, castigated both "Sarmatism" and the foppish aping of everything French. Bohomolec found an ally in the person of the king, Stanisław August Poniatowski, who, among his other accomplishments, counted a knowledge of English and who ordered a statue of Shakespeare to be placed on the premises of his palace (Łazienki) in Warsaw among those of other great men of the theater. At Poniatowski's inspiration, a magazine, *The Monitor*, was founded in 1765, and from that moment, stage and press worked hand in hand. Like his predecessors, the King maintained an Italian opera troupe, and performances were given by French and Italian actors for the public at large. The precedent for such a practice had been set by the Saxon kings, August II and August III, but Stanisław August gave orders to create, in addition, a team of professional Polish actors; the history of the Polish professional theater begins in 1765 with the first performance of that troupe before a paying audience. For several years the King retained ownership of that company, but after many financial complications, the question was debated in the Diet, and the Warsaw Theater was reorganized as a national enterprise.

Bohomolec, the editor of and a frequent contributor to *The Monitor*, introduced on its pages comic figures for satirical purposes. He used these same figures in his comedies. Both the periodical and Bohomolec's plays alienated those at whom he aimed his satire. In one of his comedies, entitled *The Monitor*, therefore, he applied a curious (almost Pirandello-like) procedure: we see a tavern in a little town where various Bohomolec characters, familiar to the viewers, have gathered upon hearing that the "Monitor" has come to town. Imagining it to be a person, they decide to take vengeance. Some are for cutting off his fingers, while others advocate more lawful methods. Finally, a man enters who says he is pleased that they take him for *The Monitor*

The Monitor [margin note]

but he is only one of its contributors. The man, an alter-ego of Bohomolec, gently disarms his enemies. He tells the character who incarnates drunkenness, for example, that drunkenness in general was being castigated in his satirical articles and he hopes no one recognizes himself in such a picture. To which he receives the reply: "Of course I drink, but I'm not a drunkard." In the same way a superstitious character does not concede that he is superstitious, etc. Thus, the author is saved, thanks to the blindness of his antagonists.

Some articles about the theater in *The Monitor* were directly suggested by the King, who was not a partisan of French dogmatic adherence to the three unities. But the King, who enjoyed reading Samuel Johnson, was rather isolated in his penchants, and Polish drama moved toward a concise, clear-cut, French-style comedy of manners, usually in verse (though Bohomolec himself wrote in prose). Certain comic figures, introduced by various playwrights, were to have a long life on the Polish stage and were further elaborated by the heir of eighteenth-century Polish theater, Alexander Fredro (1793–1876).

Franciszek Zabłocki (1754–1821)   Extremely prolific, with a talent for satire, Franciszek Zabłocki wrote some sixty comedies and aimed his invective, of which he was a master in prose as well as verse, at representatives of "Sarmatian" mentality. He borrowed plots from various foreign authors—from Beaumarchais, Diderot, Romagnesi—but he possessed a rare gift for creating purely native types. This is the greatest merit of his best-known comedies in verse, such as *Sarmatism* and the *Fop-Suitor* (*Fircyk w zalotach*). But besides his ability to observe, Zabłocki, as a poet, also possessed great skill in applying the thirteen-syllable verse line to realistic, and especially humorous, situations. He was not the only playwright to use that most common meter of Polish Classicism, but his liveliness, due to the insertion of common idioms, won him favor in the eyes of the eighteenth-century public and makes him quite readable today. Echoes of Zabłocki's comic types and colloquial verse can be found in Mickiewicz's *Pan Tadeusz*.

Julian Ursyn Niemcewicz (1757–1841)   To include Julian Ursyn Niemcewicz in the chapter on the theater is an arbitrary choice, as he can be discussed with equal validity as poet, novelist, translator, or memorialist. The peak of his activity, however, is connected with the theater.

Niemcewicz is one of the most colorful personalities of Polish letters, and his long life allowed him to live through radically different phases of history.

Born into a noble family of average means, he received a good education at the military academy of Warsaw, where his enthusiasm for literature attracted the attention of the powerful Czartoryski princes. Thanks to private fellowships, he traveled widely abroad, in

Italy, France, and England. His memoirs enable us to sense the atmosphere prevalent at the time of his youth, and he is not reticent about relating his amorous adventures or amusing details such as a drinking bout in Sicily with some young Englishmen, which ends by their jumping into the fountain of Arethusa, fully clothed and appearing at the opera still dripping wet.

As a deputy to the Four-Year Diet, Niemcewicz emerged as one of the most vigorous leaders of the Camp of the Reform—a position which did not impede his mixing politics with love: the Camp of the Reform was encouraged by Luchessini, the Prussian ambassador (a maneuver which later proved to be a rather treacherous one); and Niemcewicz, a good friend of Luchessini, repaid the dubious benefits of Prussian diplomatic backing by having a child with his wife. To serve his faction he managed to write hastily, in 1790, a comedy entitled *The Return of the Deputy* (*Powrót posła*), treating it as a political pamphlet. When staged in 1791, it became one of the channels whereby the pressure of the Warsaw public was brought to bear upon the Diet to vote a new constitution. There are not many examples of spectacles having such an immediate political effect. As to its technique, the comedy is written in thirteen-syllable verse with rhymed couplets; it observes the three unities and is built on a love intrigue. The action takes place on the country manor of an average gentry family. The hosts, Mr. and Mrs. Chamberlain, are treated cordially by the author. They represent the reasonable element of the old generation of gentry, not hostile toward the changing world. Their son, Valery, is a progressive deputy to the Diet; he is in love with Theresa, who is a guest of the Chamberlains along with her parents. The latter are the target of the author's malice. In Mr. Gadulski (Mr. Talkative), a portrait of a Sarmatian Pole, the audience recognized those deputies to the Four-Year Diet who employed a filibuster tactic to oppose any changes. (One such deputy, after seeing the spectacle, delivered a speech in the Diet against subversive plays and even introduced a motion to withdraw the concession granted to the theater— fortunately without success.) Torrents of words pour from Gadulski's mouth; he discusses everything—international politics, laws, strategy— but he is a complete ignoramus. On the other hand, Mrs. Gadulski lives in the world of sentimental literature and weeps over Rousseau's *Nouvelle Héloise* and over a Polish translation of Edward Young's *Nights*. She injects French words into every other sentence, scorns her prosaic husband, and takes advantage of his stupidity by terrorizing him with swooning fits. Because sadness is fashionable, she forces herself into gloomy moods by recalling her first husband. She provokes the spectator's crueler instincts, primarily, the urge to give her a sound thrashing. Her stepdaughter, Theresa, has been promised by her to a fop, Mr. Szarmantcki (Mr. Charmer), who dresses in the French manner, takes no interest in public affairs, being preoccupied only with fashionable carriages, hunting, and women. Not long ago he was in France, and when Valery, the deputy, pronounces a speech praising the French Revolution (to the applause of the whole theater), Szarmantcki answers that he left France precisely because of the disorders. When the deputy expresses his admiration for the English parliamentary system, Szarmantcki replies that he observed their horses, not their system. Unfortunately for himself Szarmantcki unmasks the real motive behind his sentimental façade (so dear to Mrs. Gadulski)—his greed for a dowry. Thus, Theresa and the young deputy, who are in love with each other, are able to marry and all ends well.

Handsome, graced with a pleasant personality and with literary renown, Niemcewicz enjoyed the favor of Prince Adam Czartoryski, one of the few magnates who backed the Camp of the Reform. The Czartoryskis (called in Poland simply "The Family") maintained a lively cultural center on their estate of Puławy. After the Confederacy of Targowica and the Russian intervention, followed by the second partition of the country and the outbreak of the insurrection led by Kościuszko, Niemcewicz became an aide-de-camp to the latter, sharing with him all the vicissitudes of the campaign. Together with his superior, he was taken prisoner after the last battle and deported to Russia, where he spent two years in solitary confinement in the Petropavlovsk fortress. The trial proved him to be a man of strong character. In prison he kept himself in shape by playing ball, making the ball out of the only material available, i.e., his hair. Having received some books in various languages, he found solace in translating Pope's *The Rape of the Lock*.

At the time of Paul I's accession to the throne of the czars in 1796, Kościuszko and Niemcewicz were liberated and granted permission to leave Russia. Niemcewicz and his commander immediately set off on a trip to America, where they were greeted in Philadelphia by enthusiastic crowds. Yet Kościuszko soon found that he was under surveillance because of his suspected pro-French sympathies. (The Federalists, then the ruling party, nourished extreme hostility toward the French Revolution.) Kościuszko embarked clandestinely on a boat leaving for Europe, aided by his personal friend Thomas Jefferson, who charged him with a secret peace message to the French Revolutionary government. Niemcewicz remained in America and after having married a widow, Mrs. Kean, settled in Elizabeth, New Jersey, where he acquired American citizenship. His extensive travels throughout the States resulted in an interesting work, *Travels in America*. In Warsaw Niemcewicz had been a very active member of a Freemasonic lodge, *le Bouclier du Nord;* since many eminent persons in America were Freemasons or Rosicrucians, he was granted access to many circles and was received cordially on the estate of George Washington. His account of everyday life at Mount Vernon provides a valuable, detailed description of agricultural techniques, conditions of the Negro slaves, etc.

Niemcewicz spent some eleven years in America, this period interrupted once by a trip to Poland. Among his perceptive observations on life in America, some of the most amusing are those on the state of despondency and even desperation among some Americans who looked with envy toward the Revolution in Europe and complained of apathy in their own country. Niemcewicz usually answered as follows:

Oh madman, I said to myself, you don't know what you want; you have a big and comfortable house, fields four times as much as you need; you live under free and wise laws, and you pine for upheavals and blood. You are a fanatic, my friend, your brain is sick. The security and well-being in which you live weighs you down, bores you; you feel a need for sensations and shocks though it may be the ruin of your home and your country. But go to France, go to Europe, look what is going on there, and you will return cured from your madness.

Yet Niemcewicz himself returned to Europe for good, in 1807, when Napoleon created the Duchy of Warsaw. He parted in a friendly manner with his wife, who remained in America. Up to 1830, he was one of the leading personalities in Polish literary life. From Niemcewicz's pen came the first translations of English "ballads" to reach the Polish public. He was the first to translate Gray's "Elegy Written in a Country Churchyard" (1803), and the first to translate Byron. In 1816, he published *Historical Songs* (*Śpiewy historyczne*). This is a volume of balladlike poems written according to a certain plan; namely, Niemcewicz used them to illustrate the history of Poland, taking as the theme of each song eminent monarchs and leaders from the past. Music was composed for the "songs," and they became a kind of ABC of the Polish nation, remaining extremely popular for a long time and educating the people in the spirit of a national Romanticism. The book also exerted an influence on Russian literature, introducing a new genre of historical poem. This service was due particularly to Kondraty Ryleyev, later the hero of the Decembrist rebellion, who knew Polish, translated some of Niemcewicz's songs into Russian, and wrote similar poems of his own.

Niemcewicz is also the author of a few novels. *The Two Gentlemen Sieciech* (*Dwaj panowie Sieciechowie,* 1815) is written in the form of a memoir by representatives of two generations, one from the Saxon epoch, the other Niemcewicz's contemporary. It is a sociopolitical study of changes in mentality revealing the opposition between obscurantism and a new progressive spirit. *Lejbe and Sióra* (1821) is a sentimental novel in the form of letters between two Jewish lovers; here, too, Niemcewicz achieves a "first" in Polish literature with his treatment of the problem of the cultural emancipation of young Jews from the traditional ghetto. *Jan of Tęczyn* (*Jan z Tęczyna*, 1825) can be called the first Polish historical novel in the manner of Sir Walter Scott. It presents life and manners in sixteenth-century Poland and Sweden. This turning toward the glorious reign of Sigismund August is highly characteristic of Polish attitudes after the partitions. This is also a novel with a key: in the passages dealing with the insanity of the Swedish king, Eric XIV, readers discovered allusions to the crazy behavior of Grand Duke Constantine, the virtual ruler of Poland after the Russian victory over Napoleon.

Very active in the Society of the Friends of Learning (which was the name designating the Polish academy of sciences), Niemcewicz, now in his seventies, was looked upon as a patriarch of letters and was surrounded with universal respect. Yet this was not the last stage of his career. After the defeat of the Polish insurrection of 1831, he was compelled to go into exile, leaving behind his library and manuscripts. He settled in Paris, where he died in 1841 after having written his *Memoirs of My Time* (*Pamiętniki czasów moich*), a fascinating picture of a whole era and of various adventures in Poland, Italy, England, Russia, and America. Certainly, Niemcewicz cannot be called a great writer. Yet he was a man with an open mind, possessing a rare gift of moderation which served to balance the contradictory features of his nature: deeply religious and yet anticlerical, a man of society with a penchant for constant amorous involvements but a hard-working literary craftsman, avid of everything new but careful to avoid excess, a progressive but at the same time skeptical about virtue imposed by terror, as in the French Revolution, he remains an example of a writer who combined the mentality of the Enlightenment with that of budding Romanticism. The peak, undoubtedly, of his multifaceted activity was reached at the time of the Four-Year Diet with the staging of his *Return of the Deputy*.

Wojciech Bogusławski (1757–1829)   A monument to Wojciech Bogusławski in Warsaw commemorates not only an author, but a man who was the father of the Polish professional theater, who was both an actor and a stage director. He belonged to the same social stratum as Niemcewicz and Kościuszko, namely, to the gentry of very modest means. As a young man he chose a career in the army, which was then being slowly organized after a time of virtual nonexistence, but he switched to the theater for financial reasons and became a professional actor. The theater, however, has a magic of its own, and Bogusławski worked as if bewitched. He was a demon of energy—acting, staging, organizing, translating, and adapting foreign plays, as well as writing plays of his own. He was the first full-fledged director of the National Theater in Warsaw, and it was there in 1791 that he staged Niemcewicz's comedy, a fact which speaks clearly for his political sympathies. Later, during the Russian intervention, he staged his own play (adapted from an English novel), *Henry VI, Hunting*, which under an innocent and exotic appearance concealed revolutionary undertones. As he belonged to the political conspiracy which was preparing the insurrection of 1794, he wrote and staged that year an original play in the form of a vaudeville or a comic opera, called *A Supposed Miracle, or Krakovians and Mountaineers (Cud mniemany, czyli Krakowiacy i Górale)*. The music was composed by his close collaborator, Jan Stefani. At that moment, the insurrection under the command of Kościuszko was spreading northward from Kraków, and the spectacle itself became a revolutionary event. To explain why this was so it is enough to say that the play introduces masses of people on the stage. The plot is simple. A constant quarrel has marred the relations between a village near Kraków and the mountain folk from the Tatras. The two groups fight each other over a trifle: a love affair which offends the dignity of the mountaineers. They are reconciled thanks to a "miracle" which is nothing but the work of a student who makes use of his knowledge of electricity. For the audience both the Krakovian peasants and the mountaineers represented popular forces and untapped national reserves exactly at the moment Kościuszko was forming his peasant militia and arming it with scythes. The feudal manor is nonexistent; all characters belong to the lower classes; the one intellectual who appears is a poor student. Through him a certain anticlerical element is introduced, as the supposed miracle is, in fact, a triumph of science. The songs in the play, either by alluding more or less directly to politics or by stimulating the audience's projection of their own current political sympathies into the events occurring on stage, provoked a great emotional response. A German writer present at the spectacle relates the event as follows:

A few chief actors, probably by arrangement, were singing textual variations to the melody, and these parodies soon overshadowed the original text. They were repeated by everybody with joy. They spread quickly from the theater to the street, and after the events at Kraków, the battle of Racławice, they changed all the Warsavians into opera singers.

Russian officers present at the performance were bursting with laughter, not understanding the real implications. But Russian diplomats showed more insight, and after three evenings the play was forbidden. In our century, an eminent theater director, Leon Schiller, highly skillful in the use of large masses on the stage, brought out the revolutionary contents of the play and made it a permanent part of the repertoire of the Polish theater.

Even after the fall of the state, Bogusławski succeeded in keeping his troupe together. For a few years he worked in Lwów, where, among other plays, he staged *Hamlet*, in his own adaptation from the German. In 1799, he returned to Warsaw, making it his permanent headquarters while he gave visiting performances in many towns throughout Poland. Thanks to his efforts, a special law was passed: a tax was levied on all spectacles in Warsaw to help subsidize the National Theater. His initiative also led to the creation of the Theatrical Commission, which elaborated the "Bylaws of the National Theater" defining the privileges and duties of the director, the actors, members of the orchestra, etc. The tax, in addition to those laws, explains why throughout the nineteenth century the efforts of the czarist police to curb and Russify the theater in Warsaw proved to be in vain. In 1825, again thanks to Bogusławski, a building was erected in Warsaw to house the National Theater, and volumes containing the complete works of Bogusławski were sealed in its foundations. Through his activity, Bogusławski brought about a change in status for the actor in Polish public opinion. Formerly, when an actor died in Warsaw, it was only thanks to the intervention of the king that his body was laid to rest in a cemetery. Largely because of Bogusławski's impressive example, public opinion began to accept the actor as a man engaged in a highly honorable profession.

MEN OF LETTERS

Ignacy Krasicki (1735–1801)   "Prince of Poets," as he was called by his contemporaries, Ignacy Krasicki was, in many respects, a typical man of the Enlightenment, not only because he combined a literary profession with a clerical one. As a man who believed natural religion to be in accord with that most human of attributes, Reason, he had words of praise for all religions, and from his literary work it would be difficult to guess that he wore a cassock. Though he fulfilled his duties as a clergyman excellently, acquired a bishopric, and gathered dignity after dignity, he knew how to enjoy life. His high income hardly sufficed for all his pleasures. As to those pleasures, they included, first of all, a passion for rare books, for gardening and rare species of plants, a delight in an excellent cellar, and a fondness, especially in his old age, for exotic sweets and jams. He was a man of the golden mean, a smiling, skeptical sage praising moderation and despising extremes. His was a mentality which returned to Horatian ideals of the Renaissance, to a life of contemplative retirement. This did not interfere with his talents as a courtier: he was a favorite of the king, Stanisław August, and, after the first partition, when his bishopric of Warmia became the property of Prussia, he was a favorite of King Frederick the Great. As was fitting during his century, he was a cosmopolitan and owed his imposing literary knowledge to his readings in foreign languages, yet without a doubt he was indebted to the mentality of the Polish "Golden Age," and, in this respect, his admiration for Erasmus of Rotterdam is significant. As a poet, he was responsible chiefly for that distillation of the language which for a while toned down the chaotic richness of the Baroque. In a way, he returned to the clear and simple language of Kochanowski, and his role in Polish poetry may be compared to that of Alexander Pope in English poetry. A hard worker, he conceived of literature as a specific vocation, namely, to intervene as a moralist in human affairs. Since he was not pugnacious by temperament (contrary to one of his masters, Voltaire), his moralizing, rarely distinguishable from sheer play, lacks vitriolic accents.

His long mock-heroic poem, *Mouse-iad* (*Myszeidos*, 1775), by its very title alludes to glorious exploits (not unlike Voltaire's *Henriade*, for instance). It is written in *ottava rima*, a verse form used earlier in Polish translations of Tasso and Ariosto. In humorous verses, it sings of a war between cats and mice which takes place in a remote time under the rule of the legendary King Popiel, who, because of his misdeeds, was devoured by mice. The local Polish background induced some readers to look for political allegories, but the author's playfulness is uppermost here, and it is hard to see any political message, although many details are taken from Polish political life.

Krasicki wrote a second mock-heroic poem, entitled *Monachomachia, or the War of the Monks* (*Monachomachia albo wojna mnichów,* 1778). The subject of that work (also composed in *ottava rima*) recalls Boileau's *Le Lutrin*. The action takes place in a little town which possesses "three inns, four remnants of gates, nine monasteries, and, here and there, a few little houses." The monks lead a delightful, if not too edifying, life which consists mainly in sleeping and drinking. Unfortunately, they are not deprived of ambition where the superiority of their respective establishments is concerned. A dispute between the Dominicans and the Carmelites reveals that neither side is too strong in theology, but as they are robust and well-rested men, the argument is soon transformed into a brawl (described in Homeric terms), which, however, ends peacefully the moment an enormous drinking cup, *vitrum gloriosum*, is brought in, and the combatants are reconciled in their common worship. For a clergyman, the poem was somewhat strange, and it provoked many attacks, to which Krasicki replied by writing a companion poem, *Anti-Monachomachia*

(1780), where he seemingly retracts his insinuations but is even more malicious in his irony. The ironic poem with digressions written in *ottava rima* will be introduced into the Romantic movement by Byron in his *Don Juan*, but in Polish literature it will stem also from Krasicki.

Among Krasicki's works employing the shorter poetic forms, his *Satires* (*Satyry*, 1779) fills a prominent place. Here the author shows himself to be an observer and psychologist of human folly, which is presented in the form of human types: drunkards, fops, wives crazy about the latest fashions, etc. Many details of everyday life, revealed through dialogue, verge on the grotesque, and much that is effective in the presentation of various patterns of social behavior is achieved through the device of parody. One satire, using a somewhat different device, "Felicitations" ("Powinszowania"), praises lavishly the most common human vices. Krasicki in his *Satires* practices the difficult art of presenting vivid characters while using only the simplest words.

But the most durable among Krasicki's poems are those in his *Fables and Parables* (*Bajki i przypowieści*, 1779). Here particularly we feel the "light touch" of a man of the Enlightenment. The ambition of such a writer was not to force his way toward the formulation of a newly discovered truth, but, since Reason is universal, to give form to a general, commonly known wisdom. Poetry for him was a more concise and elegant prose, and originality of subject had no importance. Thus, Krasicki unhesitatingly borrowed the subjects of his fables from the enormous body of fabular literature starting with Aesop and finishing with his own French contemporaries. He also borrowed from La Fontaine, especially in the second volume of his collection *New Fables* (*Bajki nowe*), published after his death, but whatever he took was always completely transformed. His extreme conciseness is best seen if one counts the number of words in the original author's version and compares it to that of Krasicki's on the same subject. The pleasure not only for the poet but for the reader as well is probably due to the squeezing of a whole story, sometimes even a novella, into a few lines, and among Krasicki's best are those fables which consist of only one quatrain where the author's pen moves in one rush toward the final *pointe*. The title *Fables and Parables* is explained by the division into parts, the first dealing with presumed animals, the second with people. Krasicki's philosophy is dry and sober. His is a world where the strong win and the weak lose in a sort of immutable order recognized as such without protest. A certain cynicism seems to be an ingredient of eighteenth-century thinking, and some fables are even cruel. Reason is exalted as the human equivalent of animal strength: the wise survive, the stupid perish. The thinkers of the Enlightenment saw a perfect parallel between the order of the world and the operations of

Reason, and this analogy constituted a source of optimism. To give a few samples of Krasicki's fables in a literal translation:

The Wagon Driver and the Butterfly

A wagon got stuck in the mud and couldn't move.
The driver was tired and the horses exhausted.
A butterfly then sitting on the wagon
Believing he was a burden, thought: "Compassion is not a bad
    habit."
He flew away and said to the man: "God bless you, go on your
    way."

Ugrzązł wóz, ani ruszyć już się nie mógł w błocie;
Ustał furman, ustały i konie w robocie.
Motyl, który na wozie siedział wtenczas prawie,
Sądząc, że był ciężarem w takowej przeprawie,
Pomyślił sobie: "Litość nie jest złym nałogiem."
Zleciał i rzekł do chłopca: "Jedźże z Panem Bogiem!"

The Lamb and the Wolves

You will always find a reason if you want something enough:
Two wolves suddenly fell upon a lamb in the wood.
They were about to tear it apart;
It asked: "By what right?"
"You are tasty, weak, and in the wood." Soon they had eaten it all.

Zawsze znajdzie przyczynę, kto zdobyczy pragnie:
Dwóch wilków jedno w lesie nadybali jagnię.
Już go mieli rozerwać; rzekło: "Jakim prawem?"
— "Smacznyś, słaby i w lesie" . . . Zjedli niezabawem.

Birds in a Cage

"Why do you weep?" a young siskin said to an old siskin.
"You are better off now in a cage than you were in the fields."
"You were born in it," said the old one, "so I forgive you;
I was once free but now I'm in a cage and that is why I am
    weeping."

"Czego płaczesz? — staremu mówił czyżyk młody —
Masz teraz lepsze w klatce, niż w polu, wygody."
"Tyś w niej zrodzon, — rzekł stary, — przeto ci wybaczę;
Jam był wolny, dziś w klatce, i dlatego płaczę."

Krasicki wrote a great deal in prose as well. Fiction in Poland, as we have seen, had not yet begun to develop, and what can be called the first Polish novel is due to the pen of Krasicki. *The Adventures of*

Nicolaus Doświadczyński (*Mikołaja Doświadczyńskiego przypadki,*
1776) combined many varieties of fiction. It may be called a novel
of adventure, like *Robinson Crusoe,* and a philosophical tale in the
Voltairian sense where details of life serve a definite satirical aim.
There are also elements of the educational novel, like Rousseau's *Emile,*
and even of the utopian novel in the Swiftian spirit. In part one, little
Nicolaus, after a typical Sarmatian childhood, is placed in the care
of a French tutor, Damon, who initiates him into roguery. The boy
then travels to Paris, where he lives a dissipated life, but after falling
into debts, he sets sail from Amsterdam to Java to escape his creditors.
The ship is wrecked during a storm, and Nicolaus, clinging to a
board, is flung by the waves onto an unknown island. This first section of the work fulfills what we would expect of a satirical novel of
manners, while the next part presents a utopia in the form of the
island of Nipu. Its inhabitants are peaceful and happy; they live on
farms all of which are of equal size. They have no government, no
army, no police, no written laws, no money, and are ruled by their
elders. The wise Xaoo, for whom Nicolaus works as a farm hand,
teaches him some simple virtues and can scarcely believe the stories
of the viciousness of so-called civilized man. In spite of their gentle
character, the inhabitants of Nipu are resolute enough to apply radical
means against subversion. They stone a few young men contaminated
by one who had left the island and had brought back news of the
glamour of the manufacturing and trading countries. In this part,
Krasicki seems to blend a Rousseaulike dream of the "noble savage"
with the memory of the rural, self-sufficient, patriarchal life of Old
Poland. In the third and last part the hero escapes from the island,
to his later regret, as he is captured and made a slave by Spanish
pirates, sold somewhere in Latin America, ransomed and freed by a
good American Quaker, and reaches his native land only after many
trials, all of which allow the author to write a kind of picaresque
novel.

More than once, however, Krasicki showed his fondness for literary
mixtures of novelistic genres. In his *History Divided into Two Books*
(*Historia na dwie księgi podzielona,* 1779), he pretends to be publishing a manuscript found in Poland by accident and written by none
other than Grumdrypp (one of the immortals whom Gulliver had met
in the country of Luggnagg). Krasicki refers openly to Swift, and
the manuscript tells the story of Grumdrypp, who not only was immortal, but possessed a miraculous elixir for making him young again,
after living the full human cycle. Grumdrypp relates how he traveled
back in space and time and how he found Greece at the time of Alexander the Great, Rome in its decline, Gaul, China, medieval Poland,
Byzantium, etc. He presents a "revisionist" picture of history, quarrel-

ing with historians because they praise victorious nations, while he himself discovered that peoples depicted by historians as barbarians were nothing of the sort. For instance, he sings the praises of the druids in Gaul who were defeated by the Romans. This "science fiction" of Krasicki's is permeated by a humanitarian spirit, seen in his exhaltation of those figures who fostered a rule of law, education, philosophy, and science over figures who were powerful rulers and creators of empires.

Another prose work of Krasicki's, *Mr. Pantler* (*Pan Podstoli*, 1778), can hardly be called a novel, as the action consists entirely of conversations presumably reproduced by the narrator, who was once a guest at the estate of a nobleman with the honorary title of Pantler of the King. The hero is a virtuous, wise man, a model of good husbandry; thus, the "novel" is, in fact, a treatise on the best way to live and on the rules of enlightened farming. In many ways, the work induces one to think of the ideals cherished by Polish Renaissance writers. At the same time, since basic "economic endeavors" are stressed as more important than broader ideological or political considerations, there is something of a foreshadowing here of the "organic labor" program later advanced by the so-called Positivists. Always eager to study and make himself useful, Krasicki, as befitted a man of the Enlightenment, managed his literary affairs skillfully; and, in addition to his creative activity, he wrote literary criticism, adapted foreign works, collected data on writers of the past, and wrote biographies of poets. He was also a devotee of the theater and even managed to write a couple of comedies.

A clergyman (the bishop of Smolensk) and a poet, Adam Naruszewicz was one of the closest friends of the king and an assiduous frequenter of the so-called "Thursday dinners" at the court, which brought together the cream of Polish intellectuals. As a poet, he wrote satires, often modeling them upon Boileau. In spite of a somewhat heavy style, they are pungent, sarcastic pictures of Warsaw life and abound in realistic details. Yet Naruszewicz owes his place in Polish literature not to his poetry, but to his historical works. At the instigation of the king, he undertook the enormous task of writing a history of Poland based on modern research methods and using available archives in Poland and abroad. The result was his *History of the Polish Nation from the Times of Its Conversion to Christianity* (*Historia narodu polskiego od przyjęcia chrześcijaństwa*), which became the second attempt of such broad scope, the first being Jan Długosz's fifteenth-century chronicle. Between 1780 and 1785 he published six volumes, and to give an idea of his meticulousness and capacity for work we should add that his history does not extend beyond the year 1386 (i.e., the date of the union between Poland and

Adam Naruszewicz (1733–1796)

Lithuania). The rationalistic, moralistic, and didactic approach of a man of the Enlightenment is clearly distinguishable in his treatment of the past. His presentation is slightly flavored with the ideology of the Camp of the Reform (which stressed the necessity for a strong central power and a hereditary monarchy), a bias which can be explained by his cordial relations with the king.

Stanisław Trembecki (1735–1812)

Together with Krasicki, Stanisław Trembecki must also be called one of the most gifted poets of Polish Classicism, and the esteem in which he has been held even by poets who seem to have nothing in common with him is somewhat striking, especially if we consider that the entire bulk of his output could be contained in one thin volume. He himself cared little about publishing and treated his talent simply as a means of ingratiating himself with powerful protectors. If Krasicki was the embodiment of "smiling rationalism," Trembecki exemplified another side of the eighteenth century: the headlong pursuit of pleasure and of mad enjoyments. He called himself "one of the boldest trouble-makers, one of the most assiduous drunkards, one of the most zealous lovers, and one of the best gamblers." As his era favored cosmopolitanism, young Trembecki squandered his fortune in Paris on women and cards, but he also satisfied there his passion for philosophical debates, being personally acquainted with Diderot, d'Alembert, and Holbach. For a while he earned his living in Belgium by giving lessons in fencing. During his stay abroad he involved himself in constant duels. For the rest of his life he was condemned to be a perennial hanger-on at the courts of magnates or at the royal court, and in the choice of his protectors he showed little fastidiousness. As his wit was highly appreciated, he was a well-received guest at the king's "Thursday dinners." He resided for many years on the Ukrainian estate of one of the most ominous figures among the Polish magnates, Szczęsny (Feliks) Potocki, one of the chief organizers of the Targowica Confederacy.

Present in every line of his poetry is Trembecki's philosophy: materialistic, sensual—a kind of gourmet's enthusiasm which sees the world as something tangible, rich in color, movement, and shapes and which reflects this perception in language. Most of his poems are circumstantial odes, epigrams, and letters in verse, but his pen also produced a certain number of fables. Although mostly adapted from La Fontaine, they present a contrast to the classical elegance of the French writer, for Trembecki through his language, full of colloquialisms and often folk idioms brutal in their conciseness, introduces live, elemental forces of nature. His fables are one of the best examples of a realistic style in poetry and illustrate, perhaps, the conflict between the sensual character of Polish and the intellectual character of French, a trait we have already observed in Morsztyn's translation of Corneille. The French specialist in Polish literature, Paul Cazin, wrote: "Trembecki's *Fables* are masterpieces of which Théophile Gautier would have been jealous." Trembecki's admiration for everything lush, vigorous, abundant, fertile found expression in his longer descriptive poems, above all, *Sofjówka*, a name which referred to the Ukrainian Versailles, i.e., the magnate Potocki's estate designed and built in French style to honor one of society's celebrities of that period, Sofia Potocka (who, incidentally, began her career as a Greek harlot in Constantinople). Written in rhymed couplets of thirteen-syllable verse lines, it praises the fertility of the Ukrainian soil, its luxurious vegetation, fat sheep and cattle; while, at the same time, it extols man's will, victorious in transforming the world, and his mastery over nature. *Sofjówka* first appeared in a periodical in 1806 and was published later on in 1822 with a commentary by a young Romantic poet, Adam Mickiewicz, who throughout his life was to remain an admirer of Trembecki. Although Trembecki practiced occasional poetry, which would seem to make him a rococo poet, he remains, above all, a representative of vigorous Classicism in construction. An excellent translator of Voltaire, Trembecki was closer in many ways to that philosopher than Krasicki, since he was an avowed deist, if not an atheist. We have mentioned already that he was careless about the fate of his poems. Thus some of them were ascribed to other authors, as he sometimes published under pseudonyms. Once in a game of chess he even forfeited a fragment of his translation of *Jerusalem Delivered* to a friend, who then published it under his own name.

A close friend of Trembecki's, Kajetan Węgierski, whose life was short, had nothing in him of the slightly cynical wisdom of an epicurean, traces of which can be seen in his colleague. Of violent temperament, passionate in his loves as well as in his writing, he was moved to write by the force of indignation and malice, aiming his attacks at the powerful of this world. As a result, he was feared and detested as a master of vitriolic pamphleteering. A libertine, a deist, an anticlerical, he was brought up in an atmosphere of unbounded admiration for French philosophical culture. He was a brilliant realistic poet; his verse is as concise as if constructed of epigrams, and his satirical descriptions of life and manners in Warsaw luxuriate in lifelike details. Let us add that he was the first to translate *The Rape of the Lock* of Alexander Pope, thus anticipating Niemcewicz's translation. Węgierski's writings offending influential personalities finally provoked a threat of imprisonment, and he had to escape from Poland. In 1783, he landed in the United States. His descriptions of America are full of enthusiasm for the new republic. On his way back to

Kajetan Węgierski (1755–1787)

Poland, he stopped over in London long enough to write a malicious satire on the Prince of Wales, after which he was again forced to escape. He died in Avignon in 1787 of tuberculosis, leaving this summation of his fate:

> I must die without provoking in anybody a tear of regret . . . without having done any service to my country, to humanity, to my relatives. . . . Accustomed since my childhood to follow the impulses of my fancy, I lived through my thirty-one years without any system, without any plan, dependent only upon my passions.

Jakub
Jasiński
(1761–1794)

Described in Adam Mickiewicz's *Pan Tadeusz* as "a handsome and gloomy young man," Jakub Jasiński seen in his portrait in the uniform of a general cuts the figure of a somewhat legendary hero. But he is significant also from the standpoint of the internal logic in the trends of the Enlightenment, which evolved from a critical appraisal of the existing order of things toward openly revolutionary ideals. The author of frivolous poems, Jasiński was, at the same time, a proponent of Virtue, in the Jacobin sense, and a convinced republican. For instance, in his *Poem at the Time When the Polish Court Mourned the Death of Louis XVI* (*Wiersz w czasie obchodzonej żałoby pnez dwor polski po Ludwiku XVI*) we read: "And when freedom, honor, riches have been taken from you, You weep because a king was slain three hundred miles from here!" And he concludes: "We should say, let the kings perish and the world be free." His hopes were focused on Revolutionary France, and in another poem he prophesies that soon the Revolution will spread freedom "from the Tagus to the Neva" and then:

> Forever the doors of war will be closed,
> Tribe will transfer to tribe a peaceful age,
> And only then will the world return to its primeval shape,
> When humankind will be a race of brothers.

In his poem *To the Nation*, written in 1794 on the eve of Kościuszko's insurrection, Jasiński sounded a call for a republican struggle:

> Pay no heed that you are bound by heavy chains.
> Wherever people have said "I want to be free" they have always become free!
> Keep in mind examples of the West,
> What the forces of tyrants are, and the power of a nation.

During the insurrection of 1794, Jasiński as one of the chief military commanders was responsible for the smashing of the Russian garrison in Lithuania and, later on, fought in the defense of Warsaw, where he died in battle.

SENTIMENTAL POETS

The so-called sentimental lyricists of the Enlightenment are, ob- *Franciszek* viously, the inheritors of the bucolic poetry of the Baroque. The rococo *Karpiński* madrigal profited in Poland from the general trend toward purification *(1741–1825)* and simplification of the language. Its native roots remain, however, clearly perceptible. Not without importance, perhaps, is the fact that Karpiński, the most popular among those lyricists, was born in a region where bourgeois poetry flourished during the seventeenth century, namely, the area at the foot of the Carpathian Mountains south of Lwów. He received a very old-fashioned Sarmatian education in Jesuit schools, where he proved himself skillful in theological disputes in Latin and was even tempted by his superiors to enter the Order. Later, he, like Niemcewicz, served at the court of the powerful Czartoryski family. In his memoirs, written in advanced age in the seclusion of his farm, he was to complain that he had not received sufficient remuneration because he, unlike other courtiers, had abhorred flattery and had always clung to truth. Indeed, he showed considerable independence; for instance, after his retirement from the magnates' service he personally tilled the soil along with his peasants.

Because of his poems where the name of Justina constantly recurs, he was known in his lifetime as "Justina's lover." But Karpiński's literary career was not limited to his lifetime. Some of his poems, put to music, have been sung by generations of simple people who have never cared about the name of their author. Primarily those are religious poems, either greeting the morning:

> When the morning lights arise,
> To you the earth, to you the sea,
> To you sing all the elements:
> Be praised, great God!

> Kiedy ranne wstają zorze,
> Tobie ziemia, Tobie morze,
> Tobie śpiewa żywioł wszelki,
> Bądź pochwalon, Boże wielki!

or praying in the evening:

> All our daily cares
> Mercifully receive, just God,
> And as we fall asleep
> Let even our sleep glorify you.

Wszystkie nasze dzienne sprawy
Przyjm litośnie, Boże prawy,
A gdy będziem zasypiali,
Niech Cię nawet sen nasz chwali.

One of Karpiński's Christmas carols completely lost its connection to the author and was put on the same level as much older songs of that kind. That Christmas carol, in fact, bears the traces of Karpiński's Jesuit education and makes use of the paradoxical juxtapositions so frequent during the Baroque period and the Middle Ages:

God is born; power trembles,
The Lord of heaven is naked;
Fire—congeals; glare—darkens;
He who is infinite—has boundaries.
The scorned one—is covered with glory,
The mortal one—is a king for centuries!
And the word became flesh
And dwelled among us.

Bóg się rodzi — moc truchleje;
Pan niebiosów — obnażony;
Ogień — krzepnie; blask — ciemnieje;
Ma granice — nieskończony,
Wzgardzony — okryty chwałą,
Śmiertelny — Król nad wiekami . . .
A *Słowo Ciałem* się stało
I mieszkało między nami.

Among his secular poems, one in particular, "Laura and Filon," won favor among the petty gentry (a class which lived practically like peasants). It was sung to the accompaniment of a guitar, and became a standard sentimental lay. "Laura and Filon" combines rococo artificiality with some traditions of Baroque pastoral poetry. The poem is a conversation between rustic lovers (who, however, bear the Greek names Laura and Filon). The supposedly simple characters speak in a language hardly allowing us to guess their low status.

Uneven in his literary output and a minor poet, Karpiński was cherished, nevertheless, in the first decades of the nineteenth century by the Romantic generation. Here, one is led to reflect upon the ties between Polish Romanticism and the Baroque: sentimental poets seem to provide a bridge.

Dionizy Kniaźnin (1750–1807) Many families from the Byelorussian area were shifting their national loyalties; thus the same names appear on the Russian and Polish sides (e.g., Dostoevskys, Stravinskys, etc.). While one branch of the Kniaźnin family produced a well-known Russian playwright, Jacob Kniaźnin (1742–1793), another has remained in Polish letters thanks to a sentimental poet who spelled his name Kniaźnin. The Pole received his education at Jesuit colleges in Polotsk and Vitebsk and entered the novitiate of the Order. His poetic gifts were noticed while he was still a student writing Latin verse. In 1773, when he was teaching at the Jesuit college in Warsaw, the Order was disbanded, and Kniaźnin woke up one morning a layman. At first he found a job with the Załuski Library (which had been turned into a public institution); then he was taken into the service of the Czartoryskis as a secretary and became a "client" of "The Family" for life, traveling with them abroad, teaching their children, and for years residing at their center of cultural life in Puławy. He provided their theater in Puławy with plays and wrote occasional verse celebrating important events in "The Family's" life. Of course, he was on friendly terms with other writers connected with the Czartoryskis like Niemcewicz and Karpiński. These contemporaries characterized him as a small, pale man, carelessly dressed, extremely shy, with a tender heart, passing easily from gaiety to melancholy. At the height of the French vogue in dressing, he cultivated the old-fashioned Polish attire; he wore a moustache, and, though contrary to the habits of the old Sarmatian gentry, he wore long hair falling in curls. He makes a curious figure, perhaps because of the contrast between his poems, mostly madrigals, and his tragic fate: after witnessing the effects of the partitions—namely, the barbarous destruction of the library, the paintings, even the gardens, in Puławy by Russian troops—he gradually lost his mind, and the last eleven years of his life were darkened by complete insanity.

For the theater in Puławy, where members of the princely family and their guests were performers, he wrote plays in verse, such as *The Spartan Mother* (*Matka Spartanka*), "An opera in three acts" extolling patriotic virtues, and the opera libretto *The Gypsies* (*Cyganie*), the first Polish play where the colorful gypsies are treated with sympathy.

His first poems, collected in a volume entitled *Carmina*, were in Latin. (They even included a translation of Kochanowski's *Laments* into Latin.) He translated from Latin into Polish as well, especially Horace, where his masterful use of internal rhymes and a great variety of meters recalls the poetic craftsmen of the early seventeenth century. Mostly, however, his work is composed of short poems in the Anacreontic tradition. They sing of the vicissitudes of love in a tone of "sweet melancholy," and their delicate patterns induce us to think of his biography: It seems that because of his extreme shyness he was condemned to an awestruck and distant worship of women. Graceful and lyrical, Kniaźnin, at his best, chases Venus, Cupid, and nymphs out of his poetry and achieves a subtle simplicity. It would be useless to translate any of his verse, for when deprived of its meter, it loses its appeal. His concern for perfection impelled him to revise his published work over and over. In his lifetime, he gathered the contents of his *Love Poems* (*Erotyki*, 2 vols., 1779), his *Poems* (*Wiersze*, 1783), and other works in a collection called *Poetry* (*Poezja*, 1788). An assiduous translator, he provided Polish versions not only of Horace and Anacreon (or rather Anacreon's imitators) but also of modern writers like Ossian, the presumed Homer of the North, and the Swiss poet Gessner. He reacted strongly to political events such as the Constitution of May 3 (1791), the onslaught of foreign powers, and the insurrection of Kościuszko, and this explains his growing despondency and final mental illness after the sad events of which his country was the scene.

If we observe in Karpiński evidence of a certain continuity extending from the Polish Baroque toward Romanticism, the same, and even to a greater degree, can be said of Kniaźnin, who, in his Anacreontic poems, sounds at times like a contemporary of the "poets of conceits" with the addition of a new sentimental tone.

THE REFORMERS

*Hugo
Kołłątaj
(1750–1812)*

"Only two subjects have interested me all my life: the form of public education and the reform of my nation's political system." This confession, expressed by Hugo Kołłątaj, should perhaps be qualified, as he was equally interested in acquiring wealth and position for himself. Yet it is true that he displayed unusual energy in the service of public causes, and he can be said to have been a true leader of the Camp of the Reform. His capacity for work and his multifaceted interests were astonishing. Born into an old but impoverished noble family, he made his way up combining motives of personal ambition with a struggle against the *status quo*. He studied in Lesser Poland in a high school which was under the supervision of Kraków University and whose level was somewhat higher than that of the Jesuit schools of the time. He went on to the University of Kraków, which, however, could not boast of particularly high standards. Later he donned a priest's cassock and was sent to Vienna for further study, then to Naples and to Rome, where he received a doctorate in law and theology. Well-acquainted with astronomy, chemistry, and mathematics, he remained all his life basically a commentator upon the political organization of society and a proponent of "moral sciences," which to Kołłątaj meant those studies that would lead to a social order corresponding to natural law. His stay in Italy and his excellent knowledge of the language brought him into close touch with the views of Italian lawyers and philosophers and their broad-minded interpretation of historical change. And it was through the Italians that he came into contact with the ideas of the French physiocrats, who saw in agriculture the foundation of the well-being of human societies. After his return to Poland he worked for the Commission for National Education and succeeded in thoroughly reforming the University of Kraków; he introduced a new curriculum with a stress on the sciences in spite of bitter opposition on the part of the conservatives. Moreover, as a result of his experience in Kraków, he elaborated a plan for the reform of education throughout the entire country: two universities, those of Kraków and Wilno, were each to control a certain number of high schools, which in turn were to control a network of elementary schools. Thus, it can be said that those writers born at the end of the century, who received a good intellectual foundation either in the region of Wilno or in that of Kraków, were indebted to Hugo Kołłątaj.

At the time of the Four-Year Diet Kołłątaj became the brains behind the scene. He founded what was known as "Kołłątaj's Forge" (*Kuźnica Kołłątajowska*): a group of publicists who gathered in Kołłątaj's home in Warsaw to elaborate strategy. Among his close collaborators were Franciszek Ksawery Dmochowski (a famous translator of Homer and author of an *Art of Poetry* modeled upon Boileau); Franciszek Salezy Jezierski, a priest, quite radical in his French-style rationalism; another priest, and perhaps even more radical (he was called "The Forge's Thunder"), Jan Dębowski (who was later on to become an officer in the Polish legion in Italy). The group also found occasional allies in the playwright Franciszek Zabłocki, in the young mathematician and astronomer Jan Śniadecki, and in Julian Ursyn Niemcewicz.

Kołłątaj himself, at the time of the Four-Year Diet, published two works advancing such concrete proposals as the establishment of universal taxation; the raising of the status of burghers by the creation of two chambers in the Diet, one for the gentry and one for the burghers; and the maintenance of a sufficiently numerous army. In those works— namely, *Anonymous Letters to Stanisław Małachowski* (*Do Stanisława Małachowskiego Anonima listów kilka*, 1789), written as letters to the speaker of the Diet, and *Political Laws of the Polish Nation* (*Prawo polityczne narodu polskiego*, 1790)—he was obviously drawing conclusions from French rationalist ideals of equality and of the "nation" as being not limited to one ruling class, but he reinterpreted them in the light of local needs. Accused by his adversaries of desiring to see peasants' axes put to the necks of the gentry, he was, in reality, quite moderate, envisaging the new system as an alliance of average landowners and burghers against the rule of the aristocratic oligarchy. But it is also true that the activists in Warsaw's Jacobin Club during the insurrection of 1794 had come mostly from Kołłątaj's "Forge." Appointed Vice-Chancellor to the Crown after the enactment of the Constitution of May 3 and Minister of the Treasury during the Kościuszko insurrection, Kołłątaj, after the failure of the uprising, escaped to Austrian-occupied Galicia. At the request of Russia, however, he was imprisoned as an "extremely dangerous man," spending eight years in confinement (part of that time in a fortress) while attempts of the French Government and even of Napoleon Bonaparte himself to intervene were of no avail. Liberated, thanks to the minister of foreign affairs of the Russian Empire, Prince Adam Czartoryski (then the right-hand of the czar, Alexander), he immediately plunged into activity, taking part in the organization of an excellent school in Krzemieniec, Volhynia, then writing a sociophilosophical work aimed at combatting the influence of German idealistic philosophy (especially that of Kant and Fichte), which he despised. That work, entitled *The Physio-Moral Order, or the Science of the Rights and Duties of Man, Which Are Derived from Eternal, Immutable, and Necessary Laws of Nature* (*Porządek fizyczno-moralny, czyli nauka o należytościach i powinnościach człowieka, wydobytych z praw wiecznych, nieodmiennych i koniecznych przyrodzenia*), remained unfinished, the first volume appearing in 1810. When the French-Polish Napoleonic troops entered Warsaw in 1806, Kołłątaj, who was living in a Russian-occupied province, was deported to Moscow by order of the czar. There he was covered with honors, which did not mitigate his regrets for being unable to reach Warsaw in time to play, as he had hoped, an eminent political role. At last, back in the Duchy of Warsaw, he had to content himself, as a man possessing many enemies, with the activity of publicist and, as before, of a pedagogical reformer. Attacks on him in his lifetime (and afterward, by many historians) stressed his insatiable ambitions, his greed, and the strange shifts of his political allegiance (which included a temporary placating of the Targowica Confederacy). Yet he was a politician, above all quite conscious of the necessity for maneuvering, and he should be appraised as a man extraordinary, even for the Enlightenment, in his powers of mind and will, cherishing above all clarity and precision in thought and action.

Stanisław Staszic (1755–1826)   Staszic, like his predecessor of the Renaissance epoch, Andrzej Frycz Modrzewski, whom he resembles in many respects, came from a small town (Piła, in Greater Poland) and was the descendant of an old burgher family. Fulfilling the wish of his pious mother, he became a priest. His father, however, gave him a part of the family fortune to study abroad, and Staszic devoted himself to science at the universities of Leipzig and Göttingen and at the Collège de France in

Paris. He made geological excursions into the Alps and Apennines, and geology was to be one of his main occupations. His personal acquaintance with the famous French naturalist, Buffon, led to his translation of Buffon's *Epochs of Nature*, which he published in 1786. Bitterly resenting the obstacles which confronted citizens of plebeian origin at every step in Poland, he turned to social and political writing. Inspired by his readings of French philosophers, particularly of Jean Jacques Rousseau, he formulated a radical program of reforms. Passionate not only in his presentation of the unequal and unjust treatment accorded burghers in Poland, he was fervent also in his denunciation of the fate of the peasants, which stands among the most moving pages written on that subject. It is obvious, therefore, that such works of his as *Remarks on the Life of Jan Zamoyski* (*Uwagi nad życiem Jana Zamoyskiego*, 1785) and *Warnings for Poland* (*Przestrogi dla Polski*, 1790), where he was led by practical considerations to moderate his sharp criticism of the *status quo*, fall into the category of the most influential writings of the Camp of the Reform. Staszic adhered to the idea of "nation" in the sense brought forward around that time by the ideologists of the French Revolution, although, like Kołłątaj, he saw that "nation" as composed of average gentry and burghers united to combat the oligarchy of the aristocrats. As for the peasants, Staszic proposed that they be granted ownership of the land they tilled as well as personal freedom, but he did not advocate their immediate economic emancipation, in order not to antagonize the middle-class landowners. Thus, his program corresponded, more or less, to principles underlying the Constitution of May 3. For many years Staszic was connected with a family of progressive magnates, the Zamoyskis (in Zamość), in the capacity of tutor, and he made broad use of the excellent library of that old estate. Later on, he conducted geological research all over Poland, including the Tatra Mountains. In 1808 he was elected president of the Society of the Friends of Learning (The Polish Academy of Sciences) in Warsaw, and in the last few decades of his life he also occupied high posts in the field of education. Venerated in old age by his contemporaries and having acquired some wealth despite his plebeian origin, Staszic is an example of the social transformation which had begun to take place in the country in the direction desired by him as a youth. He built a palace in Warsaw as the seat of the Society of the Friends of Learning and a monument to Copernicus, both of which still stand today. Staszic welcomed the Napoleonic constitution enacted in 1807 in the Duchy of Warsaw, which granted personal freedom to the peasants. On his own estate (which he had meanwhile acquired), he divided his land among the peasants and created a model community arranged along cooperative lines with schools, a bank, and a hospital.

His philosophy or rather his "meditation" on (to use his own words) "main epochs of change or the rise and fall of civilizations" is contained in an enormous work written in blank verse entitled *The Human Tribe* (*Ród ludzki*). This is a treatise summing up the views of a typical man of the Enlightenment seeking the causes for the departure of human societies from the path leading to justice and happiness. A materialistic approach to the analysis of social transformations won that poem a reputation as an extremely impious and subversive work. And its first edition (1819–1820), for that reason, is a rarity. After the Congress of Vienna, when Prince Constantine, the brother of the czar, Alexander I, resided in Warsaw as the commander of the Polish army, he took great pleasure in ripping the pages out of a particularly handsome edition of Staszic's poem and burning it in the fireplace. Staszic, unlike Kołłątaj, did not possess the temperament of a politician; his figure is rather that of a scholar, a philanthropist, and a defender of the oppressed, like his sixteenth-century forerunners. Just as the name Bogusławski has remained connected with the theater of Warsaw, so the name of Staszic is inseparable from what became the Polish Academy of Sciences.

THE INCREDIBLE POTOCKI

Jan Potocki (1761–1815) As we have indicated, the eighteenth century was not only an "Age of Reason" but also an age of preoccupation with mystical, pseudo-mystical, or even Satanic experiences. In view of Poland's position as a country emerging from a long sleep and threatened with complete destruction by neighboring powers, that aspect could not find adequate representation. Only one figure, that of a cosmopolitan aristocrat writing in French, is worthy of note, but in his bizarre pursuits he outdid any of his contemporaries, such as members of the French "mystical lodges." Brought up in the Ukraine and in Switzerland, he spoke eight languges fluently thanks to his many tutors. As a young man he studied in Vienna, at the Academy of Military Engineering and received an officer's commission. He saw action in the Mediterranean, where he pursued North African pirates who were threatening the island of Malta. In Warsaw he married an aristocratic young lady, Princess Lubomirski, and found himself entangled in court intrigues. Later, in southern Italy, he avidly explored the traces of Arabian influence in that area. In Turkey he became so entranced with the oriental way of life that afterward he frequently appeared dressed in the Turkish manner, and it was from that country that he brought his valet (from whom he was inseparable), Osman. In Greece he was an attentive observer of the growing clandestine movement of revolt against Turkish domination. His curiosity in regard to the world of the Levant led him on travels through Egypt, while his journey to the Slavic lands of the Adriatic and to islands of Slavic culture in Germany (the Lusatian Sorbs) engendered in him the idea of studying Slavdom as a whole—its antiquities and its common linguistic sources. He made, of course, prolonged visits to Paris and did not bypass the Netherlands, which was then the scene of feverish political activity. In 1788, we see him ascending in a balloon over Warsaw, together with the French proponent of air travel, Blanchard, the faithful Osman, and a dog, Lulu. During the Four-Year Diet, Potocki was among those deputies who favored the reform. In general, he was a popular personality in Warsaw, though accused of the eccentricity of speaking better French than Polish and suspected of having somewhat impious Jacobin tendencies; yet the truth was that Potocki, who found himself in France at the moment when the Jacobins were reaching for power, became disillusioned with those fanatics of Virtue. Spain and Morocco, not France and its social upheavals, now conquered his imagination, as before he had been fascinated by the Levant, and he made prolonged stays there.

In 1805 we see him as a scientific adviser of a Russian expedition to China. The appointment can be explained by his friendship with the Russian minister of foreign affairs, the Polish Prince Adam Czartoryski. Actually, the expedition only got as far as Ulan Bator in Mongolia and was refused admission to China.

Potocki's writings include voluminous works on Slavic prehistory, and he can be called a precursor of Slavic archaeology. Written in French, *Research on Sarmatia* was published in Warsaw in 1789–1792; *Historical and Geographic Fragments on Scythia, Sarmatia, and the Slavs*, in Germany in 1796; and *Prehistory of the Peoples of Russia*, in Petersburg in 1802. He also wrote short comedies to amuse his friends—which are staged today in Poland—and a bizarre novel, also in French, which had an unusual fate. Potocki began the novel in 1803—and in 1815, the year of its completion, he took his own life, using, for that purpose, a pistol loaded with a silver bullet. The first part of the work was published anonymously (in a printing of one hundred copies) in St. Petersburg in 1804 under the title, *The Manuscript Found in Saragossa*. The delight it provoked among connoisseurs and its circulation all over Europe in hand-written copies led to the publication, also anonymously, of other separate parts in Paris in 1813–1814, possibly without the knowledge of the author. Among the novel's admirers was Alexander Pushkin, who even intended to write a poem inspired by the plot, but only jotted down the first stanza. The novel in its entirety was translated from a French manuscript into Polish by an *émigré* writer, Edmund Chojecki (who also wrote in

French under the pen name Charles Edmond), and came out in 1847. Subsequently the French manuscript was lost, leaving the Polish version as the only complete one. If the novel fascinated its first readers, it is largely for reasons which are still valid for today's readers. It is hard to imagine such an amount of adventures in the presumed supernatural squeezed into one book. Potocki's fondness for the Islamic world is seen in what we may call the "box structure" (borrowed from Arabic literature) of the work: the first story leads to the appearance of a narrator, who tells another story, in which still another narrator appears with his story, and so on. It begins with a supposed discovery of an old manuscript in Spain in Saragossa, when it was taken by French and Polish troops in 1809. The action related in the manuscript goes back as far as the end of the seventeenth century and the beginning of the eighteenth century: a young officer of half-Spanish, half-Flemish descent, Alphonse Van Worden, heedless of many warnings, travels to Madrid through the haunted mountains of Sierra Morena and is retained there for sixty-six days by mysterious forces personified, first of all, by two beautiful Tunisian girls who, from time to time, visit him at night. The novel is divided into chapters titled according to the number of days—first day, second day, etc.

In European literature analogies can be found in picaresque novels, especially those of the French author Lesage, but *The Manuscript Found in Saragossa* is also a gothic tale of horrors. Through a fantastic mixture of humor, suspense, swiftly changing scenery—some stories take us back in time to Alexandria and Jerusalem at the time of Christ, some move in space to Sicily, Malta, Mexico—the author conveys his philosophy, which is that of a skeptic, of an eighteenth-century deist searching for a more secure basis of ethics than self-interest and yet full of curiosity about Satanic forces entangling human fates. The central stories are undoubtedly those which present figures of scholars endowed with boundless thirst for knowledge: all the enthusiasm of the author for science and all his self-irony are visible there. The novel is so rich in narratives, each one making a separate whole, that it has been plundered by imitators in various countries, taking advantage of its anonymous publication. In Polish literature, Potocki has a legend of his own, that of a buoyant, somewhat crazy, life tending toward the melancholy skepticism of mature age.

CHAPTER VII

Romanticism

BACKGROUND INFORMATION

AFTER THE THIRD PARTITION, the *Respublica* disappeared *The* from the map of Europe, but it survived in the minds of its *Napoleonic* inhabitants. To keep the three areas of the previous Polish state apart, *Aftermath* profoundly united as they were by a common language and tradition, was no easy task for the occupying powers. And it was not only in Polish minds that the *Respublica* remained alive: as late as 1848, Karl Marx called for a reconstruction of Poland based on the map of 1772, i.e., before the first partition. The fall of the Polish state coincided in time with the rise of Napoleon Bonaparte's star, and the hopes of the Poles went out toward this man. Indeed, so great was the impact of the Napoleonic legend upon the Polish mentality that it entitles us to include several decades of Polish history in this chapter.

In 1797, a Polish Napoleonic legion was created in Italy. Loyal to the French ruler, in spite of his callous treatment of Polish troops (out of several thousands of Polish soldiers who were sent to Haiti to put down the revolution of Toussaint L'Ouverture, only a few hundred returned), the commanders of the Polish Napoleonic troops saw their fidelity recompensed in 1806 when the Napoleonic army entered Warsaw (in Prussian hands since the third partition). Napoleon's victory over Prussia led to the creation (in the treaty of Tilsit) of a tiny Polish state called the Duchy of Warsaw. A constitution modeled upon France's was granted by Napoleon in 1807, and the Napoleonic Code was introduced. The constitution recognized the peasants as free and equal citizens, but did not give them ownership of the land. This should be stressed, as it explains the difference between the peasant's status in central Poland and his status in Russia and in the

Grand Duchy of Lithuania. After the Napoleonic constitution went into effect, the peasant in central Poland was still obliged to work in the fields of his landlord, but he was not a serf.

The new Duchy of Warsaw was soon engaged in a successful war against Austria on the side of Napoleon and in this way was able to extend its boundaries to incorporate the territory taken from the Austrian-occupied provinces. Later on, in 1812, the Duchy supplied Napoleon with some troops for his invasion of Russia. In his army of over a half-million men, Poles accounted for about 100,000.

Napoleon's defeat and withdrawal took the faithful Polish units west again, and their commander, Marshal Józef Poniatowski, died on the battlefield near Leipzig. When the Holy Alliance of monarchs assembled at the Congress of Vienna to redraw the map of Europe, one of the most difficult problems, in view of the subterranean tensions between the victors, was the Polish question. The powers agreed, at last, to recognize the creation of a Kingdom of Poland (known later in history as the "Congress Kingdom") bound in a personal union to Russia. The Russian czar was to be crowned king of Poland, but was to pledge that his rule would respect local law and the parliament. Thus, an autocratic czar was to be a constitutional monarch in Poland. The paradox inherent in such an arrangement proved later to be the seed of failure. Russia, Prussia, and Austria retained large areas of the old *Respublica*'s territory. Unable to settle a troublesome dispute over Kraków, the Congress proclaimed it a free city under the international supervision of the three neighboring powers. It remained thus from 1815 to 1846.

The Kingdom of Poland, whose nominal head was Czar Alexander I (crowned the Polish king), possessed a strong army, trained mostly by former Napoleonic officers who were magnanimously forgiven their fighting against Russia. The army was the "pet" of the Czar's brother, Grand Duke Constantine, an unbalanced, if not half-insane man, who resided in Warsaw and behaved not unlike a boy playing with tin soldiers. Inhuman discipline in the army led to many desperate acts, including suicide, on the parts of both officers and subordinates. Grand Duke Constantine (who appears often in Polish literature) had, probably, a kind of passion for Poland. In any case, he cannot be held responsible for the proliferation of secret police "services"—of various kinds; these were fostered by Russian civil commissars such as the famous Novosiltsov. Steadily increasing friction weakened the already tenuous connection between the administration and the parliament, not to speak of public opinion, and reflected Alexander I's gradual abandonment of a liberal policy in Russia. Yet, for a decade and a half, the precarious order of things arranged at the Congress of Vienna gave the Poles, regardless of the province they inhabited, considerable opportunities for cultural and economic development. Much was done for the economy in the Kingdom by the minister of finance, Lubecki; while the network of schools created by the Commission for National Education freely continued its activity. A new university in Warsaw was founded in 1816. The University of Wilno (situated in the territory annexed to the Russian Empire) was considered the best institution of learning in all Russia, while an excellent new *lycée* was established in Krzemieniec in Volhynia. Kraków, of course, preserved its traditions as an ancient capital, and its university profited from the reforms introduced by the men of the Enlightenment. Generally speaking, in both the Kingdom of Poland and in the Russian-occupied provinces there were no attempts to curtail teaching or publishing in the Polish language.

Around 1820, a movement among the youth, the expression of which in literature came to be called Romanticism, spread through Poland, and it took on organizational forms similar to those of the revolutionary brotherhoods in Germany. Clandestine contacts were established with young Russians, who, after their attempt at seizing power in December of 1825, were to be known under the name of Decembrists. When the new czar, Nicholas I, unleashed his rule of unmitigated police terror upon the country, the revolutionary spark was ready to flare. In November 1830, a group of young officers of the Polish army revolted and, during a dramatic November night, succeeded in bringing Warsaw over to their side. The insurrection of 1830 amounted, in fact, to a war between Poland and Russia. The parliament voted an act which dethroned the Czar as king of Poland. Military activities lasted practically throughout the year of 1831, but Poland was at last defeated. During the so-called Great Emigration which followed, several thousands of officers and soldiers and a number of the most active intellectuals left the country, migrating first to Germany, then to France. Paris, for some two decades, became the center of Polish cultural and political life. The order upheld by the Holy Alliance of monarchs was looked upon by Polish writers and political leaders as a diabolical conspiracy against the peoples of Europe. Many of them placed their stakes, therefore, on revolutionary groups in Western Europe like the Italian *Carbonari* and the French Utopian Socialists. The Emigration was divided within itself: The conservatives grouped around the so-called "Hôtel Lambert" (a private residence in Paris). They were partisans of a constitutional monarchy for Poland and members of the aristocratic Establishment. The democrats, whose main organization was the Democratic Society, placed their hopes in a revolution of European peoples against the tyrants. Still further to the left were the Polish People's Communes (*Gromady Ludu Polskiego*), composed mostly of former rank-and-file soldiers residing on the mainland of England and on the island of Jersey. They advocated a revolution in Poland that would lead to a division of landed estates among the peasants in the spirit of Christian communism. The causes of the defeat of the 1830 revolution became the subject of infinite debates among the *émigrés*. According to radical democrats, the Poles could have won by proclaiming economic freedom for the peasants, arming them, and carrying their revolutionary fervor to the Russian masses. All Polish writings of the period abound in mystical appeals to the Napoleonic myth as a force which would abolish the reactionary order oppressing Europe.

The Kingdom of Poland, after the insurrection of 1830–1831, preserved but weak vestiges of autonomy. The University of Warsaw was closed down in 1831. The University of Wilno, regarded as a hotbed of dangerous ideas, soon shared the same fate. The czarist government also began a campaign of persecution directed against the Greek Catholic Church in the former Grand Duchy of Lithuania, a church of Byelorussian peasants. The very existence of non-Orthodox Eastern Slavs was considered an offense to the principle of unity between the czarist throne and the Orthodox Church, a unity vital for the Russian monarchy.

The 1830s, in spite of the loss of the most energetic leaders, who had escaped to the West, witnessed some abortive conspiracies, which grew in force with the advent of the 1840s. A Roman Catholic priest from the neighborhood of Lublin, Father Piotr Ściegienny, succeeded in weaving a vast clandestine network among the peasants with a program of communist revolution. His propaganda booklet was conceived as a presumed letter from the Pope to the peasants, calling for banishment of the lords and for fraternity with the Russian peasant as a brother in the same fate. The participants in that conspiracy were sent to hard-labor camps in Siberia. There, some of them became Dostoevsky's cell mates, and he mentions them in his *Notes from the House of the Dead*. The unrest in Poland increased with the approach of the fateful year of 1848, the "spring of nations." Edward Dembowski, a young philosopher of aristocratic origin, a brilliant writer in the spirit of the Hegelian Left, was one of the leaders of the short-lived revolution in the free city of Kraków in 1846, and he died in a clash of the crowd with the Austrian troops. He had tried in vain to avert an antirevolutionary scheme of the Austrian authorities, namely, a peasant revolt in southern Poland. The peasants attacked the manors, massacring their owners (sometimes even sawing them in half). Their leader, Jakub Szela (a character who turns up often in the literature of the twentieth century), acted at the instigation of the Austrian officials, for whom a peasant revolt was a tool to drive a wedge into Polish solidarity based on patriotic aspirations—the gentry being frightened to death, after the peasant rebellion, of the "dark masses."

In 1848, an insurrection broke out in Prussian-occupied Poland, and, for a while, battles took place between Prussian troops and Polish volunteer detachments. The government of the Hapsburg Empire, pressured by revolutions in Vienna (and Lwów), granted Galician peasants the right to own land and freed them from obligatory duties to their lords. The revolution in Hungary attracted many Poles, among them a general of the artillery, Józef Bem, who became one of the chief commanders of the Hungarian revolutionary army and to this day has remained for the Hungarians a half-legendary figure, known as "Daddy Bem." In Italy, the leading Polish Romantic poet, Adam Mickiewicz, organized a small legion composed of artists and intellectuals that fought for the Italian cause against the Austrians in Lombardy, and then with Garibaldi in the defense of republican Rome. In 1849 Mickiewicz founded an international socialist newspaper in Paris, *La Tribune des Peuples*. The complete breakdown of the European revolutionary movement evoked despair and dejection among the Poles, but soon new hopes were born with the outbreak of the Crimean War, allying Turkey with France and England against Russia. A Polish legion was formed in Constantinople comprising Russian war prisoners of Polish descent. Adam Mickiewicz was active there, too, and together with his friend Armand Lévy, brought to short-lived fruition his idea of a Jewish legion, the first Jewish military unit in modern times. Russia's defeat in the Crimean War and the death of the "gendarme-czar," Nicholas I, released a movement of the liberal intelligentsia in Russia pressuring for decisive reforms. The emancipation of the peasants was proclaimed in 1861 (the czar's edict did not cover central Poland, where the situation of the peasant had been different ever since the Napoleonic constitution of 1807). Thwarted expectations of national autonomy in Poland resulted in increasing unrest among Warsaw's population, where a clandestine revolutionary committee had begun to act. It owed its organization primarily to a poet, Apollo Korzeniowski, father of the future English novelist, Joseph Conrad. Clashes between Warsaw crowds and Russian troops occurred more and more frequently. An unwise decision of Count Alexander Wielopolski, the civil governor of Poland and a most influential figure among the Polish conservatives, led to the outbreak of a new Polish insurrection in January 1863. Wielopolski had advised Russian military authorities to draft all young men suspected of political activity for some twenty years of service. The Provisional National Government, which grew out of the clandestine revolutionary committee, announced the economic emancipation of the peasants. The Russian troops fought throughout 1863—against detachments of guerrillas composed not only of Poles but also of some Russians, Germans, French, and Italians, followers of Garibaldi. A meeting of workers in London, organized by Karl Marx to express solidarity with the Poles, culminated in the creation of the First Socialist International. But the insurrection of 1863 was doomed in advance by lack of arms and by the nearly complete indifference of the peasants to the appeals of their compatriots. Guerrilla detachments included only the nobles, the petty gentry, artisans, and some workers of budding industrial enterprises. Only in Lithuania was peasant participation considerable. "Pacification" meant for Poland the gallows, deportations to Siberia, and ruinous taxation of landed estates. In its policy, the czarist government applied principles elaborated by certain Russian Pan-Slavists according to whom the upper layers of "Latinized" Polish society were traitors to the cause of Slavdom, as opposed to the "good" (i.e., truly Slavic) Polish peasants. The peasants were told that the insurrection was an intrigue of the nobles directed against the benevolent czar who had emancipated the peasantry. In fact, however, it had been the manifesto of the Provisional National Government that had forced the hand of the czarist authorities, who then granted Polish peasants economic emancipation with slightly better conditions than in Russia. The year 1863 closed a whole era, that of Romanticism in politics and in literature. A constant looking forward toward a mythical upheaval of European nations was to be superseded by a call for sober concentration upon small economic and cultural tasks.

Nationalism, Romanticism, Messianism   Heroic insurrections, participation in revolutionary movements all over Europe, retaliative executions carried out by the occupying powers, and deportations to Siberia unavoidably shaped the Polish mentality. These crucial events came at a time when modern nationalism was crystallizing under the impact of the French Revolution and German philosophy. In the old *Respublica* the line between "Polishness" and "non-Polishness" had been a blurred one. Skarga's *Sermons*, for instance, contained hints of a messianic vocation assigned to the Poles, but this idea can be interpreted as stemming from an attachment to the state's institutions, rather than from a worship, on Skarga's part, of the "nation" as a spiritual unit. But when Poland lost her independence, the concept of "Polishness" gradually emerged as an ethereal entity requiring loyalty and existing even without embodiment in a state. It is extremely difficult to make an impartial appraisal of the Polish mentality in the period we are dealing with. If the history of the country can be called "abnormal," its thought and literature were no less so. An old tendency to idealize "golden freedom," which had distinguished Poland from her neighbors, the autocratic monarchies, underwent a mutation: enormous talents for self-pity were displayed, and Poland was presented as an innocent victim suffering for the sins of humanity. This new version contained the additives of Napoleonic myth and Utopian Socialism. Hatred for the main occupying power, Russia, inclined the Poles to interpret the conflict between the two countries as a struggle between the forces of light (democracy), on the one hand, and those of darkness (tyranny), on the other. Russia was not "European"; it was "Asiatic," marked forever by the Tartar yoke. In all fairness we should add that such views were not the property of the Poles alone, as a leading revolutionary, Karl Marx, considered the Slavs as born slaves with the exception of two freedom-loving nations: the Poles and the Serbs.

To place Polish literature of this time in a proper perspective is a task that has never been brought to a conclusion. A jungle of criss-crossing currents, of madly daring ideas, of self-pity and national arrogance, and of unsurpassed brilliancy in poetic technique asks for constantly renewed explorations. If the term Romanticism is treacherous, denoting as it does different phenomena in each country, it would be doubly dangerous to apply its most widely accepted meaning to Polish literature. The struggle against the classical rules of good taste, which began in Poland (as in France) around 1820, concealed, from its inception, political undertones. Contrary to the brand of Romanticism which in many countries was identified with a withdrawal of the individual into his own interior world, Romanticism in Poland acquired an extremely activist character and was clearly a consequence of many ideas of the Enlightenment. Perhaps, after all, Prince Metternich, an archreactionary, an evil demon for the progressive intelligentsia of his time, gave the best definition of the new ferment in his secret memorandum written for Czar Alexander I in 1820:

The progress of the human mind has been extremely rapid in the course of the last three centuries. This progress having been accelerated more rapidly than the growth of wisdom (the only counterpoise to passions and to errors), a revolution prepared by the false systems, the fatal errors into which many of the most illustrious sovereigns of the last half of the eighteenth century fell, has at last broken out in a country [France] advanced in knowledge, and enervated by pleasure, in a country inhabited by people whom one can only regard as frivolous, from the facility with which they comprehend and the difficulty they experience in judging calmly.

In what, according to Prince Meternich, does the evil of modern time consist?

This evil may be described in one word—presumption; the natural effect of the rapid progression of the human mind toward the perfecting of so many things. This it is which at the present day leads so many individuals astray, for it has become an almost universal sentiment.

Religion, morality, legislation, economy, politics, administration, all have become common and accessible to everyone. Knowledge seems to come by *inspiration;* experience has no value for the presumptuous man; faith is nothing to him; he substitutes for it a pretended *individual conviction,* and to arrive at this conviction, dispenses with all inquiry and with all study; for these means appear too trivial to a mind which believes itself strong enough to embrace at one glance all questions and all facts. Laws have no values for him, because he has not contributed to make them, and it would be beneath a man of his parts to recognize the limits traced by rude and ignorant generations. Power resides in *himself;* why should he submit to that which was only useful for the man deprived of light and knowledge? That which, according to him, was required in an age of weakness cannot be suitable in an age of reason and vigor, amounting to universal perfection, which the German innovators designate *by the idea, absurd in itself, of the Emancipation of the People!* Morality itself he does not attack openly, for without it he could not be sure for a single moment of his own existence; but he interprets its essence after his own fashion, and allows every other person to do so likewise provided that other person neither kills nor robs him.

In thus tracing the character of the presumptuous man, we believe we have traced that of the society of the day, composed of like elements, if the denomination of society is applicable to an order of things which only tends in principle towards individualizing all the elements of which society is composed.

Presumption makes every man the guide of his own belief, the arbiter of laws according to which he is pleased to govern himself or to *allow* someone else to govern him and his neighbors; it makes him, in short, *the sole judge* of his own faith, his own action, and the principles according to which he guides them.

Metternich's memorandum could have been presented to the police for use as a miniature handbook on rebel psychology. But he gives more detailed advice too, being perspicacious enough to notice the multi-faceted philosophical, literary, and political character of Romanticism:

The real aim of the idealists of the party is *religious and political fusion,* and this being analyzed is nothing else but creating in favor of each individual an existence entirely independent of all authority, or any other will than his own, an idea absurd and contrary to the nature of man, and incompatible with the need of human society. . . . It is principally *the middle classes of society* which this moral gangrene has affected, and it is only among them that the real heads of the party are found.

If we keep in mind that the authority so praised by Metternich was, for the Polish rebels, a foreign authority, opposed to their patriotic feelings, we receive a portrait that delineates perfectly the nature of Romanticism in Poland.

A constant preoccupation with postulated political change explains the fondness Polish Romantics displayed for the philosophy of history. Their themes were elaborated sometimes in opposition to, sometimes in agreement with, Hegelian thought. In any case, Polish Romanticism was thoroughly imbued with historicism. One more observation should be made: though Shelley called the poet a lawgiver for humanity, few people in England, we may suspect, took that claim seriously. As a consequence of national misfortunes, the reading public in Poland gave literal acceptance to a similar claim on the part of their own poets. The poet was hailed as a charismatic leader, the incarnation of the collective strivings of the peoples; thus, his biography, not only his work, entered the legend. We may guess that a transference of the Napoleonic myth of a "providential man" into the realm of literature was at work here. Among foreign writers, no one more fully than Lord Byron, as a poet and a man of action, filled these deep emotional needs. Byron's fame in his native country was insignificant if we compare it with the near worship surrounding him in the Slavic countries. The three Polish Romantic poets, Adam Mickiewicz, Juliusz Słowacki, and Zygmunt Krasiński, were acclaimed as national bards, and these greatly magnified figures dominated several literary generations—a somewhat arbitrary triad, as they were not all writers of equal talent.

CLASSICISM AND PRE-ROMANTICISM

During the first two decades of the century, Warsaw dictated literary fashions. As in France, the classical principles of good taste were still the rule, not only in literature but also in theater and in the fine arts. There was a marked division into high-brow and low-brow genres. Poetry and versified drama (submitted to rigorous rules) belonged to the former class; while the sentimental novels and "bourgeois dramas" gradually invading the market were ranged in the latter. The bourgeois drama originated in Germany, and the most disparate works, starting with the so-called "horrible products of a sick imagination" like Schiller's *The Robbers* and ending with the prolific and shallow production of Kotzebue, were lumped together under this label. The Warsaw literati for a while successfully blocked the influx of such suspect novelties, which offended their rationalism and classical tastes. The classicists organized themselves into a "Society of X's" (*Towarzystwo Iksów*) and held gatherings where literary works and new plays staged in Warsaw were discussed. To exert pressure as a body, all of them signed their articles of criticism with an X. Perhaps the most important member of the X's was Kajetan Koźmian (1771– 1856), a rich landowner, a senator, a poet, a translator, and a very active participant, as were all his colleagues, in the Society of the

Friends of Learning. An excellent craftsman of late classical or, as it is sometimes called derogatorily, "pseudoclassical" Polish verse, Koźmian still makes pleasant reading, but his fate exemplifies the difficulties of writers who follow a moribund trend. For nearly twenty-five years, he worked on a long descriptive poem, *Polish Husbandry* (*Ziemiaństwo polskie*), comparable to Delille's imitations of Virgil's *Georgics* and composed in impeccable couplets; but by the time it was ready, works of that type were considered old-fashioned bores. Besides, Koźmian with his conservative and legitimist views and his extremely violent denunciations of Romanticism (much in the spirit of Metternich) made enemies for himself out of the young generation and was ridiculed by Mickiewicz as "an author of a thousand lines on planting peas."

Another luminary of the Society of *X*'s was Ludwik Osiński (1775–1838), the author of graceful odes, a literary critic, for a while director of the Warsaw Theater, and a professor of literature at Warsaw University. More tolerant and open-minded than Koźmian, he acknowledged some literary value in the Germans of the *Sturm und Drang* period, commented favorably upon the brothers Schlegel, and even moderately praised Shakespeare. Franciszek Ksawery Dmochowski (1762–1808), whom we have already mentioned in the chapter on the Enlightenment, adapter of Boileau, translator of the *Iliad* and of Milton, died in Napoleonic Warsaw; but his son, Franciszek Salezy Dmochowski (1801–1871), became one of the most zealous defenders of the classical *status quo*. Stanisław Kostka Potocki (1752–1821) exemplifies another aspect of the period. The Warsaw literati, though accused by the young of undue respect for the established order, were, in fact, loyal inheritors of the Voltairian spirit. They directed their malice at superstitions, prejudices, and human folly much like their Enlightenment predecessors. They differed from them in renouncing larger political strivings. Potocki, minister of education in the Congress Kingdom of Poland, a fervent Freemason, a supporter of the Society of the Friends of Learning, and one of the *X*'s, wrote a kind of satirical novel which he had to publish anonymously, so violent was its attack on the clergy. The novel was entitled *A Journey to Dunceville* (*Podróż do Ciemnogrodu*, 1820), and to our day *ciemnogród* in Polish has served to denote people of ultraconservative views.

The Warsaw literati were particularly concerned with the theater. They dreamed of writing tragedies in verse (a genre also honored by Voltaire) and took for the greatest authorities such French codifiers of rules (for the neoclassical tragedy) as Jean François La Harpe (1739–1803). To understand what they were looking for in that genre, one may use the example of the most famous French painter of the Napoleonic era, Louis David. His was a painting of costume and

gesture, where Frenchmen appeared as ancient Romans, or if specifically modern situations were celebrated (as, for example, in his large
canvas, "The Death of Marat"), the characters were transformed into
figures of an ancient tragedy. The Polish classicists believed that the
fusion of contents taken from local history with rigorous, French-
inspired form would result in a new literary genre, a national tragedy.
For this reason they gave unreserved applause to Alojzy Feliński
(1771–1820). A poet, a translator, a veteran of Kościuszko's uprising,
and later on a professor of literature at the *lycée* of Krzemieniec,
Feliński wrote a tragedy in verse, *Barbara Radziwiłł* (*Barbara Radzi-
wiłłówna*), performed in 1817 and even translated into French and
German. The author's metrical inventiveness, without breaking out of
thirteen-syllable rhymed couplets, proved itself within that framework.
He used various combinations consisting either in parallelism between
syntax and line or in anticlimaxes (for instance, a sentence broken by
a caesura), etc. For his subject, Feliński chose a historical event of
the sixteenth century. (As we have already remarked, the Poles turned
toward their Golden Age as a kind of compensation.) The event,
famous in its time and, for that reason, recorded copiously in literature, was not unlike the affair of Edward VIII and Mrs. Simpson in
the twentieth century: the crown prince of Poland, son of King Sigismund I and the Italian princess, Bona Sforza, clandestinely married
Barbara Radziwiłł, the daughter of a Lithuanian lord, but not of royal
parentage. After the death of his father, when the prince was to
ascend the throne as Sigismund August, violent opposition was voiced
from the Senate—a demand was made that he either divorce his wife
or abdicate. The leader of the anti-Radziwiłł faction was the queen
mother, Bona. With great difficulty, the young king overcame innumerable intrigues, finally receiving the consent of the Diet to crown
his wife, when suddenly, after a short illness, Barbara died. According to popular legend, since Bona was a vicious woman, skillful like
all Renaissance Italians in the methods of poison and the dagger, she
must have poisoned Barbara. This moving story of the royal love and
despair of a king, who in his grief supposedly turned to a magician
promising to show him the phantom of his beloved, acted powerfully
upon popular imagination. Feliński studied historical documents, but
to preserve the three unities he distilled a sort of extract, departing
somewhat from facts and dates. He constructed a tragedy of conflict
between passion and civic duty. As the action rises, the king is more
and more cornered and at the climax finds three possibilities left to
him: a civil war (his opponents are ready to attack the royal castle
in Kraków), abdication (which for him would be a cowardly act), or
divorce. He makes a very curious and very Polish decision: to avoid
pressures from the lords in the Senate and to avert a civil war, he

appeals to the Diet and promises to accept its verdict. But his victory in the Diet is turned to nothing when Barbara dies, poisoned. Throughout the five acts neither the passions of the king nor those of Barbara occupy the foreground, and the vicious Bona is perhaps the most vivid character. Contrasting figures of lords—one backs the king, another leads the rebels because of his anarchistic ambitions, still another is primarily concerned with the interests of the state as a whole—make us think of Kochanowski's *The Dismissal of the Grecian Envoys.*

The success of Feliński's play came at the time when Niemcewicz's *Historical Songs* (published in 1816) was at the peak of its popularity. The national past thus began its career as a legitimate subject for both poetry and drama. In Russia too, Kondraty Ryleyev, indebted in this respect to Niemcewicz, whom he translated, attempted between 1821 and 1823 to write a kind of lyrical history of Russia from the tenth century to the nineteenth century in a series of *dumy,* singing of such personalities as Oleg, Sviatoslav, Dimitry of the Don, Ivan Suzanin. He drew his themes from Karamzin's *History of Russia,* but made near rebels out of his heroes (for instance, the troops of Dimitry of the Don in the fourteenth century want to fight "for freedom, truth, and law").

The new Romantic fashions made their entrance slowly; at first they were visible only in low-brow genres, but some respected French writers also contributed to the opening of forbidden paths. Le Tourneur was the first to translate the collected works of Shakespeare into French (though he did it in prose), and in his preface he introduced the word *romantique:*

Whoever will want to know him [Shakespeare] let him direct his gaze on the vast sea or fix it on the aerial and *romantique* landscape.

So what is the meaning of *romantique?* Paintings of Salvador Rosa, landscapes of the Alps, untrimmed English gardens, and Shakespeare—"everything which awakens in a moved soul tender affections and melancholy ideas." Next, Jean-François Ducis rewrote Le Tourneur's version in verse, diluting Shakespeare with a sentimentalist's melancholy sweetness and expurgating all "coarseness" and "nonsense" (there is no Iago in *Othello,* for instance, because the public could not have borne such a horror of villainy; and the names of characters are changed to add a Nordic flavor: Desdemona and Brabancio become Hedelmona and Odalbert). In Poland then, Shakespeare was played according to Ducis or according to a German translator, Schröder (in whose version of Hamlet, the protagonist does not die). But the Polish literary public soon discovered true Shakespeare through an excellent German translation by August Wilhelm Schlegel.

In addition, Schlegel's Vienna lectures on "Dramatic Art and Litera-ture," published in 1809–1811, served the innovators in Warsaw as their chief weapon against pseudoclassical views on drama. The theo-retical principles of Romanticism were elaborated in Germany and spread all over Western Europe by Madame de Staël, whose book, *On Germany* (*De l'Allemagne*), had its first edition of 1810 com-pletely destroyed at Napoleon's orders—Madame de Staël being his staunch enemy. By 1813, the year of its second edition, *On Germany* had won acclaim in Poland.

Among the writers on the border line of Classicism and Romanti-cism, we should place Julian Ursyn Niemcewicz (see pp. 170–174), whose knowledge of English gave him direct access not only to the works of Pope and Samuel Johnson, but to those of Gray and Byron as well as to English and Scottish ballads. Another such transi-tional figure was Kazimierz Brodziński (1791–1835), a poet and a professor at Warsaw University. In 1818 he came out with a long treatise, *On Classicism and Romanticism* (*O klasyczności i roman-tyczności*), accompanied by an essay, "On the Spirit of Polish Poetry." Well-read in German philosophy, Brodziński took from Johann Gott-fried Herder the idea of a specific national character expressing itself in every given literature. Moderate in his judgments, he tried to see advantages in both currents and to combine them in such a way as to remain true to what he called the "essence of Polish poetry." He came to the conclusion that the idyll is the truest expression of the Polish national character. In his poetic practice, he attempted to apply that principle, particularly in his idyll, *Wiesław* (1820), where he depicts somewhat too happy Polish peasants. Brodziński's moderation not only failed to satisfy the young, but provoked the anger of the classicists. It was against him that an eminent professor of the University of Wilno, Jan Śniadecki, a mathematician, an astronomer, and a ration-alist, wrote his essay, *On Classical and Romantic Writings* (1819), in which he called Romanticism "a school of treason and plague," a danger for education and the purity of the language. Śniadecki was one of the brightest minds of his time, and his words should not be taken lightly. Yet he had to lose. Not only foreign imports, such as the poems of Ossian (treated as genuine Nordic songs) and senti-mental novels, were promoting the change in sensibility. The novel form was already being imitated by Polish authors: the most suc-cessful of such works was *Malvina, or Intuitions of the Heart* (*Mal-wina czyli domyślność serca*, 1816), by Princess Maria Wirtemberska, née Czartoryska. Perhaps the most important single phenomenon that determined the shift was the Napoleonic legend, releasing as it did new forces of feeling and imagination. Viewed in this light, Polish Romanticism came close to resembling that branch of French Ro-

manticism which was represented by Stendhal. The poetry and prose
produced by those who had served in the Napoleonic army was, thanks
to their energy and broad vistas, far removed from the placid offerings of the Warsaw literati; this is apparent, for instance, in a poem
by Cyprian Godebski, "To the Polish Legions in Italy" ("Wiersz do
Legiów polskich," 1805). It is visible in a novel by the same author, *A
Grenadier Philosopher* (*Grenadier filozof*, 1805), where we have a story
of Polish and French soldiers wandering from Italy through France,
sharing a common disillusionment with the ideals which the French
Revolution failed to bring to fruition. Besides, the conviction was growing that poetry is not just a matter of good taste as prescribed by the
educated classes. While German theoreticians extolled the Nordic genius
in opposition to the French classical genius, Polish writers began to
realize the value of Slavic folklore. In this respect, the role of Zorjan
Dołęga-Chodakowski (pen name of Adam Czarnocki—1784–1825)
should be remembered. A self-taught ethnographer and archaeologist,
he was responsible for collections of folk songs from Poland, Byelorussia, and the Ukraine.

ADAM MICKIEWICZ

(1798–1855)

Adam Mickiewicz was born on Christmas Eve in Nowogródek (or
perhaps in Zaosie, a village near that town), in the Grand Duchy of
Lithuania. His father was a small-town lawyer, a very typical representative of the petty gentry. The poet's mother, belonging to the same
class, had been a servant girl at a neighboring manor before her
marriage. The region, which had once been ethnically Lithuanian,
now had a peasant population speaking Byelorussian, and the folklore that was to mark Mickiewicz so strongly was predominantly
Byelorussian. The childhood and early adolescence of the future poet
was permeated with the cordial, warm atmosphere of local Roman
Catholic and Greek Catholic traditions. He went to a school in Nowogródek maintained by the Dominican Order. Its curriculum had been
reformed according to the principles elaborated by the Commission
for National Education and had been placed under the supervision of
the University of Wilno. Mickiewicz was a mediocre pupil, but
participated very actively in school games, theater performances,
and "moot courts" organized to resemble old Polish tribunals. A
gift for friendship and group life, so visible later on in his life, can
be traced back to these high school years. He was fourteen when the
Napoleonic army, in its expedition against Russia, entered Nowogródek and Napoleon's brother, Hieronymous, King of Naples, took up
quarters in the family house. The echoes of that event, as well as

the landscapes and human types of his native province, were, in his mature age, to become the material for Mickiewicz's epos in verse, *Pan Tadeusz*. In 1815, he entered the University of Wilno on a scholarship, studying first the sciences, then switching to literature. After graduation in 1819, he became a high-school teacher, fulfilling the terms of the scholarship, in the neighboring town of Kowno. His university years were among the happiest in his life, and he profited greatly, especially from his professor of classical philology, Groddeck, an eminent German scholar, and from his professor of literature, Borowski. His knowledge of Latin authors, which he brought from his high school and the university, was so thorough that it enabled him, later on, to lecture successfully as professor of Latin literature at the College of Lausanne in Switzerland. But his student's life was also a life of intense friendships and of participation in clandestine or semiclandestine groups, of which he was one of the most zealous organizers. One such group, the Philomaths, as they called themselves, had no avowed political goals. They gathered regularly to read and criticize each other's poems and papers on various subjects. But in fact, because of their close contact with the Freemasons, especially with one fervent Freemason, an ex-soldier of Kościuszko's army by the name of Kontrym (who was then a university librarian), the Philomaths tended to influence their colleagues in the progressive and patriotic spirit. For that purpose, they applied a model pattern of conspiracy, acting as a small, invisible lodge, creating and infiltrating larger student organizations, such as the Philareths. Much time was given to group excursions in the nearby wooded hills, to songs, and to humorous ceremonies, etc. In general, as their works and their correspondence show, Mickiewicz and his friends were joyous young men, full of a sense of humor and well deserving of the sobriquet "Sternians," Laurence Sterne being one of their favorite authors.

Mickiewicz's first poems were imitations of Voltaire, written to amuse his friends. Like his model, he took relish in irreverent themes, for instance, in his adaptation of *La Pucelle d'Orléans*. As his master in classical Polish verse he looked, above all, to Stanisław Trembecki. From these early exercises he acquired a firm, classical discipline. His first poem to be published, "City Winter" ("Zima miejska," 1818), is still an excellent example of a vigorous, classical poem. Its tone is half-humorous, its syntax Latinlike, studded with inversions; and already that manly concreteness of style, which is Mickiewicz's chief merit, is visible in this first sample.

Mickiewicz and his friends were, stylistically and spiritually, the direct descendants of the eighteenth century. They studied not only Voltaire, Diderot, and Rousseau, but also such philosophers as Condillac and Helvetius. Mickiewicz's poem of 1820, not printed but circulated in handwritten copies, "Ode to Youth" ("Oda do młodości"), which was to become popular with the whole young generation, is a kind of Freemasonic song, calling man to push the "clod of the earth" onto new paths, to join forces in altruistic love, to storm the "citadel of Fame," and to prepare for human freedom. In its style, the poem is marked by numerous references to classical mythology. It is curious to note that in the same year Mickiewicz wrote "A Hymn for the Ascension of the Holy Virgin," and that coincidence seems to confirm the definition of Romanticism as a politico-mystical current. Another poem of Mickiewicz's, "The Potato" ("Kartofla," written 1819), deserves our attention, as it is a humorous picture of the discovery of America. Written in classical couplets, this is a story of how Columbus is stopped in the middle of the ocean by the Greek gods, who, having been driven out of Europe, are jealous of their new possessions on the American continent. The fate of Columbus' expedition, however, is decided in the Christian heaven. There, certain saints strongly oppose Columbus' progress because they foresee the slaughter of the Indians. Among those in favor of allowing the discovery of America is St. Dominic, shown in a very disagreeable light as the murderer of the Albigensians. But victory goes to St. Dominic when he holds up a potato in front of the saintly company and throws it on the balance: the blessings that the plant holds for hungry populations outweigh the tears of the Indians. St. Rafael adds a prophecy as to the future of America:

> Then will a star of liberties shine over the new world,
> Virtue and learning will gather under its rays;
> The People of sovereign power will rule over equals, they
> Will bend old-fashioned tyrants to their feet and kindle
> New fires in Europe from the spark of Freedom.

The years spent by Mickiewicz as a schoolteacher in Kowno were rather grim, as he could visit his friends in Wilno but rarely; moreover, an unhappy love oppressed him. That love for Maryla Wereszczaka was to be a kind of Romantic archetype in Polish literature thanks to Mickiewicz's fame. Maryla came from a well-to-do landowning family. Despite her emotional involvement, she refused to go as far as marrying a penniless schoolteacher, preferring instead a count. It seems that she regretted it later. In Kowno Mickiewicz gradually discovered Schiller, Goethe, and Byron and started to write ballads. The appearance of his first book of poems, *Ballads and Romances* (*Ballady i romanse*), in 1822 opened for good the era of Romanticism in Poland. The preface to that volume was a manifesto of the new current, but the poems themselves spoke even more clearly:

The Romantic

"Silly girl, listen!"
But she doesn't listen
While the village roofs glisten,
Bright in the sun.
"Silly girl, what do you do there,
As if there were someone to view
   there,
A face to gaze on and greet there,
When there is no one, none, do you
   hear!"
But she doesn't hear.

Like a dead stone
She stands there alone,
Staring ahead of her, peering
   around
For something that has to be found
Till, suddenly spying it,
She touches it, clutches it,
Laughing and crying.

Is it you, my Johnny, my true love,
   my dear?
I knew you would never forget me,
Even in death! Come with me, let
   me
Show you the way now! Hold your
   breath, though,
And tiptoe lest stepmother hear.

What can she hear? They have
   made him
A grave, two years ago laid him
Away with the dead.
Save me, Mother of God! I'm
   afraid.
But why? Why should I flee you
   now?

What do I dread?
Not Johnny! I see you now,
Your eyes, your white shirt.

But it's pale as linen you are,
Cold as winter you are!

Romantyczność

Słuchaj, dzieweczko!
—Ona nie słucha—
To dzień biały! to miasteczko!
Przy tobie nie ma żywego ducha.
Co tam wkoło siebie chwytasz?
Kogo wołasz, z kim się witasz?
—Ona nie słucha.—

To jak martwa opoka
Nie zwróci w stronę oka,
To strzela wkoło oczyma,
To się łzami zaleje;
Coś niby chwyta, coś niby trzyma;
Rozpłacze się i zaśmieje.

"Tyżeś to w nocy? to ty, Jasieńku!
Ach! i po śmierci kocha!
Tutaj, tutaj, pomaleńku,
Czasem usłyszy macocha!

"Niech sobie słyszy, już nie ma
   ciebie!
Już po twoim pogrzebie!
Ty już umarłeś? Ach! ja się boję!
Czego się boję mego Jasieńka?
Ach, to on! lica twoje, oczki twoje!
Twoja biała sukienka!

"I sam ty biały jak chusta,
Zimny, jakie zimne dłonie!
Tutaj połóż, tu na łonie,
Przyciśnij mnie, do ust usta!

"Ach, jak tam zimno musi być w
   grobie!

Let my lips take the cold from you,
Kiss the chill of the mould from
      you.

Dearest love, let me die with you,
In the deep earth lie with you,
For this world is dark and dreary,
I am lonely and weary!

Alone among the unkind ones
Who mock at my vision,
My tears their derision,
Seeing nothing, the blind ones!

Dear God! A cock is crowing,
Whitely glimmers the dawn.
Johnny! Where are you going?
Don't leave me! I am forlorn!

So, caressing, talking aloud to her
Lover, she stumbles and falls,
And her cry of anguish calls
A pitying crowd to her.

"Cross yourselves! It is surely
Her Johnny come back from the
      grave:
While he lived, he loved her en-
      tirely.
May God his soul now save!"

Hearing what they are saying,
I, too, start praying.

"The girl is out of her senses!"
Shouts a man with a learned air,
"My eye and my lenses
Know there's nothing there.

"Ghosts are a myth
Of ale-wife and blacksmith.
Clodhoppers! This is treason
Against King Reason!"

Umarłeś! tak, dwa lata!
Weź mię, ja umrę przy tobie,
Nie lubię świata.

"Źle mnie w złych ludzi tłumie,
Płaczę, a oni szydzą;
Mówię, nikt nie rozumie;
Widzę, oni nie widzą!

"Śród dnia przyjdź kiedy . . . To
      może we śnie?
Nie, nie . . . trzymam Ciebie w
      ręku
Gdzie znikasz, gdzie, mój Jasieńku!
Jeszcze wcześnie, jeszcze wcześnie!

"Mój Boże! kur się odzywa,
Zorza błyska w okienku.
Gdzie znikłeś! Ach! stój, Jasieńku!
Ja nieszczęśliwa."

Tak się dziewczyna z kochankiem
      pieści,
Bieży za nim, krzyczy, pada;
Na ten upadek, na głos boleści
Skupia się ludzi gromada.

"Mówcie pacierze! —Krzyczy pros-
      tota—
Tu jego dusza być musi.
Jasio być musi przy swej Karusi,
On ją kochał za żywota!"

I ja to słyszę, i ja tak wierzę,
Płaczę i mówię pacierze.

"Słuchaj, dzieweczko!" —Krzyknie
      śród zgiełku
Starzec i na lud zawoła:
"Ufajcie memu oku i szkiełku,
Nic tu nie widzę dokoła.

"Duchy karczemnej tworem gawie-
      dzi,
W głupstwa wywarzone kuźni.
Dziewczyna duby smalone bredzi,
A gmin rozumowi bluźni."

"Yet the girl loves," I reply diffidently,
"And the people believe reverently:
Faith and love are more discerning
Than lenses or learning.

"You know the dead truths, not the living,
The world of things, not the world of loving.
Where does any miracle start?
Cold eye, look in your heart!"*

"Dziewczyna   czuje—odpowiadam skromnie—
A gawiedź wierzy głęboko;
Czucie i wiara silniej mówi do mnie
Niż mędrca szkiełko i oko.

"Martwe znasz prawdy, nieznane dla ludu,
Widzisz świat w proszku, w każdej gwiazd iskierce;
Nie znasz prawd żywych, nie obaczysz cudu!
Miej serce i patrzaj w serce!"

(1821)

It seems that the old man in "The Romantic" is none other than the rationalist professor, Jan Śniadecki. If the revolution accomplished by Mickiewicz was not an immediate victory of the spirit of Romanticism over that of rationalism, it certainly was a victory in terms of language. Classical poetry had been an exercise by the learned for the learned. Now, servant girls, valets, and people barely able to read suddenly found something close to their hearts and quite understandable without any recourse to learning. Hence the success of *Ballads and Romances* with the lower strata of the population. Mickiewicz took fantastic folk motifs and reworded them into poems, sometimes, though rarely, even imitating the rhythm of a folk song. The mixture of the miraculous and the humorous in these poems makes one think of Ovid. Also present in the *Ballads* is the region of the poet's childhood, that Lithuania of fir forests and clear lakes inhabited by nymphs.

Mickiewicz's second volume, published in 1823, contained two longer works in verse: *Grażyna*, with the subtitle *A Lithuanian Tale*, and Parts Two and Four of *Forefathers' Eve*. Grażyna is a Lithuanian woman's name meaning "graceful." The poem combines a metallic beat of lines and syntactical rigor with a plot and motifs dear to the Romantics: night, the glimmer of armor, a cloudy sky, a moon, the gates of a castle, etc. As in many of his other early writings, Mickiewicz situates the action in his native province. The setting for *Grażyna* is the castle of Nowogródek; the time, the end of the fourteenth century, i.e., the Middle Ages. The Lithuanian prince, Litawor, has concluded a pact with the Teutonic Knights, pledging to fight with them against the Grand Duke of Lithuania, against whom he bears a grudge. Grażyna, his wife, learns of her husband's deed, and while he is asleep, she puts on his armor. Disguised as the prince,

* Translated by W. H. Auden.

POEZYE

ADAMA MICKIEWICZA.

TOM DRUGI.

W I L N O.

DRUKIEM JÓZEFA ZAWADZKIEGO.

1 8 2 3.

The title page of Adam Mickiewicz's second volume, *Poems*, 1823.

she leads his warriors against the Teutonic Knights. Grażyna dies from a wound received on the battlefield, but the Teutonic Knights are defeated. Her husband, regretting his action, commits suicide by leaping into the funeral pyre which consumes Grażyna's body. The figure of a heroic woman fascinated the public (for instance, in the romances of the eighteenth-century French writer Florian); she also appeared in Mickiewicz's *Ballads* and other early samples of his talent. This is a nonerotic heroine—a wife, a commander.

To prepare himself for the writing of *Grażyna*, Mickiewicz studied old chronicles, but, in fact, he endowed the historical details with a meaning quite alien to the Middle Ages; thus, *Grażyna* can be called a poem decrying collaboration with the enemy. As for the suicide of the prince, it is just a Romantic device. Let us add here that precisely at the time he was working on *Grażyna*, Mickiewicz started to translate Byron's *Giaour*.

Another longer poem contained in the 1823 volume is the opening part of *Forefathers' Eve* (*Dziady*). Completed much later, or rather

never, since he himself looked at it as a kind of "work in progress,"
it is Mickiewicz's major theatrical achievement. It is also the most
typical theatrical work of Polish Romanticism. Its structure, of fragments joined together by a kind of dream logic, makes it difficult
for a foreigner to grasp the meaning of the sequence. Therefore, let
us explain that in Kowno and Wilno Mickiewicz wrote only a sketch
of Part One and all of Parts Two and Four, which were published in
his volume of 1823. Later on, in Dresden, he wrote Part Three,
which comes *after* Parts Two and Four. Thus, the whole drama in
verse can be basically divided into the so-called *Wilno Forefathers'
Eve* and the *Dresden Forefathers' Eve*. Only a man of extraordinary
perspicacity could have sought the revitalization of drama in a return
to the sacred spectacles of the past, still preserved in folklore. In
Mickiewicz's lifetime, peasants in the Grand Duchy of Lithuania
still gathered on All Souls' Day in remote chapels to celebrate the
pagan rite of calling on the dead and offering them food. Usually,
an elder presided or even a local priest who connived with their centuries-old customs. It was this folk ritual, known as *dziady*, that
Mickiewicz chose for the framework of his dramatic poem. Thus,
in Part Two we see peasants at night reciting incantations and encountering ghosts. The first to appear are "light" spirits—two very
rococo cherubs who cannot enter heaven because they were too happy
on earth. They ask for a mustard seed, and, before leaving the folk
gathered in the chapel, they recite the following admonition:

> For hear and weigh it well
> That according to the divine order
> He who has never tasted bitterness
> Will never taste sweetness in heaven.

> Bo słuchajcie i zważcie u siebie,
> Że według Bożego rozkazu:
> Kto nie doznał goryczy ni razu,
> Ten nie dozna słodyczy w niebie.

A "heavy" spirit enters next, a version of Tantalus adapted to the
peasant imagination, namely, the ghost of a bad landlord. He is
surrounded by predatory birds that snatch away any bit of food
offered him. Since he maltreated his serfs, no one among the living
can help him, and the predatory birds are the souls of those he once
tortured:

> Yes, I have to endure pain century after century;
> The divine sentence is just,
> For to him who has never been humane
> No human can bring any help.

Tak muszę dręczyć się wiek wiekiem,
Sprawiedliwe zrządzenia Boże!
Bo kto nie był ni razu człowiekiem,
Temu człowiek nic nie pomoże.

The third spirit belongs to an intermediate category "of those who lived neither for man, nor for the world": a young shepherdess, again from a rococo pastoral, who, being too proud, has rejected amorous offers from the lads and now does not want any food offered at the rite. She asks only that young peasants seize her by the hands and draw her to the earth, but in her phantom state she cannot be reached:

> So hear and weigh it well
> That according to the divine order
> He who has never touched earth
> Never will enter heaven.

> Bo słuchajcie i zważcie u siebie,
> Że według Bożego rozkazu:
> Kto nie dotknął ziemi ni razu,
> Ten nigdy nie może być w niebie.

Thus, the lesson of the scenes is drawn partly from folk wisdom and partly from the philosophy of the Enlightenment, while the division of spirits into categories carries an allusion, perhaps, to Pope's *Rape of the Lock*. The last spirit to appear (and he is uninvited) is the ghost of a romantic young man (Werther after his suicide?). He does not speak at all and only stares silently at one of the girls in the crowd. This figure provides a link between the rite in the chapel and the next part of the drama, to which the ceremony is a kind of overture. And, indeed, the construction of Part Two is operatic, with choruses of peasants, arias of spirits, duets, and recitatives. Its basic rhythm is a trochaic tetrameter, divided by a caesura into two equal parts. As a dramatic work permeated by an indefinable mood it is the first in Polish literature.

The next part (Part Four) relies even more upon the creation of a certain atmosphere. It is evening. A parish priest sits alone with his children (he is a Greek Catholic priest and a widower). He receives a visit from a bizarre stranger, a young man whose disjointed talk tempts the priest to consider him either a madman or a ghost. After some time, the priest recognizes him as his former pupil, Gustaw. Part Four really consists of nothing but Gustaw's monologue, spoken as if from beyond the grave, the story of unhappy love told by a creature who might belong just as well to the living as to the dead. Gustaw's story is a judgment pronounced over his own soul: how he discovered "villainous books"—sentimental literature inclining him to search for ideal love; how he encountered *her;* how he was rejected because she preferred worldly riches. The whole speech is punctuated by a clock striking first the hour of love, then the hour of despair, and, finally, the hour of warning. At the second stroke, Gustaw stabs himself but does not fall. At the third, he disappears. Nonsensical as it seems in résumé, Part Four is full of powerful poetic and dramatic effects. Its power resides in what has been called an "objective lyricism," the ability, so typical of Mickiewicz, to embody outbursts of passion in tangible images. We have to do here with a realistic diary of the heart and, at the same time, a pronounced manifesto of individualism as a revolutionary force struggling against a social order that makes love dependent upon class divisions. Since Gustaw's monologue is based upon a flow of free associations justified by his presumed madness, what results, in fact, is a display of expressionistic technique, offering great possibilities to modern stage directors.

Before we pass on to the last part of *Forefathers' Eve* (written in Dresden) some biographical information is in order. In 1823, the czarist authorities clamped down upon the youth movements in Lithuania. This coincided with Alexander I's retreat from his liberal policy, but it was also an action directed against the superintendent of the Wilno school system, Prince Adam Czartoryski, by his enemies, chief of whom was the senator Novosiltsov. Not only were several high school students (aged twelve to sixteen) arrested and sent to Russia for life as common soldiers, but also the Philomaths were detected (the police owed some measure of their success to a report from a spy in Frankfurt on the Main, who was able to learn about student organizations in Wilno because they maintained ties with similar groups in Germany). In October of 1823, Mickiewicz, like his friends, was arrested and detained for about half a year in a monastery of the Basilian Fathers that had been converted into a prison. The sentences meted out at the trial were rather mild. Mickiewicz was forbidden to live in Lithuania or in any of the so-called "western guberniyas." He was to place himself at the disposal of the authorities in Russia, where he would be given a teaching position. In November 1824 he arrived in St. Petersburg; and thus began what, for the Polish poet, proved to be a triumphant exile. Since the Philomaths had also maintained contacts with organizations in Russia, he was greeted by the young Russian intelligentsia as one of "theirs." Moreover, his Freemasonic connections were of help. It is possible that he entered Freemasonry in Russia; in any case, it was there that he became acquainted with the writings of an eighteenth-century author popular among Russian Freemasons, Louis Claude Saint-Martin, whose influence is felt in many of the poet's works.

When Mickiewicz arrived in Russia, he was already famous in literary circles, and if we add that he was a man of simple manners, of good intellectual training, with a gift for improvisation (in French, as his Russian was weak), a talent highly appreciated then, it should not be surprising that his Russian hosts found him an extremely appealing figure. His best friends in St. Petersburg were Kondraty Ryleyev and Alexander Beztuzhev, and it is possible that had he stayed in St. Petersburg, he might have shared the fate of those Decembrist leaders. But he received a position at a *lycée* in Odessa, and in the winter of 1824/1825 set out for the south of Russia, making the whole cross-country trek in post sledges. Odessa was a gay port, a center of the wheat trade, with an international colony, Italian operas, balls, and social gatherings. The teaching job was purely nominal, and Mickiewicz lived, as he said himself, "like a pasha," surrounded by women, one of whom in particular, Karolina Sobański, appears in his poetry. Karolina (nee Rzewuski), sister of the Polish writer Henryk Rzewuski, was also the mistress of General Witt, chief military commander in southern Russia (a son of famous Sofia Potocki from her first marriage). She was involved with the Russian secret service, and it seems that her report on the good behavior of her lover, Mickiewicz, was not without a positive effect on his being granted a passport for travel abroad a few years later. An excursion to the Crimea in the company of General Witt and Mrs. Sobański led Mickiewicz to write his famous *Crimean Sonnets* (*Sonety krymskie*), published in Moscow in 1826 and soon translated into Russian. The work was to have assiduous translators in Russia throughout the nineteenth century and into the twentieth. The sonnet as a literary form was revived by German Romantics, but Mickiewicz also looked to Petrarch for his model. In Odessa, he wrote a cycle of twenty-two love sonnets, to which *Crimean Sonnets* proper is the sequel. Taken together, the love sonnets and the *Crimean Sonnets* form a diary of internal experience expressed through what we might call today "objective correlatives." If Mickiewicz, in many respects, is a poet on the border line of Classicism and Romanticism, here he transcends those classifications thanks to the calm limpidity of his style and a complete domination of his material. The love sonnets retrace his ideal love for Maryla, pass to sensuous loves in Odessa (having nothing of the ethereal quality connected with the Romantic treatment of love), and end with a bitter rejection of his transitory ties with women. The *Crimean Sonnets* can be seen as a strongly symbolical presentation of the poet's feelings through the corresponding landscapes. He uses two basic symbols: the sea—as an expanse of life, a distance, travel to an unknown destination, storms of passion; and the mountain—as a place above the daily turmoil of mortals, as elevation and elation. Mickiewicz was justly called a "poet of transformations," and the rush to reach forward, beyond the given moment, to a new stage of internal development is already visible in the whole sonnet cycle. Daring metaphors go together with a manly vigor of lines. When describing a gallop, he says:

> As in a broken mirror, so in my torrid eye
> Pass phantoms of woods, valleys, and rocks

> Jak w rozbitym źwierciedle, tak w mym spiekłym oku
> Snują się mary lasów i dolin, i głazów.
>> ("Bajdary")

Or he says, speaking of the sea:

> The light in its rustling plays as in the eye of a tiger

> W jego szumach gra światło jak w oczach tygrysa.
>> ("Ałushta in Daytime" ["Ałuszta w dzień"])

Looking down on the sea from a mountain he sees "fleets and flocks of swans" and an "army of whales," i.e., breakers:

> A na głębinie fala lekko się kołysa
> I kąpią się w niej floty i stada łabędzi
>> ("Ałushta in Daytime")

> Jak wojsko wielorybów zalegając brzegi.
>> ("Ajudah")

The whole Crimean peninsula becomes for him a boat, and he apostrophizes its highest mountain peak:

> O mast of the Crimean boat, Great Chatyr Dagh!

> Maszcie krymskiego statku, wielki Chatyrdahu!
>> ("Chatyrdah")

Through references to Islamic poetry he introduces local, oriental color into the *Crimean Sonnets*, and his use of many Turkish words not found in Polish dictionaries aroused the ire of the Warsaw classicists. Thus, Mickiewicz paid tribute to the fashion for oriental motifs in literature, as did Goethe and Byron, not to mention Delacroix in painting. The Orient is very much present in his sonnets on the ruins of the Moslem past in Crimea, where the tomb appears as an important symbol of the transience of human passions, and the image of night, when

> the air is full of scent, that music of flowers

> Powietrze tchnące wonią, tą muzyką kwiatów,
>> ("Ałushta at Night" ["Ałuszta w nocy"])

brings to mind Arabic poetic motifs of sensuous contemplation.

The *Crimean Sonnets*, like the poems written later on in Rome and Lausanne, has been justly ranked among the highest achievements in Polish lyricism.

Tranferred by order of the authorities to Moscow, Mickiewicz arrived there in the beginning of 1826 at a time when a mood of depression, the aftermath of the Decembrist revolt, prevailed among the intelligentsia. He lived amid the society of literary salons, where he made new friendships—particularly with Baratynsky; Pogodin; the *Lubomudry* ("friends of wisdom") group: Venevitinov, Khomyakov, Ivan Kireyevsky; with Serge Sobolevsky, a close friend of Pushkin's; and at last with Pushkin himself when he came to Moscow in the fall of that year. This meeting marks a separate chapter both in Polish and in Russian literature, as the two poets were to allude to each other, later in their respective works. Among Mickiewicz's friends, we should also mention Caroline Jaenisch, a young poetess. She was the first to translate his poems (as well as Pushkin's) into German, and she came to occupy an honorable position in Russian poetry under the name of Pavlova after she married the novelist Pavlov.

In 1828, Mickiewicz published a long poem, *Konrad Wallenrod*, in St. Petersburg. Completely different from his sonnets and the most "Byronic" of his works, it is a tale in verse with a subject presumably taken, as in *Grażyna*, from old Lithuanian chronicles. An American reading this tale would inevitably think of romantic stories about Indians brought up in a white settlement but who, responding to the call of the wild, return to their tribes to take vengeance upon the white man. Konrad, the hero, born a pagan Lithuanian, has been raised a Christian by some Teutonic Knights who captured him during one of their raids on Lithuania. By dint of valor, he has climbed to the top of the hierarchy of the Order and has been elected the Grand Master and Commander-in-Chief. But one day an old Lithuanian minstrel is permitted to entertain the Knights. His singing, in a language incomprehensible to the others, arouses the hero's awareness of his origins. To avenge the misfortune suffered by his native country at the hands of the Order, he conducts a military expedition in such a way that the Teutonic troops suffer utter disaster. In addition, the poem was supplied with a motto from Machiavelli that counseled being a fox and a lion at the same time. Although the political content was evident to every Polish reader, it was apparently not so clear to the Petersburg censorship because the work was passed. Novosiltsov, however, read it in Warsaw and sent in an alarm report containing an analysis that could have been envied by any literary critic. But because the chief of the political police, Beckendorff, detested Novosiltsov, the second edition of *Konrad*

Wallenrod appeared in 1829—with some prefatory remarks, it is true, in which Mickiewicz paid homage to the "father of the peoples," Czar Nicholas I. The most committed politically of all Mickiewicz's poems, *Konrad Wallenrod* exerted strong influence upon the young generation, although many in the name of Christian ethics objected to it for glorifying treason.

A second edition of Mickiewicz's poems, published in St. Petersburg in 1829, bore an introduction entitled "On Warsaw Critics and Reviewers," where, with unrestrained irony, the leader of the victorious Romantic trend crushed his opponents in the Warsaw periodicals "of good taste."

Mickiewicz's efforts to obtain a passport for travel, avowedly for a health cure, finally succeeded with the help of several friends. In the spring of 1829, he set sail from Kronstadt just in time to avoid the revocation of his passport which was in the offing. From Russia he brought another type of poem, a token of his interest in Arabic poets, whom he read in translation. *Faris* (written in Petersburg in 1828 and published in 1829) is modeled upon the "kasida" (a lyrical form with panegyrical content). It praises a lonely Bedouin rider rushing intrepidly through the desert. An anecdote would have it that the idea came to Mickiewicz while speeding through Petersburg streets in a troika. The mad movement forward has, of course, a symbolic meaning and expresses a striving toward a mystical union with divinity. The last two lines are:

> As the bee sinking her sting buries her heart with it,
> So I have sunk first my thought, then my soul in heaven!

> Jak pszczoła topiąc żądło i serce z nim grzebie,
> Tak ja za myślą duszę utopiłem w niebie!

While traveling through Germany with a friend, Edward Odyniec (a minor poet), Mickiewicz paid his respects to Goethe in Weimar, where he was received cordially; then, crossing the Alps, he went to Rome. There he found an international society not unlike Moscow's; even some of his Russian friends were on hand—the Princess Volkonsky and Sobolevsky, also Poles (among whom a young, pure girl, Henrietta Eve Ankwicz, seemed to be his platonic love), and some Americans like James Fenimore Cooper, with whom he liked to ride in the Roman suburbs. The period of his sojourn in Rome was marked by a return of intense and even devout religious feelings, and the profundity of the so-called "Roman lyrics" is somewhat reminiscent of the English metaphysical poets. Like the poems written not long after he left Rome, they go to the core of Mickiewicz's internal contradictions: a descendant of the Enlightenment, the poet turns violently against the pride of Reason and opposes to it the humility of Faith. Mickiewicz undoubtedly was by temperament an intuitionist, and not by chance was he the first to introduce Emerson to the Parisian public. But, despite his belief in the truth of the heart, a conflict between his personal pride and the humility required by religious orthodoxy was no less acute, and his religious lyrics bear traces of a constant tension between those two poles.

The news of the outbreak of the insurrection in Warsaw reached Mickiewicz in Rome, but he lingered quite a long time before he decided to join his compatriots; his travel expenses were paid in part by the Russian friend, Sobolevsky. For some reasons that are unclear, instead of going straight to Poland, he went to Paris—perhaps carrying a message from Italian *Carbonari* to French radicals. Deeply disillusioned by French politicians, he traveled across Germany to the Prussian-occupied part of Poland near the border guarded by Russian troops. By then it was the middle of August 1831; the Poles had clearly lost the war, and he could not, or did not want to, reach Warsaw. A love affair with a bluestocking (Konstancja Łubieński, who later on pestered him with letters asking him to marry her), receptions, and hunting parties at the moment when Poland was suffering a military defeat seemed to remain with Mickiewicz as a permanent font of remorse. That very remorse, perhaps, released a tremendous force of inspiration when he landed in Dresden, then full of Polish refugees. Indeed, the period between 1832 and 1834 was one of incredible productivity for Mickiewicz. It was in Dresden that he wrote the continuation of *Forefathers' Eve* (Part Three). The drama thus completed (though Mickiewicz planned to write other parts) can be called a morality play revived as well as a Promethean poem. It is the story of a man surrounded by supernatural powers and struggling for his salvation. At the same time, through a strong autobiographical element and its loose, fragmentary character, it is a typically Romantic work. In the preceding parts we saw Gustaw with his unhappy love; here we find him in a czarist prison, an alter ego of Mickiewicz during his half-year imprisonment in Wilno. There comes a night when the prisoner is transformed from a man preoccupied with his personal problems into a man dedicated to the cause of his nation and of humanity. To mark it, he even changes his name to Konrad—Mickiewicz had given the name before to his Lithuanian hero. Politics is introduced in a series of realistically treated scenes, making any application of a formula to such a work of disparate techniques extremely difficult. The problem of the prisoner, Konrad, is that of human suffering, and of God's permitting it. If God is indifferent while he, Konrad, is not, it means that he is morally superior to God. His monologue of defiance addressed to God in magnificent verse is known in Polish literature as "the Great Improvisation." Prompted by evil spirits, he is ready to insult God: "You are not the father of the world but a. . . ." He is saved from pronouncing "czar" by the intervention of good spirits. He undergoes one more transformation: from proud rebel into humble fighter for the collective cause, but not in revolt against Providence—a foreshadowing of Mickiewicz's future activity as a Christian Socialist. As befits a morality play, earth, heaven, and hell are present on the stage. Good is represented by the prisoner's guardian angel, by choruses of night spirits on the right side, by angels, by a humble Roman Catholic priest (Father Peter), by an innocent girl (Eve), by Polish and Russian revolutionary youth; while evil is personified by devils, night spirits on the left side, czarist officials, Senator Novosiltsov in person, and Polish "good society"—collaborationists and opportunists. This is, in a sense, also a poem of the night. In dreams, the veil hiding a deeper, supernatural reality is lifted and man enters into contact with mysterious powers. The main characters—Konrad, Father Peter, Eve—live through their most intense experiences in visions. Into Father Peter's vision, Mickiewicz inserts a messianic prophecy that holds out the hope of a great man who will lead Poland and humanity toward bright destinies. Even a cabalistic cipher, to designate him— forty-four, an equivalent of the Hebrew letters *DM*—is introduced. (Does it stand for Adam, for Mickiewicz himself? We do not know, and the author confessed that he had known only at the time of writing.) Whatever its meaning, it is an obvious reflection of eighteenth-century Illuminism and cabalism in a new Romantic setting. Written extremely fast—*Forefathers' Eve*, Part Three, sometimes sounds as if it had been dictated to a medium—and published in Paris in the same year as it was composed (1832), it remained a splendid dramatic poem until 1901, as only modern stage directors dared to present it on the stage. Mickiewicz, in his sixteenth lecture of 1843 at the Collège de France, which was to become a kind of gospel for Polish theater directors of the twentieth century, spoke of the essence of the Slavic theater of the future as an interplay of the natural and the supernatural; thus, the Slavic drama, in his intention, was to be an heir to Greek religious tragedy and the medieval religious theater. As to staging, he anticipated a flowering of architecture, painting, and music that would make possible the presentation of such dramas. In his own time, he saw only one building that seemed suitable for the purpose: the Olympic Circus in Paris. *Forefathers' Eve* was first introduced into the repertoire of the Polish theater by the reformer Stanisław Wyspiański (1869–1907). Afterward it became a kind of national sacred play, occasionally forbidden by censorship because of its emotional impact upon the audience. The most complex and rich among the products of Romanticism, combining dreams with brutal, realistic satire, it has been looked upon as the highest test of skill for theater directors.

When *Forefathers' Eve* appeared in print, it was accompanied by a long descriptive poem entitled *Digression* (*Ustęp*), written sometime before Part Three and summing up Mickiewicz's Russian experiences. Logically, it is connected with the drama as a picture of the country to which Gustaw-Konrad (Mickiewicz) is taken after his imprisonment in Wilno, and it follows Mickiewicz's itinerary, as the titles of the chapters indicate—"The Road to Russia," "The Outskirts of the Capital," "Petersburg," "The Monument to Peter the Great," "Military Review," and "The Day Before the St. Petersburg Flood of 1824." Here again, as so often in Mickiewicz, we move from an ultra-Romantic drama to a sharp, biting classical verse which could have been envied by the eighteenth-century satirists. The whole poem portrays czarist Russia as a huge prison, but is full of pity for the oppressed Russian nation and meditates upon the future of this country frozen in a despotic system. The imagery is that of winter. Even the inhabitants of that snow-covered land are depicted as bearing in themselves souls like pupae awaiting the spring:

> But when the sun of freedom will shine,
> What insect will fly out from that envelope?
> Will it be a bright butterfly soaring over the earth,
> Or a moth, dirty tribe of the night?

> Ale gdy słońce wolności zaświeci,
> Jakiż z powłoki tej owad wyleci?
> Czy motyl jasny wzniesie się nad ziemię,
> Czy ćma wypadnie, brudne nocy plemię?

The city of St. Petersburg stands as a symbol of despotism for Mickiewicz. Built by order of the czar in a most unsuitable place, it rests on the bones of thousands of serfs who perished during the construction. The slow, organic growth of Western European cities is compared with that urban monument to the sheer will of one man. In the chapter entitled "The Monument to Peter the Great," Mickiewicz shows two poets under the statue: one is himself; the other, Pushkin. Into the Russian's mouth he puts a long speech similar in content to the Pole's (his own) meditation. The Russian poet compares the czar on his horse to a waterfall suddenly frozen solid and suspended over a precipice:

> But when the sun of freedom will throw its rays
> And the western wind will warm these states,
> What will happen to the waterfall of tyranny?

Lecz skoro słońce swobody zabłyśnie
I wiatr zachodni ogrzeje te państwa,
I cóż się stanie z kaskadą tyraństwa?

The chapter called "Military Review" expresses the horror of army pageants in St. Petersburg, which last for hours and leave in their wake frozen bodies of soldiers on the enormous, empty squares of the capital. The last chapter, on the flood, bears a second title: "Oleszkiewicz." The name refers to a friend of the Polish poet, a painter, a Freemason, and a mystic who introduced him to the works of Saint-Martin and to the cabala; in the poem, Oleszkiewicz prophesies the doom of the czarist empire, that kingdom of evil incarnate. The great flood with its unleashing of elemental forces brings to completion, thus, the symbol of winter present throughout the poem. For Russia, spring will be a calamity, a time of immense suffering. The *Digression* can be called a summation of Polish attitudes toward Russia in the nineteenth century, and Joseph Conrad, who of course had read that poem, seems to repeat its contents line for line in some of his writings, especially in *Under Western Eyes*. Pushkin was prompted by it to write a reply to Mickiewicz, and the outcome was his masterpiece, *The Bronze Horseman*, set just at the time of the St. Petersburg flood and centered around the statue of Peter the Great. Pushkin attempted to convey his love for the city and his ambivalence—his feelings of fascination and fear—toward Peter as the epitome of a ruler. The dialogue between the two poets was probably also provoked by the poem placed at the very end of *Forefathers' Eve*, after the *Digression*, and entitled "To My Muscovite Friends." In it, Mickiewicz deplores the fate of the Decembrists—Ryleyev executed, Beztuzhev condemned to hard labor—and castigates those who dishonor themselves by accepting "honorary" distinctions and high positions from the czar or by singing his triumphs with mercenary pens:

> Whoever of you will raise a complaint, for me his complaint
> Will be like the barking of a dog, so accustomed
> To wearing his collar long and patiently,
> That he is ready to bite the hand which tears at it.

> Kto z was podniesie skargę, dla mnie jego skarga
> Będzie jak psa szczekanie, który tak się wdroży
> Do cierpliwie i długo noszonej obroży,
> Że w końcu gotów kąsać—rękę, co ją targa.

Yet Mickiewicz stressed perfect frankness in his relations with Russian literati—"crawling in silence like a snake," he deluded the despot, but for his Russian friends he always had a "dovelike simplicity."

Forefathers' Eve in the shape we know it today appeared in Paris in 1832, and at the end of the same year we see Mickiewicz himself in Paris, deeply involved in the political quarrels and intrigues of the Great Emigration. The *émigrés* were split into two factions: democratic, and conservative monarchist. Those on the left side of the spectrum were represented, first of all, by Joachim Lelewel, an eminent historian, an ex-professor at the University of Wilno, whom Mickiewicz as a student once honored with a poem; and Maurycy Mochnacki, the leading literary critic of Romanticism, author of the book *On Polish Literature of the Nineteenth Century* (*O literaturze polskiej wieku dziewiętnastego*, 1830). Mochnacki was the first in exile to explain the failure of the Polish revolution by the reluctance of propertied classes to call all the people to arms. On the right, the conservatives rallied around Hôtel Lambert, the residence of Prince Adam Czartoryski, onetime foreign minister of Alexander I and later superintendent of the Wilno school district. Mickiewicz was closer to the democrats, but he took no sides. He maintained: "The Pole is a natural democrat and republican." Besides many articles, he wrote *The Books of the Polish Nation and of the Polish Pilgrims* (*Księgi narodu polskiego i pielgrzymstwa polskiego*) in 1832, and sent it immediately to the printer. A strong conviction that truth is accessible not to the wise men of this world but to simple-souled, humble people endowed with intuition inclined him to address the Polish exiles in as simple a style as possible. The form of the work copies the gospel parables and their Polish imitations by Skarga. It is also possible that Saint-Martin's rhythmically modulated sentences influenced him. As to its contents, *The Books* develops the messianic idea put forward in *Forefathers' Eve*. Poland was to redeem the nations through her suffering, and the mission of the Polish pilgrims was to announce to the materialistic Western nations a new world spiritually transformed. Rural, patriarchal Poland is contrasted to the West, contaminated by the diabolical forces of money, much as Russian Slavophiles opposed their country to the West. Mickiewicz talks with the authority of a prophet. He, as a Pole, has been charged to warn Frenchmen and Englishmen of a despotism that will subjugate all Europe if it is connived with and tolerated in one part of Europe:

. . . and you, tradesmen and merchants of two nations, avid for gold and paper with the value of gold, you used to send money for the crushing of freedom, but indeed, the days will come when you will lick your gold and masticate your paper and nobody will send you bread and water.

In another passage:

And to the Frenchman and the Englishman the Pole says: If you, children of freedom, do not follow me, then God will reject your tribe and will rouse defenders of freedom out of stones, that is, out of the Muscovites and the Asiatics.

The Books encountered the hostility of both the Catholic clergy and the Polish democrats, for whom it was too mystical. It found a considerable response, though, when translated into foreign languages. The French writer Lamennais, a Catholic priest whose socialistic-religious ideas had led to a clash with the Vatican, and who was a close friend of Mickiewicz's, was clearly indebted to *The Books* in his *Paroles d'un croyant*.

As we said, the years 1832–1834 were years of creative vigor for Mickiewicz. Notwithstanding the turmoil of journalistic chores (being the editor of a periodical, the *Polish Pilgrim*), he wrote during this time a work of pure poetry. *Pan Tadeusz* had very little to do with the ideological conflicts of the day. Indeed, when starting that long poem, he treated it as an island to which he could escape, "closing the door on Europe's noises." According to his original intention, it was to be a modest idyll somewhat in the genre of Goethe's *Hermann und Dorothea*. Gradually, it grew into an imposing whole, divided into twelve books, where the Polish Alexandrine (thirteen-syllable couplets) was put to a use which Mickiewicz's eighteenth-century masters would never have suspected. *Pan Tadeusz* is something unique in world literature, and the problem of how to classify it has remained the crux of a constant quarrel among scholars. Is it a "novel in verse"? an epos? a fairy tale? In it Mickiewicz returned to the country of his childhood and adolescence—Lithuania of 1811/1812. Because the world he was describing was gone forever, he could achieve a perfect distance, visible in the kind of humor which permeates the lines. Indeed, the painting of a provincial microcosm was an extremely attractive undertaking for an exile in Paris who looked for solace in "the remembrance of things past." The American scholar, Professor George R. Noyes, was probably close to the truth when he spoke of the "childish freshness" with which Mickiewicz endowed his landscapes and his people—a childish freshness and amazement of the kind best expressed in English in some lines of the British metaphysical poet, Thomas Traherne. A fragment of a letter written much later by Mickiewicz (at the end of his life, when he was in Turkey) also provides a clue to his ability to see beauty in most trivial things:

I have heard that in Smyrna there is a supposed "Grotto of Homer" but I am not curious! I looked at something else. A pile of manure and rubbish was lying there, all the remnants together: manure, trash, slops, bones, broken pots, half a sole of an old slipper, some feathers—this I liked! Long did I stand there because it was just like the front yard of an inn in Poland!

Translated into prose, *Pan Tadeusz* often sounds like a Walter Scott novel. In verse, the amount of faithfully reproduced details from everyday life takes one by surprise because it seems hardly credible that these can be the material of poetry. Even involved lawsuits are true to what we know of the juridical quarrels of the period. Yet *Pan Tadeusz* does not tell the story of a "problematic hero" in conflict with his surroundings and, for that reason, is a long way from nineteenth-century novels. In fact all of its characters are mediocre, average people immersed in their society and not suffering from alienation. Such perfect harmony between the characters and the world they are destined to live in is an essential trait of the ancient epic, and this is why *Pan Tadeusz* has been called "the last epos" in world literature. Like the *Iliad* and *Jerusalem Delivered*, which begin with an invocation addressed to the Deity, *Pan Tadeusz* begins with an invocation to Lithuania, whose strongly personified nature in all its mornings, sunsets, storms, and serene skies gives to small human affairs a kind of benevolent blessing. On the other hand, there is much of the mock-heroic epic in *Pan Tadeusz*; the poet's eighteenth-century training comes out in an inclination to literary parody—where Homeric lines are applied to a skirmish between squires and Russian soldiers or a magnificent centerpiece is described in the terms Homer used for Achilles' shield. At the same time, some books of the poem are just idylls, revealing Mickiewicz, in addition, as an inheritor of the whole bucolic trend that started with Rej. But the modern reader is also justified if he plunges into *Pan Tadeusz* as into a fairy tale, with its aura of remoteness and its simplified psychological portraits. For those who are acquainted with Polish literature of the Enlightenment, *Pan Tadeusz* appears to owe a good deal to eighteenth-century comedy; some characters act as if they came straight from the plays of Zabłocki or Niemcewicz. In *Pan Tadeusz* Mickiewicz, a Romantic poet, returned to his classical beginnings but with infinitely greater skill. Only one figure can be regarded as slightly "Byronic"—Father Robak, a monk with a tragic past. Otherwise, the "sentimentalists" such as the Count and Telimena, are gently ridiculed. Laurence Sterne, so appreciated by Mickiewicz and his friends when they were students, even lends a few devices, and the "hobbies" of some of the characters in *Pan Tadeusz* are no less strange than Uncle Toby's in *Tristram Shandy*. As in Sterne, certain lines referring to those hobbies create leitmotifs and recur with the same rhymes every time a given person enters the action.

Pan Tadeusz is also a vast panorama of a gentry society at the moment it is living through its last days. One of Mickiewicz's contemporaries, Stanisław Worcell, leader of the most radical Polish *émigrés* (*Gromady Ludu Polskiego*), described it as "a tombstone laid by the hand of a genius upon our Old Poland." The richness of human types, taken as they are, without any bile or moralizing, so conquers our attention that we forget about the limited field of observation. A manor, a village of gentry farmers, a half-ruined aristocratic castle quite suffice while peasants move somewhere far in the background and tradesmen appear only in the person of wise Jankiel, a Jewish innkeeper famous for his skill in playing the dulcimer. The element of politics is not lacking, for the action takes place on the eve of the Napoleonic expedition against Moscow and is completed by it. But it is politics of a not very complex sort. At the end of the poem the young generation dons the uniform of the Polish Napoleonic army and in response to the spirit of the day proclaims the peasant a free citizen.

Pan Tadeusz, after its appearance, was not highly praised by those simple people whom Mickiewicz desired for his readers. The Polish exiles found its tone not elevated enough, and no wonder, if they compared it with a gospel-like tract, *The Books of the Polish Nation*, by the same author. A handful of writers saw it as a masterpiece, although Mickiewicz himself did not. After having put the last touches to the poem, he said: "I hope I will never again use my pen for trifles." But *Pan Tadeusz* gradually won recognition as the highest achievement in all Polish literature for having transformed into poetry what seemed by its very nature to resist any such attempt. In it, Mickiewicz's whole literary training culminates in an effortless conciseness where every word finds its proper place as if predestined throughout the many centuries of the history of the Polish language.

After *Pan Tadeusz*, Mickiewicz wrote nothing more in verse, except for a few lyrical poems of rare perfection. His silence has been variously interpreted. A teacher, a prophet, a publicist, an organizer, he chose the life of action as if to confirm what he had once said, paraphrasing German mystics: that it is more difficult to live honestly through one day than to write a book. He was devoured by a need for shaping history directly, and poetry did not seem to him powerful enough; it lost out in a struggle with reality. Some scholars explain his silence by suggesting that he simply ran out of talent. Perhaps, living in France where the literary scene was rapidly changing, where the novel was growing—and nothing is more characteristic of the fate of Polish literature than that Mickiewicz, unlike Pushkin, did not attempt to write prose fiction—he realized that to continue in his accustomed style was impossible. He said once himself that he saw a promised land of future poetry, but he would never enter it.

He settled down in his life as an exile. His books were smuggled into Poland, but even the mention of his name was forbidden by censorship. He married a young girl whom he had known in Moscow as a teen-ager, Celina Szymanowski, brought up several children in that far from happy marriage, taught Latin literature with success at the College of Lausanne, and held the first chair of Slavic literatures at the Collège de France in Paris during the years 1840–1844. His courses in Slavic literatures given there fill several large volumes, and, though obsolete today from the point of view of modern scholarship, they are full of daring insights. In his courses, he paid tribute to his Russian friends, the writers, especially to Pushkin. He spoke to the Paris public on an unknown American writer, Ralph Waldo Emerson, and translated some of his essays. The similarity between the views of the two men is sometimes striking. But practically all his life, Mickiewicz longed for a "providential man" matching Napoleon. Perhaps at times he assigned such a prophetic role to himself; for a while, when he was a professor in Paris, he became a true believer in a certain Andrzej Towiański, the founder of a religious sect. In Towiański's teachings it is not difficult to uncover the heritage of eighteenth-century mystical lodges; and since Mickiewicz, thanks to Saint-Martin, was imbued with the same spirit, he was ready to recognize in Towiański's magnetic personality his spiritual master. He carried his enthusiasm to the classroom, transforming his university chair into a pulpit for preaching the new politico-religious creed, thereby driving the French Government to despair, and as a consequence he was finally deprived of his position. The poetry after *Pan Tadeusz*, mentioned above, is limited to exquisite, gnomic poems, extremely short and concise, just "thoughts" adapted from the German mystics, Jakob Boehme and Angelus Silesius, and from Saint-Martin. When in Lausanne, he wrote a few verses, the so-called "Lausanne lyrics," untranslatable masterpieces of metaphysical meditation. In Polish literature they are examples of that pure poetry which verges on silence.

The year 1848 for Mickiewicz marked a passage into direct political action. He went to Italy and organized a Polish legion there to fight for the liberation of the northern Italians from Austria. His plan was to attract to that nucleus soldiers of Slavic descent from the Austrian army and to pave the way for the breakdown of the Hapsburg Empire by appealing to Slavic nationalism—an idea that materialized at the end of World War I. Mickiewicz himself proclaimed a set of "principles" (*Skład zasad*) for the legion, a sort of political manifesto outlining the system that would underlie the independent Slavic states of the future. A Christian and progressive interpretation of equality, liberty, and fraternity, it declares for example:

Everybody in the nation is a citizen. All citizens are equal before the law and before the administration. . . . To the Jew, our elder brother, esteem and help on his way to eternal good and welfare, and in all matters equal rights. . . . To every family, a plot of land under the care of the community. To every community, common land under the care of the nation.

Equal rights for women were also proclaimed, and a fraternal hand was extended from Poland to brothers Czech and Russ. Certain features of Utopian Socialism are distinguishable in that credo, and although Mickiewicz and his legion were greeted by enthusiastic crowds in Rome, Florence, and other Italian towns, he let himself in for violent attacks from the *émigré* Polish Right, especially after he committed the indiscretion, at his audience with Pope Pius IX, of grabbing the Pontiff by the sleeve and shouting: "Let me tell you that the Holy Spirit resides today under the shirts of the Paris workers." The pan-European revolution of 1848 soon proved a failure; yet the next year, 1849, Mickiewicz was editing an international socialist paper in Paris, *La Tribune des Peuples*, whose contributors included French followers of Fourier and Proudhon, Russian followers of Bakunin, Italian followers of Mazzini, one German, Ewerbeck (a personal friend of Marx and Engels), and some Poles from the democratic Left. The enterprise did not last long, being soon killed by censorship. Mickiewicz, for the next few years, held a modest job as librarian at the Library of the Arsenal. But the Crimean War again drew him into organizational activity. Polish and Cossack legions were being formed in Constantinople, and Mickiewicz left for the Near East in 1855 to aid the cause of struggle against Russia. With his friend Armand Lévy, who under the poet's influence returned to the faith of his Jewish ancestors, Mickiewicz set about organizing a Jewish legion and applied to the Turkish Government for permission to enlist not only Russian Jews (prisoners of war) but also Jews from Palestine. Mickiewicz's strong pro-Jewish feelings throughout his life and his messianic philosophy based upon an analogy between the history of the Jews and that of the Poles led some Jewish scholars to conjecture about the partly Jewish origin of Mickiewicz. His mother's name was that of a Frankist (see pp. 164–166) family, but there are no documents to corroborate such a thesis. His interest in the Bible and the cabala seems to be due mainly to his penchant for eighteenth-century Illuminism, which itself was strongly influenced by Jewish religious writings.

Mickiewicz, while visiting a military camp near Constantinople, contracted cholera and died suddenly in the arms of his faithful Armand Lévy. His body was taken to France, and a few decades later, in 1890, his remains were transported to Poland and buried in the royal crypt of Wawel Castle's cathedral in Kraków.

Mickiewicz is for Poles what Goethe is for Germans and Pushkin for Russians. There is an additional element, that of his biography as pilgrim, leader, and fighter. Thus, if Byron after his death in Greece fired the imagination of the early Romantics (and of Mickiewicz himself), Mickiewicz through his life of service to the Polish cause grew into the embodiment of a "national bard" and a spiritual commander for the generations to come. If the phases of his activity seem bizarre to us today, they were not in the context of an era marked by the most wild *élans* of the European mind. We can, however, admire the soberness that we find at least in his poetry. By virtue of his upbringing he was certainly a man close to the Enlightenment. The poetic discipline he acquired through modeling his early poems on the classics puts him at the opposite pole from such Romantics as Shelley or Musset or Alfred de Vigny. For Poles, Kochanowski's estate "Czarnolas," like Parnassus in Greece, is a metaphor for poetry; after Mickiewicz, Lithuania also became a kind of seat of the Muses. Curiously enough, Poland's greatest poet never set foot in Warsaw or Kraków. He was a posthumous child of the old *Respublica.*

JULIUSZ SŁOWACKI
(1809–1849)

Juliusz Słowacki was born in Krzemieniec, Volhynia, where his father, Euzebiusz Słowacki, was professor of literature in the town's famous *lycée.* Later the family moved to Wilno when the father received the chair of literature at the university there. After his death, the poet's mother married another professor from the University of Wilno, Bécu, a medical doctor; and the only child from her first marriage grew up in the company of two stepsisters. It was an effeminating atmosphere; his mother was a hypersensitive, exalted woman who devoured French novels and was not devoid of some literary talents herself. Young Słowacki was a fragile boy with bad health, brilliant, arrogant, and filled with immeasurable ambitions. An introvert, well-read in Polish, French, and English literature, he was to be a lonely man all his life, the epitome of a melancholy Romantic. He was very young when he received his diploma in law at the University of Wilno. His biography does not lack an unhappy love: for Ludwika Śniadecki, daughter of an eminent professor of chemistry, Jędrzej Śniadecki. A strong-willed and somewhat masculine type of girl, she was in love with a Russian officer, Rimsky-Korsakov; after his death in a battle in the Caucasus, she married a Polish novelist, Czajkowski, a colorful figure who settled in Constantinople, embraced Mohammedanism, and, aided by his wife, became a wizard at diplomatic intrigues. The same Czajkowski

(Sadik Pasha) organized the Polish legion in Turkey in 1855, already mentioned in connection with Mickiewicz. Słowacki's first love is present throughout practically all of his ethereal poetic work, which is somewhat analogous to Shelley's. Besides his unrequited love, the other passion running through Słowacki's life was his desire first to equal, then to compete with, Mickiewicz for the position of "national" poet. During the years 1829–1830 he worked as an employee in the ministry of finance in Warsaw, and his first poems were published after the outbreak of the insurrection against Russia. He made a trip to London as a diplomatic courier for the revolutionary government and after Poland's defeat joined the Great Emigration in Paris. There, in 1832, he published two volumes of poetry, followed by a third in 1833. His works evoked a slighting remark from Mickiewicz —young Słowacki's poems, according to the former, were fine but empty, "a church without God inside." Yet at least one of his early poems does give a measure of Słowacki's talent: "An Hour of Thought" ("Godzina myśli") is the purest example of a melancholy, meditative trend in early Polish Romanticism. It captures the mood of adolescent despair and inability to face life. Through the subdued light of evenings in Wilno and its environs wander the figures of Ludwika and Słowacki's youthful friend, Ludwik Szpicnagel, who took his own life even though a brilliant career awaited him. The poem still retains a certain classical rigor of form, but some presages of Słowacki's future development are visible. His poetry was to move toward an ever greater exuberance of sound and colors, toward what may be termed a revival of the Polish Baroque. Even though it is often difficult to say why, the overwhelming visual sensation of his writings is that of the colorful Polish seventeenth century. Słowacki's life was uneventful, dedicated exclusively to creative work; and when he died at the age of forty, he left behind a poetic structure of huge dimensions. In his last phase, he passed beyond the boundaries delimiting Romanticism and was, in fact, a symbolist poet, with his own mystical doctrine of poetry as capturing the ineffable through the music of verse and images.

Słowacki's plays in verse belong to the main body of Polish Romantic drama and reveal not only the extraordinary breadth of his talent but also its weakness. Contrary to Mickiewicz, he seems to have drawn little from his life experience and much from his reading and hallucinatory dreams. He was a master of what Professor Backvis has called "amazing literary cocktails," mixtures of Shakespeare, Calderón, Lope de Vega, and old Polish poetry. His was a quite deliberate attempt to compensate for what Polish drama lacked in the past, and in his search for models he did not scorn folklore. A reference to his childhood theatrical experiences in Volhynia is significant in this respect: he speaks of the *wertep* (Ukranian Christmas puppet show) of Krzemieniec "to which, perhaps, I am indebted for all my Shakespearean fervor." In Paris, he was an assiduous theater- and operagoer, just at a time when daring Romantic innovations in the art of *mise en scène* were being tried out. Action was presented, for instance, against a panorama of the Alps so contrived as to give an illusion of reality; ghosts and fairies soared over the stage lifted by machinery in the flies. In general, theater directors showed a predilection for the fantastic and the bizarre. Encouraged, as we may surmise, by his impressions as a theatergoer, Słowacki wrote the drama *Kordian* (1834), which was also an attempt to oppose and rival Mickiewicz's *Forefathers' Eve*. Intended as the first part of a trilogy (never completed), it is composed of a series of fragmentary scenes—phases in the evolution of a hero. Kordian, an adolescent in a swallowlike flutter of anxiety, cannot find an aim in life and tries to kill himself, since his unhappy love offers no relief. Later on, we meet him in meditation on the cliffs of Dover and in St. James Park in London; we see him in Italy, where he searches in vain for oblivion in the arms of a courtesan, and at an audience with the Pope (whose attitude toward the Polish cause is attacked), and on the summit of Mont Blanc, where he discovers his inner vocation: to serve the national cause (and in this way to prove his own ability to act?). Next, we are transferred to the oppressive climate of Warsaw, ruled by the Grand Duke Constantine. Kordian, as a member of a clan- destine organization, is party to a plot to assassinate the czar, Nicholas I, who has come to Warsaw for his coronation as king of Poland. Unable to draw other conspirators over to his side, Kordian decides to commit the murder himself. Since he is an officer of the Polish army, and has been assigned to stand guard at the door of the Czar's bedroom, he has only to make use of the opportunity; but he is inhibited by his moral scruples and faints after a struggle with Fear and Imagination. Kordian is banished to an insane asylum first, then sentenced to death. But at the personal request of Grand Duke Constantine, he is granted a reprieve after passing a test of valor (a leap on horseback across raised bayonets). Czar Nicholas, however, issues an order for his execution. At the end, it is uncertain whether an officer bearing a reversal of the Czar's order will arrive in time to stop the execution.

Like Mickiewicz's *Forefathers' Eve* and Krasiński's *Undivine Com- edy, Kordian* exemplifies that type of Romantic drama which is most specifically Polish, dealing as it does with history in the making. Central to all three dramas is the problem of action versus poetry and the spiritual transformation of the hero. Against Mickiewicz's exaltation of the individual savior, Słowacki, who was politically close to the radical democrats, pitted his skeptical views of the "providential man," reflected in his treatment of Kordian. Kordian, a neurotic, a Hamlet (in the way Romantics conceived Hamlet), can hardly be called a leader, though we do not know how he would have evolved in the subsequent parts of the dramatic trilogy, which, in Słowacki's intention, were to have dealt with the whole history of the Polish insurrection of 1830–1831. In *Kordian* Słowacki magnifies the emotional capacity for revolutionary *élan* displayed by the Warsaw crowds, but the mob's political immaturity and the general lack of wise leaders comes in for sharp satire. Politically, the play conveys the radical democrat view as to who was responsible for the defeat: since the leaders of the uprising were convinced from the very start of the victory of the established order, this, together with their hopes for a compromise with Russia, led them to betray the masses. Performed often on the Polish stages of our time, *Kordian*, although its fragmentary structure and its central theme epitomize the Polish Romantic imagination and its verse is brilliant, cannot be compared to that national mystery and morality play, *Forefathers' Eve*.

Among Słowacki's other works for the stage, *Balladyna* (written 1834, published 1839) contains every technique he learned from the Paris theater, and above all what he learned from Shakespeare. (*Les balladines* was a term which the Parisian press applied to eerie female dancers in Meyerbeer's opera, *Robert le Diable*.) Słowacki creates a country of make-believe, something like prehistoric Poland, but he mischievously mixes epochs, employing all sorts of anachronisms. In the preface, he explains that his play is written in an "Ariostic style," which presupposes a light, slightly mocking treatment of all the motifs. It is a dramatized fairy tale, or ballad, with freely invented folklore elements. There is a queen of fairies in love with a peasant drunkard who, when she changes him into a willow, sheds tears of vodka, and a young peasant heroine who kills her sister out of rivalry for the affections of a nobleman. Having become the lady of the castle, she commits a series of further murders, aided by a sinister Von Kostryn (even in the old Slavic world, a German was synonymous with evil-doing!). There is even a peasant transformed by his disillusioned mistress (the queen of fairies again) into a king . . . of diamonds. (No apologies to the yet unwritten *Alice in Wonderland* by Lewis Carroll, born 1832.) In all, *Balladyna* is one of Słowacki's "cocktails," blending characters and situations from Polish ballads, *A Midsummer-Night's Dream*, *Macbeth*, *King Lear*, etc.

Quite another thing is the comedy in verse, *Fantazy*, completed around 1841. The ethereal poet could also wield an extremely malicious pen, and this play, which is considered the most realistic of his works, contains a vitriolic satire of contemporary Polish life. The action takes place on an estate in the Ukraine. Count Fantazy, melodramatic and Romantic, has returned from a voyage to Italy. He pays a visit to his neighbors, Count and Countess Respekt, who have two daughters with fine-sounding names: Diana and Stella. Fantazy, who speaks in an inflated, Byronic style, is a poseur and a complex scoundrel. He knows that Diana hates him, he admires her character, her moral purity, but he wants to commit a base act and to buy her. Since he is rich and his neighbors are ruined, he calculates on a successful outcome. The Respekts are extremely dignified members of the Establishment, very lofty in their words, but perfect scoundrels too. They decide to sell their daughter to him, but before the marriage is concluded, a second visitor, an old Russian major, reverses everything. We learn that the Respekt family had been deported to Siberia and there had met the major. Meeting him had been providential for them, and he had become their best friend. Also, in Siberia, Diana had been betrothed to a deported Polish revolutionary, Jan, and is still in love with him. Accompanying the major now is Jan, disguised as a common soldier. Słowacki confronts the complete artificiality and pretense of the Polish aristocrats with the simple manners and deep humaneness of the Russian major. To help Jan and to foil the marriage between Diana and Fantazy, he maneuvers with great ingenuity. It is impossible to outline the extremely intricate details of the plot; in any case, a duel results between the major and Fantazy in the form of a card game played for the highest stakes: the loser is to commit suicide. Fantazy, who loses, experiences his moment of truth, but unexpectedly it is the old major who kills himself, having become tired of life and wishing to arrange Jan's marriage. The parents agree to the marriage because another *deus ex machina* is introduced: a rich relative dies and leaves them a fortune. Thus, not only all "right-thinking" members of Polish society, but phonies like Count Fantazy in his Byronic cloak are Słowacki's target, while the figure of the major, an ex-Decembrist, "an old, stupid liberal," as he calls himself, is one of the most moving ever created by the poet. He speaks a peculiar language, a mixture of Russian, Ukrainian, and Polish words, and his speeches delivered in verse constitute a tour de force.

Among Słowacki's plays on historical subjects, a very Shakespearean tragedy, *Maria Stuart*, a youthful work, has its admirers. More often staged, though, is another tragedy, *Mazeppa*, completed in 1839. Mazeppa, a colorful personality, was, at that time, a part of European literary lore, a kind of European Buffalo Bill. His adventures were related in the eighteenth century by Voltaire, later on, he showed up in the poetry of Byron, Victor Hugo, and others; and popular drawings presented him being dragged, naked, by a wild horse. This refers to an anecdote noted down by Polish memorialists such as Jan Chryzostom Pasek (whose memoirs in their entirety were published in 1836). Mazeppa, a Ukrainian nobleman, educated at a Polish Jesuit college and sent by King Jan Casimir to study artillery in Holland, became, upon his return, a courtier in Warsaw; then he joined the Ukrainian cause and reached the highest dignity in the land, that of Hetman, in which post he was a successor of Bohdan Chmielnicki. Although he was a vassal of Peter the Great, he turned against him and sided with the Swedes, only to see all his political hopes ruined at the Battle of Poltava. As a young man, famous for his love affairs, he was once punished by an angry husband, who stripped him of his clothes, bound him to his horse, then lashed the beast into a gallop. In Słowacki's play, however, Mazeppa is neither a savage Cossack (as imagined by Western poets) nor a villain (as in Pushkin's *Poltava*). He is a young, noble-minded courtier and a confidant of King Jan Casimir. To cover up for the King, who aspires to the favors of the beautiful wife (Amelia) of an old governor (Wojewoda), in whose castle the action is placed, he takes the blame upon himself and is about to die at the hand of the jealous old man; meanwhile, the exposure of a real love triangle reveals that Amelia is the mistress of the governor's son (Zbigniew) from his first marriage. The situation is "resolved" by the deaths of these three. Słowacki's tragedy, thus, gives a Romantic treatment to the mores of the seventeenth century.

Lilla Weneda, written the same year as *Mazeppa*, is interesting only as an attempt to fill in, by imagination, the details of an epoch unreported in any chronicles—prehistoric Poland. Giving credit to the theory that a conquest lay at the origin of Polish state, Słowacki invented a desperate war between pure-hearted, peaceful aborigines (the Wenedzi) and vicious conquerors (the Lechici). The former incarnate Poland's "angelic soul"; the latter embody all the vices of the nobility (including a "taste for pickled cucumbers and yelling"). Another "literary cocktail," with components taken mostly from Shakespeare, the tragedy is of doubtful value because of its rather gratuitous horrors.

Throughout his life Słowacki was emotionally dependent upon his mother, and the letters that were continuously exchanged between mother and son not only provide a valuable commentary on his entire work but are one of the highest achievements of Polish Romantic prose. Salomea, or Sally, as he called his mother, was his true love affair. His involvements with other women were largely literary inventions. When he lived abroad, his mother would send him from Poland modest sums of money, which he quite skillfully invested in stocks. Thus, he was free to devote all his time to literature.

His stay in Switzerland from 1833 to 1836 (in Geneva, then in Vevey, near Lausanne) appears to have been especially fruitful. He moved there mainly because of the lack of recognition from the *émigrés* in Paris and because of his feud with Mickiewicz: in *Fore-fathers' Eve* Słowacki had been shocked to find his stepfather, Dr. Bécu, depicted in the blackest colors, the very image of a servile collaborator. It was in Switzerland that he wrote *Kordian*, *Balladyna*, and an ethereal idyll of love under the title *In Switzerland* (*W Szwajcarii*), where the Alpine countryside fuses with the poet's own "inner landscape."

In 1836 we find him in Rome. From there he set off in the company of some friends on a journey through Greece, Egypt, and Palestine. The voyages, especially to the countries of the Levant, satisfied the Romantic longing for a constant change of scenery and fresh impressions. In one of his letters to his mother, Słowacki wrote: "A voyage gives us many, many images; only it's a pity that it shows everything to be less beautiful than it was in our imagination; and then two images persist in our memory—one, such as it *should be*, painted with our eyes; the second, more beautiful, created previously by our imagination. Sometime in the future, the third and most beautiful will be created, out of our imagination and dreamy recollections —and it will combine in itself everything that was most beautiful in those images. I cannot understand how Byron could write on the spot." And in another letter: "If poetry did not exist in the world, the very thought that man walking on the earth gathers so many bright, enchanting images and, together with them, has to go down to the grave would have given birth to it." In his poem, *A Voyage to the Holy Land*, reconstructing the impressions from this voyage, Słowacki proves himself a rare virtuoso. He takes pleasure in devising the most unexpected rhymes; his lines sparkle with wit and lyricism, colorful descriptions of places, satirical and humorous remarks—all this set in a casual style so that the reader has the feeling of complete ease and an effortless flow. But, of course, Słowacki did not relinquish his ambitions to become national bard and to surpass Mickiewicz. His stay in Greece returned later in "Agamemnon's Grave" ("Grób Agamemnona"), a short poem meditating upon the fate of Greece and Poland. Some lines that have become proverbial show Słowacki's typical aggressiveness in his attitude toward his country. He conceived it his patriotic duty to castigate Poland for being "the peacock and parrot" of other nations, and he searched for her "angelic soul" imprisoned as it was in the skull of a drunken guffawing nobleman. From his sojourn in a monastery in Lebanon, Słowacki brought the first draft of a long poem in prose, *Anhelli* (published in 1838). If *Kordian* is, to a large extent, a counterpart of *Fore-*

fathers' Eve, Anhelli parallels Mickiewicz's *Books of the Polish Nation and of the Polish Pilgrims.* The scenery of the poem is the forests and wastelands of Siberia, the home of many Poles deported there by the czarist authorities. But it is not a real Siberia; it is a place of exile per se, with its symbolic snow, symbolic cold, and the splendid lights of the aurora borealis. And the deportees, who, in the author's intention, stand for the Polish *émigrés,* are not at all pure and sympathetic even though they are martyrs for a cause. They are divided into three political parties—monarchist aristocrats, democrats, and a religious sect—which combat each other with vicious hatred. While Mickiewicz was inclined to treat the *émigrés* as apostles, Słowacki attributed to them no effectiveness whatsoever, and in his poem he has them die a sterile death in exile. The hero, Anhelli, also one of the deportees, is singled out by a shaman (from a local Siberian tribe) and initiated into the mystery of acceptance of his suffering and death; he becomes, in his way, a kind of passive redeemer. In the final scene, a symbolic knight on horseback, illumined by the fiery glow from the northern lights, announces the hour of universal revolution; but by then Anhelli is dead. Thus the poem suggests the idea of a sacrifice not recompensed by any immediate fulfillment, yet not useless, since in some mysterious way it is spiritually necessary for the sake of a future regeneration. The language is deliberately archaic, the tone is biblical. Słowacki succeeds in conveying his idea through striking and, as usual, ethereal images. His strivings for recognition among the *émigrés,* however, remained unsuccessful. Very few of them reacted to his art. Słowacki's only comfort was his friendship with another poet, Zygmunt Krasiński, who understood him well. His books, which Słowacki had published at his own expense, either passed unnoticed or were met with little malicious notes in *émigré* periodicals. A scandal finally brought him, if not applause, at least notoriety; it was connected with the publication of *Beniowski* in 1841. (Only the first five songs of the long poem were printed; the others appeared posthumously.) Written in *ottava rima*—a verse form with an old tradition in Polish poetry, going back to Krasicki's mock-heroic epics and Piotr Kochanowski's version of *Jerusalem Delivered*—*Beniowski* is a poem of digressions, obviously competing with Byron's *Don Juan.* The plot traces the vicissitudes undergone by a Hungarian-Polish nobleman, an authentic figure who took part in the military campaigns against Russia in the Ukraine during the so-called Confederacy of Bar (1768–1772) and then was deported to Kamchatka. He escaped from there, in a boat built by himself and some companions, to Japan, went to France, and ended his life commanding the tribes of Madagascar in a war against the French. But the main character was merely a pretext, and the poet did not get beyond young Beniowski's adventures in the Ukraine. He deals with every topic of the day, settles accounts with his enemies, and displays breath-taking acrobatics in passing from lyricism to sarcasm, from sarcasm to fireworks of images. Słowacki had a predilection for the Ukraine, and it forms the backdrop of many of his plays, but nowhere is it so alive as in *Beniowski*. In terms of color, it is blue, gold, vermilion; at least these are the dominating shades. Praised, despised, provoked even to a duel, Słowacki, after *Beniowski*, was recognized as a major literary figure.

But a new turn in his life directed him again into paths which were to be scorned by his contemporaries. After settling for good in Paris, in 1839, the author of *Kordian* and *Anhelli* was marked by more and more pronounced mystical tendencies. In 1842 he met Andrzej Towiański, who convinced him of his special mission as a poet and persuaded him to enter the sect where Mickiewicz was a leader second only to Towiański. This required Słowacki to humiliate himself in the name of a religious principle. Quite soon, however, he discovered that the sect was jealous of any independence on the part of its members, and he left it the next year, in 1843. Out of Słowacki's mystical phase, especially from 1842 on, came works which, neither in his lifetime nor for decades after his death, exerted any influence, as they were completely out of step with prevailing literary fashions. The labors of his last stage foreshadow and often surpass French symbolism, but as a rule, the works are even more difficult for the average reader than those of the *poètes maudits*. And it was not until the generation of the 1890s, with its perception of correspondences between states of soul and landscapes, sounds, and colors, took over the literary scene, that the late Słowacki was really discovered. In the short, mystical lyrics written in this period he attains the highest perfection of his art, and they alone would have assured Słowacki a position as one of the best Polish poets. He spent the last years of his life building up the enormous structure of his mystical system. As befitted a Polish mystic, he raised historical events to cosmic dimensions and saw in history superhuman, mystical forces shaping the fate of mankind. Słowacki's "system" is no easier to grasp than William Blake's and affords as many interpretations.

An extraordinary poem in prose, *Genesis from the Spirit* (*Genesis z ducha*), written in 1844 in Pornic on the Atlantic seacoast, is an exposition of his philosophical credo. In it he combined his readings in the natural sciences, especially in the theory of evolution as elaborated by Lamarck, with his spiritualism and his radical democratic sympathies. Meditating on the ocean, the cradle of life, he sees in the evoution of animal forms a travail of the Spirit throughout millions of years:

On the rocks of the ocean you put me, my Lord, in order that I might recollect centuries-old deeds of my spirit, and suddenly I felt a son of God, immortal in the past, creator of the visible things, and one of those who render to you a voluntary tribute of love on garlands of suns and stars.

* * *

You, old ocean, tell me how the first mysteries of organisms appeared in your depth. The first developments of nervous flowers into which the spirit was blooming. . . .

* * *

I smile today, Lord, seeing an unburied skeleton which does not possess any name in the present language (as it is effaced from among the living forms). I smile seeing the first lizard with the head of a bird, provided with a wing at its foot, starting a flight to explore the world and to find a place for those heavy monsters which were later on to devour whole meadows, whole forests.

"Everything is created by the Spirit and for the Spirit; nothing exists for physical aims." Through its own efforts the Spirit ("to a book filled by You he has affixed the seal of his duration") moves from lower forms toward higher and higher forms, but when it reaches man, the travail is not over. The Spirit, "eternal revolutionary," shapes History through revolutions which are spasms of birth, until humanity, transformed, approaches Christ. Notes of messianism are not absent: the Spirit incarnates itself in some exceptional individuals or in whole nations, like Poland for instance, purified by her suffering. In its main lines, Słowacki's vision of a cosmic evolution is strangely similar to the thesis proposed some hundred years later by a French Jesuit anthropologist, Teilhard de Chardin.

A poem of grandiose proportions, *King-Spirit* (*Król-Duch*) remained unfinished. Only the first part was published in 1847; the rest of the manuscript contained serious gaps. No other such attempt exists in Western poetry: though the poem is primarily concerned with the history of Poland, it presents the wandering of the Spirit as it informs the bodies of leaders, kings, and saints throughout the centuries of European civilization. It begins with the story of a certain Her, a heroic soldier mentioned by Plato who, after his death, is resurrected in the body of Poland's legendary first prince, Popiel. Słowacki portrays Popiel as a ruthless ruler with a well-defined goal: to immunize his nation against all future suffering by forcing upon it a system of deliberate cruelty. The scenery is mostly that of the Middle Ages, but it is not an "authentic" Middle Ages. Like Albion in Blake, this is a vision without a bit of pretense to "reality." *King-*

Spirit, with its traditional *ottava rima*, goes far beyond anything the symbolist poets dared to do later on. It unites the cosmic and the historic, and probably only a Pole, fascinated in the extreme with the philosophy of history, could have written it. To himself, Słowacki assigned a special mission. He wanted to conjure up Poland and its history out of his imagination like a God-creator, to postulate it through *Słowo*, the Word.

Calderón (whom he translated) influenced Słowacki in his last dramas, where a fusing of the natural and the supernatural produces a splendid Baroque chaos. In *Father Marek* (*Ksiądz Marek*) and *The Silver Dream of Salomea* (*Sen srebrny Salomei*), both written in 1843, he returned once again to the Ukrainian scene, choosing plots from the political events of the eighteenth century (the Confederacy of Bar, the massacres of Polish nobles by the Ukrainian peasants). The characters, however, and their adventures are bigger than life; their monumentalism has nothing to do with earthly reality. Also the unfinished historical drama *Samuel Zborowski* runs counter to the traditional realism of plays like *Boris Godunov*, for example. The action takes place in a cosmic dimension, beyond time and beyond space. Zborowski, a magnate of the sixteenth century, appears before the tribunal of Christ, asking to be tried a second time. At his first trial on earth he was sentenced to death, and was beheaded for his completely anarchic deeds. In Słowacki's drama, Zborowski personifies the strength of a spirit struggling against all forces seeking to constrain it, while Chancellor Zamoyski (who sent him to death) represents the obstructing power of the established social order. Songs relating the experiences of spirits in successive incarnations (beginning in ancient Egypt) parallel in their penetrating beauty the perfection of Słowacki's mystical lyrics from the same period.

In 1848, Słowacki went to the Prussian-occupied part of Poland at the news of a revolution there. The revolutionary movement proved abortive, but he did spend a few weeks in Dresden, where he met his mother after an eighteen-year separation. In 1849, tuberculosis, aggravated by his feverish poetic efforts, took his life in Paris. He was buried at the cemetery of Montmorency, where, six years later, the body of his rival, Mickiewicz, was laid. In 1927 his remains were brought to Poland and buried in the royal crypt of Wawel Castle.

What is most characteristic of Słowacki's poetry is his fondness for pure colors—silver, gold, red, blue—and for iridescent, nacreous light. For this reason, he has been compared to such painters as Turner. Or he has been called a "centrifugal" poet, as opposed to Mickiewicz, whose work is "centripetal." While the latter, even in his most Romantic poems, tends toward concreteness and tangibility,

Słowacki dissolves every object into a kind of fluid maze of images and sonorities. As a whole, Słowacki's work, which is extremely abundant, is uneven. It can be sublime in its depth of thought and breath-taking in its virtuosity or irritating in its nearly automatic writing. After his death, his fame grew, but he was still not considered equal to Mickiewicz. Only the generation of the symbolists began to see in Słowacki their master, the number-one poet, a predecessor of French symbolism and, in some aspects of his thought, a precursor of Friedrich Nietzsche. Today, we take a more sober view, for we are, perhaps, less prone to consider the "music" of verse as one of the strongest sides of Słowacki's talent, or, for that matter, as the major quality of any poet.

ZYGMUNT KRASIŃSKI
(1812–1859)

Unlike Mickiewicz, who came from the poor gentry, and Słowacki, who came from the intelligentsia, Zygmunt Krasiński descended from an old aristocratic family, bore the title of count, and possessed a fortune. His father was a military man; he had been a general in the Napoleonic army and after the Congress of Vienna had entered the army of the Polish Kingdom with the same rank. As a reactionary of strong convictions, ultraloyal toward the czar, the general was looked upon by the radicals as an ominous personality. In Mickiewicz's *Forefathers' Eve*, one of the most satirical scenes (the Warsaw salon) alludes precisely to gatherings held in the home of old Krasiński. While Słowacki had a mother fixation, Zygmunt Krasiński trembled practically all his life before the authority of his father. In that intellectual, there was a surprising blind compliance with paternal commands, to the extent that in his mature age he married a woman picked out for him by his father at the same time swearing eternal love to another. As a young student in Warsaw, Krasiński upheld his father's political views in the teeth of opposition from his colleagues. During a students' demonstration he was the only strike-breaker, and for his breach of solidarity he received a slap in the face from a fellow student. Soon, however, he left to study at the University of Geneva, where he made several foreign friends. His friendship with a young English journalist, Henry Reeve, in particular, proved intellectually fruitful—for both. When the uprising of 1830 broke out, General Krasiński took the side of the Russians and categorically forbade his son to return to Poland, denouncing the whole movement as the folly of a mob thirsting for the blood of aristocrats. And when the hostilities were over, he brought his son, to the latter's shame and despair, to St. Petersburg in 1832 and presented him to the czar. It was not long, however, before Krasiński went abroad again, and much of his life thereafter was spent either in France or in Italy. Since he had not been compromised, he could travel freely from country to country, and if he spent more time abroad than in Poland, it can be explained by the fact that the center of Polish literary life was in the Great Emigration. To protect his huge estates in Poland from confiscation, he published his books anonymously and was known as Poland's "anonymous poet." Krasiński was a man endowed with a brilliant mind, excellently educated, well-read in several languages, and able to write with equal ease in French or Polish. His political acumen and his knowledge of intricacies of European politics were quite exceptional. Not only his works bear testimony to this but also his letters. Indeed, the extent and quality of his correspondence alone would have sufficed for other writers as a serious literary accomplishment. He suffered, as was not uncommon in that epoch, from a true epistolary mania, promoted by his amorous attachments to highly intelligent women, especially to an aristocratic divorcée, Delfina Potocki. Famous also for her romance with Frédéric Chopin, Delfina was, for many years, Krasiński's mistress, confidante, first reader of his works, and a recipient of his letters, which he often wrote daily, touching on all the current intellectual and political problems. The date of his marriage (1843) had been fixed in advance by his father, who had also chosen the bride: a rich, aristocratic girl, Eliza Branicki, completely alien to the bridegroom; after his marriage, Krasiński continued his love correspondence with Delfina.

As an adolescent, Krasiński had written historical novels in the style of Walter Scott, glorifying the feudal chivalry of the Middle Ages. The two dramas of his young manhood were also written in prose and one of them is undoubtedly a masterpiece not only of Polish but also of world literature. Written in Vienna and Venice in 1833, *The Undivine Comedy* (*Nie-Boska komedia*) is the product of a twenty-one-year-old. Even if we take into account Krasiński's brilliance, it is difficult to understand how a young aristocrat could conceive the only European work of the period that dealt with the class struggle in nearly Marxist terms. (At the time, Karl Marx was fifteen!) Perhaps the drama grew out of some mysterious recesses of fear in the young man's subconscious. He was shaken by the French revolution of 1830 and by the workers' riots in Lyon. He had also been impressed by his father's view of the Polish insurrection. The events of his time, together with his meditation on the French Revolution of 1789, fused in his mind into an idea of revolution in general. For him, it was clear that a revolution in Europe had to come and that he and people of his sort would be wiped out by it. The central problem of the drama is a universal, not only a Polish, one, and the action takes place in an indefinite country. The characters have a symbolic dimension, and Mickiewicz, analyzing *The Undivine Comedy* in his courses at the Collège de France, saw in it the highest achievement of the Slavic theater. Like Mickiewicz in *Forefathers' Eve*, Krasiński takes up first the personal life of his hero, Count Henry, then shows him as a politically committed man, in command of the reactionary forces defending themselves on the ramparts of the Holy Trinity castle against the atheistic, revolutionary forces led by a professional revolutionist, Pancras. However, Mickiewicz's drama on the transformation of a personality is basically optimistic—as the hero, through his falls, gropes toward a fuller awareness of the place of the individual in a community; while in Krasiński's drama Count Henry tries in vain to become another type of man, but his unhappy marriage, his pursuit of The Maiden (Art), and his political activity reveal only his internal worthlessness. A strange Romantic drama: Count Henry is not satisfied with the quiet life of the social Establishment, scorns his wife, and drives her to madness by pursuing Art. Later, he discovers that his son is touched by blindness (the mark of a seer ever since Homer), while Art, a beautiful maiden, lures him to the edge of a precipice over the ocean, where she unveils her body—a decaying corpse. Thus poetry's demoniac side is denounced in terms reminding us of Thomas Mann's novel, *Doctor Faustus*, where Esmeralda contaminates Adrian Leverkühn with a deadly disease and, in that way, releases his musical genius. It is a strange Romantic drama, also, in that it is a reversal of the optimistic faith in the upheaval of the masses. Count Henry scorns those whom he commands; he knows that they are rotten, that they have to perish and he himself with them; but the assaulting plebeians are also a blind crowd whose passions of hatred and revenge are coolly exploited by Pancras. The exchange of vitriolic remarks during the meeting between Pancras and Count Henry (Pancras feels an irrational attraction for Count Henry) is the most powerful passage in the drama. Pancras' philosophy is nothing other than dialectical materialism. Here, Krasiński went beyond the nineteenth-century image of the revolution as a spontaneous movement and approached the twentieth century in that he envisaged a revolution as something organized by professionals and controlled from the top. Pancras is a man of iron will, clear thinking, fanatical, using a new discipline to go straight to his goal, which is the salvation of the oppressed. His total awareness, however, adds a touch of melancholy to Pancras' character. When the fortress of the aristocrats is taken and Count Henry commits suicide (belying once again his role as defender of Christianity),

Pancras has a vision; he sees a cross in the sky and exclaims: "Galilaee vicisti!" (Galilean, you have won!) These are his last words. Whether Krasiński added such an ending because he could not find a way out of the dilemma is immaterial; actually, he was influenced by Hegel, and his drama, through such an ending, achieves much more than it would have, had Krasiński concluded with a prophetic trumpet blast foretelling the post-mortem rehabilitation of the aristocratic class. If the traditional Christian (and aristocratic) order is the thesis, and atheistic materialism the antithesis, then a synthesis can only be brought about in the future, after the reactionary order has been abolished. We find similar ideas much later in twentieth-century Russian poetry, for instance, in Alexander Blok's *The Twelve*, where Christ appears at the head of Red Army soldiers. This does not mean that Krasiński felt any sympathy for the radical, plebeian trends which he combatted his whole life. His drama seems to have come from neurotic fears, and the figure of Orcio, Count Henry's blind son, may be especially significant in this respect. Orcio lives in the underground chambers of the Holy Trinity castle and, perhaps, personifies Count Henry's guilt. *The Undivine Comedy* is a truly pioneering work in its treatment of an unusual subject and in its visual elements. The conflict between higher and lower classes is dramatized as a struggle between forces occupying the castle of Holy Trinity, which dominates an enormous valley, and the masses swarming in the lowlands. The introduction of crowds into the action confirms what Mickiewicz said about the impossibility of staging such products of the Slavic imagination with the means then at the disposal of the theater. And like Mickiewicz's *Forefathers' Eve*, only in the twentieth century did Krasiński's drama reach the public in a theater. Above all, one suspects that it would make an excellent film scenario.

Another drama of Krasiński's, *Iridion*, was conceived earlier than *The Undivine Comedy* but actually written a little later. Here, too, he is fascinated with the decay of a society. Iridion, the hero, is a Greek who lives in Rome at the time of its decline under the rule of Heliogabal. His dominating passion is hatred of Rome for having subjugated his native country. To take vengeance he prepares a revolution, enlisting the help of the barbarians (which were then so numerous in Rome), gladiators, and proletarians, while counting on the participation of the Christians. His counselor is the demoniac Massinissa, who personifies the principle that the end justifies the means. At the decisive moment, though, the Christians obey their bishop, who advises winning not with arms but with meekness and martyrdom freely accepted. As a result, Iridion fails and must lie for centuries in a lethargic sleep, awaiting a new struggle against the empire of evil. Then, he will be resurrected in, or rather incarnated by, the Polish nation. And in the ensuing struggle with czardom, methods other than Massinissa's will be used. Krasiński's attitude toward democratic movements, which he accused of Massinissa-like leanings, is evident here. *Iridion* (and later Krasiński's poetry) contributed to the Poles' morbid preoccupation with their martyrdom, which they came close to identifying with that of the early Christians. Like *The Undivine Comedy*, *Iridion* is written in prose, only it is more ornate and rhythmical, typically Romantic, and today we find it rather irritating. Although a work of considerable talent, especially in its perspicacious analysis of the decadence of Rome, it is inferior to *The Undivine Comedy*.

In his mature age, Krasiński turned to poetry, but he deplored in himself his lack of "that angelic measure which is the sign of a poet." His poems are treatises on his philosophy of history, written in verse, and they reflect his preoccupations with Hegel, Schelling, and with those Polish philosophers who, though they stemmed from Hegel, opposed him on many points: August Cieszkowski (a representative of the Hegelian Right, but having some influence on the Hegelian Left in Germany) and Bronisław Trentowski. *The Dawn* (*Przedświt*), published in 1843, idolized the division of mankind into nations as necessary and predetermined by God, likening these divisions to the parts of an immense chorus. Viewed in such a light, the partition of Poland became a crime against humanity. But Poland would be resurrected, because the blame for her fall did not lie within; her sufferings had been preordained as a redeeming sacrifice. Similar ideas are developed in *The Psalms of the Future* (*Psalmy przyszłości*, 1845; enlarged edition, 1848). Słowacki, a personal friend of Krasiński's and a democrat, came out with a versified attack on *The Psalms*. His anger as a democrat reached the boiling point when he read Krasiński's call for harmony between social classes and his warning against democratic slogans that incited the masses to bloody upheavals such as the peasant rebellion of 1846. Poland's "anonymous poet" was popular in the declining phase of Romanticism, which came to a rather abrupt end with the insurrection of 1863; but today we cannot accept his being placed on an equal footing with Słowacki, much less so with Mickiewicz.

THE UKRAINIAN SCHOOL

The name "Ukrainian School" is used to designate three poets who were born in the Ukraine and who found in it a nourishment for their Romantic imaginations. Antoni Malczewski (1793–1826) came from

a wealthy family, was a brilliant student at the *lycée* of Krzemieniec
in Volhynia, served with the Napoleonic Polish army of the Duchy
of Warsaw, then spent a few years traveling in Western Europe. An
avid sportsman, in 1818 he climbed l'Aiguille du Midi of Mont Blanc,
but while abroad he did not neglect literary heights either. In 1816, it
seems, he met the renowned Lord Byron, whose poetry he greatly admired. After his return to Poland in 1820, he became entangled in a
mysterious emotional affair with a woman whom he attempted to cure
from a nervous illness by using mesmerism. It seems that this unfortunate tie precipitated his death at the age of thirty-three. His long poem,
Maria, published in 1826, constitutes his whole literary output, but
its place in Polish literature is exceptionally high. It is written in a
verse that is still classical and that contrasts with its content, which
is pervaded by moods of nostalgia and gloom. Rich, complex, and
extremely original, Malczewski's versification was a major contribution to the victory of Romanticism, and as such was matched only
by Mickiewicz's. The poem itself (subtitled *A Ukrainian Tale*) can
be looked upon as a tragedy. It has a logically structured action
which is compressed into twenty-four hours. The plot is based on a
real event of the eighteenth century: Count Potocki, a Polish artisto-
crat residing in the Ukraine, enraged by his son's marriage to Ger-
truda Komorowski, of noble but not of aristocratic parentage, had
the girl drowned in a pond. Malczewski moved the action further
back—to the seventeenth century, when the Ukraine was constantly
harassed by Tartar raids. In the poem the young husband goes
off to fight the Tartars; he returns home unexpectedly only to find
his wife, Maria, dead. The melancholy atmosphere of the vast Ukrainian steppes, the traditional virtues preserved on the small manor
where Maria lives with her father, the bravery of Polish soldiers,
ever ready to pursue the Tartars, form merely a backdrop for the
impending tragic event: the manor is invaded by a gay parade of
masked figures singing songs about Venetian carnivals and celebrating Shrovetide; these are the heroine's murderers and, ironically,
just happen to be disguised as executioners. A very diversified
rhythm, carefully chosen rhymes, and a tone of pessimism in regard
to all human affairs make *Maria* an unforgettable experience for a
Polish reader. This particular tone makes one think, above all, of
Joseph Conrad's prose. And perhaps in some way Conrad, since he
knew Polish Romantic literature well from his childhood, was
indebted to *Maria*.

Józef Bogdan Zaleski (1802–1886) is a minor poet, but remains
part of Poland's literary heritage thanks to his early works of pure
lyricism. His idyllic, songlike poems on his childhood in the Ukraine,
which he called *dumki* and *szumki*, present the life of the Ukrainian

peasants among whom he grew up, but they are unconcerned with any wounding realities. His humans are somewhat miraculous creatures; girls are undistinguishable from little divinities inhabiting groves and streams. Full of charm, Zaleski's poems appealed to readers because of their somewhat monotonous melodiousness. This singsong quality, in contrast to the more fastidious musicality of Słowacki, was to plague Polish verse throughout the late Romantic period. Yet Zaleski, whom many, including Mickiewicz, called a nightingale, was perhaps the most graceful among the practitioners of this type of meter.

Though Seweryn Goszczyński (1801–1876) enjoyed renown in his lifetime, it was, we may suspect, rather for political than for purely literary reasons. His childhood in the Ukraine, where he grew up in a very poor Polish family, bore no resemblance to that of Bogdan Zaleski, and early in life Goszczyński showed signs of being a born rebel. He belonged to a revolutionary, clandestine organization and later became one of the "Belvederians" who set off the insurrection of November 1830 in Warsaw with their attack on Belvedere Palace, the residence of Grand Duke Constantine. After this, he functioned as a radical writer and activist in the Galicia of the Hapsburgs, and finally, he joined the Great Emigration in Paris, where he allied himself with the radical democrats. His main literary work, a long poem entitled *Castle of Kaniów* (*Zamek kaniowski*, 1828), praises the Ukrainian peasant rebellion and the vengeance taken against lords and oppressors (the action takes place at the time of the Humań massacres in the eighteenth century). Its chaotic construction and its amassing of horrors in the worst Romantic fashion make it barely readable today. Goszczyński was also active in literary criticism, and possessed the doubtful merit of terrorizing Aleksander Fredro, the most important Polish comedy writer of the nineteenth century, into a long silence by reproaching him for complete indifference to the national cause.

ALEKSANDER FREDRO
(1793–1876)

In a period of revolts, martyrdom, and flights of the imagination, Polish literature saw the birth of works that stand as the purest incarnation of Polish humor—Mickiewicz's *Pan Tadeusz* and the comedies of Aleksander Fredro. Fredro was born into a wealthy family residing south of Lwów in the foothills of the Carpathian Mountains. The family name had already made a mark in literature thanks to Maksymilian Fredro in the seventeenth century. As an adolescent and young man, Fredro showed no literary leanings at all. He led the life of a healthy puppy. At the age of sixteen he joined the Napoleonic army of the Duchy of Warsaw, and he served Napoleon faithfully until the fall of his empire. He fought in Russia, and for a while he was a prisoner of war there; in France he was a messenger for the general staff and used to ride the country roads a few steps behind Napoleon himself. A soldier of great physical endurance and bravery, decorated several times, he linked his own fate to that of Napoleon's, not because he was enthusiastic about the person of his leader, but out of a sense of duty. He visited practically all of Europe on horseback, and after Napoleon's defeat he returned to his native province in Galicia, where he assumed the management of his family's affairs and, as a veteran whose active life was over, started to write merely for self-amusement. Fredro was a man of bitter and smiling wisdom, acquired not through books, but through life experience. His formal education was almost nil, and in his memoirs he tells how once he asked a friend to explain the meaning of "caesura." And yet comedies in verse were to become his specialty. Fredro was not a Romantic. His plays (though sometimes compared to Goldoni's) stemmed directly from the Polish comedy of the eighteenth century. With Fredro, therefore, the genre of Polish comedy in verse, whose origins go back to the *komedia rybałtowska*, reached its peak. In all probability, some works of the Polish Baroque theater were also known to him. He should not be regarded solely as an heir of the didactic Enlightenment trend. Fredro did not trouble with any thesis; he was simply possessed by a demon of laughter. In contrast to eighteenth-century comedy writers, who conceived of characters as types, Fredro built his as temperaments, individualizing them, making them visceral, as it were, and left the actor many possibilities to impersonate a given role through gestures, little signs, peculiar tics. Writing for the theater in Lwów, he was able to test on the spot public reaction to a sentence or a passage. His verse has a classical clarity and neatness, but even though he adopted the versification of eighteenth-century comedy, he put it to quite a different use. He molded his meter perfectly to everyday speech—which explains why his idioms have become so much a part of the Polish language that they are quoted even by people who know nothing of their origin.

In a way, it would be true to say that Fredro was the last writer of the old *Respublica*. In his plays he introduced figures taken from the Polish gentry, a milieu he knew well, and he sometimes chose the pre-partition era as the time of action. Amid the flux of historical change going on in his own century, he probably sought an anchor in the past.

Fredro left about thirty comedies, some twenty of which were written before 1835, when, attacked by Seweryn Goszczyński for being no more than a jester, he took offense and fell silent for ten years. His most well-known are *Ladies and Hussars* (*Damy i Huzary*, 1826)—a trifle, very popular with stage directors; *Maiden Vows* (*Śluby panieńskie*, written 1827); *Vengeance* (*Zemsta*, 1833); and *Mister Jowialski* (*Pan Jowialski*, 1832)—one of Fredro's few plays in prose.

In *Maiden Vows, or Magnetism of the Heart*, the comic situation results from a vow never to marry, made by two young girls, Klara and Aniela. Their hesitation, induced by the strategy of a young man (Gustaw) and by "magnetism," culminates after many *quid pro quos* in their breaking the pledge. All together, this is a gentle raillery at sublime Romantic concepts of love.

Vengeance, not only for the theatergoer but for the reader, is a real treat. Rhymed lines in trochaic tetrameter give the play its quick tempo. Fredro rarely contrived his plots and characters; rather, he transformed artistically what he had heard from others or seen for himself. For instance, a few years before starting work on *Vengeance*, he acquired an old castle as part of his wife's dowry. By perusing the family archives, he learned its story. It seems that already in the seventeenth century, the castle had fallen into ruins; moreover, it stood on the border line between two estates. Each owner obstinately claimed his right to the castle, and they kept up a constant feud, annoying one another, playing malicious pranks, and spending money on lawyers and lawsuits. Fredro was not concerned with historical exactitude; he did not aim at recreating the atmosphere of the seventeenth century, so he moved up the action in time to the eighteenth century, an era still very much alive. He introduced characters taken from his own surroundings, who were behaving then no differently from the gentry at the time of the original feud. There were many such survivors. The rest was theatrical craft. The succession of scenes is so rapid that, as a critic has remarked, the figures seem to pop up as in a puppet show.

There are two main protagonists: Raptusiewicz the Cupbearer (*Cześnik*)—every nobleman had to have a title—is turbulent, quick-tempered, noisy, spontaneous, forever clutching at his saber as the universal cure-all. In the past, as we learn, he had been all too prone to use that remedy at dietines (local elective assemblies), where he scarred many a face in duels. His adversary, Milczek the Notary (*Rejent*), is soft-spoken, sly, always master of himself, a petty lawyer well versed in all the tricks of his trade, and something of a pharisee, since his piety never interferes with his not especially lofty deeds. He has a saying which he repeats incessantly: "Let heaven's will be done—we must agree with it always." He probably believes he is carrying out "heaven's will" when he concocts the scheme of marrying his son, Wacław, to a rich widow, Podstolina (from Podstoli, another honorary title), whose very appearance provokes hilarity. After having been widowed three times, she is "on the look-out" for a fourth mate, and states unequivocally that "not to have a husband pains mightily." Podstolina is the object of the old duelist's (Raptusiewicz's) affections. In the figure of Papkin, we meet our old acquaintance, the *miles gloriosus* (Albertus) from *komedia rybał-towska*, yet Papkin is something more. If other characters are painted realistically, this penniless hanger-on is just a clown, a sort of toy with a little mechanism inside that makes him talk, talk, talk about himself, his fantastic military exploits, his successes with women, his important connections, etc., only to cover up his miserable status, his cowardice, and his lack of any earthly possessions except for an English guitar and a collection of butterflies. There is the standard couple of young lovers, Wacław and Klara, Raptusiewicz's niece. They are not, however, involved in a romantic way, as Klara is quite a sober young person. The action is limited to a few hours, and takes place sometimes in the Raptusiewicz's house, sometimes in Milczek's. Through a window in each house, the audience sees a garden with a wall under construction, to separate the two properties. Raptusiewicz orders his men to drive away the masons who are building the wall (at the notary's request). The notary, in turn, meticulously writes up some imaginary testimony in the form of complaints from the masons, supposedly beaten up by Raptusiewicz's servants, with the intention of using that document in court. Meanwhile, Wacław steals into Raptusiewicz's house to see Klara and there falls into a deadly trap: he finds Podstolina, one of his "old flames"; at that moment such an amorous female is not at all to his liking. When the notary subsequently forces Wacław into consenting to marry Podstolina, Raptusiewicz in fury conceives his own vengeance. Just to play a foul joke on the notary (and deprive him and his son of Podstolina's dowry), he commands his servants to seize Wacław, and he marries him under duress to Klara; the young people, of course, submit to that inhuman treatment with delight. Everything ends well. Both parties come to an agreement, and further complications of the dowry problem turn to the profit of the young couple. The play is dominated throughout by the buffoon, Papkin, whose speeches are a constant interlude, and whose personality is, perhaps, the most complex, hinting of Fredro's interest in somewhat pathological beings like the hero of his play *Mister Jowialski*.

Written in prose, *Mister Jowialski* employs the old device of disguise in a way that is reminiscent of the seventeenth-century *komedia rybałtowska*, in particular, *Peasant into King* by Piotr Baryka. Ludmir, a poet, and Wiktor, a painter, roam the countryside paying homage to the Romantic interest in folklore. Ludmir, who has fallen asleep under a tree, is found by the inhabitants of a neighboring manor, who take him for a country boor. They decide to have some fun at his expense by dressing him up as an exotic potentate and playing clown before him. All such pranks are instigated by the dictator of the manor, Jowialski, a senile and scatterbrained old man who imposes a requirement of laughter upon his entourage. He shows considerable inventiveness in avoiding anything serious by changing everything into a joke. He speaks in proverbs and little versified fables. His humor has an undercurrent of indecency and cynicism and some leaning toward the macabre. But the manor is inhabited by other crazy people as well. Jowialski's son (who is called throughout the play by his title, Mr. Chamberlain) is plainly weak-headed. While his father is a compulsive joker, he is completely indifferent to the world except for one thing: birds and bird cages, which he constructs incessantly. His wife, Mrs. Chamberlain, talks only of her first husband, Major General Tuz, who drowned in the Vistula during a flood. The niece of the imbecile bird lover, Helen, is a romantic girl whose head is full of sublime novels and who is able to talk only in the language of the soul—here Fredro directs his humor at the fashionable Romantic language of "metaphysics." She has a suitor, a healthy, ruddy-cheeked squire, but unfortunately he does not understand the soul. Ludmir, disguised as an oriental king, pretends to be a simple-minded boor not to spoil the fun, but he also profits from the opportunity to court Helen—and with great success, since, as a poet, he knows how to speak to her. He is sober enough to know that the fondness for poetic language is a temporary illness of young girls; besides, Helen is to his liking and is a rich heiress. He himself is a pauper. After many twists and turns of the plot, Ludmir proves to be Mrs. Chamberlain's son from her first marriage, to General Tuz—it had been assumed that the baby had perished in the flood together with his father. Thus, there is a happy ending: the engagement of Helen and Ludmir. The silly plot notwithstanding, *Mister Jowialski* is an enigmatic play, especially if we take into account the date of its writing, 1832, soon after the disastrous events of 1831. Some scholars see in it an indictment— a play on the decadence of the nobility as a class. Others see in the character of Jowialski more complexity; perhaps he is a wise old man wearing a clown's mask; indeed, the play's dominating figure can be interpreted by an actor in various ways. According to a literary critic (Jerzy Stempowski) who devoted a long philosophical essay to the hero, Jowialski represents "a state of satisfaction in dementia and idiocy." He differs from the insane in that he is active and he imposes upon others his own vision of the world, in which there is no place for sadness. "His negative judgment on the serious affairs of this world prevents him from being engaged in any of them, even in those which seem to concern him the most. Obviously, he expects nothing good from the world. He has decided to make a selection among the phenomena, and, brushing aside all the others, he concentrates his attention only upon those which provide an opportunity for laughter and games." Jowialski is always staging a spectacle. He is like Prospero with his magic wand except that Prospero did not laugh, just as the gods do not laugh. "Laughter as a systematic gesture," says Stempowski, "is, among other things, an expression of the helplessness of the laughing man in the face of the world of phenomena impenetrable to reason and deprived of sense. Laughter, so conceived, resembles, to some extent, what O. W. Holmes calls 'the terrible smile,' a smile betraying in the laughing man a consciousness of his own impotence and uneasiness." The critic is inclined to believe that "Mr. Jowialski's laughter expresses the awareness of the inertia felt by his caste thrown into a world which takes on unpleasant and incomprehensible forms."

Fredro's position as a major Polish comedy writer is well established, and his plays have formed an integral part of the repertoire of the Polish theater ever since the nineteenth century.

PROSE IN THE ROMANTIC PERIOD

The proliferation of minor poets writing in partitioned Poland, in exile, even in deportation to the steppes and mines of Siberia, was such that a mere register of the names would cover many pages. Prose, which developed mostly in Poland itself, encountered serious obstacles. Censorship was severe. Even more deleterious was the downward trend in education, resulting from the policy of the occupying powers. The universities of Warsaw and Wilno and the *lycée* of Krzemieniec were forced to shut their doors soon after 1831. Access to high school was made more and more difficult for plebeian youth, and was clearly cut off in 1847. Prussian and Austrian policy consisted in the progressive Germanization of schools. Obviously, in such conditions, books had to take on utilitarian tasks, filling in for the interdicted publicism and manuals of national history. The obligations thus imposed upon writers prevented them from analyzing contemporary life in a sufficiently detached way. The disasters undergone by Polish society inclined writers to look for a collective identity in the past, to retreat, so to speak, into the womb of tradition. This explains the reappearance of the *gawęda* style, the predecessors of which were the memorialists of the seventeenth century. *Gawęda* may be roughly defined as a loose, chatty form of fiction (not unlike what the Russians call *skaz*) in which a narrator recounts episodes in highly stylized, personal language. Both the language and the mentality of the storyteller are usually those of an average, old-fashioned squire. The most adept at this genre was Henryk Rzewuski, brother of Karolina Sobański (already mentioned in Mickiewicz's biography). A picturesque personality, he worshipped Old Poland in its most Sarmatian, obscurantist aspects, and showed nothing but contempt for all the trends stemming from the Enlightenment. A capricious and self-contradictory publicist, he contributed for a long time to a Polish review published in Russia, the *St. Petersburg Weekly* (*Tygodnik Petersburski*). He advocated complete fusion of Poland with Russia—politically at least—and as a loyal servant to the czar scorned any dreams of independence. His first book, *The Memoirs of Mr. Seweryn Soplica* (*Pamiątki imć pana Seweryna Soplicy*), was published in 1839 in Paris, and though it was called a novel, it is, in fact, a *gawęda*. Episodic anecdotes taken from the life of the eighteenth century are related in humorous essays connected by the personality and colorful speech of the narrator. The work hypnotized its readers with the vividness of its style and was admired by Mickiewicz, who knew it in manuscript form long before its publication. Another of Rzewuski's works of fiction, *November* (*Listopad*, 1845–1846), deals again with the eighteenth century and gives a panorama of social and political life. The author's obvious sympathy for the old-fashioned Sarmatians and his antipathy to French-borrowed ideas are somewhat mitigated by his effort to preserve an artistic balance between the opposites. *November* is, perhaps, more of a historical novel than a *gawęda*, though the "gabbiness" of its style with all its Baroque humor and prodigality of colloquialisms links it to the author's preceding work. The vein of Sarmatian gentry buffoonery that runs throughout all Rzewuski's writings was also typical of other writers, who like him, cannot be said to have contributed anything to the formation of a disciplined, economical language in fiction.

Henryk Rzewuski (1791–1866)

Another representative of the *gawęda*, Ignacy Chodźko, was a teller of tales about the life of the petty gentry in Lithuania. The flavor of this life on the banks of the rivers Wilia and Niemen can be especially enjoyed in his *Lithuanian Sketches* (*Obrazy litewskie*). The *gawęda* remained popular up to the second half of the nineteenth century.

Ignacy Chodźko (1794–1861)

A prolific historical novelist, Zygmunt Kaczkowski introduced a

Zygmunt
Kaczkowski
(1825–1896)

narrator similar to Rzewuski's Soplica in his series of narratives, *The Last of the Nieczujas* (*Ostatni z Nieczujów*, 1853–1855); and like Rzewuski, he set the action in the eighteenth century. But the *gawęda* was not confined exclusively to prose; it wandered on into poetry.

Władysław
Syrokomla
(1823–1863)

Władysław Syrokomla (pen name of Ludwik Kondratowicz), a native of Lithuania, who spent most of his life in Wilno, was a somewhat tragic figure. He possessed considerable talent, but was forever struggling against his lack of education and his poverty. A translator from Latin (Sarbiewski's odes), he was also a poet who felt most deeply about the sad fate of the Byelorussian peasant and wrote some folkish poems in the local dialect (i.e., Byelorussian). His *gawędas* in verse depict with a mixture of sentiment and humor scenes from the life of the petty gentry in remote provinces.

Józef Ignacy
Kraszewski
(1812–1887)

The historical novel is best exemplified by Józef Ignacy Kraszewski. This most prolific of Polish novelists left a work encompassing some seven hundred volumes—which must be reckoned among the highest outputs ever on a world scale. He is still widely read in Poland. Born in Warsaw, he studied at the University of Wilno before it was closed down. His student days did not lack a period spent in prison. Though Warsaw-born, he was so fascinated by Lithuania that he began to gather material on its myths and its history. Some of his scholarly studies and fiction on Lithuanian subjects contributed to the rebirth of Lithuanian national feeling, as did works by other authors published in Polish, such as the first *History of Lithuania* (1835–1841) by Teodor Narbutt. But this was only the first stage of Kraszewski's multifaceted activity. While living in Volhynia as a tenant farmer and landowner, he became thoroughly acquainted with the lot of the peasant. For a while, he contributed to the *St. Petersburg Weekly*, then for some eleven years edited his own literary review, called *Athenaeum* (sixty volumes), printed in Wilno. Afterward he was appointed superintendent of schools and at the same time directed a Polish theater in Zhitomir, in the Ukraine. Next, he edited a newspaper in Warsaw, but was dismissed and black-listed by the authorities. He emigrated to Dresden and lived there for a long time, until his presence came to the attention of Bismarck. Pronounced a dangerous individual, he was sentenced in 1883 to a three-and-a-half-year imprisonment but served only over a year, during which time he continued to write novels. As an old man with ruined health, he settled in Italy, in San Remo—only to lose all of his belongings during an earthquake there. He died in Geneva.

Kraszewski was a committed writer in the full sense of the word. In his journalism, his historical studies, his essays, and his fiction, he pursued one aim: he wanted, as he used to say himself, "to provide the reader with ordinary bread." He did not limit himself to historical subjects. For instance, his "peasant novels" (*Ulana* [1843], *Ostap Bondarczuk* [1847], *The Hut Beyond the Village* [*Chata za wsią*, 1854]) made use of his observations gathered in Volhynia. Extremely popular, they have a strong antifeudal edge, and may be said to have paved the way for the emancipation of the peasants, although Kraszewski by no means could be classified as a radical. He did not bypass contemporary problems preoccupying the intelligentsia, but his historical novels constitute his chief merit. In Polish literature, Kraszewski founded, in fact, a new genre of fiction based upon documents and other sources where the faithful presentation of a given epoch is the main goal, and plot and characters are used simply as a bait for the readers. Novels such as *Rome Under Nero* (*Rzym za Nerona*, 1866) are meticulous reconstructions of ancient history. He conceived the monumental plan of writing a series of novels that would encompass the entire history of Poland starting from its earliest beginnings. *An Ancient Tale* (*Stara baśń*, 1876), about a prehistoric and pre-Christian community, goes the furthest back in time. The numerous volumes of this series take the reader up to the eighteenth century, the period of the Saxon dynasty. Written earlier than the rest, his "Saxon novels," *The Countess Cosel* (1874) and *Brühl* (1875), are considered to be his best. Even if the historical novel is a very risky genre, as the interpretation of historical sources tends to get mixed up with attitudes proper to the author's own time, Kraszewski can be said to have achieved a great deal, being primarily a historian making careful use of his materials. His novels, intended as "ordinary bread," had little to do with the lofty Romanticism of his contemporaries and were an active factor, even as they are today, in the spread of literacy. Perhaps it would not be out of place here to bring in historical painting, especially the work of Jan Matejko (1838–1893), the success of which paralleled the popularity of Kraszewski's novels. Through a similar use of themes taken from Polish history the works of these two men can be considered as artistic and ideological counterparts.

The realistic novel, mainly under the influence of Balzac, made its way slowly and is best exemplified by Józef Korzeniowski. A native of Galicia, educated at the *lycée* in Krzemieniec and, for a while, a professor of rhetoric and poetry there, he went on to become professor of Latin literature in Kiev, a high-school principal in Kharkov, and later on, chairman of the Commission for Public Education in Warsaw. Korzeniowski was also successful at playwriting, and some of his plays were performed in his lifetime by the theater in Lwów. His best-known play, *Carpathian Mountaineers* (*Karpaccy górale*,

Józef Korzeniowski (1797–1863)

1843), is a drama focused on the figure of a young Ukrainian peasant who avoids being drafted into the Austrian army and becomes one of those Carpathian brigands who, together with the Tatra brigands, were the heroes of folk songs and legends throughout the latter part of the eighteenth and the first half of the nineteenth centuries. In his novels, *The Speculator* (*Spekulant*, 1846), *Collocation* (*Kollokacja*, 1847), and *Relatives* (*Krewni*, 1857), he proves himself a sharp-sighted observer of a society in flux, paying close attention to the economic aspects of his characters' daily existence. He traces the decay of the traditional "gentry village" and the attempts of that class of the gentry to win a new status by migrating into the ranks of the *bourgeoisie*. Korzeniowski's realism heralded the "social novel" as it was to be practiced by Polish authors in the last decades of the nineteenth century.

Teodor Tomasz Jeż (1824–1915)   The example of Teodor Tomasz Jeż (the pen name of Zygmunt Miłkowski) can explain to a large extent the lack of "normal" literature in Poland under the partitions. His fate was by no means unique. While studying at the University of Kiev, he became a radical democrat and belonged to a clandestine group. In 1848, he went to Hungary and served as a soldier in the revolutionary army throughout the campaign; after that he lived in Turkey; next he took a job in London as a manual worker and wrote journalism; then he lived in the Balkan countries as an emissary of the *émigré* Democratic Society. During the Crimean War he acted as a secret agent there for Turkey and its Western allies. Afterward, he resided in Constantinople for a few years, then went back to London, and finally settled in Romania. During the Polish insurrection of 1863, however, he was once again one of the organizers. After a short interval as a prisoner of the Austrians, he spent the rest of his life engaged in *émigré* politics in Belgrade, Brussels, and Geneva. He took to writing novels rather late, and is known mainly as a writer who introduced a new theme into Polish literature: the Southern Slavs and the history of their struggle against Turkish oppression.

Maurycy Mochnacki (1804–1834)   Prose in partitioned Poland, though modest in scope, served sometimes as a vehicle for refined essayists. This was especially true of the period before 1830, when the ideology of the budding Romantic movement found its most brilliant expression in Maurycy Mochnacki's *On Polish Literature in the Nineteenth Century* (*O literaturze polskiej w wieku dziewiętnastym*, 1830). Mochnacki has been called the most daring literary critic of the nineteenth century. A keen political journalist during the Polish-Russian war of 1831, the intellectual leader of the radical democrats, he managed, while in France, to produce what is still his most durable work, a political and social analysis in two volumes: *The Uprising of the Polish Nation in*

1830–31 (Powstanie Narodu Polskiego w r. 1830–31, 1834). Tuberculosis took his life prematurely.

After the fiasco of 1830–1831, Warsaw was a cultural desert until around 1840, when a new movement of young intellectuals began to gather momentum. These young people were connected with a progressive, even cryptorevolutionary, periodical, *The Scholarly Review (Przegląd naukowy)*. Hegel's philosophy had an overwhelming influence on these circles, and it especially marked a highly promising young philosopher, Edward Dembowski, an aristocrat with the title of castellan. Unfortunately for posterity, Dembowski, who developed the ideology of the "Hegelian Left," put his ideas into practice. He was killed in a clash with Austrian troops near Kraków at the age of twenty-four. Such young men and women in Warsaw, bound by a common passionate interest in new ideas, by platonic loves and friendships, were called "enthusiasts"— *entuzjaści* (masculine) and *entuzjastki* (feminine), in Polish. *Edward Dembowski (1822–1846)*

Narcyza Żmichowska, an emancipated woman, one of the "moving spirits" among these groups, was a private teacher all her life in the employ of rich families. Frustrated in her strivings for personal happiness, a political prisoner for two years, she kept herself together thanks to exalted friendships with other women thrown into a similar situation. Her novel, *The Heathen Woman (Poganka*, 1846), written in Romantic lyrical prose, is a half-fantastic portrait of an evil heroine; in this portrayal the author settled an account with a lady from high society with whom there had been a past involvement. *Narcyza Żmichowska (1819–1876)*

Another sign of new life in the 1840s was the young poets and painters who gathered in Warsaw cafés and salons. They were known as *Cyganeria* (Bohemians). Some of them, like Cyprian Norwid and Teofil Lenartowicz, became eminent writers.

HISTORIANS AND PHILOSOPHERS

The biographies of Polish historians and philosophers show constant wanderings across the European continent. Joachim Lelewel, the descendant of a Polonized German family (Loelhoeffel de Loewensprung) and the most important figure in Polish historiography since Jan Długosz, was born in Warsaw. A scholar to the core, he completed his studies at the University of Wilno and received an assistant professorship there, which he filled between 1815 and 1818, then a full professorship in European history, which he held from 1822 to 1824. He was beloved by students as a man of democratic convictions, and his virtues were celebrated by Adam Mickiewicz in one of his earlier poems. Deprived of his chair after the trial of the *Joachim Lelewel (1786–1861)*

Philomaths, he moved to Warsaw, where he engaged in fervent political activity. But politics was not one of his strong points, and he proved himself an inefficient leader during the war of 1831 against Russia, when he served a short span as member of the revolutionary government. After the defeat, he set out on foot across Germany to France, where his fame as a scholar and his radical views assured him the spiritual leadership of the *émigré* democratic wing. Expelled from France, after the intervention of the Russian Embassy (the czarist police feared him as a dangerous instigator of revolutionary ideas), he took to the road, again on foot, walked through France, and settled in Brussels in 1833 for the rest of his life. He led a solitary existence, maintaining himself solely by his books, which he began to write in French. He left behind a tremendous work that embraces twenty volumes of Polish and European history. His *Historica* (*Historyka*, 1815) was the first book in Polish dedicated to questions of methodology in historical studies. *Numismatics of the Middle Ages*, written in French and published in 1835, contained his own illustrations, as did his *Geography of the Middle Ages* (1852–1857), also in French. His monumental work in four volumes, *Poland of the Middle Ages* (*Polska wieków średnich*, 1846–1851), in Polish, testifies both to his striving toward objectivity and to his Romantic spirit. Like Michelet in France and Ranke in Germany, he searched for that which was indigenous, unique to national institutions. In Poland, he found that originality in the primitive communities of the Slavs; but those indigenous tentatives had been stifled by the emergence of an aristocracy and by the impact of the Roman Catholic Church. Thus, in the history of Poland, he saw a struggle between the Slavic-Republican-Democratic-Pagan element and the Monarchic-Christian-Feudal element. In the parliamentarism of the gentry, he divined a survival of the former and tended to ascribe the misfortunes of the country not to the weakness engendered by the principle of unanimity in the Diet but to the abuse of a basically healthy system. Such theses were not just the opinions of a publicist, for Lelewel induced a true revolution in historical scholarship through his meticulous examination of sources, his use of numismatics, and his stress on the material aspects of change in societies. Under his pen, history definitely ceased to be a story of rulers and was transformed into the story of successive phases.

Julian Klaczko (1825–1906)   Quite an opposite direction was taken by Julian Klaczko. A native of Wilno, born into a Jewish family, he wrote in Hebrew as a growing boy and was connected with the Jewish "Haskalah" (Enlightenment) movement, but soon switched to Polish. After finishing his university studies in Germany (where he published in German), he moved to Paris and there won fame for his mordant publicism, written in excellent French, which exerted considerable influence on public opinion. For many years he was a contributor to the most influential Parisian review, *La revue des deux mondes*. He did not abandon Polish and lent his support to the conservative *émigrés*, that is, the monarchists grouped around Prince Adam Czartoryski in the Hôtel Lambert. Of his studies on poetry, art, and politics, perhaps the most significant are the following, written in French: *Causeries florentines*—on Dante; *Rome et la Renaissance*—on Michelangelo; *Les deux chanceliers*—on the foreign policies of Bismarck and Gorchakov.

Messianism, so devoutly celebrated in Polish Romantic poetry, had just as much of a sounding board in voluminous works of philosophical prose. August Cieszkowski, a rich landowner from the province of Poznań and a philosopher, after completing his studies in Berlin, entered into serious polemics with Hegelian thought. He took much from the German philosopher, but at the same time attempted to give the main lines of his system a new twist. In his *Prolegomena zur Historiosophie*, published in Berlin in 1838, he reproached Hegel for giving insufficient place to the idea of will and free human action. *Prolegomena* exerted some influence in Germany and also upon Hegelians in Russia. Later on, he developed his philosophy of will in a work of several volumes called *Our Father* (*Ojcze nasz*), the first part of which appeared in Poznań in 1848. This is a kind of sentence-by-sentence meditation on the Lord's Prayer. Cieszkowski, a personal friend of Zygmunt Krasiński, predicted a phase in human history when freedom throughout the world would be achieved through human action; this phase would be characterized by the ascendancy of the Slavs, and, of course, the Poles, who have been especially called to that final task.

August Cieszkowski (1814–1894)

Somewhat similar ideas were expressed by Bronisław Trentowski. A teacher who came from a petty-gentry family in Mazovia, he joined the Polish uprising as an active combatant in 1831, then migrated to Germany. In Freiburg im Breisgau, he lectured on philosophy and published scholarly studies in German. Returning to Poland later on, he settled in Prussian-occupied Poznań and there was able to publish his books in Polish. Though dependent upon Hegel, he elaborated a historiosophical system of his own, and, like Cieszkowski, he also stressed action: "All my teaching, all my politics, is the teaching of *Deed*." According to Trentowski, history's final stage was to be marked by the victory of the Slavs. The Poles were assigned the mission of preserving God in their souls, for the occidental world had rejected Him. Central to his view is his treatise on pedagogy, *Upbringing, or A System of National Pedagogy* (*Chowanna, czyli system pedagogiki narodowej*, 1842), which out-

Bronisław Trentowski (1808–1896)

lines his plan for a basic reform in education so conceived that it would prepare Poles for their future obligations: Polish psychology should be transformed, as it is overwhelmed by a powerful and quite oriental imagination that works to the detriment of such purely intellectual qualities as are dominant in the Western mind.

J. M. Hoene-
Wroński
(1778–1853)

　　Józef Maria Hoene-Wroński up to this day has not ceased to attract dedicated interpreters both in Poland and abroad. An officer of the artillery, he served under Kościuszko in 1794, then in the Russian army. After a short period of study in Germany, he joined up with the Polish Napoleonic legion in Marseilles, and from that year (1800) until his death, he preferred to remain in France, publishing his books there. (They were written exclusively in French.) A mathematician, a physicist, a theoretician of law and economics, Wroński sought to deduce mathematically all the rules of human knowledge and behavior from one underlying principle. This principle eludes definition, as it is the source of all being and all knowledge and is, thus, inaccessible to man's intellect. He named it the Absolute. He was convinced that all religious and metaphysical truths could be proven by correct reasoning and, thus, would become as universally acceptable as mathematical equations. As soon as mankind recognizes a doctrine (his own) that "incarnates absolute philosophy, fulfills religion, reforms sciences, explains history, discovers the goal of nations," it will move from the stage of chaos and conflict to a stage of perfect reasonableness. Opposing to Hegel's his own system, he saw the law of creation (*la loi de la création*) as a movement which stems from the Absolute and tends toward greater and greater diversity of being through a struggle of opposites; in place of Hegel's triad he introduced duality as the motor of change. In history he distinguished four periods, characterized by the goals pursued in their respective civilizations: material (the East), moral (Greece, Rome), religious (the Middle Ages), and intellectual (modern Europe). The final stage will come back as the result of a union between the good and the true, between science and religion. This will be accomplished by the Slavic nations, who will supplant the Latin and Germanic nations in their role as spiritual leaders. He designated his absolutist system "messianic" because it was the fulfillment of the Slavic mission in the world. He divided philosophy into two separate disciplines: one, devoted to cognition; another, to tracing directives for politics, law, and economics in accordance with the rules of justice and progress, deduced from the Absolute. The stress Wroński laid upon the second of these disciplines places him in the current of Polish Romantic activism. Though acclaimed by a few as a mathematical genius, he did not win, either among his French or his Polish contemporaries, wider recognition. The extreme intricacy of his system has forced his interpreters and disciples to employ a style no less obscure than their master's own. He left a voluminous *œuvre* consisting of some one hundred titles. His most important books are *Philosophie des mathématiques* (1811); *Prodrome du messianisme, révélations des destinées de l'humanité* (1831); *Métapolitique messianique* (1839); *Messianisme ou réforme absolue du savoir humain* (1847); *Philosophie absolue de l'histoire* (1852).

STORY OF A FAMILY

Apollo Korzeniowski (1820–1869) was one of three sons in a family of soldiers and adventurers from the Ukraine. His father had served under Napoleon and later took part in the uprising of 1830–1831. Apollo's elder brother was deported to Siberia for membership in a conspiracy; his younger brother perished on the battlefield in 1863. As a young boy, Apollo himself was constantly suspended from high school on account of his "freethinking." He is described by his contemporaries as ugly but witty, the possessor of a malicious tongue with which he terrorized society. His plays in verse are marked by a similar propensity toward vitriolic satire. Throughout his life, he was obsessed by a deeply felt dichotomy between the Ideal and the hoggish life which surrounded him. An inveterate hater of the Establishment, he combined a somewhat hazy radicalism with a religious frame of mind—which impelled him toward active participation in the political struggle. In 1855, he witnessed a rebellion of the Ukrainian peasants, which arose as a result of the weakening of czardom during the Crimean War. His sympathy went to the peasants, who offered only a passive resistance to the troops and were crushed with artillery. For a while he was a student of oriental languages in St. Petersburg, then a tenant farmer in the Ukraine; but Apollo Korzeniowski's real interest was literature and politics, which for him went hand in glove. In 1861, he moved to Warsaw and there plunged into conspiratorial activity. He became one of the founders of the clandestine City Committee, the nucleus of the provisional government that directed the uprising of 1863. By that time he was married to a girl whom he had won after many years of opposition from her family, as he was poor, a poet, and of unsettled character.

Evelina Bobrowski was a girl with great merits of mind and character. Although the Bobrowski family was proud of its sober, realistic approach to life, only one of its representatives, Evelina's elder brother Tadeusz Bobrowski, fulfilled the expectations. All his life, he stayed away from politics; an excellent administrator of his family's estates, he was enlightened, moderately progressive, and businesslike. He left behind one of the most interesting memoirs of the Polish nineteenth century. Another brother of Evelina's was the exact opposite. Fervent, enthusiastic, romantic, radical, during the insurrection of 1863 he displayed a genius for guerrilla logistics; a leading figure among the so-called "Reds," he was killed in a duel that was set as a trap for him by his more conservative enemies. Evelina, through her marriage with Apollo Korzeniowski, embarked on a similar road, and her loyalty to her beloved husband was unshakable. An only son was born to them in 1857, and was given the two Christian names, Józef and Konrad. (His father highly revered Mickiewicz's works.) Their boy was to become a novelist, writing in English under the pen name of Joseph Conrad.

Apollo Korzeniowski was arrested in Warsaw in 1861, spent nine months as a prisoner in the Warsaw fortress, and, subsequently, was deported to Vologda in northern Russia. Evelina and the child accompanied him. They made the journey from Warsaw in a carriage under police escort. In such circumstances the saving of the child's life when he fell ill with meningitis verged on a miracle. In Vologda, where the climate was so severe that, in one of his letters, Korzeniowski spoke of there being only two seasons: "white winter and green winter," he wrote a political treatise, *Poland and Russia* and had it smuggled abroad, where it was published by an *émigré* periodical in Leipzig in 1864. The treatise totally rejects Russia, depicting it as a monstrous organism that feeds on slavery and as a tyranny whose czar unites in his own person all functions: commander-in-chief, legislator, and priest. A state religion is idolatrous; it spreads fatalism and fanaticism. And Western Europe, by avoiding a confrontation with Russia, is preparing a defeat for itself: "At the Congress of Vienna, European governments, freed from their fear of Napoleon, that man of destiny, were already trembling at the sight of the czarist empire, that implacable machine of destruction. . . . Europe was exhausted by twenty years of war; its governments were ready to tolerate the most terrible violence and crime among themselves if only not to endanger peace. Their slogan was *Peace!* but their hidden, torturing thought was how to placate Muscovy." According to Korzeniowski, England bore the burden of responsibility for Russia's strength because in the name of the balance of power she did not wish to see a revolt in Poland or the Ukraine lest it strengthen France.

The climate finally undermined the health of Evelina, and Korzeniowski, after many attempts, obtained permission to move to Chernigov. But Evelina soon died there from tuberculosis. A childhood spent in the company of a gloomy, desperate father probably explains much in the work of the future English novelist. Allowed to leave the Russian Empire because of his poor health, Apollo Korzeniowski took his son and moved to the Austrian-occupied part of Poland. He died in Kraków in 1869. The attendance of large crowds at his funeral turned it into a manifestation of respect for the gallant fighter. After his father's death, the adolescent Józef Konrad was placed under the care of the sober-minded Tadeusz Bobrowski. For many years after, even when Joseph Conrad was roaming the seas, Bobrowski provided paternal advice and kept up a cordial correspondence with his charge.

Korzeniowski's poems circulated anonymously during his lifetime, and were sometimes ascribed to the "anonymous poet," Zygmunt Krasiński. They are typical of late Romanticism in their form and in their stress upon martyrdom as the destiny of those men who do not accept the egoistic pursuit of money and pleasure. But it is thanks to his two plays in verse that Apollo Korzeniowski remains in literature. The first, entitled *Comedy* (*Komedia*), was strongly attacked by critics upon its publication in Wilno in 1856. The author was rebuked for the brutality with which he satirized "good society" and for modeling some of the situations too closely on Griboyedov's *Woe from Wit*. Though a critic conceded: "His wit bites to the bone; his irony kills; his laughter is similar to the growling of a dog followed by a deep sinking of teeth." The play remained unstaged until 1952, when it was called "the most progressive, the most savage, the most vitriolic work of literature from the fifties of the last century." His second play, *For That Sweet Money* (*Dla miłego grosza*), came out in 1859 in St. Petersburg with many lines of dots (indicating the censor's slashing). It was performed, however, in Korzeniowski's lifetime by Polish theaters in Zhitomir and Kiev. The action of both plays takes place in the wheat capitals of the Ukraine—Odessa and Kiev; both plays treat the same theme—the corruptive power of money. Even the plots are similar. A young man's emotional involvement with a girl fails to end in marriage because the young man is a "proletarian," an intellectual, and a revolutionary, while the beautiful and intelligent girl is completely in the power of the societal set of values, which in this case means the selling of oneself to whoever possesses money. Marriage, thus, turns out to be legalized prostitution, and such monsters as those plays uncover are seldom to be met with even in the novels of Balzac. The same character, Henry, appears in both plays—in the first, it is Henry's marriage plans that are frustrated; in the second, his friend's. Henry is a bitter, disillusioned man, compelled to live in a milieu which he hates and in which he must mask his true feelings; his friend, Joseph, a revolutionary who has returned from deportation, tries to win the hand of a young girl, but the result is only an inextricable tangle of misunderstandings, because she believes Joseph is rich. Henry acts as adviser, endeavoring to cure his friend of his illusions as to girls of good society. The third play, a short tragedy entitled *Act One (Akt pierwszy)*, is inferior to the two preceding; it was written at the end of Korzeniowski's life and traces the workings of fate, which reveals itself as an inherited propensity to treason; political treason and betrayal in marriage are somewhat equated. Apollo Korzeniowski holds an honorable place in Polish letters, and his dual attitude as an ironic realist and an indomitable knight cannot be ignored by any student of the writings of Joseph Conrad.

CYPRIAN NORWID
(1821–1883)

The peculiar fate of Cyprian Norwid, who remained practically an unknown poet throughout the nineteenth century but whose influence, since about 1900, has grown stronger in every decade, cannot be understood unless we describe the situation in Polish poetry at the time of his appearance on the literary scene. Norwid reached manhood when Polish poetry was under the domination by the great poets of the Emigration, and the sheer weight of their talent crushed all newcomers. Although access to the works of Mickiewicz and Słowacki was either difficult or (in the Congress Kingdom) forbidden, copies from abroad steadily found their way into Polish hands. The poets who imitated those two authors and who constituted, thus, the second wave of Romanticism tended to dilute the primary accomplishments of the "Great Romantics." They moved, as we have already mentioned, toward a facile melodiousness. Basically syllabic, Polish verse is a pliable instrument, because within its patterns, "feet" can be composed of accented and nonaccented syllables; syllabic verse is thus turned into "syllabotonic." Mickiewicz and Słowacki, while applying in some poems trochaic, dactylic, or iambic "feet," did not use them rigidly; thus, their verse was never monotonous. Their successors, however, developed a liking for a pounding rhythm, and the poets who became most popular with the public in the middle and second half of the nineteenth century exemplify that predilection. Thus, one of the most widely read, Wincenty Pol (1807–1872), employed a pattern that verges on nursery rhyme. Pol (actually Pohl), a Polonized son of an Austrian functionary in Galicia, produced a kind of patriotic "treatise" in verse (a work full of charm, incidentally) on the geography and customs of various Polish provinces: *A Song About Our Land (Pieśń o ziemi naszej,*

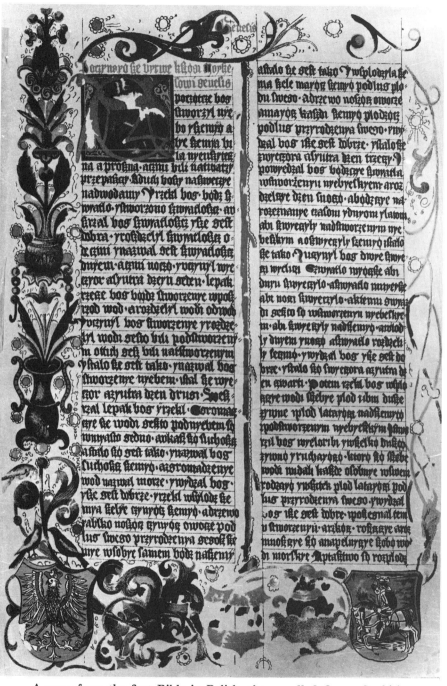

A page from the first Bible in Polish, the so-called Queen Sophie's Bible. Illuminated manuscript, 1455.

Mikołaj Rej (1505–1569). Portrait dated 1550.

The title page of a novella in verse, *The Game of Chess*, by Jan Kochanowski (1530–1584).

Jan Zamoyski, Chancellor of Poland. Portrait from the Uffizi Gallery, Florence.

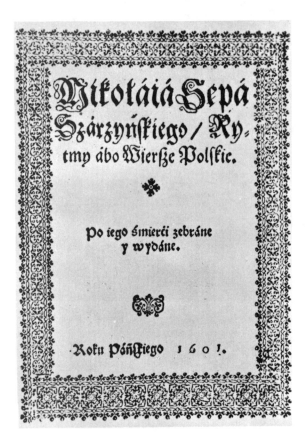

The title page of *Rhythms*, a collection of poems by Mikołaj Sęp-Szarzyński (ca. 1550–1581).

Jan Andrzej Morsztyn (1613–1693).
Portrait by Hyacinthe Rigaud.

Wespazjan Kochowski (1633–1700). Anonymous portrait from the Church of Goleniów.

Stanisław Herakliusz Lubomirski (1642–1702). Portrait by an unknown artist.

Ignacy Krasicki (1735–1801). Portrait by Per Krafft.

Jakub Jasiński (1759–1794). Portrait by an unknown artist.

Grave é à Paris par Croutelle, 1828.

Adam Mickiewicz (1798–1855). Steel engraving.

Juliusz Słowacki (1809–1849).

Zygmunt Krasiński (1812–1859).
After a portrait by the French artist
Ary Scheffer.

Cyprian Kamil Norwid (1821–1883).

Józef Ignacy Kraszewski (1812–1887).

Bolesław Prus (1845–1912).

Henryk Sienkiewicz (1846–
1916). Portrait by Jadwiga
Janczewska.

Jan Kasprowicz (1860–1926).

Stefan Żeromski (1864–1925).

Stanisław Wyspiański (1869–1907). Self-portrait.

Illustration by Stanisław Wyspiański for the *Iliad:* Apollo shooting
an arrow of plague (1897).

Straw-men (mulches), painted by Stanisław Wyspiański in 1899.

Drawing by Bruno Schulz (1892–1942) for the cover of his book *Cinnamon Stores*.

Stanisław Ignacy Witkiewicz (1885–1939).

Witold Gombrowicz (1905–1969).

1835). Geography was Pol's passion, and as a teacher and specialist, he made several research voyages throughout Poland (the Tatra Mountains included), leaving valuable and picturesque prose accounts of his expeditions. Most of his life was spent in Galicia—in Lwów and Kraków. After the uprising of 1831, in which he had taken part, he joined the Great Emigration, but his stay abroad was relatively short, and he soon returned to Galicia. His experiences of war and exile are reflected in his *Songs of Janusz* (*Pieśni Janusza*, 1831–1833). His long poem, *Mohort* (1852), pays tribute to the genre of *gawęda* in verse, and in it, he duly returns to the days of the old *Respublica*. Mohort is the family name of a brave and modest nobleman-soldier who combats the Tartar raids on the southeastern borders of the country.

Another poet, of considerably greater talent than Pol, was Teofil Lenartowicz (1822–1893). The son of a master mason, he was born in Warsaw. As a youth he frequented circles of the Warsaw *Cyganeria* (Bohemians) but, in fact, did not belong to them. He was just beginning his career as a government official when, threatened with arrest because of his political connections, he escaped from Russian-occupied Poland in 1848. He lived in Kraków, in Brussels, then in Paris, and from 1856 on, in Italy. He settled in Florence, where, besides writing poetry, he practiced sculpture. For a while, he taught the history of Slavic literature at the University of Bologna. He died in Florence, but his body was brought back to his native land for ceremonial burial in Kraków. Lenartowicz's years of childhood, spent in a village in the province of Mazovia near Warsaw, marked him forever; and in his best poetry he returns to the landscape of the Mazovian plain as seen through the eyes of a peasant child. Naïve, idyllic, and presumably "folkish," a few of the poems contained in his two volumes, *The Small Lyre* (*Lirenka*, 1855) and *The New Small Lyre* (*Nowa lirenka*, 1859), can be counted among the most graceful of Polish lyrics. His longer poems, published in 1855, *Rapture* (*Zachwycenie*) and *The Blessed One* (*Błogosławiona*), contain a curious treatment of religious themes: for a soul after death, heaven has all the outward features of a Polish landscape and a Polish village. Among Lenartowicz's abundant works are some interesting poems on the Italy of his time; they were published under the title *Italian Album* (*Album włoskie*, 1870). He also tried his hand at historical poetry, and the verses in which he returned to the heroic past appeared in the volume *Old Armor* (*Ze starych zbroic*, 1870). But Lenartowicz, above all, remained in his readers' memories as the "Mazovian lyre player" (*lirnik mazowiecki*).

His contemporary, Kornel Ujejski (1823–1897), came closer to the Romantic idea of a bard. Born in Podolia, he studied in Lwów, then in 1847 went to Paris to attend the Sorbonne and the Collège de France. There, he met Mickiewicz, Słowacki, and Chopin. In 1848, he returned to Galicia, where he earned his living as a gentleman farmer and even received a deputyship to the State Council in Vienna. His poetry is a response to the collective misfortunes of the period. Thus, his poem "Marathon" (1845), describing the struggle of the Greeks against the Persians, refers, in fact, to the struggle of the Poles against the occupying powers. For his cycle, *Lamentations of Jeremiah* (*Skargi Jeremiego*, 1847), he drew on the Bible and Krasiński's messianic poetry to convey the tragedy of fratricide, i.e., of the 1846 rebellion, encouraged by the Austrian authorities, of the Polish peasants against their Polish lords. One of the poems from this cycle, called "Chorale," was set to music and, for a while, was on the point of becoming a national anthem. But Ujejski was not only attracted to the Bible because Polish messianism took its inspiration from the Old Testament; he also paraphrased the Song of Solomon and published a whole cycle of *Biblical Melodies* (*Melodie biblijne*, 1852). In his *Translations from Chopin* (*Tłumaczenia Szopena*, written in the late fifties) he attempted to render the Polish composer's music in verse. Though venerated in his lifetime, Ujejski is a minor poet and less a "bard" than a mourner; he can claim few lyrics to his credit as pure as those of Lenartowicz.

Norwid admired the "Great Romantics"; he knew Mickiewicz personally, and enjoyed the friendship of both Słowacki and Krasiński. He also counted Lenartowicz and Zaleski among his intimates. Yet both his philosophy and his literary technique went beyond the Romantic trend. At the start of his career, he was hailed as a poet of considerable promise; as he matured, critics rebuked him more and more frequently, bewailing the impenetrable obscurity of his style and his jarring syntax, until no one would publish him. If measured by the standard of public opinion, his poetic life ended as a failure. Only subsequent transformations in sensibility brought about a reappraisal that assigned him the position of precursor of modern Polish poetry.

His biography was responsible, too, for his estrangement from the tastes of his contemporaries. Born near Warsaw into an impoverished noble family and orphaned at an early age, he was brought up by relatives. His somewhat erratic education consisted of a few years of high school in Warsaw and some courses in painting and sculpture. Later on, he acquired great erudition on his own, especially in history and archaeology. Young Norwid, whose first poems had made him famous in circles of the Warsaw Bohemians, was fascinated, as it was the fashion of the day to be, by folklore. With a friend, he set off on foot across Poland, jotting down, along the way,

the texts of folk songs and making drawings of human types, architecture, and landscapes. When he was twenty-one, he left for Germany and Italy to study sculpture on a privately provided scholarship.
He was never to return. The Russian Embassy in Berlin, owing to
an incident (he had lent his passport to a political suspect and had
been imprisoned), withdrew his passport, and Norwid, willingly
or not, found himself part of the Great Emigration. He spent several
years in Italy, living in Florence and Rome and traveling there—once
he made a trip along the Mediterranean—and all this, including his
keen interest in the history of art, went into the making of his poetry.
Norwid is, in a way, a poet of the Mediterranean, of its many-
layered past—Egyptian, Jewish, Greek, Roman. In Rome he was a
frequent visitor at the Café Greco, a gathering place for writers
that was also patronized by Gogol. In 1848, he witnessed Mickiewicz's activity in Italy, though he took a rather critical attitude
toward it. An unfortunate, unreciprocated love for one of the high-
society lionesses of the period, the beautiful Mrs. Maria Kalergis, a
lady of Russian-Polish origin married to a Greek shipowner, proved
to be a disrupting factor throughout many years of his life. Norwid,
as a young man, was somewhat of a delicate dandy, a timid, reserved
introvert, veiling the depth of his feelings with irony. Moreover, he
was penniless. While in exile, he was condemned to earn his living
as a draftsman and sculptor, but was too proud to confess his utter
misery. From Italy he went to Paris, where he often worked as a
simple manual laborer. Out of a desire to escape from poverty and
his memories of unhappy love, he migrated to America at the end
of 1852, traveling in the steerage amid crowds of immigrants. The
voyage, by frigate, lasted sixty-three days. In New York, he found
a job as illustrator for the catalogue of the so-called Crystal Palace
exposition of 1853–1854. Yet his stay in the New World was made
unendurable by his complete solitude in New York and what he felt
to be the lack of history in America, of the kind that speaks to man
through the permanent traces—no matter if they are ruins—left by
human hands. He returned to Europe in 1854, going first to London,
then to Paris, where he lived until his death. His appraisal of America was a complex one, as positive as it was negative, and his two
poems on John Brown show an intense spiritual participation in the
abolitionist movement. Solitude pursued Norwid not only in America.
More and more isolated by his reputation for eccentricity, he was
given up for lost by literary critics as a man who had squandered
his talent writing incomprehensible things. Without family, growing
old and deaf, he communicated less and less with the Polish *émigré*
milieu. He succeeded in publishing only one large volume in his
lifetime: his *Selected Poems*, which appeared in the famous "Brock-
haus Collection" of Polish literature printed in Leipzig in 1863.

Without means of support, in the last years of his life he found
refuge in the St. Casimir House in Paris, a home for the aged
maintained by Polish nuns. When he died, there was no money for
a separate tomb, and he was buried in a pauper's grave. The contents of his trunks, filled with manuscripts and drawings, reached
posterity only in part, because the nuns at St. Casimir's had censored
them and some things were destroyed (though it is doubtful whether
they contained anything offensive, as Norwid had been a practicing
Roman Catholic all his life). Some twenty years after the poet's
death, Zenon Miriam Przesmycki, one of the first Polish "modernists"
and the first translator of Arthur Rimbaud, began collecting Norwid's
manuscripts and publishing them in his review, *Chimera*.

"Censorship," a pen-and-ink drawing by Cyprian Kamil Norwid, 1841.

Norwid's destiny led him into a singlehanded confrontation with his
Polish contemporaries and with the new industrial civilization of the
West, the leviathan of the Big City, in whose belly he spent many
years. Toward his elders in Polish poetry he defined his attitude as
follows:

> Laurels, I have not taken, then or now,
> A single leaf from you, nor a leaf's notch,
> Only perhaps a cool shade on my brow
> (And that's not yours but comes with the sun's touch);

Nor did I take from you, giants of stardom,
Anything save your roads all overgrown
With wormwood, and your curse-scorched earth and boredom.
I came alone, I wander on alone.*

Dlatego od was . . . o laury! nie wziąłem
Listka jednego, ni ząbeczka w liściu,
Prócz może cieniu chłodnego nad czołem
(Co nie należy wam—lecz słońca przyjściu . . .);
Nie wziąłem od was nic, o! wielkoludy,
Prócz dróg zarosłych w piołun, mech i szalej,
Prócz ziemi klątwą spalonej i nudy . . .
Samotny wszedłem i sam błądzę dalej.

Though he was well-read in Western European literature, he preserved complete independence from the literary currents of the day. Even though some of his poems bring to mind works of Théophile Gautier and the budding French symbolists, basically he was against aestheticism. As a man and as a poet, Norwid aspired to be like Don Quixote, a knight of truth (his poem on Don Quixote is one of his best). His weapon was a subtle irony so hidden within symbols and parables that his first readers hardly noticed it. To break the monotony of regularly repeated "feet" within the syllabic pattern, he deliberately made his verse sound roughhewn; often he would just abandon the syllabic system for free verse. In a letter (to Bronisław Zaleski) of November 1867, he revealed that he was completely aware of what he was doing:

What Karol says about the number of syllables is *the most hideous barbarism* and *shows complete ignorance of even Horace himself.*

When my *Vade-Mecum* comes out in print, they will see, they will recognize what the true lyric of the Polish language is like because as yet they do not know it at all, nor have they the flimsiest notion about it.

There is no prose; there was never any prose in the world—all that is complete nonsense. *What is a Period in Prosody?* There never was any prose—and number, which the writer cannot hide in long-and-round-sounding words, is nothing but a total *destruction of the nature of rhythm.*

Perfect lyric poetry should be like a cast in plaster; the slashes where form passes form, leaving crevices, must be preserved and not smoothed out with a knife. Only the barbarian takes all this off of the plaster with his knife and destroys the whole, but I swear before you that what Poles call lyric poetry is just *a pounding and a mazurka.*†

Norwid's imagery also put him on the opposite shore from the current fashion. His training as a sculptor and as a draftsman inclined him to flee the colorful and the picturesque. He uses subdued colors,

* Translated by Christine Brooke-Rose.
† Translated by Jerzy Pietrkiewicz.

a chiaroscuro transfixed with shafts of light (he particularly admired Rembrandt), but this is not an art for art's sake. Every line serves to bring the reader closer to the philosophical goal of the poem, and Norwid, undoubtedly, is the most "intellectual" poet ever to write in Polish.

Norwid's encounter with industrial civilization somewhat recalls the experiences of his American contemporaries, writers with a rural background. When Emerson, formulating the program of the transcendentalists, said, "It is better to be alone than in bad company"; or, "All that is clearly due today is not to lie"; or, "This is not a time for gaiety and grace. His [the transcendentalist's] strength and spirits are wasted in rejection"—Norwid could have accepted these maxims as his own. But an even more striking analogy can be found with Herman Melville. Both writers made similar use of irony. In the world which the industrious white man created and which he called a Christian world, Melville saw nothing but brutality, callousness, greed, and misery. He was an Ishmael, wandering over the face of the earth in search of primeval innocence, and he seemed to locate that innocence beyond the pale of the materialistic civilization of the nineteenth century. Norwid, as a newcomer, from a preindustrial society, thrown into the jungle of Western Europe, was alien to all the bustle of buying and selling. Images of ghastly London and Paris streets which appear in some of Norwid's poems parallel the American writer's descriptions in prose. Although Norwid probably never read Melville, in one of his short stories, entitled "Civilization," he employed the symbol of a ship similarly to the way Melville handled it in his *Confidence Man*. But Norwid's solutions were not Melville's. If we were to search for the reason, we might make conjectures about the collectivist tradition in Poland versus the isolation of the individual in America or about Roman Catholicism versus Protestantism. Whatever the reason, Norwid could not simply reject civilization, hypocritical and pharisaical though it may be, in the name of an innocent, natural pre-Christian man. While Melville was mainly concerned with the problem of Man and Nature (an obsession for many American writers), Norwid concentrated upon the problem of Man and History. He has been called a "poet of ruins" because he went to the sources of European history in the Mediterranean region and listened to the echoes of its past. For Norwid, History was a continuity, a process tending in a certain direction, a constant accomplishment of God's hidden plan through mankind. A given civilization was just a phase between the past and the future; the present could not simply be cast aside, because it was the place where the future was being engendered. The materialistic civilization of the nineteenth century worshiped financial and political power, condemning those who were true to the conscience of history, be they individuals or groups, to martyrdom. The goal of history, according to Norwid, was "to make martyrdom unnecessary on the earth," and the achievement of this was, therefore, the only criterion of progress. As he said himself:

A man is born on this planet to give testimony to the truth. He should, therefore, know and remember that every civilization should be considered as a means and not as an aim—thus, to sell one's soul to a civilization and at the same time to pray in church is to be a pharisee.

Because he was convinced that Christ had led man out of the realm of fatality and into the realm of freedom, Norwid's attention constantly turned to early Christianity both in verse and in prose. His long poem *Quidam* is, for instance, a vision of Rome in the second century. Historical meditation cannot be separated from Norwid's poetry. It is its very core. And some of his views are striking: his stress on the role of "peripheries"—Samaria for Judea, Gaul for the Roman Empire, America for Europe—and the gradual movement from the centers toward the peripheries; or his theory of "stumbling blocks": for America—the Negro, for England—Ireland, for the old Polish *Respublica*—the Ukraine, for Russia, Prussia, and Austria—Poland, for France—continuous revolutions; or his principle of "things passed over in silence": every epoch passes over something in silence, and that which remains beneath the surface, inadmissible to the consciousness of one era, becomes a motive power in the next.

Norwid was not a politician, and he maintained his distance from all the political groupings of the Great Emigration. He believed that an artist participates in history through his art. His conception of art is closely connected with his respect for human labor. While he elaborated his philosophy of labor and art independently from Ruskin and Morris in England, he resembled them in some respects. He was not a socialist, though some of the writings of French socialists combined with his own life experience as an artisan may have gone toward shaping his pious approach to human toil. His theory of art is set forth in the long poem *Promethidion* (published in Paris, 1851), written in the form of a conversation among a few characters and provided with footnotes in prose. The title means "Prometheus' child." To Norwid, Prometheus was more a giver of crafts to mankind than a rebel; thus, labor, whether a peasant's, a sailor's, or an artist's —or that very poem—is Prometheus' child. As a Christian, Norwid saw in labor the result of original sin. Before his Fall, man lived in harmony with God and the universe. Through sin, he entered the path of history, and to redeem himself, man must work throughout innumerable millennia. But work is redeeming only if it is accepted with love and not as a scourge imposed by the fear of starvation or punishment. Work accepted with love is the highest manifestation of human freedom. However, in modern times manual labor has become a scourge, and the only work performed with love and joy is that of the artist. This means that a complete cleavage exists between the work of "the people" and the work of the creative and educated circles. Only if these two branches of human endeavor are united will it be possible for toiling people to share the joy known by the artist. If the highest forms of art were to be united with the humblest objects of everyday life, the chasm separating those who live *by spirit alone* from those who live *only by their hands* would disappear. The artist should be an "organizer of the national imagination." Norwid was drawing upon his observations of his native country when he said:

Those nations which forgot about the uplifting function of art, which failed to establish *their own* art, and so failed to bring forth a chain of handicrafts—either lost their real existence or are just toiling; their work, disconnected from the *work* of the *spirit*, is not more than a fatality and a penance imposed upon one social layer. The "people," whose very souls are shaped by *manual* work, must, by necessity, grow further and further from those higher circles of the nation who perform only mental work. For the *contents of thought* obtained through manual work are different from those obtained by *pure thinking*. The result is that abstract thought, deprived by degrees of its ties with humble labors, returns in difficult moments (i.e., politically difficult) to folk wisdom, peasant motifs, proverbs, legends, or songs—and even technological folk traditions. Often, it is too late, and the backbone with its marrow uniting the total sum of work in a given nation disintegrates into *remembrances of the past* and *longings for the future*.

Art must come from a dialogue between the popular imagination and the "learned" imagination of an artist. To quote Norwid again: "The best musician is the People, but the composer is their fiery tongue." This means that the composer transforms his native music into an art that is more than national, and, in fact, it is universal. Frédéric Chopin (a personal friend) was for Norwid an ideal example of such a composer. Norwid's revolt against mazurkas in poetry is, therefore, nothing other than a revolt against a shallow interpretation of folk tradition. As for his negative opinion of "art for art's sake," it can be summed up in one line from his *Promethidion:* "Art is a banner on the tower of human labors."

Because of his forward-looking treatment of Polish verse, Norwid's role has sometimes been compared to Mallarmé's in French poetry. It would be a mistake, however, to draw analogies with French symbolists. On the one hand, Norwid was rooted in the Romantic preoccupation with History. On the other, he overcame his isolation as an individual through an understanding of the complex links between a work of art and the collectivity; unlike Mallarmé, he did not limit himself to "purifying the language of the tribe," but always strove to convey a message. One is tempted to say that the social orientation, which is so noticeable in Polish literature from Kochanowski on, culminated in Norwid, and his influence in the twentieth century has been to act as a counterbalance to the overbearing presence of the French symbolists.

Norwid is not an impeccable poet. The nearly complete absence of an audience, and thus, the lack of any controls, permitted him to indulge in such a torturing of the language that some of his lines are hopelessly obscure. But his poems are never just a translation of philosophy into verse. His philosophy seems to grow organically with his images, although the weight of intellectual contents is so great that sometimes it threatens to break the artistic structure. Several of Norwid's poems put him on a level with Mickiewicz and have become part of Poland's classical heritage. One of the most famous, "To the Memory of Bem, A Funeral Rhapsody" ("Bema pamięci rapsod żałobny," 1851), honored a Polish hero—an insurrectionist in 1830–1831, and a leader of the revolutionary Hungarian army in 1848–1849. Under Norwid's pen, Bem's funeral takes on features of an old Slavic pre-Christian rite, and this march of primitive tribesmen and women is itself transformed into a march of all humanity over the obstacles of tyranny toward the future. The poem has a very intricate metrical pattern and is one of the examples of the "Polish hexameter." But what proved to be most fruitful for modern Polish poetry was Norwid's collection of short poems, *Vade-Mecum*, which remained unpublished in his lifetime and dates probably from before 1866. Although Norwid is so difficult to translate that an idea of the original can scarcely get through to an English reader, here are two rather successful English versions by Christine Brooke-Rose:

Marionettes

How can one help being bored, when silently
A million stars shine in the silent skies,
Each one glittering quite differently,
And everything stands still—and flies . . .

And the earth stands still like the abyss of time,
Like those who are living at the moment, whose
Last small bone will vanish into slime
Though men will be—as always . . .

How can one help being bored on so restricted
A stage, so amateurishly set,
Where mankind's each ideal has acted,
And life is the price of a seat . . .

I rack my brains to kill another hour,
For I am wrapped in boredom's deadening curse.
I ask you, madam, what can be the cure?
To write some prose perhaps, or verse?

Or not to write? Just to sit in the sun
And read that interesting romance
The Deluge wrote on grains of sand, for fun,
To amuse mankind, perchance!—

Or better still—I know a manlier way
With boredom: to pass PEOPLE by
But visit PERSONAGES—and display
An exquisitely knotted tie . . . !

Marjonetki

Jak się nie nudzić? gdy oto nad globem
Miljon gwiazd cichych się świeci,
A każda innym jaśnieje sposobem,
A wszystko stoi—i leci . . .

I ziemia stoi—i wieków otchłanie,
I wszyscy żywi w tej chwili,
Z których i jednej kostki nie zostanie,
Choć będą ludzie, jak byli . . .

Jak się nie nudzić na scenie tak małej,
Tak niemistrzowsko zrobionej,
Gdzie wszystkie wszystkich Ideały grały,
A teatr życiem płacony—

Doprawdy nie wiem, jak tu chwilę dobić,
Nudy mię biorą najszczersze;
Coby tu na to, proszę Pani, zrobić,
Czy pisać prozę, czy wiersze—?

Czy nic nie pisać . . . tylko w słońca blasku
Siąść czytać romans ciekawy:
Co pisał Potop na ziarneczkach piasku,
Pewno dla ludzkiej zabawy(!)—

Lub jeszcze lepiej—znam dzielniejszy sposób,
Przeciw tej nudzie przeklętej:
Zapomnieć LUDZI, a bywać u OSÓB,
—Krawat mieć ślicznie zapięty . . . !

Nerves

They die of hunger in a certain place
Where I went yesterday— bchind each door
A coffin-room. I tripped over the staircase
On some uncountable uncounted floor.

It must have been a miracle—it was
A miracle, that I should grasp a splay
And mouldered beam (as on the cross
A nail was stuck in it). I got away.

I got away with half my heart—no more.
Barely a trace of my old gaiety.
The crowd like market cattle bore
Me along. The world was loathsome to me.

Today I must visit the Baroness
Who will be sitting on her satin sofa,
Receiving everyone with such finesse.
What shall I say? What shall I say to her?

The mirror will crack. The candelabra
Will have convulsions at such REALISM.
The painted parrots on the long macabre
Ceiling beak to beak will shriek: SOCIALISM!

So—I shall take a seat, holding my hat
In my hand, putting it down next to me . . .
Then I shall return home—just like that—
After the party—a dumb Pharisee.

Nerwy

Byłem wczora w miejscu, gdzie mrą z głodu,
Trumienne izb oglądałem wnętrze;
Noga powinęła mi się u schodu
Na nieobrachowanym piętrze!

Musiał to być cud—cud to był,
Że chwyciłem się belki spróchniałej . . .
(A gwóźdź w niej tkwił,
Jak w ramionach k r z y ż a!)—uszedłem cały! .

Lecz uniosłem pół serca—nie więcej;
Wesołości? . . . —zaledwo ślad!
Pominąłem tłum, jak targ bydlęcy;
Obmierzł mi świat . . .

Muszę dziś pójść do Pani Baronowej,
Która przyjmuje bardzo pięknie,
Siedząc na kanapce atłasowej—
Cóż powiem jej?

. . .Zwierciadło pęknie,
Kandelabry się skrzywią na   r e a l i z m,
I wymalowane papugi
Na plafonie, jak długi,
Z dzioba w dziób zawołają: "S o c j a l i z m!"

Dlatego: usiądę z kapeluszem
W ręku—a potem go postawię.
I wrócę milczącym faryzeuszem
—Po zabawie.

Norwid, in attaching so much importance to *Vade-Mecum* (as seen from his letter, quoted above, to Zaleski), was not mistaken. That collection gives us a sampling of his qualities at their best. And today's readers may see in his controlled irony a foreshadowing of the kind of poetry Jules Laforgue or T. S. Eliot were to write.

The long poem *Quidam*, already noted in connection with Norwid's philosophy, analyzes the interplay between three basic societal factors in second-century Rome under the rule of the Emperor Hadrian—the Jews, the Greeks, and the Romans. It can be placed beside those versified dramas in which Norwid reconstructs the life of ancient Egypt (*Cleopatra*) or harks back to the era when pre-Christian folk myths were born in Poland (*Krakus, Wanda, Zwolon*). In an unfinished play bearing a double title, *In the Wings: Tirteus* (*Za kulisami: Tyrtej*), he effectively uses the device of a "play within a play": at a masquerade ball, contemporary "good society" is prattling in a salon; simultaneously in another room a tragedy is performed about a Greek hero. The tragedy is a flop; the salon is insensitive to heroism. Norwid's play was meant to highlight the decay of the nineteenth century; heroism, not the garish, obvious kind but rather a silent and concealed virtue, was really his concern as a dramatist. The same applies to his comedies with a strong satirical bent: *The Ring of a Grand Lady* (*Pierścień wielkiej damy*), *Pure Love in a Spa by the Sea* (*Miłość czysta u kąpieli morskich*). In the first of these, the main character, Mak-Yks, is a poor young man who lives in a garret provided for him by his relative, a countess. He is not unlike Norwid himself: proud, wounded, pure-hearted, living in the company of his books. Barely tolerated by his artistocratic benefactress, Mak-Yks is the only true human being in the surrounding display of vanity and frivolity.

Norwid's plays are sometimes performed in Poland, but they are difficult to stage on account of their reliance upon innuendos and their deliberate avoidance of blatant effects. They could more aptly be called dramatic poems.

Norwid also left several prose studies on art and a few short stories. There is nothing about the latter that recalls the realistic stories of the nineteenth century, and, indeed, they are modern parables. In "The Secret of Lord Singleworth" ("Tajemnica Lorda Single-worth"), for instance, a rich Englishman travels around Europe— which is nothing extraordinary, except that in every city he goes up in a balloon. We learn at the end that he suffers from an obsession with impurity, intensified by what he sees in various capitals. In "The Stigma" the central motif is our lack of independence due to a "stigma" imprinted on us by a convention, or by civilization, or by a circumstance, so that we act a role and are not ourselves. In "Civilization" ("Cywilizacja") the line between reality and dream is blurred, and a journey in a ship across the Atlantic gradually takes on the aspect of an expedition of civilized but half-crazy mankind into the unknown and toward shipwreck. Perhaps the best single piece of Norwid's prose is "Ad Leones," written at the end of his life in 1881. This is a story of a dignified, healthy, highly talented sculptor in Rome. He spends every evening at the Café Greco, attracting admiring glances because of his nonchalant elegance, his beard, and his beautiful grey-hound bitch. He is working on a huge group sculpture representing Christians being thrown to the lions, hence the title "Ad Leones." The work happens to attract an American banker, who wishes to buy it immediately, under one condition: that some details be changed and that it be renamed "Capitalization." The sculptor readily complies and, with a few movements of his chisel, transforms the central figure of the lion into a coffer. This story, one of Norwid's most biting satires, grew out of his reaction to current exhibitions of art in Paris.

Norwid's extant correspondence, painstakingly gathered by Zenon Miriam Przesmycki at the beginning of our century, not only elucidates his artistic work, but, taken together, forms a kind of philosophical diary. The correctness of his judgments on events and, in particular, his negative appraisals of the Polish mentality, which he regarded as warped by political oppression, have been corroborated by subsequent developments, and today he sounds astonishingly up-to-date.

Norwid's intense historicism, his refusal to practice a narrowly utilitarian poetry, and, at the same time, his rejection of "art for art's sake" paved the way for a specific kind of literature that meditates on history and art and that is, perhaps, uniquely Polish. His reflections on work inspired one of the most original Polish thinkers of the twentieth century, Stanisław Brzozowski. Let us notice, too, that Norwid marks the transition from the concept of the writer or artist as a purely spiritual creature to one which sees him as a good craftsman whose labor should be recompensed by society. Thus, Norwid left his imprint upon the Polish literary scene both as a poet and as a philosopher; but as one of our contemporaries, Mieczysław Jastrun, justly stressed in his introduction to the *Selected Poems* of Norwid (Warsaw, 1949):

It is being said that Norwid is first of all a thinker, a philosopher. This is incorrect. Norwid is, first of all, an artist, but an artist for whom the most interesting material is thought, reflection, the cultural experience of mankind.

Or, to put it another way, one may use the words of an eminent literary critic, Kazimierz Wyka, according to whom "the poetic world that is natural to Norwid is the objective world of culture."

CHAPTER VIII

Positivism

BACKGROUND INFORMATION

THE UPRISING OF 1863 in Poland strained Russia's relations with France and England. French and English involvement, however, was limited to diplomatic notes that sustained the vain hopes of the Poles and infuriated the czarist government. The event was greeted with enthusiasm by revolutionaries in both Western Europe and Russia. Italian volunteers (Garibaldi's), Frenchmen, Hungarians, Germans, Serbs, and Czechs joined the Polish guerrilla units, and a few hundred Russian officers and soldiers fought on the Polish side. A young Russian intellectual, Andrei Potebnya, went to Poland from London and gave his life in one of the battles. Marx and Engels hailed the uprising as the beginning of a new era of revolution. A meeting held by workers in London to express sympathy for the Poles, and at which Marx was the main speaker, resulted in the creation of the First Socialist International. But the consequences of the uprising were felt, first of all, in Russia. The diplomatic intervention by the Western powers had angered the Russian intelligentsia and actually contributed to a loss of influence on the part of the liberals. Chauvinism proved strong enough to combat anyone who dared take the side of the Poles; such people as Herzen were branded as "traitors" and "Western agents." In fact, the Polish uprising spelled the end of Herzen's influence, which had seeped into Russia clandestinely with his London newspaper, *Kolokol*. On the Right, Russian Pan-Slavists found themselves in an awkward position. Their main argument in addressing the Czechs and the Southern Slavs had always been that Russia was the protector of all the Slavs, but the revolt in Poland seemed to belie this claim. In their writings, therefore, the

Pan-Slavists had to resort to intellectual tightrope walking in order to reassure both themselves and their fellow Slavs outside Russia. According to them, Poland was a traitor to the Slavic family, because she had become "Westernized" and "Latinized." Yuri Samarin wrote: "Poland is a sharp wedge which Romanism has thrust into the very heart of the Slavic world with the aim of shattering it into bits." Samarin elaborated a detailed program of how to deal with Poland. He distinguished three elements in the "Polish Question": the Polish people as a national concept, the Polish state as a political concept, and "Polonism" as a cultural concept. He attributed the strength of the Poles to a fusion of those three elements and advised Russia to separate them. While the right to a national life should not be denied the Poles, a separate Polish state could not be tolerated, and "Polonism," as a Latin culture, foreign to the Slavic spirit, should be destroyed. The Pan-Slavists—Samarin, Aksakov, Pogodin—further distinguished two components within "Polonism": "the people" and "society." For them, the only true Slavs in Poland were the peasants, while "society," composed of the gentry, the Catholic clergy, the Westernized intelligentsia, and the urban middle class, should be suppressed by every possible means as a true enemy. The Pan-Slavist program was, to a large measure, eventually adopted by the czarist government. The peasants were favored and granted land (following the policy proclaimed by the insurrectionist Polish government), while the severest measures were applied against other classes—mass deportations, heavy taxation of landed estates, and the confiscation of property belonging to those suspected of having sympathized with or participated in the uprising. Whatever remnants of autonomy the Kingdom of Poland possessed were liquidated; even a new name was designated for official use, "Vistula land" (*Privislansky Kray*). The Russian language was rendered compulsory in all schools, and pupils were punished for speaking Polish among themselves. Heavy taxation and the difficulties of adapting to a system of hired labor (unavoidable, since the peasants were freed from their duties toward the manor) ruined a great number of gentry farms. As a consequence, an intense migration began from the countryside to the towns. The descendants of the gentry were taking up new places in society, either as part of the urban intelligentsia or as manual workers. The Polish proletariat absorbed great numbers of the petty gentry, and such people often became leaders in workers' movements. The aftermath of the uprising could be compared to the post-Civil War era of Reconstruction in America. Poland was gradually being transformed into a capitalist country. Her system of railways, in the second half of the nineteenth century, grew into the densest in the whole of the Russian Empire. Along with this, however, went a sharp decline in the maintenance of roads and waterways. The years 1870–1880 witnessed a steep increase in industrial production. The enormous market possibilities in nearby Russia attracted investments of foreign, mostly German and French, capital. A cotton textile industry was responsible for the mushrooming industrial city of Łódź. A French-owned linen textile works thrived in Żyrardów. In the northeastern tip of Silesia (then an area within the Russian Empire), coal mining and metallurgy prospered. But this rapid expansion meant an inhuman exploitation of native workers: the workday lasted 11 to 13 hours, some days up to 15 hours; for minors it was 8 hours.

THE POSITIVISTS

The unsuccessful uprising brought about not only the disintegration of the nobility as a class. It meant a break with the past in other ways as well. The shock of the many deaths in battle or on the gallows was so violent that the whole complex of attitudes called "political Romanticism" was subjected to a drastic revision. Young people in Warsaw, known as "Positivists," took their name from a term introduced by the French philosopher Auguste Comte: Positive Philosophy. Comte's work was probably the high point in the nineteenth-century cult of science. But in their thinking, Polish Positivists were less indebted to Comte than to English utilitarians, above all, Herbert Spencer and John Stuart Mill. They were also avid readers of Charles Darwin, whose theory of evolution fascinated them. They believed that if nature evolves progressively, the same laws can be detected in society; and this strong tendency to look for analogies between human societies and biological organisms explains their emphasis on organic growth rather than revolutionary change. Comte's optimistic philosophy was, in fact, a theory of unlimited bourgeois progress based on a belief in the magical blessings of the Industrial Revolution. Comte divided mankind's entire history into three successive periods: theological, metaphysical, and scientific. According to him, fortunate mankind had already entered the scientific period. Comte considered himself the founder of a scientific church which would supplant all previous beliefs and religions. The Polish Positivists may have chosen the English utilitarians as their masters, but their basic optimism was characteristically Comtian. In a tragic country, they were reacting against a national past that had piled misfortune on misfortune. Without the possibility of expressing political aspirations, they had to place all their hopes in science and in economic progress. Because of strict censorship they were forced to display their ideas in literary criticism, through a system of allusions, using the literary works as points of departure for debate on larger issues. The Positivist upsurge occurred in the years 1868–1873, whereas what may be termed the "ideological phase" of Positivism extended to 1881. One has to admire the quantity and quality of periodical publications, polemicizing with each other, and the number of translations of scientific and literary works. The organs of the most radical wing of the Positivists—the *Weekly Review* (*Przegląd tygodniowy*) and *Truth* (*Prawda*)—voiced the opinion that all revolutionary dreams should be abandoned because the value of a given nation is not a function of its independence but of its contribution to the economy and to culture. A citizen's basic duty, therefore, was to develop industry and trade and to foster education. The Positivists launched the slogans of "organic work" and "work at the foundations." Treating society as an organism, analogous to animal organisms, they stressed the harmonious interactivity of all of its constituent parts. Thus, regardless of their intentions, individuals who strove to enrich themselves in the long run strengthened the organism. According to the Positivists, Poland's obsolete feudal mentality, inherited from the Polish gentry, was an obstacle to her transformation into a modern capitalistic country. A strong moralistic current permeated their publicism; they attacked obscurantism, clericalism, class barriers and advocated equal rights for the downtrodden—not only for peasants, but also for Jews and for women. The followers of the new trend were, to a large extent, inheritors of eighteenth-century Polish rationalism, and like their predecessors, they devised a program to spread literacy and popularize science, convinced that knowledge would automatically lift the moral level of the masses. Theirs was quite a task, if we remember that, owing to the lack of elementary schools, illiteracy in Poland had reached 90 per cent (there could hardly have been any solace in knowing that the figure for Russia was 94 per cent). Toward the Polish past they took a critical attitude, ascribing the fall of the old *Respublica* to that very anarchy so dear to the Polish nobles. This stance sharply opposed the Romantic view, in which Poland was presented as an innocent victim of vicious neighbors. The reappraisal of Romanticism in literature was severe, although the Positivists certainly did not refuse greatness to Mickiewicz, Słowacki, and Krasiński. They turned their anger mostly against the second wave of the Romantics, particularly against the craze for messianic ideas. Poetry was a pet peeve because it disregarded logic. For the Positivists, the first Romantics were great poets *in spite* of their being sometimes incomprehensible, while their successors seemed to accept incomprehensibility as a principle. Thus, literature was to be a kind of cognition, but inferior to scientific cognition, and the Positivists openly set for literature a utilitarian ideal. Art was to illustrate in a vivid manner the truths attained by a scientific mind. Poetry could be tolerated only if it was clear, understandable, logically analyzable, and of educational value. Some Positivists were even inclined to recognize poetry as a useful corrective: without its exaltation of the sublime, utilitarianism risked degenerating into narrow egoism. But, as the literary genre best suited to the needs of a writer-citizen and most able to convey the greatness of industry and technology, they chose the novel. They excluded, however, its historical species. One of the leading writers of the time, Eliza Orzeszkowa, explained why: "A historical novel imperfectly written is not only useless but harmful, since it gives to unprepared minds a false idea of things that it is much better not to know than to know in a distorted way." The novel was to present not the life of the nobility and aristocracy but that of the new middle class and the simple people. It should introduce, to quote Orzeszkowa again, "a burgher, a banker, a factory owner, a merchant, tails and top hats, machines, surgeon's instruments, locomotives." By developing in the reader a better grasp of social laws, the novel would serve Science. The fates of characters were not to depend, as they had in Romantic literature, on blind chance or the intervention of extrahuman forces, because any feeling of impotence in the face of destiny would destroy a reader's faith in himself. The novel should be realistic and should contain "an idea" [read "tendency"] artfully blended, however, with the form. Today, it is easy to see the internal contradiction in such a prerequisite, but for the Positivists, "Truth" was identical with the unveiling of humanity's harmonious advance toward Progress; therefore, there could be no collision, theoretically, between a tendency and realistic art. Obviously a literature that turned back with nostalgia toward feudal Poland was not to the Positivists' liking. Aleksander Fredro's plays and Józef Korzeniowski's novels were esteemed for their sober approach to reality. Russian literature, because it had been imposed by the czarist government as a means of Russianizing the young people, received, at that time, a hostile reception. In their looking westward, the Positivists did not differ from the majority of Polish society. Among Western writers they particularly cherished Dickens, Mark Twain, and Alphonse Daudet. Although the novels of Émile Zola were discussed, their brutality was felt to be unacceptable.

The Positivists, believers in a liberal ideology based on the conviction that free enterprise in industry, trade, and agriculture is a guarantee of continuous, harmonious progress, tried to console themselves when they observed the violence of the struggle for money within the growing capitalistic society. Gradually, however, they became more and more skeptical, more and more pessimistic, especially after 1881. By the eighties, social conflicts had grown so acute that new clandestine socialist parties were already formulating revolutionary programs. It was then that the first Marxist organization, "Proletariat," was founded. The socialist movement led to the creation of the Polish Socialist Party (PPS) in 1892, and its rival, the Social Democratic Party of the Polish Kingdom (SDKP), in 1893, which was later on (in 1900) transformed into the Social Democratic Party of the Polish Kingdom and of Lithuania (SDKPiL). The opposition between the two parties pivoted on the issue of national independence. While the PPS attempted to combine the struggle for socialism with the struggle for national liberation, SDKP, true to the principle that "the proletarians have no country," advocated revolution throughout the whole Russian Empire, believing that the victory of revolution would automatically resolve national conflicts. In the twentieth century, the PPS was to turn into a party of parliamentary socialists; while out of the SDKPiL and the Left Wing of the PPS the Polish Communist Party would be born. The Positivists were opposed to revolution on principle, and, paradoxically, through their opposition to the socialists, some of them were to move toward the political parties of the Right, especially toward the party of the National Democrats (ND), whose program advocated a *modus vivendi* with czarist Russia, which they saw as protector of the free-enterprise system. It was paradoxical because the Positivists could not be defined as spokesmen for "bourgeois interests." Defenders of the underdog, progressive moralists, they illustrate, through their predicament, rather an honorable weakness inherent in a moralistic position.

Aleksander Świętochowski (1849–1938)   The most eminent fighter in the ranks of the Positivists was a man of a prolificacy approaching that of Józef Ignacy Kraszewski. Primarily a publicist, Aleksander Świętochowski was also the author of novels and dramas. Like nearly all the representatives of Positivism, he was a graduate of the "Main School" (*Szkoła Główna*). Under that name the University of Warsaw functioned from its reopening in 1862 until it was closed down in 1869 to be supplanted by a Russian-language university. A brilliant man, a sharp, even violent, polemicist against the conservatives, accused by his adversaries of haughtiness and pride, he edited the periodical *Truth* (*Prawda*), signing his articles "Truth's Deputy." Świętochowski placed his hopes in education: "All the great problems hidden in the womb of mankind can be solved by education alone, and this education must be compulsory." He was not an enthusiast of capitalism: "Capitalism . . . is a beast which is still able to crush people, but time is restraining its spout with more and more effective bits." It was, after all, preferable to socialism, which would lead to universal slavery: "Everybody would be forced to comply with prescribed norms of thought and of action, to renounce his own plans, not to choose his own roads. The only originality of the individual would consist in his lesser or greater capacity to accomplish the social will, and the only freedom left would be the possibility of physical labor and the consumption of its fruits." Polemicizing with the conservative Russian press, which reproached the Poles for their revolutionary tendencies, he wrote:

If we have supposedly contributed to the rise of Russian nihilism, the question arises: who threw the socialist baby into our yard? Recently—as we learn from the Petersburg daily papers—a group of our youth studying at Russian institutions got entangled in the propagation of the revolutionary gospel and ended their careers in more or less remote localities of Siberia; while Polish institutions, like the late *Szkoła Główna*, have not furnished socialism with a single champion.

In order to show Świętochowski's political preoccupations, it would be fitting to quote his own words once again. These were written in 1883:

Two phantoms have been chilling the blood in the veins of Europe, paralyzing its work and destroying its hope of a better future: on the one hand, an immense system of political alliances established by Bismarck for enigmatic purposes; on the other hand, an equally immense and equally mysterious system of socialist associations, engendered by Marx—these are the two mines under the foundations of the world, which threaten to explode and provoke fear.

Though recognized by the most radical Positivists as their leader, Świętochowski remained, in fact, a lonely man, guarding a critical aloofness toward political causes. In the later stages of his long life, he cooperated with the party of National Democracy in combatting socialism, but its nationalism and racism were alien to him, and the ND's never really regarded him as one of "theirs." As a creative writer, he cannot be accorded a very lofty position. He seemed even in his own day excessively cerebral; and his dramas, for instance, are nothing but cold, artificial fires of dialogues. Among his works, one of the most important is a two-volume *History of the Polish Peasants* (*Historia chłopów polskich*, 1925–1928).

The worship of learning so typical of the Positivists was not mere lip service. The leading literary critic of their camp, Piotr Chmielowski, a *Szkoła Główna* alumnus, remains today an imposing example of enormous erudition, of hard work, and of intellectual integrity. By profession a historian of literature, and the author of many volumes in that field, he edited periodicals dedicated to literary criticism and was held in high regard by people of varying political opinions. He rejected a chair at the University of Warsaw because he was asked to lecture in Russian. Later on, after becoming a professor at the University of Lwów in the Austrian-occupied part of

Piotr Chmielowski (1848–1904)

Poland, he continued to encounter difficulties; as a freethinker he created many enemies in university circles. Chmielowski, in promoting the "scientific investigation" of literature, followed in the footsteps of the major figure in European literary criticism of that time, Hippolite Taine. A rationalist, or, if one prefers, a rationalistic moralist, Chmielowski believed the goal of literature was to liberate human thought and to make possible an individual confrontation with the world. It should also contribute to the forging of strong character, making a person capable of useful work and of disinterested service for the good of society. Just as Świętochowski, beginning in the eighties, condemned revolutionary socialism, Chmielowski waged war in the nineties against "decadentism," a trend which had begun to invade Polish literature. All that tangle of complaints and cries of hatred for society, that display of fallen angels, shocked Chmielowski, as it shocked other Positivists. In the words of another literary critic, Stanisław Brzozowski, who belonged to the next, anti-Positivist generation, "When the young people exclaimed, 'We cannot live!' Chmielowski answered, 'So change your way of thinking.'" And yet nobody paid greater tribute to him than Brzozowski:

Literature did not provide him with aesthetic pleasures. For him it was a duty. It seems to one sometimes that he was a builder, intent upon examining the resistance of the blocks with which the house of Polish culture was to be constructed. He took them one by one and probed them with his pick. He worked without respite, often not seeing that what he tested for strength was not a flagstone but a bas-relief, not a column to maintain a vault, but a statue.

Or again: "He served what he loved in literature, not with the rhetoric of mannerisms, but through his self-abnegation, application, and persistency."

Włodzimierz Spasowicz (1829–1906)   It would be unjust not to mention Włodzimierz Spasowicz, a precious ally of the Positivists and a man who counterbalanced, to some extent, the mutual hostility between Poles and Russians. A lawyer by education, he settled permanently in Russia, where he acquired fame as a gifted orator and one of the most effective defense attorneys (he was caricatured in Dostoevsky's *Brothers Karamazov*). Spasowicz also wrote a great deal, both in Polish and in Russian, attacking with some success what survived of the messianic mentality. A sober literary critic and politician, as a liberal he deplored the disastrous effects of the 1863 uprising in Russia proper, where it weakened the progressive camp. Although accused in Russia of being an alien and a democrat in his heart, and angering the Poles by his program of cooperation with Russia, he succeeded in maintaining his own line. In his literary criticism, he belabored those writers who represented a certain generalized state of mind; for instance, he took up Wincenty Pol's poetry and in his analysis decried the entire frame of mind which produced nostalgia for old gentry virtues and vices. Difficult to classify, Spasowicz in some respects was close to the historians of the Kraków School, while his political liberalism linked him to the Warsaw Positivists.

THE KRAKÓW SCHOOL

The city of Kraków, thanks to its university and to the rather liberal Austrian administration, was the true preserver of Polish tradition. After 1866, when Austria granted autonomy to its Polish provinces, Kraków's importance as a center of ideas increased. In the Russian-controlled part of Poland, the anti-Romantic revision was accomplished by Positivists who were strongly imbued with the discipline of the natural sciences, in Kraków, however, the reaction to Romanticism came from scholars in the humanities, particularly from historians. Convinced conservatives who proclaimed their loyalty toward the Hapsburg dynasty, they invoked the successive rebellions, which had brought down a series of misfortunes upon the country, as an example of the irresponsibility typical of a revolutionary zealot. Erudite, good writers, they meticulously investigated the history of Poland and substantiated their theses with careful, scholarly analysis. For the failure of the old *Respublica*, they detected causes rooted in a remote past. According to them all evil stemmed from the weakness of Poland's royal power and from the political anarchy born out of the gentry's parliamentary system. To these ills, some historians added religious tolerance. Provoking an uproar in the press through their collectively written column, *Stańczyk's Portfolio* (*Teka Stańczyka*)—the rubric referred to a sixteenth-century jester—they were branded "Stańczyks" or buffoons, deprecators of sacred national feelings. They condemned unequivocally the uprising of 1863 and were completely opposed to any search for guidance among the Polish *émigrés* in Paris or to any pinning of hopes on hypothetical aid from Western powers. As politicians, they voiced the opinions of the Conservative Party, which was backed by rich landowners and sent deputies to the parliament in Vienna. The leaders of the Kraków School were Józef Szujski (1835–1883), a professor of the Jagiellonian University from 1869, secretary general of the Kraków Academy of Sciences, as well as author of many valuable studies; and Michał Bobrzyński (1849–1935), professor of law and, for a while, governor of Galicia. Bobrzyński's *History of Poland* (1879) remains perhaps the best book on the subject even today, in spite of his clearly presented bias.

NATURALISM

Naturalism, as a term applied to literature, first appeared in France; it was a corollary of the emphasis on biological sciences. The naturalistic technique was built on detailed external observation of human beings, since it was assumed that man's behavior is determined by elementary instincts and, as such, is no different from that of other animals. In the eighties, Polish writers began to elaborate a theory of the novel, and they turned their attention toward the French novelist Émile Zola, who, in his *Le roman expérimental* (1880), explained the principles of the "scientific novel," which he proposed as an objective "mirror of life." Zola was combatted in Poland by the conservative ("old") press, whose arguments, pointing up his uncritical worship of the natural sciences, were valid enough. The Positivists (the "young" press) took an interest in his theories but, as we mentioned, were never able to share his extremist attitudes. Bolesław Prus, the most eminent novelist of the period, considered Zola's novels symptomatic of the times:

Poetry and aesthetics up to today have served only the tastes of a social layer living in prosperity; now, entering upon the scene is a layer of people who live in poverty and whose fate leaves much to be desired, at least in regard to aesthetic exigencies.

What was often referred to then as "obscene" French literature received the following rather sympathetic, if slightly condescending, comment from Prus:

Its themes are usually taken from life, and its language from the plebeian classes, who, for their own comfort, have always had a ready stock of bad words to offer the honorable public. Books written in that manner are a novelty in every epoch; let us add immediately—for both young persons and the well-bred. But not for the reason that such matters are absent from the salons of the nobility or the bourgeois, or that actions related to those matters do not occur; rather the more mature social classes have noticed that to insure comfort and pleasure in this life, not only soap, a comb, and a toothbrush are useful, but also one's keeping silent about certain things.

Polish theoreticians of prose were more fascinated by the artistry of Gustave Flaubert than by that of Zola. Antoni Sygietyński, for instance, held Flaubert up as a model for the novelist who wants to build up his characters through careful observation of temperaments and passions without stressing their beneficial or harmful role in society, who wants, in other words, to accomplish a purely objective study, a "mirror" of life.

Although naturalistic leanings were visible in some writers at the very end of the nineteenth century in Poland, the novel as a detached and dispassionate investigation failed to win a place of prominence. It was felt that naturalism was all right for "prosperous and happy France," but not for a nation whose very existence was in danger. Moreover, two other factors weakened the impact of the naturalistic approach: the first was the growth of "decadentism" and a new subjective art; the second was the strivings of the revolutionary socialist movement. Thus, in its Zolalike variety, naturalism had but few Polish representatives.

BOLESŁAW PRUS
(1845–1912)

Undoubtedly, the most important novelist of the period was Bolesław Prus (the pen name of Aleksander Głowacki). He was born in 1845, the son of a minor employee on a landed estate in the district of Lublin. Like many others in Poland, his father lived only on his salary, but was of noble origin. The name Prus, designating the family's coat of arms, later served his son as a pseudonym. Orphaned early and brought up by relatives, Prus had an unhappy childhood. He was a schoolboy when the uprising of 1863 broke out, and, like his comrades, he joined a guerrilla unit. This is a chapter in his life about which little is known, for he did not like to talk about it, probably because of an acute conflict between his feeling of duty and his personal convictions. After being wounded in a battle, he spent several months in a hospital and then in a prison, from which he was finally released on the grounds of being underage. (His relatives probably falsified his birth certificate.) Owing to these experiences, he matured early; but he remained an introvert, inclined to use masks. In his high school, to which he returned after his stay in prison, he was known as a wit and even a buffoon. He was mostly interested in science, and toyed with the idea of studying at one of Russia's big universities. But on the advice of his friends, he registered in the mathematics and physical science department of the *Szkoła Główna* in Warsaw. Science was surrounded, there, by an atmosphere of worship; but the ideology of Positivism, then evolving, left Prus rather cold. His stay at the *Szkoła Główna* was cut short owing to lack of money. Partly for financial reasons and partly because he took seriously the slogan that called for the intelligentsia's getting to know the life of the masses directly, he worked for a while in a metallurgical factory in Warsaw. All of his free time, however, he devoted to self-education. His reading of Herbert Spencer was crucial;

later on, he was to call him "the Aristotle of the nineteenth century." And in his mature age, he confessed: "I grew up under the influence of evolutionist Spencerian philosophy, and I heeded its counsels, not those of idealistic or Comtian philosophy." In order to learn, he needed money and time, but his factory job gave him neither. He remarked in his notebooks: "In order to learn, capital is necessary. So my aim should be as follows: to find a job that would give me as much money as possible, and that would leave me as much time as possible for learning." He tried tutoring, but at last, he found what he had been looking for, as a contributor of verse and prose to humor magazines. The public liked him, while he himself considered his occupation a defeat. He wrote: "Good humor is like a thistle which usually grows on the ruins. It wounds a delicately shaped mouth, but is a joy for asses." He acquired the dubious position of a literary buffoon; and later, when he turned to novels, it seemed somehow unnatural to his readers. Prus's mathematical mind, his love for precision and thoroughness, prompted him to approach his role as a humorist quite seriously. He had seven notebooks for gathering material; the first, for facts; the second, for relations between facts; the third, for general remarks; the fourth, for witticisms; the fifth, for scientific facts and views; the sixth, for observations and methods of making them; the seventh, for historical notes. Gradually, thanks to such material, he was engaging himself in a study of society as a whole. He passed beyond the narrow limits set by the humor magazines and began to publish short pieces on various subjects. These *Weekly Chronicles* (*Kroniki tygodniowe*), as Prus called his articles, were published in various Warsaw periodicals for about forty years, bringing him renown and exercising a decisive influence on the Polish progressive intelligentsia. The genre originated in France; *chroniques*, as they were called, dealt mostly with Parisian mores, theater gossip, scandals, artists' lives, etc., treating it all with *esprit*, wit and malicious humor. The Polish *kronika*, besides this, may have also borrowed some features from the *gawęda* (see Chapter VII, p. 255), adapting them to new circumstances. Because censorship did not allow for direct discussion of certain questions, some tiny detail from everyday life had to serve as a pretext for a discourse built of hints and allusions. Prus employed his humor as a tool. His aim was to combat and to educate. He compared the public to a fish, which can be caught only with a bait of jokes. Another time he said that every week he prepared a soup that should be nourishing, but that every good cook adds ingredients to taste, in his case—humor.

Prus was a middle-of the-roader; he cannot be ranged among the fighting Positivists of Świętochowski's ilk. Indeed he reproached them for their attachment to theories and words and for an insufficient knowledge of reality. The success of his *Chronicles* was due to Prus's genuine humor; the public guessed that behind everything he wrote was a goodhearted, compassionate man, indulgent even toward those he satirized, always ready to defend the underdog, organically incapable of hatred. His readers were won over by that blend of laughter and sentiment, so typical of Prus—a somewhat melancholy, skeptical smile and a belief in the inherent goodness of human nature. His point of departure was usually a little fact, for instance, the story of a botanist, gathering herbs outside Warsaw, who was surrounded by angry peasants demanding money—if herbs had value for him, they reasoned shrewdly, he should pay for them. To enrich a subject, Prus used many devices: he introduced human types, little scenes he observed, dialogues, humorous doggerel of his own. The *Weekly Chronicles* remain a valuable source of knowledge about everyday life in Warsaw, a city for which Prus had a strong attachment. How deeply the *Chronicles* implanted themselves in the minds of the progressive intelligentsia is indicated by the use of the same title in the years 1918–1939 to head a column written by a progressive spokesman and, in many ways, an inheritor of Prus's social philosophy —the poet Antoni Słonimski.

Prus passed to fiction gradually. This came about as a result of his disillusionment with the effectiveness of journalism. While learning the craft, he was indebted, above all, to Józef Ignacy Kraszewski, among Polish authors, and to Charles Dickens and Mark Twain, among foreign authors. He began with short stories, usually situating them in a Warsaw apartment building among its poorer tenants (whose apartments always faced onto a gloomy central courtyard). His characters usually live on the brink of starvation: the seamstress in "Ball Gown" ("Sukienka balowa"); the unemployed mason in "A Tenant in a Garret" ("Lokator poddasza"); the little blind girl in "Organ-Grinder" ("Katarynka"), whose poverty prevents her from undergoing surgery; the poor coypist in "Waistcoat" ("Kamizelka"). This last story is a good example of Prus's tenderness toward his characters. It tells the tale of a waistcoat sold to a secondhand dealer after the death of the owner. While the latter was ill with tuberculosis, he had lived with only one thought: not to depress his wife. He assured her his waistcoat had been getting too tight, while she herself in her turn had been narrowing it in the seams in order to fool him. The rich, in Prus, are not treated with any ferocity. A houseowner to whom a poor seamstress owes money turns out unexpectedly to be quite humane; or a tenement owner, a Jewish rabbi, goes in search of help for an unemployed mason; or an old bachelor, a connoisseur of music, is at first irritated by the organ-grinder in the courtyard, but when he notices the joy its sounds give to a blind girl, not only does he pay, the janitor to bring in all the organ-grinders of the neighborhood, but he contributes money for the blind girl's operation. In "Michałko," Prus depicts an illiterate young peasant newly arrived in Warsaw who is a little like a Steinbeck hero. Michael (Michałko) is extremely strong, hard-working, and so naïve that by city standards he is an idiot. After saving a man from being crushed by a wall on a construction site, he disappears into the crowd, unaware of the very notion of heroism.

The short stories date mostly from the earlier phase of Prus's work. Around 1885, he turned to the novel. As a realist, he formulated his program in opposition to both "idealism" (read "Romanticism") and naturalism, although Flaubert and Zola, who both were then called naturalists, had some impact upon him. "The aim of literature," he wrote in 1885, "is to aid the spiritual development of the individual and of society. The sciences aid thought, social sciences aid thought and will, while literature aids thought, feelings, and will, that last indirectly." Quite interesting is the parallel he drew between literature and science: "Such characters as Hamlet, Macbeth, Falstaff, Don Quixote are discoveries as valid for psychology as the laws of planetary motion are for astronomy. Shakespeare is worth no less than Kepler."

Of Prus's three best novels, his first, *The Outpost* (*Placówka*), appeared in 1886. It is a study of a Polish village. The hero, a peasant named Ślimak (which means "snail"), serves to illustrate the life of the entire village. Practically all of its inhabitants are illiterate. There is no school, and religion consists largely of magic: when one of them buys, by chance, a painting representing "Leda with a Swan," they pray to it just as they do before two old portraits of noblemen, former benefactors of the local church. The far from picturesque, poor, and hard-working village has been touched, however, by certain transformations taking place in the country as a whole. A railway is being built in the neighborhood, and the owners of a manor have sold their property to German settlers, who divide up the land into small farms. Here, Prus inserts a message, as he was deeply distressed by Bismarck's policy. German settlers were being given loans and encouraged by the German Government to move across the border into Russian-occupied Poland. The Germans were economically stronger and better organized than the Polish peasants, while the rich Polish landowners seemed to lose their patriotic spirit when money was involved. In the novel, landowners speak more French than Polish, and decided to move either to a city or abroad instead of staying in the boring countryside. The plot is built around a series of misfortunes which befall Ślimak when he refuses to sell his plot of land to the German settlers, who want to construct a windmill on it. The extremely stubborn Ślimak does not act out of self-interest, since the money from the sale of his property would buy him a better farm elsewhere. He acts out of sheer inertia and an attachment to the principle inculcated by his father and grandfather: once a peasant loses his inherited plot of land, he is headed toward the greatest of misfortunes, namely, becoming a wage earner. Ślimak himself lacks the strength of will that his wife possesses (and here, Prus seems to be a good observer of the Polish village). He hesitates. But his wife, although she is on her deathbed, asks him to swear that he will never sell the land. Far from being a hymn to the supposed vigor of the peasant, the novel exposes his conservatism. It is the only defense he can make against the inroads of a world hostile both to him and to his country.

This somber picture is enlivened by Prus's flashes of humor and his warmth. The local priest, though preoccupied mostly with dinners, drinking, and hunting parties at neighboring manors, is, under Prus's pen, not completely deprived of all semblances of a good Christian. Two of the lowliest creatures, by village standards, emerge as bearers of the most lofty ethics of selflessness. Ślimak's half-wit farm hand, upon finding an abandoned baby, carries it to his miserable quarters and takes it under his permanent care. A Jewish wandering peddler, himself a wretch, is the only one to befriend Ślimak after his wife has died and his farm has burned down. In his thoughts he does not separate himself from Ślimak, whose misfortune is felt by him as his own. Thus, *The Outpost* is different from the novels of naturalists who would have life reduced to the blind struggle for existence, in that ethical motives here have considerable weight. All told, it is, in spite of its weaknesses, an honorable achievement in the realistic, discreetly tendentious, novel.

Being a Spencerian, Prus looked at man as part of nature, but he did not see Darwin's theory of the "survival of the fittest" as the key to understanding social dynamics. Although struggle was necessary to eliminate worthless individuals, cooperation, also found in nature, was even more important. For Prus, society was an organism, whose health depended on the equilibrium and harmonious functioning of its parts. In his view, it was impossible to keep a social organism healthy without ideals toward which people might tend, for example, the ideal of being a scientist, or a technician, or a merchant. For Prus, Polish society was sick. Its model of behavior had been imposed by the nobility, and it was a model based upon worship of an outmoded code of honor, empty phraseology, and false spiritualism which forgot that it could only subsist thanks to masses of people engaged in manual labor. For centuries the *bourgeoisie* had been weak; the peasant (such as he appeared in *The Outpost*) could hardly be recognized as a force for progress.

It is this pessimistic vision that underlies the huge sociological panorama in Prus's novel *The Doll* (*Lalka*). The title is of purely accidental significance and alludes to an episode involving a stolen doll, although the public saw in it a judgment on the main female character. The author had originally intended to call the book *Three Generations*. Published in installments beginning in 1887 and as a book in 1890, *The Doll* has been considered by many people the best Polish novel because of its combination of a richness of realistic details with a simple, functional language. There are few instances in world literature of a novel's hero acquiring in the public eye all the characteristics of a live and tangible person, as did *The Doll*'s principal character, Stanisław Wokulski. Thus, between the two world wars, Prus's admirers expressed their feelings by attaching a plaque to the wall of a Warsaw apartment house (which could be identified from an exact description in the novel), with the inscription: "Here lived Stanisław Wokulski, hero of *The Doll* by Bolesław Prus."

The basic structure of *The Doll* consists of two parallel narratives: one relates the events in the 1870s, the time of action; the other, thanks to a diary written by one of the characters, shifts the reader by flashbacks to the time of the "Spring of Nations" in 1848–1849. There is an imposing gallery of characters. They come from various social classes, represent diverse mentalities and attitudes, but are always connected with the two central figures, each of whom belongs to a different generation. Stanisław Wokulski begins his career as an underpaid waiter in a Warsaw restaurant. He comes (like Prus) from an impoverished noble family. An athletically built adolescent, he leads the life of an ascetic, dreaming about making discoveries in science. Deported to Siberia because of his participation in the uprising of 1863, he spends several years there, and upon his return to Warsaw takes a job as a salesman in a shop owned by a German named Mincel. Prus's minutely detailed description of the old shop (belonging to Mincel's father) is one of the most charming passages in the novel. By marrying, though not too willingly, the shopowner's widow, Wokulski comes into money. He uses this capital to set up a partnership with a Russian merchant, whom he had met during his forced stay in Russia. Together they go to Bulgaria during the Russo-Turkish war, and Wokulski acquires a fortune selling army supplies to the Russians. Although he and his Russian partner have engaged in some not necessarily innocent financial operations (dealing in armaments for instance), Wokulski is nevertheless portrayed as a type of "positive capitalist"—hard-working, sober, calculating, a useful member of society. Yet there is a chink in his armor. In his heart he is a Romantic, a man who dreams about some undefinable "true life." It is this lack of internal unity which brings about his defeat, for he is blind to the worthlessness of an aristocratic woman with whom he is in love. Wokulski exemplifies the difficulty of abandoning what Prus looked upon as the stigma of Poland's chivalrous past. An old man, Ignacy Rzecki, a friend of Wokulski's and manager of his store in Warsaw, represents that Poland which is gradually disappearing. The warmth with which Prus treated him proves that the novelist was far from using clichés or too clear-cut divisions. Rzecki comes from the Warsaw "folk"—i.e., artisans, minor employees, petty bourgeois. He lives on memories of his bygone youth, a heroic chapter both in his life and in the life of Europe. It is from his (Rzecki's) diary that we learn about some of Wokulski's adventures, thus seen through eyes of an admirer. We also find the story of young Rzecki. A pure Romantic, he, and his friend Katz, went to Hungary in 1848 to enlist in the revolutionary army. Outbursts of lyricism accompany his battle descriptions as he reminisces over the most beautiful experience he ever lived through. For Rzecki, the whole cause of freedom in Europe was connected with the name of Napoleon Bonaparte, and the Hungarian revolution sparked new hopes of abolishing the system of reaction which had triumphed after Napoleon's fall. Rzecki never lost hope; later, he placed his confidence in Emperor Napoleon III. While he writes his diary, he still believes in Bonaparte's last scion, Napoleon III's son, Prince Loulou. However, at the end of the novel, when he hears that Prince Loulou has perished in Africa fighting in English ranks against rebel tribesmen, he is suddenly seized by the despondency of old age. Beneath his asceticism, his punctuality, his dry and pedantic appearance, Rzecki lives in constant excitement, preoccupied by the affairs which he discreetly designates in his diary by the letter *P*, namely, politics. An avid reader of the daily press, he sees indications everywhere showing that "it" has begun. Prus coddled no other figure in his work as much as Rzecki, lavishing on him all the treasure of his sentiment and humor. A shy believer in great causes, a shy admirer of women, too timid ever to confess his feelings, Rzecki makes a funny and truly moving figure. In addition to these two generations, the novel provides glimpses of the youngest one, personified by a promising scientist, Ochocki, a few students, and the young salesmen in Wokulski's store. Here, Prus's attitude seems ambiguous, expressed rather by questions than by answers. The half-starving students live in the garret of an apartment house, in constant conflict with the landlord because they do not pay the rent. They are gay, inclined to macabre pranks, rebels against the established order, and, probably, socialists. One young salesman is also attached to socialist ideas; others are only too ready to pursue sleek careers, and even their business integrity, as compared with Wokulski's or Rzecki's, is somewhat dubious.

The plot of the novel is centered around Wokulski's unhappy love for Izabella Łęcki. Perhaps depth psychology would elucidate why Wokulski's long-repressed needs and desires lead him to invest all his feelings in a person for whom he is no more than a brute, a plebeian who looks like a butcher, with huge, red hands. Izabella lives in an ideal world, untouched by the "dirt of life," convinced that people below the level of aristocracy are subhuman. She, a virgin, indulges in dreams in which she surrenders herself to famous actors and singers or to a statue of Apollo. Sometimes, though, her dreams are disquieting: dens full of smoke and soot, gigantic figures of filthy workers hammering on fiery iron; one of them tries to grab her, and he has Wokulski's face. To conquer such a woman, Wokulski must renounce his modest way of life. He begins to frequent theaters and aristocratic salons, to spend money on carriages and flowers. To help Izabella's father, a completely ruined man who keeps up only the appearances of wealth, he founds a company for trade with Russia and sets the aristocrats up in business. Izabella's milieu appears as more of a caricature than we might expect from a mild middle-of-the-roader. The facade of senatorial dignity, of grave and polite manners, hides dishonest deals in marriages, stupidity, and a complete incapacity for economic survival—a major sin in a bourgeois system. The hero's downfall—Wokulski, as the author leaves us to guess, commits suicide at the end of the novel—highlights the basic theme of *The Doll*—the inertia of Polish society. The only energetic and successful representative perishes, for private reasons it is true, but perhaps because he is just as much the bearer of a virus as the aristocratic milieu: he makes an absolute out of love and honor and, because of that, is crushed at the critical moment of his life. Wokulski and Rzecki are, in many ways, alter egos of Prus himself, a man on the border line of two mentalities. Wokulski, the frustrated scientist, is created in Prus's own image. During a visit to Paris, Wokulski reveals his "Eastern European complexes." He envies Western technology, progress, industry, and feverish work. In Paris, he meets an old scientist, named Geist, who has made the extraordinary discovery of a metal lighter than air; in the hands of those who would use it to organize mankind, it could bring universal peace and happiness. Wokulski, till the end of the novel, is torn between his love for Izabella and the idea of settling in Paris and using all his fortune to perfect Geist's invention.

Rich in episodic figures and observations of daily life in Warsaw, the novel demonstrates nineteenth-century realism at its best. It fulfills the basic exigency of the genre: to lead the hero toward a full awareness of the rift between his dream and the reality of the society around him.

After *The Doll*, Prus wrote a long novel on the emancipation of women—*The Emancipationists* (*Emancypantki*, 1894). The novel as a whole can be called an artistic failure, perhaps because Prus (not unlike Rzecki in *The Doll*) seems to have known little about women; at least he was never able to build a convincing female character (Izabella in *The Doll* is a satirical portrait).

The daring conception of his next novel, *Pharaoh* (*Faraon*), written in 1894–1895 and published in 1896, is matched by its excellent artistic composition. It can be defined as a novel on the mechanism of state power and, as such, is probably unique in world literature of the nineteenth century. Ancient Egypt had tempted the European imagination ever since the hieroglyphs had been deciphered by the Frenchman, Champollion, after the Napoleonic invasion of Egypt. Yet it was mainly its external side, its picturesque exoticism, that attracted writers. Prus, by selecting the reign of "Pharaoh Ramses XIII" (who never existed) in the eleventh century before Christ, sought a perspective that was detached from the pressures of actuality and censorship. Through his analysis of the dynamics of an ancient Egyptian society, he wanted to suggest an archetype of the struggle for power that goes on within any state. He researched his material thoroughly, and if he committed some historical errors, they were due to the level of the Egyptology of his time; besides, this is immaterial in view of his purpose. As a journalist, he had been interested in Arabi Pasha's revolution (in 1881–1883). Arabi Pasha launched his uprising with the slogan, "Egypt for the Egyptians," but was beaten back by the English and deported to Ceylon. It is probable that Prus's meditation on those events in Egypt, then a British colony, helped him to bridge the gap between the ancient world and modern politics; the old often serves him as a metaphor for the new.

The treatise on Egyptian civilization which opens the novel agrees surprisingly with Arnold Toynbee's historical thesis—that civilization arises as a response to a challenge. The inhabitants of the valley of the Nile had to regulate its flooding or perish. For the accomplishment of the former, great mathematical and astronomical skills were required—and they were provided by the priestly caste, the highest, since Egypt lived under a theocratic system. But Prus was concerned with the period of Egypt's decay. In the eleventh century B.C., the population has diminished from eight million to six million. Desert sands are relentlessly devouring the arable land. Egypt has powerful enemies; the strongest are the Assyrians. Because of financial difficulties the Egyptian army is not numerous and is composed mostly of aliens, Greeks and Asiatics. But Egypt's predicament is due, above all, to an upset class equilibrium. And here we find the idea, so dear to Prus, of society as an organism with its parts functionally adapted to the goals of the whole. The young Pharaoh, Ramses XIII, whose political maturing forms the overt subject of the novel, discovers gradually that one class, the priests, has acquired absolute power at the expense of the other layers of the population. Organized both as a church hierarchy and as a political party (with an inner party accessible only to the initiated), disposing of tremendous wealth, with a monopoly on scientific knowledge, the priests have so shackled the monarchs that they are unable to introduce any reforms, while the peasants, who nourish the entire population, have sunk into misery and must bear the burden of inhuman taxation. But the Church Party is not fully autonomous. It has international bonds and seems to be dependent on the highest of initiates, the priests of Chaldea. Another international force, the Phoenicians, exists within Egypt itself. As financiers, they control, to a great extent, the functioning of the state. Young Ramses draws up a three-point program: out-and-out war against the Church Party, which he justifies by the need to curb its power; military action against Assyria, which he considers necessary but which is opposed by the priests; radical measures to better the lot of the peasants. Pursuing that policy, he concludes an alliance with the Phoenicians and wins over both the army and the mob. Yet he fails, not only because of personal shortcomings, but because his adversaries are people of formidable stature. The Church Party, under its monolithic facade, conceals an acute struggle for power, but the high priests are extremely intelligent, disciplined men who identify the interests of the Church Party with those of the state, and are ready to use any means to foster that supreme interest; for instance, to compromise Ramses, they order the massacre of one thousand Libyan prisoners of war to whom Ramses has promised life. They maintain ubiquitous undercover agents, especially among the corrupt and plethoric bureaucracy, whose proliferation is one of the causes of Egypt's decay. The bureaucracy and the commanding posts in the army are recruited mostly from the aristocracy, whom Ramses is unable to rally in wholehearted support of his program. As contrasted with the chief priest, Herhor, Ramses is but a young fool. He is a shifting, contradictory personality, swayed by his passions, noblehearted but deluded by visions of grandeur. He dreams of acquiring the name of Ramses the Great, of conquering Assyria, and of improving agriculture with the labor of prisoners of war. This mentality is typically military-feudal (and we may suspect that in reality he is a Polish nobleman). His impulsiveness is no match for the cold, calculating minds and experience of the high priests. Moreover, he is always entangled in affairs with women, who are used as a bait by those who attempt to sway him to their side.

The first volume of the novel describes the slow awakening of moral consciousness in Ramses, then the crown prince, his loves, his drinking bouts and military feats; Volume Two traces his combat against the priests and ends with the assassination of the young Pharaoh. The direct cause of Ramses' fall is his scorn of science. He has been warned about an eclipse of the sun, known to the priests in advance through astronomical calculations, but he pays no heed. When the people rise up precisely on that fateful day, the priests are able to convince the mob that the eclipse is a punishment of the gods for an attempt to change the established order of things. After Ramses' death the chief priest, Herhor, is crowned Pharaoh. He not only carries out some of the reforms which Ramses had planned to introduce (i.e., periods of rest for the peasants every seventh day) but concludes an advantageous treaty with Assyria, and draws considerable sums from the Church's treasury for the use of the state.

The Pharaoh was received rather coolly by both critics and the public. It was understood as an attack upon the Roman Catholic clergy. Yet Prus's intention went beyond the limits of one country; he shuffled elements taken from ancient Egypt, contemporary Egypt, from Poland and the Europe of his time to convey certain views on the health and illness of civilizations. We are led to assume from the novel that general trends in history are stronger than the wishes of individuals, and whoever opposes them must fail. Young Ramses was out of step with the most important forces able to shape the fate of his country. He was rooted in the military aristocratic tradition; therefore, his understanding of the mechanism of power was somewhat naïve. Perhaps he was a cousin of Wokulski's, a romantic in his heart. At the same time, however, it is clear from the reading that a crazy individual—and perhaps only a crazy individual—is at the origin of changes. By his actions, Ramses engendered a revolutionary situation within the country and strengthened opposition against the initially planned treaty with Assyria, which would have been harmful to the interests of Egypt. The chief priest, Herhor, when crowned Pharaoh, had to take into account this new ferment unleashed by Ramses. We may also assume from *The Pharaoh* that dependence upon international centers testifies to the existence of a grave illness in a social organism, as exemplified by the reliance of Egyptian priests upon the sacred college in Chaldea and by the cancerous growth of Phoenician capital, which promoted Phoenicia's interests behind the scenes to the detriment of Egypt. Analogies could be found at will in Poland, Western Europe, and in the Egypt of Prus's time. The author's kind heart and his humor proved to be his best artistic allies in writing the novel. The anta-gonists are not simply black or white. Each of them is complex and many-faceted. They are rather personifications of social forces, neither good nor evil in themselves but comparatively, according to their rela-tionships to each other. In a sense, *The Pharaoh* can be linked up with the educational novel of the seventeenth and eighteenth centuries, like Fénelon's *Adventures of Télémaque*, in which the education of a crown prince is at stake. Other features make it a strictly realist novel of the nineteenth century, and, in its stress on the social background, it resembles the French novel as practiced by Balzac, Flaubert, and even Zola. What makes it unique is that no one had ever attempted to deal with the State as such in a novel. *The Pharaoh* is, perhaps, inferior to *The Doll*, as it lacks the same immediate observations of detail, but it is a work worthy of Prus's intellect and one of the best Polish novels.

At the time he was working on *The Pharaoh*, and even more later on, Prus was inclined to be pessimistic about Poland as a society. Instead of an organism functioning harmoniously, he saw contra-dictory interests in bitter conflict. He wrote in one of his articles: "Our society today does not look like an organism, like a net in which every interstice is connected with thousands of others, but like a heap of sand which seeps through one's fingers." He rejected all expectations of change through war or a revolution. For him the Boer War of 1900 served as a warning of the fate of small nations. The future, according to him, belonged to the Big Powers, aligning themselves into larger unions perhaps, and renouncing a part of their sovereignty. He hoped that huge states would gradually be transformed into commonwealths, which would grant autonomy to the smaller nations dominated by them. While not excluding a better mutual understanding between Poles and Russians, he was extremely sensitive to growing German nationalism and was skeptical of coexistence with Germany. A few quotes from his articles prove that already, at the turn of the century, perceptive people were able to glimpse some of the dangers yet to become a reality:

We live in the epoch when science is beginning to lose its character of uni-versal truth and is becoming a set of falsities, of instruments for a rapa-cious policy. . . . The honor of creating such a science belongs to the Ger-mans; less than a year ago, a philosopher, Hartmann, acting as a political agent, advised his compatriots to exterminate the Poles. . . . Wait a bit, and upon the stem of the once glorious German science will grow a "new chemistry" to poison unpleasant peoples, a "new medicine" to contaminate them with epidemics.

Sometimes in Prus there are even traces of Pan-Slavism:

And what if a war creates proper frames for the Slavic question which today—in reality—does not exist? And what if it happens so that all the Slavs would desire to be free, in their own lands, in order to work, within the limits of their forces, for some new civilization and not to feed upon Roman-German remnants?

The main reason for Prus's pessimism was his conflict with the young generation. Around 1900 the modernist movement in literature and art, which rejected the tenets of Positivism, was in full swing, while in politics the upper hand was being taken by revolutionary socialists who condemned political realism and the pussyfooting prudence of the old generation. Even more in Poland than in Russia, the year 1905 was marked by strikes, barricades in the streets, and sentences of death carried out by socialists upon managers or foremen of factories, officers of the czarist police, etc. Prus then wrote his novel *The Children* (*Dzieci*). From the title it is not difficult to guess the contents. Publicistic in character, intended as a warning, the novel, which is devoid of humor, is one of Prus's weakest works. The remaining products of his late period can also be characterized as the meditations of a publicist rather than as literature.

The stature of Bolesław Prus as a writer of rare integrity and high intellectual standards has never been questioned, and in recent times scholars have done much to revive interest in his activity as a publicist.

ELIZA ORZESZKOWA
(1841–1910)

If we conceive of literature in the way that most twentieth-century critics and writers are inclined to, that is, as the voice of a bitter, alienated, and despairing individual, then Orzeszkowa should be dismissed in advance as a completely uninteresting personality, the very reverse of a rebellious genius. But perhaps there is some truth in what Beethoven said when he was an old man: "The more I advance in age, the more I recognize that goodness is more worthy than genius." Orzeszkowa was a provincial. She spent all her life in the country or in small towns. She was self-taught and earned her living as a professional writer at a time when it was difficult for a woman to gain access to the working world. Her writings are permeated with a love for human beings; their technique is old-fashioned and, perhaps, not up to the level of the exceptional mind which she revealed in her correspondence with the most eminent intellectuals in Poland and Europe.

Eliza Pawłowski was born on the family's hereditary manor,

Milkowszczyzna, near Grodno, in the former Grand Duchy of Lithuania. She received her primary education from governesses; then for five years she attended a boarding school for girls in Warsaw. She was scarcely sixteen when she was given in marriage to Piotr Orzeszko, who was oldish by the prevailing standards (over thirty), but who possessed a fortune and the reputation of a good dancer. They moved to his estate in Polesie, the region of the Pripet Marshes. There Eliza engaged in clandestine political activity both preceding and during the uprising of 1863. She was among those who saw the revolt as a struggle not only for national independence but also for democracy and the emancipation of the peasants. Her attitude was a source of conflict with her conservative husband, who disagreed with her ideas. Paradoxically, she escaped imprisonment by a near miracle, while Piotr Orzeszko was arrested for joining the guerrillas and deported to Siberia. She did not follow him, as the rift between them was already an accomplished fact. Later on, after his return, she initiated long-lasting divorce proceedings. Orzeszko's estate, like many others, was confiscated, while Eliza could not maintain her inherited farm owing to financial burdens imposed by the czarist government as a general policy of retribution for Polish recalcitrance. She found herself a solitary woman, forced to pave her own way in the world. And the position of women was to be one of the central motifs in her writings. Most of her life she spent in the provincial town of Grodno, where she was a virtual prisoner. She had been placed under police surveillance because of her "organic work" in the Positivist spirit— founding schools and a Polish publishing house in Wilno. But there, in Grodno, by reading in French, Polish, and Russian, she acquired an astonishing breadth of horizons, and the very list of titles of books she managed to read is surprising. If she is ranged among the Positivists, it is not because she was directly indebted to them. Rather, she developed parallelly, sometimes coming to similar, sometimes dissimilar, conclusions. She was active both as a creative writer and as a publicist. Among her articles, an attack upon Joseph Conrad, perhaps, did not quite deserve Conrad's calling her "that hag," as she was desperate then over the country's having lost the flower of its intelligentsia in the 1863 uprising, and over the draining of men of talent to other countries. She reproached Conrad with treason for having forsaken his native tongue. Yet Orzeszkowa, out of all her contemporaries, was the most open to new intellectual trends, and until her death in 1910 she reacted with understanding to those currents which seemed to the Positivists just madness. A long-lasting friendship with a medical doctor in Grodno led to a marriage in her declining years.

Her abundant literary production could be qualified as "populist," although the term has not been used in Polish criticism. While Prus was a writer of the city (Warsaw), Orzeszkowa drew her material from her acquaintance with "little people" in her native province: Jewish families in small towns, petty gentry, farmers, and peasants. Her short stories and novels are more or less didactic, aiming at the inculcation of ethical values. Her central motif was a human being's fulfillment of himself in spite of the obstacles thrown up by social conditions—which make out of a woman, a man's toy; out of a Jew, a prisoner of ghetto superstitions; out of a peasant, a prisoner of village superstitions; out of a landowner, a prisoner of established mores. Those of her characters whom she treats with sympathy are emotionally involved in seeking the welfare of a community; they transcend the boundaries of their individual lives through empathy. By her books, Orzeszkowa exerted influence not only in Poland. Translated into other languages, particularly into Russian, German, and Czech, her novels fostered the cause of women's emancipation and of equal rights for the Jews. As typical of her short stories, we should mention "Strong Samson" ("Silny Samson," 1877) with its curiously accurate psychological insight: a miserable Jewish tailor plays the role of Samson in an amateur theater, and it transforms him for the rest of his life. The novel *Meir Ezofowicz* (1878) gives a picture of a Jewish town virtually unchanged since the time Julian Ursyn Niemcewicz wrote his *Lejbe and Sióra*. This is a poetic saga of a family which, for several generations, has stood for progress within the Jewish community. The family's last descendant, Meir Ezofowicz, a young man, revolts against the obscurantism of his milieu, but he is opposed by Rabbi Todros, the descendant of a fanatical and intolerant Sephardic family. In the end Ezofowicz is cursed and expelled from the town. The word "saga" is appropriate because the somewhat poetic tale is constructed around a family legend: every few generations (ever since the sixteenth century), a just man with a heart overflowing with love for mankind is born into the Ezofowicz family. Meir has a boundless and naïve confidence in the blessings of learning. He is a true heir to his sixteenth-century ancestor whom the Polish king nominated as leader of the Jews in the Grand Duchy of Lithuania. He is also a tribute to his more recent ancestor of the eighteenth century, politically allied with the Camp of the Reform. Strongly melodramatic and old-fashioned in its syntax, the novel seems to continue the sentimental school. The same applies to another novel on Jewish themes, *Eli Makover* (1875).

The best of her novels on peasant life are *Dziurdziowie*—the title comes from the name of a peasant family—(1885) and *The Boor* (*Cham*, 1888). The first is about a young girl who marries a blacksmith from another village and is surrounded by suspicion because the neighbors believe she practices witchcraft; this leads to her murder by the angry villagers. The second takes up the old theme of a woman killed by kindness. The hero, a simple, goodhearted peasant, marries a harlot to save her; he even takes her back when, after an "escape," she returns home, pregnant with somebody else's child. But she is unable to change, and, perhaps out of remorse, commits suicide.

Orzeszkowa's acquaintance with the life of the Jews and of the peasants was, perhaps, less profound than her acquaintance with the life of petty-gentry farmers. For that reason, no doubt, her novel *On the Banks of the Niemen* (*Nad Niemnem*, 1888) is her finest accomplishment in fiction. The region of the Niemen River is very similar to the countryside described in the pages of Mickiewicz's *Pan Tadeusz*. Orzeszkowa managed to convey the unique flavor of her native land in prose. She depicts a blessed valley, far removed from the centers of civilization, that has lived for centuries its unique, autonomous life. She also constructs a myth (which has a strangely American ring to it) about the valley's first settlers in the sixteenth century: a couple of outlaws from society, a man of low origin and a girl probably from an aristocratic family, came to the area, which was then virgin forest, cleared the land around their hut, and pioneered a new community. Those who now, i.e. in Orzeszkowa's time inhabit the village in the center of the valley are their descendants. All bear the same name—Bohatyrowicz. To distinguish each other they use nicknames. Although proud possessors of noble titles conferred on all their clan by the king, they till the soil like ordinary peasants and lead a healthy existence, not unlike their ancestors of a few centuries ago. The heroine of the novel, Justyna, inhabits a manor where she is supported as a poor relative. She meets a young man from the village, Jan Bohatyrowicz, and is torn between two conflicting patterns of behavior. She belongs to the upper class. To marry Bohatyrowicz would mean abandoning her privileges and working with her own hands on the farm. On the other hand, if she wishes to retain her upper-class status, she will have to abandon Jan, whom she loves. This dilemma, although set forth in a Positivistic way, carries an additional element usually avoided by the Positivists, namely, memories of the "mad" uprising. Across the river Niemen, in the forest, is a grave of insurrectionists killed in 1863. Among them reposes not only Jan Bohatyrowicz's father, but also the brother of the landowner in whose home Justyna is living. The grave acquires a symbolic meaning. It points to a moment of collective *élan*, of a striving toward the removal of social divisions thanks to one uniting, national, and democratic cause. People from the upper class receive rather harsh treatment in the novel. They are frozen in fearful self-protection or, indifferent to the fate of their country, dream about moving somewhere abroad. For Justyna to marry Jan is to win her dignity; in her present status she is neither fish nor fowl; she has room and board but nothing useful to do. To marry him is also to become integrated into the community, which is a true preserver of tradition. To use somewhat trite terms, the novel is about Justyna's alienation and her integration, which at last she decides to accomplish through her marriage. For Orzeszkowa, uprootedness was a great evil. One had to be rooted not only in one's small community, but also in the historical past. The village of Bohatyrowicze piously guards memories embedded in the very soil: Justyna and Jan assist at the making of a new cross for the grave of the first settlers and listen to tales about the participation of some of his family in the Napoleonic Wars and in the two subsequent uprisings. The novel can also be considered as a treatise on courage. An old, bitter spinster, Marta, also a poor relative living on the manor, exemplifies what happens when a woman is shackled by regard for her social status. Marta had loved a man from the village, but lacked the daring to defy prejudices and marry him.

On the Banks of Niemen is more serene than Prus's *The Outpost*, and no wonder: it deals not with illiterate peasants but with average farmers, a numerous and rather energetic class, especially in the former Grand Duchy of Lithuania. Also, Orzeszkowa had a better feeling for benevolent, radiant nature, and in her novel, work in the open field bathes in the aura of poetry. At the same time, there is none of the false picturesqueness that so often mars novels on folkish themes. Her world is gentle and humane, making us, who belong to an industrial civilization, not a little envious.

Religious meditation, though not in dogmatic terms, was not alien to Prus and even more strongly pervades some of Orzeszkowa's writings. That is why she was not indifferent, in her advanced age, to metaphysical crisis—a central problem of the so-called "modernists," who roused, however, her indignation by their "immorality" and rejection of "ideals." Thus, in one of her late works, a dialogue entitled *Ad Astra* (1904), she formulates both the agnostic attitude and the revolt against it, as she felt it herself:

If, as you pretend, in the far, far abysses of the universe, beyond the impenetrable tissue of suns and stars, there is but an *x*, an unknown, alien to us and ominous in its absolute solitude, cruel in its orders pronounced once and for all eternity, asking nothing from its creatures, unconnected with them by any thread of cooperation or of love, making out of their births, their deaths, their sufferings and passions a strange theater in which "it" is the author and only spectator—if this is so—where is the hope of rebirth, where are giants? What evil can there be and what good? You are right. This is logical. Where there is no supreme will, there is no opposition to it, no service to be performed; if there is no purpose and no aim, there is no guilt and no merit, no growth, no fall, no rebirth, nothing . . . Yes. But what can I do with my pain, not only my pain, but with that which is around me like a sea?

The utilitarian approach to society and literature was, in Positivist writers, but a surface hiding more fundamental ethical and even metaphysical concerns. Since Orzeszkowa added to this a warm attachment to national tradition, returning with sympathy several times in her work to the "mad" uprising of 1863, she stands somewhat apart from the main current of Positivist thought.

HENRYK SIENKIEWICZ
(1846–1916)

Although perhaps inferior intellectually to his Positivist contemporaries and exposed to their criticism, Sienkiewicz won international fame and a Nobel Prize. To appraise him objectively is quite a task, for he combined a rare narrative gift with shortcomings that are serious enough to disqualify him from the title of a truly great writer. He was born in Wola Okrzejska in Podlasie province, went to school in Warsaw, and attended the *Szkoła Główna* for a while, studying mostly history and literature. As a young man, he had a passion for heraldry, arising partly out of a snobbish pride in his family's aristocratic origins, although on his father's side he was descended from average squires of Tartar origin, who had embraced Christianity and were ennobled in the eighteenth century. Not having inherited a fortune, however, Sienkiewicz had to search for a means of earning a livelihood early. First he tried tutoring; then he became a journalist. And he was a good one. His gift of observation, his taste for adventure, his attention to detail (aided, perhaps, by his passion for hunting, which enriched his knowledge of zoology and botany) were admirably combined with an easygoing, sociable nature and a flair for style. He worked for the progressive, Positivist press and wrote as an enemy of conservatism. Later on, he changed sides, and Positivist circles came to regard him as a kind of renegade. His early literary productions were on the periphery of journalism: humorous satirical scenes aimed at the social parasitism of the gentry. He was thirty when his newspaper (*Gazeta polska*) sent him to cover the Centennial Exposition in Philadelphia in 1876. That trip was also a pretext for something else: a group of Warsaw writers and artists had decided to migrate to America and to found a phalanstery there, as an experiment in communal living. They had chosen California in advance, and Sienkiewicz was charged with locating a proper site. The project was financed by Count Chłapowski, the husband of the famous actress Helena Modrzejewska. Sienkiewicz traveled across the United States, gathering observations and material. His discovery of rich hunting grounds in California, redwood forests, and the Sierras filled him with enthusiasm. When the other members of the group arrived from Poland, they established their colony in Anaheim (future home of Disneyland). Modrzejewska served as a cook for the small community, whose members dutifully tilled the soil and planted orange trees. But it was not long before they grew bored; besides, they were in financial trouble. Modrzejewska learned English and appeared in the leading role of *Camille* in San Francisco. Thus began her successful acting career in the American theater, in whose annals she has remained as Helena Modjeska. Sienkiewicz returned to his hunting and writing, and sent articles to Polish newspapers, which brought him wide renown. These "Letters from America" read well even today and are valuable for the balanced view they provide of American life of that time. The articles describe New York, the Great Plains during the campaign against Sitting Bull, a hunting trip to Wyoming, but mostly California.

His first (if we bypass a few short stories and an early, rather weak, novel) longer work of fiction, *Charcoal Sketches* (*Szkice węglem*), was written in Los Angeles, but it had nothing to do with America. On the contrary, this is a short novel depicting a God-forsaken Polish village; the very name of the place speaks for itself— Sheepshead in the country of Jackassville. The hero is a local bigwig, a secretary of the commune, and the only literate among the surrounding peasants. He blackmails them, exploits them, and his unruly passions as a local Don Juan bring misfortune to a peasant family. As befits a realistic tale with social content, there is a message: owners of the manor bear the blame for keeping aloof from the village and leaving the peasants in the power of such petty tyrants.

During his two-year stay in California, Sienkiewicz met several Poles who served him later on as prototypes for characters. One of them was Captain Korwin-Piotrowski, then a United States inspector in San Francisco for Chinese immigration. A man of gigantic stature and immense strength, a braggart, a liar, a drunkard, he was also a gay personality and an excellent storyteller, drawing upon his rich experience in Poland, where he had fought in the Polish-Russian war of 1831, as well as upon his wanderings across the American prairies, his battles with Indians, etc. Sienkiewicz, who had a great feeling for language, admired his earthy and humorous way of talking. In all probability, Mr. Zagłoba (a kind of a Polish Falstaff) in Sienkiewicz's historical trilogy of the seventeenth century was modeled on the San Francisco inspector. Moreover, the natural scenery of the Great

Plains and the California forests made a lasting impact on Sienkiewicz, and we may suspect that his descriptions of the Ukrainian
steppes or primeval forests in Poland of the fifteenth century (in *The
Teutonic Knights*) were based, to some extent, upon his American
reminiscences.

Sienkiewicz's so-called "American short stories," written after he
had returned to Poland but inspired by themes with which he had
made himself familiar in California, leave the reader with mixed
feelings. He is good when he is a reporter; but fictional elements are
often sentimentalized to the point of becoming outright *kitsch*. The
most popular among these short stories, "The Lighthouse Keeper," is
a good illustration of how he "touched up" reality for melodramatic
effects. The hero, an old Pole, has fought in many wars and revolutions, dug gold in Australia, searched for diamonds in Africa,
farmed in California, traded with savage tribes in Brazil, and so on,
always pursued by a mysterious fatality, until, at last, he finds peace
as a lighthouse keeper in Aspinwall in the Panama Canal Zone. One
day he receives a package of books from New York among which is
Mickiewicz's *Pan Tadeusz*. As he reads, he becomes so captivated by
this vicarious return through poetry to his native land that he forgets
to light the beacon and, consequently, loses his job. Scholars have
tracked down Sienkiewicz's model for the story. He was a man who
had had similar extraordinary adventures in his life, but not because
he was pursued by a mysterious fatality. He was simply convinced
that the agents of the czarist police were following him across the
five continents. The trance he fell into while reading a book sent from
New York was not provoked by patriotic feelings, but by the extremely
lively action of a historical novel. Perhaps a story that stuck to the
facts would have been even more pathetic, although we have to concede that because of censorship Sienkiewicz could not have mentioned
the man's persecution complex.

In 1878, Sienkiewicz went to Paris, where he stayed for several
months; then he lived in Galicia for a while and appeared in Warsaw
after a four-year absence. By this time, the Positivists had already
written him off as a total loss. He had balked in the name of complete artistic freedom as to the choice of subject and its treatment.
Rules and principles bored him; politically, he was moving toward the
Polish Tories, and soon he founded a newspaper of his own, *The
Word* (*Słowo*), in the spirit of "enlightened conservatism."

Sienkiewicz was of the opinion that the aim of literature should be
to comfort the heart, and to furnish the reader with what he really
wants, not what some superior intellects contrive as supposedly healthy
nourishment. Then why not turn to history, for which the Polish
public showed a predilection? The eighties saw him publishing in

the newspapers installments of a historical trilogy, which came out in book form shortly afterward. The titles of the volumes are *With Fire and the Sword* (*Ogniem i mieczem*, 1884), *The Deluge* (*Potop*, 1886), and *Pan Michael* (*Pan Wołodyjowski*, 1887–1888). So immediate was public response that Sienkiewicz found himself under continual pressure from his readers, who begged him by letter not to harm one or another beloved character. The Trilogy reached everybody in Poland who was able to read, and became a "must" for every adolescent. Translated into other languages, it enjoyed tremendous popularity, especially in Slavic countries. Sienkiewicz was a hardworking writer; with a deadline constantly hanging over his head, he had to send in installments regardless of his personal troubles. His wife (whom he had married soon after his return to Poland) was dying from tuberculosis, and he needed money to take care of her in various sanatoriums in Western Europe. He managed, however, to do extensive historical research for his three novels, and although his interpretation of the facts can be questioned, he cannot be reproached with lack of data. Obviously, he picked the middle of the seventeenth century as the time of action because he wanted to take the reader "back to the womb," to the glorious *Respublica*, even though it was entangled, then, in disastrous wars. Besides, wartime was ideal for picaresque plots. He also attempted to reconstruct the language of the seventeenth century. As models, he used the old memorialists, above all, Jan Chryzostom Pasek; the result was a style so vivid that schoolboys, after reading the Trilogy, would speak among themselves in its peculiar seventeenth-century Polish.

The three parts of the Trilogy follow the adventures of a permanent cast of characters through the Polish-Cossack wars (Volume One); the Polish-Swedish war (Volume Two); and the Polish-Turkish wars (Volume Three). In each successive part, however, the reader finds new characters; he also finds that some of the figures who play a prominent role in the preceding volume are relegated to the background, or that previously minor figures occupy the center of the stage. The Trilogy reminds one of Alexandre Dumas's *The Three Musketeers*, and Sienkiewicz willingly acknowledged his indebtedness to the French author. It must be said, however, in Sienkiewicz's favor, that the scope of his historical vision far surpassed his model's. On the whole, these are novels of military adventure with a due proportion of love involvements and miraculous escapes. The pace is quick. The main figures are supermen or superwomen with whom the reader identifies. The element of suspense is nearly constant; but dramatic scenes are interlaced with humorous ones. Among the comic characters, the most striking is Mr. Zagłoba, an old, one-eyed nobleman with a huge belly, a kind of bumblebee buzzing with jokes, a resourceful braggart and coward, though cunning and able to perform feats of courage when cornered. There is also a lean, seven-foot-tall, Don Quixote-like Lithuanian knight, Longinus Podbipięta, who has sworn to remain chaste until he shall have cut off three Tartar heads in one stroke. So strongly did unsophisticated readers identify with the Trilogy characters that they did not conceive of them as born in the author's imagination. (Sometimes a mass was requested for the repose of the soul of a personality whom Sienkiewicz at last had let die on the battlefield!) The wild Ukrainian steppes in *With Fire and the Sword* recall the American Great Plains at a time when law was in the weapons one possessed. Already in his "Letters From America," Sienkiewicz had compared life on the prairies to that on the peripheries of the old *Respublica*, and the Trilogy does bear a resemblance to cowboy-and-Indian stories.

But the Positivists were serious people. They sought in the Trilogy an accurate image of historical events; what they found only confirmed their distrust of historical subjects. And it must be admitted that Sienkiewicz remodeled the seventeenth century to his own and his readers' liking. The Cossack wars were class wars—and Sienkiewicz showed them as such—directed against Polish magnates whose interests clashed with those of the state. The king could not be blamed, therefore, for not supporting the magnates. According to some Polish historians, Prince Jeremi Wiśniowiecki, commander of the Polish troops, was a nasty, cruel type, who followed a stupid policy. In Sienkiewicz's version he is a saintly soldier, a servant of Christ and Western civilization. Bohdan Chmielnicki, the leader of the Ukrainian revolt, was actually a man of much greater stature than he appears to be in Sienkiewicz's belittling portrayal. Although the author is obviously fascinated with a savage and brave Cossack (Bohun), in general his characters are either "good guys" (Poles) or "bad guys" (Ukrainians)—which is fine, but only from the point of view of a literary success. In *The Deluge*, the highly intellectualized segments of the population, above all, the Protestants, are either eliminated from the pages of the novel or are given roles as traitors and collaborators with the Swedes. Sienkiewicz's ideal is a pious, healthy, Roman Catholic soldier, not overburdened with ideas but endowed with a great capacity for fencing, drinking, and love-making. Bolesław Prus, who wrote a biting criticism of Sienkiewicz, noticed all this, and he also remarked that war, which constitutes the main occupation of the heroes, is treated like a fairy tale. Heads, hands are cut off, heaps of corpses are piled up, but blood is not blood, it is rather blueberry juice; and all the while that valiant knight, Podbipięta, whom Prus calls a "walking guillotine," keeps his eyes fixed piously heavenward. Most likely, all these arguments against the Trilogy are just "shooting a cannon at a sparrow," since Sienkiewicz accomplished what he had set out to do: to give readers a colorful yarn and "to comfort their hearts." On the other hand, admiration or disdain for Sienkiewicz has long been a gauge of political orientation in Poland. In general, his writings promoted a conservative mentality. His impact upon the public has been without equal; one has only to cite such instances as that of underground fighters during the Second World War, who used the names of Sienkiewicz's heroes as aliases.

Sienkiewicz's fame in the West was secured chiefly by his novel on ancient Rome, *Quo Vadis?* (1896). In the annals of French publishing, for example, it figures as one of the top best sellers of all time. The novel contrasts a decadent but vivid pagan empire under Nero with a virtuous, though somewhat pale, primitive Christian community during the era of catacombs and martyrdom. Madness like that of the emperor Nero or an effeminate relativism and skepticism like that of the elegant Petronius have to succumb, "and the basilica of St. Peter still dominates the world." Undoubtedly Sienkiewicz, just as in his Trilogy, did a good job of enlivening all the historical clichés, but his Rome was somewhat too lacking in complexity. A critic of the twentieth century, Stanisław Brzozowski, said that it would be enough to compare Cyprian Norwid's poem *Quidam* with *Quo Vadis?* to discover the superficiality of that novel which brought Sienkiewicz the Nobel Prize.

The Teutonic Knights (*Krzyżacy*, 1900) is, again, a novel on the Polish past. It takes the reader even further back than the Trilogy, to the beginning of the fifteenth century, when the very existence of both Poland and the Grand Duchy of Lithuania was threatened by the Teutonic Order. Bolesław Prus was not the only one to be seriously concerned with German nationalism and its slogans directed against the Slavs. The decades prior to World War I witnessed a continuous rise in German imperialistic dreams, and Sienkiewicz, in some of his shorter writings, dealt directly with that theme. In *The Teutonic Knights*, he exploited—and reinforced—what had been for centuries an archetype in the Polish imagination. In presenting the arrogance, racial prejudice, and cruelty of the Teutonic warrior-monks who carved a realm for themselves in East Prussia he was quite in agreement with historical data. The narrative culminates in the battle at Grunwald and Tannenberg in 1410, the biggest ever fought by the Poles and the Lithuanians. Sienkiewicz followed historical documents closely, and his interpretation of the facts is more acceptable here than in the Trilogy. The primeval forests in which his heroes live, hunt, and do battle are probably a composite of his impressions of the forests of Lithuania and the redwoods of the American West Coast.

But Sienkiewicz did not limit himself to historical subjects. *Without Dogma* (*Bez dogmatu*, 1891), in the form of a diary kept by a highly refined man of aristocratic origin, was an attempt to portray the *fin-de-siècle* despair resulting from lack of faith in anything and lack of purpose. The hero, Płoszowski, is a connoisseur of art and literature yet unproductive himself, lacking a will to live, convinced that his world of intellectual elegance, of aesthetic enjoyment is doomed. Actually, Sienkiewicz was following in the footsteps of a French writer, Paul Bourget, hailed in France during his lifetime as a novelist equal to Balzac and Flaubert. Bourget defended traditional bourgeois values against the young generation's agnosticism, the source, according to him, of all moral turpitude; these views were particularly propagated in his novel *The Disciple* (1889). Bourget recognized in Sienkiewicz a kindred soul, and the French translation of *Without Dogma* appeared with his preface. Sienkiewicz certainly did not conceive of his hero as a positive figure, yet some Polish "decadents" of the last decade of the nineteenth century were inclined, for a while, to identify themselves with him. All in all, *Without Dogma* is of rather transient importance, as is another novel on contemporary life, *The Połaniecki Family* (*Rodzina Połanieckich*, 1895), where Sienkiewicz attempted to extol the blessings of a philistine way of life: Połaniecki is a bourgeois of noble origin, who makes money from rather unsavory speculations; he combines his financial skills with the conviction that he is serving both God and Country. Unlike the Positivists' progressive capitalist, he is opposed to any change in the established order. Taken as a major offense by the progressive intelligentsia, the novel indicated Sienkiewicz's *rapprochement* with the ideology of the National Democratic Party and its program of capitalist prosperity under the "protection" of czarist Russia.

Sienkiewicz's position in Polish literature owes much to his feeling for the language. Many sentences of his have been quoted in dictionaries as examples of well-balanced prose. Perhaps the best definition of Sienkiewicz's shortcomings was formulated by Orzeszkowa in one of her letters:

If I was born with a creative faculty, it was a mediocre one. That spark was a little enlivened by considerable intellectual capabilities, and great emotional capabilities, perhaps too great for one heart. Quite the reverse with Sienkiewicz. So I often thought that could our two individualities have been united in one, they would have produced quite a writer.

OTHER PROSE WRITERS

Adolf Dygasiński was a Positivist and a worshipper of science. *Adolf Dygasiński (1839–1902)* A teacher by profession, he seemed to be more receptive than any of his contemporaries to naturalism, both as a literary technique and as a philosophy. In his short stories and novels he put to use his familiarity with the Polish countryside, its manor and its villages. Hunting, that beloved pastime of the gentry folk with its own rules and rituals, is very much present on his pages. As a naturalist, prone to throw a bridge between the animals and men, he endows the creatures of field and forest with nearly human psychology, and often shifts the perspective of his narrative from human to animal. For this reason, critics compared him to Kipling. In his last work, *The Feast of Life* (*Gody życia*, 1902), a kind of long prose poem in praise of nature's indomitable *élan*, he employed an ornate, highly stylized, and strongly cadenced language for which he was applauded by the younger generation, the "modernists."

A descendant of one of the Austrian families that moved to Gali- *Jan Lam (1838–1886)* cia and swiftly became Polonized, Jan Lam was well known in Lwów as a journalist and humorous chronicler of the provincial scene. What Prus was for Warsaw, Lam was for the eastern part of Galicia under Austrian rule. Skillful in the genre of the *feuilleton*, he also wrote novels in which Austrian, Czech, and Polish petty bureaucrats are the targets of his satire: *Miss Emily, or The High Society of Tsapowice* (*Panna Emilia, czyli wielki świat Capowic*, 1869) and *The Empty Heads* (*Głowy do pozłoty*, 1873). A somewhat extraordinary man, highly gifted and very courageous (he slipped across the border in 1863 to fight in the uprising), a person with a tragic outlook, Lam, in trying to adapt himself to a stifling provincial environment, could not develop his talent, which was ruined by alcoholism and recurring severe depressions.

Successive waves of deportation brought many Poles to Siberia. *Adam Szymański (1852–1916)* Among them were people trained in the natural sciences, and the resulting Polish contribution to the exploration of Siberia was considerable. For instance, a young professor of zoology, Benedykt Dybowski (deported in the 1860s), carried out investigations of the underwater fauna (at a depth of 3,300 feet) in Lake Baïkal and discovered many previously unknown species, for which he was awarded a gold medal by the Russian Geographic Society. He also made valuable ethnographical and linguistic observations of the tribes of Kamchatka. Aleksander Czekanowski, a geologist deported after the 1863 uprising, described areas that, until then, had been inaccessible. An organizer of expeditions beyond the Arctic Circle, he, too, received a gold medal from the Russian Geographical Society, for his research in paleobotany on the Angara River. In addition, he completed the first dictionary of the Tungusic language. Jan Czerski (only a high-school student in Wilno when he joined the uprising of 1863) was a self-taught scientist. He made a thorough study of the geological structure of Lake Baïkal, was the first to penetrate into the basins of the Yana, Indygirka, and Kolyma rivers, and discovered a chain of mountains, which today bears his name. He was thrice awarded the gold medal from the Russian Geographical Society. Bronisław Grąbczewski, the son of an 1863 exile, entered the Russian army and rose to the rank of general. He led scientific expeditions exploring Turkestan, Pamir, Hindukush, and northern Tibet.

When Adam Szymański published his *Sketches* (*Szkice*, 1887), they understandably provoked great interest, as they drew upon his experience of deportation in Siberia. *Sketches* is a collection of short stories about how average Polish deportees coped with a harsh climate, the primitive mentality of northern Siberian natives, and their own nostalgia.

Wacław Sieroszewski (1860–1945)

The theme of Siberia found a more thorough treatment in the hands of another writer, who belonged to a different generation. A descendant of a noble family ruined by the 1863 uprising, Wacław Sieroszewski became a manual worker in Warsaw. He joined the socialist movement when he was seventeen. Arrested in connection with his political activities, he spent two years in prison, then was deported in 1880 to the coldest region of Siberia, the land of the Yakuts. A man of resourcefulness and vitality, he twice attempted to escape from Siberia and twice failed. But his description of one region, in Russian, *The Yakuts* (*Yakuty*, 1896), won him a gold medal from the Russian Geographical Society and his freedom. Gradually he turned to fictionalizing his adventures; his novels and short stories, which bear the imprint of authenticity, were widely read, especially by young people, along with stories of Indians. Their number is imposing. The novels —*The Confines of the Forest* (*Na kresach lasów*, 1894), *Rishtau* (1899), *The Flight* (*Ucieczka*, 1904)—date from the period of his most intense literary activity. A socialist fighter in the revolution of 1905, a soldier of Piłsudski's legion in 1914–1915, Sieroszewski later played a fairly prominent role in the literary life of independent Poland during the years 1918–1939, when he was regarded as a kind of venerable "veteran." Sieroszewski's factual reports are, perhaps, the most durable part of his output. They provide a valuable insight into the fate of political prisoners. He was passionately interested in the mores and customs of local populations and was also a good observer of nature. In his memoir, *Beyond the Polar Circle* (*Za kołem polarnym*, 1926), he tells of his escape from Verkhoyansk, in the land of the Yakuts, and how, after some 1,200 kilometers of trudging through uninhabited expanses, he reached the Arctic Ocean. When caught, he was transferred, as a punishment, to Kolymsk.

The descendant of a noble family of German settlers in Lithuania, Józef Weyssenhoff filled most of his life with occupations befitting a gentleman, namely, social life, hunting, and travel abroad to all the fashionable spots in Western Europe. His early poems paid tribute to the blue sea and white temples of Greece. Later, he published a novel, *The Life and Ideas of Zygmunt Podfilipski* (*Żywot i myśli Zygmunta Podfilipskiego*, 1898), acclaimed as very effective in ridiculing Polish "high society" with its mania for admiring everything that is Western European and despising everything that is Polish. Podfilipski is a moron, though full of tact and skeptical, elegant maxims on all human affairs. His knowledge as to the kinds of ties one should wear or how to behave in various circumstances is unlimited. He is not completely indifferent to mankind, for he would like to transfer to posterity his philosophy of the futility of all serious endeavors. It is not certain that in creating the figure of Podfilipski, Weyssenhoff was fully aware of what he was doing. In any case, thanks perhaps to the ambiguity in the mind of the author himself, this is the best of Weyssenhoff's novels. The others too often seem to be written by Podfilipski. They lack a proper distance in their presentation of the milieu of the Polish manor in the former Grand Duchy of Lithuania. Weyssenhoff is at his best describing his true passion: hunting in the forests of his native region. His later fiction grew more and more ideological, in an attempt to uphold the tenets of the rich landowners' conservative political creed.

Józef Weyssenhoff (1860–1932)

POETRY

Neither the secondhand techniques of versification practiced by those who imitated the Great Romantics nor the Positivistic scorn for Romantic imagination favored a vital poetry, and during the second half of the nineteenth century poetry lived through a visible decline. Little images from real life or short stories put to verse achieved popularity. Poetry acceded to the request of reasonableness, and its sentences often did not differ from a rhymed prose. Verse became melodious in a rather trite way, with a constantly repeated pattern of trochees, iambs, or amphibrachs. Even very gifted poets were caught in that unfavorable ambiance and often complained of being sentenced to live in an "unpoetic age."

Recognized as a leading poet of the period, Adam Asnyk came from

Adam Asnyk
(1838–1897)

a petty-gentry family and was the son of an insurrectionist soldier who had spent two years of enforced exile in Siberia, then had become a prosperous merchant in Poland. Young Adam studied in Warsaw at the Medical Academy. After a short imprisonment for political activity he escaped abroad in 1860. Forbidden to return to the Russian-occupied part of Poland because of his political involvements in 1863, he acquired a doctorate in philosophy at the University of Heidelberg and settled for the rest of his life in the Austrian part of Poland—first in Lwów, then in Kraków. This did not prevent him from traveling all over Europe, and even to North Africa, India, and Ceylon. Asnyk was undoubtedly a disciple of the Romantics, and above all of Słowacki; but he evolved toward less ambitious, smaller forms which sometimes seem pedestrian, for they are really little more than rhymed philosophical, or even scientific, discourses. Perhaps his best poems are those inspired by the Tatra Mountains. The opening up of the Tatras fell in the 1870s of the nineteenth century, and some hitherto inaccessible peaks were conquered at that time. By the turn of the century, the mountains were tempting writers as unexplored subject matter. Asnyk himself was one of the first members of the "Tatra Society" and an enthusiastic mountain climber. A journalist, an editor, and a member of various societies, he was a man of multiple activities, and his popularity as a poet mounted steadily. Some of his short lyrics, on love and nature, were even set to music.

A cycle of thirty sonnets, *Over the Depths* (*Nad głębiami*), written in 1880–1894, blends mountain landscapes with an exposition of the author's philosophical system. The latter was strongly marked by the scientific evolutionism of the nineteenth century, by German idealistic philosophy, and, perhaps, by some of Słowacki's philosophical ideas: although movement according to immutable laws is proper to the whole universe, which is composed of atoms, there exists a spiritual force beyond matter, driving all phenomena toward perfection and, thus, endowing the blind dance of elements with meaning. Asnyk's philosophy in those sonnets strongly recalls that of Bolesław Prus. The Positivists appreciated Asnyk's progressive beliefs and often quoted one of his short poems where he said that "one must go forward with the living, reach for a new life and not to crown one's head stubbornly with a bunch of withered laurels." Undoubtedly the best craftsman of his generation, Asnyk showed some similarities to the French Parnassians, who also paid their debt to the scientific *Weltanschauung* of the epoch. His influence waned, however, with the appearance of the "modernists" in the last decade of the century, and he has never recovered his former prominence.

Maria
Konopnicka
(1842–1910)

Acclaimed at one time as a "bard" worthy to occupy the place on Parnassus that had remained empty after the passing of the Great

Romantics, Konopnicka is more interesting, perhaps, as an example of an emancipated woman than as a poet, although some of her short poems are justly included in every anthology. She was born in a small town (Suwałki), the daughter of a lawyer, Józef Wasiłowski, and brought up in a gentry milieu. While a young pupil in a boarding school run by nuns in Warsaw, she met another prospective writer, Eliza Pawłowski (later Orzeszkowa), and their friendship was of considerable consequence. They exchanged letters afterward, and Orzeszkowa sustained her in difficult moments. Married early to a much older landowner, she lived on his estate, bore him six children, and then rebelled, throwing aside all the standards of the manor, moving to Warsaw, and embarking upon a career of her own. Self-taught, she devoured the works of Montaigne, John Stuart Mill, Buckle, Ribot, etc., as well as those of the Polish Positivists. Her maturing as a poetess came at a time when Positivistic optimism had already receded and the sharpness of class conflicts was making itself more and more acutely felt. Konopnicka was very radical in denouncing the predicament of the lower classes and quite violent in her anticlericalism. For that reason, her literary career encountered many obstacles. The conservatives accused her of inciting the peasants to rebellion against their lords; the clergy called her impious; and even some liberals had reservations about her emotional shrillness. She drew the special attention of the czarist censorship, which hardly facilitated matters.

Many of her poems are novelettes in verse on the plight of the oppressed; she also tried her hand at prose short stories on similar subjects, and with success. Her lyrics, however, are marred by their sing-song, syllabotonic rhythms, and she has often been quoted to demonstrate the undesirable effects of stressing monotonous "feet" in Polish verse. But some of her lyrics, which take their tone of lament from folk songs, deserve a place together with authentic anonymous folk poetry. In general, Konopnicka can be called a "Populist" poet, particularly attentive to a Poland different from that of the educated upper classes. Her moving short stories from the lives of peasants, workers, and Jews have been standard reading in the first grades of high schools up to today. She spent some twenty years of her advanced age working on a long epic poem, *Mister Balcer in Brazil* (*Pan Balcer w Brazylji*, 1910). In its form (it is written in *ottava rima*), it follows a tradition set by other Polish poets like Krasicki and Słowacki. The topic was highly relevant in her day, for masses of Polish peasants were migrating to the Americas, and their plight in Brazil, where they had to clear untouched, primeval forests, was probably the harshest of all. Konopnicka traveled to Western Europe several times and was well acquainted with the brutal conditions of peasant migration. The hero of her poem, Mister Balcer, is a modest village blacksmith. The form of the *ottava rima*, which, for Tasso, had served to depict chivalrous exploits, was, in Konopnicka's intention, to be used to present the even crueler battlefields of modern times. Except for a few vivid passages, the poem as a whole is more a proof of Konopnicka's keen sensitivity to current problems than a literary feat. Her achievement in poetry is, in some respects, akin to Orzeszkowa's in prose. Because Konopnicka's poetry and her short stories are very accessible, even to uneducated readers, her works have, since her death, been constantly re-edited in millions of copies.

Felicjan Faleński (1825–1910)   Unlike Asnyk and Konopnicka, Felicjan Faleński was a marginal figure. Relative recognition came to him only in old age. He has been dismissed by some as merely the husband of Maria Trębicka, who exchanged letters with Cyprian Norwid; for Norwid (once a schoolmate of Faleński's in Warsaw), Trębicka was, above all, the friend and confidante of his love, Maria Kalergis. But Faleński is an interesting poet in his own right, and the author of plays in verse which reveal a vastness of intellectual horizons. A man of erudition and a skillful translator of Edgar Allan Poe, Hans Christian Andersen, and E. T. A. Hoffmann, he was able to spend whole years rendering various foreign poets into Polish and putting several books of the Old Testament into verse. His bibliography bears traces of an early estrangement from society due to his father's very energetic collaboration with the czarist authorities. Faleński was most successful in some short poems on the Tatra Mountains, where his imagery is sometimes astonishingly modern, and in the short epigrams to which he gave a Greek name, *Meanders* (*Meandry*, 1892). He was preoccupied with Greece also as a playwright, and in his *Althea*, he dealt with the theme of Meleager and Atalanta (like Swinburne in England). Ironic and embittered, Faleński was out of step with the literary scene of his time, and sometimes he vented his anger at the public by burning all the volumes of his poetry, which, incidentally, he published at his own expense.

Wiktor Gomulicki (1848–1919)   Wiktor Gomulicki, born in a small town (Ostrołęka) into the family of a prosperous surveyor, went to high school in Warsaw, then studied law at the *Szkoła Główna*. It was in Warsaw that he started off on his successful literary career. He wrote poetry, novels, short stories, essays, and literary criticism, besides translating Pushkin, Nekrasov, Victor Hugo, Musset, to name only a few. Although the compact neatness of his form approached that of the French Parnassians, he was primarily a poet of "images" from daily life in Warsaw, particularly in one of its sections, his beloved Old Town. Within the accepted syntactical conventions, using a language as transparent and as accessible as prose, Gomulicki was able to catch, in a nearly photographic way, many small details he observed in Warsaw streets; he depicts old, white-haired women going with their jugs to fetch water or milk, or a café where an old French lady is perennially ensconced reading the newspapers, or birds singing out of their cages in a garret, or old cobblers, or retired employees. There is a tenderness, seasoned with melancholy, and a smile in Gomulicki's poems, and often trite things are transformed into messengers of something great and sublime. One of his finest poems, "El Mole Rahmim," describes a Jewish wedding celebrated in a drab and dirty courtyard. For the poet, who observes the rite, these ugly surroundings, under the impact of the religious song, are transformed into a beautiful valley with the mountains of Lebanon in the distance. He sees the miserable participants of the ceremony as the inhabitants of the valley in the age of the Prophets: "And stars shone above like a golden menorah."

While we have touched upon several poets here, the discussion does not nearly exhaust the long list of those who were esteemed, published, and analyzed by literary critics. Those other names belong today, however, to a realm visited only by specialists.

CHAPTER IX

Young Poland

T HE CLOSER WE MOVE to our own time, the more difficult it becomes to present the contradictory currents that shaped the life of Europe in an era which, in many respects, has not yet come to a close. Europe, at the end of the nineteenth century, enjoyed both peace and prosperity, but underneath the buoyant expansion of capitalism, destructive forces were at work, and the more sensitive minds felt this. The enigma we have to cope with is the genesis of a new approach to reality and art, emerging simultaneously in various European countries despite their respective differences in economic and social development. Whether we speak of a mutual "contamination" or of a "natural growth" out of local conditions or simply refer to an unidentifiable *Zeitgeist*, the fact is that similar tendencies in France, Germany, Poland, and Russia sprang up more or less at the same time. Partitioned Poland was submitted to three different rhythms emanating from three different capitals: Vienna, St. Petersburg, and Berlin. Yet in literature she succeeded in blending cosmopolitan influences with her own literary past and in producing, thus, something specific and original. Cosmopolitanism is the proper word here, because European culture, in an age when one traveled without passports, was felt to be all of a piece, and young people, whether they were Frenchmen, Poles, or Russians, pored over the same Latin and Greek classics, read the same German philosophers and French poets.

Modern Polish literature begins with the generation that emerged from adolescence around 1890. The term "Young Poland" (*Młoda Polska*) was applied to certain spokesmen of that generation only in

1899. Before that date various names were used, such as "decadents" or "modernists." Yet Polish scholars seem to agree that the term "Young Poland," coined as a parallel to "Young Scandinavia" and "Young Germany," defines the new phenomena better than any term ending with -*ism* just because of its vagueness.

Like many other literatures, Polish literature today is a continuation of the gropings begun around 1890. One can say that the approximate date of 1885 (usually given as the beginning of the crisis in nineteenth-century scientism in France) marked a return to the Romantic revolt after a hiatus of several decades of naïve confidence in unlimited bourgeois progress. At first, the new movement was represented only by small groups of Bohemians. These rebels against the Establishment had no programs except negation. They combatted recognized art and literature, proclaimed the end of Parnassian poetry and of naturalism in prose, made alliances with anarchists in politics, and saw Western civilization as having reached a stage of decadence. The Parisian review *Le Décadent* explained in 1886:

Born out of the hyperblasé civilization of Schopenhauerism, the decadents are not a literary school. Their mission is not to create. Their task is to destroy, to abolish everything that is old. . . . It would be nonsense to conceal the state of decadence which we have reached. Religion, mores, justice, everything is tending toward decline.

Since everything that happened in France was followed closely in Poland, the local rebels against the Positivist utilitarian ideal were also called "decadents" at first. But, of course, the word is too vague to capture the unprogrammatic changes that took place in sensibility. The word "symbolism" is no more precise. In France, the poetry of those who worshipped Charles Baudelaire, Rimbaud, Verlaine, Mallarmé, Jules Laforgue was called, from 1886 on, "symbolist." And it was exactly in 1886 that a review called *Le Symboliste* began to appear, edited by Jean Moréas and Gustave Kahn. Symbolism, if we keep to the definition used in France, designated not the masters but minor poets, and to believe French historians of literature, it came to an end in 1900. In a larger sense, a great number of poets writing in the nineteenth and twentieth centuries could be called "symbolists," and a new awareness of the role of symbols ("correspondences") in poetry stems from Baudelaire, who borrowed the notion from Emanuel Swedenborg. In Poland, although we find writers who were "symbolists" in this larger sense, they published no "symbolist" manifestos; thus, it would, perhaps, be an abuse to introduce the term as the title of a given chapter. However, what Arthur Symons says in his book on French symbolists applies equally to their Polish contemporaries:

Here then, in this revolt against exteriority, against rhetoric, against a materialistic tradition; in this endeavor to disengage the ultimate essence, the soul, of whatever exists and can be realized by the consciousness; in this dutiful waiting upon every symbol by which the soul of things can be made visible; literature, bowed down by so many burdens, may, at last, attain liberty, and its authentic speech. In attaining this liberty, it accepts a heavier burden; for in speaking to us so intimately, so solemnly, as only religion had hitherto spoken to us, it becomes itself a kind of religion, with all the duties and responsibilities of the sacred ritual.

Had decadentism and symbolism been the only labels applied to this chaotic movement, the affair would have been relatively simple, but other -*isms*, like naturalism and impressionism, vied for supremacy. Relatively short-lived as a method applied to the novel by Émile Zola, naturalism as a pessimistic vision of man, seen as subject to biological or social fatalities (which were conceived as a sort of counterpart to the biological struggle for life), bore fruit in a literature of cruelty and pity, and only at the turn of the century do we notice its impact in Poland. As a literary technique, it often went together with impressionism—and it is no wonder, since the mania of the naturalistic writer for collecting detailed observations led him to rely upon his eye and, thus, to reclaim fleeting impressions or sensations and to substitute subjective sensory data for a reality ordered by his reason.

The movement of "Young Poland" can be traced back to the innovative activity of a few isolated, energetic individuals interested primarily in poetry and philosophy. Already in 1887, Zenon Przesmycki (pen name: Miriam) was editing a literary magazine in Warsaw, called *Life* (*Życie*), that was moderate in tone but published many translations of such "wild" poets as Edgar Allan Poe, Baudelaire, Verlaine, and Swinburne. Arthur Rimbaud's *The Drunken Boat*, translated by Przesmycki and published in 1892, became a literary event and laid the foundations for one of the generation's two poetic myths— one being of Baudelaire, another of Rimbaud. Edward Porębowicz, a modest scholar, had been specializing in Romance languages since 1880 and published excellent translations of Provençal poetry. His later translations of Celtic, Germanic, and Scandinavian folk songs provided some fine poets, like Bolesław Leśmian, with abundant material. Antoni Lange, a poet in his own right, introduced Baudelaire's *Flowers of Evil* in the early 1890s. In addition, there were literary critics who popularized the new dramas constructed out of a web of symbols, especially those of the Belgian, Maurice Maeterlinck (whom a critic, Ignacy Matuszewski, called "the Shakespeare of the *fin de siècle*"). Henrik Ibsen also found many followers. In Kraków, between 1897 and 1900, a little magazine called, like its Warsaw predecessor, *Life* (*Życie*) attracted both theoreticians and practitioners of "Young Poland" (it was in this journal that the name "Young Poland" was applied for the first time). Later on, between 1901 and 1908, a sumptuous review, *Chimera*, edited by Zenon Przesmycki (already mentioned), was the main propagator of the already victorious innovations.

But we would be wrong to reduce the new ferment to literary fashions. It was a true crisis of the scientific *Weltanschauung*, lived through by those who had been imbued with it and who were searching for a way out in philosophers that offered some hope to the individual. Arthur Schopenhauer and Friedrich Nietzsche were read for that purpose: the first, because he advised the individual to withdraw from the infernal circle of immutable determinism; the second, because he reclaimed the individual as a self-sustaining entity creating values in a universe without metaphysical sanction. Polish readers first learned about Nietzsche from the then famous Danish critic, George Brandes, who had been translated into Polish in the early nineties; also from enthusiastic references in Ola Hanson's book, *Young Scandinavia*, which appeared in Polish in 1893; and finally, from a Pole, Stanisław Przybyszewski, who spread the word about Nietzsche as early as 1892. The first book on the subject of Nietzsche's philosophy (by Maria C. Przewóska) was published in 1894, and from 1900 on, his works were published in translation. To this list of philosophers should be added the names of Max Stirner (1806–1856), who exalted the Self, freed from any obligations toward society, and Eduard von Hartmann (1842–1906), who, combining Schopenhauer and Schelling, built up a system of his own, stressing the role of the Unconscious (*Das Unbewuste*). In the decade preceding the outbreak of World War I, Henri Bergson and Søren Kierkegaard were translated and commented upon. If we add that the socialist movement carried with it sometimes superficial, sometimes thorough, acquaintance with Feuerbach, Marx, and Engels, we would complete the picture of that multifaceted intellectual aggression which assailed the young minds of Poland. It is more difficult to assess the inroads made by Russian thought. They were limited to the Russian-occupied part of Poland, since people from the Austrian and German sections did not know the language, and if they read Dostoevsky, for instance, it was in German translations. Moreover, if any affinities with contemporary Russians existed, few Poles would confess to it publicly because of an unwritten code of behavior. But there were exceptions: the leading literary critic of the period, Stanisław Brzozowski, was steeped in Russian literature and kept track of all the new developments in Russia until his death in

1911; Marian Zdziechowski, a partisan of Schopenhauer's pessimistic philosophy, considered pessimism a necessary ingredient for the renewal of Christian religion and also felt a kinship with the Russian philosopher Vladimir Solovyev, whom he admired. Another movement of the time should be mentioned in connection with Zdziechowski, and that is the so-called "Modernism" within the Roman Catholic Church. Religious Modernism, stressing subjective experience, whose main representative in France was Loisy, had in Poland a defender in the person of Zdziechowski, even after its condemnation by Rome in 1907.

Apart from these literary and philosophical borrowings from abroad, the movement in Poland was shaped by the situation there and by native traditions. Although the generation of the Positivists was publishing its most mature works precisely then, nonetheless, in the last decade of the nineteenth century and the first decade of the twentieth, Positivism seemed to the young a reflection of defeat. They objected to its having compromised itself by a timid utilitarianism and by a faith in harmonious progress that was belied by the violence of social conflicts. Bolesław Prus, clear-thinking enough to see Polish society as a heap of sand, was still clinging to some hope of gradual improvement, but this hope was rejected by the young. The pendulum was swinging back to a Romantic dream of independence and revolution. Then came 1905, the year that shook the Russian Empire in the wake of the Russo-Japanese War, and a crucial date in the history of "Young Poland": the weakness of czardom manifested itself; censorship in Warsaw relaxed; national independence ceased to be just a crazy idea.

Of course, the Great Romantics were interpreted anew, and the order of their importance was somewhat reshuffled; it was Słowacki (in his late mystical phase) who became the number-one poet for "Young Poland." For more, perhaps, than purely anecdotal reasons, let us note here that Feliks Dzierżyński (1877–1926), a militant in the Social Democratic Party of the Polish Kingdom and of Lithuania (SDKPiL), whom Lenin was to choose for his right hand and who was to organize the most powerful police apparatus in modern history, the Cheka, used to recite from memory stanza after stanza of Słowacki's *King-Spirit*. Also of more than anecdotal significance is the fact that another socialist (from the Polish Socialist Party), the founder of the independent Polish state in 1918, Józef Piłsudski, had exactly the same predilections. Even rejuvenators of messianism were not lacking in the new movement. Such a reaching back to the Romantics was understandable in view of the enormous wealth of their poetry and thought as compared with the somewhat pedestrian work of the Positivists. And this makes it clear why some Polish scholars speak of "Neo-Romanticism" rather than of "Young Poland." Yet the term does not embrace all the aspects of that new version of the battle between Classicists and Romantics.

If we try to apply a concise formula, we might say that at the center of "Young Poland's" preoccupations was a religious crisis. These were people imbued with a scientific, evolutionist *Weltanschauung*, and their revolt against it did not spell their rejection of its basic tenets. Yet science could not give them any foundation for Value. Although their religious beliefs were undermined, they could not renounce the search for the meaning of life and death. The universe was a self-perpetuating mechanism with no room for pity and compassion. Somebody had to be accused, so they accused God, with a nearly Manichean intensity, and their bitterness at times sounded like a renewal of the Byronic revolt. In some, we find even a peculiar Satanism, an identification with the fallen angel. In poems and in thematic painting, images of *dies irae*, of God's wrath, abound. As Arthur Górski, one of "Young Poland's" spokesmen, wrote:

Over all souls a terrible darkness is spreading in which even doubt is extinguished; nothing is certain but horror and pain; all the walls between the real and the incomprehensible are broken. There is nothing but a dust of souls tossed by fate and crashing against each other over the abysses.

Such writers, like their French counterparts, decried the decadence of European society. Theirs was a call to revolt against the trite and meaningless life of a being whom they called a "philistine" or a "bourgeois" (later on, the name for this figure changed, as we know, to "organization man" or "bureaucrat"). Arthur Górski (quoted above) defined the situation thus:

As disillusionment with the life of society and with its typical product, a modern philistine, grew, ties between the individual and that society loosened; disgust and protest against the banality and soulless existence of the organized mass increased. . . . More sensitive and profound minds, after having lost their respect for the philistine and their sympathy with social movements, began to withdraw from life and look for its other, more durable values. . . .

What values? The central myth of "Young Poland" was that of the artist who enters into contact with the ineffable essence of reality and, in a certain sense, redeems all those who do not dare to reach deeper than the superficiality of the daily grind. Art that creates values in a world deprived of values became for "Young Poland" an object of worship, and it was not by chance that they considered music the highest art, closest to expressing the inexpressible. As to their attitude toward life (which they opposed to art), it was characterized, especially in the years 1890 to 1900, by a desperate hedonism and by dreams of Nirvana; many poems were dedicated to the lady Death (we might recall that "death"—*śmierć*—is feminine in Polish), who liberates mortals from the pain of existence.

The Positivists greeted the new writings with indignation and a cutting irony; for instance, one of them said, about the young writers:

Above all, everything in them is faked: faked sufferings, faked or very cheap pessimism, an artificial scorn, and even more artificial monstrosities of spirit and of instinct. Young men, healthy as fish, do not sleep and drug themselves with black coffee in order to acquire a more decent, namely, "modernistic," taint and to write hymns in honor of the absinthe which they cannot swallow; a weakling pretending to be a superman in order to cover his own nothingness; a philistine posing as a Nero or a Marquis de Sade.

Or further:

If a Prometheus cries, "I suffer" we vibrate with compassion. But if a student to whom a girl refuses a dance cries out thus, our heart does not change its ordinary rhythm.

These attacks were largely justified if we consider the average output of the young poets. One of them was able to write:

> Amid the ocean of black coffee
> I sail toward an island of bliss.
> A clown full of boredom and dreams,
> I hold the heavy rudder of my funny ship.

And:

> My soul in a wreath of thorns,
> On the white cross of your body,
> Nailed with the nails of my desires,
> Bowing her head slowly expires.

The Positivists were ready to recognize the shortcomings of their generation, yet felt they had been justified, and they reproached the young for their lack of memory. Orzeszkowa, in one of her letters, said:

In the battles of the uprising [of 1863] an immense stream of the best blood was spilled. The uprising here [Lithuania] was more fierce and more obstinate than in the Kingdom. The bravest, the noblest, the most loving perished either from a bullet or during deportation, or in exile. . . . Throngs of noble-minded democrats were felled by bullets, died in the northern steppes, were hanged on gallows—spiritual brothers of my early youth, I know how many, how promising, how inflamed with Holy Spirit.

But the quarrels between the Positivists and the modernists were joined by other camps. Marxist literary critics, who began to appear in the nineties, resented the image of the artist as a kind of superman, ascribing it to a fear of the masses which soon, according to them, were to take over the rule of a doomed society; and after this, social duties would be *imposed* upon the artist. Yet it was "Young Poland" that emerged the victor, with consequences for literature unforeseen by any of the combatants. The change in sensibility and style did not lead to an art that would proudly close itself in an ivory tower. On the contrary, it brought about a re-evaluation of the national heritage and a renewal of the spirit of commitment to the collectivity, but not in the simple, utilitarian terms of Positivism.

Linguistically, it was a period of chaos. The subjectivism of indefinite moods was an invitation to license both in poetry and in prose, which is understandable if we keep in mind that the Polish language had never been as rigidly disciplined as, for instance, French; in fact, it had been constantly menaced by upsurges of the Baroque. Over-embellishment and rhythmicality at the expense of the normal syntax made the style of "Young Poland," a few decades later, a synonym for bad taste. And yet, if the majority of those writers bore a stigma that diminished their stature, a few of them did manage to achieve greatness, perhaps owing to this very freedom in experimentation.

THE INITIATORS

Przybyszewski's role, which was due to his intellectual daring and magnetic personality, can hardly be exaggerated. Memoirs and diaries of his contemporaries reveal a universal fascination with that master of Bohemian ceremonies. A hard drinker, hard talker, a pianist, and a proponent of "satanic" doctrines, he was born in Greater Poland (then part of Germany), the son of a schoolteacher. After finishing a German high school, he went on to study, first architecture, then psychiatry, in Berlin, where, for some time, he was also an editor of a Polish socialist newspaper. His involvement in socialism, however, was short-lived. His first works, written in German—*Zur Psychologie des Indyviduums, Chopin und Nietzsche, Totenmesse, Homo Sapiens* —brought him fame in the circles of Berlin Bohemians, who considered him a genius. "Young Germany" was closely intertwined with "Young Scandinavia," one of whose leaders was August Strindberg (1849–1912), and Przybyszewski, through personal friendships, was very much "in" with both movements. (In 1893 he married a Norwegian girl, Dagny Juel.) Przybyszewski returned to Poland in 1898, settled in Kraków, and took over the editorship of *Life* (*Życie*), which we have already mentioned, a little magazine constantly on the verge of disappearance. owing to financial troubles. His dynamism at once focused all the disparate tendencies, which up to then had remained nameless, and the movement, before it received the label of "Young

Stanisław Przybyszewski (1868–1927)

Poland," became known as Przybyszewski's *Moderna*. Today, scholars use the term *Moderna* to designate the first phase of "Young Poland," culminating around 1900. In *Life*, on January 1, 1899, Przybyszewski published his manifesto entitled "Confiteor," which openly defied the codes of Positivist commitment. The somewhat doubtful precision of the manifesto in no way diminishes its interest. Among other things it stated:

Art has no aim, it is aim in itself; it is the absolute because it is a reflection of the Absolute—the Soul. And since it is the absolute, it cannot be enclosed within any frame, it cannot serve any idea, it is dominant, it is a source from which all life comes.

Art stands above life; penetrates the essence of the universe; reads to the ordinary man a secret, runic writing; interprets all that exists from one eternity to the other; it knows neither limits nor laws; it knows only the duration and power of the soul; it binds men's souls to the soul of universal nature and considers the soul of the individual as a phenomenon of that other soul.

Tendentious art, art-pleasure, art-patriotism, art possessing a moral or a social aim ceases to be art and becomes a *biblia pauperum* for those who do not know how to think or who are not educated enough to read proper textbooks. For such people, wandering teachers are necessary—not art.

To act upon society in an instructive or moral sense, to foster patriotism or social instincts through art means to humiliate art, to throw it down from the summits of the Absolute into the miserable accidentality of life, and the artist who proceeds that way does not deserve the name of artist. A democratic art, an art for the people, is even lower. An art for the people is a hideous and platitudinous banalizing of the means used by the artist; it is a plebeian act of making accessible what, by the nature of things, is not easily accessible. The people need bread not art; when they get bread, they will find their path themselves. . . .

Art so conceived becomes the highest religion, and the artist becomes its priest. He is personal only by an internal power with which he re-creates states of soul. Besides that, he is a cosmic, metaphysical force through which the absolute and eternity express themselves. He is holy and pure, regardless of whether he presents the most terrible crimes, uncovers the most hideous dirt, or raises his eyes toward heaven and penetrates the light of God.

These lofty words were interpreted not only by Przybyszewski's enemies but also by many of his followers as an invitation to license, to a special, Bohemian style of life. He himself was not overburdened with moral scruples, even in respect to his professional obligations. Every friend who visited him in Kraków, before being allowed to embark upon "serious" conversation, was given an assignment: he was confronted with one or two pages of a book Przybyszewski happened to be translating and a bottle of cognac. This detail illustrates a certain pattern of behavior which, together with his violence in argument, his sarcastic laughter, and the philosophy he proposed, earned him the name of "Satanist." But Przybyszewski's was a profound mind, more serious than one can judge from his disorderly style of life and writing. All those who found themselves in his orbit were forced by him to go to the most radical, uncompromising conclusions, and many of his contemporaries expressed gratitude to him for his liberating influence. In spite of his boundless admiration for Nietzsche, the path he set out to tread was his own.

His manifesto, quoted above, made an appeal to what he often called in his writings the "naked soul." If man is a part of a chain of evolution, like amoebas, fish, birds, then what he thinks and wills is determined by instincts, by blind forces. Przybyszewski was obsessed by the illusory character of man's freedom. Even love was a trick played upon the individual by the need of the species for biological survival, and he often returned to a dream of Androgyne, uniting both sexes in one body. In order to discover the true human being, it was necessary to go deeper than consciousness, to those elements which bind man to his animal ancestors. He spoke derisively of "poor, poor consciousness." To quote him:

What can we know of a power eternally begetting unhappiness, of a demon in ourselves who, similar to a medieval prince of darkness, lives in the eternal night of ourselves, in whose hands we are helpless somnambulic tools?

Or again:

There is no free will at all, and, consequently, there is no responsibility; our acts of will are willed yet not by us, but by a carnal man in ourselves over whom we have no power. There is no good and no evil because we ascribe these qualities, strictly speaking, to nature only, which rules over man; yet to praise it or to blame it is nonsense.

The "naked soul" is a substratum, independent, in a sense, of external accidents and endowed with a physiological memory. The "naked soul" reveals itself, not through consciousness, which is accidental, dependent upon a milieu or an epoch, but

. . . in psychic actions which are on the limit between sensation and thought, which last a fragment of a second, and which have no definition in human language.

The "naked soul" makes its presence known in so-called "abnormal" psychic states—hysteria, hallucination, possession. Przybyszewski praised those epochs of history when the "naked soul" released all the brakes, as in the Middle Ages with their devils, collective psychoses, and witches' Sabbaths. He deserved the name of "Satanist" in that Satan was for him a symbol of primordial, hidden forces in man. Reaching for the true core of man, he saw it in a demon who is nothing other than sexual desire. In his words: "In the beginning there was lust." Today this sounds very familiar, as Freud has accustomed us to the notion of libido, but Freud, who was twelve years older than Przybyszewski, was hardly known at the turn of the century except within a narrow circle of specialists in Vienna. Przybyszewski, we might say, was capturing those same fluids in the air that crystallized in the work of the founder of psychoanalysis.

An interdependence between the materialistic outlook of the nineteenth century and the worship of Art can be clearly traced in Przybyszewski's thinking. Since man is in the power of forces he cannot control, there is no value. Only art is capable of creating value and, thanks to this creation of value, is the only accessible absolute. As to how the "naked soul" expresses itself through art, Przybyszewski's ideas are quite unclear. In any case, he addressed litanies to art as to a deity (a female deity, since "art"—*sztuka*—is feminine in Polish):

As your name was holy to me and I have never used it in vain, listen to me, Lady! As I took upon my shoulders without complaint the heaviest burden of pain, as I bore in bloody toil the terrible cross of sufferings up the hill of death and damnation, redeem me, Lady! Eleison, eleison!

So extremist was he in his position that even Nietzsche seemed to him too "literary"; and Przybyszewski exposed himself to many misunderstandings, since his disciples interpreted his pronouncements as a call to uncontrolled spiritualism and individualism. He himself wanted to be a "naturalist of psychic phenomena" and always remained true to his psychiatric studies in Berlin. The following confession could have come from the pen of Freud:

Naïve critics looked for the origin of my "naked soul" in the marvelous dreams of Novalis; they suggested as sources Maeterlinck or D'Annunzio . . . oh, no. My "naked soul" is a product of a natural, "strict" science, of the kind of science that does not consider phenomena that occur supposedly beyond accepted natural laws as something highly undesirable, but, on the contrary, is favorable to them, as it sees in them facts in disagreement with theory, facts which can advance our knowledge by a century. And it just happens that in everything where a role of the soul has hitherto been denied, I saw its most powerful signs. I proclaimed this with youthful daring, going against all existing laws, norms, and certainties permitting of no doubt. I stated that the "naked soul" exists beyond all the external acts of that little normal soul, of our poor, infinitely poor consciousness.

A prolific writer, first in German, then in Polish, Przybyszewski was known during his lifetime not only in Poland; he enjoyed singular renown also in Russia. Today, we are inclined to look at him more as a kind of "witch doctor" of the *Moderna* than as an author of artistically valid poems-in-prose, novels, and plays. His psychological dramas—*For the Sake of Happiness* (*Dla szczęścia*, 1900), *The Golden Fleece* (*Złote runo*, 1901), *The Snow* (*Śnieg*, 1903), and others—suffer because of his philosophy; the characters thrash around in the clutches of fate (libido) but succumb without provoking our feeling of pity, as tragedy is possible only when there is a clash between Will and Fate. Today, their somewhat gratuitous murders and suicides too often look like a deliberate parody, and, indeed, his technique was parodied by theatrical experimenters in the 1920s (like Stanisław Ignacy Witkiewicz). Przybyszewski's novels lack a unity of style and, again, are more interesting as illustrations of his philosophical views than as literary achievements. Perhaps, of all his writings, some pages dedicated to medieval demonology are his best. His autobiography, *My Contemporaries* (*Moi współcześni*, Vol. I, 1926; Vol. II, 1930), written at the end of his life, provides some of the most valuable clues, if not always to the literary figures of the period, as he was prone to distort data in his own special fashion, then to its most typical attitudes.

One may ask why, instead of Przybyszewski, Zenon Przesmycki was not acclaimed the leader of the *Moderna*. The merits of this poet, who used the pen name of Miriam, were considerable. He translated authors whose names became a rallying cry of the new movement—Maeterlinck, Rimbaud, and others. A man of means, he spent quite a fortune publishing a richly laid out magazine; *Chimera* presented not only literary works, but also drawings and reproductions of paintings. But Miriam lacked the Przybyszewski fist. Of a calm, contemplative temperament, he was often accused of enclosing art in an ivory tower and of excessive aestheticism, while really he was concerned with the metaphysical contents of literature and tried in vain to destroy the labels glued to him. As a poet, he was rather a Parnassian, and this, of course, served to confirm the general opinion of his Buddhalike impassivity. But Miriam's name will remain forever connected with his discovery of Cyprian Norwid. Works of Norwid's that had been completely forgotten, or were never published at all, appeared in *Chimera*, and Miriam furnished the first collected edition of the neglected poet's writings with numerous footnotes, the result of truly "Benedictine labors." Miriam was not a fanatic of one trend. He had a feeling for very different kinds of literature. As to his discovery of Norwid, only some aspects of that poetry were accessible to the sensibility of "Young Poland." It was only after World War I that Norwid's influence began to acquire greater proportions.

Zenon "Miriam" Przesmycki (1861–1944)

POETRY

Poetry disengaged itself with difficulty from limitations imposed upon it by Positivistic soberness. These efforts filled the 1890s and issued, around 1900, in a flood of verse that reconquered for poetry the rank of most honored literary genre. Lists of poets provide us with an insight into a changing social structure. During the nineteenth century, practitioners of literature, with few exceptions, had come from the intelligentsia of gentry descent. Now, however, underdog groups—peasants and Jews—began to produce well-educated and talented individuals; also the number of women writers continually increased. As to what names should be given particular credit, the picture is still somewhat blurred. Criteria change, and the re-evaluation of "Young Poland" is still on the agenda. One thing is certain: that analogies with what was going on at the same time in France or even in Russia would be deceiving, though the era was an extremely cosmopolitan one. Only those elements that corresponded to specific needs determined by Polish literary traditions were assimilated from foreign imports; and as we mentioned, the spirit of Polish Romanticism pervaded the modernistic imagination.

Antoni Lange
(1861–1929)
    The role of precursors, as we all know, is a somewhat awkward one. Antoni Lange was very active as a poet and translator, long before Przybyszewski's manifesto, but he remained somewhat on the margin. He was born in Warsaw; from 1886 to 1890 he studied linguistics, philosophy, and literature in Paris while furnishing news articles to the Warsaw press and contributing (under an assumed name) to a socialist periodical published abroad, *Clarion Call* (*Pobudka*). After his return to Poland, he became one of the leading personalities in Warsaw literary circles.

    In his poetry, he did not depart from the logical structure of discourse, even though in theory he upheld the dignity of pure art. A virtuoso of rhyme, his verse tending to be somewhat cold and cerebral, he was akin to French Parnassians. His intellectual curiosity was unlimited. One of the first to popularize Indian philosophy and literature, he published many articles on the subject as well as his own translations from Sanskrit (*Nal and Damayanti, Bhagavat-Gita*). He also followed the latest developments in the sciences, which led him into a science-fiction prose, for instance, in his collection of short stories *In the Fourth Dimension* (*W czwartym wymiarze*, 1912). He edited anthologies of world literature, but as a creative author he was surpassed by the proliferation of new talents, and the last phase of his life was poisoned by a feeling of bitterness. Today, Lange is valued above all as a translator of poetry. He was constantly learning new languages in order to enlarge his sphere as a translator, and he introduced the Polish public to Czech poets like Jaroslav Vrchlicky, Hungarian poets, and modern Greek poets. No editor of Théophile Gautier or Stéphane Mallarmé or Edgar Allan Poe in Polish can ignore the translations made by . Antoni Lange in the nineteenth century.

Lange was, after all, recognized in his lifetime as an authority. His contemporary, Wacław Rolicz Lieder, was less fortunate. Lieder remained completely unknown, even long after his death, and was discovered only in the 1930s. Today he occupies an honorable place. Born in Warsaw, the son of a well-to-do bank official, Lieder attended, unwillingly, a Russian high school where his resentment expressed itself in rebelliousness, for which he was eventually expelled. He finished high school in Kraków, and studied at the Jagiellonian University. Between 1888 and 1897, he lived abroad, in Paris at first, where he obtained a diploma from the École des Langues Orientales; then in Vienna, where he studied law; and again in Paris. His acquaintance with Near Eastern languages resulted in a textbook of Arabic and in translations of Persian poets. He was accepted in Parisian literary circles, knew Paul Verlaine, and was a habitué of Café François I (located where the Gare de Luxembourg now stands). He also kept up a friendship with the Czech poet Julius Zeyer, whom he visited in Bohemia. Most fruitful, however, was his fervent and lasting bond with the German poet Stefan George (1868–1933), who, in 1892, began to edit his *Blätter für die Kunst*, which marked a most significant date in German letters. George translated and published many of Lieder's poems; thus, when Lieder was unknown in his own country, he was already highly regarded among the German avant-garde. But not only the Polish reading public should be blamed for this neglect, as Lieder, an extremely proud and sensitive man, took offense when his volume was badly received by the critics. Subsequently he published his volumes in an extremely small number of copies, sometimes only twenty, and forbade the critics to review them. Moreover, the literary path he followed differed from that usually pursued by poets in Poland. The poetic license to which readers had become accustomed in the work of the *Moderna* was of no help to the reader in grasping Lieder's somewhat stern expression. Lieder's poetry grew out of three interacting components: the influence of Western poets, French Parnassians and French symbolists and, of course, Stefan George (a reciprocal influence); Near Eastern poetry; and his boundless admiration for old Polish poetry, especially for that of Jan Kochanowski, to whom he dedicated some fine poems. Lieder's experimenting with the poem-in-prose, encouraged, no doubt, by his

Wacław Rolicz-Lieder (1866–1912)

reading of Arthur Rimbaud, anticipated by many years the "innovations" of the 1920s. There is still another reason why Lieder could not appeal to Polish "decadents." He lacked the apocalyptic ardor, being rather stoical, hieratic, and restrained, and this is exactly what brought him and Stefan George together. On the other hand, his seignorial individualism and his disdain of trivia allied him with "Young Poland." Nearly all his poetic work was written in the 1890s; for he abandoned literature shortly after his return to Warsaw to spend his energy and money gathering material for his linguistic studies on Old Polish. (In the end, his scholarly efforts were not well received by the Academy of Sciences.) Lieder's poems addressed to Stefan George, as well as George's poems to Lieder, and their translations of each other constitute one of the most striking instances of Polish-German literary exchange. Those close to Stefan George called Lieder "Callimachus"; the name refers to an Alexandrian poet and was used by an Italian humanist who lived in Poland in the fifteenth century—Philippo Buonacorsi.

Kazimierz Przerwa-Tetmajer (1865–1940)   With the publication of his first volume of poems in 1891, Kazimierz Tetmajer was hailed as "The Poet" by the "decadents," and it must be said that he accurately mirrored all their modes. Born into a landowner's family from the region south of Kraków at the foot of the Tatra Mountains, he studied philosophy in Kraków and Heidelberg; later, he became closely connected with Bohemian circles and lived, off and on, in Kraków, Warsaw, and Zakopane. At the time, Zakopane, a mountain village, was swiftly becoming not only a fashionable resort, but nearly the cultural capital of Poland, as it was a meeting place for leading personalities from all three parts of the partitioned country. Tetmajer's best lyrics were inspired by the landscape of the Tatra Mountains, but his poetry owed its immediate recognition to his having given shape to the standard *fin-de-siècle* motifs, namely, the melancholy of decadence, and escape through sensuousness (e.g., bold descriptions of women's bodies). A poet of transition, he employed a logic that presented no difficulties to common sense. For instance, his poem "End of the Century" ("Koniec wieku") sounds like an article set to verse:

> A curse? Only a savage when he hurts himself curses his god hidden in space.
> Irony? But can the worst of jeers be compared with the irony of the most ordinary things?
> Ideas? But thousands of years have passed and ideas are always no more than ideas.
> Prayers? But not many today are still deluded by an eye framed in a triangle, gazing out at the world.
> Scorn? But only an idiot feels scorn for that burden which he could not take upon his weak shoulders.

Despair? Do we have to imitate the scorpion that kills itself
  when surrounded by burning coals?

Struggle? But can an ant thrown upon the rails fight a train
  approaching at full speed?

Resignation? Do we suffer less when we place our head sub-
  missively under the knife of a guillotine?

Future life? Who among men looks into the secrets of stars,
  who can count extinguished suns and who guesses the limit
  of light?

Sensuous pleasures? Yet there is something in our soul that
  thirsts amid the pleasure and asks for something else.

So what is there? What remains for us who know everything,
  for whom none of the old beliefs is enough?

What is your shield against the spear of evil, man of the end of
  the century?

He hung his head silently.

Przekleństwo? . . . Tylko dziki, kiedy się skaleczy,
Złorzeczy swemu bogu, skrytemu w przestworze.
Ironia? . . . Lecz największe z szyderstw czyż się może
Równać z ironią biegu najzwyklejszych rzeczy?

Idee? . . . Ależ lat już minęły tysiące,
A idee sa zawsze tylko ideami.
Modlitwa? . . . lecz niewielu tylko jeszcze mami
Oko w trójkąt wprawione i na świat patrzące.

Wzgarda? Lecz tylko głupiec gardzi tym ciężarem,
Którego wziąć na słabe nie zdoła ramiona.
Rozpacz? . . . Więc za przykładem trzeba iść skorpiona,
Co się zabija, kiedy otoczą go żarem?

Walka? . . . Ale czyż mrówka rzucona na szyny
Może walczyć z pociągiem, nadchodzącym w pędzie?
Rezygnacja? . . . Czyż przez to mniej się cierpieć będzie,
Gdy się z poddaniem schyli pod nóż gilotyny?

Byt przyszły? . . . Gwiazd tajniki któż z ludzi ogląda,
Kto zliczy zgasłe słońca i kres światłu zgadnie?
Użycie? . . . Ależ w duszy jest zawsze coś na dnie,
Co wśród użycia pragnie, wśród rozkoszy żąda.

Cóż więc jest? Co zostało nam, co wszystko wiemy,
Dla których żadna z dawnych wiar już nie wystarcza?
Jakaż jest przeciw włóczni złego twoja tarcza,
Człowiecze z końca wieku? . . . Głowę zwiesił niemy.

But Tetmajer was not always so rhetorical. His lyrics written in traditional meters, and rhymed, were praised for their melodiousness and

perception of sensuous detail. As befitted a period aspiring to a translation of visual images into auditory impressions and vice versa, he interfused data from all the senses to convey a state of the soul. His technique was basically impressionistic. Mountain landscapes, the most permanent ingredient of his lyricism, often appear as forms given a substance by the play of light and mist. But his despair may have been a tribute paid to fashion, as his poems do not completely conceal an undercurrent of mad passion for life. Tetmajer, being a native of the Tatra foothills, was attracted by the mountain region with its folk music and rural architecture, just then being discovered by poets and painters (in the fine arts a "Zakopane style" came into being), and with its past preserved in the oral tales of old mountaineers. He knew some of the storytellers who remembered a bygone epoch of valiant mountain bandits (Robin Hoods of a sort). But Tetmajer, although he was a prolific prose writer, had no success with novels, either on contemporary or on historical subjects; he was very good, however, in his stories, written in a mountain dialect, where shepherds, poachers, and bandits reach the stature of nearly Homeric heroes and local yarns are transformed into chronicles of some fantastic history: *In the Rocky Highlands* (*Na skalnym Podhalu*) was the title of his huge cycle of short stories, appearing between 1903 and 1911.

Tetmajer's fame as a poet waned gradually, while he himself was touched by mental illness. His verse bears many traces of that easy melodiousness which marred Polish poetry during the Positivistic era, and today he is not assigned a very high place in letters. He is rather a minor poet.

Jan Kasprowicz (1860–1926) The son of a peasant from the Prussian-occupied part of the country, a native of the same region that once produced a Latin poet-humanist, Klemens Janicki (Janitius), also of peasant origin, Jan Kasprowicz, despite many obstacles, made his way to the top of the social ladder thanks to his strong character. After a German high school, he studied philosophy and philology in Leipzig and Breslau, spending half a year in prison for his political activity. In 1899 he moved to Lwów in the Austrian part of Poland, and there, supporting himself by journalistic work, he managed to obtain a doctorate at the university. In 1909, he became professor of comparative literature. A man of volcanic temperament, both in his private and professional life, of great avidity for learning, he fought against serious handicaps due to his initial lack of refinement, and entered the literary scene quite late, as his early poems were below the accepted standards. He was an indefatigable translator, particularly of English poets, very uneven and exuberant, and, as in everything he wrote, at times in poor taste, but in some of his versions of Keats and Shelley he still remains unsurpassed. Kasprowicz's early poetry clung to Positivistic attitudes and techniques, although, owing to his origin, his poems on the miserable life of the peasants sounded genuine. Moreover, he had already introduced the religious motifs so typical of his later work. Not a native of the mountain region, Kasprowicz nevertheless shared his contemporaries' infatuation with the Tatras. He spent most of his free time in Zakopane, and the volumes of poems which brought him renown all bore the mark of his deep feeling for the nature of the highlands.

He mastered the symbolist style, and upon the appearance of *Love* (*Miłość*, 1895), and *A Wild Rosebush* (*Krzak dzikiej róży*, 1898) he was acclaimed by Przybyszewski's circle as a major poet. Kasprowicz's peculiar qualities, which made him, in many ways, a unique phenomenon, found their best expression in his free-verse hymns contained in two volumes: *To the Perishing World* (*Ginącemu światu*, 1902) and *Salve Regina* (1902). Shrieks of pain at the sight of suffering in the universe and accusations of God, the creator of evil, were rather standard themes, but Kasprowicz's originality consisted in his fusion of old religious laments of the peasants with his own philosophical ponderings. Thus, the tragedy of existence received a background of Polish fields and fallows; universal evil was transformed into particular calamities falling on villagers. There is something medieval in Kasprowicz's hymns—a sound as if of an organ, images of peasants' processions over a half-sterile earth. Nature in these hymns yields symbols for human despair, and perhaps for that reason, Kasprowicz was called a pantheist. If the term "expressionism" has any meaning, it can designate a will to find artistic means for violent emotions, and in this sense, Kasprowicz's hymns could be called expressionistic. At the same time, they are rooted in a typically Polish, religious, peasant sensibility. The hymn entitled "Dies Irae" is a poem of apocalyptic terror. The hymn "O Holy God" borrows its title and leitmotifs from a mournful litany and is centered around a vision of plague. "My Evening Song" and "Salve Regina" seem to announce a reconciliation through a childlike faith in the Holy Virgin, who (perhaps identified with Mother Earth) averts the wrath of God. Because of the intensity of his revolt against God, combined with a nonetheless Catholic acceptance, Kasprowicz was highly regarded by Catholic journalists and, for the same reason, proclaimed by the so-called "national camp," i.e., the political Right, as a "truly Polish" poet. Today, we can go beyond such classifications. He was unruly, often self-contradictory, alternately tempted by pathos and irony.

A stay in Paris and London brought about a volume of poems-in-prose with a title which somewhat surprised the critics: *On a Heroic*

Horse and on a Tumble-down House (*O bohaterskim koniu i walącym się domie*, 1906). The "heroic horse" had once taken part in glorious charges of the English cavalry, then had served in a circus, and finally ended as a ragpicker's nag. As for the tumble-down house, perhaps it symbolized the whole of Western bourgeois civilization. Its irony and avant-garde technique make this volume more appreciated today than in the author's lifetime.

Yet Kasprowicz did not cease to write poetry of reconciliation. In *The Book of the Poor* (*Księga ubogich*, 1916) he devised his own form to convey his humility before the splendor of creation. This is one of the rare instances in Polish poetry of purely tonic quatrains, based not upon the number of syllables but on the number of accents in every line. *The Book of the Poor*, written during World War I, is a meditation in verse with a recurring motif of mountain nature; it focuses on the human sufferings, accepted as inevitable. His heroes are poor lumberjacks barely earning a living, shepherds, or wandering musicians. In his last volume, Kasprowicz, who was then residing in Zakopane, went even further in simplicity, sometimes adding a touch of affection. *My World* (*Mój świat*, 1926), with the sub-title *Songs for the Fiddle and Little Paintings on Glass*, as it is easy to guess, consists of variations on themes from folklore. Kasprowicz also wrote verse plays, which are, rather, dramatic poems, as their theatrical value is slight. He attempted to revive medieval mystery and morality plays; for instance, in his *Marchołt the Fat and Bawdy* (*Marchołt gruby a sprośny*, 1920) he took as his hero a popular figure of sixteenth-century pulp literature.

The place of Kasprowicz in Polish letters today is not as high as his enthusiasts predicted. Hampered not only by his Positivistic heritage and the linguistic license of the *Moderna*, he, for all his daring, also suffered from his lack of sophistication. Yet even his roughness and occasional lapses of taste strike us as more convincing than the tidy elegance of Tetmajer's lines.

Tadeusz Miciński (1873–1918)

"Young Poland," as we have tried to indicate, willingly returned to Polish Romantic thought with its mystical concepts, especially to Słowacki's last, occultist and "symbolist" phase. One should keep in mind that ever since the era of Romanticism, many Poles had been attracted by crazy flights of half-philosophical, half-poetic imagination; and certainly Tadeusz Miciński surpassed them all. His work, at first sight, gives the impression of a madhouse where various epochs of history are incongruously jumbled together and notions of time and space are blurred.

Miciński, born in Łódź, studied philosophy in Kraków and in Germany; he traveled extensively all over Europe and, inevitably, chose Zakopane in the Tatra Mountains as one of his permanent homes. During World War I (in 1918), he was killed in Russia by a mob who mistook him for a czarist general because of his beard and bald pate. A thorough investigation of his writings has never been undertaken, as their alloys of stupendous richness have discouraged scholars. The aura of his work is that of Słowacki's *King-Spirit*. He was fascinated by Hindu religious philosophy, by gnosis, the cabala, occultism, and his central theme is that of Lucifer as the personification of divine wisdom trying to penetrate itself in the chaos of the evil world. Lucifer is a necessary polarity to Christ, who personifies divine love, but at the same time is somewhat identical with him. We mention this not to give an idea of Miciński's meandering thought, which is impossible here, but to provide a hint as to the realm in which he moved. He marks the revival of a metaphysical historiosophy. Roman Catholicism he rejected as a distortion of true religious feeling. This he saw at first in India; then he moved toward a kind of syncretistic religion. In his desire to supplant Catholicism (which, according to him, was nefarious to the Polish nation), he was a curious descendant of Polish anticlericals—of old-time Protestants and of Juliusz Słowacki.

Miciński wrote a few short poems. They are contained in his volume *The Darkness of Stars* (*W mroku gwiazd*, 1902) and secured him a place among those poets who explored the feeling of metaphysical terror in the face of infinity. He is also the author of amorphous, weird works that are sometimes called novels, sometimes dramas, but, in fact, are enormous poems-in-prose. In *Knyaz Potemkin, A Drama in Four Acts* (1906), the revolt of Russian sailors on the ship *Potemkin* in 1905 acquires symbolic dimensions as a struggle between Lucifer and Christ for the soul of Russia. Miciński's Eastern orientation accounts for his choice of Constantinople as the setting of *In the Dusk of a Golden Palace, or Brazilissa Teofanu, A Tragedy from the History of Byzantium in the Tenth Century* (*W mrokach złotego pałacu, czyli Bazylissa Teofanu*, 1909); while in *Nietota, A Novel from the Secret Book of the Tatra Mountains* (1910), the resort village of Zakopane is transformed into a cosmic arena where demoniac, superhuman powers struggle for the soul of Poland. In the novel *Father Faust* (*Ksiądz Faust*, 1913), a provincial priest (whose wild biography is revealed through flashbacks) preaches sermons about a new syncretistic religion to a crowd of Catholics, Orthodox Christians, and Jews; he acts as a master of mystical initiation for a political prisoner and predicts that Polish-Russian brotherhood will come through revolution. We are not concerned here, though, with tracing Miciński's concepts. The very texture of his works, with their fantastic symbolism pushed to a frenzy, attracted certain of his contemporaries, and was a serious factor in destroying the fashion for photographic realism. His Byzantine sumptuousness, uninhibited gibberish, and complete disregard for literary conventions did not remain without influence; and the novels of Stanisław Ignacy Witkiewicz, whom we will take up later, borrowed many aspects of Miciński's historical *opera buffa*.

Jerzy Żuławski (1874–1915) A native of the highlands of southern Poland, Jerzy Żuławski, after finishing high school in Kraków, studied philosophy in Switzerland, where he obtained a doctorate. He spent a great deal of time in Zakopane, where he was famous as an excellent mountain climber, traveled widely in Europe, and in 1914 volunteered his service to the first Polish military unit created by Józef Piłsudski. He died in a military hospital during the war. A philosophical poet, a translator of old Hindu poetry and of some books of the Old Testament, he was also a brilliant essayist and playwright. The most important of his dramas is, perhaps, *Eros and Psyche* (1904), tracing the story of a couple's eternal love throughout many reincarnations. Żuławski was also the first successful author of science fiction, following the example of Jules Verne and H. G. Wells. His three poetic, tragic novels concern the fate of the first human settlers on the moon: *On the Silvery Globe* (*Na srebrnym globie*, 1903), *The Victor* (*Zwycięzca*, 1910), and *The Old Earth* (*Stara ziemia*, 1911).

Maria Komornicka (1876–1948) The feminine invasion of literature produced but few valid works, yet the women writers of the period were a leaven contribution to the refinement of taste, and their role as translators and propagators of new trends can hardly be exaggerated. Maria Komornicka was unique for the passion and even fanaticism with which she embraced the philosophy of Friedrich Nietzsche. Born near Warsaw, she received a good education in Poland and then, as a very young girl, went to England to study for four years. Her poems, often in free verse or in prose, were quite savage vindications of total freedom for the individual, in this case, for a superwoman. It is striking that even her personal life was to follow a pattern similar to Nietzsche's, as in 1907 she fell mentally ill and was forced to abandon literature. She had no time to develop her gifts, and if, perhaps unjustly, we speak of her while bypassing a multitude of other names, her figure was at least very characteristic of the mores of the period.

Bronisława Ostrowska (1881–1928) Among the various centers of Polish literary life (at the turn of the century), due place should be given to Paris, where a permanent colony of Polish writers and painters resided. Bronisława Brzezicka was born in Warsaw, received her secondary-school training there, then married an eminent sculptor, Stanisław Ostrowski (who lived mostly in Paris), and spent much of her time in the Latin Quarter. She achieved maturity in her own poetry late, shortly before her death, but she was a skillful translator of French poetry and prose. She reacted to all novelties, even if they were known to very limited circles in Paris; thus, she published in 1907 her version of Marcel Schwob's *Le livre de Monelle*, which, today, is recognized as one of the landmarks in the development of the poetic novel. Her translation of Oscar V. de L. Milosz's mystery play, *Miguel Mañara* (in O. W. Miłosz, *Poezje*, translated by B. Ostrowska, 1919), is perhaps one of her highest achievements, and it was done when that poet was virtually unknown in Paris, except for a small coterie of friends. Of Lithuanian origin (a relative of the author of this book), Oscar V. de L. Milosz is now ranked among the best French poets of the twentieth century.

Leopold Staff
(1878–1957)

We can regard "Young Poland" as a moment of crisis, as a watershed from which many rivers flowed in varying directions, or we can say that the despondency and despair, which culminated in Przybyszewski's *Moderna*, was subsequently overcome as several ways that would lead out of that blind alley were discovered. Critical of pessimistic ravings as being too far from any classical, Western tradition, Leopold Staff was, by temperament perhaps, a Renaissance humanist. Born in Lwów into a family of Polonized Austrians, he went through high school there and received a good background in Greek and Latin, then studied philosophy and Romance languages at the university. His professor, Edward Porębowicz, was a renowned translator of Romance literatures. Staff's thorough scholarly preparation allowed him to pursue effectively his humanistic ideal of a life dedicated exclusively to letters. Of a rare industriousness, he was constantly publishing volumes of his poetry as well as both prose and verse translations; between 1909 and 1914, he worked for a Lwów publishing house as editor of an important series (*Sympozjon*) of philosophical works, among which appeared selected writings of Cardinal Newman and Søren Kierkegaard. Indeed, were we to bypass Staff's own poetry, his activity as a translator and editor would assure him of a place in Polish literature. His range was wide—from Friedrich Nietzsche, whose several works he rendered into Polish (including *The Joyful Knowledge*, 1906), to St. Francis of Assisi, the Latin poems of Jan Kochanowski, Heraclitus, the Greek Sophists, and Old Chinese poetry (through French versions). Today, the Roman Catholic liturgy employs several of Staff's translations of the Psalms and centuries-old Latin hymns.

Staff defined himself in one of his poems as a "joyful pilgrim," and his first volume bears a title that is already very far from the moods of the *Moderna: Dreams of Power* (*Sny o potędze*, 1901). To Staff, poetry was a quest for wisdom, and wisdom resided in the joy of the quest. Critics, in trying to pin down the sources of his thought, hesitated between Nietzsche, the Stoics, and St. Francis of Assisi. In fact, Staff, as befitted a humanist, took a somewhat smiling approach to his teachers; he drew from each of them whatever happened to suit his needs and, beelike, knew how to suck sweetness from various flowers. From Nietzsche he acquired *gaia scienza*, energy, a free breathing-in of the air of the summits; from the Stoics, an acceptance of human limitations; while St. Francis helped him to combine Christianity with an affirmation of the flesh, of man, who can be seen as a brother to all living creatures. The clear colors of Staff's poetry recall the Horatian poetry of the Renaissance; but, undoubtedly, he was also in harmony with certain turn-of-the-century philosophical trends. His notion of life as wiser than any intellectual constructs echoes Henri Bergson's theory of *élan vital*.

Daylight, noon, fertile fields in the sun are recurrent images in his poetry. The technique of his verse cannot be characterized briefly. Staff's proteanism confounded his contemporaries because he was nearly always up-to-date; and at the very end of his life, after World War II, he fell under the influence of very young poets.

The collections of verse which he published between his debut in 1901 and World War I, though different in tone from the poetry of "Young Poland," nevertheless bore the stigma of its vocabulary and metrics. These were *Day of the Soul* (*Dzień duszy*, 1903), *To the Celestial Birds* (*Ptakom niebieskim*, 1905), *The Blossoming Bough* (*Gałąź kwitnąca*, 1908), *Smiles of the Hours* (*Uśmiechy godzin*, 1910), *The Swan and the Lyre* (*Łabędź i Lira*, 1913). Acclaimed as one of their masters by a postwar poetic group, "Skamander" (also in revolt against "Young Poland"), Staff so modified his style as to make it difficult to distinguish from "Skamander's", especially in his collections *High Trees* (*Wysokie drzewa*, 1931) and *The Color of Honey* (*Barwa miodu*, 1936). During the Second World War, Staff lived in Warsaw under the Nazi occupation, working on translations from Latin and contributing his poems to clandestine publications. Lauded by the literary press in People's Poland as the dean of Polish poets, he underwent one more metamorphosis; rejecting meter and rhyme, he achieved a high degree of sophisticated simplicity, which made his poems sound at times like Chinese ideograms, especially in the slim volume, *Osiers* (*Wiklina*, 1954)—perhaps his highest accomplishment. Yet, despite his transformations, he always remained true to himself, and his work can be viewed as a constant progress in his "joyful quest." He had the good fortune to have been always accepted, sometimes admiringly, sometimes reluctantly. Since his death in

1957, many scholarly treatises on Staff and his work have appeared, but the assessments of his position in the history of Polish poetry vary. In all probability, Staff will be assigned the place of a model humanist, a perfect craftsman, one of the major influences shaping poetry in Poland, but not himself a major poet, unless we consider the great bulk of his output a necessary preparation for a relatively small number of lyrics which figure in every anthology of Polish poetry. Two poems of his old age tell much about what he was concerned with throughout his life:

The Bridge

I didn't believe,
Standing on the bank of a river
Which was wide and swift,
That I would cross that bride
Plaited from thin, fragile reeds
Fastened with bast.
I walked delicately as a butterfly
And heavily as an elephant,
I walked surely as a dancer
And wavered like a blind man.
I didn't believe that I would cross that bridge,
And now that I am standing on the other side
I don't believe I crossed it.

Most

Nie wierzyłem
Stojąc nad brzegiem rzeki,
Która była szeroka i rwista,
Że przejdę ten most,
Spleciony z cienkiej, kruchej trzciny
Powiązanej łykiem.
Szedłem lekko jak motyl
I ciężko jak słoń,
Szedłem pewnie jak tancerz
I chwiejnie jak ślepiec.
Nie wierzyłem, że przejdę ten most,
I gdy stoję już na drugim brzegu,
Nie wierzę, że go przeszedłem.

Duckweed

In an old, deserted park
I stood at a pond
Covered with the thick fur of duckweed.
Thinking

That the water here had once been transparent
And that it ought to be so now.
With a dry twig picked up off the ground
I began to rake away the green patina
And conduct it to the outlet.

I was found at this activity
By a quiet wise man
Whose brow was incised by thought,
And he said with a gentle smile
Of condescending reproach:
"Don't you regret wasting the time?
Every moment is a drop of eternity,
Life is the twinkling in eternity's eye.
There are so many matters of the utmost importance."

Ashamed, I walked away
And all the day long I thought
Of life and death,
Of Socrates,
Of the immortality of the soul,
Of the pyramids and Egyptian wheat,
Of the Roman Forum and the moon,
Of the mammoth and the Eiffel Tower . . .
But nothing came of it.

Returning the next day
To the same place
At the pond
Covered with thick green fur,
I saw the wise man with his brow now smooth.
Gently,
With the twig I had left,
He raked the duckweed from the surface of the water
And conducted it to the outlet.

The trees rustled,
In their branches, birds were singing.

Rzęsa

W starym zapuszczonym parku
Stałem nad stawem
Pokrytym grubym kożuchem rzęsy.
Myśląc,
Że woda była tu niegdyś przejrzysta
I dziś by być taka powinna.
Podjętą z ziemi suchą gałęzią

Zacząłem zgarniać zieloną patynę
I odprowadzać do odpływu.

Zastał mnie przy tym zajęciu
Mędrzec spokojny
O czole myślą rozciętym
I rzekł z łagodnym uśmiechem
Probłażliwego wyrzutu:
"Nie żal ci czasu?
Każda chwila jest kroplą wieczności,
Życie mgnieniem jej oka.
Tyle jest spraw arcyważnych."

Odszedłem zawstydzony
I przez dzień cały myślałem
O życiu i o śmierci,
O Sokratesie
I nieśmiertelności duszy,
O piramidach i pszenicy egipskiej.
O rzymskim Forum i księżycu.
O mamucie i wieży Eiffla . . .
Ale nic z tego nie wyszło.

Wróciwszy nazajutrz
Na to samo miejsce
Ujrzałem nad stawem,
Pokrytym grubym zielonym kożuchem,
Mędrca z czołem wygładzonym,
Który spokojnie,
Porzuconą przeze mnie gałęzią,
Zgarniał z powierzchni wody rzęsę
I odprowadzał do odpływu.

Wkoło szumiały cicho drzewa,
W gałęziach śpiewały ptaki.

Bolesław Leśmian
(1878–1937)

Leśmian, considered today by many people as the most accomplished Polish poet of the twentieth century, is, in many ways, unique in world literature. In his lifetime, however, he had but few fervent admirers, and, in general, was looked upon as a marginal author of charming, folklike ballads.

He was born in Warsaw into a Jewish middle-class family, obtained a diploma in law at the University of Kiev, and except for a few years spent in Paris, he led the uneventful life of a minor public official, including, after 1918, some lucrative posts as a notary public in provincial towns. Shortly before his death in 1937, he was elected a member of the Polish Academy of Literature like his colleague and rival, Leopold Staff.

He began to publish his poems around 1900, occasionally also in Russian: some can be found in the excellent Russian symbolist reviews, *The Golden Fleece* (*Zolotoye Runo*) and *The Scales* (*Vesy*). The similar Polish review, *Chimera*, favored Leśmian, and he was encouraged by its editor, Zenon Przesmycki. In all the mannerisms of his early phase, he was undoubtedly a poet of "Young Poland"; one cannot say that he ever abandoned that style, but slowly through linguistic experimentation he did elaborate a language of his own. He thus had good reason for not hurrying with the publication of his books. His *Crossroads Orchard* (*Sad rozstajny*, 1912) and *Meadow* (*Łąka*, 1920) revealed him as a poet whom it was difficult to compare to any of his contemporaries. *Shadowy Drink* (*Napój cienisty*, 1936) and *Forest Happenings* (*Dziejba leśna*, published posthumously) appeared at a time when Leśmian was regarded as a leftover from "Young Poland," owing to the stir caused by new techniques. True recognition of Leśmian's originality came only in the late 1950s and in the 1960s.

He is nearly untranslatable on account of his experiments with the language, in which he took advantage of the extremely flexible Slavic morphology, inventing, for instance, verbs out of nouns, and nouns out of verbs. Since, for him, rhythmical incantation and rhyme were features that distinguished the "lyrical language" from what he called the "scientific language" (of prose, of everyday communication), he employed metrical patterns borrowed from folk songs and ballads. Reading his lines, one enters a strange world having little to do with real human beings or landscapes as an ordinary observer would perceive them. Both the fantastic creatures which inhabit Leśmian's poems and nature are metaphors of his very personal and tragic outlook. Leśmian's was extremely well-read in philosophy and in anthropological studies on primitive religions. His central problem can be defined as that of man who is a born worshipper, *homo adorans*, in perpetual need of contact with God; yet that God is so weak that he seems to depend on the worshipper for his very existence. Or to put it another way, the existence of man and nature is a function of the existence of God and vice versa, but both are illusory. Perhaps only man-as-poet maintains both through his creative act. Leśmian can be called the purest symbolist—yet his symbols are not so much correspondences as autonomous, myth-creating images. It would be hopeless, for instance, to ask what "Ineffable" Leśmian was trying to convey in the verse where the poet sees God, who has fallen down with the morning dew and slumbers, stretched out on the grass in a ravine under a shuttered-up shadow of a hazel bush. Superficially, Leśmian is mostly fascinated with nature. He took much from Henri Bergson, his notion of flux, of *élan vital*, and thus, in his poems, nature stands for a continuous transformation, since its very essence is a passage from shape to shape, from existence to nonexistence. Bucolic images are put to a perverse use, and beneath is the tremor of a religious mind deprived of religion and forced to cope with that lack. In this respect, Leśmian's myth-creating activity can be compared to William Butler Yeats's. In his poem "The Soul Went Awandering" ("Wyruszyła dusza w drogę"), the soul, bitter about being torn by death from the beauty of the world, goes to heaven, but is not consoled by the presence of God, as she desires His death. In another poem, two fairy-tale characters wander through the forest in search of an herb that gives immortality; they overcome the dragon guarding it, but on their return they meet a weeping God (*Płaczybóg*—here is an example of Leśmian's word-coining), and out of compassion they give Him the herb (since the one immortality He possesses is less secure than two). They themselves accept their mortality and soon die. Because of his submergence in nature, Leśmian has sometimes been called a pantheist, but this term hardly elucidates anything. His last tragic poems on religious themes provide the key to the whole of his work, for instance, his "God in Heaven, Full of Glory" ("Boże pełen w niebie chwały"), where the poet asks whether, at the moment his soul perishes, God secretly weeps or perishes together with him. With his images of nature, Leśmian, in fact, was weaving a semantic web, a world of make-believe, man's only solace. Contrary to some of his contemporaries for whom death was a blessed Nirvana, he constantly returned to the indefiniteness of any state, even the state of death, since everything is in movement. The following poem, "A Graveyard" ("Cmentarz"), can be quoted (in a very inadequate translation, as all its music and its rhymes are gone):

> A wanderer, looking askance at existence,
> Entered a graveyard: death, grass, oblivion, and dew.
> It was a graveyard of Ships. Sails under the earth
> Fluttered, seething, driven by a posthumous tempest.
> The wanderer sensed eternity upsprouting from the grass
> And adding his own silence to the silence of the place
> He crossed what was near: a few bees, two bushes
> And on the first tomb he read the following inscription:
> "I perished not by chance but by the will of the gale
> And I believed I would not have to die again,
> That I would find a harbor in death, and in that harbor, Death.
> But Death deluded me! For Death I am not dead!

The contrary wind is here, and the terror of shipwreck
And fear and ignorance, everything but life!
My subterranean remains, though tired by nothingness,
Still are worthy of a rudder, worthy of a storm!
No one knows what wind it is that fills the sails,
Whoever puts to sea will never stop.
I know that depth where struggles the post-mortem Ship.
No sleep! Eternity is watching! The corpse is not happy!
For the endurance of my sails, swelled by death
Say, passer-by, three times Hail Mary!"
The wanderer plucked a few young leaves for no one
And knelt down to say the requested prayers.

Wędrowiec, na istnienie spojrzawszy z ukosa,
Wszedł na cmentarz: śmierć, trawa, niepamięć i rosa.
Był to cmentarz Okrętów. Pod ziemią wrzał głucho
Trzepot żagli, pośmiertną gnanych zawieruchą.
Wędrowiec czuł, jak wieczność z traw się wykojarza,
I ciszę swą do ciszy dodając cmentarza,
Przeżegnał to, co bliżej: pszczół kilka, dwa krzaki
I na pierwszym grobowcu czytał napis taki:
"Zginąłem nie na ślepo, bo z woli wichury—
I wierzyłem, że odtąd nie zginę raz wtóry,
Że znajdę przystań w śmierci, a śmierć w tej przystani,
Ale śmierć mię zawiodła! Umarłem nie dla niej!
Trwa nadal wiatr przeciwny i groza rozbicia,
I lęk, i niewiadomość, i wszystko prócz życia!
Szczątki moje podziemne, choć je nicość nuży,
Jeszcze godne są steru i warte są burzy!
Nikt nie wie, gdzie ten wicher, który żagle wzdyma?
Kto raz w podróż wyruszył—już się nie zatrzyma.
Znam tę głąb, gdzie się Okręt mocuje nieżywy.
Snu—nie ma! Wieczność—czuwa! Trup nie jest szczęśliwy!
Za wytrwałość mych żagli, które śmierć rozwija,
Przechodniu, odmów—proszę—trzy Zdrowaś Maryja!"
Wędrowiec dla nikogo zerwał liście świeże
I ukląkł, by żądane odmówić pacierze.

What is peculiar to Leśmian is his intense Polishness, in the sense that he was steeped in the tradition of old Polish bucolic and folk poetry. But his philosophical preoccupations gave the motifs he took from those sources a new twist. He was also indebted to folk songs and ballads of other nations, and some formal similarity can be found between his verse and the translations of Celtic, Scandinavian, German, and French ballads made by his contemporary, Edward Porębowicz. How two poets—William Butler Yeats and Leśmian— both born around the same time, coped with the same dilemma of agnosticism would make a challenging subject for some future study.

In his articles on poetry—for instance, in his *Treatise on Poetry* (1937)—Leśmian deplored the so-called "impurity" inherent in that art. Contrary to other artistic mediums like color and sound, "the word is condemned to live a life of painful and tragic duality, since it has to fulfill no less than two diametrically opposed tasks. On the one hand, in the highest poetic achievements, it is itself a 'word for its own sake.' On the other hand, in everyday life, it circulates in colloquial speech as a common, colorless, soundless notion." In periods that are favorable to poetry, the word is free; it is sheer rhythm; it is a dance. But in periods when people expect "commitment" and contents from poetry, the word is conceptual. In such unpropitious times, says Leśmian (referring to a Polish fairy tale), a poet's words wear a "cap of invisibility." Poets are ashamed of a sacred dance; they want to be recognized as sober, useful members of a community. According to Leśmian, a poet is like a mime who adapts his song to an imaginary instrument he holds in his hands. Often, that instrument (lute, flute, cithara, etc.) symbolizes a whole literary school. The instrument is different in Classicism, different in Romanticism, and so on. The dramatic situation of poets born in "bad periods" (the Positivist era, for instance) consists in their attempting to sing to an instrument inadequate for the needs of any poetic temperament.

In the last phase of his life, Leśmian was critical toward poetic groups known as the Vanguard, which were gathering more and more followers. Yet it was exactly out of the Polish Vanguard of the twenties and thirties that there grew a new awareness of the myth-creating function of the language, which, in turn, contributed to Leśmian's posthumous fame. Judging from some of his theoretical pronouncements, he should have been a partisan of "pure poetry," such as that advocated by Henri Brémond in France in 1925, but his poetry is something more—it is a code which, when deciphered, unveils its richness in infinite layers of meaning. No other poet issuing from "Young Poland" equals Leśmian's stature, and he should be ranked with the great figures of modern European literature.

THE THEATER

Stanisław Wyspiański
(1869–1907)

Stanisław Wyspiański, the reformer of the Polish theater, was born in Kraków in 1869, the son of a sculptor. He wrote in one of his poems:

> At the foot of Wawel Castle my father had his workshop,
> A huge white, vaulted room
> Alive with a big crowd of the dead;
> There, a little boy, I used to wander and what I felt
> I chiseled later into the shapes of my art.

After he finished high school, he studied at the Jagiellonian University and at the School of Fine Arts, where his professor was Jan Matejko, then a renowned painter of gigantic historical canvases. From Matejko he learned respect for a meticulous study of details of dress, shoes, weaponry, etc. Later on, thanks to scholarships, he visited Italy, Germany (where he became a fervent admirer of Richard Wagner), and France. He studied in Paris for some time, and in his painting moved quite far away from his early teachers. Very original in his decorative approach, he is, perhaps, somewhat akin to Gauguin.

Drawing of a plant by Stanisław Wyspiański.

As a man of the theater, he can be understood only if we keep in mind his passion for drawing anything he observed—architecture, human figures—and for making constantly new projects for theatrical set designs. "The thought of Wyspiański never expressed itself through words; he did not think in words, he thought with tensions of his will and with emotions expressed in color, movement, and sound. He thought in theatrical terms" (Stanisław Brzozowski). Though he lived only thirty-eight years, through his plays he accomplished a real revolution. The factors which are at the source of his work can be listed in a few points:

1. His native city, Kraków, was one solid museum, preserving the glory of Poland's past. It was also subject to the inertia typical of provincial towns of the Hapsburg Empire. Wyspiański both loved the museum and revolted against it.

2. The contrast between his provincial Poland and Western Europe, which he clearly perceived during his travels, provoked in him a not altogether conscious urge to redeem the sad present through the splendor of art.

3. The museumlike quality of life surrounding him in Kraków was enhanced by the preponderance of Greek and Latin in the curriculum of his high school. Disgusted by the present, he continually strayed in his thinking to Greece and Greek tragedy.

4. Richard Wagner's theater in Bayreuth convinced Wyspiański that the theatrical spectacle should form a unity of word, color, music, and movement.

5. If Wyspiański was in any way indebted to Friedrich Nietzsche, it was, above all, to Nietzsche's theory of the Dionysian origin of tragedy and to his praise of energy.

6. He deeply felt the essence of tragedy to lie in its power to arouse feelings of pity and terror. He said himself:

> There is only one eternal trend of truth
> That there is no life except through sin:
> The fate given to mortals is to weigh the burden of mutual crimes.

7. His admiration for Corneille (he made a new translation of *Le Cid*) shows that human will was for him the most important component of tragedy. To quote him again:

> You go through the world and you give a shape to the world by
>   your actions.
> Look at the world, the shape of the world, and you will see your
>   guilt.

8. He was directly and strongly influenced by Mickiewicz's vision of the future of Slavic drama, as presented in the poet's sixteenth lecture of 1843 at the Collège de France. In drama, Mickiewicz explained, "poetry is transformed into action before the audience. . . . The destiny of that art is to stimulate, or rather, if it is possible to say so, to force lazy spirits into action." Mickiewicz believed that the Slavic drama was called to continue the only valid theatrical line, begun in the Greek tragedies and carried on in medieval mystery

plays. The Slavic drama was to combine all the elements of national poetry—lyricism, discussion of current problems, historical images— into a blended unity thanks to a typically Slavic gift for grasping the supernatural. Drama was a means of bringing to life the solemn figures of saints and heroes. But Mickiewicz also foresaw a completely new method of staging, which announced the theater of the twentieth century. Wyspiański probably found the first embodiment of Mickiewicz's hints in the stagecraft of Richard Wagner. At any rate, his was a conscious turning against the theater as conceived then by the actors and by the public, and his strivings parallel the program of the reformer of the English theater, Gordon Craig.

Wyspiański cannot be classified simply as an author of plays (written mostly in verse). Those plays, the language of which bears the trace of mannerisms proper to "Young Poland," have been justly defined as librettos deliberately intended as material for a stage director. His true successors were not writers, but men of the theater, such as Leon Schiller, who elaborated his theory of the "monumental theater" between the two wars. Schiller himself said of Wyspiański:

. . . the theater was the only means of expression for him; on the stage he solved the most personal problems, and they were always the nation's problems. He went further than the postulates of Craig . . . he wished to oppose that theater which had been destroyed by literature, demoralized by a cult of actors and was trying to save itself through pseudo-pictorial spectacles. He created the idea of "pure theater," an autonomous theater which possesses its own aesthetics and its own craft and where literature has no more right than the actor, while the actor is as much a component of theatrical art as the décor. The only master of such a theater is an artist of the theater endowed with all its skills and crafts.

Schiller voiced the opinion, now well established, that Wyspiański continued where the Polish Romantic theater left off and that his theatrical work expanded a trend that could boast of such monumental plays as Mickiewicz's *Forefathers' Eve* (staged for the first time by Wyspiański himself in 1901), Słowacki's *Kordian*, and Krasiński's *Undivine Comedy*. In Schiller's words: "He fulfilled the last will of Mickiewicz." Moreover, since Schiller was a Leftist, he considered Wyspiański a precursor of the "fighting" or political theater and claimed that Wyspiański, in this respect, was ahead of the German theatrical vanguard, represented by directors like Piscator (and out of which, let us note, issued the theater of Bertolt Brecht).

In order to facilitate the task of the reader, we may divide Wyspiański's plays according to theme and ignore chronology. His Greek cycle embraces *Meleager*, *Protesilaus and Laodamia*, *Achilleis*, and *The Return of Odysseus*. Though interesting for a student of Wyspiański, they are rather marginal to his main work.

In his two tragedies on contemporary themes, he took his subjects from the most obscurantist milieu. *Curse* (*Klątwa*) takes place in a remote Polish village; the peasants have been terrified by a drought lasting several months, and they seek the sinner among themselves for whose sins they suffer. Their search ends as they accuse the mistress of the village priest; and they stone her to death in order to bring rain. Characteristically, the play could not be performed in pious Kraków, and it was staged in Warsaw only when the censorship office was assured that posters would relegate the time of action to the Middle Ages. A similar backward village is the scene of *The Judges* (*Sędziowie*) except that the characters are members of a family of Jewish innkeepers; the play deals with a murder committed by one of them and the vengeance of destiny.

In his Slavic cycle, Wyspiański reverted to the remote past of his native city: to its pagan times, as in *The Legend* (*Legenda*), a dramatic fantasy; or to medieval Kraków and the assassination of Bishop Stanisław, as in *Bolesław Śmiały* and *Skałka* (i.e., Little Rock, the site of the royal castle).

Then there is a cycle dedicated to the uprising of 1830. *November Night* (*Noc listopadowa*) is a particularly good example of Wyspiański's technique. Warsaw, on the night the revolt breaks out, is no ordinary city; it is a scene where mythical forces are brought into play, where statues of Greek gods and goddesses come to life in the city's parks, and where the call to arms mingles with the Greek myth of resurrection through the return of Persephone to the surface of the earth. Thus, a symbolist treatment, usually associated with extremely individualistic art, is applied here to the fate of a whole community. *Varsovienne* (*Warszawianka*) takes its title from a revolutionary song and is a short play about two girls during a battle, raging in their neighborhood, in which their dear ones are engaged. This is strictly a work of mood, not unlike some of Eugene O'Neill's plays. The third play of the cycle, *Lelewel*, centers around a somewhat confused political leader, the scholar Joachim Lelewel, and is less satisfactory from the artistic point of view.

Wyspiański's full stature is seen in his cycle on national problems, which includes *The Wedding* (*Wesele*), *Liberation* (*Wyzwolenie*), *The Legion* (*Legion*), and *Acropolis*, the first of these being the best. In the autumn of 1900, Wyspiański's friend, the poet Lucjan Rydel, married a peasant girl. The wedding was held in the girl's village, Bronowice, near Kraków (now part of the city), and Wyspiański attended. It was a curious gathering, a motley crowd coming from all social classes: journalists, painters, poets, peasants, aristocrats, bluestockings. Wyspiański, observing all this, was struck by a singular vision. In February of 1901, the manuscript of *The Wedding* was ready; and in March, the theater dared to stage it. Some slashing by the censor did not do much harm. (Kraków was a rather idyllic city in that the censor, present in the audience, was tactful enough to escape when the actors delivered forbidden lines.) The play's powerful emotional impact sparked a new era in Polish theater. Notwithstanding what has been said about the factors shaping Wyspiański, to understand the form of *The Wedding* one must look for its source in the traditional Polish Christmas puppet show (*szopka*). The puppets were moved on sticks; they would pop up, utter a few lines, and disappear. In Wyspiański's play, the stage represents a room in a peasant's cottage where characters enter, either singly or in twos and threes, converse or meditate aloud, then return to an adjoining room from which the sound of music and dancing is heard. Short dialogues, confrontations of various social classes and mentalities occur in quick succession as characters disappear and reappear, as in a puppet show. There is no central figure. The real subject is the very night of the wedding, progressing, as is usual at evening parties, from relatively sober beginnings toward the weird atmosphere of predawn hours. The music, ever present, helps to build up a peculiar, spellbinding mood that is difficult to convey in words. As the night advances, fantastic creatures make their entrance; they are, if one prefers a rationalistic explanation, projections of the characters' own thoughts. A journalist meets the royal jester Stańczyk from the sixteenth century; an aristocrat sees the ghost of a magnate famous for his pride and for his betrayal of the national cause; and a mulch from the garden (visible outside the window) is inadvertently called in by a poetic and sophisticated girl, Rachel. The personified mulch takes over as a kind of maestro, and the play ends as the company begins a somnambulic dance under the spell of the straw man and his fiddle. Thus, there are two groups of characters: "living persons" and "persons of the drama" (i.e., the embodied dreams and desires of the wedding guests). Viewed as a whole, the play offers a pitilessly exposed cross section of a Polish society that is touched by a strange paralysis of the will: a peasant's saying—"They do not will to will" —applies, above all, to the intelligentsia. But peasants do not fare much better in the drama. If we have to delineate a plot in *The Wedding*, it consists in the growing expectation of some tremendous, extraordinary event, which remains unnamed (an uprising? miraculous recovery of the country's independence?). The phantom of an eighteenth-century wandering lyre player and minstrel, Wernyhora (a purely legendary figure), gives a peasant lad a golden horn at the sound of which the "spirit will be fortified; Fate will be accomplished." The lad is sent to signal from afar the coming of the big event. All those present are ordered to prepare themselves and to strain their ears toward the road from Kraków. Yet the lad returns empty-handed; he has forgotten about his mission and has lost the golden horn. The big event never comes; instead, the play closes with a dreamlike dance of "hollow-men" that symbolizes the inertia of Polish society.

Both the characters and their sayings impressed the play's first audiences so much that some expressions entered the journalistic idiom as convenient catchwords for certain attitudes, while many of the lines from the verse play became part of everyday Polish speech, for instance:

> Let there be war the whole world over
> As long as the Polish countryside is quiet,
> As long as the Polish countryside is calm.

> Niech na całym świecie wojna,
> Byle polska wieś zaciszna,
> Byle polska wieś spokojna.

Even some of the characters became proverbial; for example, Rachel, the young woman who invites the mulch in from the garden, typified the female admirers who adulated the poets of the *Moderna* (her Jewish name is significant of the ascendancy of new social groups). With her crimson shawl, her dark beauty, her somewhat ethereal refinement, she has been evoked, since then, by many poets of the twentieth century.

Liberation (*Wyzwolenie*), with its symbolism, also applies to national problems. Contrary to what one might expect, the title denotes not a political upheaval, but an act of triumph over the Polish morbid infatuation with martyrdom, which had been exalted by Romantic poetry. The drama depicts a symbolic struggle against a stone monument to a Genius (who resembles Mickiewicz in every feature). Theatrically it is no less daring than *The Wedding*. When the curtain rises, we see a stage on which the actors have just finished a performance. They joke, take off their costumes, and leave the theater. Only one, Konrad (the name obviously refers to the hero of *Dziady*), remains in the supposedly empty theater building; he engages in a solitary battle with a crowd of Masks, who are but the shapes of his own contradictory thoughts, then passes on to a duel with the Genius himself.

The Legion dramatizes a polemic with Polish Romantic literature, and the play is often too allusive even for the Poles. Yet nowhere in Wyspiański did an invasion of the fantastic reach such proportions as in *Acropolis*, an enormous call for faith in Life and Action, a parable on night and dawn, death and resurrection. This is a dream about night happenings in the royal castle of Wawel in Kraków, when human figures step down from old tapestries and engage in dialogues or statues move about, and a meeting of many centuries of history takes place. Mythological deities, Greek heroes, and Polish personalities of the past communicate with each other before the play ends with the sunrise and the triumphal entry of Christ, who rides in a chariot; he is identified somewhat with Apollo. In the play's imagery, the Vistula River, on which Wawel Castle stands, merges with the Skamander, on which Troy stood (it was because of *Acropolis* that a principal poetic group of the 1920s called its magazine *Skamander*).

Apart from his theatrical imagination, not matched by any of his contemporaries in Europe, Wyspiański also made another significant contribution: he introduced new elements to the thought of "Young Poland" by overcoming the *Moderna*'s worship of Art as an absolute, and by suggesting a return to a new variety of commitment. This role of Wyspiański's was stressed by the most eminent literary critic of the period, Stanisław Brzozowski, who belabored the *Moderna* with judgments such as this: "The art of people who want to escape into it from life is but the state of soul of those individuals who consider their lives worthless, feel their lives are worthless." Wyspiański, according to Brzozowski, conceived of the theater as a historical activity, and this vision was already "a revolt against decay, a search for health, life, energy." Yet, it would be erroneous to look for any clearly formulated philosophy in Wyspiański or any "program." His was a pure striving toward energy, yet, as Brzozowski said, "he spiritually overcame the world to which he belonged, but which he could not leave." And "Wyspiański does not know what the life of a new Poland will be, but he knows that the death of the old Poland is death indeed." Or: "The most profound meaning of Wyspiański's work consists in this: The world that emerges in his work *negates itself*, undermines its own foundations. A structure of thought is erected, but only in order to be destroyed. Yet Wyspiański cannot leave that world of ruins and rubble because he possesses nothing else besides this." Brzozowski, using Hegelian terms, suggested that Wyspiański should be "forgotten in a good way," which means he should be preserved in order to be superseded by new vistas. There is no doubt, however, that Wyspiański's plays in verse are the cornerstone of the modern Polish theater.

Naturalistic and Psychological Drama

The Polish theatrical repertoire during the era of "Young Poland" embraced many contemporary plays translated from foreign languages, above all, those of the Scandinavian authors Henrik Ibsen, August Strindberg, and Knut Hamsun, and of the Germans Hermann

Sudermann and Gerhart Hauptmann. Among French works, the most popular were the symbolist dramas of Maeterlinck and the picturesque, heroic dramas of Edmond Rostand, while Oscar Wilde, Bernard Shaw, and William Butler Yeats represented the English language. In addition, a great number of Polish poets wrote symbolist plays (Kasprowicz, Żuławski, Staff, etc.), but nobody could equal Wyspiański in this field. Besides the symbolist offerings, however, this period left another valid contribution to the Polish theater, namely, naturalistic drama.

A "woman in revolt," surrounded by scandalous gossip, Gabriela Zapolska (1857–1921) was an actress, a playwright, and a novelist. She was also an extremely bitter person, detesting not only males, whom she accused of regarding women as their prey, but also females engaged in competitive chases for men. Her novels, characterized by naturalistic brutality and melodrama, had a strong publicist slant. They were aimed at exposing the hypocritical morality of the *bourgeoisie*, while taking up the defense of its victims. Garish and sensational, they are relegated today to pulp literature. Although Zapolska's lack of serious intellectual training condemned her to crude oversimplifications, her predatory eye led her to produce in some of her plays more than transitory effects. *Mrs. Dulska's Morality* (*Moralność pani Dulskiej*, 1907) unmasks a respectable woman from a bourgeois milieu along lines familiar to English readers from G. B. Shaw's *Mrs. Warren's Profession*. Mrs. Dulska has since become proverbial, and the play has never been left out of Polish repertoires. Another play, *Miss Maliczewska* (*Panna Maliczewska*, 1912), in which the heroine is a kept woman, owes its force to the passion with which Zapolska unveils the disgusting behavior of the masculine part of mankind. Actually, if it were not for her artistic success in these two dramas, Zapolska, once considered a leading exponent of naturalism, would be forgotten.

Not a prolific author, Jan August Kisielewski (1876–1918) was very promising, but he failed to develop his talent. He created a sensation with his first drama, *In the Net* (*W sieci*, 1899), which took up a theme very much debated then, namely, the rebellion of a young girl, "crazy Julietta," against a stifling, anti-intellectual way of life at home. This was the classical conflict of the time between youthful aspirations and the petty, everyday routine of the philistines; to the author's credit is his not especially favorable portrayal of Kraków's artistic, coffeehouse society, to which he himself belonged. His comedy *Caricatures* (*Karykatury*, 1899), on the Kraków snobs and the bourgeois, is regarded as an example of a good naturalistic play.

Tadeusz Rittner (1873–1921), an official in one of the ministries of Vienna, provided both Polish and Viennese theater with his plays, which were brittle, somewhat lacking in dramatic force, but well constructed. They deal mostly with conflicts between eroticism and ethics. They can be characterized as naturalistic with some reliance upon mood and symbols. Among them, *In a Little House* (*W małym domku*, 1904) and *Silly Jack* (*Głupi Jakub*, 1910) are still performed today.

Karol Hubert Rostworowski (1877–1938), who spent practically all his life in Kraków, wrote rambling dramas, and, like Wyspiański's, they were in verse. He was fond of taking historical personalities as his heroes, for instance, Judas Iscariot or the Emperor Caligula. Yet he is most remembered for his naturalistic tragedy in prose, *Surprise* (*Niespodzianka*, 1928), subtitled *A True Event in Four Acts*. The "true event" is a peasant woman's crime committed against a stranger who comes to her hut. On hearing he has just returned from America, she kills him to get his dollars for the education of her younger son. The man who was murdered, however, proves to be her elder son, whom she did not recognize, as he arrived late at night.

Some good craftsmen furnished new versions of the "slice of life" technique. Włodzimierz Perzyński (1877–1930) was an elegant writer, apt at handling paradoxical situations, an ironist who preferred above everything a well-placed epigram. These qualities come to the fore in the concise prose of his short stories and novels, and because of them he differs greatly from the overlyrical stylists of "Young Poland." His three comedies make him one of the best psychologists in Polish dramatic writing. *The Lighthearted Sister* (*Lekkomyślna siostra*, 1904), *Ashanti* (*Aszantka*, 1906), and *Frank's Happiness* (*Szczęście Frania*, 1909) explore, much more deeply than Zapolska did, the hypocritical morality of the middle class.

If psychological imbroglios resulting from the relations between the sexes frequently preoccupied the writers of "Young Poland," by the end of the period, as well as after the First World War, the theme was given a more ironic treatment. Thus, Wacław Grubiński (born 1883), in his playfulness, was closest to the Polish classicists of the eighteenth century or, among his foreign models, to Oscar Wilde and Anatole France. He specialized in paradoxical short stories and comedies. *The Innocent Sinner* (*Niewinna grzesznica*, 1925), a comedy involving a love triangle, or rather a quadrangle, is merely a pretext for the author's adroit juggling of the unexpected reactions on the parts of both the betraying and the betrayed.

From what we have said, the obvious conclusion is that in spite of Wyspiański's innovating spirit, the Polish theater was also paying due tribute to the more traditional dramatic forms. A truly successful continuation of Wyspiański's discoveries would come only later.

A NEW OPPOSITION TO THE "MODERNA"

Tadeusz Żeleński ("Boy" was a humorous pen name), the son of a well-known composer, was born in Warsaw. He received a diploma in medicine from the Jagiellonian University in Kraków, then engaged in scientific research, and soon was embarked on a promising academic career. However, he met Przybyszewski and other writers of the "Moderna," and his life took a different turn. In Poland, at the beginning of the century, there was a craze for "literary cabarets" modeled after those in France; and Żeleński became one of the most witty script writers for the "Green Balloon," a cabaret founded in Kraków in 1905 (it lasted until 1912) by poets and painters. The outcome of that type of creativity was Żeleński's volume of satirical verse and songs entitled *Little Words* (*Słówka*, 1913). Yet what appeared to be mere frivolity became an important landmark for the history of Polish poetry, precisely because of its unpretentiousness and its colloquial language; it was a real relief after the high-strung and maudlin poems of the modernists. Boy's epigrammatic terseness was such that many of his expressions entered the everyday idiom. It was humor, therefore, that prepared the way for a radical change in poetry: the use of words designating the most trivial objects, a practice rather frowned upon by the seekers after the Absolute, was soon to come into its own.

During World War I, as a military physician stationed in Kraków itself, Żeleński, out of boredom, struck another vein of his talent; namely, he started to translate systematically from the French, a language he knew to perfection. Out of this came his gigantic plan of bringing to the Polish reader the best works of French literature in a new or first Polish version. For Żeleński, the task carried an almost ideological burden. He admired French literature for its down-to-earthness, for its never losing sight of the basic powers ruling human life: sex and money. This he opposed to the excessive spiritualism of Polish literature. Little by little, throughout the several decades of his career, Żeleński succeeded in translating around one hundred volumes. Never before or since has French literature in Poland had such an excellent interpreter, able to adapt his style to various authors totally different from each other. When translating Villon, Rabelais, Brantôme, he applied the language of old Polish authors, especially that of Mikołaj Rej. Polish memorialists and Kochanowski

Tadeusz "Boy" Żeleński (1874–1941)

served him in the reconstruction of Montaigne. But with equal ease he passed to the classical style of Racine and Molière, to Voltaire, Diderot, Rousseau. He also rendered nearly the whole of Balzac's *Human Comedy* and the major works of Stendhal. When he met his death (he was executed by the Nazis in Lwów in 1941), he was completing his translation of Marcel Proust.

Between the two wars, Boy (as he was popularly known) was one of the leading theatrical critics, essayists, and publicists. Endowed with a rare capacity for work, brilliant, witty, widely read, he was regarded as a major force by all liberals and anticlericals. He was what might be termed in America a radical. He engaged in "revisionist" campaigns, combatting everything that was solemn and pompous. His literary studies on French writers had a clear pedagogical purpose. He coined a special word—"gilders" (*brązownicy*)— for those Polish literary historians who had bypassed the scandals in writers' private lives in order to obtain effigies of saints. His passion for debunking sometimes led him into outright crusading, for instance during his famous campaign in the thirties for sexual freedom and "conscious motherhood." Compared with such deep and intricate thinkers among his contemporaries as Stanisław Brzozowski, Boy often sounds shallow. Liberal ideology has its pitfalls exactly where it seems to be most realistic, and this was precisely where Boy ran into trouble. Yet Boy was greatly needed in a country where, as a satirical poet used to say, "there was too much holy water, and too little ordinary soap." Certainly his monumental achievement as a translator will never be forgotten.

Karol Irzykowski (1873–1944)   Born and educated in Lwów, where he studied German literature at the university, Karol Irzykowski had nothing of the colorfulness which characterized Boy-Żeleński. Hyperintellectual, reproached for dryness and causticity, he was not highly appreciated by his contemporaries. He longed to be a creative writer, but his fate was to become a literary critic. One exception is his huge novel, *The Hag* (*Pałuba*), written in the years 1891–1903 and published in 1903. In many respects, this is an extraordinary work; it bucked the stream of the *Moderna* both in its philosophy and in its technique, while, at the same time, it was equally opposed to the realism and naturalism of the nineteenth century. It is a psychological study of a few characters who go through the motions of their roles in a trivial plot. The novel proper has less importance than the digressions on novel writing and the inserted essay containing the author's ideas on man as reflected in literature. Irzykowski deliberately rejects any claim to omniscience. He does not pretend, as the Positivists, for instance, did, to understand what is going on in the minds of his heroes. He merely makes conjectures, and often confesses that he simply does not know. His attention is focused on the web of words in which his characters embroil themselves. Influenced by some contemporary philosophers, especially by the empiriocriticism of Ernst Mach and Richard Avenarius, he makes a sort of semantic exploration. Man, according to him, is a poseur; he falls into a trap of ready-made notions that are produced by a given society and that shape, in their turn, all interhuman relations. Nothing about the characters of the novel is authentic. They are prisoners of such concepts as love, fidelity, poetry, beauty, etc., which in fact are simply masks assumed by their subconscious, for the unavowable, which exists deep inside them, cannot come to the surface except in forms borrowed from the society of a specific time and place. In the essay parts of his novel, Irzykowski classifies man's various subterfuges. For instance, what he calls "the wardrobe of the soul" is an area of the mind where self-compromising thoughts put on a decent dress. And he gives an example: a girl being seduced manages to convince herself that this is Love and, thus, cannot refuse anything to the seducer. What Irzykowski names "touchy points" are insignificant, small details of one's own biography which cannot be admitted because they seem not up to the level of our lofty requirements. "Blind spots" occur when we try to preserve our psychological well-being by feigning ignorance of some uncomfortable knowledge about ourselves. The word *pałuba* (roughly, "hag") holds for Irzykowski symbolic meaning. It stands for all those moments when, to quote him, "you lose, mentally, the ground under your feet, moments that are best and most precious in your life, moments of the greatest annoyance and the greatest concentration, when your horizon broadens suddenly"—in other words, when, for a short instant, authenticity penetrates a basic inauthenticity. The author, who cruelly dissects his characters in a detached manner, does not assume that they are exceptions; they exemplify human behavior in general. Neither does he believe in his own ability to get rid of inauthenticity. In the essay, he seems to suggest rather that the analysis applied to the characters could be applied to himself too.

If viewed from the perspective of its own time, the novel makes fun of all the shibboleths of the *Moderna*: Art as Absolute, the antagonism between male and female, torrents of lyrical descriptions, confessions of internal tragedies. All these, for Irzykowski, are just masks characteristic of the period. The weaponry of his attack consists in parody—for instance, he parodies the style in which one of his heroes, a poet, writes—or in outright literary criticism (as in the essay part) of prevailing maladies. The extraordinary technique of *The Hag* (an author discussing his troubles in writing a novel) is, on the one hand, a throwback to Laurence Sterne and, on the other, an anticipation of the experimental European novel of the late twenties. The place allotted to the subconscious has led many critics to speak of a "pre-Freudian intuition" or to connect the work with the psychology of Alfred Adler. Yet notwithstanding Freud's first book on psychoanalysis, which appeared in 1900, ideas such as these were "in the air" of the epoch. *The Hag*, because of its austere, even pedestrian, language, was unique in the literature of "Young Poland," and because of this, as well as because of its cerebral quality, it was received rather disdainfully. In the decades to follow, however, its impact upon a few prose writers was considerable; and as they were often more talented, if not as perspicacious as Irzykowski, their works overshadowed his.

In the years 1918–1939, Irzykowski was a leading literary critic, but in such dead earnest that he often deserved the name of a pedant. He led a many-pronged attack, starting from his premise that literature is basically fictitious, and thus out of the reach of any "mirror-of-life" theories. For him, so-called realism or naturalism was a mere pretense. What he said about Émile Zola is significant:

Realism is not difficult for Zola because he does not try to fathom man; he considers him only as a product of nature, like a flower or a fruit. This would have been justified if only Zola had been God and not a man; man can write objectively about plants but not about man.

He also attacked "the cult of life," which he labeled "vitalism." In his opinion, "the principle of complication" was essential for cultural phenomena, while admirers of Life kneel before it, entranced by its very chaos. One of the most significant volumes of Irzykowski's criticism bears the title *The Struggle for Contents* (*Walka o treść*, 1929). He was for striving toward a literature free from masks and subterfuges even if this is a hopeless task. "Contents," in his interpretation, is exactly this: an effort to go beyond the network of unquestioned "meanings." One of his targets was Boy-Żeleński, who sounded somewhat hollow to Irzykowski because of his sweeping generalizations; of course, the ascetic and self-tormenting Irzykowski, less concerned with beliefs and ideas than with the way they are handled in literature, had much less appeal for the public than his picturesque antagonist. Irzykowski died from wounds received in Warsaw during the uprising of 1944. His diaries—*Observations, Motifs and Notes from Life* (*Notatki z życia, obserwacje i motywy*)—were published for the first time in 1964.

IN THE SATIRICAL VEIN

The popularity of the literary cabaret and Boy-Żeleński's *Little Words* marked the revival of a humorous literature in Poland, which has acquired since then many brilliant representatives. Already, in 1902,

Adolf Nowaczyński (1876–1944) made his debut with his *Monkey's Mirror* (*Małpie zwierciadło*), where the "academic prophets" and "alcoholics" of the *Moderna* received a rather unkind treatment. Skillful in prose as well as in verse, Nowaczyński subsequently showed his talent for pastiche, performing linguistic acrobatics with sixteenth-century Polish. His turning to old Polish jocularity and ribaldry was not accidental, for this very choice was an antidote to the ravings of suffering souls. For his unorthodox laughter he was feared and detested by many in his native Kraków. Later, he furnished the Kraków stage with colorful, successful plays, built with characteristic bravado around intriguing historical figures, such as *The Czar Pretender* (*Car samozwaniec*, 1908), *Frederick the Great* (*Wielki Fryderyk*, 1910), *Pułaski in America* (*Pułaski w Ameryce*, 1917), *The Commander of Paris* (*Kommendant Paryża*, 1926—about one of the leaders of the Paris Commune, Jarosław Dąbrowski), *The Spring of Nations in a Quiet Corner* (*Wiosna narodów w cichym zakatku*, 1929—a comedy about the city of Kraków in 1848). Nowaczyński's plays bear some resemblance to his pamphleteering; garish, though intelligent, they are more like dramatized *feuilletons* than works of true dramatic force. After World War I, Nowaczyński put his pen to work for the cause of the National Democratic Party (Rightist and anti-Semitic) because it afforded him the most space for taking his stand as an unruly, anarchistic freelancer and jester, somewhat akin to the turbulent polemicists of the Polish Counter Reformation.

A satirical poet, Jan Lemański (1866–1933), resurrected the old form of the fable in verse, applying it to modern situations. The animals enact strictly human scenes; they often stand for figures which the author observed in the literary cafés. For instance, a romance between a goose (who dreams about an ideal life of art and poetry) and a fox (who deplores his subjection to evil heredity) comes to a sad end when the fox makes a meal out of the goose. The fable goes on to suggest the carnivore's philosophical despair over the implacable mechanism of nature. The fox's parting words are: "Ha, our existence is a mystery." Such poems testified, of course, to the ebbing of the respect for the somewhat gratuitous profundity of "Young Poland."

NOVELISTS

Stefan Żeromski
(1864–1925)

Called "the conscience of Polish literature," Stefan Zeromski was born in central Poland near the town of Kielce, the son of an impover-

ished nobleman. His native region at the foot of the Holy Cross mountain chain had been a battleground during the 1863 insurrection, and
this theme was to receive a new treatment under Żeromski's pen. His
biography exemplifies the fate of those country gentry who migrated
to the cities, as well as all the transformations undergone by the progressive intelligentsia in its political attitudes. Żeromski studied veteri-
nary medicine in Warsaw, worked as a private tutor, and endured
much financial misery while writing his first stories. For a while, he
was a librarian at the Polish museum in Rapperswil, Switzerland—
an occupation which proved to be fruitful for his creative work, for he
was to make use of his research, later on, in his historical novels. From
1904 on, once he had achieved public recognition, he was able to dedi-
cate all his time to literature. In his early stories, both short and long,
Żeromski was a good pupil of the Positivists, applying a realistic style
that leaned somewhat toward naturalistic brutality. Yet he was a Neo-
Romantic in spirit. His obsession both with social injustice and with
the armed struggles of the past carried revolutionary innuendos.

His first novel, *Sysyphian Labors* (*Syzyfowe prace*, 1898), was
largely autobiographical. It is a story of Polish students in a Russian-
administered high school of a provincial town (Kielce) at a time when
the czarist authorities were using all the methods at their disposal to
obliterate the very notion of Polish nationality. The characters, though
under the spell of great Russian literature (which also served as an
instrument of Russification), organize themselves into little groups
to oppose the pressure, and it is characteristic that one of the leaders,
Andrzej Radek, is the son of an agricultural laborer, a proletarian for
whom the struggle to maintain his national identity and rebellion
against the social system are inseparable.

Żeromski's early period, during which he produced mostly short
stories, culminated in the novel *Homeless People* (*Ludzie bezdomni*,
1900). The hero, Dr. Judym, son of a Warsaw cobbler, is presented
as a man who is fully aware of how wretchedly the Polish masses live.
This consciousness is both his pain and his call to duty. Dr. Judym
says:

I am responsible for everything here! I am responsible before my spirit
which cries out within me: I protest! If I, a doctor, will not do it, who
will? I have received everything that I need. I must give back what I
have taken. That damned debt! . . . I can have no father, no mother, no
wife, not a single thing that I might press to my heart with love, as long
as those nightmares [Warsaw slums and workers' towns in the mining district of Silesia] exist. I must renounce happiness. I must be alone.

The hero of *Homeless People* represents that part of the intelligentsia
at the turn of the century that felt guilty because of its privileged posi-

tion due to education. Instead of quietly pursuing his career, he constantly risks, and loses, his jobs, since he dares to speak out the cruel truth. In the final chapter of the novel, he rejects the love of a woman (whose love he returns), as in his battle for social justice he would be weakened by founding and caring for a family. Such an idealistically minded figure accounts for the term *Żeromszczyzna*, or, the quality of being like Żeromski's heroes; the word was used ironically by the novelist's adversaries. Those adversaries were mostly on the political Right. All those who rallied to the Polish Socialist Party or who were sympathizers of it, like Zeromski himself, did not seem to mind this rather sentimental approach to social problems. *Homeless People* is a cruel novel which spares no image of abjection or misery. For this reason, and also because of his naturalistic leanings in his short stories, Żeromski was often attacked as a "sadomasochist," and, in a much graver reproach, as "contaminated" by Russian prose writers.

Extremely sensitive to the changes of mood in Poland, Żeromski reacted to the rising wave of Neo-Romanticism by writing a huge historical novel, *Ashes* (*Popioły*, 1904). As for most Polish writers, his choice of the epoch to be treated was highly significant. While Sienkiewicz in his Trilogy had re-created the *Respublica* of the Counter Reformation, Żeromski attempted a reappraisal of the Napoleonic period. For the Poles, this era summed up the ferment of the Enlightenment: radicalism, struggle for independence, and faith in the French Revolution. The main characters in *Ashes* leave Poland to join the Polish Napoleonic army, combat on battlefields all over Europe, including Spain, only to return as broken men with ashes in their hearts; and yet, to believe the passionate tone of the work, not in vain, as the legend of the deed will sustain national hopes. Some of them are sophisticated intellectuals who take their pledges as Freemasons very seriously but are thrown into tragic conflicts of conscience when confronted with the *desastres de la guerra*. As to cruelty, Żeromski rewarded his detractors fully, especially in the scenes of guerrilla warfare in Spain and the siege of Saragossa. In *Ashes* both the virtues and weaknesses of that uneven writer come to the surface. Compassion, humanity, wisdom, vastness of historical vision, go together with an exalted lyricism (which perhaps is not well suited to the tasks of the novel as a literary genre) and a penchant for melodrama. Indeed, the relaxation of unimaginative discipline in writing, so necessary for poetry, which had been stifled by Positivism, proved nefarious to many prose writers, especially for Żeromski, who was, in his mature age, rather too inclined toward poetry disguised as the narrative of novels.

The solitude of fighters, be they noble-minded intellectuals, soldiers, or professional revolutionaries, was one of Żeromski's basic themes, and he was obviously a Neo-Romantic in his counterposing of a "redeemer" to the inert mass hardly capable even of following. This is especially noticeable not only in his works dealing with the Napoleonic era (besides *Ashes* he wrote a tragedy entitled *Sułkowski*) but also in his treatment of the Revolution of 1905 (in *The Rose* [*Róża*, 1909], a drama published in Kraków under a pseudonym) and of the 1863 uprising. In fact, the contrast between the bravery of the guerrilla units and the apathy, even hostility, of the peasant was, in 1863, particularly depressing. Besides short stories on the theme of 1863, he wrote a novel, somewhat Faulknerian *avant la lettre;* it was called *The Faithful River* (*Wierna Rzeka*, 1913). This is a story of a wounded insurrectionist who is hidden and cared for by a young heiress on her parents' estate, of their love affair and parting. Clerical circles reproached Żeromski for demoralizing youth through the role which he assigned to sex in his plots. A scene in *The Faithful River* somewhat shocked them: when Cossacks searched the house, they discovered a bed with bloodstains on the sheet. The blood was that of the wounded man, who had been whisked into a safe place, but the girl, when asked whose blood it was, did not hesitate to answer, "Mine." So accustomed are we to bluntness in novels today that we may only reflect about the influence of naturalism on Żeromski. Among the remainder of his novelistic works, the last, published the year of his death, in 1925, is, perhaps, one of the most significant. *Before the Spring* (*Przedwiośnie*) tries to cope with what was a crucial problem for the progressive intelligentsia after 1918, when Poland emerged as an independent country. Enthusiasm for the goal achieved, a goal that had been pursued by several generations, could not hide the unpleasant reality: the old injustices still existed, and the heritage of backwardness was such that slow democratic evolution seemed to some intellectuals inapplicable to the needs of the people. Perhaps a revolutionary change was needed? Russia had its revolution—but the Polish army in 1920 stopped the march of that revolution toward the West by routing the Soviet forces in a battle at the gates of Warsaw. There were many in Poland like Cezary Baryka, the hero of the novel. Since he is the son of a Polish engineer working in the oil fields of Baku, on the Caspian Sea, he lives through the Russian Revolution as an adolescent. In spite of his revolutionary ideas, he returns to Poland because of his patriotically minded father, fights as an officer in the Polish-Soviet war of 1920, but later on, when invited to the estate of his friend from the regiment, a rich boy, he discovers "the eternal Poland" of the gentry: good life at the expense of the illiterate peasant masses. The novel concerns Cezary Baryka's search for both a moral and a political solution. He is repulsed by the fanaticism and the destructive spirit of Polish Communists, but not quite convinced by the perspectives unfolded by an old liberal, Gajowiec, who often sounds like a mouthpiece of Żeromski himself. The novel ends with Baryka's spontaneous act: he joins a march of the unemployed heading toward the president's palace and walks in the first row.

Żeromski, besides being a novelist, wrote a great deal of publicism. He consciously continued the whole progressive tradition in that genre, extending from the Arians and Frycz Modrzewski through the journalists of the Enlightenment like Staszic and Kołłątaj.

Among his theatrical plays, one in particular enjoyed great success: *A Quail Escaped Me* (*Uciekła mi przepióreczka*, 1924—the title alludes to a folk song). The play is true to what was called *Żeromszczyzna:* A castle is to be transformed into a cultural center designed to spread a love of the theater and fine arts throughout the surrounding region. The project is the accomplishment of one man who has convinced the aristocratic lady who owns the castle of the justness of his cause; soon he gathers a group of enthusiastic supporters. But everything falls to pieces because of his sudden love for the wife of the local teacher. Not only the quail escapes, but real motives of behavior are unveiled: the rich lady's civic spirit was in truth but a hidden passion for the man. Yet his idea will be carried on by others.

During the first quarter of the century, nobody, not even his enemies, questioned Żeromski's position as the most important Polish fiction writer. He was called "an insatiable heart," "the conscience of Polish literature," and the awarding of the Nobel Prize to Reymont for his *Peasants* provoked some indignation among the Poles. It was felt Żeromski should have received it. His extraordinary gift for compassion, his open-mindedness, and the dramatic plots of his books account for that worship. Today, there is a tendency to regard the stories of his early period as better constructed artistic wholes than his novels. In the former, which are closer to the prose of the nineteenth century, he did not indulge in the unrestrained lyricism that later entered his style under the impact of modernism and symbolism; moreover, he merely presented the sad social reality without proposing solutions (in truth, he had never had solutions for the pressing issues of the day). Yet Żeromski was, first of all, a public figure of great stature; this, together with his feeling for the unexplored resources of the Polish language—and his vocabulary is of a stupendous richness—secures him a place apart in Polish literature.

Władysław Reymont
(1867–1925)

Reymont's fiction stemmed, to a large extent, from his youthful wanderings and changes of profession. Son of a village church organist, he refused, to the despair of his parents, who wanted to make a priest of him, to go through school; and then, when trained as a tailor, he did not join the ranks of steady craftsmen. Instead, he became a member of a traveling company of actors, sharing their life of poverty, and acquiring, through his wanderings in provincial towns, real familiarity with the lot of the downtrodden and the uneducated. For a while, he worked as a minor railway employee, as a factory hand in Łódź, and finally, as a railroad switchman living in a small village on the line; this was when he started to write. His first short stories, where he depicts the fates of poor peasants and agricultural laborers with a naturalistic crudeness, drew the attention of both public and critics alike; and his first novel, *Comedienne* (*Komediantka*, 1896), confirmed their expectations. This is a study of the hopeless conditions crushing wandering actors, a milieu that was somewhat exotic for the average reader. The term "study" is even more applicable to a novel on the most capitalistic city in Poland, Łódź, entitled *The Promised Land* (*Ziemia obiecana*, 1899). During the last decade of the nineteenth century, Łódź, thanks to rapid investments in the textile factories, grew from a small town into a kind of Manchester of eastern Europe, exporting its products all over Russia's enormous expanses. It was a city of speculation, of fortunes won in a few days, of bankruptcies, and of the inhuman exploitation of working people. In his novel, Reymont compared it to a monstrous tumor and described it with all the hostility of an alien, migrant villager.

The early writings, however, were but a prelude to his huge novel in four volumes, *The Peasants* (*Chłopi*, 1904–1909). He knew the Polish village well, but this time he did not confine himself to a severe bluntness; instead, he envisioned a vast epic. Naturalism looked at man as a biological being; from this, there was but one step to the celebration of those qualities of man which make him a splendid animal: spontaneity, strength of passion, vitality, endurance. In Poland the early years of our century were a time of so-called *chłopomania* ("peasant mania"), which was not deprived of political undertones. The village signified the untapped resources of the nation, the gauge of the future. What the intelligentsia lacked themselves, they willingly saw in the illiterates or half-literates, "unspoiled" by any cultural decadence. Reymont's work also parallels those Scandinavian novels where a certain idealization of primitive characters was the rule. Divided into four volumes (entitled, respectively, *Autumn*, *Winter*, *Spring*, and *Summer*), *The Peasants* is an epic of a community that celebrates its Catholic feasts, drinks, dances, and works in harmony with the rhythm of nature. The main characters (upon whom Reymont confers the half-legendary stature of Homeric heroes) exemplify the community's virtues and vices. The basic plot, however (a love affair between Antek Boryna and his young, beautiful stepmother, Jagna, plus the vengeance of old Boryna), could have just as well been set in an urban milieu. Praise of primitive passions and of peasant vigor entranced Reymont's readers no less than the language of the novel, which abounds in descriptions of nature and agricultural labors, and which was judged as highly poetic. Like Żeromski, Reymont started with a restrained prose learned from the Positivists, but later on felt encouraged by the general temper of "Young Poland" to experiment with conveying various moods of landscapes, seasons, and human encounters. Torrents of words were admirably suited to his ebullient temperament, but it is exactly his overpicturesque language that lowers the value of that ambitious work. *The Peasants* brought Reymont the Nobel Prize in 1924, and his energy seems to have been spent on that major endeavor of his literary career. He wrote a historical trilogy, *The Year 1794* (*Rok 1794*, 1913–1918), but the very subject was beyond the scope of his self-taught craft.

Wacław Berent
(1873–1940)

Born in Warsaw, Wacław Berent studied life sciences at the University of Zurich, where he received his doctoral degree in ichthyology. A writer with passionate philosophical interests, well acquainted with Schopenhauer and Nietzsche (whom he was one of the first to translate into Polish), he managed to embody in a few novels the successive stages of his changing *Weltanschauung*.

The first, entitled *The Specialist* (*Fachowiec*, 1895), was a reaction against the advice given to the young intelligentsia by the Positivists. The hero of the novel goes to work in a factory and becomes a skilled laborer only to discover that manual labor, as imposed by modern industry, is dehumanizing and that the worker's useful economic role does not protect him from the disrespect shown to people of low social status. The novel, thus, by implication, attacked the Positivists' optimistic faith in the blessings of technology.

In his next novel, *Rotten Wood*, (*Próchno*, 1903), Berent depicted the Bohemian international milieu in one of Europe's large cities. It might have been Munich or Berlin. The characters— one poet, one actor, one playwright, one journalist, one painter, one musician—are all affected by the despair of the *fin de siècle*. They consider themselves "decadents" and nurse along a hopeless vision of Western civilization. Analyzed with great perspicacity, the Bohemians engage in interminable, subtle conversations in which Schopenhauer, a dream of Nirvana, and Buddhism constantly return. They are sterile, entangled in personal complications without issue, and suicide seems the only way out. Although intended as a protest against the "rotten wood" of Bohemian circles in the name of a Nietzschean call to energy, the novel by its style belongs totally to the *Moderna* current and was not only received as such by Berent's contemporaries, but praised by the *Moderna* for what it condemned. Yet the author's identification with his characters is so strong, his language so true to the fashion of the day that the responsibility for the misunderstanding must be laid at his own door.

Berent's third novel, *Winter Wheat* (*Ozimina*, 1911), describes Warsaw on the eve of the Russo-Japanese War, the consequences of which led, in both Poland and Russia, to the Revolution of 1905. In a way, the framework of the novel as well as its pitiless images of inertia reminds one of Wyspiański's *The Wedding*. As in the latter, the action lasts only one night and the scene is a party. People of various backgrounds with various pasts are gathered in the rooms of a rich Warsaw financier, and through revelations of their life stories, their personal conflicts, we receive a panorama of a society debased by political enslavement, moral hopelessness, the pursuit of money and trifling pleasures. Perhaps the most positive figure in the novel is an old Russian colonel who looks at the Poles with an ambivalent mixture of scorn and fascination. In Wyspiański's *The Wedding*, as the night wears on, the atmosphere becomes more and more charged with expectancy and longing for an extraordinary event. In Berent's novel, an "event" actually does occur: the news of general mobilization is announced in the middle of the night. At dawn, some of the party guests take a stroll through working-class districts in Warsaw; they are drawn into a mob demonstration against the police. An armed clash results, and in the rifle fire one of the protagonists is killed. Again, as in *Rotten Wood*, the burden of the novel is a call for vigor, health, and self-renewal; the title is, of course, symbolic: winter wheat seeds sleep under the snow, but begin their growth with the coming of spring. Thanks to its excellent composition and a real insight into the state of society, it could be called a great novel, if not for its language bearing the stylistic stigma of the period. In trying to convey a mood by filling out scenes with glimpses of heavy draperies and faces, disembodied voices heard through cigar smoke, Berent applies a tortuous, one might say, expressionistic, language that often violates what is felt to be the natural flow of Polish prose.

A striving toward excessive ornamentation is even more pronounced in *Living Stones* (*Żywe kamienie*, 1918), an extraordinary work which has often been defined as a medieval ballad in novel form. Here, the reader finds himself in an unidentified town in the Middle Ages. Every type of medieval character is introduced: conformist burghers, monks (divided internally between fear of hell and love for old Latin poetry), jesters, wandering comedians. The story is centered around the arrival of a carefree, joyous troupe of actors to the town; they represent freedom, buovancy, and a release from stifling everyday routine. Here, too, Berent remained true to Nietzsche. The language is heavily stylized in an effort to inject everything with a medieval flavor; yet it is exactly this stylization that constitutes the novel's weakest point and reveals a certain disparity between Berent's sophistication (in the best sense of the word) and his artistic means; his prose, like so much of what "Young Poland" produced, was excessively contaminated by poetry. Precious as it is in style, though rare in its understanding of the Middle Ages, *Living Stones* marks the end of one phase in Berent's work, and its date of publication, 1918, coincides with the end of "Young Poland's" hegemony.

All his novels could be called historical studies, even if they are mostly preoccupied with the history of the present. With such concerns, it is no wonder that, at the end of his life, he turned to scarcely fictionalized biographies (written in a rather severe, simple style). He chose the epoch of the Polish Enlightenment with its upsurge of energy exemplified by the militants of the Camp of the Reform and by their successors, the Napoleonic officers. His *The Current* (*Nurt*, 1934), *Diogenes Disguised as a Nobleman* (*Diogenes w kontuszu*, 1937), *The Twilight of the Commanders* (*Zmierzch wodzów*, 1939) might be defined as portrait galleries of publicists, scholars, and generals in the Napoleonic army—works on the very border line of fiction. A member of the Polish Academy of Literature, a solitary man who shunned the literary and political battles of the day, Berent has been and still is esteemed as a thinker and has maintained his position as an author for the elite.

CRITICISM AND PHILOSOPHY

Stanisław Brzozowski
(1878–1911)

"Young Poland" won its battle, not a little aided by gifted critics who allied themselves with its cause. The names most often heard were those of Ignacy Matuszewski and Wilhelm Feldman. Yet it was another essayist and critic who remained uppermost in the minds of subsequent generations. Stanisław Brzozowski's life was short. He lived only thirty-three years, but he succeeded in leaving a voluminous work, which is being constantly subjected to new exegeses. The son of a squire who lost his fortune, he studied in Russian high schools, first in Lublin, then in Nemirov in the Ukraine, where he belonged to a "circle" of students who discussed current issues. He discovered literature through great Russian prose writers and later voiced his gratitude especially to Turgenev, Uspensky, and Belinsky. He became a fervent "Darwinist," in revolt against his traditional Roman Catholic, Polish milieu. At Warsaw University, owing to his oratorial talent, he was acclaimed by his fellow students as one of their leaders, and soon was suspended by the czarist authorities for a year because of his political activity. An unfortunate misdemeanor committed when he was nineteen (he took some money from the treasury of the students' union) ruined, in effect, his whole life. When, for political reasons, he was soon arrested, the police used this affair to blackmail him, and this was the source of subsequent rumors that he had been enlisted as an agent of the Okhrana (the czarist secret political police). In the light of all available documents, the accusation was false, but the rumors were spread both by the Okhrana and by Brzozowski's political enemies. He was a socialist, though not a member of the Polish Socialist Party, and his vitriolic articles infuriated the whole political Right. The complexity of his brilliant mind was such and his evolution so rapid that it is extremely difficult to follow all the transformations of that man, who was incessantly digesting new ideas and devouring books in several languages (Polish, Russian, German, French, later Italian and English). Soon he ceased to be a "Darwinist." Nietzsche liberated him from the worship of a scientific *Weltanschauung*. To Przybyszewski (whose weaknesses, however, he understood well) he ascribed a particular role in his "conversion." Finally, he was dazzled by Karl Marx, and he remained faithful to him, although he was never an orthodox Marxist; in his view, Marx's true philosophical thought was blurred by Marx himself in his advanced age and, above all, by Engels. Incredible as it may seem, Brzozowski actually reconstructed by intuition certain theses that appear only in Marx's early writings, which had not yet been published then (i.e., *Economic-Philosophic Manuscripts*, 1933). His lack of orthodoxy made it nearly impossible for him to find defenders on the Left in order to stave off the attacks from the Right. He was forced to be a one-man army. In the spring of 1905, he left Russian-occupied Poland for Galicia, under Austrian rule, but soon the tuberculosis he had contracted in a Warsaw jail forced him to move to Italy—first to Nervi, then to Florence. In his absence, accusations of his being an agent of the czarist police caused an uproar, and he returned twice to Kraków to submit himself to an open hearing arranged by the Socialist Party. It yielded no conclusive results. His feverish literary activity was hindered neither by illness nor by slander, but these, combined with poverty, ended his life prematurely in 1911. He is buried in Florence.

Highly original as a philosopher, Brzozowski was misunderstood in his lifetime because the problems that preoccupied him only moved into the limelight in Polish and European intellectual circles after World War II, under the impact of existentialism and the "back to young Marx" trend. He had hoped to reach the larger public through his novels.

Flames (*Płomienie*, 1908), his first novel (if we bypass the youthful *Whirlpools* [*Wiry*]), dealt, however, with too unfamiliar a subject: the moral conflicts of the members of the Nechaev group of professional revolutionaries in Russia. Much later, such professional revolutionaries were to fascinate Malraux, then Camus, in France. The author leads his main character, a Pole, through several revolutionary cells in Russia, through the Paris Commune, and then through revolutionary milieus in Italy. The work was judged by some critics as suspect, unpatriotic, and as harboring pro-Russian leanings. Hastily written, too publicistic, it is nevertheless a display of the author's intellectual power.

But Brzozowski's second novel, *Alone Among Men* (*Sam wśród ludzi*, 1911), confirms his gift for novel writing and is one of the most fascinating Polish works of fiction. The author intended it to be the first volume of a series on, as he defined it, "the philosophical-political transformations of European consciousness" between the years 1830 and 1878. He wrote:

I can hardly understand why novelists have been so little interested in changes in the type of the historical leader. Even in Western Europe not enough is known about that break which separated the pre-1830 generation from everything that happened after that date, and not enough is known about the big psychological crisis of 1848 that changed the entire thinking of Europe's intelligentsia. These are subjects full of dramatic tensions. Such figures as Philippo Buonarroti, Blanqui, Mazzini are infinitely superior, by the power of their internal spiritual unity, even to the human types created by great masters like Balzac and Stendhal.

In his intention the cycle would have concentrated on the Paris of Heine, Saint-Simonists, Fourierists, Polish *émigrés*, etc. *Alone Among Men* is a story of the spiritual maturing of a young man, Roman Ołucki, whose adolescence occurs during the early 1830s. By origin a Polish nobleman from the Ukraine, he lives first there, then migrates to Berlin, where he finds himself in the milieu of the Hegelian Left. This volume is obviously but a preparation, a glimpse of the author's plan to portray figures who exemplify the most vital ferments of European thought in the nineteenth century. Yet the novel, just as it stands, abounds in unforgettable characters. In a Catholic country, Brzozowski was the first to provide such profound and complex portraits of priests: Father Rotuła, son of a peasant, a Voltairian, a Jacobin who carries in his heart the childish faith of his peasant ancestors; and Father Giava, a demoniac Jesuit, whom the hero of the novel meets in Berlin. Giava has intellectual certainty of the truth contained in Catholic dogmas but lacks faith (in the sense of emotional assent). He moves among the Berlin revolutionaries as a self-appointed *agent provocateur*. His reasoning: the sooner a revolution, the sooner the Left will compromise itself, and from this the Vatican can draw a neat profit. (Some ten years later Thomas Mann was to create a similar Jesuit figure, Naphta, in his *Magic Mountain.*) The most "Dostoevskian," perhaps, of Polish novels, *Alone Among Men* also grappled with the conflict between Polish and Russian attitudes. With rare courage, Brzozowski mercilessly dissected his protagonists, both Poles and Russians. He went to the core of the tragedy of Russian progressivism under autocratic rule, and of the Polish refusal to recognize evil as an integral part of the universe. One of his characters, Reitern, an ex-liberal and a Russian officer, exclaims:

If it were not for the Muscovites, all of this world would be fine; you Poles are now behind us as though you were behind a mountain: the Russians have screened the sun from us (you say), but it exists. Well, we *are* Muscovites, good only for screening the sun. Oh! I hate you, innocent lamb's blood of Abel.

In the part of the novel that takes place in Berlin, Brzozowski exhibits no less insight into the German mentality. A philosopher who bears a somewhat ironic English name, Truth, is modeled on Hegel himself (in some of his essays Brzozowski made deep character studies of Hegel as a man). It is surprising that such a rich work was not hailed upon its appearance as a great literary event, but Brzozowski had been defamed and his novels were surrounded (except for a few admirers) by a conspiracy of silence.

His third novel, *A Book About an Old Woman* (*Książka o starej kobiecie*), which centered around a revolutionary of 1905 who is killed by his own (socialist) party, remained unfinished.

As a literary critic, Brzozowski either captivated the young or infuriated them. He shared the adventures of "Young Poland," first as a fervent supporter of the *Moderna*, then as its detractor in a book that created quite a stir called *The Legend of Young Poland* (*Legenda Młodej Polski*, 1909). His *volte-face* cannot be understood without delving into his philosophy. The most important of his philosophical essays were gathered in the volumes *Ideas* (*Idee*, 1910), *Voices in the Night, Studies on the Romantic Crisis of European Consciousness* (*Głosy wśród nocy*, published posthumously in 1912), and *Diary* (*Pamiętnik*, also published posthumously). Brzozowski's whole thought was a call for energy and for faith in unlimited human possibilities. Although the inspiration may have been initially Nietzschean, it was completely modified by the Polish thinker's meditation on history. Brzozowski proposed that European rationalism, which had begun in the Renaissance, reached its final conclusion in the Hegelian system; after Hegel, philosophy as taught in university classrooms was dead. At the turn of the eighteenth century new directions had been forged by the Italian philosophers of history, above all by Giambattista Vico. Proudhon and Marx were the legitimate heirs of that line. The future belonged, in Brzozowski's opinion, to a philosophy that would recognize human struggle through labor against the forces of nature as the basis of freedom. The image of the world which man possesses at a given moment is always a reflection of the state of technology at that given moment. He reproached professors, preoccupied with the questions of the theory of knowledge, for wanting to know "in what climate locomotives are born, and in what tree galoshes ripen"; the problem of subject versus object is solved exclusively through human praxis.

It would not be an exaggeration to say that the crux of Brzozowski's thought is his dialectical reappraisal of Romanticism, including Polish Romanticism. The latter, activist and voluntaristic, is, as redefined by Brzozowski, different from what is commonly signified by that term. Brzozowski, thus, revindicated certain of Mickiewicz's and Norwid's pronouncements (especially the latter's) whenever those writers contended against standard Romantic attitudes. He regarded the scientific *Weltanschauung* that infatuated the second half of the nineteenth century as the outcome of a duality born within the Romantic man. He was fond of saying that "the world of Darwin is but one of the shapes taken on by the world of Rousseau." Romanticism brought about a split between the interior world (of the soul), endowed with values, sensibility, etc., and the exterior world, cold, indifferent, cruel, and subject to the iron laws of necessity. The worshippers of science did not remove the dichotomy; they simply put the stress on the second part: "The superstition, scientific, naturalistic, intellectualistic, positivistic, etc., retains the reality of the Romantics but stripped of values; it rejects their internal world, their spiritual, otherworldly reality." How can the duality be overcome? Only through a denial, on the one hand, of the supposedly immutable laws in historical development which are indifferent to human values and, on the other, of a shameful withdrawal into one's subjectivity. Man is a maker; he makes and incarnates values ("the measure of value is value itself; the existential act is the only reality"). Brzozowski criticized Marxists who, contaminated by the natural sciences, envisaged a socialist society as the product of a necessary, somewhat metaphysically predetermined, process. To quote him again: "Whoever is a creator and inventor of value, whoever conceives the future not as a stream carrying strengthless human puppets but as a task, connects everything with value." The meaning of history, for Brzozowski, consisted in an increase of human freedom, because only in freedom could a greater quantity of human values be incarnated. This is why he ascribed such a role to a philosophy of labor. He wrote: "The only foundation of human freedom is the power of human hands over nature; if that power diminishes, the pressure of cosmic necessity over us increases." More strongly than the orthodox Marxists, he opposed mankind to Nature and to the Universe. This specific feature of man's—his creative transcending of blind Nature in which no value resides—was nearly an obsession with him. So anthropocentric was his vision that his fascination with Roman Catholicism in the last years of his life and his devotion to the memory of Cardinal Newman (which increased the number of his enemies, this time on the Left) is, perhaps, not so surprising. After all, Christianity, because of its concept of a God-man, is strongly anthropocentric. Brzozowski, of course, did not attempt to build up any "system." His thought, in constant movement, dazzling in its dialectical jumps, cannot be neatly arranged into a chain of premises and conclusions. But many of its apparent incongruities have lost their wild aspect over the tragic decades which separate us from his death. He was ever attentive to the tie that binds the lowest human being—regardless of his status or his capabilities—to the highest, and addressed his reader as a fellow sharer in the responsibility for everything that happens to mankind as a whole: "Our life is a post; if we abandon it, mankind will lose it forever." For him, all of humanity was one community uniting the dead and the living, a church on the march through millennia toward freedom.

We have presented, of course, only the sketchiest outline of Brzozowski's philosophy, but it suffices, perhaps, to explain his attack upon the *Moderna*, which covers the six hundred pages of his *Legend of Young Poland*. He detested decadence, aestheticism, and saw in the *Moderna* an acute relapse of the Romantic "illness." The writers of the *Moderna* were disgusted by Positivistic platitudes, yet in their hearts were convinced that man is in the power of a determinism discovered by Science. They took flight into their souls. But for Brzozowski this revolt was also important through its irony and melancholy, as a reaction against an ugly, bourgeois society and the so-called scientific laws invented by it. He labeled the poetry of the *Moderna* the "revolt of a flower against its roots." In Polish Romanticism of the nineteenth century, he praised the reliance on will, while in the *Moderna* he discovered a decay of the will. "Young Poland," in his eyes, was guilty of laziness and of a scornful grimace which constituted a blasphemy in the face of the holiness of life, of love, of the creative faculties of man. Literature, according to him, should strengthen in its readers such attitudes as would help to transform society—in the case of Poland, to change it into a society of "free workers" (Brzozowski's political program was marked by the thought of French syndicalism). This does not mean, though, that he was for a tendentious literature serving "causes." He searched for a much deeper connection between the features of a given society and the style of its art. He said:

The social analysis of experience as expressed in art still uses very primitive procedures. It looks for a tendency. It forgets that the social element shapes what is the most personal in us; our physical and mental physiology; it forgets that in these most personal features the structure of a given society, its hidden life, is most strongly reflected.

His disagreement with tendentiousness in literature was categorical:

Neither Byron nor Shelley did as much for the real maturing of freedom as, for instance, Robert Browning or Balzac. And it is certain that those who cannot be classified from the point of view of political struggles are the true educators of a nation, since they serve real life and not a goal consisting in organizing mirages, superstitions, and political fictions.

Within Brzozowski's lifetime, the *Legend of Young Poland* was his only book to have the effect of a bombshell. His other works were almost inaccessible, even to educated readers. Here, however, he was chastising recognized literary "greats," and a scandal always seems to attract attention. Brzozowski dealt a decisive blow to the fashionable sobbing over the cruelty of existence, and his attack paralleled, on the intellectual plane, Wyspiański's spontaneous rebellion or the instinctive mockery of humorists such as Boy-Żeleński or Nowaczyński.

Because of his frankness, his audacity, and the slanderous campaigns against him, Brzozowski was, for the vast majority of his contemporaries, an enigmatic, if not unpleasant, personality. He did not lack, however, supporters among the young intelligentsia. During his hearings in Kraków there was even an exchange of blows in the hall. Yet for several decades after his death, his work was judged as dangerous, and the notoriety attached to his person persisted in many circles. He terrified Marxists by his unorthodox views, and liberals suspected him of totalitarian, perhaps prefascist, leanings. A complete edition of his writings was begun, however, shortly before World War II; it was interrupted by the outbreak of hostilities. After World War II, in People's Poland, he was again taboo as the most ominous deviationist (had he not launched a call: "Revisionists of all churches unite"?). Yet his influence upon literary criticism has been permanent, and after 1956 he was recognized in literary circles as a major force in Polish literature of the twentieth century.

CHAPTER X

Independent Poland: 1918-1939

BACKGROUND INFORMATION

Polish political émigrés of the Romantic era longed for, in Mickiewicz's words, a "war of peoples," which would restore the independence of their homeland. While the war of 1914–1918 was not necessarily a "war of peoples" and while Poles, drafted into Russian, Austrian, and German armies, shot at one another, its outcome proved favorable to Poland as well as to a few other subjugated nations. Russia was in the throes of revolution; Germany was beaten; and the Hapsburg Empire had disintegrated. A small nucleus of Polish military forces, which had been created in 1914 by Józef Piłsudski in Kraków and had fought on the side of Austria, grew into an army that took possession of the territories abandoned by the occupants. Piłsudski, a professional revolutionary and a Socialist, had distinguished himself by his bravery in holdups of trains carrying czarist funds and as the editor of the clandestine organ of the Polish Socialist Party, *The Worker* (*Robotnik*). He spent a few years as a deportee in Siberia, only to resume his revolutionary activity at the end of his sentence. In 1905, he traveled to Japan in an effort to establish an anticzarist mutual aid agreement. While sincere in his radical convictions, he was hardly a Marxist. Brought up in Lithuania on the hereditary estate of his parents in a spirit of fidelity to the memory of the 1863 fighters, Piłsudski set as his primary goal the liberation of his country. Such a man, endowed with the magnetism of a born commander, was able to draw to his own person all the nation's energies, which until then had had an outlet only in literature. He swiftly created an efficient army, and he himself soon became a living symbol of national independence. Poland was torn by an

Formation of a New State

internal conflict between the Left, which viewed Piłsudski as their man, and the Right, which treated Piłsudski with distrust, if not outright hatred. Yet, in view of the common goal, a kind of uneasy cooperation was established, and a leader of the National Democratic (Rightist) Party, Roman Dmowski, devoted his diplomatic talents to winning recognition for Independent Poland at the Versailles Peace Conference. "The Polish Question" was one of the first to be solved at Versailles within the framework of President Wilson's Fourteen Points, but the borders of the new state gave rise to innumerable international intrigues and bickerings.

As the German army retreated from Byelorussia and the Ukraine, it left behind a void where Polish forces, advancing from the west, met Soviet forces moving in from the east. Piłsudski, however, had no intention of cooperating with either Denikin's or, later, Wrangel's counterrevolutionary Russian armies. As a faithful son of the Grand Duchy of Lithuania, he cherished federalist dreams to which a "one and indivisible" Russia, claiming all that had been former czarist territory, was a threat. Foreseeing that Russia would be weak for a long time because of the Revolution, he set out to recover the eastern territories of the old *Respublica*. In the spring of 1920, his army occupied Kiev, but soon had to retreat. As for the Bolsheviks, they cared little about territorial possessions, convinced that the Revolution would spread all over Europe. For them a war with Poland meant merely an advance toward Berlin (a city then seething with revolutionary ferment). After the Soviet army, commanded by Trotsky, had driven the Poles out of Kiev, it advanced rapidly, stretching itself out along a large front, from the Dnieper to the Vistula. A major battle took place in August 1920 on the outskirts of Warsaw. Profiting from a strategic blunder on the part of the Soviet command, Piłsudski executed the classical maneuver of outflanking the enemy and inflicted a crushing defeat on the Soviet forces, which in a few days were pushed back several hundred kilometers. The peace treaty of Riga (1921) delineated a border between the Soviet Union and Poland that cut through the middle of ethnically mixed areas with large Byelorussian and Ukrainian-speaking populations on both sides.

The first national assembly, which issued from free elections, voted a constitution defining Poland as a republic with a neat division of the legislative, executive, and judiciary powers. The system was modeled upon France's, and the unfortunate result was a similar proliferation of small political parties. Piłsudski held the provisional title of chief of state. After having coped with the border question, he withdrew from public life. The first president of the country, Gabriel Narutowicz, was considered, however, his man. He was elected in 1922 by the votes of Socialists, liberals, and national minorities. The hatred of the Right for this man was such that he was soon assassinated by a nationalist fanatic.

The parliament (composed of two chambers) and the constantly changing cabinets faced tremendous tasks. The partitions had left their imprint in the form of different laws and different administrative systems in each of the three parts of the state. Money was not stable, and Poland went through severe inflation. Large areas had been devastated by war. In spite of interparty quarreling, of which the Diet was the scene, most of the problems were solved in a very short time. Not, however, those which inhered in the very economic structure of society. The extent of industrialization in the country was insufficient to absorb the potential labor force from the countryside, which was disastrously overpopulated. Foreign capital, which controlled many of the key industries, was invested unwillingly and at high interest. The price gap between industrial products and agricultural products was enormous, and the majority of the population, employed in agriculture (around 80 per cent), lived on a level of bare subsistence. This caused a mass migration of workers abroad, mostly to France. In addition to economic difficulties, a very high percentage of national minorities, who spoke Yiddish, Byelorussian, Ukrainian, or German at home, led to acute conflicts aggravated by the fanaticism and intolerance of the powerful National Democratic Party. Relations with neighboring countries carried the threat of future frictions. The peace treaty of Versailles had not conceded Gdańsk (Danzig) to Poland; instead, a "free city" of Danzig had been created, so that the Poles had to build a new seaport, Gdynia, on a small strip of the Baltic coast in their possession. Both the corridor separating East Prussia from Germany proper and the "question of Danzig" were to serve Hitler as a pretext to unleash World War II. Silesia, which had been the scene of guerrilla warfare between Polish and German units in the wake of the First World War, was cut in two by a plebiscite held in circumstances unfavorable to Poland. In 1920 Czechoslovakia took for herself the region of Cieszyn (Tesin), which action Poland was to repay in a dishonorable way in 1938 at the moment when Czechoslovakia was succumbing to Hitler's troops. In the northeast, Poland observed a common border with the newly independent Baltic states, Lithuania and Latvia; but the Lithuanians claimed Wilno (Vilnius) on the grounds that it was the centuries-old capital of the Grand Duchy and therefore, according to them, was being retained by the Poles illegally. The question was a thorny one, as the majority of inhabitants spoke Polish; and the outcome of it all was a break of diplomatic relations between the two countries. The proximity of the Soviet Union hardly facilitated the tasks of the Polish leaders. The Polish Communist Party, born out of the Social

Democratic Party of the Polish Kingdom and of Lithuania, was very unpopular, since it was viewed as representing the interests of Russia. Its status was at first semilegal, then illegal, and its following very limited; but in the eastern provinces of the state the Communist Parties of Western Byelorussia and Western Ukraine operated from just across the border. They found considerable response, owing to a newly awakened nationalism in those territories. In the Ukrainian-speaking provinces, the Communist Party competed with a strong Ukrainian nationalist movement which looked to Germany for inspiration and alliance. One may well wonder how, in those conditions, Poland could get through several years of relative internal peace and normalcy.

The multitude of small political parties, the instability of the governments (which fell every few months if not weeks) brought Piłsudski out of his retirement and convinced him of the necessity of intervening. In 1926, that part of the army supporting him took power in Warsaw after a short exchange of gunfire with the troops who remained faithful to the president. Piłsudski, however, was not cut out for the role of dictator. He did not envision an authoritarian rule, and was rather inclined to consider himself as a kind of "lord protector." His *Putsch* was welcomed by Socialists, liberals, and even a section of the Communists, as it seemed to present a barrier to the encroachments of the powerful Right. In the beginning, their hopes seemed to be fulfilled, but soon Piłsudski revealed himself as a man of whims and resentments, acting more by instinct than by any clearly formulated principles. He founded a concentration camp, where he sent several members of the Diet. He appointed his beloved officers to positions of power and, thus, paved the way for rule by a military junta. Later, these so-called "colonels" curtailed the freedom of political parties and, by means of a "national front," rigged elections. As long as Piłsudski was alive, they were hindered in their maneuvers, but after his death in 1935, they made an opening to the Right and pursued a policy that veered more and more toward fascism. Contamination from neighboring Germany was responsible for anti-Semitic regulations, for instance, at the universities. Nevertheless, in spite of an ominous political climate in the years 1935–1939, Poland was not yet totalitarian, and the opposition press vitriolically denounced the abuses of the ruling junta.

Piłsudski's Putsch

A competent and energetic teaching profession succeeded in rapidly organizing a unified school system composed of elementary schools, eight-year *gymnasia* (after which the student passed a centrally administered *baccalauréat* exam), and universities. While the elimination of illiteracy in the countryside was making swift progress, economic difficulties, in practice, closed the doors of the *gymnasia* to

Education and Social Reforms

peasant and working-class youth. This flaw was hardly compensated for by the high level of research institutes and of academic instruction. Besides schools teaching in the Polish language, there were many that taught in Yiddish, Hebrew, and German, although very few taught in the languages spoken by the majority of the population in the eastern provinces, i.e., Ukrainian and Byelorussian.

The efforts of the teachers were paralleled by those of a traditionally strong professional group, namely, men of the theater. They founded a network of repertory theaters and, later on, a theatrical school in Warsaw on a university level (The State Institute of Theatrical Art). A diploma from that school was required from all candidates for the profession.

The agrarian reform voted by the Diet in 1920 envisaged the parceling out of estates over a certain size among the peasants, with compensation to the owners. Its implementation was very slow; besides, no amount of land could have absorbed the masses of poor peasants forced to remain in the countryside, owing to lack of industrial development in the towns. A strong trade-union movement resulted in very progressive legislation on social security and medical care. Yet agricultural laborers were, in practice, excluded from its benefits. All together, if the average standard of living in Poland was lower than in neighboring Czechoslovakia with its more balanced and more industrial economy, it was still bearable because of the low cost of food. Poland, however, was sorely afflicted by the American economic crisis of 1929, and for a few years there were great numbers of unemployed living on doles. The major problem, though, was still "hidden unemployment" in the countryside.

The Dividing Line   The joy, even euphoria, that followed the recovery of independence in 1918 was faithfully noted by literature. Around 1930, the tone changed. The economic crisis, the violation of the constitution by the military junta, the emergence of fascist groupings on the Right, propagating anti-Semitism and announcing "a night of long knives" for "Jews and intellectuals," converged with Hitler's grab for power in neighboring Germany. Marxist publications began to attract writers, although few felt able to place their trust in Stalin. The Communist Party of Poland, considered a foreign agent and, thus, illegal, was given a low rating in Moscow because of its efforts to adapt itself to specific local conditions; its leaders were called to Moscow in 1938 and executed by order of Stalin, while the party itself was disbanded under the pretext that it was infested with traitors. In intellectual circles a feeling of impotence and presentiments of an imminent European catastrophe prevailed. It is no wonder, then, that the literature of the thirties was marked by apocalyptic or humorously macabre visions.

POETRY

"*Skamander*"

At the end of World War I, several eminent writers of "Young Poland" were alive and active. Such was the case of Jan Kasprowicz, of Bolesław Leśmian, of Stefan Żeromski, and of Władysław Reymont. Tadeusz Boy-Żeleński and Karol Irzykowski were to remain the most prized pens in literary publicism for two more decades. But new voices were already heard in 1918. These voices belonged to a group of young poets who read their poems in a Warsaw literary café called "Under the Picador" and who were published in a periodical, *Pro Arte et Studio*; in January 1920 they issued their own review, which they called *Skamander*. The title referred to the river of Troy in Wyspiański's *Acropolis*, which "glittered with a Vistula wave." The young poets emitted a shout of triumph: they were the first generation of free and independent Poland, but, above all, they were free from commitment. Poetry, which had had to serve a cause for so long in Poland, could at last recover its lightheartedness and could perform a spontaneous dance without recourse to compulsive justifications. One of those poets, Jan Lechoń, in his poem "Herostrates," exclaimed:

> And in the spring let me see spring, not Poland.

> A wiosną niechaj wiosnę, nie Polskę, zobaczę.

Equally exuberant and triumphant was their manifesto published in the first issue of *Skamander*. Here are some fragments:

We believe deeply in the present, we feel we all are its children. We understand there is nothing easier than to hate this "today" of ours, not acknowledged by anybody as his own. We do not wish to pretend that evil is nonexistent, but our love is stronger than all evil: we love the present with a strong first love. We are and we want to be its children. And this day is not only a day of the seven plagues, it is also a day when a new world is being born. That new world has not yet emerged from the earth; its shape is still a guess, but the trembling we feel under our feet proves it is rising already. . . .

We cannot hate the world, the earth is dear to us and we do not disavow it because by doing so we would disavow ourselves. We are bound too strongly to this blood-drenched globe to be able to fly away into realms of a "beautiful illusion." We believe that the kingdom of spirit is a kingdom of this world, that it will, must be, of this world.

Referring to the Polish Romantics, the manifesto says:

When raising the old claims, we are aware that we are a hundred years older, that our words are different though they sound the same, that new times will see and must see in a symbol another meaning. We are aware that owing to a turn of history we have to incarnate what those men of the past announced. . . .

We want to be poets of the present and this is our faith and our whole "program." We are not tempted by sermonizing, we do not want to convert anybody, but we want to conquer, to enrapture, to influence the hearts of men, we want to be their laughing and their weeping. . . .

We know that the greatness of art does not appear in subjects, but in the forms through which it is expressed, in that most light and elusive game of colors, of words transforming a rough experience into a work of art. We want to be honest workers in that game, through our efforts hidden under frivolous shapes. . . .

We believe unshakably in the sanctity of a good rhyme, in the divine origin of rhythm, in revelation through images born in ecstasy and through shapes chiseled by work.

The belief in the "sanctity of a good rhyme" indicates the rather traditional leanings of the "Skamander" group. Perhaps because of that it won more favor with the reading public than other competing groups. *The Source (Zdrój)*, a journal attracting writers related to "Young Poland," on the one hand, and those related to German expressionism, on the other, seemed too verbose and too chaotic. Warsaw futurists (or, rather, Dadaists) such as Aleksander Wat and Anatol Stern, who played with "liberated words"—i.e., liberated from the tyranny of syntax—were too odd. "Skamander" poets responded well to the demands of the public. Into their verse they introduced words taken from everyday life, colloquial idioms, and an urban setting. They were lyrical, tender, and ironic toward themselves. In all of this they differed from their solemn predecessors of "Young Poland." Analogies with poets in Western Europe or America would be misleading. The "Skamandrites" were attached to Polish poetry of the past, especially to the Romantics, but at the same time, they were cosmopolitan, open to both Russian and French influences. (They belonged to the same generation as the Russian Acmeists, and certain similarities may be found between the two.) We have been speaking of a group, but it embraced men of strong individuality who eventually went their separate ways. They are usually put under the same label, however, even if their initial alliance was relatively short-lived.

Born into a Jewish, middle-class family in the industrial city of *Julian Tuwim (1894–1953)* Łódź, Julian Tuwim began to write poetry a few years before World War I, encouraged by a poet whom he admired, Leopold Staff. As a student of Warsaw University, he provoked a scandal by publishing a brutal poem, "Spring," obviously inspired by his reading of Rimbaud. From the start, he revealed himself as a virtuoso of lyricism and humor. He produced numerous texts for light theatrical revues and cabarets, which earned him a good deal of money and, thus, left him time for more serious pursuits. He is also the author of delightful poems for children. As a poet, he went through a long evolution. Drunk with life (and the entire group worshipped Life), bursting with energy and jokes, he liked to appear in print as a prankster; for instance, he published in 1921 (together with his colleague, Antoni Słonimski) *The Busy Bee, A Farmer's Almanac*, liable to drive any real farmer insane. With age he became a poet of metaphysical terror veiled under linguistic brilliance. A permanent feature of Tuwim's poetry was what one might call his passion as a hunter in pursuit of words. He delved into dictionaries, collected rare books written by madmen and graphomaniacs, experimented with roots of words (a whole poem as well as its title, "Słopiewnie," conveys no meaning other than an aura of some invented proto-Slavic language). This sensual, amorous relationship with word stems, their prefixes and suffixes, makes Tuwim somewhat akin to Leśmian.

The devil was another fascination of Tuwim's, and he appears often in his poems. Perhaps the poet looked upon himself as a little possessed or as a half-joking, half-tragic demon. In any case, he not only gathered works on demonology but compiled a book himself, from old sources, on witches and devils in Poland. Fond of everything bizarre, he loved provincial towns, their barbershops and apothecaries, restaurants in provincial railroad stations, posters and illustrations from the 1880s, amulets, talismans, miraculous elixirs. His first volumes—*Ambushing God* (*Czyhanie na Boga*, 1918), *Dancing Socrates* (*Sokrates tańczący*, 1920), *The Seventh Autumn* (*Siódma jesień*, 1922), *The Fourth Book of Poems* (*Wierszy tom czwarty*, 1923), *Words in Blood* (*Słowa we krwi*, 1926)—were an assault on a reality that was unbearably palpable, and a pervasive dream of a word so intense that it would be one with the thing it designated. This was also a dream of identifying himself with what can be touched, smelled, seen. In a poem, "Grass," he says:

> Grass, grass up to my knees!
> Grow up to the sky
> So that there won't seem to be
> Any you or I.

So that I will turn all green
And blossom to my bones,
So that my words won't come between
Your freshness and my own.

So that for the two of us
There will be one name:
Either for both of us—grass,
Or both of us—tuwim.*

Trawo, trawo, do kolan!
Podnieś mi się do czoła,
Żeby myślom nie było
Ani mnie, ani pola.

Żebym ja się uzielił
Przekwiecił do rdzenia kości
I już się nie oddzielił
Słowami od twej świeżości.

Abym tobie i sobie
Jednym imieniem mówił:
Albo obojgu—trawa,
Albo obojgu—tuwim.

But Tuwim is untranslatable in all his poems, not only in those poems where, true to the macaronic tradition of the Polish Baroque, he uses Latin to rhyme with Polish, for instance, in his poem about frog Latinists who croak "qua-qua" and "quam-quam."

In his mature phase, which includes the volumes *Czarnolas Speech* (*Rzecz czarnoleska*, 1929—a reference to the estate where Jan Kochanowski lived), *Gypsy Bible and Other Poems* (*Biblia cygańska i inne wiersze*, 1933), and *The Burning Essence* (*Treść gorejąca*, 1936), he achieved a classical conciseness, along with the metallic ring of his line. He was an excellent translator of Russian poets, not only of contemporaries like Boris Pasternak, but, above all, of Pushkin, under whose spell he had fallen completely. Tuwim's admiration for the great Russian poet went together with his love for Polish poetry of the Renaissance and for Mickiewicz's *Pan Tadeusz*. This classical framework, however, served only to make more poignant his obsession with the precariousness of all things human.

Tuwim had an ambiguous attitude toward society. A liberal, and an enemy of the anti-Semitic Right (which he derided in many poems), he showered irony on the bourgeois:

* Translated by Lawrence Davis.

Horrible dwellings. In horrible dwellings
Horribly live horrible dwellers.

Straszne mieszkania. W strasznych mieszkaniach
Strasznie mieszkają straszni mieszczanie.

But, in fact, his denunciations were addressed to all human society as such. Tuwim was a mystic confronted with a vanity of vanities built upon an abyss. In him dwelt the fear of a society seen as Plato's Great Beast. However, it was political anger that forced Tuwim to write his powerful long poem, *Ball at the Opera* (*Bal w operze*, written 1936, published in its entirety only after World War II). Here, Tuwim's abilities as an author of light verse, as a satirist, and as a tragic poet converge. The fury in his description of generals, diplomats, bankers, whores, and plainclothesmen at a ball in the palace of a fascist dictator, Pantokrator, is matched by the nervous dazzling rhythm of his verse. Toward dawn, as the ball reaches its height, the scene moves to the outskirts of the capital (Warsaw), where peasant carts carrying fresh produce to town pass city sanitation trucks on their way to dispose of sewage in the country. It is an apocalyptic poem where Tuwim's horror of a corrupt society's filthy doings fuses with a foreboding of genocide. Originally, the poem bore a motto from the Apocalypse of St. John, and the end of the ball is nothing other than the end of the world.

After Poland's defeat by the Nazis in 1939, Tuwim managed to escape abroad; he lived in Rio de Janeiro and New York and while in exile, wrote a very extended poem—a whole book in verse—*Polish Flowers* (*Kwiaty polskie*, published in 1949). It is a rare instance in our century of a work set in iambic verse with a plot interspersed with digressions and reminiscences from childhood. Its Romantic sources are obvious: Słowacki's *Beniowski*, Pushkin's *Eugene Onegin*. A nostalgic exile, Tuwim turned back to his native Łódź and to the Polish countryside as he remembered it from childhood and adolescence. Although invaluable as a supplement to and a commentary on Tuwim's whole poetic work, it is inferior to some of his short poems and to the *Ball at the Opera*.

After the war, Tuwim returned to Warsaw and declared in prose and in verse his new-found loyalty to People's Poland; but all Polish critics agree today that he wrote nothing more of value. Between the two wars, his position in Poland was that of number-one poet. Although some of his verses were subsequently overshadowed by new schools and literary fashions, there can be no doubt as to his high place in Polish literature.

Son of a Polish white-collar worker in the Ukraine, Iwaszkiewicz went through high school there; from 1912 to 1918 he studied law

Jarosław Iwaszkiewicz (1894–1980)

at the University of Kiev and music at the local conservatory. Ukrainian landscapes, avant-garde music, and his readings, particularly of Oscar Wilde and Vyacheslav Ivanov (both as poet and as essayist), left strong imprints on his early youth. In 1918, he migrated to Warsaw. His first works were stories in a poetic prose imbued with a sensuous perception of the Ukraine and its many Levantine aspects: *Escape to Bagdad* (*Ucieczka do Bagdadu*, written 1916–1918), *Legends and Demeter* (*Legendy i Demeter*, written 1917–1918). Exoticism, or, more accurately, a propensity for blending the cultures of Greece, of the Middle East, of Eastern and Western Europe, can be traced throughout much of his writing.

His early poems puzzled everybody by strangely combining the technique of an ironic madrigal with a rush of colors and sounds. In this, Iwaszkiewicz resembled some "Young Poland" poets such as Miciński; there was also a touch of Wilde's aestheticism and of Russian symbolism. *Octostichs* (*Oktostychy*, 1919) was a daring experiment with metrics and assonance. *Dionysiacs* (*Dionizje*, 1922) was, perhaps, the only truly expressionistic volume of poems published in Poland after World War I. In these poems, the myth of Dionysus, so crucial for European literature of the turn of the century, found a violent, very personal expression, for it was deeply engrained in Iwaszkiewicz's personality, in his internal conflicts and in his eroticism. Fantastic, musical landscapes of colors, wild and unexpected breaks in rhythm, dissonant tones of ferocity and sweetness in this volume destined Iwaszkiewicz to be a "poet's poet" and, thus, less popular with the public than others of his group. But none of them could rival his voracity for color and his ability to re-create an aura of once-seen but half-forgotten, almost magical, lands and cities. Although reproached for his intuitionist, nonintellectual, and nonsocial art, he fascinated several younger poets. With his early publications he had already left a mark upon the history of Polish poetry.

His maturity brought poems reflecting not only his deeper internal experience, but also his travels in Western Europe, his preoccupation with the mythical aspects of cultures (two mythical centers for his imagination are Sicily and Venice), and his fascination with certain Western European poets like Stefan George and Jean Cocteau. Those were *The Book of Day and the Book of Night* (*Księga dnia i księga nocy*, 1929), *Return to Europe* (*Powrót do Europy*, 1931), *Summer 1932* (*Lato 1932*, 1933—a small volume of metaphysical poems considered as his peak), and *Another Life* (*Inne życie*, 1938).

For the larger public, Iwaszkiewicz was primarily the author of novels. The early ones, strongly autobiographical, meandering, and subjective, could be compared to Russian symbolist prose and to the poetic prose of the French literary vanguard of the time. *Hilary, Son of a Bookkeeper* (*Hilary, syn buchaltera*, 1923) refers to the author himself, an *émigré* from the Ukraine, in Warsaw. *The Moon Rises* (*Księżyc wschodzi*, 1924) is a sensual story of vacations on a Ukrainian estate, on the eve of turbulent historical events. The subject of young men and young girls in summer was very much to Iwaszkiewicz's liking, and with it, he proved, more than once, his master's hand, choosing it again later on for his long story, *Maidens from Wilko* (*Panny z Wilka*, 1933). His huge historical novel, *Red Shields* (*Czerwone tarcze*, 1934), completely ignored the traditional technique of meticulous reconstruction based on documents. On the contrary, this is a fantasy, a lyrical report on the adventures of a Polish crusader, a medieval prince, who visits all of Europe, including Sicily, is attracted by Arabic civilization in the Holy Land, and returns home, where he loses in his struggle for the crown. Prolific, endowed with a rare vitality, Iwaszkiewicz also wrote about music and provided his friend, the composer Karol Szymanowski, with librettos, besides contributing plays to the theater: *Summer in Nohant* (*Lato w Nohant*, 1936) is built around an episode from the life of Chopin; *Masquerade* (*Maskarada*, 1938), around the final episode in the life of Pushkin.

During the war, Iwaszkiewicz was the only "Skamander" member who remained in Poland, and his home near Warsaw was a meeting place for intellectuals engaged in the underground movement. At that time he wrote some of his finest long stories such as *Battle on the Plain of Sedgemoor*, about the Monmouth rebellion against James II in England, and *Mother Joan of the Angels*, based on documents relating to a seventeenth-century French convent (in Loudun) whose nuns were possessed by the devil. In the latter story, Iwaszkiewicz took no more than the initial idea from the sources; he shifted the scene to a convent in the eastern territories of the old *Respublica* and gave the characters Polish names. (Later on, Aldous Huxley made use of the same sources for his *Devils of Loudun*.)

After the war, Iwaszkiewicz became one of the leading literary personalities in People's Poland; he served as president of the Writers' Union and has had the merit of editing, since 1956, a literary review, *Creative Work* (*Twórczość*), a high-caliber monthly. Several volumes of stories, poems, and criticism that came from his pen during this postwar period did not hinder him from producing a three-volume novel, *Glory and Vainglory* (*Sława i chwała*, Vol. I, 1956; Vol. II, 1958; Vol. III, 1962), where his characters, representatives of the intelligentsia, are conducted through several decades of wars and social changes. It is doubtful, though, whether such a socially oriented enterprise suited his talent. But even here, he remained true to his belief in the ever-renewing and beneficent *élan* of Life. One of his poems, "To My Wife" ("Do żony"), may serve to illustrate the hunger for life and an ecstatic immersion in its current so typical of him as a man and as a writer:

> When, tired by beauty that everyday anew
> I caught into my ears and eyes greedily open,
> I die, do not weep. I will go sated
> With life which is great, difficult, and tempestuous.
> A deity, a running fire in my limbs
> Will fly away or will dissolve.
> The heart so strongly beating will stand still.
> This voice will then become a frozen letter.
> You may then feel that I left behind
> No more than fragments of insufficient words.
> But you should know that often there were hours
> When speech was strangled in my too narrow chest.
> The world was far too beautiful to give my poems
> Only to you. O my beloved,
> I looked into unconfinable spaces,
> I was transported by unconfinable feelings.
> Yet when people down here and stars in the sky
> Rushed through my heart in their endless swirling,
> You endured, faithful like water, unchangeable,
> The only one in the world who loved me.

> Strudzony pięknem, którem co dzień łowił
> W rozwarte chciwie uszy i źrenice,
> Gdy umrę, nie płacz. Usnę, syty życia,
> Które jest wielkie, trudne i burzliwe.
> Bóstwo, co ogniem przez me członki biegło,
> Odleci wyżej albo się rozwieje;
> Serce bijące tak żywo—zastygnie,
> A głos umarłą stanie się literą.
> Wtedy pomyślisz sobie, że zbyt drobne
> Zostają po mnie ułomki wyrazów.
> Lecz wiedz, że nieraz godziny zachwytu
> Słowo dławiły mi w piersi za ciasnej.
> Świat był zbyt piękny, abym tylko tobie
> Oddał me wiersze. O najukochańsza,
> W nieogarnione patrzałem przestrzenie,
> Nieogarnione brały mnie uczucia.
> Lecz gdy tu ludzie, tam gwiazdy na niebie
> Serce me wiecznym pruły kołowrotem—
> Ty trwałaś wierna jak woda, niezmienna,
> Jedyna w świecie, która mnie kochałaś.

Iwaszkiewicz's many-sidedness is also visible in his translations. One of the best to render Arthur Rimbaud into Polish, he also translated a few plays of Paul Claudel's, a novel of André Gide's, a play of Jean Giraudoux's, Andersen's fairy tales (from the Danish), as well as some Tolstoy and Chekhov stories.

A native of Warsaw, from a Jewish family that produced several *Antoni* scientists and medical doctors, Antoni Słonimski completed his studies *Słonimski* at the Academy of Fine Arts in Warsaw; then for a while he lived *(1895–1976)* in Munich and Paris. In 1913, he made his literary debut. His first volume of sonnets (1918) revealed his fondness for a chiseled, somewhat Parnassian form. But he differed from his colleagues in his temperament, that of a pure intellectual, always maintaining a distance between his feelings and their expression either in poetry or in prose. While the "Skamander" poets reacted to current events rather haphazardly, Słonimski, a rationalist, a liberal, a pacifist, could well be described as an heir to the progressive Positivists. Not by chance was he attracted by English writers such as H. G. Wells. His poetry, even though he often wrote pure lyrics, cannot be separated from his commitment as a liberal fighter. Bolesław Prus had been a friend of the Słonimski family, and Antoni, having grown up to be a writer himself, borrowed Prus's title, *The Weekly Chronicle*, for his own column, which ran for several years in a leading literary weekly, *The Literary News* (*Wiadomości literackie*). Feared by obscurantists, whom he scathed with ridicule, he, like Prus before him, used trivial events, theatrical spectacles, or clippings from the press as points of departure for his witty arguments.

Słonimski's poetry confirms our proposal of 1930 as a dividing line. Before that date, a joyous traveler, he brought back from his trips to Palestine and to Brazil poems saturated with sun and sea: *Road to the East* (*Droga na wschód*, 1924), *From a Long Journey* (*Z dalekiej podróży*, 1926). Later on, a new somber tone in his poetry registered the ominous signs of a world cataclysm: the economic crisis, the burning of surplus wheat for which there was no market, mass unemployment, rising totalitarianism, and the threat of war. When the Japanese were conquering Manchuria, when "a fat jester roared from the Capitoline, 'Romani,'" when newsreels showed military maneuvers and suicide leaps from the fifteenth floor, Słonimski addressed posterity: "I earnestly ask you to remember that I was against" ["Bardzo proszę pamiętać, że ja byłem przeciw"]. In 1932 he visited the Soviet Union, and his articles from that journey satisfied neither the admirers of the Russian Revolution nor its detractors. In Leningrad he met his cousin, a zealous Communist, but Słonimski himself deemed it more honest to be Hamlet. The following poem, "Hamletism" ("Hamletyzm"), was the fruit of that encounter:

Long did I look into the dark eyes of my brother,
Into eyes well-known, although the face was not,
As he spoke, as he cautiously weighed out each word
In Leningrad, on somber Marat Street.

Michał, Aunt Fanny's, Uncle Ludwik's son,
Names which awake the wistful taste of childhood,
Sternly and gravely concludes the discussion.
And yet he's my cousin. A very close relation.

Magnitogorsk and Urals. With us or against.
Stalin, the Party, vast, incessant toil.
The Five-Year Plan. As children five years old
We used to exchange letters. Michał looks ill.

Light of young eyes, yet hair untimely gray.
Calm, but intent, faithful in what you do,
You serve and want to serve your country well
And you say: "Good night, prince"—"Good night, Horatio."*

Długo patrzałem w ciemne oczy mego brata,
W oczy znajome, choć na obcej twarzy,
Gdy mówił, gdy ostrożnie każde słowo ważył.
W Leningradzie na smutnej ulicy Marata.

Michał, syn cioci Fanny i stryja Ludwika.
Imiona, które budzą smak dzieciństwa rzewny,
Surowo i poważnie dyskusję zamyka.
To przecież brat stryjeczny. Bardzo bliski krewny.

Magnitogorsk i Ural. Z nami albo przeciw.
Stalin i partia. Ciągły trud, niezmierny.
Plan pięcioletni. Jako pięcioletnie dzieci
Pisywaliśmy listy. Michał jest mizerny.

Blask młodych oczu przeczy przedwczesnej siwiźnie.
Spokojny, lecz namiętny i wierny swej pracy,
Służysz i pragniesz wiernie służyć swej ojczyźnie,
Mówisz: "Dobranoc, książe"—"Dobranoc, Horacy."

He was aware of the madness seizing Germany, and his poem "To the Germans" is really a poem about Archimedes, who stands for intellectuals of all times: Archimedes was tracing his figures on the sand when the Romans conquered Syracuse, and he said to a Roman mercenary, "Do not touch my circles," only to be killed in the next instant.

* Translated by C. M. and P. D. Scott.

As a weapon against the forces of darkness, which were strong in Poland too, Słonimski chose comedy. For instance, his play *Family* (*Rodzina*), staged in 1933, has a plot centered around the figures of two brothers, young totalitarians. One is a fervent Communist, the other an enthusiast of "Aryan purity." At the climax, both receive an unpleasant surprise when they discover that they are the sons of a prosperous Jewish miller, and, thus, neither proletarian nor "Aryan."

Shortly before the war, a satirical novel of anticipation by Słonimski appeared: *Two Ends of the World* (*Dwa końce świata*, 1937), which, unfortunately, proved to be all too prophetic. In the novel, Warsaw is utterly destroyed by the bombs of a dictator by the name of Retlich (read in reverse, it approximates "Hitler"). Out of all its inhabitants only two remain alive, but when they meet amid the ruins of the city, they cannot find a common language, as one is a sophisticated Jewish boy (a former bookstore salesman) and the other is a moronic brute from a workers' district who speaks an unintelligible slang. Eventually, an army of Lapps in their reindeerskins occupies Warsaw and puts both of them into a concentration camp.

During the war, Słonimski, escaping the Nazis, went to France, then to England, where he lived until 1951. After his return to Poland during the Stalinist period, he was forced to remain on the sidelines, but since around 1956, he has been in the forefront as leader of a liberal coterie of writers.

It has been said that every one of Słonimski's poems can be "translated" into prose, so logical is his syntax and so prominent is a "story." Yet, he is not a journalist in verse; he is a true descendant of the Polish Romantics, able to combine commitment with inspiration. He is distinguished from the Neo-Romantics of the *Moderna* by his sober colloquial idiom. His metrical inventiveness made him one of the best craftsmen of "syllabotonic" verse. Though rhymed in a traditional way, his lines were often quoted by younger poets who abandoned both rhymes and regular meters. In his old age he often abandoned rhyme himself, but his attachment to "syllabotonic" patterns has persisted. His volumes of poetry published after World War II are true to his vocation of a pacifist and of a somewhat melancholy and sentimental humanist.

"Skamander's" youthful buoyancy was perhaps best exemplified by Kazimierz Wierzyński. Son of a railway employee from southern Poland, he studied at the universities of Kraków and Vienna, made his literary debut in 1913, fought during World War I in Piłsudski's legion, then, as a draftee in the Austrian army was taken prisoner by the Russians. He spent three years in Russia. At the café "Under the Picador" and in the review *Skamander*, he conquered the public with poems that were pure shouts of joy. (He celebrated "the green

Kazimierz Wierzyński (1894–1969)

in my head where violets grow.") The titles of his first volumes give an idea of his themes: *Spring and Wine* (*Wiosna i wino*, 1919), *Sparrows on the Roof* (*Wróble na dachu*, 1921), *Diary of Love* (*Pamiętnik miłości*, 1925). A robust young man, well built and handsome, he was one of the few European poets who wrote odes about athletics. A volume of his, *The Olympic Laurel* (*Laur olympijski*, 1927), which includes titles such as "One Hundred Meters," "The Pole Vault," "The Discus Thrower," won first prize at a literary contest of the Ninth Olympic Games in Amsterdam.

Around 1930 his work began to voice his growing concern with public issues, and through its high-strung rhetoric was a return to the Polish Romantic heritage. The new note of bitterness in his volumes was that of a writer who, more than anybody in the "Skamander" group, remained loyal to his adolescent devotion to Piłsudski. Here, again, the titles are significant: *Fanatical Songs* (*Pieśni fanatyczne*, 1929), *Bitter Harvest* (*Gorzki urodzaj*, 1933), *Tragic Freedom* (*Wolność tragiczna*, 1936). After the outbreak of the war he emigrated first to France, then through Portugal and Brazil to the United States, where he settled. His wartime poems testify even more strongly to a return to the patriotic commitment of the Romantics.

His book in prose, *The Life and Death of Chopin*, published in New York in 1949, was a best seller in the United States. In the difficult predicament of a poet in exile, deprived of a public in his native tongue, Wierzyński seemed to draw strength from an intimate contact with nature on the American east coast. His sixties brought a resurgence of creativity, and his late, short lyrics are among his best. He somewhat relaxed in them and abandoned the self-imposed discipline of traditional meters. Throughout his career he remained attached to the image of a poet as a man who writes under the dictation of a demon. One of his late poems, "A Word to Orphists" ("Słowo do orfeistów"), catches the attitude well:

> Who is standing behind me I don't know, but I know he is there,
> What he is saying I don't know, but I repeat after him,
> I don't hear the words, but I am able to write them down
> And this is so important that I ask no questions.

> Kto za mną staje, nie wiem, ale wiem że tam jest,
> Co mówi, nie wiem, ale powtarzam to za nim,
> Nie słyszę tych słów, ale napisać je umiem
> I to jest tak ważne że o nic więcej nie pytam.

Maria Pawlikowska-Jasnorzewska (1894–1945)   Born in Kraków, the daughter of the well-known painter Wojciech Kossak, Maria Pawlikowska-Jasnorzewska grew up in an artistic and intellectual milieu, and after the appearance of her first volume of poems, *Fiddle-Faddle* (*Niebieskie migdały*, 1922), she was warmly accepted by "Skamander" poets as one of their own. Subsequently, *Pink Magic* (*Różowa magia*, 1924), *Kisses* (*Pocałunki*, 1926), *Dancing* (1927), and *Fan* (*Wachlarz*, 1927) won her the position of best Polish poetess. Her apparently effortless verse, set in a filigreed form, often not unlike Japanese haiku, gives the impression of playfulness, where the author toys with themes such as a woman's loves, dresses, balls, disillusionments. But, in fact, Pawlikowska had a sophisticated mind, nourished by extensive readings in philosophy, and underneath the frivolity one can discern a pessimistic and gravely serious outlook. This is even more characteristic of her later volumes— *Paris* (1928), *A Profile of the White Lady* (*Profil białej damy*, 1930), *Raw Silk* (*Surowy jedwab*, 1932), *A Sleeping Crew* (*Śpiąca załoga*, 1933), *A Ballet of Bindweeds* (*Balet powojów*, 1935), and *Crystallizations* (*Krystalizacje*, 1937)—where, in a most poignant manner, she expresses her obsession with the transience of the flesh. That she was, in her sly way, a philosophical poet did not hinder her from writing several comedies. During the war she emigrated to France, then to England, where her latent pessimism, aggravated by her brooding over the catastrophe of her country and of Europe, as well as by her illness, resulted in a few moving poems before she died in Manchester.

The youngest of the "Skamandrites," Leszek Serafinowicz (Jan Lechoń is his pen name) was born in Warsaw into a poor white-collar worker's family, went through high school there, and studied literature at the university. He published two volumes of poems when he was fourteen and fifteen years old (1913, 1914) that he later destroyed. In the café "Under the Picador," his recitations were permeated with a wry, caustic humor. His volumes published after World War I—*A Crimson Poem* (*Karmazynowy poemat*, 1920), *The Silver and the Black* (*Srebrne i czarne*, 1924)—were acclaimed as revelations of an accomplished master. The first comprises a series of variations on themes related to recent Polish history in which Lechoń's skill, obviously learned from the Romantics, makes for rare limpidity and control over meter; one of these poems collides, however, with the others in that volume, which is so seriously concerned with public issues: "Herostrates" extolls rebellion against any form of commitment. The second volume sings, in equally impeccable verse, of love, death, and the seven deadly sins. A poem on Beatrice, which best summarizes Lechoń's tormented personality, ends with the following words:

Jan Lechoń (1899–1956)

> There is no earth no heaven no abyss and no hell.
> There is only Beatrice. And she doesn't exist.

Nie ma nieba ni ziemi, otchłani ni piekła,
Jest tylko Beatrycze. I właśnie jej nie ma.

Later on, following the path of Lechoń's destiny, his readers often remembered those lines; they might be the key to many of his misfortunes. Eaten up by skepticism as to all values and ideas, with his hopelessly involved personal life, with the premature fame of a genius, he tried to keep up his high standards, but was too proud and too critical to publish anything. During the long years of his silence, he wore the mask of a diplomat, serving as attaché at the Polish Embassy in Paris. After France's defeat, he left, together with Julian Tuwim, via Brazil for the United States. The war untied the knots that had bound him, and he published several poems in *émigré* periodicals; the author of "Herostrates" had reverted to a style of commitment proper to the 1830s. Only a few poems of his last phase, the most personal and the most desperate, matched his early volumes, however. He killed himself in 1956 by jumping from a New York skyscraper. In the whole of modern Polish poetry, his crystalline, cold verse seems to come the closest to classical rigor. Lechoń had an unbounded admiration for Mickiewicz, and in his craft one can always recognize the ear attuned to *Pan Tadeusz*'s thirteen-syllable (seven plus six) line.

Revolutionary Poets

Bruno Jasieński (1901–1939)   The futurist movement in Poland was short-lived. The revolt of the futurists against the established rules of orthography as well as of politics was disorderly and chaotic; some of them turned it into a kind of emotional Marxism and a praise of the Russian Revolution. Such was the case of Bruno Jasieński, who, after his first volume, *A Boot in a Buttonhole* (*But w butonierce*, 1921), switched to social-protest poetry. He published *Song on Hunger* (*Pieśń o głodzie*, 1922), *Earth to the Left* (*Ziemia na lewo*, 1924, together with Anatol Stern), and *Song on Jakub Szela* (*Słowo o Jakubie Szeli*, 1926, a dramatic poem on the leader of the peasant rebellion of 1846). This last work appeared in Paris, where Jasieński lived as a journalist and where his second novel, *Je brûle Paris* (his first was *The Legs of Izolda Morgan*, 1923), was printed in the Communist daily *l'Humanité* in 1928. The novel can be called vicarious vengeance upon gay, bourgeois Paris, and it anticipates the city's downfall. Expelled as an undesirable alien from France, Jasieński moved to Moscow, where he wrote one of the first Socialist Realist novels, *Man Changes His Skin* (*Chelovek menyaet kozhu*, 1932), and became a member of the executive committee of the Soviet Writers' Union.

Arrested in 1936, he died near Vladivostok in 1939 on his way to a concentration camp in Kolyma. (He was "rehabilitated" in the Soviet Union in 1956.) A gifted, though uneven, poet, he is remembered particularly for some powerful passages in his poem on Jakub Szela.

Władysław Broniewski was born into an intelligentsia family living in a small town (Płock) on the Vistula, left high school in 1915 to enlist in Piłsudski's legion, was decorated many times for his bravery, and fought as an officer in the Polish-Soviet war of 1920. Afterward, he became a supporter of the Russian Revolution. His internal development corresponds in an astonishing way to that of the hero in Żeromski's novel, *Before the Spring*. *Władysław Broniewski (1897–1962)*

After his first volume, *Windmills* (*Wiatraki*, 1925), he published, together with Ryszard Stande and Witold Wandurski, a Communist manifesto in verse, *Three Salvos* (*Trzy salwy*, 1925). His two friends were not destined to leave a durable trace. Stande, an underground activist for the Communist Party, wanted by the police, escaped to Moscow, where he did not produce any valid poems, was arrested in 1938, and soon died in prison. (He also was "rehabilitated" in the Soviet Union in 1956). Wandurski, full of interesting ideas as an avant-garde playwright and a theater director, also an activist for the Communist Party, migrated to the Soviet Union in 1933 and died in prison sometime after 1934 ("rehabilitated" in the Soviet Union in 1956).

Broniewski, since he was not engaged in direct political activity, remained in Poland. His mature poetry—*Smoke over the City* (*Dymy nad miastem*, 1927), *Paris Commune* (*Komuna paryska*, 1929), *Heavy Heart and Song* (*Troska i pieśń*, 1932), *The Last Cry* (*Krzyk ostateczny*, 1938)—is virile and concise; it is carried forward by the rush of his anger and, with its division into rhymed quatrains, is quite traditional, although he injects new vigor into this verse form through a meter based on the count of accents rather than syllables. Clearly understandable, even to unsophisticated readers, to workingmen and -women, Broniewski's poetry was capable of swaying audiences when recited aloud. Its tone is, perhaps, closer to the revolutionary *élan* of 1848 than to the mood of our century. He himself was a picturesque personality, with his drinking bouts during which he managed to recite from memory, hour after hour, from the Polish Romantics and from Russian poets. In whatever he wrote he combined an essential "Polishness" that stemmed from his intimate tie with tradition with a summons for a revolutionary upheaval; and it is no wonder that he found a tremendous response among his readers. Protected from persecution by his former comrades in arms, Piłsudski's officers, he enjoyed the exceptional position of a great Communist poet in anti-Communist Poland. In 1939 his poem "Fix

Bayonets!" ("Bagnet na broń") was on everyone's lips. It called for readiness to fight the Germans. As the Nazi army advanced through the country, Broniewski went east to Lwów, which was soon taken over by the Soviet Union. Treated with respect at first, he was arrested in the beginning of 1940 and detained at Lubianka prison in Moscow, until Hitler's attack upon the Soviet Union in 1941 persuaded Stalin to grant an amnesty to the Poles. With the Polish army of General Anders, organized in the Soviet Union, he left for Iran, Iraq, and Palestine. In 1945, on his return to Warsaw, his anti-Stalinist poems, written after his stay in prison, were tactfully passed over in silence. Proclaimed "the national poet," a recipient of many prizes, decorated by the government for revolutionary merit, Broniewski composed an ode to Stalin in 1949. His output during the postwar years is inferior to his prewar and wartime work. His unhappiness, arising out of his ill-fitting role as poet of the established order, and out of personal misfortunes, expressed itself in the last phase of his life in short nostalgic lyrics on his native region near Płock by the Vistula River. When a new literary generation came to the fore around 1956, he was completely out of step, and to them he appeared to be no more than a relic. His paradoxical biography illustrates especially clearly the difficulties of Polish Leftists both in politics and in literature.

Close to the "Skamander" poets in his craft, Broniewski not only shared their tastes but was bound to them by ties of mutual esteem and friendship. He should be ranked with the best of them, and his stature will probably be better perceived as critics gain more perspective in time.

The First Vanguard

The Vanguard of the 1920s is usually distinguished from that of the 1930s, with the former referred to as the First Vanguard and the latter as the Second Vanguard. As early as 1918, a few poets and painters in Kraków who frequented a café called "The Nutmeg" had formulated some programs and had given themselves the name of "Formists." They stressed pure form as the essence of art; thus, in painting, their movement led to a deformation of represented objects or even a nonfigurative composition.

Tytus Czyżewski (1885–1945) One of them, though he is valued today as a painter, was also a poet, and his works have a right to a place in every anthology. Tytus Czyżewski wrote very little, but his *Pastorals* (*Pastorałki*, published in Paris in 1925), for instance, are of great beauty. In it, he applied a procedure then current among composers of music like Stravinsky and Béla Bartók, or Karol Szymanowski in Poland. In these naïve and purposely awkward Christmas carols he gave an avant-garde treatment to motifs from old Polish poetry—of shepherds who bring little Jesus gifts of cheese, butter, or pears and who play the fiddle and bagpipe to amuse him. Czyżewski, a native of the Tatra foothills, was thoroughly familiar with the region's folklore, and as an avant-garde poet he completely rejected nineteenth-century metrics; he was able, thus, to invent new verse instrumentation for old melodies.

Kraków, though one of the most conservative towns in Poland, The Switch witnessed the birth of yet another avant-garde group. In 1921, Tadeusz Peiper (born 1891), after a long sojourn in France and Spain, returned to his native Kraków, where he founded a little review, *The Switch* (*Zwrotnica*), which he edited in the years 1922–1923 and 1926–1927. Peiper was the first theoretician of a new poetry opposed to "Skamander," and he found talented collaborators, who were both poets and theoreticians, in the persons of Julian Przyboś and Jan Brzękowski. *The Switch* reproached "Skamander" for its passive submission to a lyrical flow. They derided inspiration and exalted a controlling mind that conveys an emotion by translating it into equivalent images (we might say "objective correlatives"). As their main instrument, they chose metaphor, aiming for a line that was as dense as possible: "a little plain nourished by one breast of a hill"; "immense eyes of air look at you"; "you cannot disengage yourself from the arms of a horizon thrown about your neck"; "every night fear grew up, the mountain of a rising scream" (all quotations from Przyboś). For them, a poem that could be grasped easily at first reading was trite and hardly differed from a night-club song. They opposed magical incantation through repetitive rhythms. They broke with "syllabotonic" verse and derisively referred to "Skamander" poets as "organ-grinders." Instead, they modulated their phrases with no interest in feet or syllable count. "Skamander" in their view was too garrulous and too autobiographical; what they asked of the poet was "the least possible number of words" and "an emotional reticence." "Skamander"'s manifesto consisted in a programmatic denial of any program. This corresponded well to what the critics called a "vitalism" of that group. According to the group calling themselves (after the name of their review) "The Switch," worship of life was simply the outcome of a programmatic anti-intellectualism. Because they were, in fact, rationalists, admirers of technology, of the machine, as opposed to those who looked to spontaneity, biology, nature, they constantly felt compelled to justify the role of poetry, which, by its very form, was supposed to affect the mentality of the reader. Being socialists, they hoped that a disciplined mind composing a poem would "infect" the reader with a similar orderliness.

Peiper even spoke of a "socialist rhyme" (a rhyme spaced so meticulously at long intervals that, at first reading, it is imperceptible). Yet a poem was for them an autonomous object, valid by its very existence and not dependent upon any message translatable into prose. By their emphasis on the specific language of poetry, they were the successors of French symbolism. In Poland the symbolist tree put forth two branches: one representing a lyrical flow, incantation, sonority; the other representing a controlled construction, as in the group of "The Switch." The exploitation of the subconscious or the use of a "meta-language," nonsensical by the standards of reason, was alien to the constructivists of "The Switch." Dadaist and surrealistic elements were found rather in the works of the so-called futurists of the early twenties and in some poems of "Skamander."

The editor of *The Switch*, Tadeusz Peiper, influenced many of the young more by his uncompromising articles than by his poetry, which is interesting only as an example of unflinching attachment to principles. The same applies, perhaps, to Jan Brzękowski (born 1903), who lived mostly in France and edited there an international avant-garde magazine, *L'art contemporain*, in 1929–1930. His views differed from Peiper's and thus introduced an indispensable variety into the program of the group. Only Julian Przyboś gained wider recognition, both as a poet and as a theoretician.

Julian Przyboś (1901–1970) A native of a village in southern Poland, Przyboś, in spite of the poverty of his peasant family, went through high school in a provincial town and studied Polish literature at the Jagiellonian University in Kraków. Afterward, he worked as a high-school teacher for many years. In 1922, he started to publish and to cooperate actively with *The Switch*, to be connected later on with another avant-garde review called *Line* (*Linia*, 1931–1933), edited in Kraków by Jalu Kurek. Engaged in the battle for new architecture and nonfigurative painting, Przyboś also belonged, from 1930 to 1935, to a group known as "a.r." ("revolutionary artists") in Łódź. Architecture, as an art that organizes space, occupied a central place in his essays (not only the bulk of concrete but also the space around it is shaped by the will of the architect). This preoccupation with spatiality corresponded to Przyboś's visual sensitivity, and as a poet he was, more often than not, an apparatus made of huge lenses that absorbed and deformed visible things. But he was also a socialist for whom artistic creativity signified a man's *élan* toward universal happiness through the realization of all human potentialities. But an artist's first duty toward mankind is to create good art and not to renounce high standards in the name of any supra-artistic goal.

Przyboś's poetry seems to be built upon two obsessions: the first has to do with concentrated strength and tension, the titanic effort of tearing off words from their trite dependences in everyday language; the second, with imminent explosion and consuming flames. His landscapes, whether urban or rural, are dynamic, charged with an energy of their own, ready to burst forth. This represents Przyboś's distrust of a passive submission to nature (he regarded nature as only a potential extension of man's will). A materialistic and rationalistic *Weltanschauung* directed him toward a peculiar metaphysics of tangible forms. By striking one word against another, he attempted to kindle the spark of a new apprehension of reality. Since he explored all the resources of Polish grammar for that purpose, his poems are rarely translatable. Even the titles of his volumes can hardly be rendered: *Screws* (*Śruby*, 1925), *Twin Grasp* (*Oburącz*, 1926), *From Higher Than* (*Z ponad*, 1930), *Into the Deep Forest* (*W głąb las*, 1932), *Equation of the Heart* (*Równanie serca*, 1938). The following version does not pretend to exactitude:

They strangled the air with banners.
Under all the triumphal arches
the rebels put dynamite!

Who am I? An exile of birds.

The table under my pen, having swollen up to its edges
exceeds itself
like a tank about to attack.
Already today the house burns with tomorrow's fire,
faster my heart assaults me.

Shrapnel bursts from poles of street lights:
the lamps were lit in the streets all at once.
The day passes in an armed song of soldiers and gives its last rattle.

From the rusty grass the ribs of the fallen ruffled the sod.

Alive, I walk in this present and yet bygone city.

Who am I? An exile of birds.

The gardens—the new moon like a thorn rising from the boughs—
The world without me fulfills itself, motionless and free
and only the laurel of autumn leaves falls on my head.

. . . so that I never keep silent.

Gentle,
I would turn my every pocket into nests for swallows
flying away from people.

Powietrze uduszono sztandarami.
Pod wszystkie triumfalne bramy
zbuntowani podkładają dynamit!

Kim jestem? Wygnańcem ptaków.

Stół pod moim piórem wezbrawszy do samych krawędzi
przebiera swoją miarę,
jak czołg, gdy ma ruszyć do ataku.
Dom już dziś płonie we mnie jutrzejszym pożarem,
serce atakuje mię prędzej.

Szrapnel pęka ze słupów latarni:
lampy zapalono na ulicach jednocześnie.
Dzień mija w zbrojnej pieśni żołnierskiej, rzęzi.

Z rudej trawy zjeżyły żebra poległych darń.

Żywy idę miastem będącym, a już tylko byłym.

Kim jestem? Wygnańcem ptaków.

Ogrody—Nów jak cierń wschodzący z gałęzi—
Świat beze mnie się spełnia wolny i bezczuły,
i tylko liści jesiennych opada na głowę laur.

. . . abym już nigdy nie ucichł.

Łagodny
Każdą kieszeń obróciłbym w gniazdo dla jaskółek
odlatujących od ludzi.

During the war, he lived for a while in the Soviet zone, in Lwów, then after 1941 in his Nazi-occupied native village, where he worked as an agricultural laborer and wrote poems for the resistance movement. Immediately after the war, he served as the first chairman of the Writers' Union; in the years 1947–1951 he acted as legate of the People's Republic of Poland to Switzerland. He was never a partisan of Socialist Realism in poetry, as this meant a compulsory revival of nineteenth-century metrics, and would have violated his fanatical avant-garde principles. His prolific production, especially after 1956, embraces both poetry and studies in the history of Polish literature; especially valuable are his treatises on the poetics of Mickiewicz.

Toward the Second Vanguard

The notion of the Second Vanguard is a vague one; many names and groups may be cited, but their claim to solidarity was based on a certain intellectual climate rather than on any common programs. All of them assumed a certain independence from both "Skamander" and the Kraków Vanguard, and all groped for new solutions. These solutions, however, were not sought in the realm of literary techniques. The optimism proper to the first decade of independence was over. Everyday existence, threatened by "warnings and portents and evils imminent," was precarious. Marxism, totalitarian fascist regimes, a renewed interest in metaphysics (if only through the intermediary of phenomenology) forced the asking of too many questions and estranged poets from a neat, well-ordered craft. The Second Vanguard, neither neat in its thought nor well ordered in its verse, was rich, complex, chaotic, conscious of a disparity between the fate of modern man and the artistic means at his disposal. Experimentation went together with a certain skepticism as to aesthetic values. "Skamander" and the First Vanguard were reproached for the narrowness of their concerns. Cosmic visions of a doomsday made their appearance in poems, treated sometimes with solemnity, sometimes with macabre buffoonery. To some of these poets, the term "catastrophism" has been applied. An eminent contemporary literary historian and critic, Kazimierz Wyka, has defined it as

an intellectual-artistic phenomenon in Polish poetry of the second decade between the two wars, which consisted in a symbolist-classicist elaboration (sometimes with a surrealist or expressionist tinge) of themes suggesting and announcing the approach of an inevitable historical and moral catastrophe.

No single poetics can be ascribed to the Second Vanguard. Its poets employed many techniques. Some applied traditional meters, while others completely rejected syllabotonic "feet." Their merit lay in opening up new, if dark, vistas; postwar poetry with its philosophical contents can be said to have stemmed more or less directly from them. Some of these poets became leading figures after World War II, and, thus, belong to two periods.

To include Ważyk in this chapter is somewhat risky, since he made *Adam* his literary debut quite early, with the volumes *Semaphores* (*Sema-* *Ważyk* *fory*, 1924) and *Eyes and Lips* (*Oczy i usta*, 1926), and was not *(1905–)* associated with any schools. He could have been just as correctly ranked with such First Vanguard poets as Tytus Czyżewski; nevertheless, poets of the Second Vanguard were inclined to treat him as an ally.

Born in Warsaw, of middle-class Jewish parents, endowed with a brilliant mind, he fascinated young Bohemians with his early poems where influences of French "cubist" painting and poetry predominated and with his excellent translations of Guillaume Apollinaire. In the thirties, too conscious perhaps of a crisis in poetic form, he kept silent,

writing only fiction, i.e., stories—"Man in the Dark Gray Suit" ("Człowiek w burym ubraniu," 1930)—and novels—*Lamps Are Lit in
Karpów* (*Latarnie świecą w Karpowie*, 1933) and *Family Myths*
(*Mity rodzinne*, 1938). He spent the war in the Soviet Union and
returned to Poland as an officer of the Polish Communist Army. A
volume of his wartime poems was one of the first books published
after the war in Lublin: *The Heart of a Grenade* (*Serce granatu*,
1944). It contained, among other poems, "Sketch for a Memoir"
("Szkic pamiętnika"). Fragments of this farewell to and summation
of a bygone era are quoted below. The poem catches particularly
well the atmosphere which produced the poetry of the Second Vanguard.

Years of affliction,
lacunae in memory,
between one war and another
my brother, unemployed, went crazy and jumped out the window.
I did not visit him in the morgue,
I wept only when I knelt before his drawer,
looking at the trifles as useless as he was:
a lighter out of order, little inventions,
magic tricks which he liked very much—
for him they took the place of assonance and rhyme.

Not only that disturbed me—
furniture too, sumptuous draperies,
pederasts writing poems about angels,
everything in society that announced new war,
beautiful mythomaniacs with platinum hair,
dressed in the style of the Viennese Secession,
novels not written, stillborn,
boredom and emptiness foretelling war.

Conversations at supper or over vodka in bars,
iridescent words in which the chaos drones.
For in those years people of not quite bad will
had their minds filled with noise, a camouflage for reaction,
ideas got entangled like gods in the era of syncretism,
I knew a painter who for three hours
was able to talk nonsense without stopping,
others composed crosswords,
waited for a cataclysm
as for a monstrous group photograph in a flash of magnesium,
read Nostradamus.

A liar was among us disguised as a journalist,
an informer was a Schöngeist or a bohemian poet,

a pimp and a German agent posed as snobs,
no one knew what were other people's sources of income,
ten just men were dying in Spain.

Lata zgryzoty,
luki w pamięci,
pomiędzy jedną wojną a drugą
mój brat bezrobotny, obłąkany wyskoczył z okna.
Nie oglądałem go w kostnicy,
płakałem tylko, kiedy ukląkłem przed jego szufladą,
gdzie leżały drobiazgi nieużyteczne jak on:
Zepsuta zapalniczka, drobne wynalazki,
sztuczki magiczne, które lubił bardzo—
to zastępowało mu rymy i asonanse.

Niepokoiło mnie nie tylko to—
meble, draperie sute, ozdobne,
pederaści piszący wiersze o aniołach,
wszystko, co w obyczajach wróżyło nową wojnę,
piękne mitomanki o platynowych włosach,
w sukniach z epoki secesji,
powieści nienapisane,
obumarłe przed narodzeniem,
nuda i czczość zwiastujące wojnę.

Rozmowy przy kolacjach czy w knajpach przy wódce,
słowa tęczujące, w których dudni chaos.
W tych latach bowiem w ludziach nienajgorszej woli
reakcja maskowała się zgiełkiem w umysłach,
pojęcia gmatwały się jak niegdyś bogowie w epoce synkretyzmu,
pewien mój znajomy malarz
przez trzy godziny bez przerwy potrafił mówić od rzeczy,
inni układali krzyżówki,
czekali na kataklizm
jak na upiorną fotografię zbiorową w wybuchu magnezji,
czytali Nostradamusa.

Kłamca był między nami, przebrany za dziennikarza,
szpicel był pięknoduchem albo poetą-cyganem,
alfons i ajent niemiecki był snobem,
nie wiedziano, kto z czego żyje,
dziesięciu sprawiedliwych ginęło w Hiszpanii.

In the Stalinist years, Ważyk, with his dialectical mind, convinced himself of the justness of the new line imposed upon writers and became one of the most feared "terroreticians" of Socialist Realism. But he was clever enough to publish but few poems himself, dedicating his time to a high-quality translation of Pushkin's *Eugene Onegin*. In 1955, his *Poem for Adults*, deriding totalitarian abuses, found a wide response and marked the overt beginning of the "thaw." The unorthodox and liberal Ważyk, after that date, wrote what are probably the best poems of his career, permeated with a somewhat melancholy serenity and wisdom.

A connoisseur of French poetry, a poet with a scholarly interest in Polish metrics of various centuries, he has exerted a beneficent influence, which counterbalances the linguistic excesses of the very young, through his practice of strict economy of means. Not the least of his achievements are his translations of Horace into the idiom of modern poetry.

Mieczysław Jastrun (1903–) Mieczysław Jastrun is placed in the chapter with equal reservations. He developed far from any schools or groups. Born in southern Poland of a Jewish family, he received his doctorate in Polish literature at the Jagiellonian University. His first poems showed an almost complete dependence upon "Skamander": *Meeting in Time* (*Spotkanie w czasie*, 1929), *Another Youth* (*Inna młodość*, 1933); but his next volumes, *Smoldering History* (*Dzieje nieostygłe*, 1935) and *A Stream and Silence* (*Strumień i milczenie*, 1937), though not a break with "Skamander" in their versification, revealed an individual and independent poetic personality through his choice of a basic theme: a meditation on time in relation both to the individual and to history. It was in the thirties that Cyprian Norwid, from among the poets of the past, was brought to the fore—understandably, in view of the acute historical anxiety afflicting this generation—and Jastrun was a writer who had an affinity for Norwid's thought.

Jastrun survived the war, remaining in hiding in Warsaw. His wartime poems, first printed in clandestine anti-Nazi periodicals, were published under the title *A Guarded Hour* (*Godzina strzeżona*) in 1944. His best poems, perhaps, are those of his mature age, and date from after 1956. By temperament a contemplative, Jastrun has always felt strongly drawn to the German poet, Rainer Maria Rilke. In addition to his poetry, he is the author of many essays on literature, and of a slightly fictionalized biography of Mickiewicz, which has been translated into many languages.

Quadriga During the years 1926–1931, a few young poets in Warsaw edited a poetry review called *Quadriga* (*Kwadryga*). Their somewhat hazy program called for a socially responsible poetry, criticized "Skamander" for its lack of commitment and its self-complacency. Their pacifism, their sympathy for the underdog, their acknowledgment of Norwid as a patron testified to a groping toward some undefined seriousness of purpose. The most radical in his stern factuality was Stefan Flukowski (1902–), but he has remained an experimenter appreciated only by the very few. More widely known were Władysław Sebyła (1902–1941) and Lucjan Szenwald (1909–1944), whose paths were destined to diverge radically. After his early pacifist poems, *Songs of a Pied Piper* (*Pieśni szczurołapa*, 1930), Sebyła became more and more preoccupied with a poetry of metaphysical discourse, thus taking over the heritage of the Polish *Moderna*. His *Egotistic Concert* (*Koncert egotyczny*, 1934) and *Images of Thought* (*Obrazy myśli*, 1938), are characteristic of the philosophical anxiety of the thirties. Mobilized as a reserve officer during the war, then interned in the Soviet Union, he perished in the massacre of Katyn Forest.

Szenwald, on the other hand, oriented himself toward Marxism and, after having become a political activist, rejected his best early works (among which was a long poem of rare depth and complexity of thought, a kind of materialistic cosmogony, entitled *My Mother's Kitchen*) and started to write committed poetry. In spite of his wide literary background, however, few of these works are first-rate. A political officer in the Soviet army during the war, he perished in an automobile accident near Lublin in Poland in 1944.

Gałczyński certainly would have laughed to find himself ranged with any "vanguard." It was one of his favorite pastimes to stick his tongue out at various hopelessly literary trends. Born in Warsaw, the son of a railway employee, he spent a few years during World War I in Moscow because his family had been evacuated to that city. When back in Warsaw as a student, he added to his familiarity with Russian poetry and with Latin, English, German, and French poets. It is said that he wrote for his professor a learned dissertation with many quotations and footnotes on a nonexistent minor English poet. Later on, in the same vein, he liked to include in the list of his works the entry *"Introduction to Cannibalism: Lecture Notes* (out of print)." A jester, he started publishing humorous verse under the pseudonym Karakuliambro, as well as whimsical, somewhat surrealistic prose. But his long poem, *The End of the World: Visions of St. Ildefonse, or a Satire on the Universe* (*Koniec świata: Wizje świętego Ildefonsa czyli Satyra na Wszechświat*), which appeared in *Quadriga* in 1929, although it is extremely amusing, belongs, in fact, to the apocalyptic genre under the guise of *opera buffa*. Fond of urban folklore, of slang, of kermesses with their merry-go-rounds and trite melodies, of everything which smacked of *kitsch*, he managed to transform this raw material into real poetry, drawing from Warsaw street humor and from "Skamander." Add to this his playing with classical mythology and his worship of Horace, and the result is a crazy mixture, which he brought off with astonishing skill. His *End of the World*, the scene of which is a somewhat fantastic city

Konstanty Ildefons Gałczyński (1905–1953)

named Bologna (in Poland, Bologna and Padua ever since the Renaissance have been symbols of students' towns), was not only a joke. It corresponded to the catastrophist mood of those years, as did another work of Gałczyński's, composed of short, seemingly light verses, *Playland* (*Zabawa ludowa*, 1934) which is about workers and clerks spending Sunday at the shooting galleries, drinking beer, and dancing at the fairgrounds on the outskirts of a big city. The poem ends with a reference to Virgil's fourth eclogue, which, according to a legend, was a foreboding of a giant turn in history; Gałczyński hints of machine guns and the approach of an iron age.

He always derided avant-garde poets who wrote verse that was incomprehensible to the larger public. He wanted to be like the poets of old who were loved and remunerated on the spot for their services. Thanks to his absurd humor, he could always count on applause, and with his recitations he succeeded in magnetizing every audience. Politically amoral, he soon left his *Quadriga* friends and moved in with the periodicals of the extreme Right because they, especially a Warsaw weekly, *Straight from the Shoulder* (*Prosto z mostu*), had a wide circulation thanks to their anti-Semitism. Gałczyński wrote some poems announcing "a night of long knives" for Jews and intellectuals; but when drunk he would visit poets whom he admired, like Julian Tuwim, kissing their hands and begging forgiveness. Yet he was sincere in his collaboration with the Right because of its closeness to folkish and plebeian elements. In his technique, he brought the syllabotonic verse of "Skamander" to its self-destroying fulfillment. About the time Tuwim was writing his *Ball at the Opera*, Gałczyński finished his *Ball at Solomon's* (*Bal u Salomona*). The poem is an oppressive dream where places, characters, and situations are blurred, but where the sinister situation of Poland and of Europe is always recognizable.

Taken prisoner as an ordinary soldier, Gałczyński spent the war in a prisoner-of-war camp in Germany, then for a short time tasted exile in France and Belgium, but being a poet who could not write without applause, he returned in 1946 to People's Poland. His career there as a minstrel of socialism is a wonder, if we consider that Apollo, Zeus, Stalin, Johann Sebastian Bach all danced a ballet in his poems. He achieved his goal: he was both widely read and well remunerated. Besides his poems, he invented a new way to reach the public: a *feuilleton* in a weekly with a large circulation, *Cross Section* (*Przekrój*). The column was called *The Green Goose—The Smallest Theater in the World* (*Teatrzyk "Zielona Gęś"*) and consisted of short "plays" sometimes of no more than two sentences (for instance, a "play" entitled "Gluttonous Eve" obviously must come to a swift end because the protagonist, Eve, eats a whole apple, leaving nothing for Adam and thus destroying the foundation of the entire Bible). Tracked down as a "petty bourgeois in socialist garb," Gałczyński, at the peak of Stalinism, switched for a while to translations, the result of which was a fine version of Shakespeare's *A Midsummer-Night's Dream*. The response he found among the public was too genuine for the bureaucrats; in the midst of universal grayness, he provided his readers with color and fantasy. Yet there is no doubt that his attachment to People's Poland was real. If his taste for everything plebeian had sent him before in the direction of the Right, he now fulminated with equal fervor, and a sly grin, against the bourgeois and the reactionary. And the mass audience he acquired was much larger than that he could have hoped for through his previous commitments to the Right. The everyday idiom with all its ironic short cuts, which so attracted some of the "Skamander" poets, found its ideal interpreter in Gałczyński. And the whole tone of Polish poetry in the last decades, that blend of seriousness and macabre humor, would be unthinkable without him. Praying to Apollo and to the Holy Virgin, Gałczyński was not only a buffoon; he assigned to himself the role of the medieval *jongleur de Notre Dame*, of a weak man, a drunkard, a vagabond thrown into a world alien to the true desires of his heart, but trying to survive and to bring people something of beauty. Through his grotesque blend of poetic trappings gathered from various epochs and his fondness for classical mythology, Gałczyński may be said to have reactivated Polish Baroque poetry.

Józef Czechowicz came from a poor family in Lublin. He studied pedagogy in a school for elementary teachers, after which he worked as a teacher in small towns and villages. His wide literary background was gained through self-education. He made his literary debut with a volume of poems entitled *Stone* (*Kamień*, 1927), which was already free from the influence of "Skamander." Although Czechowicz was unorthodox in his approach to metrics and rhyme, all of his poetry was intrinsically linked to the so-called "bourgeois lyricism" of the seventeenth century and to folk songs. The qualities that characterize the verse of these two traditions—a somewhat childish tenderness, a subdued melody, a shunning of any rhythmical staccato (which is alien to the very essence of the Polish language)—were revived in Czechowicz's poetry with great success, and like Tytus Czyżewski, he proved what a vivifying effect folklore can have upon avant-garde poets. While he was the first to translate some of the little-known foreign poets of the avant-garde (Mandelstam, Joyce, T. S. Eliot), he knew how to take from old madrigals and folk songs their emotional tone without imitating either their rhymes, which he used sparingly, or their stanza divisions. Bucolic, awkward, rural Poland is present throughout his lines even when he deals with city scenery.

Józef Czechowicz (1903–1939)

The voice of the poet himself, murmuring, hardly audible, is not similar to anything heard in Western poetry, and since he was exploiting hidden sonorities proper to one language only, he is untranslatable. His lyrics can be likened to chamber music made poignant by the counterpoint of dark philosophical and metaphysical problems. His volumes of verse where sensual dreams and poetic myths express his anxieties—*a day like everyday* (*dzień jak codzień*, 1930), *a ballad from beyond* (*ballada z tamtej strony*, 1932), *in lightning* (*w błyskawicy*, 1934), *nothing more* (*nic więcej*, 1936), *a human note* (*nuta człowiecza*, 1939)—can be included in the "catastrophist" trend. (Czechowicz did not use capital letters or punctuation.) His foreboding of a universal conflagration and of his own imminent death lent a peculiar light to his bucolic landscapes. He was killed by a bomb in his native Lublin at the age of only thirty-six.

"Żagary"   In 1931, a group of students at the University of Wilno founded a little review whose name, Żagary, they borrowed from the Lithuanian for "brushwood," or, in a more local meaning, for dry twigs half charred in fire but still glowing. Their group best exemplified all the contradictory strivings that were propelling the young generation beyond accepted artistic forms. Because of their dark visions in which the political was translated into the cosmic by means of a new kind of symbolism, they were soon recognized as the instigators of a "school of catastrophists." Basically antiaesthetic, they hesitated between their sympathies for Marxism and their metaphysical frame of reference. They declared their independence from both "Skamander" and the First Vanguard, confining themselves to no single poetics. In the sphere of social responsibility, their attitude was ambivalent, oscillating between commitments of one sort or another and the defense of their freedom as poets who reserved the right to reject commitment if it threatened their artistic liberty.

One of the three original founders of the group, Teodor Bujnicki (1907–1944), was killed during the war by a Right-Wing underground organization and left no important work. Jerzy Zagórski (1907–   ) wrote significant poems before 1939. They are contained in the volumes *A Blade of a Bridge* (*Ostrze mostu*, 1933), *Expeditions* (*Wyprawy*, 1937), and particularly in his *Coming of the Enemy* (*Przyjście wroga*, 1934), with the subtitle *A Poem–Fairy Tale*. This captivating chaos of fragments in prose, surrealistic songs, and biblical verses is used to convey an anticipated immensity of the disaster awaiting the earth. Armies moving from the Caucasus to the North Pole, the birth of a man-monster who perhaps is Antichrist, Asiatic steppes exploding with human masses, make for one of the weirdest sets of symbols in modern poetry, the key to which was not provided by the author. During the war, Zagórski lived in Warsaw, editing underground publications—among which was an anthology of anti-Nazi poems. After the war he remained active as a poet and a translator of poetry, associating himself with Roman Catholic intellectual circles.

The youngest of the founders, Czesław Miłosz (1911–   ) is the author of this book, and he feels embarrassed to characterize his contribution. Born in the heartland of Lithuania, son of a civil engineer whose professional wanderings brought the family to Siberia and the banks of the Volga, he received his master's degree in law from the University of Wilno. His first slim volume of poetry, *A Poem on Time Frozen* (*Poemat o czasie zastygłym*, 1933), was spoiled by social ratiocinations; but the next, *Three Winters* (*Trzy zimy*, 1936), is considered by literary historian and critic Kazimierz Wyka the most representative work of "catastrophism." Its rush of symbols, set unexpectedly into lines with a classicist ring, alludes to calamities of cosmic amplitude. Critics have tended to see a myth of the Earth, a protective deity ever renewing herself, as the core of Miłosz's poetry, or have been calling him the only true pantheist in Polish poetry. It is not certain whether this is true, since Christian elements are also strong. There is no doubt, however, that his poetry is permeated with the nature of his native Lithuania. During the war, Miłosz lived in Warsaw, where he edited a clandestine anthology of anti-Nazi poems. His poetic work, collected in a volume called *Rescue* (*Ocalenie*, 1945), and published as one of the first books in postwar Poland, marked a new approach to historical tragedy and, together with the volumes of Ważyk, Jastrun, and Przyboś, left its stamp upon the development of Polish poetry in the next two decades.

As for other members of the "Żagary" group, Jerzy Putrament (1910–   ) published two volumes before the war, *Yesterday the Return* (*Wczoraj powrót*, 1935) and *Forest Road* (*Droga leśna*, 1938), an interesting cross between his sensitivity to the landscape of his native region south of Wilno and his Marxist, revolutionary commitment. However, except for a few war poems published after his return from the Soviet Union as an officer of the Polish Communist Army, he developed as a writer of less than first-rate fiction. Aleksander Rymkiewicz (1913–   ), intimately bound, as were all of his colleagues, to a northern nature of forests, lakes, and marshes, produced before the war quite an extraordinary poem, "The Pathfinder" ("Tropiciel," 1936), a fairy tale about an eerie polar expedition that, in fact, translates the same fears common to the whole group into images of snow, ice, and frost. After the war, Rymkiewicz, one of the numerous Poles who had to migrate from Wilno, found a substitute homeland in the forests of East Prussia taken over by Poland.

Polish poetry of the war and postwar period was to evolve under the tutelage not of "Skamander" but of the First Vanguard and to an even greater extent of the Second Vanguard, and here the place of Józef Czechowicz and "Żagary" is substantial. While the First Vanguard demonstrated the possibilities of a freely modulated phrase liberated from a count of syllables or accents, the Second Vanguard opened up a larger philosophical dimension.

THE THEATER

All Polish theaters were of the repertory type, and some were subsidized by municipalities. Although this arrangement did not exempt them from the necessity of commercial success, and, therefore, of staging plays able to attract large audiences, their choice of plays, both native and foreign, not to mention their stagecraft, often revealed a high degree of sophistication. G. B. Shaw was one of the most applauded contemporary authors (to the extent that some of his plays had their world or Continental première in Warsaw), and daring spectacles of the Polish Romantic drama became known as major feats of stagecraft. The most talented theater director of the period between the wars, Leon Schiller, elaborated his theory of a "monumental theater," basing it upon Wyspiański's pioneering work and Mickiewicz's Paris lecture on the Slavic drama. Schiller assigned to the director a role similar to that of an orchestra conductor: one who controls masses of actors moving together in a balletlike rhythmic pattern. Mickiewicz's *Forefathers' Eve*, Krasiński's *Undivine Comedy*, and Słowacki's fantastic dramas could be presented with the help of a revolving stage and with the collaboration of the best artists, who designed sets and costumes. Polish theater moved away from a photographic imitation of life enclosed in a box of a room with one wall removed; this does not mean, of course, that realistic comedies by contemporary playwrights, often quite silly, did not fill the house. There was, however, one man who drew radical conclusions from the decay of nineteenth-century drawing-room comedy and who initiated a new trend in the Polish theater, a trend which drew acclaim from the Western public only much later through the plays of Ionesco and Beckett.

Stanisław Ignacy Witkiewicz
(1885–1939)

Born in Warsaw, the only son of an eminent art critic, Witkiewicz spent his childhood and adolescence in what was then the capital of

Polish arts, Zakopane. Then, in 1904–1905, he studied painting at the Academy of Fine Arts in Kraków, traveled in Western Europe, and in 1914 went on a scientific expedition with his family's friend, the anthropologist Bronisław Malinowski, to New Guinea and Australia via India and Ceylon. Holder of a Russian passport, he was compelled to take a ship to Russia at the outbreak of World War I, entered an officers' training school in St. Petersburg, then fought as an infantry officer in an elite regiment. Decorated with the Order of St. Anne for bravery, he always remembered the minutes before an attack as the most terrible of his life. When in Russia, he started to study philosophy and tested hallucinatory drugs—among others, peyote. At the outbreak of the Revolution he was elected commissar by his soldiers, but the Revolution was a trauma for him which determined many of his later ideas. In 1918 he returned to Poland, settled down in Zakopane, and cooperated with the Kraków Vanguard ("Formists" and "The Switch"). In an essay written in 1919, *On New Forms in Painting and on the Resulting Misunderstandings*, a whole theory of art was sketched out. Witkiewicz was a philosopher, and his views on art are closely related to his personal *Weltanschauung*, which he constantly subjected to debate in his plays, novels, and essays. One deliberately dry treatise, *Notions and Assertions Implied by the Notion of Being* (1935), he destined for professionals only.

According to Witkiewicz, all that we can say about the world is that it is composed of "Particular Existences." Every human Particular Existence feels astonishment at itself; it asks:

Why am I exactly this and not that being? at this point of unlimited space and in this moment of infinite time? in this group of beings, on this planet? Why do I exist if I could have been without any existence? Why does anything exist at all?

This feeling Witkiewicz calls a "Metaphysical Feeling of the Strangeness of Existence." Mankind, he says, looked for answers first in religion, then in philosophy, but in modern times philosophical systems have shown their bankruptcy: "Throughout the entire struggle Mystery veils dropped away one by one, and the time has come when we see a naked, hard body with nothing more to be taken off, invincible in its dead statue's indifference." Philosophers then behaved like the fox who pronounced the grapes to be sour because they were too high. They proceeded to explain away metaphysical problems as illusory notions imposed by the structure of language. Witkiewicz detested Logical Positivists, but he also was an enemy of Bergson, who preferred intuition to intellect, and of the Pragmatists and Marxists because instead of a search for ontological truth they extolled ethics. According to Witkiewicz, it was enough to discern the direction of the twentieth-century history to make a prediction: mankind was headed toward "happiness for all," a victory of ethics which would spell death to religion, philosophy, and art. Man will be happy but deprived of that which made his greatness in the past: "Ethics will devour metaphysics"; "From a herd we came and to a herd we shall return." In many of Witkiewicz's pronouncements, there are proofs of a good acquaintance with Marxism, but he envisaged social revolution not only as inevitable, but as an inevitable disaster. Yet, for the moment, art was still alive. For him, it remained the only possibility of expressing and soothing the anxiety that comes from the "Metaphysical Feeling of the Strangeness of Existence" due to the demise of religion and philosophy. The work of art achieves this through its "unity in multiplicity," i.e., through its form. A work of art is Pure Form, and its "contents" are but accidental. In the past, when man was able to soothe his metaphysical anxiety through religion or philosophy, Pure Form profited indirectly; it was well ordered and harmonious. Such serenity is inaccessible to the modern artist. He relies only upon art and, therefore, must fuse into a unity more and more disparate and dissonant elements; otherwise his feeling at the moment of creation would not be sharp or intense enough. Thus, modern art tends toward a perversity which feeds on everything that is strident, ugly, jeering. If it sometimes achieves simplicity, it is but a perverse simplicity. Witkiewicz distinguished between "homogenous" and "composite" arts according to their more or less homogenous media. For example, the former included music (uses sound) and painting (uses line and color); the latter, poetry and the theater. Nevertheless, he believed that theater could achieve Pure Form, though with some reservations:

If we can imagine a painting composed of completely abstract forms that, unless we indulge in an obvious autosuggestion, would not provoke any associations with objects of the external world, no such theatrical play can even be thought of, because a pure becoming in time is possible only in the sphere of sounds, and the theater without actions performed by characters, even the most strange and improbable characters, is impossible, as the theater is a composite art.

However:

In painting, a new form—pure and abstract, without direct reference to a religious background—was achieved through the deformation of our vision of the external world, and, in a similar manner, a Pure Form in the theater can be achieved at the price of a deformation of psychology and action.

Witkiewicz's views on the subject were presented in his book *The Theater* (*Teatr*, 1923). He even gives an example of what a play, constructed according to his recipe, should be:

Thus: three persons dressed in red enter and bow, we do not know to whom. One of them recites a poem (which should make the impression of something necessary exactly at that moment). A gentle old man enters, with a cat he leads on a string. Until now everything has been going on against a background of a black curtain. The curtain is drawn apart and an Italian landscape appears. Organ music is heard. The old man talks with the three persons. He says something which corresponds to the mood which has been created. A glass falls off the table. All of them, suddenly on their knees, are weeping. The old man changes into a furious brute and murders a little girl who has just crawled out from the left side. At this, a handsome young man comes running and thanks the old man for that murder while the persons in red sing and dance. The young man then weeps over the corpse of the little girl, saying extremely funny things, and the old man, chuckling on the sidelines, changes again into a good-hearted character. As a finale, he pronounces sentences that are sublime and lofty. The costumes can be of any kind, stylized or fantastic—and music may intervene in various parts. So, you would say, a lunatic asylum, or rather the brain of a madman on the stage. Perhaps you are right, but we affirm that by applying this method, one can write serious plays, and if they are staged in the proper way, it would be possible to create things of extraordinary beauty. They may be dramas, tragedies, farces, or grotesques but always in a style not resembling anything that exists. When leaving the theater, one should have the impression that one wakes up from a strange dream in which the most trite things have the elusive, deep charm characteristc of dreams, not comparable to anything. . . .

Witkiewicz added:

Our aim is not programmatic nonsense; we rather try to enlarge the possibilities of composition by abandoning lifelike logic in art, by introducing a fantastic psychology and fantastic action, in order to win complete freedom of formal elements.

Witkiewicz wrote around thirty plays, his first at the age of eight. (It was called *Cockroaches*, about a city invaded by these hardy insects.) Their very titles testify to the unity between his theory and his practice: *Mr. Price, or Tropical Nuttiness; Gyubal Wahazar, or On the Passes of Nonsense: A Non-Euclidean Drama in Four Acts; Metaphysics of a Two-headed Calf; The Ominous Bastard of Wermiston; A Madman and a Nun, or Nothing Is So Bad That It Can't Be Made Worse: A Short Play in Three Acts and Four Scenes—Dedicated to All the Madmen of the World* (y compris *Other Planets of Our System as Well as Planets of the Milky Way and of Other Galaxies*) *and to Jan Mieczysławski.* Those plays, some of which were staged in the twenties and thirties, caused dismay among the average theatergoers but were fully appreciated in the late fifties, two decades after Witkiewicz's death. His pursuit of Pure Form in the theater was in a sense a failure, since action deprived of any kind of logic can hardly be called action at all. But his fantastic psychology, his language bearing little resemblance to ordinary speech, his inventiveness in devising improbable situations, in juxtaposing costumes of various epochs, in coining new words, and in the naming of his characters (for instance, "Doña Scabrosa Macabrescu") made him, certainly, one of the most interesting phenomena in modern theater. It is even more important to note that Witkiewicz gave vent in his most nonsensical plays to his own traumas and fears, which perhaps betrays Pure Form, but provides enough material for those who search for contents. His pessimism as to the future of civilization, his fear of soulless "bliss" in a mechanized society led him to concentrate upon madmen, misfits, and maniacs as his characters. To him they were specimens of a doomed world and through their frenzy and folly the only individuals deserving of an author's attention. Witkiewicz's orgies for the stage consist of unbridled sex and murder, which, however, comes off as rather gratuitious and inoffensive, since the victims rejoin the other actors after a few minutes. The plays are also orgies of philosophy, since even the humblest figure knows by heart the most complicated treatises on ontology.

Discouraged by the frigid reception awarded his plays, Witkiewicz all but abandoned the theater after 1930, producing only one dramatic work after that date: *The Cobblers* (*Szewcy*, written 1931–1934). Probably the closest of any of his works to a normally constructed drama, it is a fantastic parable on intellectual and moral decay and on two successive revolutions, one fascist, the other Marxist. It need not be added that the work does not rely on naturalistic technique; it tells the story through macabre metaphors.

As a theoretician and practitioner of the theater, Witkiewicz was more indebted to native than to foreign sources. It is easy to discern an echo of Przybyszewski's dramas, whose murders and suicides he often seems to parody. Above all, however, he was influenced by Wyspiański's dreamlike plays. He himself acknowledged the metaphysical and chaotic Tadeusz Miciński as one of his masters.

Though trained as a painter, Witkiewicz did not pretend to have much talent; he treated his "psychological portraits" as a way of earning a living. He was also experimenting with drugs and usually marked at the corner of the canvas whether he had taken any drug while working on that particular portrait, and if so, its name. Out of those experiments grew his book *Nicotine, Alcohol, Cocaine, Peyote, Morphine, Ether + Appendix* (*Nikotyna, alkohol, kokoina, pejotl, morfina, eter + dodatek*, 1932).

Witkiewicz is also the author of novels, although he refused to acknowledge the genre as an artistic form. He called it "a bag," a catchall, a pretext for an exposition of the author's opinions on various matters and for settling accounts with one's contemporaries. Therefore, his novels are completely free from any attempts to compete with nineteenth-century writers of fiction. On the one hand, they are akin to the eighteenth-century novel with its game of extraordinary adventures and author's digressions; on the other hand, they were harbingers of the new novel that won its freedom as a philosophical fantasy. Stylistically, Witkiewicz was a descendant of "Young Poland." But writers of "Young Poland" were solemn, while Witkiewicz pressed the pedal all the way to the floor in order to achieve grotesque effects of humorous bathos; woman as demon visited the writings of "Young Poland," but nobody went further than Witkiewicz in humorous-pathetic descriptions of sexual acts. His style, however, presents a serious obstacle to translating him into foreign languages.

Witkiewicz, through his philosophy, his plays, and his novels, was the most "catastrophist" among Polish writers, and poets of the thirties borrowed much from him, not vice versa. His novel *Farewell to Autumn* (*Pożegnanie jesieni*, 1927) is a work of anticipation. The action takes place in the future, in some unreal country (which is meant, however, to be a very real Poland). A revolution of the "levelers" is in the offing, having been preceded by another revolution (like Kerensky's?). The hero, Atanazy Bazakbal, one of those crazy intellectuals and artists who create degenerate art, tries to draw as much "Metaphysical Feeling of the Strangeness of Existence" from his sexual adventures; sex, in this respect, was for Witkiewicz related to art. In the universal grayness after the revolution (described many years later in the same terms by Orwell) he suffers at his desk in some obscure office, escapes across the border, but at the last moment has an illumination: the course toward depersonalization of human beings can be reversed by launching a warning. He retraces his steps, is caught by frontier guards, and executed.

Another novel, *Insatiability* (*Nienasycenie*, 1930), takes place within a nearly identical setup, except that the future is more remote. Western Europe has gone through Communist upheavals, Russia has renounced Communism, while Poland is ruled by a dictator of genius, Kocmołuchowicz (from *Kocmołuch:* "a dirty face"), who is able to maintain neutrality, and is even believed to be the man who will save Communist Europe from the onslaught of Communist China. Witkiewicz, parodying fiction about "a yellow peril," gave a new, more convincing version. The Chinese army, animated by faith in the supreme ideologist, Murti-Bing, has conquered Russia and is approaching the borders of Poland. The adventures of the hero, Genezyp Kapen, gradually becoming a schizophrenic, provide a pretext for unfolding a panorama of a doomed society; obviously the author had in mind European and Polish society around 1930. The term "insatiability" stands for the impossibility of satisfying metaphysical craving. Art has become sheer insanity. Panaceas are proposed from all sides, for instance, by sophisticated Neo-Catholicism. Also mysterious peddlers make their appearance, distributing pills of oriental origin which, when taken, provide the individual with a feeling of blissful harmony with the universe and rid him of metaphysical anxiety. The pills corrode all will to resist. Just before the battle of Kocmołuchowicz's army against the Chinese, the unpredictable chief, at a crucial juncture, submits to the invaders, who proceed to behead him with the greatest honors. A new order is established, and the characters of the novel are permitted to continue their inoffensive occupations as "has-beens" under the auspices of a Ministry of the Mechanization of Culture.

Witkiewicz, who escaped toward the east from the advancing Nazi army in 1939, committed suicide when the Soviet army moved forward to meet the Germans according to a pact of neutrality. His work was taboo for many years in postwar Poland, but in the late fifties literary critics of the young generation recognized him as one of the most fascinating figures in modern Polish literature, and his plays became a permanent feature of the theatrical repertoire.

THE NOVEL AND THE SHORT STORY

The book market in independent Poland was not very large, but it was sufficient to absorb works of Polish authors as well as numerous translations. Among the latter, priority seems to have gone to French authors such as Romain Rolland, Georges Duhamel, Paul Morand, Roger Martin du Gard. American and English writers were represented by Upton Sinclair, Theodore Dreiser, Dos Passos, D. H. Lawrence, Aldous Huxley. German novelists of the Weimar Republic were widely read, especially Thomas Mann. Soviet literature of the twenties was well-known; Boris Pilnyak, Konstantin Fedin, Feodor Zoshchenko, Ilya Ehrenburg (then an *émigré*), won particular favor. Among the foreigners, of course, Joseph Conrad had a prominent position, thanks to his Polish origins and to the translations done by his cousin, Aniela Zagórska, often revised by Conrad himself. Żeromski's authority among Polish novelists was uncontested, but in 1918 new talents were already invading the scene, and gradually they gained in stature.

Maria Dąbrowska (1889–1965) Critics maintained unanimously (and their opinion has been upheld today) that the best epic narrative was due to the pen of a woman, Maria Dąbrowska, who began by writing unassuming stories for children. Coming from a family of impoverished landowners, she studied natural sciences in Switzerland and Belgium, then social sciences and economics, also in Belgium. Her devotion to the cause of social and national progress, her activities in public affairs, and her lively participation in the movement to found cooperatives indicate her adherence to the theory of "organic work" so extolled by the Positivists. Her short stories, and not only those for children, are fairly traditional in their composition, and their simple language is closer to the nineteenth century than to "Young Poland." Two early volumes are entitled *Branch of a Cherry Tree and Other Stories* (*Gałąź czereśni i inne opowiadania*, 1922) and *A Smile of Childhood: Recollections* (*Uśmiech dzieciństwa: Wspomnienia*, 1923). But of greater significance was the appearance of her *Folks from Over Yonder: A Cycle of Tales* (*Ludzie stamtąd: Cykl opowieści*, 1926). The heroes of these tales are agricultural laborers, farm hands, and poor peasants, both men and women. Dąbrowska's characters are not a pretext for either sentimentality or protest. They are human, complex, rich in spiritual strivings, and therefore their dramas deeply involve the reader. Firsthand knowledge of the Polish countryside and of the peasant dialect makes these tales a work of realism deprived of any condescension.

Dąbrowska was an intellectual, touched by all the philosophical and political currents of the time, capable of debating various issues in her essays, but in her fiction she was restrained and transmitted her message through her sympathy for certain human types. A message? There was one of course. Dąbrowska, an agnostic, a partisan of "ethics without sanction," was through and through an ethical being. She had faith in people confronted every moment of their lives by small tasks and chores. A certain heroism, hardly noticeable, with which people assume their duties was for her a gauge of perpetual renewal, and an undying hope for the species. Perhaps this heroism of duty is a link between her and Joseph Conrad, who occupied her thoughts for many years. Her book *Essays on Conrad* (*Szkice o Conradzie*, 1959) is valuable for those who take an interest in Conrad's ties with Polish Romantic literature. Her philosophy, less bitter than Conrad's, seems to translate her feeling of submersion in the human mass which, in spite of its defeats and failures, creates something constantly through its network of small labors and commitments. For Dąbrowska, that mass was the Polish nation.

Folks from Over Yonder was permeated by the same attitude which compelled her to write the major work of her life, a huge novel in four volumes: *Nights and Days* (*Noce i dnie*, 1932–1934). The title aptly indicates the nature of the work, where days and nights succeed each other in the stream of time, introducing a rhythm of irreversible change into human life; thus, man is forced to face ever new components both within himself and in the world around him. If it is true that a prerequisite for an epic is the description of customs and mores that are forever past, then Dąbrowska's novel fulfills this condition. As her heroes, she chose a gentry couple living on an estate in Poland at the end of the nineteenth century. The nights and days of Bogumił and Barbara Niechcic make up the very texture of Dąbrowska's narrative. Their financial troubles, their conflicts with each other, with other people, and with their daughter, who already follows another way of life, illustrate the transformations of a social structure over a few decades, ending on the eve of World War I. The four volumes (each with a separate title: Vol. I—*Bogumił and Barbara*, Vol. II—*Eternal Trouble*, Vol. III—*Love*, Vol. IV—*Against the Wind*) can be related to the genre of the *roman-fleuve* or "family saga" popularized by Galsworthy in England and by Roger Martin du Gard in France, but they also differ from it in the author's concentration upon two main figures who assume, each according to his or her temperament, the burdens of a conjugal life made lighter by tenderness and forgiveness. Dąbrowska's quiet, well-controlled prose with its rich but simple language has been recognized as exemplary, and quotations from her novel have been used copiously in dictionaries of the Polish language. An avant-garde poet, Julian Przyboś, said in one of his essays: "When I want to breathe in the very essence of Polish in poetry, I bend over *Pan Tadeusz;* when I want to drink from the stream of Polish in prose, I immerse myself in *Nights and Days*."

Besides authoring several articles on the cooperative movement, Dąbrowska published in 1937 *Crossroads* (*Rozdroże*), a study on the peasant question, demonstrating the necessity of an agrarian reform. During the war, she lived in Warsaw, and her behavior under the Nazi occupation served as a model for the whole community of writers. Later, in People's Poland, her prewar works were reprinted in mass editions. Courted by the Communist Party, she preserved her aloofness; her position toward revolutionary change could not be reduced to a clear yes or a clear no, which was in accordance with her usual care to avoid the extremes of either praising or condemning. During the Stalinist period Dąbrowska kept silent, but in 1955 she re-entered the literary scene with her volume of stories, *The Morning Star* (*Gwiazda zaranna*). The story "A Village Wedding" ("Na wsi wesele") is especially typical of her thought: the Polish village has passed through war, enforced collectivization, the terror of petty bureaucrats, and yet life is going on, people survive, work, marry, have children, and all have a feeling of being small parts of some large whole that is more persistent than the plagues inflicted upon them by historical fate. A current of metaphysical faith runs throughout Dąbrowska's work, though it is very difficult to seize because of her great discretion. She, like many writers before her, seemed to draw her strength from her reflections on Polish history. Her two theatrical plays, published in 1957, take up problems of the Polish past: *Stanisław and Bogumił* deals with the defeat of the policy advocated by King Bolesław the Bold in the eleventh century; *The Orphaned Genius* (*Geniusz sierocy*), with the defeat of King Władysław IV's efforts to prevent the Polish-Cossack wars in the seventeenth century by curbing the Polish magnates. Both dramas, though centered upon a defeat, contain optimistic undertones. Finally, Dąbrowska as a translator gave the Polish public an excellent version of Samuel Pepys's *Diary* (1948).

The war, which lasted on Polish territory from 1914 until the end of 1920, and the adventures of both soldiers and civilians, who found themselves in various countries of Europe, could not fail to produce a crop of books, in the form of either memoirs or fiction. Ferdynand Goetel (1890–1960), as an Austrian citizen, had been interned in Tashkent, then served for a while in the Caucasus with a Red Army detachment. He won success overnight with his stories and a novel, *Kar-Khat* (1923), set in the turbulent time of the civil war in the Caucasus Mountains. Goetel, later on, had the distinction of writing an experimental novel, *From Day to Day* (*Z dnia na dzień*, 1926), where the author functions in a double role: within the novel he writes a diary on writing a novel, and, thus, becomes one of its characters. *War Literature*

Many years were to pass, however, before the best book on fighting appeared. This was Stanisław Rembek's (1901–   ) *In Action* (*W polu*, 1937). A brutal, sober, and concise account, it barely fictionalizes the adventures which befell a Polish artillery unit in the summer of 1920 during the Polish-Soviet War.

Not war itself but the bewilderment of man, who becomes involved in it against his own will, is the subject of Józef Wittlin's *Salt of the Earth* (*Sól ziemi*, 1936), originally intended as the first volume of an unwritten cycle, *A Tale of a Patient Infantryman*. Having been translated into many languages, the novel retains an honorable place in European pacifist literature. Wittlin (1896–1976) attended high school in Lwów, the capital of his native province, then studied philosophy and philology at the University of Vienna. During World War I, he served for two years as a soldier in the Austrian infantry. In 1914, he embarked upon his huge project, a new Polish version of Homer's *Odyssey* in verse, which he published in 1924, but has subsequently revised over and over. If the magazine *Source* (*Zdrój*), published in Poznań in the years 1917–1922, constituted an important link between the late phase of "Young Poland" and the postwar literary trends, it was more because of its programmatic defense of expressionism than because of the stature of the poets associated with it—except for Józef Wittlin. The poems in his *Hymns* (*Hymny*, 1920), written in free verse, are indebted for their style to the expressionistic largesse of Jan Kasprowicz, but, instead of metaphysical torment, they voice a humanist's protest against the debasement of man, a victim of powerful states and social systems. They can be likened to the woodcuts of a Flemish rebel against war and oppression, Frans Masereel, one of the most eminent representatives of expressionism in European art. As such, they hold a position of their own, even if Polish poetry veered toward the greater formal discipline of "Skamander" and the First Vanguard. For the hero of his *Salt of the Earth*, Wittlin chose an illiterate peasant from the Carpathian Mountains who has been drafted into the Austrian army and must bear the brunt of military action, without understanding why men have to kill each other and who the people are who have decided his fate. He bears a symbolic name, Niewiadomski ("Unknown"), and, indeed, the novel is a kind of monument to the average, unknown soldier, torn out of his village and caught up in an incomprehensible mechanism.

Not prolific, basically an essayist, only occasionally writing verse or fiction, Wittlin left Poland in the summer of 1939, and since 1941 has been living in New York. He dedicated a warm book of recollections to his native city—*My Lwów* (*Mój Lwów*, 1946).

The Political Novel   The socialist movement attained the peak of its influence during the revolutionary outburst of 1905. It had its own writers, who were more directly involved in it than, say, a sympathizer like Stefan Żeromski. Such a socialist writer, active both in "Young Poland" and in the postwar period, was Stefan Gałecki (1873–1937), publishing under the pen name Andrzej Strug. As a student arrested for a political offense he spent a year and a half in a Warsaw prison, was deported to Archangelsk, and upon his return joined the PPS (Polish Socialist Party). An underground militant in 1905, at the outbreak of World War I he enlisted in Piłsudski's legion, having been a member of the socialist *fraction* that supported the revolutionary leader. Later on, he was disillusioned by the lack of radical reforms in Independent Poland and became the standard-bearer of those Socialists who opposed Piłsudski. His novels about terroristic assaults on czarist officials, conspiracy, and heroic students and workers are permeated with revolutionary romanticism: *Underground People* (*Ludzie podziemni*, 1908), *A Story of One Bomb* (*Dzieje jednego pocisku*, 1910), etc. His participation in military action during the war, together with internal self-questioning and political disenchantment, resulted in his postwar novel, *The Generation of Marek Świda* (*Pokolenie Marka Świdy*, 1925). Strug devoted himself after World War I to writing antimilitaristic and pacifist novels presenting war as an outgrowth of imperialistic international capital—*The Tomb of the Unknown Soldier* (*Mogiła nieznanego żołnierza*, 1922), *The Key to the Abyss* (*Klucz otchłani*, 1929), and a trilogy, *The Yellow Cross* (*Żółty krzyż*, 1933). When he died, his funeral turned into an occasion for a huge demonstration by the whole political Left.

It was not a Socialist, however, who was to leave the most precious novelistic documents on Polish political life during the years 1918–1939. Juliusz Kaden-Bandrowski (1885–1944), born in southern Poland, the son of a medical doctor and publicist, went through high school in Kraków and Lwów, studied music in Brussels, where he also acted as a correspondent for the Polish press, and made his literary debut with a volume of experimental prose, which revealed a passion for naturalistic meticulousness. The "stories" in this volume, entitled *Professions* (*Zawody*, 1911), examine the workaday world of a laundress, a glazier, a dogcatcher, a butcher, etc.

In 1914, Kaden-Bandrowski enlisted in Piłsudski's legion and became a chronicler and propagandist of his commander's deeds. One of the staunchest supporters of Piłsudski's *Putsch* in 1926 and of the resulting new regime, he was very influential, and, for that reason, hated by the political opposition. His adversaries underestimated his seriousness of purpose as a novelist, and it was only in the late fifties that due tribute was paid to his art. As a writer, he inflicted upon himself a self-torturing discipline. He conceived of the novel as a mirror which should show a truth objectively. To do this an author must use documentation. Kaden-Bandrowski traveled all over Poland, collected notes and statistics, and prepared briefly sketched character studies of public figures with whom he mixed—all this with the sole intent of grasping the intricacies and interdependences of what was happening. In his novels, he advanced no thesis; he was deliberately ambiguous— he would have said, like reality itself. Since many of his characters were modeled upon known political figures, cries of malice and slander were heaped upon the author. His novel *Arch* (*Łuk*, 1919) rather unceremoniously depicted life in Kraków during World War I. *General Barcz* (1923) portrayed a "strong man," an army officer with political ambitions, aspiring to rule with an "iron fist," i.e., to create a perfect order, which, as is universally known, can only be introduced by a military junta.

Out of Kaden-Bandrowski's professional research in the Dąbrowa mining basin in Silesia, where he stayed in 1923–1924, grew his huge novel in two parts, *Black Wings* (*Czarne skrzydła*, 1925–1929). The work spares no one—neither French capitalists (owners of the mine), nor their servile Polish executives, nor socialist politicians catering to workers' demands and tiptoeing between one compromise and another. Perhaps the only sympathetic character is a young miner, a Communist activist. The gloomy landscape of the mining country, the misery, and the exploitation are present in *Black Wings* in all their ugliness. A fire in the mine, one of the key episodes in the plot, is scarcely fictionalized: here Kaden-Bandrowski described with great exactitude a real event, changing only the name of the company. The two volumes of *Black Wings* were followed by a three-volume sequel, *Mateusz Bigda* (1933), which was met with scoffs because of its incredible size. In general, Kaden-Bandrowski had more good fortune with his short stories, which were praised by critics, favored by the public, and translated into foreign languages, than with his novels. *Mateusz Bigda* is, in fact, an expedition into a political jungle, into behind-the-scenes intrigues, dirty deals, and demagoguery masking personal ambitions. Only an author no less persuaded than Émile Zola of his vocation to note down the ungainly and the malodorous could have applied himself to such a task. And we have not brought in the name of Zola accidentally. Kaden-Bandrowski was often called a naturalist. To back up this judgment, critics cited his nearly scientific method of gathering data as well as the means he used to characterize his heroes. He centered his attention upon physical details—little tics, aging flesh, resemblances to various kinds of animals. But it would be equally true to say that the extreme intensity of his attack upon reality, his deformations and caricatures, resulted in a style that was close to expressionism. Perhaps analogies could be established between him and some Soviet writers of the twenties.

In spite of his close relations with ruling circles, Kaden-Bandrowski was a rather solitary man devoted to one endeavor only; one might call it the inquiries of a social naturalist. Amid quarreling ideologies, he was isolated in his rather outmoded conviction, which he himself formulated as follows: "I believe that to be able to say everything about man means to unshackle him from all his fetters."

Utopias and Antiutopias   The catastrophe of World War I, the Revolution in Russia, which opened a new era, and the fluidity of political forms inclined some writers to ironical and paradoxical predictions. Polish futurists (whose role in poetry was slight, owing to the preponderance of "Skamander" and the constructivist First Vanguard) liked to thumb their noses at the public in their prose. Thus, Bruno Jasieński in his first novel, *The Legs of Izolda Morgan* (*Nogi Izoldy Morgan*, 1923), prophesied, much as did the Czech writer Karel Čapek, the end "we are moving toward with mathematical precision," namely, the rule of machines, which, having won their independence, will crush human beings. The same Jasieński, in his *Je Brûle Paris*, for which he was expelled from France in 1928, depicted a rather un-Marxist destruction of bourgeois French civilization by revolutionaries who provoke a fatal epidemic by contaminating the water.

Another futurist, Aleksander Wat (1900–1967), published his sarcastic tales of anticipation under the title *Lucifer Unemployed* (*Bezrobotny Lucyfer*, 1927). To give an idea of its contents it is enough to say that one of the tales is entitled "Long Live Europe (from the memoirs of an ex-European)," or that in another tale, "The Wandering

Jew," we are introduced to the third millennium of our era, marked by the triumph of the Roman Catholic Church on a planetary scale. Due to the conversion of the Jews to Christianity, all the clergy are Jewish, while anti-Semites learn Hebrew, discover the cabala, and become enemies of the Papacy. A link between these works and Stanisław Ignacy Witkiewicz's antiutopias, which we have already mentioned, is obvious. In the late fifties, Wat was to re-emerge as an important poet.

Writers on the Left were sensitive to the "newspaper-clippings technique" of Dos Passos, to realistic films, and to discussions on literature taking place in the Soviet Union. In addition, Polish sociologists gathered volumes of written reports from people directly concerned with their own economic plight; these were *Memoirs of Migrants* (Polish workers in France and Latin America) and *Memoirs of Peasants*. Such authentic testimonies found a vivid response among the public and were often rated higher than fiction. The trend increased in momentum around 1930, under the impact of the economic crisis. For example, a Communist review, *The Literary Monthly* (let us note here that although the Communist Party was banned, Communist-oriented periodicals managed somehow to appear), edited by Aleksander Wat in 1929–1931, favored "the social document" and increased interest in it by announcing a contest for the best description of a given milieu by nonprofessionals. The contest met with massive response from the review's readers. In 1933, several writers with Leftist sympathies, ranging from noncommitted to Communist, joined together to form a writers' group project under the name of "City Outskirts" (*Przedmieście*). They set as their goal the focusing of attention upon facts little or never touched upon in fiction. They wrote about average people, who were treated as representatives of a given social group or of a profession, and tried to catch the very social climate of certain streets or town districts. The promoters of the project were Helena Boguszewska (1886–   ) and Jerzy Kornacki (1908–   ), who often signed their works together. Their joint novel, *The Vistula* (*Wisła*, 1935), is a report on the life of workers who earned their living from the river as sand-diggers and boatmen. Thus, a "literature of fact" competed in the thirties with standard fiction, which was losing its foothold—at least, literary circles were debating among themselves the difficulty of building imaginary characters and plots due to an awareness of the changes brought about by psychology and the social sciences. While the "literature of fact" has doubtful artistic merits, it left its imprint upon the generation of novelists making their debut shortly before the outbreak of World War II.

Nobody exemplifies better than Leon Kruczkowski (1900–1962) the trend toward the "social document." A native of Kraków, he completed his technical studies there, was employed in the chemical industry for

On the Borderline between Social Document and Fiction

a few years, then taught in professional schools. A socialist activist and publicist, he provoked a stir with his first novel, *Kordian and the Boor* (*Kordian i cham*, 1932), acclaimed by the whole Left as a major literary event. A debate on certain crucial issues of Polish history, especially those of the nineteenth century, has always been characteristic of the Polish literary scene, and an author's interpretation of these issues has ranged him with one or another of the camps vying for influence with writers. The title of Kruczkowski's novel refers to Juliusz Słowacki's dramatic hero, Kordian, a revolutionary of noble origin, one of those who prepared and brought about the uprising of 1830. Contrasting a "boor" to Kordian, Kruczkowski made use of an authentic document, namely, the diary of a certain Deczyński, a plebeian who fought against the Russians in 1830–1831, but always felt his goals and his outlook were different from those of his noble commanders. Under Kruczkowski's pen, the diary was enlarged and embroidered upon, becoming a testimony of social resentment and an act of accusation. It juxtaposed two Polands and two notions of patriotism—each delineated along class lines. There is no doubt that Kruczkowski's master was Stefan Żeromski, whose *Ashes*, together with its sequel— a long story, *Everything and Nothing* (*Wszystko i nic*, 1919)—tells a story of fighters for national independence and contrasts the sad lot of simple soldiers issued from the peasantry with the noblemen's life of bravado. Because Kruczkowski provided the theme with a more radical twist, *Kordian and the Boor* was credited with opening up in literature a re-evaluation of Polish history in purely Marxist terms, and was received as a highly relevant political manifesto. The novel also revealed both the strong and the weak sides of its author's talent. A seriousness of purpose, visible throughout his whole career, was not coupled with creative inventiveness, and his clinging to documents or literary motifs introduced by others probably resulted from an awareness of his own limitations. He was less successful in his next novels: *Peacock Feathers* (*Pawie pióra*, 1935), a further probing of the same historical subject, and *A Trap* (*Sidła*, 1937), a gloomy, gray chronicle from the life of unemployed white-collar workers. As one of those writers who opposed most energetically the growing fascism in his country, he wrote an anti-Nazi play, *An Adventure with Vaterland* (*Przygoda z Vaterlandem*, 1938). After the September 1939 campaign, in which he was involved as a Polish officer, he spent five years in a prisoner-of-war camp in Germany. Upon his return in 1945 he became a leading literary figure in People's Poland. At that time, he abandoned fiction for the drama.

Quite a stir was evoked by a young author, Zbigniew Uniłowski (1909–1937), whose works were read as firsthand reports on various milieus. His premature death interrupted a career that might possibly have been that of a major novelist. *A Shared Room* (*Wspólny pokój*, 1932), is a scarcely fictionalized portrayal of the life of young Warsaw Bohemians connected with the "Quadriga" vanguard group; *Twenty Years of Life* (*Dwadzieścia lat życia*, 1937) used the form of memoirs to present the narrator's childhood in a proletarian district of Warsaw. Uniłowski's rough and vigorous talent, his colloquial, slangy language, make him the most convincing practitioner of documentary realism.

Born in the predominantly Jewish town of Drohobycz, near the oil fields in Galicia, Bruno Schulz studied architecture in Lwów, specializing in lithography and drawing, and for most of his life remained in his native town, where he earned his living as a teacher of drawing at a high school. A solitary artist, condemned to live in provincial surroundings, he also wrote—but only for himself, because he was too timid to approach publishers. He was formed intellectually by "Young Poland" and by German literature of the first decades of the century. He found his way into the literary circles of Warsaw belatedly. In 1933, he joined the group project "City Outskirts," and the next year he published his first book, *Cinnamon Stores* (*Sklepy cynamonowe*, 1934). Once acclaimed by young literati and accepted by editors of magazines and by publishers, he came forward with his second book, *The Sanitarium under the Sign of the Hourglass* (*Sanatorium pod klepsydrą*, 1937). His complete output is limited to those two books, as a manuscript of a novel, *Messiah*, which he worked on afterward, is lost. A Jew, Schulz was driven into the ghetto of Drohobycz by the Nazis and killed there.

Bruno Schulz (1892–1942)

The name of Kafka comes to mind whenever Bruno Schulz is spoken of. The latter admired Kafka, and his translation of *The Trial* appeared in 1936. His prose, no less than Kafka's, breaks with what is usually called a novel or a short story. Schulz's two books consist of tales, unified by the person of a narrator who is a somewhat phantasmagoric "I" of the author. The narrator relates his adventures in a provincial town where everything is transfigured, magnified, distorted, and changed into a dream by his imagination. The adventures disclose certain incongruous properties of matter. Because of its fluidity, matter was a constant wonder for Schulz. Shapes burgeon into shapes, disappear, then mutate again into something unexpected. Although certain similarities between Schulz and Kafka do exist (such as the obsessive presence of the father, who ends his fabulous existence under the guise of a cockroach), Schulz's talent is original, and his kinship with the writer from Prague went much deeper than literary influences could reach. He drew both his originality and his strength from his native town. Through his power of enveloping the simplest things in a web of metaphors, he made the salesmen in his father's store,

a servant girl, Adele, and his father mythological figures, the heroes
of a parable on existence. It was not in the "literature of fact," but
in Schulz's weird phantasmagories that the Jewish town found its
reflection, though it was a distorted one, emanating from the concave
and convex mirrors of his mind. His humor, his intuition (one is surprised by his image of Drohobycz's most modern street in the "Street
of Crocodiles," which might equally well be a study on man's alienation in big American cities), the metaphorical richness of his language
confirm the judgment of the young literati in the thirties who praised
Schulz and that of the Polish Academy of Literature, which crowned
him with a "golden laurel." Today, Schulz is regarded as one of the
most important prose writers between the two wars.

Maria   Literary critics were puzzled by the invasion of women novelists
Kuncewicz who secured for themselves positions as the most widely read authors
(1899–) of fiction. Whether the often advanced economic explanation is valid or
not (women supposedly had more time to write, while their husbands
were busy being the breadwinners), the list of female writers is considerable. Few of them, however, equaled Maria Kuncewicz in neatness and elegance of style or in carefulness of construction. Her university studies—French literature in Nancy, Polish literature in Kraków and Warsaw, singing at the conservatories of Warsaw and Paris
—seemed to have prepared her well for her task. She made her debut
in 1918 in the same magazine, *Pro Arte et Studio*, where the poets of
"Skamander" took their first steps, and circulated in the same Warsaw
literary milieu. While the "Skamandrites," at least initially, wanted to
restore "normalcy" to Polish poetry, which too often had been forced to
serve national and social causes, Maria Kuncewicz attempted to pursue
a similar aim in fiction. This meant a detached investigation of human
psychology, without regard for political commitments. Her numerous
short stories and two novels—*The Face of the Male* (*Twarz mężczyzny*,
1928), *The Foreigner* (*Cudzoziemka*, 1936)—qualify her for the title
of the most "Western" among her Polish contemporaries, in the sense
of focusing upon the individual. The heroine of *The Foreigner* behaves
strangely when judged by the standards of her middle-class family
because of her psychogenic "otherness." The novel is, thus, a thorough
study of "character," as predetermined by the laws of heredity, of a
secret core in the human being which distinguishes him from all
others. It is a somewhat melancholy reflection that the novel appeared
at a time when the very existence of the character as an independent
entity was being questioned by those Polish novelists who, beginning
with Irzykowski, were dissolving it into its psychological or social
prehistory.

Maria Kuncewicz was also the author of the first Polish "radio
novel." Enacted before the microphone once a week, it enjoyed tremen-

dous popularity. The title can be rendered into English as *The Every-day Life of Mr. and Mrs. Jones* (*Dni powszednie państwa Kowalskich*, published in 1938). She left Poland after the Nazis overran it, went to France, lived in England from 1940 to 1955, then settled in the United States. Since then, however, she has made prolonged trips to Poland. It is difficult to refrain from a remark here, which throws some light on the Polish writer's predicament: the best of Maria Kuncewicz's psychological novels written abroad—*The Forester* (*Leśnik*, 1952) is set in the Polish countryside at the time of the 1863 uprising.

Brought up in a sophisticated family, the daughter of a noted War- *Zofia* saw scholar and publicist, Wacław Nałkowski, Zofia Nałkowska in her *Nałkowska* youth was one of the blue stockings so numerous at the time of "Young *(1884–1954)* Poland." In her novels published prior to World War I, beginning with *Women* (*Kobiety*, 1906), she committed successively all the sins of that era: aestheticism, oversophistication, and psychological sham profundity. After the war, Nałkowska was praised as the most accomplished representative of the psychological novel, and was translated into several languages. But her most mature work came later. This was *Boundary Line* (*Granica*, 1935). The whole thought of the author, who had run the gamut of intellectual fashions as they had succeeded each other in Europe, culminated in that novel, but it was submitted to a new discipline. Characters she had investigated before as detached from their roles, which society had imposed upon them, are here set against a solid background of their social status. This is a novel on prisoners of "patterns" that are so strong they not only modify the behavior of the protagonists but penetrate to the core of their internal motivations. It is also a major analysis of the Polish intelligentsia, especially of the progressive and socialist intelligentsia, of all those readers of Żeromski or Strug who, after 1918, believing in their own good intentions, were slowly sucked in by the established order and enacted what was dictated by a given "pattern." A dramatic plot, entangling a multitude of secondary characters, serves to indicate a boundary line which human beings try to pass in vain even if they strive hard to attain their true selves. This line is fixed neither by their own will nor by their notions of good and evil. It depends upon the place they occupy in a network that predetermines their relations with other people, it depends upon their social origins, profession, and money. Thus, Nałkowska questioned the very idea of the character as a certain autonomous entity preserving his essence through all vicissitudes, no matter how oppressive or threatening. For her the "pattern" is so corrosive that it eats up from inside any intended continuity in behavior, and, perhaps, man is nothing more than what he is in the eyes of others. The philosophical and political implications of such a thesis were noticed with satisfaction by critics sympathetic to Marxism. *Boundary Line* had, of course, significance as a novel of social analysis, too, and the date of its appearance makes it one of the milestones of the "sombre thirties." After 1945, Nałkowska was active on the editorial staff of the literary weekly *Forge* (*Kuźnica*), was a deputy to the Diet, and was a member of the Commission for the Investigation of Nazi Crimes. Besides a political novel, *Knots of Life* (*Węzły życia*, 1948), she published a collection of factual stories on the Nazi genocide, entitled *Medallions* (*Medaliony*, 1946).

Witold Gombrowicz
(1904–1969)

A writer who was to win international renown after World War II and simultaneous acclaim from his younger colleagues in Poland, for whom he is a recognized master, even though he lived abroad since 1939, Witold Gombrowicz started out as the son of a well-to-do gentry family. To invoke one's genealogy was very unpopular in literary circles, but just because of this, he always stressed it, and such a reversal of the accepted codes of behavior has been typical of his "method." He completed his studies in law at the University of Warsaw, then studied philosophy and economics in Paris, but abandoned his budding legal career when he made his literary debut with some crazy short stories— *Memoirs from the Time of Immaturity* (*Pamiętnik okresu dojrzewania*, 1933). No less crazy were his novel *Ferdydurke* (1938) and his play *Yvonne, Princess of Burgundy* (*Iwona księżniczka Burgunda*, 1938). If we have employed the word "crazy," it is because Gombrowicz exhilarated the public with his buffoonery. In fact, he proceeded by a game of constant provocation, cornering the reader into an admission of unpalatable truths. Of a philosophical mind, but completely free from any respect for the sort of philosophy taught in universities, he had no reverence whatsoever for literature. He derided it as a snobbish ritual, and if he practiced it, he attempted to get rid of all its accepted rules.

Along with Stanisław Ignacy Witkiewicz and Bruno Schulz, his close friend, Gombrowicz broke radically with the nineteenth-century "mirror of life" novel. His works are fables composed to communicate his thought on existence, which is too involved to be expressed in treatises; the plots he invented for his various works allude to each other in counterpoint fashion. To explain Gombrowicz, quotations from Heidegger and Sartre have been used, but there was no borrowing of ideas, only a convergence. (Sartre's books, for example, came out later.) Gombrowicz's whole work consists in a chase after authenticity, hence his fascination with adolescence. An adolescent is a set of contradictions which may be envisaged as possibilities; he can take one or another form. When he is caught by the world of adults, he assumes a form not his own but pre-existing, elaborated through mutual relationships between adults.

Ferdydurke is a story of a thirty-year-old whom a malicious school-master-magician, Pimko, transforms into a schoolboy. The first part deals with the hero's adventures in high school, where the teaching is frozen into formulas repeated *ad nauseam* and where the youngsters are forced to admire such and such a great poet only "because he is great." Moreover, the youngsters, when they are by themselves, submit to a frozen convention of "boys will be boys" (dirty words, bragging, etc.). The hero, who is also the narrator, loses his battle for self-liberation, since his escape from high school "patterns" merely lands him in a Warsaw family of young intelligentsia, and this means a new serfdom: progressivism, lack of prejudices, a daring approach to sex, everything that seems to be "anti-Establishment," but, again, is frozen in forms, rules, and canons. The hero escapes a second time, with the vague hope of recovering his authenticity in the countryside, not through any union with nature but through fraternization with a fellow man who personifies primitive health, the country lad. The third part recounts a new disaster, as on the estate where the hero lives, both masters and servants repeat automatically the gestures and attitudes prescribed for masters and servants. A recurring motif in the novel is the pandemonium of a wriggling "heap" (*kupa*) of bodies as the characters throw each other to the floor in a kind of frenzy. That writhing mass is perhaps an image for the only authentic human contact. The opposition of immaturity and adulthood, authenticity and form can also be phrased as an opposition of nature and culture. For Gombrowicz, men, "those eternal actors," are shaped by each other, by their mutual seeing of each other. Man is "adapting" every instant to what is expected of him, according to his role—thus, schoolboys expect dirty words and bragging from each other. True individuality is unattainable, for man is always enmeshed in interdependences with other human beings. Gombrowicz even speaks of an "interhuman church," by which he means that we create one another; we are not self-existing. People whom we meet in a given situation infect us with their behavior, and even if we oppose that behavior, we are not free, since our very opposition is a pattern we fall into. And vice versa: if the behavior of one person, introduced into a group, differs from the group's, the discrepancy unleashes a chain of patterned reactions. Gombrowicz proves this in his play *Yvonne, Princess of Burgundy:* a crown prince walking in the park rebels against the pattern demanding that a young man run after beautiful, enticing girls. He notices Yvonne on the bench. She is a very ugly girl who suffers from such slow blood circulation that she never utters a word, to the despair of her aunts, who chaperone her. The prince decides to marry her and brings her to the royal palace as his fiancée. There, her numb presence soon begins to act with explosive force. The dignified court, as well as the king and queen themselves, reacts to Yvonne's numbness first through patterns of irritation, then through sadistic impulses, and at last, an unboned fish is served to Yvonne in the hope that she will choke to death, which she does. The play says a great deal about Gombrowicz's method of provocation. Anything which destroys "the form" is good, but Gombrowicz has never solved his nature-culture dichotomy. By doing so he would have to concede that man can get rid of the "interhuman church." For Gombrowicz, there is always both a striving toward liberation from "the form" and a necessary submission to it, since every antiform freezes into a new form. Each book of his, however, is a renewed attempt to capture one variety of striving and to smash one more sacrosanct rule of art. In his *Diary* and in the essays built into his novels, he attacks the inauthenticity, for instance, of people who incite each other to admiration at a concert or an art exhibit, or before masterpieces of literature. Everything he published before the war voiced his scorn for phony relationships reduced to the assuming of roles. The same premeditated arrogance helped him in his subsequent exploits.

In the summer of 1939, Gombrowicz went on a cruise to Latin America and was stranded in Buenos Aires by the outbreak of the war. During the many years he lived in Argentina, he stuck to Polish, and no wonder, as linguistic playfulness is a vital part of his craft. His novel *Transatlantic* (*Trans-Atlantyk,* 1953), has an Argentinian setting but is written in a language that parodies Polish seventeenth-century memorialists. Many consider it his most accomplished work, as it brings into the open a theme underlying all his writings: how to transform one's "Polishness," which is felt as a wound, an affliction, into a source of strength. A Pole is an immature human being, an adolescent, and this saves him from settling in a "form."

For Gombrowicz himself the key to his thought is his play *The Marriage Ceremony* (*Ślub*, 1953). On its most superficial level, that of the plot per se, it presents the dream of a soldier (Henry) in World War II who, in his nightmare, returns home to confront there a debased reality—his father is a drunken innkeeper, his fiancée a whore. The idea of the play is explained by the author in his Introduction:

Man is subject to that which is created "between" individuals, and he has no other divinity but that which springs from other people.

This is exactly what is meant by that "earthly church" which appears to Henry in his dream. Here, human beings are bound together in certain forms of pain, fear, ridicule, or mystery, in unforeseen melodies and rhythms, in absurd relations and situations, and submitting to these forms, they are created by what they themselves have created. In this earthly church the human spirit worships the interhuman spirit.

Henry elevates his father to the office of king so his father might bestow the sacrament of marriage upon him, after which he proclaims himself king and seeks to confer the sacrament upon himself. To this end, Henry compels his subjects to invest him with divinity: he aspires to become his own God.

But all of this is accomplished by means of Form. Being united, people impose upon one another this or that manner of being, speaking, behaving. . . . Each person deforms other persons while being at the same time deformed by them.

The vistas opened by such a philosophy appear clearly in a great monologue pronounced, partly in verse, by Henry in the second act:

Even though I was the most healthy . . . the most rational . . .
The most balanced person,
Others forced me to commit
Atrocious acts, murderous acts,
Insane, moronic, and yes, licentious acts. . . .
This raises a simple question: If in the course of several years a person fulfills the function of a madman, is he not then really a madman? And what does it matter that I am healthy if my actions are sick—eh, Johnny? But those who forced me to commit those insanities were also healthy
And sensible
And balanced. . . . Friends, companions, brothers—so much
Health
And such sick behavior? So much sanity
And yet so much madness? So much humanity
And yet so much inhumanity? And what does it matter if, taken separately, each of us is lucid, sensible, balanced, when altogether we are nothing but a gigantic madman who furiously
Writhes about, screams, bellows, and blindly
Rushes forward, overstepping his own bounds,
Tearing himself out of himself. . . . Our madness
Is outside ourselves, out there. . . . There, there, out there
Where I myself end, there begins
My wantonness. . . . And even though I live in peace
Within myself, still do I wander outside myself,
And in dark, wild spaces and nocturnal places
Surrender myself to some unbounded chaos!

Even more explicit is the following fragment from Henry's monologue in the third act:

I reject every order, every concept,
I distrust every abstraction, every doctrine,
I don't believe in God or in Reason!
Enough of these gods! Give me man!

May he be like me, troubled and immature,
Confused and incomplete, dark and obscure,
So I can dance with him! Play with him! Fight with him!
Pretend to him! Ingratiate myself with him!
And rape him, love him, and forge myself
Anew from him, so I can grow through him, and in that way
Celebrate my marriage in the sacred human church!*

After *The Marriage Ceremony* (*Ślub*) came the novels *Pornografia* (1960) and *Cosmos* (*Kosmos*, 1965), plus volumes of *Diary* (*Dziennik*, 1953–1968). Each book developed and deepened Gombrowicz's philosophy. *Cosmos* opens up a terrifying dimension where any laws ruling human behavior as well as those ruling matter are dissolved—since they are dependent upon an observer who arbitrarily picks this and not that point of departure for a whole series of reasonings. This principle of "it might have been otherwise" applies not only to the world in Gombrowicz's novel but to his literary procedures as well. To quote from the third volume of his *Diary* (the entry for April 1966):

I establish two points of departure, two anomalies quite distant from each other: a) a hanged sparrow, b) an association of Catherine's with Lena's lips. Those two enigmas will ask for a meaning. One will penetrate another, tending toward a totality. Guesses will emerge, associations, circumstantial evidence; something will create itself, but it will be a rather monstrous embryo . . . and that dark, incomprehensible puzzle will call for a solution, will search for a clarifying, ordering idea. . . . What adventures, what trouble with reality, when it is breaking out of the mist in such a way. . . .

Gombrowicz's destructive talent has always been directed toward depriving the reader of his certainties and his presumed values. In *Cosmos* he cast doubt upon the very nature of the act by which we apprehend the simplest objects. To quote again from the same passage of his *Diary:*

From a superabundance of phenomena which appear around me, I pick up one. I notice, for instance, an ashtray on my table (the rest of the objects on the table recede into nothingness).

If I succeed in proving to myself why I noticed exactly the ashtray ("I want to get rid of the ashes from my cigarette"), everything is fine.

If I noticed the ashtray by chance without any intention and I do not return to that perception, also everything is as it should be.

But if, after I have noticed a phenomenon without importance, I return to it—woe! Why did you notice it again if it is without importance? So it means something to you if you returned to it? That's how, by the very fact that you illegitimately concentrated your attention upon a phenomenon a second longer, that thing begins to distinguish itself, becomes signifi-

* All quotations from *The Marriage Ceremony* in Louis Iribarne's translation.

cant. No, no (you defend yourself), this is a common ashtray! Common? Why do you protect yourself if it is common?

That is how a phenomenon becomes an obsession.

Is reality obsessional by its nature? Since we build our worlds by associating phenomena, I would not be surprised to discover that at the beginning of time there was a *twice-made association*. It traces a direction in chaos and is at the origin of order.

With translations of his works into French, German, Swedish, English and the staging of his plays in Paris during the sixties, recognition came to Gombrowicz from Western European critics. At that time he left Argentina, lived for a while in West Berlin, then settled in the south of France. In 1967 he received for *Cosmos* the Publishers' International Literary Award of twenty thousand dollars (Prix Formentor).

While Gombrowicz, at the outbreak of World War II, was already a mature writer, the same cannot be said about those whose names were often mentioned around 1935–1939 as the most promising in the field of prose. These were Adolf Rudnicki (born 1912), Jerzy Andrzejewski (born 1909), Tadeusz Breza (born 1905), and Teodor Parnicki (born 1908). Rudnicki was the most productive: he published five books. But he was to reach the peak of his creativity later, during the war and postwar years, under the impact of the tragedy of the Polish Jews. Andrzejewski, awarded a prize by the Polish Academy of Literature in 1939 for his *Mode of the Heart* (*Ład serca*, 1938), which bears traces of George Bernanos' influence, was ranged among Catholic novelists, but he subsequently took quite a different path. Breza, author of an experimental psychological novel, *Adam Grywałd* (1936), also changed his orientation later on. As for Parnicki he set off on his long journey as a historical novelist in 1937 with his *Aetius, the Last Roman* (*Aecjusz, ostatni Rzymianin*), on Rome in the fifth century. We shall discuss these authors in the chapter on postwar literature (see Chapter XI).

The Novelists of the Late Thirties

Janusz Korczak
(1878–1942)

An extraordinary man, most active in the years 1918–1939, should be mentioned in this chapter. Korczak is the pen name of Henryk Goldszmit, born in Warsaw and a successful medical doctor and writer there. After a few years of practice, he abandoned his medical career to become director of a Jewish orphanage in his native city, dedicating himself to the care of the children. He instituted his own innovative pedagogical method based on self-government. His love and respect for the child as a person permeates everything he wrote: fiction for young people and about young people, short articles, and radio talks. Children in his works are endowed with an innate sense of justice and in many cases are more serious than adults. Korczak's humor and his humanizing philosophy are best exemplified by his fablelike novels. In *King Matt the First* (*Król Maciuś Pierwszy*, 1923) a boy-king wants to change the world misgoverned by the adults, but is dethroned and deported to a desert island. *When I Am Little Again* (*Kiedy znów będę mały*, 1925) is a charming tale of an adult who through magic becomes a child (the same idea later appears in Gombrowicz's *Ferdydurke*).

Korczak's selfless life and heroic death have made him into a myth, a model of a lay saint. A Jew, he was offered a safe escape from the Warsaw ghetto during World War II by his non-Jewish friends, but he refused their offer and remained at the orphanage. Together with his children, he was taken by the Nazis to the Treblinka extermination camp.

THE ESSAY AND INTERMEDIARY GENRES

Much favored by the Polish reading public, nonfiction occupied a significant place in Polish literature, encroaching upon the domain which, in other countries, was often reserved for fiction. Between the two wars, books of literary essays, especially those by Tadeusz Boy-Żeleński or Karol Irzykowski, provoked heated controversies in the press. Around 1930, a new generation of critics brought fresh insights to the literary scene. On the one hand, they were open to the theories of Russian formalists, whose works—some accessible in translations—were debated in university seminars. On the other hand, their preoccupation with Stanisław Brzozowski's thought paralleled their interests in phenomenology (as set forth by Max Scheler) and in French "personalism" (as expounded by Emmanuel Mounier). In postwar Poland the survival of some gifted critics of that generation and their active participation in literary life contributed much to a sense of continuity, more noticeable in Poland perhaps than elsewhere in Eastern Europe.

Mention should be made here of a very typical phenomenon in Poland prior to the tragic events of 1939. A considerable number of people were brought up before World War I in a spirit of antinationalism and of respect for "European civilization" as a whole, but at the same time they were rooted in their own regional traditions. When such people wrote, they knew how to preserve an equilibrium between their "Europeanism" and their fidelity to the heritage transmitted through many centuries of Polish history. Such, for instance, was the case of the essayist Jerzy Stempowski (1894–   ), whose finesse impressed several young apprentices. A native of the Ukraine, the son of a publicist, he studied humanities in Kraków, Munich, and Zurich, where, in 1914, he presented a dissertation entitled *Antike und christliche Geschichtsphilosophie im I–V Jahrhundert*. An accomplished humanist, a connoisseur of the Roman world in its decline, he seemed to revert in his essays to the unhurried, serene pace of Old Polish diaries and written "talks" (*gawędy*), with their meandering construction. The charm of his sly, apparently effortless ruminations nourished by erudition consisted in their being so completely at variance with the frenzied rhythm of the twentieth century and with all kinds of fanatically embraced new creeds. A skeptic, very much in the manner of the eighteenth century, he punctured the belief in the exceptional quality of modern times through his game of analogies with the past, and saw the craze for nationalism, for military rule, for anti-Semitism as the sign of a hubris usually punished by destiny. At the beginning of World War II, he emigrated, reaching Switzerland after many narrow escapes, and settled there. His essays of the postwar decades, signed with the pen name Paweł Hostowiec, were published mainly in a Paris *émigré* monthly, *Kultura*, many of them under the title *Meditations of an Unhurried Wanderer*. Several were gathered in a book, *Essays for Cassandra* (*Eseje dla Kasandry*, 1961).

The most true to Stempowski's spirit among the young essayists was Bolesław Miciński (1911–1943), a poet and philosopher of great promise, whose work was interrupted by his premature death. His *Journeys to Hell* (*Podróże do piekieł*, 1938) is a collection of essays on symbolic descents to the world of the subconscious in literature: it takes its title from Ulysses' expedition to the land of the dead. In his *Portrait of Kant* (*Portret Kanta*, 1947) he approaches the thought of the German philosopher obliquely through a sympathetic description of his ordered, pedantic everyday life.

Somewhat similar to Stempowski in background, education, and outlook is Stanisław Vincenz (1888–1971). Descended from a family of French settlers who, several centuries before, had abandoned their native Provence for the Carpathian Mountains, where they became assimilated into the Polish gentry, Vincenz grew up in a miraculous world which still preserved its patriarchal, pastoral civilization. Before the partitions, that remote corner of Europe had belonged to the Polish *Respublica*, then (during Vincenz's childhood and youth) to the Austrian Empire, and between 1918 and 1939 to Poland. It was inhabited by a mixed population professing various creeds and speaking several different idioms. Known as the Country of the Hutzuls, it owed its name to a tribe of sheepherders who spoke a Ukrainian dialect. Polish and Yiddish were also used, and it was in this region that Baal-Shem, the founder of Hasidism, once lived and taught. Vincenz, after completing high school in his native province, studied at the University of Vienna, where, in 1914, he received a doctorate for his dissertation on Hegel's philosophy of religion. Yet his subsequent work is indebted not to Hegel but to his love for his homeland. *In the Upper Highlands* (*Na wysokiej połoninie*, Vol. I, 1936; Vols. II, III, published only in fragments) is a nearly unique record of the rites, customs, and legends of the Hutzul country, that now obliterated island of ancient lore that once existed in the midst of modern civilization. The book defies definition. It is part anthropological saga, part reminiscence, and part poem-in-prose. It captures the rhythm of a hieratic, solemn way of life which enabled different races and faiths to live together peacefully and harmoniously. The religious current is represented chiefly by numerous stories on the Hasidim; despite the tenderly humorous tone, they convey in parable form serious theological probings—for example, the story on *Bałaguły*, Jewish wagon drivers, who engage in a debate on whether God will forgive Samael (Satan) at the end of the world. Perhaps one of Vincenz's hidden aims was to counterpoise his world, so swiftly receding into the past, to the divisive hatreds of exacerbated nationalism and to totalitarian slogans. The completion of *In the Upper Highlands* took many years. During World War II, Vincenz crossed the Carpathian Mountains into Hungary, where he lived for a few years (his essays on the Hungarian landscape deal with Hungarian history as present in the landscape); later, faithful to his mountain heritage, he established his residence in the French Alps. Vincenz is also the author of essays on Dante and on ancient Greece.

Pre-World War I European high-school education, with its stress on classical languages, favored what we might call civility in the approach to human affairs. Both Stempowski and Vincenz read Homer in the original. So did another essayist of the period, Jan Parandowski (1895–   ), a native of Lwów and a graduate of its university, where he studied classical philology. His essays are dedicated mostly to ancient Greek literature and history; his novel *Olympic Discus* (*Dysk olympijski*, 1933) reconstructs the attitudes of the Greeks toward their Olympian games. Another novel, *Sky in Flames* (*Niebo w płomieniach*, 1936), has something about it of a theological treatise. It explores a young boy's religious crisis on the eve of World War I when he encounters the books of German "liberal Protestants" on Jesus and Christianity. Parandowski's greatest success in Poland after World War II was his translation of *The Odyssey*. Its limpid prose made it one of the best sellers.

These few figures have been brought to the reader's notice to support what we have said about a certain cultural continuity in Poland, which extends from the beginning of the century through the present postwar period.

CHAPTER XI

World War II and the First
Twenty Years of People's Poland

BACKGROUND INFORMATION

THE GERMAN INVASION of Poland, begun on September 1, *A Few* 1939, drew Poland's Western Allies, France and England, to her *Data on* side and, thus, unleashed World War II. Fine weather during that *Wartime* "memorable September" was of help to Hitler's army, permitting his planes to bomb the cities and strafe the roads relentlessly. The Nazi advance was rapid. It bypassed and surrounded Warsaw, which defended itself until the end of the month. The Soviet army moved forward from the east on September 17, and both powers met on a line which had been predetermined, along with their zones of influence, in their agreement of August 21. The Soviet Union took over the eastern provinces of Poland, traditionally designated by the Russians as Western Byelorussia and Western Ukraine because of their ethnic composition. After a few weeks, Wilno was offered to Lithuania by the Soviet Union, but in June 1940 the three Baltic states, Lithuania, Latvia, and Estonia, were absorbed by their powerful neighbor, who had established military bases on their territory. The Polish Government and some units of the Polish army withdrew to the vicinity of the Polish-Romanian border. At the news of the Red Army advance, they crossed into Romania and were interned there. A new government-in-exile, created in France by General Sikorski, opponent of the regime of "the colonels," was recognized as legitimate by the Western Allies because it issued from a mandate of the Polish president, Mościcki, who had also managed to escape into exile. The new government, which had taken up residence in Angers, France, proceeded to organize an army composed of Polish residents in France and those who arrived from Poland through Hungary, Romania, and Yugoslavia. This Polish army fought against the Nazis during their onslaught on France in 1940. What remained of it was transported, together with the government-in-exile, to England. Polish units also took part in the English landing at Narwik in Norway, and Polish pilots suffered heavy losses when participating in the Battle of Britain.

The Nazi policy in Poland differed from that applied in other occupied countries. Their goal was to exterminate as much as possible of the population and to turn what would remain of "the inferior race" into slaves. This program was applied with greater and greater boldness. There were mass executions of hostages; in the summer of 1940 the concentration camp at Auschwitz was founded, and human round-ups in the streets of Warsaw were to continue throughout the Nazi occupation. Ghettos for the Jews were ordered in the same year—at first under the pretext of "sanitary measures." All universities and high schools were closed, and a group of leading professors at the Jagiellonian University was deported to the concentration camp at Dachau. No periodicals and no books in Polish were allowed to be published. Rations of food allotted to city-dwellers were insufficient for survival even on a level of semistarvation. The outcome of these Nazi measures was the spontaneous growth of a resistance movement and a black market. In a very short time the resistance movement had at its disposal an organizational network, a true "underground state," with its own guerrilla Home Army and numerous, clandestinely printed, periodicals —dailies, weeklies, and monthlies.

Mass migrations of people looking for their relatives or fleeing Nazi persecution in their home towns and villages characterized the beginning of the period. Many escaped to the Soviet part of the former state in the hope that survival there would be easier. Yet for the Poles, the regime introduced by Stalin was incomprehensible. Old anti-Russian resentments were revived, and there was a tendency to forget that the Russian people had suffered as much as those who were making a belated discovery of the totalitarian Stalinist system. The confrontation was particularly difficult for Leftists who had not imagined the Soviet Union to be what it was in 1939–1940. They were dismayed by the mass deportations to labor camps and remote kolkhozes of Asia. According to rough estimates, around a million and a half Polish citizens —Poles, Jews, Byelorussians, Lithuanians, Ukrainians—left their homes in this manner. Fulfilling her agreement with Germany, the Soviet Union recognized neither the existence of Poland nor that of the government-in-exile. Polish Communists, though many of them fought in the defense of Warsaw in 1939, were at first absent from the resistance movement; their party had been disbanded in 1938, and, besides, the official line presented the war as a struggle of the imperialists among themselves.

The situation changed after Hitler's surprise attack on the Soviet Union. Moscow now recognized the Polish "London Government," and an amnesty opened the gates of Soviet prisons for the release of Polish citizens. A Polish army in the Soviet Union, under the command of General Anders (discharged from Lubianka prison), began to recruit soldiers from among ex-prisoners of labor camps. Tension between Soviet authorities and the Polish army, whose attitude toward the Soviet state was increasingly hostile, led to the withdrawal of that army from Russia in 1942 through Iran and Iraq and Palestine, where it merged with the Carpathian Brigade, veterans of the battle of Tobruk. The same army joined up with the Allied forces invading Italy, and the storming of the monastery of Monte Cassino, one of the fiercest battles of World War II, fell largely to the credit of the Polish soldier.

In January 1942, the underground Polish Workers' Party (*Polska Partia Robotnicza*, PPR) was created in Warsaw by the former members of the Polish Communist Party. Its program envisaged close cooperation with the Soviet Union in the struggle against the Germans and questioned the legitimacy of the Polish London government-in-exile. The role of the PPR increased in 1943 when diplomatic relations were again broken off between the Soviet Union and the exile government after the latter appealed to the International Red Cross for an investigation of the so-called Katyn Massacre; the Germans had announced a discovery of mass graves of over ten thousand Polish officers in a wood near Katyn in the region of Smolensk, then in their possession, and had exploited this for propaganda reasons. These were the bodies of Polish servicemen who had been interned after the campaign of 1939 by the Soviet Union. Most certainly one of Stalin's crimes, it envenomed Polish-Soviet relations. The PPR was the only political group in Nazi-occupied Poland that was ready to pass it over in the name of a common combat against Nazi Germany and the revolution. Attracting other Leftist elements, it formed in 1943 the Country's National Council (*Krajowa Rada Narodowa*), which amounted to a nucleus for a new government. The guerrilla units of the PPR, the People's Guards (*Gwardia Ludowa*), were reorganized as the People's Army. The majority of the guerrilla troops, the Home Army (*Armia Krajowa*), remained, however, loyal to the London government-in-exile. Thus, the underground in Poland was internally divided into two camps, if we do not count the units of the National Military Forces (*Narodowe Siły Zbrojne*), the army of the extreme Right, which suspected "London" of being too democratic.

Polish Communists in the Soviet Union founded in 1943 the Union of Patriots, which proceeded to organize a new Polish army, the Kościuszko Division, composed mostly of former deportees. This army was to fight its way to Poland at the side of the Red Army.

Meanwhile, in Poland, the Nazis, besides Auschwitz, organized other extermination camps (e.g., Majdanek, Treblinka) and stepped up the planned murder of the three million Polish Jews trapped in their ghettos as well as of the Jews brought to those camps from all over Europe. The Warsaw Ghetto was practically depopulated when, in April 1943, the survivors, commanded by heroic underground fighters, decided to die gun-in-hand rather than to submit passively to certain death. To quell this now famous Ghetto Uprising, the Germans not only used artillery but razed every building to the ground, turning the huge ghetto area in the heart of Warsaw into a desert of rubble.

In the summer of 1944, a Polish tank corps that had been trained in England was sharing the fate of the Allied forces invading Normandy, while from the east, Polish troops formed in the Soviet Union entered Polish territory together with the victorious Red Army, reaching the Vistula in July. The Polish National Liberation Committee was constituted in the town of Chełm, and on July 22 its manifesto announced agrarian and other reforms in accordance with the Polish Communists' program. On August 1, when the rumble of the Red Army's heavy guns was heard in Warsaw, the clandestine Home Army, loyal to the London government-in-exile, rose against the Germans, who then withdrew their divisions of elite SS troops from the front and in savage battles succeeded in surrounding and isolating the quarters of the city held by the insurrectionists. The uprising lasted for sixty-three days; its cost was around 200,000 dead in soldiers and civilians, as well as the almost total ruin of Warsaw, bombed every few minutes from the air and battered by heavy artillery. The Polish regiments which came from Russia attempted to cross the Vistula to bring help but were decimated by German gunfire, suffering exceedingly heavy losses, and only a few soldiers reached the other bank. After the surrender, the city's entire population was deported, and German destruction squads systematically burned and dynamited street after street. The immobility of the Red Army, which, during those events, stood on the right bank of the Vistula in the suburb of Praga, has since been attributed by the Poles to political motives. The blame, however, has usually been attached to the losers, i.e., the London government-in-exile, which gave the order for the Home Army to fight without taking full account of political circumstances.

The eastern borders of the new Poland as well as its status as an appurtenance of the Soviet bloc were settled upon at the Yalta Conference in 1945. In exchange, Poland received, by the consent of the

Soviet Union, western territories which extended up to the Oder River. Once they had been Polish provinces, but for several centuries they had belonged to Germany. Poland received, in addition, the greater part of East Prussia, onetime seat of the Teutonic Order.

Prewar Poland numbered thirty-four million inhabitants. Its war losses reached some six million; Jews made up half of that figure, and those who survived the massacre could only be counted in tens of thousands. Moreover, the population of the lost eastern provinces should be deducted from the prewar count. However, owing to an extremely high birth rate, Poland's population at this writing has already surpassed thirty million.

With the escape of many writers to Western Europe and America or to the east, Polish literature once more, as in the preceding century, found itself divided into an *émigré* wing and a domestic wing. In spite of the fact that no press or publishing enterprise could exist legally in Nazi-occupied Poland, intellectual life was intense. This was due to clandestinely printed publications, clandestine poetry readings, and even clandestine theatrical performances. Literature reflected the considerable change in attitudes which took place between 1939 and the end of the war. Despair and anger at the prewar government, which was held responsible for a rapid defeat, gave way to a critical reappraisal of the twenty-year period between the wars, its social and literary problems. While most in the resistance movement allowed themselves to be guided by the London government-in-exile, the intellectual circles regarded it with a certain skepticism, if not hostility, as the mentality it stood for was a little too reminiscent of attitudes they had satirized and combatted in the thirties. However, the atrocious conditions of Nazi rule, during which everybody sought to cling to some hope of victory, hardly spurred clear thinking about the shape of the future. Literature registered emotional reflexes ranging from pain, hatred of the occupiers, through horror, pity, sarcasm, and irony. Although the suffering was many times worse than in the nineteenth century under foreign occupation, the emotional patterns left over from Romanticism automatically reasserted themselves. Polish writers, however, had come a long way from Romantic concepts of "holy martyrdom"; they resented those patterns, the strength of which they felt themselves, and reacted with devastating self-ridicule. Clandestine literature can be characterized, thus, as oscillating between pathos (once again in favor) and ironic restraint. This makes for its interest from an artistic point of view.

Innumerable "colporteurs" for the underground press paid with their lives for what not always justified such a high price, in view of frequently poor contents. In Warsaw, those writers who shied away from journalism attempted to compensate for the lack of book publish-

Literature during the War

ing. For instance, already in 1940–1941, a literary magazine was being typed in a limited number of copies and distributed fairly regularly to little "clubs" where it was read aloud and commented upon. Volumes of poetry were usually mimeographed, sometimes printed. Poetry (because it took up less space than prose) was the mainstay of the literary Resistance. Seven clandestinely printed anthologies testify to its popularity. The first was a slim pamphlet edited by K. Kwiatek (1941). The others were of a more conspicuous size: *The Independent Song* (*Pieśń niepodległa*, 1942), edited by C. Miłosz, which also included some poems smuggled from abroad, such as a fragment of Tuwim's *Polish Flowers; The Spirit Free in Song* (*Duch wolny w pieśni*, 1942), editor unknown; *A Word That Does Not Lie* (*Słowo prawdziwe*, 1942), edited by J. Zagórski and others; *Faithful Flames* (*Wierne płomienie*, 1943), editor unknown; *Anthology of Poetry* (*Antologia poetycka*, 1944), edited in Kraków and containing some poems by Przyboś; *Out of the Abyss* (*Z otchłani*, 1944), edited by T. Sarnecki, an anthology on the Jewish tragedy which included, among other works, poems by Jan Kott (later known as an eminent literary critic), M. Jastrun, and C. Miłosz.

A handful of very young men, students at the clandestine Warsaw University and militants of the Resistance, edited from 1942 to 1944 a mimeographed monthly, *Art and the Nation* (*Sztuka i Naród*); all four of its editors perished: one in a concentration camp, one from wounds received during an exchange of gunfire with Nazi police, one before a firing squad, and one in battle. Curiously enough, the monthly was politically bound to Rightist circles. In other countries of Europe, the extreme Right tended to collaborate with Hitler, but not in Poland, even though it was suspicious of the London government-in-exile. Stylistically, the poets who contributed to *Art and the Nation* combined a dependence upon the First Vanguard with what perhaps was an even greater reliance upon the catastrophic and apocalyptic symbols devised by the Second Vanguard, whose prophecies were then seeing their fulfillment. The most gifted among these poets, Tadeusz Gajcy (1922–1944), from a Warsaw lower-class family, published two mimeographed volumes of poetry and wrote, at the end of his short life, a play in verse on Homer's blindness. He was the last of the editors of the monthly, and he died a soldier's death in the Warsaw Uprising.

A colleague of those young men from *Art and the Nation*, though he did not associate with them, Krzysztof Kamil Baczyński (1921–1944), coedited another literary monthly, *The Road* (*Droga*). Son of a literary critic, as an adolescent an admirer of Marxism, and as a young man a sophisticated, frail intellectual, Baczyński distrusted the fuzzy ratiocinations found in the articles and essays of *Art and the Nation*.

He developed in his own manner, though obviously under the spell of the Second Vanguard. In many ways his poetry resembles Gajcy's. But what was said about the recurrence of Romantic patterns applies particularly to Baczyński's poetry, whose rich imagery served more and more overtly, as he developed, to point up his central theme of self-immolation for the sake of an ideal Poland. Those critics were right who maintained that he strangely resembled Juliusz Słowacki in his concept of redemptive martyrdom. Baczyński, within a few years, produced a copious poetic work. He died as a platoon commander during the Warsaw Uprising.

Still different was Tadeusz Borowski (1922–1951), another young man from the same crop of students who was also connected with the monthly *The Road*. From a Polish worker's family in the Ukraine, he spent his childhood in the Soviet Union and in 1933 moved to Warsaw. Tough and soberly realistic, he pushed what he had inherited from the catastrophism of the Second Vanguard to its dark extreme. His two first mimeographed volumes of poems are full of self-derision. He says in one of his poems:

> What will remain after us will be scrap iron
> And the hollow, jeering laughter of generations.

> Zostanie po nas złom żelazny
> I głuchy, drwiący śmiech pokoleń.

Arrested in 1943 and deported to Auschwitz, he was to write one of the most truthful testimonies on concentration camps in world literature.

Reality so far outdistanced the imagination that writers felt a gap between the artistic means at their disposal and the raw material of facts. But this was not the only difficulty. They were aware of the traps awaiting a "literature of commitment," which all too often is nothing more than journalism in prose or verse. French poets of the Resistance, such as Paul Eluard, Louis Aragon, and René Char, had to cope with the same dilemma.

Among novelists, Jerzy Andrzejewski, whom we mentioned in the preceding chapter, was the first who dared to give a fictionalized version of current events. In his story "On Trial" ("Przed sądem," 1941) the protagonist is a young boy, condemned to death for possessing weapons, who betrays his beloved friend to the Nazis because he is afraid to die alone. The short story "Roll Call" ("Apel," 1942), based upon oral accounts the author heard from escapees of Auschwitz, registers the experience of prisoners who are kept standing for hours in temperatures below freezing. A long story (or short novel), *Holy Week* (*Wielki Tydzień*, 1943), reconstructs the moral conflicts of the

Warsaw intelligentsia, including those of its Jewish members who lived in hiding on the "Aryan side," during the Ghetto Uprising at Easter 1943, when the entire city was lit up by the glare from the burning ghetto. Because he reacted immediately to what was going on, Andrzejewski's stories that date from the last phase of the war reflect the transformations within the Warsaw intellectual milieu which occurred during the occupation. For example, he treats the mania for conspiracy with humor and, in doing so, turns, by implication, against the chivalrous patriotism extolled by the London government-in-exile and its resistance movement at the expense of clearly defined political and social goals. Andrzejewski's stand may explain why he and many of his colleagues were to accept the revolutionary changes in Poland with a favorable prejudice.

The *émigré* press, in its publications for the Polish armed forces in the Middle East, Italy, and England, lent much space to literary works, especially to poetry. These were poems not only by reputed authors such as Słonimski, Wierzyński, Tuwim, or Broniewski but also by unknown poet-soldiers. A measure of the interest in poetry is provided, for example, by an anthology of Polish poetry written in the Middle East and printed in Palestine: *Asia and Africa* (*Azja i Afryka*, 1944). It includes the work of those who began to write in their barracks or tents as well as that of known writers.

Among the soldier-writers the most outstanding personality was Ksawery Pruszyński (1907–1950), a figure who seemed to come straight out of the annals of the Napoleonic wars. Of noble origin, a gifted, energetic journalist, he worked before the war for the conservative press of the Polish "Tories," who disliked both the Left and the nationalistic Right. His travels resulted in enthusiastic articles on the kibbutzim in Palestine and in a compassionate, warm book on Loyalist Spain. During the war he fought at Narvik, Norway, served as a diplomat with the Polish Embassy in the Soviet Union, landed in Normandy as an officer of the Polish Tank Corps, and was gravely wounded at Falaise. His stories on Polish soldiers' wanderings are still highly popular. Another writer with a colorful biography is Aleksander Janta (1908–   ), a roving reporter and poet. An officer of the Polish army organized in France, he was taken prisoner by the Germans in 1940 but was clever enough to assume the name of a French infantryman. His dramatic and comic adventures as a prisoner in Germany provided him later on with material for two books. Released "home," i.e., to France, he escaped from there to England, joined the army again, and fought on the Continent in 1944.

The Polish press in the Soviet Union was of two kinds: one sponsored by the embassy of the London government-in-exile between 1941–1943, the other sponsored by the Communist Union of Patriots, which numbered among its members a few poets, such as Adam Ważyk, Jerzy Putrament, Lucjan Szenwald. Mention should be made of the anthology *Polish Poetry, 1939–1944* (*Poezja polska, 1939–1944*), edited by the Union and published in Moscow in 1944.

The Soviet offensive of January 1945 finally crushed the Germans who had been holding the left bank of the Vistula River, and the National Liberation Committee, which, in Lublin, had become the provisional government, moved to the outskirts of destroyed Warsaw. Its decision to remain in the capital against all odds was to contribute to the rebuilding of the city, a feat which otherwise might have required more time, in view of the devastation of the country and the lack of necessary machinery. Under concerted pressure from Washington, Moscow, and London, the provisional government was enlarged to include some *émigré* leaders, and this new formation was known as the Government of National Unity (RJN). The political parties it represented, besides the PPR (Polish Workers' Party), were the Peasant Party, whose leader, Mikołajczyk, prime minister of the London government-in-exile, had returned to Poland; the PPS (Polish Socialist Party), one wing of which refused to enter the coalition; and the insignificant Democratic Party. There was no doubt, however, as to who maintained control, and in a few years, the rival parties lost what little say they had. Mikołajczyk fled to America, while the Polish Socialist Party was forced to merge with the Polish Workers' Party in 1948.

In order to understand how public opinion reacted to the new setup, one should keep in mind the utter exhaustion after the war and the terrible bloodletting. The country had to be rebuilt. The London government-in-exile was compromised because it had lost its political game, which had been staked upon the United States and England. And it must be acknowledged that if the Nazi plan for exterminating the Poles as an "inferior race" had failed, it was primarily because of the heroism of the Red Army. Moreover, Poland's new border on the Oder River could be protected only by the Soviet Union against probable future German claims. The more sober-minded among the citizenry invoked Poland's geographical position as a factor that predisposed the country toward reliance upon the Soviet Union.

The revolution, though imposed from above, was relatively "mild." Nationalization of factories and mines did not meet with any obstacles; besides, they had already been expropriated by the Nazis. The long-awaited agrarian reform was greeted, however, with considerable distrust on the part of the peasantry, whose great fear was the collectivization of agriculture, planned, as they correctly suspected, for the near future. Yet great opportunities in the cities opened up for the peasant youth because of the stress upon industrialization; there were plenty of empty farms in the newly acquired western territories, while

Liberation and Revolution

Territorial changes after World War II.

the status of both peasant and worker rose rapidly as the program of universal education strove to meet the mass influx of peasant and worker children to the schools. There were also innumerable and sometimes tragic conflicts that accompanied the birth of People's Poland. Many topics and many personalities fell under a taboo strictly observed by the officials and the official press. Thousands of ex-soldiers from the Home Army, who had fought against the Nazis, were tracked down and imprisoned because of their wartime oath of loyalty to the London Government. A virtual civil war between units of the security police and the former Resistance guerrillas, who had not handed in their arms, dragged on in the forests of some regions. The repatriation of

Poles who dwelt in areas now belonging to the Soviet Union entailed great moral and physical misery. Warsaw, the capital, had to be cleared of rubble with shovels and horse-drawn carts. Elections to the Diet, far from free, disgusted even many partisans of the revolution as a sham. All this fostered a somewhat morbid atmosphere, even though the first years of the People's Republic, 1945–1949, may be called relatively easy as compared with the years which followed.

After the Socialist Party's merger with the Polish Workers' (Communist) Party, the membership of the latter increased numerically, and soon the fall of Władysław Gomułka, the first secretary of the Party, who was dismissed from his post and, shortly after, imprisoned, announced the end of the "mild revolution." Collectivization of agriculture was proclaimed and enforced by purely administrative measures. Stalinist doctrine was imposed upon intellectuals, and the enormous apparatus of the security police intensified its rule of terror. The turning point came in the year 1949, when the world of Orwell ceased to be a literary fiction in Poland. At the same time, the first Five-Year Economic Plan stepped up the process of industrialization, which was fed by the masses of peasants streaming to the cities to escape the collective farm. The resulting displacement wrought radical changes in the social structure. Poland, the majority of whose population had, until then, been employed in agriculture, acquired little by little the features of an urban and industrial society.

Ideological indoctrination shaped the thinking of at least the most active segment among the young. The "system" seemed to be established for many decades to come; yet it was only the surface, the lid of a boiling caldron. At the end of 1955 ("the thaw"), some steam was let off, and soon after, in June 1956, came an explosion: the bloody riots of workers in Poznań, which ominously hinted at the danger of a more general upheaval. Factions within the Party adopted various maneuvers to withdraw from the Stalinist line with which the Party had had to identify itself. The security police, shaken by the spontaneous riots, was disintegrating from within. October 1956 could well have seen an equivalent of the Hungarian uprising. The Poles, however, were more wary, as the Warsaw Uprising of 1944 had left durable, traumatic traces. Moreover, the Polish Communist Party proved to have more elasticity than its Hungarian counterpart, and the Soviet leaders who arrived in Warsaw by plane at a critical juncture showed more tact than they did in the case of Hungary. Władysław Gomułka, released from prison, was returned to power, backed now by a population who regarded him as a symbol of independence. In his effort to decrease tensions, he was given a helping hand by the Roman Catholic Church, which had been badly persecuted during the so-called "bygone" era and whose head, Cardinal Wyszyński, had been, like Gomułka, imprisoned. Peasants, now permitted to leave the collective farms, reverted, with few exceptions, to their traditional way of life on privately owned land. Numerous taboos were lifted, and no topic was avoided in freewheeling discussions, though attention centered mainly upon the absurdities of an overcentralized economy as well as upon terms of trade with the Soviet Union and other socialist countries. The Stalinist doctrine collapsed and became, especially for the young, a subject of derision. Public polls, a thing unheard-of in the preceding period, gave an inkling of the moods of the population. What prevailed was an acceptance of socialism but a hostility toward totalitarian dogmas and toward Poland's position of dependence on the Soviet Union. Hopes for a more democratic system within a nationalized economy created enthusiastic support for Gomułka. Gomułka's policy, however, was to save his party from utter disintegration. This he accomplished. The decade 1956–1966 was characterized by an uneasy truce between divergent Party factions combatting each other behind the scenes, between the Party and the Roman Catholic Church, and between the government and public opinion. The most daring intellectuals, who inclined toward a rethinking of all the current issues in Marxist terms, were branded "revisionists" and gradually forced into silence; while those officials who resented their loss of totalitarian controls were labeled "dogmatists" and were curbed in their ambitions. Empiricism and makeshift strategy supplanted a unified doctrine. Literature and art, though no longer submitted to directives from above, had to move cautiously among many bureaucratic obstacles.

Twenty years after the end of hostilities Poland bore little resemblance to her former self. In spite of inefficiencies inherent in a centrally planned economy, the country had advanced quite far along the road to industrialization. Its devastated capital, as well as other cities, had been rebuilt; while its numerous high schools and universities had formed a new generation of intelligentsia who came from peasants' and workers' families. Censorship of literature was compensated for by a tremendous book market, much larger than in prewar Poland. Some one hundred repertory theaters catered not only to the needs of an older, highly sophisticated public but also to those of the younger, plebeian audiences; new foreign plays (Dürrenmatt's, for example) were often staged in Warsaw earlier than in the West. Film production, which had its heyday immediately after October 1956, withered considerably because of reimposed controls, but still was able to produce works of value. In art and music, avant-garde painters and composers were winning international renown. All this went together with low salaries, hard living conditions, and a multitude of economic, political, and social puzzles that cannot be solved in a system deprived of any legal framework for public control.

POSTWAR LITERATURE—GENERAL CHARACTERISTICS

The life story of a Polish writer who published in the literary periodicals of 1945 would fill many life spans of people in less turbulent times. The Nazi occupation had cast doubt on all presumed certainties regarding human behavior. Society disclosed its frailty and ceased to appear as something external to man, existing of itself like nature. The sight of Polish Communists molding it like clay inculcated a new perception of the extent to which relationships between human beings are malleable. The status of the writer was affected. His profession was now well remunerated; in exchange, he was held to account for every word. Like the rest of the nation, he was torn by contradictory feelings and urges.

The two decades of Polish postwar literature are usually divided into three distinct periods, whose limits were determined by politics. The first extended from 1945 to 1949 and was marked by debates on what literature should be in a country aiming at socialism. Writers were left free to find their own methods. A considerable liberalism characterized their relations with the Party, and as for censorship, a watchful eye was kept out only for some clearly defined forbidden topics. Those were fecund years for literature, and while writers who had made their way before the war played a leading role, its organic growth was not hampered. The situation deteriorated in 1949 when the doctrine of Socialist Realism was imposed by Party decree. Works that deviated from the line had not the slightest chance of publication. Sterilized, reduced to an imitation of Soviet models, literature went stale and gray. The period from 1949 until the end of 1955 left few books deserving of attention. The third period, beginning in 1956, rich in achievements, cast an arch over the void separating it from the literature of spontaneous gropings immediately after the war and from modern literature in general, and thus restored the continuity in experimentation which had temporarily been lost.

"I would rather go with the devil than with you," wrote a satirical *1945–1949* poet, Janusz Minkiewicz. He had in mind all those who longed after the old order of things, including the "London Government." His emotional option was that of the majority of writers. Less motivated by pro-Marxist sympathies than by a rejection of a certain Polish mentality, they hoped that the revolutionary reshaping of the social structure would destroy that mentality's roots. A specifically Polish mixture of noble, chivalrous sentiments and nationalism in its most virulent form was held responsible by writers for the failures of the prewar system and for a foreign policy that relied solely upon the Western Allies. The readiness of writers to condemn the old regime might be dismissed as simply a desire to please the new rulers, yet the political novels which appeared shortly after the war had been written earlier, during the Nazi occupation. These novels exploited discoveries in psychology (and in novelistic technique) which had been made in the thirties. *The Walls of Jericho* (*Mury Jerycha*, 1946) and its sequel, *The Sky and the Earth* (*Niebo i ziemia*, 1949), by Tadeusz Breza are analyses of the Warsaw intelligentsia milieu in the years preceding the outbreak of the war. His ambition was to combine a psychological novel with an exploration of the intelligentsia's sellout to groups of the extreme Right aspiring to power. Breza's dominating passion in his novels is his curiosity as an observer who records complex social processes. His books, therefore, cannot be dismissed as merely a response to the needs of the moment. So, too, the aged Zofia Nałkowska had worked throughout the war years on a novelistic picture of the Warsaw prewar political elite connected with the regime of the "colonels." This was her novel *The Knots of Life* (*Węzły życia*, 1948).

The role of the narrator in these novels diverges from the role he played in the "mirror-of-life" prose of the nineteenth century. Although not written in the first person, these works reserve for the author a position similar to that of a memorialist, who proceeds through sly references to his direct knowledge of the people involved. In addition, Breza and Nałkowska made wide use of social "patterns" as forces hostile to the characters' intentions, a device which had already been employed before the war.

Writers were aware that the traditional novel had outlived its applicability. Kazimierz Wyka, one of the most active literary critics, advanced the thesis that the terrible experience of the Nazi occupation and the existential depths visited by practically everyone in Poland could not be communicated through any traditional narrative. Why invent a reality, he asked, if no writer's imagination could match the incongruous, the macabre reality itself? He predicted a "border-line novel," which would be a mixture of genres and in which the person of the narrator would predominate as a participant in events. Wyka was right. The most convincing works by authors who had descended into the abyss of genocide, such as Tadeusz Borowski, Adolf Rudnicki, or Kornel Filipowicz, are not novels at all but groups of stories connected by the figure of the narrator where fiction and eyewitness reporting are scarcely distinguishable.

While Warsaw was being rebuilt, Kraków and Łódź became the centers of literary life. In Kraków, two influential periodicals began their existence: *Creative Work* (*Twórczość*), a monthly, and *Renaissance* (*Odrodzenie*), a weekly; in Łódź a group of writers founded a weekly called *The Forge* (*Kuźnica*). The title they chose indicated their purpose: they wanted to link themselves to the traditions of the Polish Enlightenment, to its "Camp of the Reform" and especially to its spearhead, the political club called "The Forge." Literary critics Stefan Żółkiewski and Jan Kott, poets Adam Ważyk, Mieczysław Jastrun, and Paweł Hertz, along with several prose writers, engaged in a battle for realism in literature. Applying Marxist criteria, but not in a constricted, dogmatic sense, they opposed the "narrow realism" of photographic verisimilitude and advocated a "broad realism" such as Balzac or the English novelists and French encyclopedists of the eighteenth century had practiced. Although inspired mainly by Georg Lukács, they avoided his exaggerations. For them, an interdependence between the fate of the individual and the history of a given society was all-important. As to literary models, they more or less scorned the second half of the nineteenth century, preferring to admire Defoe, Fielding, and Marcel Proust. They held Soviet Socialist Realist literature in low esteem and published, instead, translations of unorthodox Russian poets like Boris Pasternak and Anna Akhmatova.

It was *The Forge* that gave much space to a debate on a literature of self-criticism, known as the "intelligentsia's settling of accounts." The term designated a critical approach to certain mental habits and conventions proper to the intelligentsia and referred to the spiritual surgery that authors who resented the code of behavior prescribed by the prewar Establishment performed on themselves.

Thus, Stefan Kisielewski (1911–   ), one of the most independent intellectuals (he was not connected with *The Forge*), who preserved his position of *enfant terrible* throughout the postwar decades, in his novel *Blood Brothers* (*Sprzysiężenie*, 1947), written during the war, tells a mocking tale of three young intellectuals who have taken an oath to accomplish great things, but whose strivings miscarry in the indefinite, paralyzing climate of the late thirties. In that parable, constructed with no attempt at verisimilitude, the main protagonist is sexually impotent, and only after he wakes up as a soldier in a beaten army, after the entire prewar order has collapsed, does he recover potency.

Also written during the war was a novel called *Bodensee* (*Jezioro Bodeńskie*, 1946), by Stanisław Dygat (1914–1978), who had begun to publish before 1939 as one of Gombrowicz's pupils. Dygat, a French citizen, was interned for a while near Bodensee in one of the mildest Nazi camps for people of undetermined national status. Spitefulness and a passion for debunking clichés led him to transform his adventures into an antiheroic novel. The narrator presents himself as uncertain, unauthentic, vacillating between his role as patriotic Pole and his flirtations with French girls in the camp. He is both attached and opposed to his Polish Romantic complex.

Autobiographical elements are also easily distinguished in *Sedan* (1948), by Paweł Hertz (1918–   ), who made his debut in the late thirties as a sophisticated poet. *Sedan* is a group of stories told by a first-person narrator who undergoes psychoanalytical treatment in Vienna and, later, quite a different treatment at the hands of History. All the certainties of his bourgeois milieu fall to pieces; he hews trees in a labor camp of the Urals, returns to Poland, receives permission, thanks to a wise Communist friend, to visit Paris, where he has lived as a student, and is repelled by the sight of bourgeois life continuing as if nothing had happened. This time he goes back to Poland convinced that even if Communism is bad, it is at least historically right.

Also narrated in the first person is the novel by Kazimierz Brandys (1916–   ), *Hobby Horse* (*Drewniany koń*, 1946). This was the first published novel (written in 1943–1945) of an author who was to become one of the officially extolled prose writers of People's Poland. It is a sarcastic portrayal of the childhood and youth of a well-intentioned man from the intelligentsia who, when he is confronted with the Nazi occupation and the conspiratorial movement of the Resistance, is morally and intellectually disarmed. To Brandys, a man of the Left, the Polish Resistance directed by "London Poles" meant the perpetuation of latent unconsciously fascist tendencies, and he shows its leaders in an exceedingly unfavorable light.

Formally, all the enumerated works contain many features of the "border-line novel."

As for poetry, the most talented young beginners had perished, and the line they represented found no heirs. Their heroic deaths gave rise to a legend that still surrounds their poetry; but the protest against inhumanity, as critics agree today, was better expressed by poets already mature at the outset of the war. Not the "Skamander" poets (all were absent from Poland except for Iwaszkiewicz) had the greatest impact upon young readers, but the poets of the First and Second Vanguards—Przyboś, Ważyk, Jastrun, and Miłosz.

1949–1955   *The Forge* was called to task for its propagation of "broad realism" and soon ceased to appear. "Socialist Realism," the dissection of which does not belong here, since it was a phenomenon not limited to Poland, thrived on simplistic thinking. It enforced a reversion to techniques of the second half of the nineteenth century and prohibited any avant-garde experiment. Literature was subjected to recipes imposed by watchdog officials and "terroreticians." The stress was upon the so-called "production novel" with a factory or collective farm setting. Escapes abroad and suicides of writers speak all too well for their moral torment in a country once again suffering under a rule of terror. Some of them, however, took the dogma very seriously, especially "the pimpled ones"—young men, many of whom had been members of the London-oriented resistance movement and whose zeal was that of recent converts. Used to living dangerously, with guns at their sides, they harbored romantic notions of the revolution and seemed not to realize that Mayakovsky, whom they adored, was somewhat out-of-date in view of the quite different circumstances. They heckled older writers, accusing them of flabby, bourgeois liberalism, but their own output was inferior in quality. Paradoxically, out of their ranks came, later on, the most violent detractors of the (to use post-1956 terminology) "period of errors and mistakes."

Nineteenth-century models were also obligatory in poetry. Mass editions of the Polish Romantics flooded the book market, but critics had to avoid the too intricate problems raised by their thought and their art. Metrical and rhymed verse was advised as the most suitable for the proletarian reader. Avant-garde art was accused of being tainted with decadence. The author of this book, who had translated some poems by the Chilean Communist poet, Pablo Neruda, was even accused of "Nerudition." Since Polish poetry had been experimenting for several decades, such a strait jacket now paralyzed it so much that few poets succeeded in maintaining their standards.

The tumbling down of what had been for several years proclaimed *1956–1966* as the Truth provoked renewed soul-searching among writers, and the intensity of their self-accusations was proportional to their previous commitment. The literature of angry men, who felt themselves deceived by a new Establishment, was distinguished by a high intellectual and artistic level; it underwent a mutation, after a short phase of ideological discussion, into a general probing of man's fate in the twentieth century. With the rejection of the dogma, Marxism was reappraised and the stress shifted to the thought of the young Karl Marx and his theory of alienation. Brilliant young philosophers, among whom Leszek Kołakowski won the greatest reputation, defended humanistic and humane socialism. Polish literature woke up to find itself one of the most philosophical in Europe, making use of philosophical parables in prose, poetry, and the theater. A flow of translations from English and French brought to Polish readers and theater audiences Albert Camus, Jean-Paul Sartre, Faulkner, Beckett, Ionesco, as well as avant-garde poetry. Several Polish writers whose names had been forbidden came to the surface, sometimes in spite of considerable resistance from the censor's office. Stanisław Brzozowski was at least partially restored to his due place. The plays of Stanisław Ignacy Witkiewicz were published in two volumes and frequently performed. Bolesław Leśmian emerged in criticism as a major Polish poet of the twentieth century. A multitude of writers came to the fore whose debuts had been delayed because of their refusal to bow to ideological exigencies during the preceding period; their independence of mind surprised the pessimists who had foreseen durable effects of intimidation. Polish poetry, now freely profiting from the experiments of two prewar decades and from its precursor, Cyprian Norwid, was one of the most vigorous in Europe through its intellectual and existential grasp of tragic political choices. Marxist training, when combined with an openness to existential philosophy and to anthropology of the Lévi-Strauss brand, revealed its usefulness both in literary criticism and in the scholarly investigation of the past. These self-perpetuating outbursts could hardly make the administration happy, however, and its renewed attempts to curtail the freedom of writers bore marks of an uneasiness not always unfounded. The normalcy of development that literature had recovered was, thus, accompanied by a growing disparity between intellectual and political life in the country.

The complexity arising from issues that belong to the present and not the past should incline the historian of literature to be wary in his judgments. For the same reason, it is impossible to do justice to all those authors whose names one encounters on book covers and on the pages of periodicals but whose work must await posterity's more detached examination. We shall, therefore, limit ourselves to those authors who best exemplify certain main currents. Although such a selection obviously presupposes a certain bias—that of the literary critic—it will correspond, at least roughly, to the provisional hierarchy distinguishable in critical essays published between 1956 and 1966 in Poland.

Poetry

Poetry and Inhumanity   Those poets who had been formed before the war and who survived the Nazi occupation lived through an ordeal that challenged the very basis of poetic art. Poetry, after all, is embedded in the humanistic tradition and is defenseless in the midst of an all-pervading savagery. The act of writing a poem is an act of faith; yet if the screams of the tortured are audible in the poet's room, is not his activity an offense to human suffering? And if the next hour may bring his death and the destruction of his manuscript, should the poet engage in such a pastime? A nearly superhuman effort to answer those questions while juggling with despair is seen in the volumes published in 1944–1945. In Przyboś's *As Long as We Live* (*Póki my żyjemy*, 1944), in Jastrun's *Guarded Hour* (*Godzina strzeżona*, 1944), and in Miłosz's *Rescue* (*Ocalenie*, 1945), the remains of "catastrophism" are overcome by an awareness that relapses into chaos, though ever-recurring, are not ultimate. A polemic with the bleak outlook of Stanisław Ignacy Witkiewicz seemed to haunt those poets, whose struggle for equilibrium was borne up by that current of Polish literature where history tended to be deciphered according to the pattern of an ascending spiral. In Miłosz's short, ironic "Song on the End of the World," Armageddon is permanent, but it is always accompanied by trees in bloom, kisses of lovers, the birth of babies. His spokesman in the poem, an old man, "who would be a prophet but has another job," since in spite of everything he must cultivate his tomatoes, says: "No other end of the world will there be." *The World*, a long poem of Miłosz's, written in 1943, is one of the most serene in modern Polish literature. Its "primerlike" quatrains describe the beauty of the simplest things and exemplify the effort to resist the temptation of utter despair.

When a poet is overwhelmed by strong emotions, his form tends to become more simple and more direct. This happened during the war to many poets who had formerly enveloped themselves in an intricate syntax. The Second Vanguard had been, to a considerable extent, "antiaesthetic"; it had often seasoned its verse with prosaisms, striving toward a certain nakedness. This tendency to be as direct as possible was revived in many poems by Przyboś, Miłosz, Jastrun, and Ważyk. Ważyk's poem "Sketch for a Memoir" has already been quoted in part. The fabric of their verse was woven of elements inherited from various avant-garde schools, including surrealism. These elements were, however, put to quite a different use. An instance of this is Miłosz's "A Poor Christian Looks at the Ghetto" ("Biedny chrześcijanin patrzy na Ghetto," 1943):

> Bees build around red liver,
> Ants build around black bone.
> It has begun: the tearing, the trampling on silks,
> It has begun: the breaking of glass, wood, copper, nickel, silver,
> foam,
> Of gypsum, iron sheets, violin strings, trumpets, leaves, balls,
> crystals.
> Poof! Phosphorescent fire from yellow walls
> Engulfs animal and human hair.
>
> Bees build around the honeycomb of lungs,
> Ants build around white bone.
> Torn is paper, rubber, linen, leather, flax,
> Fiber, fabrics, cellulose, snakeskin, wire.
> The roof and the wall collapse in flame and heat seizes the
> foundations.
> Now there is only the earth, sandy, trodden down,
> With one leafless tree.

Slowly, boring a tunnel, a guardian mole makes his way,
With a small red lamp fastened to his forehead.
He touches burned bodies, counts them, pushes on,
He distinguishes human ashes by their luminous vapor,
The ashes of each man by a different part of the spectrum.
Bees build around a red trace.
Ants build around the place left by my body.

I am afraid, so afraid of the guardian mole.
He has swollen eyelids, like a Patriarch
Who has sat much in the light of candles
Reading the great book of the species.

What will I tell him, I, a Jew of the New Testament,
Waiting two thousand years for the second coming of Jesus?
My broken body will deliver me to his sight
And he will count me among the helpers of death:
The uncircumcised.

Pszczoły obudowują czerwoną wątrobę,
Mrówki obudowują czarną kość,
Rozpoczyna się rozdzieranie, deptanie jedwabi,
Rozpoczyna się tłuczenie szkła, drzewa, miedzi, niklu, srebra, pian
Gipsowych, blach, strun, trąbek, liści, kul, kryształów—
Pyk! Fosforyczny ogień z żółtych ścian
Pochłania ludzkie i zwierzęce włosie.

Pszczoły obudowują plaster płuc,
Mrówki obudowują białą kość,
Rozdzierany jest papier, kauczuk, płótno, skóra, len.
Włókna, materie, celuloza, włos, wężowa łuska, druty,
Wali się w ogniu dach, ściana i żar ogarnia fundament.
Jest już tylko piaszczysta, zdeptana, z jednym drzewem bez liści
Ziemia.

Powoli, drążąc tunel, posuwa się strażnik-kret
Z małą czerwoną latarką przypiętą na czole.
Dotyka ciał pogrzebanych, liczy, przedziera się dalej,
Rozróżnia ludzki popiół po tęczującym oparze,
Popiół każdego człowieka po innej barwie tęczy.
Pszczoły obudowują czerwony ślad,
Mrówki obudowują miejsce po moim ciele.

Boję się, tak się boję strażnika-kreta.
Jego powieka obrzmiała jak u patriarchy,
Który siadywał dużo w blasku świec
Czytając wielką księgę gatunku.

Cóż powiem mu, ja, Żyd Nowego Testamentu,
Czekający od dwóch tysięcy lat na powrót Jezusa?
Moje rozbite ciało wyda mnie jego spojrzeniu
I policzy mnie między pomocników śmierci:
Nieobrzezanych.

A theme that consistently returns in the work of all these poets is doubt concerning the dignity of art. Jastrun neatly formulated that dialectical tension in "Remembrance" ("Wspomnienie," 1944):

> For whom is delight? Revelation of strength?
> For whom is the nightingale in the tangle of young trees?
> Its song erupts, breaks off, as if fountains
> Of light were gushing up against the sky—
>
> And far more hostile, more indifferent
> Than all that common and inhuman grave
> Is the beauty of the earth. And he that lost himself
> In the beauty of words as in some longed-for face—
> His songs are pure, too pure. They will be overbalanced
> By blood mixed with earth.

> Dla kogo rozkosz? objawienie siły?
> Dla kogo słowik w gąszczu młodych drzew?
> Zanosi się i zrywa jego śpiew,
> Jakby fontanny światła w niebo biły—
>
> I bardziej wrogie, bardziej obojętne
> Od tej masowej nieludzkiej mogiły
> Jest piękno ziemi. A kto w słowa pięknie
> Zatracał się, jak w niewidzianej twarzy,
> Tego dźwięk czysty, zbyt czysty, przeważy
> Zmieszana z ziemią krew.

The same obsession is visible in Miłosz's "The Poor Poet" ("Biedny poeta"):

> I pose the pen and it puts forth twigs and leaves, it is covered
>   with blossoms
> And the scent of that tree is impudent, for there, on the real earth,
> Such trees do not grow, and like an insult
> To suffering humanity is the scent of that tree.

> Stawiam pióro, i puszcza pędy i liście, okrywa się kwiatem,
> A zapach tego drzewa jest bezwstydny, bo tam, na realnej ziemi
> Takie drzewa nie rosną i jest jak zniewaga
> Wyrządzona cierpiącym ludziom zapach tego drzewa.

While very young underground poets were borrowing a tangle of pessimistic symbols from their Second Vanguard models, these very models turned, in a way, against themselves, trying to maintain an equilibrium between the sense of tragedy and an approval of life. Their rage, often self-directed, was mitigated by a latent humanistic rationalism.

Tadeusz Różewicz (1921–)   The most talented among those who began to publish immediately after 1945 rejected equilibrium. Tadeusz Różewicz issued from a white-collar worker's family in a provincial town and during the war was a soldier in a guerilla unit of the Home Army. His desperate tone of derision, critics like to explain, expressed the reaction of a whole generation "contaminated by death." His first volumes, *Anxiety* (*Niepokój*, 1947) and *The Red Glove* (*Czerwona rękawiczka*, 1948), received immediate notice. By contrasting the scenes of war he had witnessed, which asked for the brush of a new Goya, with the entire heritage of European culture, he arrived at a negation of literature because it seemed to be no more than a lie covering up the horror of man's brutality to his fellow man. Thus, if poetry could be practiced at all, it should seek to destroy all literary conventions. Różewicz's opposition to metrics, rhyme, and even metaphor had a moral meaning. He built his verse with simple words, sometimes scarcely bound to each other syntactically; this practice led critics to compare his technique of construction to building with blocks. His corrosive irony (not deprived of self-pity), deforming the beautiful phrase, signified an awareness that one epoch in the history of mankind had come to an end. He wanted to be naked, to shed the security provided by creeds or philosophical systems. Thence his predilection for re-evaluating words, which makes his poems sound like a primer. He says, for instance, in a poem called "In the Middle of Life" ("W środku życia"):

> After the end of the world
> after my death
> I found myself in the middle of life
> I created myself
> constructed life
> people animals landscapes
>
> this is the table I was saying
> this is the table
> on the table are lying the bread the knife
> the knife serves to cut the bread
> people nourish themselves with bread
>
> .   .   .   .   .
>
> the man talked to the water
> talked to the moon
> to the flowers to the rain

he talked to the earth
to the birds
to the sky

the sky was silent
the earth was silent
if he heard a voice
which flowed
from the earth from the water from the sky
it was the voice of another man

Po końcu świata
po śmierci
znalazłem sie w środku życia
stwarzałem siebie
budowałem życie
ludzi zwierzęta krajobrazy

to jest stół mówiłem
to jest stół
na stole leży chleb nóż
nóż służy do krajania chleba
chlebem karmią się ludzie
              .   .   .   .   .

człowiek mówił do wody
mówił do księżyca
do kwiatów deszczu
mówił do ziemi
do ptaków
do nieba

milczało niebo
milczała ziemia
jeśli usłyszał głos
który płynął
z ziemi wody i nieba
to był głos drugiego człowieka

Różewicz, by drawing the inference that man is alone in a universe without metaphysical justification and that the only reality is his exposure to other men, hit upon (without realizing it at first) the central theme of French existentialists. His poetry is a moralist's search to define himself through his relationship with another man, yet the moment he seems to establish an agreement with the world, he annihilates it with a self-destructive passion. In "Conversation with a Prince" ("Rozmowa z księciem"), he has this to say about the modern poet:

Indifferent he talks
to the indifferent
blinded he makes signs
to the blind
he laughs and
barks in his sleep
waked
he weeps
he is composed of rungs
but is not a ladder of Jacob
is a voice without echo
burden without weight
a fool without a king

Obojętny mówi
do obojętnych
oślepiony daje znaki
niewidomym
śmieje się i
szczeka przez sen
obudzony
płacze
składa się ze szczebli
ale nie jest drabiną Jakubową
jest głosem bez echa
ciężarem bez wagi
błaznem bez króla

Różewicz is a poet of chaos with a nostalgia for order. Around him and in himself he sees only broken fragments, a senseless rush. True, he wrote a certain number of tender poems on the most innocent people—children, very old men—but his world is situated between the holocaust of the last war and the threat of future annihilation by nuclear weapons.

His poems of 1949–1955, though unorthodox in form, could be printed because of his genuine abhorrence of atomic armament and his defense of peace, which he identified with the cause of the Communist bloc. They are often sentimental and inferior in quality to his other works. (We shall not consider them quoting material.) Self-contradictory, an antipoet writing poetry, defending man, to whom he refuses dignity, Różewicz sees the poet as a carrier of protest for its own sake. His "Deposition of the Burden" ("Zdjęcie ciężaru") asserts:

He came to you
and said

you are not responsible
either for the world or for the end of the world
the burden is taken from your shoulders
you are like birds and children
play
and they play

they forget
that modern poetry
is a struggle for breath

Przyszedł do was
i mówi

nie jesteście odpowiedzialni
ani za świat ani za koniec świata
zdjęto wam z ramion ciężar
jesteście jak ptaki i dzieci
bawcie się

i bawią się

zapominają
że poezja współczesna
to walka o oddech

During the decade 1956–1966, his poetry, prose, and plays moved toward an ever darker vision. As a traveler in France, Italy, or West Germany, he seemed offended by "normal" life there. For him, it was but a surface hiding the horror of existence. Whenever he brings culture into his poetry by referring to specific masterpieces of literature or painting, his interpretations are usually a reversal of the accepted versions. For instance, "Nothing in Prospero's Cloak" ("Nic w płaszczu Prospera") shows a gentle, humane Prospero, from Shakespeare's *The Tempest*, as bearer of culture and, therefore, a deceiver of poor Caliban:

Caliban a slave
taught human speech
waits

with his snout in manure
his legs in paradise
sniffs at man
waits

nothing arrives
nothing in a magic cloak
of Prospero
nothing from streets and lips
from pulpits and towers
nothing from loudspeakers
talks to nothing
about nothing

Kaliban niewolnik
nauczony ludzkiej mowy
czeka

z pyskiem w gnoju
z nogami w raju
obwąchuje człowieka
czeka

nic nadchodzi
nic w czarodziejskim płaszczu
Prospera
nic z ulic i ust
z ambon i wież
nic z głośników
mówi do niczego
o niczym

Choosing the Second World War as a touchstone for European civilization, he went so far in his despair over modern man's condition that even Albert Camus's existentialist ethics struck him as unfounded. The following excerpts from his poem "Falling, or On the Vertical and Horizontal Elements in the Life of Contemporary Man" ("Spadanie czyli o elementach wertykalnych i horyzontalnych w życiu człowieka współczesnego") will give the reader an idea of his train of thought:

Once upon a time	Dawniej
long long ago	bardzo bardzo dawno
there was a solid bottom	bywało solidne dno
on which a man could roll	na które mógł się stoczyć
down	człowiek
a man who happened to fall	człowieka który się znalazł na dnie
owing to his light-mindedness	dzięki swej lekkomyślności
or to the help of his fellow-men	lub dzięki pomocy bliźnich
was looked upon with horror	oglądano z przerażeniem
with interest	zainteresowaniem
with hatred	nienawiścią
with pleasure	radością

he was pointed at	wskazywano na niego
while he sometimes lifted himself up	a on czasem dźwigał się podnosił
stained dripping	splamiony ociekał
that was a solid bottom	
one could say	Było to solidne dno
a bourgeois bottom	można powiedzieć
	dno mieszczańskie
a different bottom was destined	inne dno było przeznaczone
for ladies a different for gentlemen	dla pań inne dla panów
in those times there were	w tamtych czasach bywały
for instance fallen women	na przykład kobiety upadłe
disgraced	skompromitowane
there were men who went bankrupt	bywali bankruci
a species now nearly	gatunek obecnie prawie
unknown	nieznany
a politician had his special bottom	swoje dno miał polityk
as did a priest a merchant an officer	kapłan kupiec oficer
a cashier and a scientist	kasjer i uczony
. . .	. . .
La chute the fall	La Chute upadek
is still possible	jest możliwy jeszcze
only in literature	tylko w literaturze
in a dream in a fever	w marzeniu gorączce
you remember that story	pamiętacie to opowiadanie
about an honest man	o porządnym człowieku
he did not leap to the rescue	nie skoczył na ratunek
about a man who practiced "debauchery"	o człowieku który uprawiał "rozpustę"
lied used to be slapped in the face—	Kłamał bywał policzkowany
for that confession	za to wyznanie
a great dead man maybe the last	wielki zmarły może ostatni
contemporary French moralist	współczesny moralista francuski
received in 1957	otrzymał w roku 1957
a prize	nagrodę

Quotations from St. Augustine and Dostoevsky ensue. Różewicz plays with them for a while; then he comes back to Camus:

That fighter with the heart of a child	ten bojownik z sercem dziecka wyobrażał sobie
imagined	że koncentryczne kanały Amsterdamu
that concentric canals of Amsterdam	są kręgiem piekła
are circles of hell	mieszczańskiego piekła
of a bourgeois hell	
. . .	. . .

from his childhood he had faith in the Bottom He certainly believed strongly in Man loved Dostoevsky he certainly suffered because there is no hell no heaven no Lamb no lie it seemed to him that he discovered a bottom that he was lying there that he fell	wyniósł z dzieciństwa wiarę w Dno Musiał głęboko wierzyć w Czło- wieka musiał głęboko kochać Dostojew- skiego musiał cierpieć nad tym że nie ma piekła nieba Baranka kłamstwa zdawało mu się że odkrył dno że leży na dnie że upadł
However	Tymczasem
there was no bottom anymore . . .	dna już nie było . . .
Falling we cannot take on a form a hieratical posture the insignia of power fall from our hands . . .	spadając nie możemy przybrać formy postawy hieratycznej insygnia władzy wypadają z rąk . . .
the word falling is not the proper word it does not explain that movement of body and of soul in which passes and wanes contemporary man	słowo spadanie nie jest słowem właściwym nie objaśnia tego ruchu ciała i duszy w którym przemija człowiek współczesny
revolted men damned angels were falling headfirst contemporary man falls in all directions simultaneously down up sideways like a weather vane	zbuntowani ludzie potępione anioły spadały głową w dół człowiek współczesny spada we wszystkich kierunkach równocześnie w dół w górę na boki na kształt róży wiatrów
once upon a time one used to fall and ascend vertically nowadays we fall horizontally	dawniej spadano i wznoszono się pionowo obecnie spada się poziomo

The reader may prefer to take Camus's side against Różewicz, since the latter, like many of his Polish contemporaries, seems to jump to conclusions. In any case, the poem is a good illustration of Różewicz's premeditated devices aimed against the "purity" of poetry: quotations from various writers and from press clippings, enumerations, polemical jabs, etc. "Falling" shows Różewicz, perhaps, at his most programmatic, because many of his short poems rely upon metaphors with many layers of meaning, a procedure which he repudiates in theory. But as we have said, Różewicz is ensconced in a permanent contradiction. Not the least paradoxical is his stance as an "antipoet," who invented a style that begot a crowd of imitators. He would be a thoroughgoing nihilist if not for the juxtaposition which, though seldom stated directly, permeates his whole work: "normal" existence is negated in the name of a postulated "full and authentic" existence. The first is the "nothing" which civilization offers to poor Caliban; the second is unattainable. Here lies the crux of Różewicz's conflict.

It was not accidental that after 1956 he became a mainstay of the Polish "theater of the absurd." His poetry, which programmatically oversteps the limits between genres, tended naturally toward monologue and dialogue, and his fury at "normal" existence found ample opportunity in the theater to lash out at the superficiality beyond which human beings are unable to go in their everyday relations. Some of his plays have been staged, some not; often they exceed the means at the disposal of even the most daring theater directors: here, too, Różewicz seeks to efface the lines between genres, in this case, between his antipoetry and his antidrama. His plays are not concerned with action in the traditional sense; his characters, as in medieval morality plays, are symbols of common humanity, everymen, although they move within a given time and place. Thus, the protagonist of *Personal File* (*Kartoteka*, 1961), who witnesses the whole of his phantomlike life, is recognizable as a Pole of Różewicz's generation, while human memory functions like the medieval post-mortem tribunal, sitting in judgment and passing sentence. *The Witnesses, or Our Little Stabilization* (*Świadkowie czyli nasza mała stabilizacja*, 1962) has a two-part construction. In the first, we assist at the morning routine of an apparently happy couple, only to be led to the realization that their relationship is a sham, that the smiling landscape beyond the window is full of horror (children play a game of burying a kitten alive). In the second, two gentlemen are seated in armchairs in such a way that they can neither reach out and touch one another nor see each other (an obvious metaphor for steady office jobs). Their dialogue reveals the impossibility of communication, and when both notice something dragging itself by and whining—a wounded dog, or perhaps a wounded man—they limit themselves to a few remarks, but they do not risk moving from the chairs.

Różewicz is a writer in the process of evolving. In spite of his acquired mannerisms he is still changing, so it is too early yet to classify him. His boldness compensates for his faults, the chief of which is crudeness. Sometimes it is difficult to distinguish whether his lack of taste is deliberate or not. Some critics have compared his poetry to collages made of paper scraps, rope, and other haphazardly gathered objects. What we mean, thus, by crudeness does not apply to his material, but to its organization, which is often not exacting enough.

Zbigniew Herbert (1924–)

Although Zbigniew Herbert is only a few years younger than Różewicz and although his biography is quite similar, he belongs to the "new wave" of poets who made their debuts in 1956. He is, perhaps, the most representative among the young poets of the second postwar decade. A native of Lwów, he attended a clandestinely operated high school during the war, besides participating in underground military training classes run by the Resistance and earning his living at odd jobs. He saw action in a guerrilla unit; after the war he obtained a diploma in law, studied philosophy and history of art, worked as a minor employee in various stage enterprises, wrote poetry, but published practically nothing throughout the period of obligatory orthodoxy. He was, thus, over thirty when his first volume, *String of Light* (*Struna światła*, 1956), appeared in print. It was followed by *Hermes, a Dog and a Star* (*Hermes, pies i gwiazda*, 1957) and *A Study of the Object* (*Studium przedmiotu*, 1961). Herbert's treatment of the basic theme of Polish postwar poetry—the tension between an artist's concern with form and his compassion for human suffering—places him at the opposite pole from Różewicz. In his outlook, he is a poet of civilization, not a rebel decrying the "nothing in Prospero's cloak." His good training in the humanities has made him somewhat wary of the longing for a state of perfect innocence. The tragedies of our century pervade his crystalline, intellectual, and ironic poetry, but they are counterbalanced by his reflections on historical situations from other ages, and are rather alluded to than approached directly. Hamlet, Marcus Aurelius, the soldiers of ancient Greece, Roman proconsuls, or deities of classical mythology are the heroes of his poems. This procedure assures him a perspective on his own time. Some of his poems, it is true, pervert the great images of Christian civilization by irony: "At the Gate of the Valley" suggests that the angels dividing the damned from the saved behave like guards in a concentration camp. It is also true that in the poem "Apollo and Marsyas" the problem of imperturbable art versus howls of pain is given a solution inimical to the former: Marsyas is a satyr who dared to challenge Apollo to a contest of flute-playing. As a punishment, he was bound to a tree and flayed. The howls of the tortured Marsyas disgust Apollo, but also make him uneasy. He departs:

> wondering
> whether out of Marsyas' howling
> there will not someday arise
> a new kind
> of art—let us say—concrete
>
> suddenly
>
> at his feet
> falls a petrified nightingale
>
> he looks back
> and sees that the hair of the tree to which Marsyas was fastened
>
> is white
> completely

> zastanawiając się
> czy z wycia Marsjasza
> nie powstanie z czasem
> nowa gałąź
> sztuki—powiedzmy—konkretnej
>
> nagle
>
> pod nogi upada mu
> skamieniały słowik
>
> odwraca głowę
> i widzi
> że drzewo do którego przywiązany był Marsjasz
> jest siwe
>
> zupełnie

Yet Herbert, in most of his other poems, rehabilitates art much as he rehabilitates the perfection of objects we see and touch. Perhaps this clinging to inanimate things is a little desperate; however, they stand for the purity of a universe independent of human suffering. For instance, he writes in a short poem, "The Stone" ("Kamyk"):

> The stone
> is a perfect creature

equal to itself
obedient to its limits

filled exactly
with a stony meaning

with a scent which does not remind one of anything
does not frighten anything away does not arouse desire

its ardor and coldness
are just and full of dignity

I feel a heavy remorse
when I hold it in my hand
and its noble body
is permeated by false warmth

stones cannot be tamed
to the end they will look at us
with a calm very clear eye

kamyk jest stworzeniem
doskonałym

równy samemu sobie
pilnujący swych granic

wypełniony dokładnie
kamiennym sensem

o zapachu który niczego nie przypomina
niczego nie płoszy nie budzi pożądania

jego zapał i chłód
są słuszne i pełne godności

czuję ciężki wyrzut
kiedy go trzymam w dłoni
i ciało jego szlachetne
przenika fałszywe ciepło

—Kamyki nie dają się oswoić
do końca będą na nas patrzeć
okiem spokojnym bardzo jasnym

Herbert's poetry might be defined as a distillation of the crushing experiences shared by everyone in Poland. Through its universalized meaning, it makes a valid contribution to the world poetry of this century. Herbert also fulfills the wishes of those Polish poets who searched, during the war, for a balance between an all-out protest against man's crime and faith in man. If his wisdom is bitter, at least he assigns the present human conflicts a place in a larger frame of reference, as he does, for instance, in his "Elegy of Fortinbras":

Now that we're alone we can talk Prince man to man
though you lie on the stairs and see no more than a dead ant
nothing but black sun with broken rays
I could never think of your hands without smiling
and now when they lie on the stone like fallen nests
they are defenseless as before The end is exactly this
The hands lie apart The sword lies apart The head apart
and the knight's feet in soft slippers

You will have a soldier's funeral without having been a soldier
the only ritual I am acquainted with a little
There will be no candles no singing only cannon-fuses and bursts
Crape dragged on the pavement helmets boots artillery horses
        drums drums I know nothing exquisite
those will be my maneuvers before I start to rule
one has to take the city by the neck and shake it a bit

Anyhow you had to perish Hamlet you were not for life
you believed in crystal notions not in human clay
Always twitching as if asleep you hunted chimeras
wolfishly you crunched the air only to vomit
you knew no human thing you did not know even how to breathe

Now you have peace Hamlet you accomplished what you had to
and you have peace The rest is not silence but belongs to me
you chose the easier part an elegant thrust
but what is heroic death compared with eternal watching
with a cold apple in one's hand on a narrow chair
with a view on the anthill and the clock's dial

Adieu Prince I have tasks a sewer project
and a decree on prostitutes and beggars
I must also elaborate a better system of prisons
since as you justly said Denmark is a prison
I go to my affairs This night is born
a star named Hamlet We shall never meet
What I shall leave will not be worth a tragedy

It is not for us to greet each other or bid farewell we live on
        archipelagoes

and that water these words what can they do what can they do
Prince

Teraz kiedy zostaliśmy sami możemy porozmawiać książę jak
    mężczyzna z mężczyzną
chociaż leżysz na schodach i widzisz tyle co martwa mrówka
to znaczy czarne słońce o złamanych promieniach
Nigdy nie mogłem myśleć o twoich dłoniach bez uśmiechu
i teraz kiedy leżą na kamieniu jak strącone gniazda
są tak samo bezbronne jak przedtem To jest właśnie koniec
Ręce leżą osobno Szpada leży osobno Osobno głowa
i nogi rycerza w miękkich pantoflach

Pogrzeb mieć będziesz żołnierski chociaż nie byłeś żołnierzem
jest to jedyny rytuał na jakim trochę się znam
Nie będzie gromnic i śpiewu będą lonty i huk
kir wleczony po bruku hełmy podkute buty konie artyleryjskie
    werbel werbel wiem nic pięknego
to będą moje manewry przed objęciem władzy,
trzeba wziąć miasto za gardło i wstrząsnąć nim trochę

Tak czy owak musiałeś zginąć Hamlecie nie byłeś do życia
wierzyłeś w kryształowe pojęcia a nie glinę ludzką
żyłeś ciągłymi skurczami jak we śnie łowiłeś chimery
łapczywie gryzłeś powietrze i natychmiast wymiotowałeś
nie umiałeś żadnej ludzkiej rzeczy nawet oddychać nie umiałeś

Teraz masz spokój Hamlecie zrobiłeś co do ciebie należało
i masz spokój Reszta nie jest milczeniem ale należy do mnie
wybrałeś część łatwiejszą efektowny sztych
lecz czymże jest śmierc bohaterska wobec wiecznego czuwania
z zimnym jabłkiem w dłoni na wysokim krześle
z widokiem na mrowisko i tarczę zegara

Żegnaj książę czeka na mnie projekt kanalizacji
i dekret w sprawie prostytutek i żebraków
muszę także obmyślić lepszy system więzień
gdyż jak zauważyłeś słusznie Dania jest więzieniem
Odchodzę do moich spraw Dziś w nocy urodzi się
gwiazda Hamlet Nigdy się nie spotkamy
to co po mnie zostanie nie będzie przedmiotem tragedii

Ani nam witać się ni żegnać żyjemy na archipelagach
a ta woda te słowa cóż mogą cóż mogą książę

Describing Prince Hamlet's Denmark, Herbert knows what he is talking about. Yet a genuine bond with the predicament of the Polish

community, which is the strength of poets like Herbert, will probably grow weaker in much younger writers, who will lack the intensity of a firsthand acquaintance with terror, either during the war or in the years 1949–1955. Whether they will be as indulgent to Fortinbras as Herbert is, or completely indifferent to his troubles, is unknown. In any case, Herbert's mature vision is matched by very few of the younger generation. Critics have described his poetic idiom as "classical"—not in the sense that he uses syllabotonic meters or rhyme, which he does rarely, but in the sense of the clarity and logical structure of his work.

The same qualities characterize his short plays, like *The Second Room* (*Drugi pokój*) or *Lalek*, regarded as the best of the miniature theater forms written in the years 1956–1966, and also his essays. Herbert traveled much in Italy, France, and Greece, and out of his journeys, undertaken in the spirit of humanism, arose a book of essays, *A Barbarian in the Garden* (*Barbarzyńca w ogrodzie*, 1962). The topics include the Albigensians, the Knights Templars, Greek geometry as applied to building temples at Paestum, the preserved data of medieval Masonic guilds. Herbert's passionate interest in the civilization of the Mediterranean owes much to Cyprian Norwid.

Wat, once a futurist, then author of weird stories of anticipation, and for a while the editor of Communist *Literary Monthly*, made a surprise comeback as a poet in 1956. Before the war, he had published poems that disgusted every critic by their Dadaist rather than futurist syntactical liberties; they appeared under the title *I at One Side and I at Another Side of My Pug-Iron Stove* (*Ja z jednej strony i ja z drugiej strony mego mopsożelaznego piecyka*, 1920). The trend of "liberated words," which Wat propagated then, was to remain without adherents for a long time. Meanwhile, he acted as an editor and a literary director of a publishing house; during the war he escaped from the Nazis to the Soviet-occupied Lwów, where he was soon accused of being both a Trotskyite and a Zionist and was imprisoned. It was only in 1946 that he returned to Poland from Soviet Asia. At that time he re-entered literary life, but again, with the enforcement of orthodoxy after 1949, was attacked as a political deviationist, pronounced an outcast, and forbidden to publish anything. A sudden spurt of inspiration in 1956–1957 resulted in some poems that revealed him as one of the young, and indeed, his style answered perfectly to the aspirations of the "new wave" in poetry. Jotting down his dreams and fleeting perceptions in a seemingly automatic way, he engaged in the buffoonery of a man who has lived through many sufferings, on whom history had played bad jokes, and who had been tossed around by all the intellectual and political currents of modern times. What made him so contemporary was his lack of respect for the conventional boundaries of poetry as a

Aleksander Wat (1900–1967)

self-contained literary genre and his reliance on the dictates of the subconscious; while modern Polish poetry, owing to a self-imposed discipline, tended to shrink from autobiographical confessions, Wat, with his uninhibited blubbering, brought to it a patch of color. *Poems* (*Wiersze*, 1957) was awarded a prize by the then leading weekly, *New Culture* (*Nowa Kultura*).

Owing to his bad health, Wat went to the south of France, and out of his stay there came a new volume, *Mediterranean Poems* (*Wiersze śródziemnomorskie*, 1962). He settled for good in France, and because of his "treason," silence suddenly engulfed his name in Poland. He died in Paris. But his poems remain significant for the post-1956 revival of "vanguardism." The following quote from "A Damned Man" ("Potępiony") will give an idea of his technique:

First in my dream appeared a coffee mill.
Most ordinary. The old-fashioned kind. A coffee-brown color.
(as a child I liked to slide open the lid, peek in, and instantly
   snap it shut. With fear and trembling! so that my teeth chattered
      from terror!
It was as if I myself were being ground up in there! I always
   knew
I would come to a bad end!)
So first there was a coffee mill.
Or perhaps it only seemed so, because a moment later a windmill
   stood there.
And that windmill stood on the sea, on the horizon's line, in its
   very center.
Its four wings turned creaking and cracking.
They probably were grinding up somebody.
And at the tip of every one of them
An equilibrist in white revolved to the melody of "The Merry
   Widow."

Najpierw przyśnił się młynek do kawy.
Najpospolitszy. Taki sobie staroświecki. Ciemnokawowy w ko-
   lorze.
(Dzieckiem lubiłem odmykać klapkę, zajrzeć i natychmiast zatrzasnąć. Z trwogą, z drżeniem! Aż zęby
dzwoniły ze strachu! Było mi tak, jakobym ja tam
był w środku kruszony! Zawsze wiedziałem, że muszę
źle skończyć!)
Najpierw zatem był młynek do kawy.
A może to się tylko tak zdawało, bo w chwilę potem stał już tam
   młyn z wiatrakiem.
A stał ten młyn na morzu, na linii horyzontu, na samym jej
   środku.
Cztery skrzydła obracały się z trzaskiem. Pewno kogoś kruszyły.
A nad szczytem każdego

ekwilibrysta w bieli
obracał się w takt melodii z "Wesołej wdówki."

Wat's casual and random "jottings," though obedient to the moment, often have the precision of simplified drawings where a few lines suffice to grasp a scene, for instance, in this poem from the cycle *Songs of a Wanderer:*

So beautiful the lungs
are breathless. The hand remembers:
I was a wing.
Blue. The peaks in ruddy
gold. Women of this land—
small olives. On a spacious saucer
wisps of smoke, houses, pastures, roads,
interlacing of roads, O holy diligence
of man. How hot it is! It returns,
the miracle of shade. A shepherd, sheep, a dog, a ram
all in gilded bells. Olive trees
in twisted goodness. A cypress—their lone shepherd. A village
on Cabris cliff, castellated
by its tiles. And a church, its cypress and shepherd.
Youth of the day, youth of the times, youth of the world.
Birds listen, intently silent. Only a cock crowing
from somewhere below in the hamlet of Spéracèdes. How
hot it is. To die on foreign soil is bitter.
It's sweet to live in France.

Pięknie aż tchu brak
płucom. Ręka wspomina:
byłam skrzydłem.
Niebiesko. Szczyty w zaróżowionym
złocie. Kobiety tej ziemi—
małe oliwki. Na spodku rozległym
dymy, domy, pastwiska, drogi,
przeploty dróg, święta pilności
człowieka. Jak gorąco! Powraca
cud cienia. Pastuch, owce, owczarek, baran
w dzwoneczkach pozłacanych. Oliwki
w krętych dobrociach. Cyprys—ich pastuch samotny. Wieś
na perci kabryjskiej, obronna
dachówkami. I kościół, jej cyprys i pastuch.
Młodość dnia, młodość czasów, młodość świata.
Ptaki milczą zasłuchane. Tylko kogut
z dołów przysiółka Spéracèdes. Jak
gorąco. Gorzko umierać na obcym.
Słodko jest żyć we Francji.

It would be a mistake to bypass another aspect of Wat's poetry, namely, that it is an unashamed scream of pain. He is not afraid of using trite exclamations, quite prosaic parentheses, or even footnotes, as if to stress his nonchalant directness. To quote the opening from "Before Breughel the Elder":

Work is a blessing.
I tell you that, I—professional sluggard!
Who slobbered in so many prisons! Fourteen!
And in so many hospitals! Ten! And innumerable inns.

Work is a blessing.
How else could we deal with the lava of fratricidal love toward
    fellow man?
With those storms of extermination of all by all?
With brutality, bottomless and measureless?
With the black-and-white era which does not want to end
endlessly repeating itself *da capo* like a record
forgotten on a turntable
spinning by itself?
Or perhaps someone invisible watches over the phonograph?
    Horror!
How, if not for work, could we live in the paradise of social
    hygienists
Who never soak their hands in blood without aseptic gloves?

Horror!

Praca jest dobrodziejstwem.
Ja wam to powiadam, ja—leń zakuty!
który przebarłożyłem się w tylu więzieniach! W czternastu!
I w tylu szpitalach! w dziesięciu! W gospodach—bez liczby!

Praca jest błogosławieństwem.
Jakżebyśmy bez niej dali radę lawie bratobójczej miłości bliźniego?
nawałnicom eksterminacji wszystkich przez wszystkich?
brutalności bez dna i miary?
Dobie biało-czarnej, która nie chce się skończyć,
ciągle da capo powtarza się jak płyta,
którą zapomniano zdjąć z tarczy,
a ona sama się kręci?
albo ktoś niewidzialny nakręca patefon? Okropność!
Jakżebyśmy bez niej mogli żyć w raju społecznych hygienistów,
którzy rąk nie unurzą we krwi bez aseptycznych rękawic?

Okropność!

New Trends
of the
Second
Postwar
Decade

Poetry after 1956, with its "laboratory privileges" restored, was free to experiment. With few exceptions, it moved toward a complexity of expression, which reduced its appeal to the larger public. The average volume of poems sold about a thousand copies, a very low figure in a country where ten thousand copies of even a quite difficult nonfiction work would disappear from bookstores within a couple of days. This state of affairs contrasted with the wartime period, when poetry enjoyed a massive response, and also with the short but violent period of upheaval in 1956 when verse provided a common idiom for universally shared feelings; in those days every metaphor had political overtones. Yet even if the number of its readers fell, poetry's influence did not diminish. In this new phase of Polish literature, the lines separating one genre from another became blurred, so that philosophy invaded the drama, the novel was sometimes barely distinguishable from the essay, and verse dropped its specific features of meter and rhyme. But it was poetry that spearheaded the exploration of new territories, and its influence was noticeable even in science fiction. In the theater, where the impact of poetic experiments was especially strong, dramatists were drawing conclusions from the theories of Stanisław Ignacy Witkiewicz, from Gałczyński's *Green Goose*, and from the Western European "theater of the absurd." Realistic "action" was abandoned for the metaphorical structure of the fable, the parable, or the morality play. To expose language as a very imperfect tool of communication between human beings became the fad of the day; thus, it is not surprising that "semantic poetry" with its exploding of grammatical syntax received much attention.

Before 1956 Miron Białoszewski (1922–   ) was an outcast and an eccentric living in utter poverty. Together with a few friends, he used to stage his absurd plays in a private apartment in Warsaw. When he was at last able to publish his first book of poems, *Turns of Things* (*Obroty rzeczy*, 1956), he provoked quite a stir. His grotesquely oriented imagination exploits the most undignified objects—kitchen utensils, rusty pipes, dirty staircases—as if he wanted to stick his tongue out at all great ideas, which are made to appear pompous when juxtaposed with inert matter and the difficulty man has in confronting it. From the linguistic jokes of his first volume, he evolved toward a radical brand of antipoetry in *Erroneous Emotions* (*Mylne wzruszenia*, 1961), wringing and torturing words, squeezing them into a pulp of inarticulate sounds. Conversations heard in the street, idioms of unclear origin provide him with the material for his operations. He tracks down "meanings" to aboriginal mutterings and mumblings. So-called "reality" disappears, supplanted by language as the only cosmos accessible to man.

Similar to Białoszewski is another "semantic" poet, Zbigniew Bieńkowski (born 1913), author of a few powerful poems on the Resistance. Unlike his colleague, however, he is obsessed with the superabundance of meaning in words and with the resulting ambiguity in language.

Tymoteusz Karpowicz (1921–   ) is sometimes ranked among the debunkers of syntax, but this subtle poet, striving for utter conciseness (in the footsteps of the First Vanguard), excels at transforming objects into metaphors through tongue-in-cheek descriptions. For instance, in "The Pencil's Dream" ("Sen ołówka"):

> when the pencil undresses for sleep
> he firmly decides
> to sleep stiffly
> and blackly
>
> he is helped in it
> by the inborn inflexibility
> of all the piths of the world
> the spinal pith of the pencil
> will break but cannot be bent
>
> he will never dream of
> waves or hair
> only of a soldier standing at attention
> or coffins
>
> what finds its place in him
> is straight
> what is beyond is crooked
> good night

> gdy ołówek rozbiera się do snu
> twardo postanawia
> spać sztywno
> i czarno
>
> pomaga mu w tym
> wrodzona nieugiętość
> wszystkich rdzeni świata
> rdzeń pacierzowy ołówka
> pęknie a nie da się zgiąć
>
> nigdy nie przyśnią mu się
> fale albo włosy
> tylko żołnierze stojący na baczność
> lub trumny
>
> to co w nim się układa
> jest proste
> co poza nim krzywe
> dobranoc

Surrealism, stifled in Poland during 1918–1939 by the rationalistic First Vanguard, took belated revenge in the poetry of Jerzy Harasymowicz (1933–   ). Dream and a fairy-tale world perceived by our senses make up his realm, where no sober advice of logic interferes with his "liberated" imagination. Yet his poetry has its roots in a definite region: the nature of the foothills at the base of the Carpathian mountains, old wooden village churches, icons, the toylike towers of Kraków (where he lives), the amusing paraphernalia of the 1900s and of the Hapsburg Empire are woven into his fabric of "wonders," which is the title of his first volume. Sometimes tenderly, sometimes cruelly, humorous, always impervious to ratiocinations, he travels through a fairyland of his own, which we may illustrate by the following verse, entitled "A Green Lowland of Pianos" ("Zielona nizina fortepianów"):

> in the evening
> as far as the eye can see
> herds
> of black pianos
>
> up to their knees
> in the mire
> they listen to the frogs
>
> they gurgle in water
> with chords of rapture
>
> they are entranced
> by froggish, moonish spontaneity
>
> after the vacation they cause scandals
> in a concert hall
> during the artistic milking
> suddenly they lie down
> like cows
>
> looking with indifference
> at the white flowers
> of the audience
>
> at the gesticulating
> of the ushers
>
>
> Wieczorem
> jak okiem sięgnąć
> stada
> czarnych
> fortepianów

po kolana
w bajorze
żab słuchają

w wodzie
akordami zachwytu
bulgocą

zachwyca je
żabia
księżycowa spontaniczność

po wakacjach
w koncertowej sali
skandale czynią
podczas artystycznego dojenia
kładą się
naraz
jak krowy

patrząc obojętnie
na białe kwiaty
publiczności

na woźnych
gestykulacje

In connection with the poetry of Stanisław Grochowiak (1934–1976) critics coined a new term: "turpism"—from the Latin *turpis*, for "ugly." The whole "new wave" showed an abhorrence of everything "nice," of everything "beautiful," favoring, instead, trenchant, crisp irony. Grochowiak went, perhaps, the furthest in his cult of the unsavory and the ill-smelling, which he conceived as a remedy for any mental laziness imprisoning man in a fool's paradise. In his love poems, for example, sex is always associated with images of raw meat, of quartered fish, of decaying bones; and human flesh is shown in its agonizing transience. An old theme in European poetry, the inseparable alliance of love and death, is recast here in a way that more than once recalls Charles Baudelaire's preoccupation with original sin. At the same time, Grochowiak is a socially oriented writer whose satirical, moralistic intent is clearly formulated, for example in "Clean Men" ("Czyści"):

> I prefer ugliness
> It is closer to the blood circulation
> Of words when they are X-rayed
> And tormented

It molds the richest shapes
It redeems with its soot
The walls of charnel houses
It gives the chilliness of statues
A mousey smell

There are people so cleanly scrubbed
That when they pass
Even a dog wouldn't growl
Though they are neither holy
Nor humble

Wolę brzydotę
jest bliżej krwiobiegu
Słów gdy prześwietlać
Je i udręczać

Ona ukleja najbogatsze formy
Ratuje kopciem
Ściany kostnicowe
W zziębłość posągów
Wkłada zapach mysi

Są bo na świecie ludzie tak wymyci
Że gdy przechodzą
Nawet pies nie warknie
Choć ani święci
Ani są też cisi

A no less sharp attack is the poem entitled "The Breasts of the Queen Are Turned Out of Wood" ("Piersi królowej utoczone z drewna"):

The hands of the queen are smeared with grease
The ears of the queen are plugged with cotton
In the mouth of the queen gypsum dentures
The breasts of the queen are turned out of wood

And I brought here a tongue warm with wine
In my mouth rustling sparkling saliva
The breasts of the queen are turned out of wood

In the house of the queen a yellow candle withers
In the bed of the queen a water bottle grows cooler
The mirrors of the queen are covered with tarpaulins
In the glass of the queen a syringe is rusting

And I brought here a vigorous young belly
Also teeth tensed like instruments
The breasts of the queen are turned out of wood

From the hair of the queen leaves are falling
From the eyes of the queen a spider web slips down
The heart of the queen bursts with a soft fizzle
The breath of the queen yellows on the windowpane

And I brought here a dove in a basket
And a whole bunch of golden balloons
From the hair of the queen leaves are falling

Ręce królowej posmarowane smalcem
Uszy królowej pozatykane watą
W ustach królowej sztuczna szczęka z gipsu
Piersi królowej utoczone z drewna

A ja tu przyniosłem język ciepły winem
W ustach szumiącą musującą ślinę
Piersi królowej utoczone z drewna

W domu królowej więdnie żółta świeca
W łożu królowej termofor ziębnieje
Lustra królowej zakryte brezentem
W szklance królowej rdzewieje strzykawka

A ja tu przyniosłem młody brzuch napięty
Zęby napięte niby instrumenty
Piersi królowej utoczone z drewna

Z włosów królowej opadają liście
Z oczu królowej spada pajęczyna
Serce królowej pęka z cichym sykiem
Oddech królowej żółknieje na szybie

A ja tu przyniosłem gołębia w koszyku
Całą wiązankę złotych baloników
Z włosów królowej opadają liście

But equally interesting are his poems where he catches the essence of the Polish geographical and spiritual landscape. Like a great deal of postwar poetry, they are untranslatable, woven as they are out of a web of allusions to Polish literature of the remote and most recent past. It is curious to note that Grochowiak, along with a few others, reversed the Vanguard trend of playing down literary conventions. In his effort to bring back meter and rhyme, he even went so far as to write cycles of sonnets. Prolific, both as a poet and as an author of prose narratives, Grochowiak has also written plays, which rank him among the experimenters with antinaturalistic theatrical forms.

The intellectually sophisticated poets of the "new wave" remolded the genre once called the "love lyric." Among women poets, Wisława Szymborska (1923–) especially captivated readers with her volume, *Salt* (*Sól*, 1962), the very title of which is an apt comment on the sting in her verse. It would be unjust to present her as a poetess of narrow range; her discipline enables her to practice philosophical poetry with a conciseness matched only by Zbigniew Herbert. Yet she often leans toward preciosity. She is probably at her best where her woman's sensibility outweighs her existential brand of rationalism, as in "I Am Too Near:

> I am too near to be dreamt of by him.
> I do not fly over him, do not escape from him
> under the roots of a tree. I am too near.
> Not in my voice sings the fish in the net,
> not from my finger rolls the ring.
> I am too near. A big house is on fire
> without me, calling for help. Too near
> for a bell dangling from my hair to chime.
> Too near to enter as a guest
> before whom walls glide apart by themselves.
> Never again will I die so lightly,
> so much beyond my flesh, so inadvertently
> as once in his dream. Too near.
> I taste the sound, I see the glittering husk of this word
> as I lie immobile in his embrace. He sleeps,
> more accessible now to her, seen but once
> a cashier of a wandering circus with one lion,
> than to me, who am at his side.
> For her now in him a valley grows,
> russet-leaved, closed by a snowy mountain
> in the bright blue air. I am too near
> to fall to him from the sky. My scream
> could wake him up. Poor thing
> I am, limited to my shape,
> I who was a birch, who was a lizard,
> who would come out of my cocoons
> shimmering the colors of my skins. Who possessed
> the grace of disappearing from astonished eyes,
> which is a wealth of wealths. I am near,
> too near for him to dream of me.
> I slide my arm from under the sleeper's head
> and it is numb, full of swarming pins,
> on the tip of each, waiting to be counted,
> the fallen angels sit.

Jestem za blisko, żeby mu się śnić.
Nie fruwam nad nim, nie uciekam mu
pod korzeniami drzew. Jestem za blisko.
Nie moim głosem śpiewa ryba w sieci.
Nie z mego palca toczy się pierścionek.
Jestem za blisko. Wielki dom się pali
beze mnie wołającej ratunku. Za blisko,
żeby na moim włosie dzwonił dzwon.
Za blisko, żebym mogła wejść jak gość,
przed którym rozsuwają się ściany.
Już nigdy po raz drugi nie umrę tak lekko,
tak bardzo poza ciałem, tak bezwiednie,
jak niegdyś w jego śnie. Jestem za blisko,
za blisko. Słyszę syk
i widzę połyskliwą łuskę tego słowa,
znieruchomiała w objęciu. On śpi,
w tej chwili dostępniejszy widzianej raz w życiu
kasjerce wędrownego cyrku z jednym lwem
niż mnie leżącej obok.
Teraz dla niej rośnie w nim dolina
rudolistna, zamknięta ośnieżoną górą
w lazurowym powietrzu. Ja jestem za blisko,
żeby mu z nieba spaść. Mój krzyk
mógłby go tylko zbudzić. Biedna,
ograniczona do własnej postaci,
a byłam brzozą, a byłam jaszczurką
a wychodziłam z czasów i atłasów
mieniąc się kolorami skór. A miałam
łaskę znikania sprzed zdumionych oczu,
co jest bogactwem bogactw. Jestem blisko,
za blisko, żeby mu się śnić.
Wysuwam ramię spod głowy śpiącego,
zdrętwiałe, pełne wyrojonych szpilek.
Na czubku każdej z nich, do przeliczenia,
strąceni siedli anieli.

Some younger poets reacted sharply against Różewicz, and in their poetry, it is precisely the artifices of culture that they make the object of their veneration. It was Baudelaire who once wrote in praise of powder and rouge. What he wanted to say—that man is never naked, since not only his dress but his gestures always bear the imprint of his epoch—could be quite suitably applied to these poets' fondness for the changeable and the transitory. Out of compassion for the frailty of man, who, despite nature's cruel treatment, i.e., death, maintains his culture through a creative effort, they try to capture the aura of various historical periods as it permeates costumes and styles. Thus, their poetry often has recourse to an imitation of past literary procedures which verges on pastiche. Quotations from foreign and Polish poets inserted into their lines make this a learned poetry, as if the Classicism of two centuries ago were celebrating its revival.

Jarosław Marek Rymkiewicz (1934–   ) and Jerzy S. Sito (1934–   ) have been the most vocal in this group. They are, and it is not surprising, also assiduous translators of poetry, mostly from English. Whether this trend will be fruitful is, for the moment, a matter of conjecture.

The term "poetry of culture" would not be out of place in a discussion of the volumes of Artur Międzyrzecki (1922–   ). A soldier of the Polish army in Italy, then for a long time a resident of France, he is, like his elder colleague, Adam Ważyk, one of the most "French" poets in contemporary literature, both because of his familiarity with modern French poetry, from Apollinaire to Queneau, and because of his "elective affinities." His output also embraces essays on modern poetry, an autobiographical narrative, *Tales of a Tent-Dweller* (*Opowieści mieszkańca namiotów*, 1957) and numerous translations from French.

Poetry and studies on poetry have performed a special function in intellectual life because of their particular sensitivity to all the currents of contemporary thought. New tools of investigation have permitted the revision of many opinions on old and modern Polish literature, and in the years 1956–1966 laid the foundations for future inquiry in this domain. Enigmas of Romanticism began to be unraveled, but poets and scholars turned with even greater zeal to the neglected poetry and theater of the Polish Baroque. If we group together poets and scholars, it is because of the constant interflow of ideas and cooperation between them. Credit should be given here to literary critics and university professors, above all, to Kazimierz Wyka (1910–   ), who combines both professions. Once an ally of the Second Vanguard, Wyka, through his essays on poetry and his university lectures, formed a generation of gifted investigators, unwilling to withdraw into a narrow scholarly field, always open to new literary phenomena.

Several publishing houses, though state-owned and, thus, prone to bureaucratic cautiousness, were quite energetic in defending a policy of their own and fostered a literary revival, as did some reviews, such as *Creative Work* (*Twórczość*), founded in 1945 and edited for a while by Wyka, then by the "Skamander" poet Jarosław Iwaszkiewicz. It is characteristic that the first pages of every issue of that leading monthly have been consistently taken up by poems. Though the poems may often be too difficult for the average reader, they have influenced an elite. Thus, contemporary poetry, by goading the students of hu-

manities and invading the stage (we might mention the mass response
to verse recitation contests), preserved the exceptional position it has
had in Polish letters since the sixteenth century.

Prose

Tadeusz
Borowski
(1922–1951)

Clandestinely published volumes of poetry, two years of Auschwitz
concentration camp, a meteoric rise in literature after the war, cut
short by a suicide before he reached thirty—such are the components
of Borowski's legend. From a Polish worker's family in the Ukraine,
born in Zhitomir, he went through a Warsaw high school after his
family moved from the Soviet Union, but he finished his secondary
studies in the underground-operated school system in 1940. Subsequently he became a student of literature in the underground Warsaw
University, earning his living at the same time as night watchman for
a building supplies firm, which gave him the opportunity to engage in
a multitude of black-market activities. Critical toward all the Polish
complexes of "martyrdom" and toward the resistance movement, he
preferred to write poetry, and his mimeographed volume, *Wherever
the Earth* (*Gdziekolwiek Ziemia*, 1942), differed radically from the
work of his contemporaries and colleagues such as Baczyński or the
group of *Art and the Nation*. Like them, however, he took much from
the Second Vanguard, but while they dissolved images into a sort of
emotional mist, he strove for sharpness, even harshness. Yet, though
the strong metrical patterns give the impression of manly vigor, his
poems are the most desperate of those produced during the Nazi occupation. In them, the torture and death of "us slaves" (Poles) is
stripped of all meaning, even of an anticipated meaning for posterity,
and the catastrophe acquires all the earmarks of a macabre prank
played by blind and indifferent forces of history, similar to a cataclysm
of nature. As if to corroborate Borowski's postulation of an absurdity
in which one draws lots with death, the Gestapo arrested him acci-
dently: Worried about his fiancée's long absence, Borowski went to
look for her. The Nazis had set a trap for members of the Resistance
in the apartment where she had been, and Borowski fell into it. But
Borowski's decision was also a moral one, for he wanted to share her
fate in the event she had been seized. In fact, he found her later on,
in the women's camp at Auschwitz, and was able to help her by sending medical supplies. Both survived. Transferred from Auschwitz to
Dachau, where he was liberated by the Americans, Borowski then
lived in Munich for a while, and there wrote his most daring stories
on Auschwitz. They were first published in Munich in 1946 in a book
signed jointly with two other former prisoners. Borowski returned to
Poland and published a selection of his stories under the title *Farewell*

to Mary (*Pożegnanie z Marią*, 1948). The treatment of the subject puzzled and even caused indignation among the critics. No such presentation of life in a concentration camp yet existed in literature, where there is no clear division into victims and criminals. The camp is shown as an infernal machine, forcing prisoners, its victims, into a struggle for survival at any price, be it at the expense of the weaker among them. All notions of good and bad behavior tumble down; "good" equals toughness and resourcefulness; "evil" equals lack of cunning or of physical strength. The narrator, who bears the author's first name (Tadeusz), is one of those tough fellows who organize their life in the camp quite well, steal, barter, know how to avoid overexertion while laboring, and look on with detachment, if not with a sarcastic grimace, at the daily processions of thousands destined for the gas chambers. The moral ambiguity is emphasized by the tone of the narrative, which is a bragging one; connivance of prisoners with their overseers is evoked in a matter-of-fact way. No overt moral judgment is passed. Borowski thus achieves an effect of cruelty which remains unsurpassed by any testimony on Nazi camps.

In his craft, he learned much from Hemingway, especially how to outline a situation through idiomatic dialogue without author's commentary. Actually, Borowski was a desperate moralist. His stories place on trial our entire Western civilization, which made such crimes possible. The stories set in Germany after the entrance of American troops betray a deep sense of outrage at the "normalcy" that will soon relegate Nazi genocide to the sphere of vague recollections or, more probably, of silence. We refer here to another book of short stories: *The World of Stone* (*Kamienny świat*, 1948).

As a moralist, Borowski searched for an ideology strong enough to transform the world and to prevent a future release of bestiality in man. Skeptical as to Marxism during and immediately after the war, he later let himself be convinced by his friends, the "pimpled ones," and then, as befitted his fervent temperament, outdid them in his will to serve and to be useful. He put his talent at the disposal of the Party, writing mostly journalism. His style was forceful and often brilliant, in spite of an unceremonious twisting of facts. His friendships with young German Communists, whom he believed to be the only Germans who fully understood what happened, contributed to his evolution. After *Farewell to Mary*, which Marxist critics denounced as the work of a nihilist, tainted with the American literature of violence, Borowski plunged into an aggressive campaign for Socialist Realism. His sudden suicide in July 1951 was a shock for all political and literary Warsaw. The reasons for that act were, as is usual in such cases, a tangle of many strands: an ideological crisis when he realized that he was an abettor of the terror came together with a personal drama of involvement with two women, and this, combined with what must have been a latent self-destructive urge, got hold of him at a moment of weakened resistance.

In spite of its apparent contradictions, Borowski's work stands as a whole, unified by his chase after some unshakable moral values. The bitterness of his early poems grew out of his disagreement with the belief in the redeeming virtue of Polish heroism. His Auschwitz stories, seemingly written in cold blood, are actually a most hot-blooded protest. He embraced a dogmatic Marxism because of the same stubborn search, as he found in it a promise of rescue for mankind. And since he was a man of scrupulous integrity, he was doomed to fail in his new duty as a "politically reliable" writer.

Jerzy Andrzejewski (1909–1983) Andrzejewski's name has recurred several times in the preceding chapters. He was born in Warsaw into a lower-middle-class family. As a young man he worked for a Rightist weekly, *Straight from the Shoulder* (*Prosto z mostu*), and the same periodical published his first volume of stories, *Unavoidable Roads* (*Drogi nieuniknione*, 1936). Soon, however, he broke with his sponsors over their anti-Semitism. His first novel, *Mode of the Heart* (*Ład serca*, 1938), awarded a prize in 1939 by the Polish Academy of Literature, revealed him as a portrayer of dramatic moral conflicts. It is possible that he has always been a potential playwright, forced by the uncertainty of the genre's destiny in our century to try his hand at the novel. In any case, *Mode of the Heart* makes an impression because of the author's effective build-up of dramatic tensions, not because he placed his characters against any convincingly described background. Andrzejewski chose night for his setting. This choice was due partly to his penchant for decors of grandeur and solemnity and partly to his admiration for Joseph Conrad and George Bernanos. The protagonists of the work are a village priest and a murderer, and during one night of decision, sin and salvation are weighed upon the balance of conscience. Not surprisingly, the novel was also hailed in the Catholic press.

Very active in the literary resistance movement during the war in Nazi-occupied Warsaw, Andrzejewski, as we have already noted, attempted to transpose actuality into fiction. This sensitivity to his immediate environment impelled him to touch upon the most drastic problems of postwar Poland in his novel *Ashes and Diamonds* (*Popiół i diament*, 1948). The idea for the novel came in the spring of 1945, when Andrzejewski, like many writers, was living in Kraków, after the destruction of Warsaw. He placed his characters in that provincial capital (although it is not named) as well as in that crucial year of 1945, the year People's Poland was born. At that time, practically every family, with its sons and daughters who had been in the Resistance, was in the throes of an agonizing decision: owing to the new government's policy toward members of the Home Army, all previous commitments to the London Government were now declared a grave political misdeed. Nor were those who returned from concentration camps free from internal conflicts. Often they had bought their survival at the price of inhumanity toward their fellow prisoners. Andrzejewski's novel revolves around these two major causes of moral strife. His hero, Matthew, a young man, an ex-soldier of the underground Home Army, would like to efface his now condemned past and return to a normal life. Yet he is loyal to the memory of his comrades who fell in battle and to his superiors. Those superiors, depicted by the author as relics of the military-junta mentality, are intransigent in their opposition to the new regime. Matthew agrees to accept a last order from them: to kill the local district secretary of the Communist Party. After that he will be free. This assignment coincides with his meeting a girl and falling in love, but he has no choice except to obey his orders. His victim, the Party secretary, whom he has seen only once, is an old Communist fighter who has suffered a great deal in various prisons and concentration camps; he is a man of hard principles, but full of compassion. The absurdity of Matthew's act, resulting in the old Communist's death, is followed by the absurdity of Matthew's own death. After shooting the secretary, he withdraws unnoticed, but is seized with panic on another street where militiamen are routinely verifying the documents of passersby. He begins to run, is ordered to stop and refuses, is fired upon and perishes from a policeman's bullets. It is obvious that both Matthew and the old Communist have the author's sympathy; their tragedies enlist the reader's compassion for those people caught in the trap of a historical situation. To complete this picture of a country torn by civil war, Andrzejewski introduces his second theme: a venerable citizen, a judge by profession, who has recently returned from a Nazi concentration camp, is unmasked by one of the characters as a former blockwarden who, as such, was ready to go very far in torturing his fellow prisoners. Should he be denounced to the police? And where are the boundaries separating crime from honesty? The judge is now an honest man, as he was before he found himself in the camp. Should he be punished if he failed once in living up to the highest, maybe unattainable (under certain conditions), standards of behavior? The novel has a twofold ambition: to capture the chaotic reality of Poland in 1945; to focus upon instants of human choice, upon "limit situations" which force one to live his moment of truth. From its first edition until today, hundreds of thousands of copies have seen print, furnishing the young with an insight into the first few months of People's Poland; but *Ashes and Diamonds* (the title alludes to a poem by Norwid) is more powerful in its aspects of tragic conflict than faithful to factual data. In making his hero a

Home Army Resistance veteran, Andrzejewski broke a taboo, since the Home Army was only referred to then as a "gang of bandits." However, he was hampered, to some extent, by censorship, which compelled him to modify many details. The film version by Andrzej Wajda, made in close cooperation with the author (after 1956, when censorship was lifted), proved to be freer.

A moralistic zeal, similar to Borowski's, propelled Andrzejewski toward the Party, which he entered in 1949; he became one of the first writers to propagate Socialist Realism in his publicism. But his attempt to practice what he propagated in a satirical-optimistic novel, *An Effective War* (*Wojna skuteczna*, 1953), was a failure. An ideological crisis in 1954 prompted him, again as one of the first, to react against political dogma. He wrote a charming tale, *The Golden Fox* (*Złoty lis*), in the same year, about a little boy who firmly believed that a golden fox had come to live in his wardrobe and who stubbornly resisted the "reasonableness" of adults and other children. The tenderhearted boy felt great pity for the heroes of Socialist Realist literature for children, such as the dog who had served capitalists all his life but in his useless old age was thrown into the street; yet even such convincingly edifying stories could not bring the boy back to conformity. At last, however, he is "integrated" and denies he has ever seen the golden fox.

In the novel *Darkness Covers the Earth* (*Ciemności kryją ziemię*, 1957), known in its English translation as *The Inquisitors*, Andrzejewski settled a bitter account with himself. Faithful to his basic concern with moral decisions, he took up the problem of an individual's responsibility in the face of terror justified by a sublime aim. The novel gives shape to his own torments and to those of his contemporaries; in an allusion to Dostoevsky's "Legend of the Grand Inquisitor," it is set in Spain of the fifteenth century. Its protagonist, a young monk, Fra Diego, is converted to the cause of the "holy terror" by the "Grand Inquisitor," Torquemada, to whom he is bound by a deferential, nearly amorous, friendship. On his deathbed, Torquemada finally wavers in his convictions, and Fra Diego is so outraged that he slaps the face of his master's corpse.

A self-analysis from a different angle can be perceived in Andrzejewski's *The Gates of Paradise* (*Bramy raju*, 1961). Written in a stream-of-consciousness style, without punctuation (except for commas), the novel is woven out of the mutual confessions of adolescents who depart from medieval France for the Holy Land as participants in the Children's Crusade. What is at the root of all mass movements storming "the gates of paradise"? the author seems to ask. Judging from the adolescents' confessions, we may presume it is the individual's fear of loneliness, his urge to be united with others in the pursuit of a common great cause, an urge which may be nothing other than libido. Inhibited until now by his Catholic and then Marxist scruples, Andrzejewski in this novel for the first time allows himself free rein in describing nuances of homosexual and heterosexual involvements. All his adolescents, both boys and girls, relate to each other in that peculiar sphere where friendship, passions of the flesh, and attachment to a cause are indistinguishable. Andrzejewski's early fondness for solemn landscapes, for the glitter of sumptuous dresses in darkness, found in *The Gates of Paradise* a territory well suited to its display. Medieval armor, cloaks, and battle horses, glimpsed from time to time in the enveloping night, lend a quality of sensuous vision to the novel, and, indeed, it was originally intended as a film scenario.

Internationally recognized, translated into foreign languages, Andrzejewski traveled to Western Europe, and after a long stay in Paris, he left his inhibitions still further behind, in the novel *He Cometh Leaping upon the Mountains* (*Idzie skacząc po górach*, 1963; its American version is entitled *A Sitter for a Satyr*). A mixture of buffoonery and melodrama, this is a display of the author's bravado in parodying the style of Western best sellers and in jousting with the artistic and intellectual milieu. The central figure, an old French painter, who spends most of his time in Provence and whose genius is revived, according to gossip, by affairs with young girls, resembles Picasso.

Ever since the start of his career, critics have labeled Andrzejewski a moralist; his metamorphosis and curious literary adventures are not untypical of many novelists in Poland and other areas of Eastern Europe.

Already before the war, Adolf Rudnicki was recognized, along with Andrzejewski, as one of the most promising prose writers. Born in Warsaw into a Jewish family, he entered the literary scene with two novels that belonged to the much debated trend of documentary literature—*Rats* (*Szczury*, 1932) and *Soldiers* (*Żołnierze*, 1933). Rudnicki's early technique of barely fictionalizing his observations is especially visible in the latter, where he depicts the everyday routine of the army barracks (he had just completed his military service). By temperament, however, he inclined in the opposite direction. His sophistication, his curiously involved style, his latent narcissism predisposed him rather to psychological probings. Yet far from detracting from the strength of his talent, this internal contradiction (which marks his entire output) was to add to its interest. The publication of his novel *Unloved* (*Niekochana*, 1937) and a long story, *Summer* (*Lato*, 1938), encouraged critics to classify him as a psychological novelist. It also paralleled his acceptance into the overrefined, artistic, and aristocratic Warsaw high society. The shock of the Second World War added a new tone to Rudnicki's writing. A combatant in the September 1939 cam-

Adolf Rudnicki (1912–)

paign, he was taken prisoner by the Germans, escaped, crossed into the Soviet-occupied zone of the country, and in Lwów contributed to a Polish Communist literary monthly, *New Horizons* (*Nowe widnokręgi*). After Hitler's attack on the Soviet Union and the occupation of Lwów by the Nazis, he returned in 1942 to Warsaw, where he lived on false documents outside the ghetto and was active in clandestine publishing enterprises. He took part in the Warsaw Uprising of 1944 as a soldier and after the liberation settled in Łódź, where he joined the group of "The Forge" (*Kuźnica*). During the war he had already embarked upon what was to become the major project of his life: to leave a testimony to the "nation of Polish Jews" and how they died. Abandoning the novel form, he wrote long stories on the subject. Gathered into a huge volume and published under the title *The Dead Sea and The Living Sea* (*Żywe i martwe morze*, 1952), they are, indeed, a monument to the memory of the Nazis' victims. Had Rudnicki been a reporter, he would have produced a factual chronicle, but nothing was further from the author's intent. Rudnicki created a fictional form to explore the personal relationships between highly individualized characters caught up in an infernal machine: regardless of their virtues and vices, the Jews are crushed for the sole reason that they belong to a race condemned to die. Thus, Rudnicki turned the refinements of his aptitude for psychology to an unexpected use. He also reinstated his early tendency to shuffle factual data. Although he stuck faithfully to the details of the historical situation, which he had witnessed, he often transformed the biographies of real persons to fit a particular thesis or lend emphasis to his over-all compositional design. An example of this is the story "The Great Stefan Konecki." In order to portray an intellectual of Jewish origin who, in the process of "assimilation" into Polish society, had become estranged from the Jewish masses, Rudnicki took an eminent literary critic (Ostap Ortwin) as his model; but for the sake of enhancing the tragedy of a man who was just a Jew for the Nazis and who ended by perishing together with those he scorned, Rudnicki endowed him with all the features of a Rightist. In reality, Ortwin had been a liberal and had never had such leanings.

Not all the stories in the volume are directly concerned with the fate of the Jews. Some are political polemics in the spirit of Marxism as it was conceived by "The Forge." From the stories of this type, another instance of Rudnicki's shuffling of data may be cited. In "Escape from Yasnaya Polyana" he combines details from the biographies of Thomas Mann and Leo Tolstoy to present the moral defeat of his character, a great German writer who, after spending the war years in exile, lacks the courage to return to the only part of his country where Nazism is being effectively eradicated, namely East Germany. Some of Rudnicki's stories are accounts settled with himself as well as with the whole intelligentsia. All told, the collection is an embodiment of "The Forge's" program calling for a renewal of narrative techniques through efforts to apply them in so-called "border-line genres." Rudnicki was most typical of the trend in prose during the years 1945–1949. In his attempt to leave a testimony to the era of the cremation ovens and gas chambers he lacks Borowski's savage thrust; his tone is lyrical, his sentences meandering, like those of a diarist. Yet while the postwar decades saw abundant literature on the subject, written in many languages, when compared with Rudnicki's work, all the rest strikes one as relying too often upon secondhand data. Only a man of avowed duality, a Pole and a Jew, could grasp all the complex sets of relationships between Jews and Jews, Jews and Poles, as well as between the victims and their Nazi executioners.

There is no point in reducing Rudnicki's stature to that of a skillful contriver of short narratives. His is a work in progress, conceived as a groping toward some over-all image; he prefers to multiply fragments instead of writing a novel, which genre he seems to dismiss because of the artificiality of its devices. In all probability, posterity will look upon him as the author of one complex mosaiclike composition in several volumes.

After 1956, Rudnicki continued to add new narratives to his medley of stories on the Jewish theme and began publishing in periodicals very personal diary notes, which are sometimes undistinguishable from fiction, on people, travels, and readings. They have been collected into several volumes under the title *Blue Pages* (*Niebieskie kartki*). His human warmth, the capriciousness of his views and of his style, even his excessive subjectivity, for which he has been attacked by some critics, make *Blue Pages* a genuinely artistic chronicle superior to journalism.

Known as a writer of "light" novels and short stories, Dygat, a native of Warsaw, issued from a family of French origin and studied at Warsaw University. He started to publish shortly before the war. In the section on main trends in postwar literature, we called him a pupil of Gombrowicz's because of his nose-thumbing at shibboleths. His stance is one of deliberate naïveté; when he narrates (usually in the first person), he likes to identify himself with a starry-eyed, disorganized, and helpless human being. As holder of a French passport not living in France, he was arrested by the Nazis shortly after the occupation of Poland and interned in a camp near Bodensee for persons who eluded the categories set forth by the German bureaucracy. After his return, having spent a year there, he wrote his novel *Bodensee* (*Jezioro Bodeńskie*) in 1942–1943; it was an act of rebellion against the tragic mood prevailing. The camp was a rather funny place, and figures as such

Stanisław Dygat (1914–1978)

on Dygat's pages. Moreover, he did not hesitate to ridicule himself (though gently) as a young man who dreams of heroic deeds, yet who, in reality, is yawning from inactivity and whose only diversions are reading or flirting with the female inmates.

His next novel, *Farewells* (*Pożegnania*, 1948), is another gentle satire. Out of a real situation of drama and misfortune, Dygat draws mostly its comic aspects: in the fall of 1944 after the destruction of Warsaw, the city's western suburbs were thronging with survivors; it was a bizarre world of black-market dealings, of guerrilla warfare, of routine manhunts organized by the Nazi police, and it was then obvious that the Red Army, encamped along the Vistula, was going to overrun the entire territory of Poland as it carried its offensive into Germany. Fear of Communism compelled many people from the intelligentsia to cast about for means of escaping from Poland to the West. The mental habits of those who "ran scared" are satirized in *Farewells*. For the characters with whom the author sympathizes, the old order of things is gone forever; they decide to stay and to begin a new life.

Though prolific in his humorous *feuilletons* and short stories, Dygat did not write any novels in the years of Socialist Realism. He returned to this form only after 1956. His two great successes were *Journey* (*Podróż*, 1958) and *Disneyland* (1965). In the first, the narrator is, as usual, a rather comic failure. During his childhood, he was so stifled by the domineering personality of his brother that he has remained forever convinced of his inferiority and has pursued no career, finding himself more or less by chance in the job of an insignificant office worker. In secret, he has been cherishing a plan to go abroad for the first time in his life, and after a long internal struggle he writes to his brother, a famous film producer in Italy. He idealizes his brother and believes the laudatory articles written about him in the international press. In Rome, he finally discovers the truth about the pettiness and moral turpitude of his idol. Moreover, the narrator, bored by his not too successful marriage, has also been dreaming about a true "great love" he would encounter somewhere in Italy. Since this does not happen, he accepts the offer of a street-girl he meets in Naples, who, out of disinterested friendship, promises to stage an enactment of love at first sight. The next day in Capri, she pretends to be a young Scottish lady whom the hero meets by chance. Both feel they are predestined for each other. After promenades together, pure kisses (and the hero is now uncertain whether she is the disguised street-girl or really a new acquaintance), the illusion falls to pieces; the girl has incarnated the role so well that the contrast with her usual behavior makes her desperate; she gets drunk, sobs inconsolably, and goes back to her profession. The narrator journeys back to Poland, back to his uneventful, gray existence, bereft of his fantasies about his superior brother, and about a great love adventure. There is a certain childishness about Dygat's characters that provokes humor mixed with pity, and imparts much freshness to his writings; yet in constructing his stories he does not scorn even the oldest devices of romance fiction, such as disguise and recognition.

Disneyland is a novel on the young generation. At a masquerade ball held by the Academy of Fine Arts, a track star meets a girl, then loses her. After searching for her in vain, he is told that she was an Australian of Polish descent on a temporary visit to the old country. He begins to go with another girl, but continues to dream of the presumed Australian, only to discover at the end of the book that the two are identical. The very title, *Disneyland*, suggests that the author is playing a prank; although Dygat's story is a fairy tale, it captures the way of life of Polish youth. Dygat's casually structured plots go together with a colloquial, nonchalant language which appropriately conveys his abhorrence of literature treated as a "sacred cow."

A composer, a music critic, a publicist, Stefan Kisielewski, a native of Warsaw, was one of the most colorful personalities of the first two postwar decades. His novel *Blood Brothers* (*Sprzysiężenie*, 1947), though uneven in two of its three parts (i.e., in those dedicated to the psychology of its heroes before 1939), is excellent in the third, which contains some of the best pages on the campaign of September 1939 (the author himself fought as an officer against the invading troops). He wrote his novel during the Nazi occupation in Warsaw. A convinced and avowed non-Marxist, openly stressing his disbelief in economy based upon Marxist premises, after the war he tried to maintain his line of "loyal opposition" to the new authorities. With his humorous pen and disarming buffoonery, which masked a penetrating mind, he became a pillar of the leading Catholic periodical, *Everybody's Weekly* (*Tygodnik powszechny*), edited in Kraków. Silenced in the years 1949–1956 because of his sarcastic remarks on Socialist Realism, he shared the fate of his colleagues from the magazine's staff when they were superseded by journalists more inclined to obey the instructions from the censor's office. After October 1956, Kisielewski jubilantly returned to *Everybody's Weekly*, hopeful as to the effects of liberalization on the economy and on intellectual endeavors, and ready to resume his weekly jabbing at the absurdities of bureaucracy. For a couple of years, he was one of the very few Catholic members of the Diet.

In his fiction, he never pretended to be a "serious" writer, and his resistance to orthodoxy was no less pronounced in his literary judgments than in his political opinions: the detective story was then held in low esteem, so Kisielewski wrote one—*Crime on the North Side*

Stefan Kisielewski (1911–)

(*Zbrodnia w Dzielnicy Północnej*, 1948). Reviving the old device practiced by Daniel Defoe, he published an "authentic" memoir of an alcoholic, *I Had But One Life* (*Miałem tylko jedno życie*, 1958), under the assumed name of Teodor Klon. This is a witty and amusing confession of a man who has reached a piteous state by slowly increasing his daily doses of vodka. But the novel is also a tragicomic description of Warsaw, chiefly during the Nazi occupation, as seen through the eyes of a permanently drunk observer. The enormous nonsense of the Nazi system, apart from its criminal side, seems to be a particularly fitting sphere for an alcoholic's vision. Kisielewski's style, without pretense to artistry, combining playfulness with a pursuit of didactic aims, inadvertently restored a robust kind of eighteenth-century health to Polish prose. His viewpoint is that of a liberal and, he himself likes to stress, that of a rationalist and materialist combatting the irrationality of the Marxists and their idealistic handling of economy. His defense of the Roman Catholic Church is motivated by the Church's present role as protector of individual freedom against the state. Although not necessarily in agreement with the Church's hierarchy, he has been allowed more freedom to express his views in the Catholic press than have his colleagues who write for state-owned papers.

Kazimierz Brandys (1916–)   A native of Łódź, from a Jewish middle-class family, Brandys received his master's degree in law from Warsaw University on the eve of the war. As a student, he belonged to a leftist organization and published political articles. He lived in Warsaw during the war, though not in the ghetto, and, at that time, wrote two novels, the second of which, *Hobby Horse* (*Drewniany koń*, 1946), was his first literary offering. In 1946, he joined the staff of *The Forge* as fiction editor and the same year published a fictionalized account of the 1944 Warsaw Uprising, *The Invincible City* (*Miasto niepokonane*), which was subsequently translated into several languages. For the next few years, he worked on his novel in four volumes, *Between the Wars* (*Między wojnami*): I—*Samson* (1948); II—*Antigone* (1948); III—*Troy, The Open City* (1949); IV—*Man Does Not Die* (1951). As an attempt to portray the intelligentsia with its political delusions and vacillations, the tetralogy may be ranged with the literature of "settling accounts." It also testifies to Brandys' gradual acceptance of Socialist Realism. The "positive heroes" of *Between the Wars* are Communsts, who alone are fully aware of the danger of fascism as the natural outcome of capitalism. At times, the novel brings to mind Maxim Gorky's *Life of Klim Samgin*, that prototype of anti-intelligentsia literature.

Brandys went even further in his novel *Citizens* (*Obywatele*, 1954), which was acclaimed for a short while as a full-fledged Socialist Realist work. In dead earnest Brandys contrived a plot that was probable only in a climate of collective psychosis. Basically, it deals with high-school teen-agers acting as vigilantes. Their suspicion of everything that smacks of "bourgeois" decadence in their teachers leads to the successful unmasking of a vile class enemy, a foreign agent.

In the post-Stalinist era, Brandys, a top writer for the Party, took a new tack and started to help bail out the bilge of "errors and mistakes." He now directed his attacks against the very same psychosis to which he had earlier contributed. In a long story, *The Defense of the Granada* (*Obrona Grenady*, 1956), and a short novel, *Mother of Króls* (*Matka królów*, 1957—American translation: *Sons and Comrades*), he presented the tragedies of disciplined, enthusiastic members of the Communist Party who were victimized by a wrong policy adopted by their superiors. *The Defense of the Granada* introduces us to a group of young believers in the revolutionary theater who want to stage Mayakovsky's *The Bath*. On the advice of a Party official with a symbolic name, Dr. Faul (pronounced *foul*), they abandon the project in favor of a worthless Socialist Realist "production play." This not only ruins their comradeship, but, because of the mutual distrust engendered by Dr. Faul, it disintegrates them morally. In *Mother of Króls*, a proletarian woman, Mrs. Król, loses all her sons, devoted Communists, who either perish at the hands of fascist regimes or are liquidated by their own party. Brandys always tried to remain faithful to the principle that the means used by Communists have sometimes been bad, but the cause is sacred. Thus, his yielding to pressures of the literary milieu after 1957 could not but seem strange. In any case, after this date, Brandys' pen skillfully elaborated existential themes in numerous short stories and narratives in the form of letters. These were gathered into a few books, under the title *Letters to Madame Z.* (*Listy do pani Z.*). They form a kind of sophisticated, verbose diary where travels, readings, and conversations are used as pretexts for philosophical meditation. Together with his plays and film scenarios in the vein of the "theater of the absurd," they curiously exemplify the change of mood in post-1956 Polish literature, with its disregard for the nineteenth-century barriers between genres.

The path of Tadeusz Konwicki followed even more zigzags than Brandys'; but from the beginning, the former's was a much more tormented and less cerebral personality. Born near Wilno into a worker's family, he finished a clandestinely run high school there during the Nazi occupation and, from July 1944 to the spring of 1945, was a soldier in a guerilla unit of the Home Army fighting against the Soviet troops who had taken over Lithuania after chasing out the Germans. Later, he succeeded in moving to Poland from his native province, which was incorporated into the Soviet Union; but as a writer he was shaped by its landscapes and people, as well as by his adventures in the forests of Lithuania during his guerrilla activities.

Tadeusz Konwicki (1926–)

His first novel, *Marshes* (*Rojsty*, written 1948), is comparable in its bitterness to the literature of "settling accounts." Because of its risky subject, it was published only in 1956. It presents the dramas of young men deceived by their well-intentioned, anti-Soviet patriotism. Convinced of the justness of the Party line in its stress on industrialization of the country, Konwicki became a Communist and dedicated a few stories to the heroic workers who were building socialism. He also wrote a Socialist Realist novel called *Power* (*Władza*, 1954). Allied, for a while, with the young romantics, "the pimpled ones," Konwicki, like most of them, became disillusioned and embarked on his individual search, far from the beaten track. A gifted author of film scenarios, he also revealed himself as a film director (*The Last Day of Summer*—a short; *Salto*—a feature-length film).

Several years later, he produced one of the most terrifying novels in postwar Polish literature. *A Contemporary Dream Book* (*Sennik współczesny*, 1963) was greeted upon its appearance as a major literary sensation. Everything uncanny that happened to the author as well as to his country finds its place in that work, only, like a dream, it is all in code. At the outset of the story, the narrator (and hero of the novel) wakes up from a coma in a Godforsaken provincial town; he had taken poison but survived. His past, which returns in flashbacks juxtaposed against the life of the poor townsfolk, who belong to a new religious sect, constitutes the fabric of the book. This is a novel about guilt, and since the feeling of guilt oppresses men with distorted, even monstrous, recollections, everything bathes in an aura of torment; situations, people, landscapes create a nightmarish web of metaphors. By taking poison the hero had wished to punish himself, and, indeed, his main characteristic seems to be his search for punishment. But if there is no God, a self-tormenting man has only himself to rely on and only he can carry out a self-pronounced sentence on himself. As we may guess from the logic of the nightmare, which blurs biographical data, the hero had fought in a guerilla unit against NKVD troops (few pages in postwar literature match Konwicki's descriptions of mutual massacres in the snowbound, frosty Nordic forest); out of a sense of guilt, he then embraced a new political ideal, only to discover, many years later, that because he served that ideal, he bears the responsibility for many crimes. Two decades of history, which is also the personal history of each character, storm the hero's conscience. He is estranged from the townsfolk, who, in their misery and dejection, seek solace in ecstatic meetings presided over by the founder of an undefined, neither Christian nor non-Christian, religion. At the climax of the book, the hero is lynched by the townsfolk as a "diabolical" Communist, but he escapes dying by a hairbreadth, only to continue once again his unreal, phantomlike existence. The impossibility of touching reality, which eludes all sensual, moral, and intellectual grasp, is conveyed through eerie images of nature, through the sexual impotence of the characters, and through the spooky ambience of a town inhabited by losers and half-wits. Many a reader has found in *A Contemporary Dream Book* if not an indictment, at least a complaint which, although not directed against anybody in particular, is raised in the name of all those in Poland who acted out of best moral motives, only to get bogged down in a quagmire of an all-pervading ambiguity where good and evil lose their clear distinctions. Konwicki's integrity, his passion as a moral-seeker, and his talent seem to predestine him for a major role in Polish letters.

The intermixing of genres so typical of postwar literature can also be seen in science fiction, which is sometimes difficult to distinguish from philosophical treatises. Stanisław Lem, a native of Lwów, moved to Kraków in 1946, and there he completed his medical studies at the Jagiellonian University. Taking advantage of his knowledge of biology and his extensive reading in physics, chemistry, and modern philosophy, he chose science fiction as a means of expression; the genre was also one of those least shackled by changing political requirements. His novels *Astronauts* (*Astronauci*, 1951), *Time Unforfeited* (*Czas Nieutracony*, 1955), *Magellan's Cloud* (*Obłok Magellana*, 1955), as well as his volumes of short stories, *Sesame* (1954) and *Notebooks from the Stars* (*Dzienniki gwiazdowe*, 1957), have been re-edited several times in Poland and translated into other Eastern European languages. Lem's sophistication, the product not only of his scientific training but also of the phases of history he has witnessed, often makes him profound.

Stanisław Lem (1921–)

His books written after 1957 place him within the general trend of existential exploration. For example, his novel *Solaris* (1961) combines a fantasy of scientific investigation with a probing of man's moral relation to the universe. Solaris is the name of a planet which, though visited generation after generation by Earth scientists, has not ceased to puzzle the specialists. Without continents, it is covered by an ocean in which no life has been found; the ocean itself, however, behaves as if it possessed a life, and even an intelligence, of its own. Periodically, geometrical structures of great beauty emanate from the surface, reach maturity, and after a brief instant of perfection, decay, topple down, and disappear, just as living organisms do. A young astronaut arrives by spaceship at a scientific station permanently supended at a certain height above the ocean. Instead of the three colleagues he had expected to find, there are only two; one has committed suicide. The two who remain seem to have been strangely affected. An atmosphere of unspeakable fear and horror pervades the whole station. But it is not long before the young astronaut discovers the reason.

Entering his cabin, he finds a guest seated on his bed: a girl with whom he had been in love on Earth and who had committed suicide a couple of years ago. As he soon learns, the other inhabitants of the station have also had guests of their own, beings of flesh and blood, who were, however, only exact replicas of persons who had entered their biographies. The ocean on Solaris acts as a creating brain, able to register human feelings and thoughts and bring to life the shapes of the subconscious. The girl recalls everything that happened to her before her death. She continues to love the man. Yet realizing at last that she is not herself, she asks for only one thing: annihilation. A molecular analysis of her blood reveals its composition to be different from that of human beings, and her wish is fulfilled. Thanks to the station's scientific instruments, in one second she is turned into nothing. The horror of the enigmatic ocean, the nights and days in the station with two moons in the sky, the personal dramas brought from Earth, is such that *Solaris* plunges the reader into dread. The real subject of the book is not man's encounter with a new form of life—the ocean—which escapes his understanding, but his encounter with himself, with his transitory existence. The beautiful geometric structures emanating from the ocean, their growth, maturity, and decay, paraphrase the stages of a human life span, and intensify that anguish within us which is usually veiled by a routine acceptance of the unavoidable.

Tadeusz Breza (1905–1970)   Tadeusz Breza came from an aristocratic family in the Ukraine; he was a novice for one and a half years in a Benedictine monastery in Belgium, a student of philosophy in Warsaw and London, where he wrote a dissertation on Hume, a diplomat, and the author of a psychological novel published in 1936 (*Adam Grywałd*). His work belongs, however, to the literature of People's Poland. In his novels about the extreme Right, *The Walls of Jericho* and its sequel, *The Sky and The Earth*, already mentioned in the section on general trends, he observed, with skeptical detachment and an outsider's curiosity, the human ambitions which, in the realm of politics, act as an unwholesome leaven distorting moral judgment. Except for his novel *Balthazar's Feast* (*Uczta Baltazara*, 1952), which is hardly more than an intellectual's exercise in handling Socialist Realist conventions, with a duly extolled "positive hero," he published little in the years of compulsory literary doctrine, dedicating himself mostly to drama criticism. Beginning in 1955 his qualifications as a former diplomat served him in good stead, and he spent several years in Rome, then in Paris, as cultural attaché for the Polish Embassy. His stay in Rome (for which his former theological studies also had been a good preparation), together with his gift as a keen observer, bore fruit in his best-selling book on the Vatican, *The Bronze Gate*

(*Spiżowa brama*, 1960). Not only lauded by the Party, it also met with a rather sympathetic reception from the Catholics. Breza's work has always hovered on the border line between essay and fiction, and the topic of *The Bronze Gate*—the Vatican and its Curia—provided him with material that was fascinating enough to allow both approaches without loss of artistic unity. *The Bronze Gate* is the report of a journalist; it is a treatise on a centuries-old, well-established institution; it is also a diary with fictionalized meetings and conversations. And a thesis is not lacking either. Breza traces the historical slowness with which the Vatican has reacted to the surrounding world. In the Middle Ages, it acted as a mainstay of the feudal order, which it tried to shore up against the onslaught of capitalism; yet when feudalism crumbled, the Vatican adapted itself to the new system and soon emerged as an ally of all forces combatting a new subversion of society, i.e., a proletarian revolution. Although the Vatican answered with hostility to the Communist seizure of power in Russia and in other countries, historical analogies allow us to suppose that slowly it will find the means of coexisting with noncapitalist regimes. Breza's report deals with Rome in the last years of Pius XII's pontificate and outlines the struggle between progressive and conservative currents within the Vatican. But it would be unjust to dismiss his book as mere journalism, even if the author, for reasons of expediency, seems to say less than he knows or understands of theological issues. His extreme cautiousness in pronouncing opinions and his well-bred elegance incline him to show the issues as personified by various Vatican dignitaries rather than to argue. He is neither for Catholicism nor against it. His stance is similar to that of an anthropologist who has discovered an ideal specimen of a culture for research. His treatise on the Vatican thus becomes a treatise on energies solidifying into established and self-perpetuating social structures.

The same topic served Breza for his next book, which was more conventional; *The Office* (*Urząd*, 1961) is a novel on the maze of bureaucratic machinery in the Vatican and the duality of its officials, who perform their functions impersonally but in private are quite humane. The plot centers around the adventures of a young lawyer from Poland who comes to Rome on behalf of his father, also a lawyer. The father seeks to recover his job as attorney at a bishop's curia; he had been deprived of his position by Polish bishops because of his too compromising attitude toward the lay authorities.

Roman Catholicism in Poland has remained a social force, outweighing, by virtue of its mass appeal, the political influence of the Communist Party. The Church's intellectual centers, such as the Catholic University of Lublin, a few periodicals edited under the auspices of the Church hierarchy, and a few monasteries counter-

The "Catholic" Novel

balanced a predominantly emotional attachment to religion on the part of the peasant population. And one should not overlook an ambiguous Catholic organization known as "Pax" with its publishing house and many business enterprises. An organization with roots in the prewar fascist Right, "Pax" has been given a free hand in its multiple endeavors and has been used by the authorities as a pawn in their moves against the Roman Catholic Church. It has usually sided with the most totalitarian elements within the Party. Disdained by both the liberal intelligentsia and Catholics loyal to the Church hierarchy, "Pax" has been very efficient in the publishing field.

The task of defining who is a "Catholic" writer is a hard one. Is he a man who belongs to a given denomination or one whose ideas, as expressed in a literary form, are in agreement with Church dogma? Instead of losing ourselves in subtleties, we may apply a purely external criterion and call Catholic those writers who cooperate with Catholic magazines and publishing houses. Those writers have shown an obvious predilection for the historical novel, perhaps explainable by their longing for larger perspectives on human time.

Antoni Gołubiew (1907–)

Thus, Antoni Gołubiew, in his enormous novel *Bolesław the Brave* (*Bolesław Chrobry*), returned to the period immediately after Poland's acceptance of Christianity, around the year 1000. The novel, whose volumes appeared between 1947 and 1955, is an attempt to reconstruct the conditions of life at that time, the half-pagan mentality of the people, battles, religious rites, and even the language, as all the dialogue is in archaic Polish.

Teodor Parnicki (1908–)

Yet undoubtedly the most inventive historical novelist is Teodor Parnicki. Even his biography seems to have predisposed him toward voyaging in time and space. Born in Berlin, the son of a civil engineer, he lived in Russia, went to school in Manchuria, where he published his first article in a Polish newspaper, then studied Polish, English, and oriental literatures at the University of Lwów. He won recognition with his novel *Aetius, the Last Roman* (*Aetius ostatni Rzymianin*, 1937), on declining Rome in the fifth century A.D. Deported, during the war, from Lwów to the Soviet Union, Parnicki departed, after his release from prison in 1941, for Teheran and Jerusalem, then lived for a while in England, and then in Mexico. After going back to Poland several times for prolonged stays, he at last returned there for good.

In his *Silver Eagles* (*Srebrne orły*), published in Jerusalem in 1944–1945, Parnicki took up exactly the same epoch that Gołubiew chose for *Bolesław the Brave;* it was not accidental that both novels were written during the war (the former in Jerusalem, the latter in Wilno). The tenth and eleventh centuries witnessed Poland's emergence as a state strong enough to inflict defeats on the German

Empire. Parnicki, however, has always been attracted by seldom explored and enigmatic areas of history, and in his novel, he plunges with relish into the international schemes of all medieval Europe. He has also tended to focus his gaze upon heroes of mixed national and racial origins, the hybrids of various civilizations. As if to prove that he could outdo any novelist in the intricacy of his historical plots, he placed the action of his *The End of the "Covenant of Nations"* (*Koniec "Zgody Narodów,"* 1955) in Bactria, a Hellenistic state of Asia between India and the Seleucid empire, in the second century B.C. "Covenant of Nations" is the name of a fantastic ship furnished with the most advanced technological devices; in the second century it is considered an "ultimate weapon." The story unravels, by means of letters, flashbacks, innuendos in conversations, and the action itself (an inquest into a political assassination), the plans of Heliodor, a high officer of the Security Police, who is reaching for control of the state. Appearance and reality seem to play a game of hide-and-seek in this work, aided by a nearly Joycean style and references to Jungian cultural archetypes; it all makes for difficult though rewarding reading.

The same purpose is discernible in *The Word and The Flesh* (*Słowo i ciało,* 1959), namely, to enter through empathy into a "hybrid" civilization. The narrator, Chozroes, son of a Persian king and a Greek woman, writes a book of meditations during the years 201–203 A.D. in Alexandria, where he is detained as a hostage of the Romans. Memoirs concerning, letters to, and imaginary dialogues with six women who have played a role in his life lead the reader throughout the whole Hellenic, Semitic, Roman, and Asiatic world, including China. Less an account of events than a dream, Chozroes' book reveals his interest in Buddhism and in gnosis. It is not accidental that the novel is dedicated to Jerzy Stempowski, connoisseur of Greek literature and essayist with an exceptional feeling for "crossbreeds" of various cultures.

The composition of Parnicki's novels is so involved and the analysis of the subconscious is given such prominence that it is nearly impossible to disengage their particular plots from this tangle, which seems to delight the author for its own sake. In *The Face of the Moon* (*Twarz księżyca,* 1961), the story of Mitroania, daughter of the king of Choresm (a country near the Caspian Sea), reveals itself gradually in three tales: one told by her when she was young, one by a physician who took notes of what she said when in a delirium, and the last, again, by her when she is old. The action takes place at the end of the third and the beginning of the fourth centuries A.D. in Choresm, in Illyria under Roman rule, and also in Rome.

In the preface to another novel, *Only Beatrice* (*Tylko Beatrycze,*

1962), the author tells us that the book was preceded by a five-year study of documents relating to the epoch with which the novel deals. It is based upon the record of a fire that destroyed a Cistercian monastery in Poland in 1309; presumably it was an act of vengeance on the part of oppressed peasants. Parnicki introduces the fictionalized arsonist, a brilliant, young, and resentful Cistercian monk of uncertain origin (a half-Polish, half-Tartar bastard), and traces his search for identity. During the trial, his self-delusions are brought to the surface. The novel has no narrator—it consists of dialogue and the hero's written confessions. A psychological study is interwoven with an exploration of a disturbing riddle from Scholastic philosophy: whether *essentia* without *existentia* is possible—more precisely, whether the soul can be an entity if deprived of the body. Some thinkers maintained that the soul, after man's death, sleeps until the day of resurrection, and this reasoning seems to have the author's sympathy. *Only Beatrice* (with epigraphs from J. Lechoń and N. Gumilev) is one of the most highly praised of Parnicki's novels.

A *New Fairy Tale* (*Nowa baśń*, 1962) deals with the eleventh and twelfth centuries in Poland, Byzantium, the principality of Novgorod, the city of Kiev, Hungary, Germany, Ireland, and England. As the title suggests, the book toys with historical motifs and legends. There is even a Toltecan myth about a red-bearded man who believed in one God. The legend was sparked by one of the characters, Eric, who was shipwrecked off the coast of Mexico. His presence among the Indians gave rise to the cult of the Feathered Serpent, or Serpent-Dove. A web of allusions to Celtic and Scandinavian tales, to chronicles and medieval literature endows the work with more symbolism than in any other Parnicki novel and suggests several possible interpretations of interlacing plots. The novel's second volume (1963) skips over a few centuries, but the biographies of characters that emerge are symbolically related to those in the first volume. They are grouped around the story of Jeanne d'Arc, who, in the author's version (which accords with a hypothesis of some modern historians), was not burned at the stake but whisked away with the consent of her judges.

All of Parnicki's novels, except the first, *Aetius, the Last Roman*, were written abroad, mostly in Mexico City, and were published in Poland starting only in 1959. His intention seems to be to revindicate the man of the past by opposing the clichés which tend to diminish him as less sophisticated than modern man. The scope and the intellectual complexity of his sagas on universal history are such that the tragic dilemmas of our time shrink to a minuscule part of a majestic whole. In place of the clichés about the West and the East (Greece-Rome versus India, Western Christendom versus Byzantium) and about national cultures as closed compartments, he proposes his inter-weaving of many religious-cultural patterns, personified by his "hybrid" heroes. No contemporary Polish prose writer can rival Parnicki in the scope of his vision and in his "hall of mirrors" technique. Events come to light only as reflected by the consciousness (or the subconcious) of a character, then acquire a different shape in the eyes of the same person in another phase of his (or her) life. Thus, the historical novel under Parnicki's pen becomes something radically different from its nineteenth-century predecessors.

Another author belonging to the same spiritual family is Hanna Malewska. After completing her studies at the University of Lublin, she worked as a high-school teacher and during the war was active in the Resistance. After 1945 she was connected with the Catholic *Everybody's Weekly* in Kraków, where she also coedited a Catholic monthly, *Sign* (*Znak*). As the subject of her first novel, *Greek Spring* (*Wiosna grecka*, 1933), she chose the Olympian games in ancient Greece; for her next, *The Iron Crown* (*Żelazna korona*, 1937), she found a hero in the last Holy Roman Emperor of the Germanic nation. *Stones Will Bear Testimony* (*Kamienie wołać będą*, 1939), for which she gathered material in France, brings to life the people who built the medieval cathedrals in the thirteenth century. During the war, she wrote a fictionalized biography of the poet Cyprian Kamil Norwid—*Harvest on the Sickle* (*Żniwo na sierpie*, 1947). Next came stories on ancient Rome, a novel on Christianized Rome at the time of the barbarian invasions, *Fleeting Is the Shape of the World* (*Przemija postać świata*, 1954), and much later, a novel, *Family Apocrypha* (*Apokryf rodzinny*, 1965), which caters to the Polish readers' craze for memoirs. Malewska traces the encounters of several generations of Polish petty squires with the embroiled history of their country in the nineteenth and twentieth centuries.

It is obvious that for writers such as Malewska an interest in history is not limited to unraveling the causes and effects of events. The central problem of such authors is that of evil in the world, which almost seems to be abetted by a blind Fate thwarting the best human intentions; yet Providence is also active, both in the life of individuals and in that of kingdoms, throughout the web of time. Is Providence identical with blind Fate? Or is it something else? To introduce God as a *deus ex machina* would be to weaken the artistic impact of the novel as a genre. Thus, Catholic writers are confronted with a difficult dilemma, and their basic intent seems to be a theodicy, i.e., a justification of God in spite of all the evil which a novelist should neither disregard nor dilute. Though the characters are mostly losers—since to lose is an integral part of the human condition—their strivings, be they of a bishop in Rome at the time of barbarian invasion, or of

Hanna Malewska (1911–)

a builder of cathedrals, or of a Polish king, are not completely fruitless and suggest the workings of some providential plan hidden in the very fabric of the universe.

The names of Gołubiew, Parnicki, and Malewska do not exhaust the list of authors who can be included under the term Catholic; but though some of them enjoyed popularity and even were copiously translated into foreign languages, they were behind in their literary techniques and often dependent upon French Catholic literature of a conservative or Rightist slant.

Jerzy
Zawieyski
(1902–1969)

Jerzy Zawieyski, a public figure, should be placed somewhat apart. His spiritual adventures, registered in plays, novels, and diaries, are moving in their evocation of the authentic torment of a modern Catholic. An actor by profession and an effective organizer of theaters on the grass-roots level, he was influenced by the "Catholic Left" in France, especially by the "Personalism" of Emmanuel Mounier, founder of the "Esprit" group and the review of the same name. Among the Catholic writers of the elder generation, he was probably the closest in outlook to the young Catholic intellectuals who were trained by the Catholic University of Lublin and who cooperated with *Everybody's Weekly* (*Tygodnik Powszechny*) and *Sign* (*Znak*).

Peasant
Themes

Considerable enrichment was brought to literature in the late thirties by young, gifted writers of peasant origin, who uncovered a terrain that was still exotic to the intelligentsia. Some of them formed a poetic group advocating "authenticism," that is, a faithfulness to the images of their rural childhood. The organ for this movement was the periodical *Poets' Region* (*Okolica poetów*), edited in 1935–1939 by Stanisław Czernik, himself a poet and a novelist. The activity of the most talented writers of peasant stock—such as Stanisław Piętak (1909–1964) and Jan Bolesław Ożóg (born 1913), who made their debuts before the war and built up reputations in both poetry and prose—continued into the postwar period.

The revolutionary change of 1944–1945 signified the end of the village as a purely agricultural community whose contact with the surrounding world was minimal. Mass migration to cities and to new industrial centers transformed the young members of practically every peasant family into workers, civil employees, teachers, or journalists. In addition, the proximity of factories engendered a new type of peasant—that of a worker who still preserved his small farm. All this social flux seemed to announce new topics for the novel, especially in view of the insistent call to realism broadcast by Marxist critics.

But there were many reasons why the village, or rather the end of the old village, entered literature belatedly. With few exceptions, the vocal novelists were of urban background and very timid in approaching the peasant, who, for them, was a strange animal. Then Socialist Realism, with its compulsory division of characters into all-black and all-white, hardly created a climate suitable for understanding the pragmatic peasant mentality. Thus in 1955, the story "A Village Wedding," by Maria Dąbrowska, a writer of nonpeasant origin, was greeted as the first unfalsified report on the village.

It was only after the upheaval of 1956 that the village, with its new conflicts and problems, found willing spokesmen in those writers who had preserved an emotional tie to their rural beginnings. Although they were already established in towns and belonged to the intelligentsia, they often felt not quite integrated into their new surroundings, yet were no longer able to return to the land. When they wrote, they drew, of course, on their first, most durable perceptions, gathered on their families' farms. For them, the village was not something to be treated with condescension, nor was it to be extolled as "picturesque" because of its folklore—a sin of which many a writer had been guilty. The village was part of themselves, the substratum of all their experience. At the same time, they viewed it, as well as their childhood, from a distance, like anthropologists. Poets especially, in search of their personal mythology, were inclined to use ancestral peasant myths, folk songs, archaic modes of behavior as their sources. Both Piętak and Ożóg, mentioned above, followed this course in their poetry. So did a younger writer, Tadeusz Nowak (born 1930), sometimes called a "peasant surrealist." A similar tendency can be seen in prose—for instance, in Nowak's charming short novel, *Ballad of an Alien Tribe* (*Obcoplemienna ballada*, 1963), where to a country boy, the village on the other side of the river is inhabited by a savage, alien race and his expeditions across the river to meet a girl from that dangerous tribe have the peculiar excitement of penetrating into a forbidden realm.

Nowak's book is but one instance of a whole trend. After 1956, when the possibility opened up for more truthful accounts of the transformations within the village, writers of peasant origin began to try their hand at the realistic novel. This was, in a way, a resumption of the efforts started in the thirties, though under new circumstances. Józef Morton (born 1911), a prolific novelist, came out with his *My Second Wedding* (*Mój drugi ożenek*, 1961), an obvious attempt to controvert all the shibboleths and didacticism, whether of Positivist or of Socialist Realist origin; instead of marionettes, he showed characters of complex psychology and a hopelessly entangled erotic life.

Julian Kawalec (born 1916), part of the "new wave" after 1956, and the recipient of several literary prizes, is a good example of the increasing sophistication in the treatment of rural themes. Critics analyzing his novels—*Pathways among the Streets* (*Ścieżki wśród ulic*, 1957), *Scars* (*Blizny*, 1960), *The Felled Elm* (*Zwalony wiąz*, 1962), *Bound to the Land* (*Ziemi przypisany*, 1962), *In the Sun* (*W słońcu*, 1963), *Dancing Hawk* (*Tańczący jastrząb*, 1964)— reproached him for his convoluted, circuitous expression. Kawalec, rebelling against the traditional "peasant novel" (of Reymont, for instance), had fallen under the spell of Faulkner, Hemingway, Camus. The core of his subject matter is the moral decisions which confront country people living through a breakdown of their inherited patterns.

One of the most authentic testimonies on the village can be found, however, in a straightforward, simply written novel which, though not narrated in the first person, resembles a memoir. This is *Stations of Memory* (*Postoje pamięci*, 1965), by Urszula Kozioł (born 1935), who is also a gifted poetess. A village, seen before the war, during the war, and immediately after the war through the eyes of a little girl, Mirka, daughter of a local schoolteacher, is the subject of her novel. Mirka's first discoveries of the world, her entrancement with nature, rites, and folk songs, are soon overshadowed by the tribulations of wartime. Misery, hard work, visits by day from the Gestapo, who terrorize the villagers and execute the entire family of a Jewish shopkeeper, visits by night from "the people of the forest (guerrillas) constitute the background for a personal drama of a little girl in love with her schoolmate, little Daniel, who is the son of German settlers and, therefore, an enemy who must be rejected. It is a warm book about the personal relations of three children: Mirka, her elder sister (paragon of courage and the highest authority), and Daniel. But *Stations of Memory* is also much more. It conducts the reader in space (escapes to other villages from the Gestapo) and in time (up to the postwar period, when the heroine is a high-school student in a provincial town) and provides a rather vast panorama of a rural region which has borne the brunt of history. Unassuming, modest in purpose, avoiding a discussion of any large political ideas, the novel inadvertently acquires an epic breadth. What is even more rare in modern literature, it is also a hymn of praise to family love. The heroine's grandparents had been illiterate peasants. Before the war, at the price of enormous self-sacrifice, her own parents, both enthusiasts of education, received their diplomas from a teacher's college. The author herself, no doubt identified with the heroine, had easy access to learning, as did most of her generation, and her novel seems to be dictated by a sense of guilt, a feeling not untypical of all "peasant" literature.

The Theater

During the war, actors and theater directors in Poland had a clandestine organization of their own, which was very efficient in bringing help to members of their profession, in enforcing rules of behavior, in arranging illegal performances of plays (the German-licensed music halls were boycotted), and also in organizing poetry readings. Blueprints for a postwar administrative reform of the theater were being drawn up, and some of them proved to be of use after the liberation, when the financial burdens were taken over by the state. A new and heroic chapter was added to the history of the Polish theater, a theater which, since the end of the eighteenth century, had been accustomed to providing much more than entertainment; among the most cherished names of its wartime leaders are those of Edmund Wierciński and his wife Maria.

The theaters which opened in 1945 throughout the devastated country had no competition from the cinema or from television as yet nonexistent, and they attracted enthusiastic audiences. The period 1945–1949 was marked by the strong personality of director Leon Schiller (1887–1954). He survived his imprisonment in Auschwitz, while his colleague, Stefan Jaracz (1883–1945), famous as both an actor and a director, succumbed to the aftereffects of his own similar imprisonment. Schiller's "monumental theater," which took over the tradition founded by Mickiewicz and Wyspiański, had been the most important development in the art of staging between the two wars, and it now found new scope for growth, as Schiller, respected for his Leftist views, was given almost free rein in his productions. He knew how to draw substance even from trifles such as the eighteenth-century *Krakovians and Mountaineers* by Wojciech Bogusławski, which he transformed into a fascinating display of rhythmic movement, light, and color. Whether following in Schiller's footsteps or rebelling against him, every director who began his career during the postwar decades bears the imprint of his influence.

Few new plays were staged in the first years after the war, and talents were chiefly put to work developing a "classical" repertoire chosen from both Polish and foreign literatures. On the whole, Polish Romantic drama was avoided as too inflammatory; Mickiewicz's *Forefathers' Eve*, for instance, reached the stage only in 1955. The imposition of Socialist Realism in 1949 meant the demise of the Schiller approach, which was considered too "Western" (he himself turned to teaching), and a relapse into a photographic naturalism in settings, costumes, and acting, as well as an influx of hastily concocted "realistic" plays with a political message.

Praised by the Left before the war as a novelist (we have already
dealt with his fiction in the section on the novel in 1918–1939),
Kruczkowski, now an officially extolled playwright, wrote dramas
whose characters exemplified political attitudes. Guided by his belief
that taking sides in politics reveals the moral nature of a given man,
he tried hard to seek for roots of political decisions, identifying the
"reactionary" with the corrupt and the "progressive" with the un-
tainted. In effect, he produced an equivalent of the literature on sin
and salvation, with the addition of an intermediary zone—those who
are tainted but manage to escape from the devil's snare. The fruits of
his efforts paralleled similar attempts in Soviet drama and in some of
the plays of Jean-Paul Sartre. Although it is easy to dismiss such
procedures as artistically doubtful, Kruczkowski's preoccupation with
what happened in Germany (he spent five years there as a prisoner
of war) gives them a certain validity; for in Germany, to be pro-Nazi
or anti-Nazi was, indeed, a moral decision. In his most popular play,
The Germans (*Niemcy*, 1949), Professor Sonnenbruch and his
family hold themselves aloof from politics, guarding a strict neutrality
toward the Nazi regime. They are forced to say yes or no, however,
when an old friend, a Communist wanted by the Gestapo, asks for
their help. The pharisaic detachment of the middle-class German
intellectual is exposed when only one member of the family, a young
woman, dares to break the sacrosanct German rule of loyalty toward
any government. At the end of his life, Kruczkowski succeeded in
going beyond dramatized political commentary. His *Death of the
Governor* (*Śmierć gubernatora*, 1961), the idea for which was borrowed from a story by Leonid Andreyev, is a tragedy on the exercise
of power. The evil resides not in the governor, who is a rather well-
intentioned man, but in the very division of people into rulers and
ruled. Caught up by a situation, the governor orders the police to
shoot at a crowd storming his residence and afterward bravely assumes
the moral consequences, recognizing that the hatred people feel for
him is justified. This play, by a former Socialist Realist author, testifies to the general reversal of literary trends after 1956—from "realism" back to metaphor.

The discarding of dogmas in 1956 allowed Leon Schiller's disciples
to turn their energies, now unhampered, to the staging of dramas
from the neglected Romantic era, to Old Polish plays (e.g., the
sixteenth-century *Story of the Most Glorious Resurrection of Our
Lady* directed by Kazimierz Dejmek was acclaimed as a major theatrical event), and to Shakespeare; audiences were electrified by the
interpretation of *Hamlet* and *Richard III* as tragedies on twentieth-
century politics. Among contemporary playwrights, Bertolt Brecht,
Samuel Beckett, and Friedrich Dürrenmatt were given special promi-

nence. Much support came from an energetic monthly, *Dialog*, which introduced new texts of plays by both Polish and foreign authors.

A Polish variety of the "theater of the absurd" was developed by poets Tadeusz Różewicz, Stanisław Grochowiak, and Zbigniew Herbert, for whom it was a natural extension of the themes underlying their poetic work and stemming from their war experiences. It was not a poet, however, but a satirical feuilletonist who won the position of leading playwright.

Born in the vicinity of Kraków, the son of a mailman, Mrożek began his career in that city as a cartoonist and an author of short humorous articles for the newspapers. Around 1956, he revealed himself as a master of the satirical short story. His fierce, absurd humor makes use of comic techniques from satirical works of modern Polish literature, from Boy's *Little Words* to Gałczyński's *Green Goose*. The result is akin to Gogol's achievement in stories like *The Nose*. The vagaries of the bureaucratic Establishment, together with the specifically Polish mixture of industrialization and backwardness, of sophistication and parochialism, have been a boon to Mrożek's talent for concocting uncanny, surrealistic transformations of reality. For instance, in the title story from *The Elephant* (*Słoń*, 1958; English versions published in 1962, 1965), economy-minded directors in a small-town zoo fret over the lack of an elephant to display. They finally decide to "do-it-themselves" by inflating an immense, elephant-shaped balloon. Some school children happen to witness the inevitable failure of the ruse when the gigantic balloon, propelled by a strong gust of wind, rises into the sky and punctures its "hide" on the treetops in the neighboring botanical gardens. Their severe disillusionment turns the children into hooligans. "Wedding in Atomice" pretends to be a picture of country manners, but, while the traditional peasant wedding always ended in a drunken brawl, Mrożek's peasants fight each other not with knives and sticks but with atomic weapons.

One of his favorite devices is a sly parody of styles; thus, to use but one example, "En Route" starts out as a nineteenth-century narrative: "Just after N———, the road took us through flat, damp meadows. . . . Our carriage bowled along at a brisk rate," etc., but culminates in the narrator's discovery of a "substitute telegraph line," that is, men standing in the fields at calling distance from each other and transmitting a telegram: "Faaaaaatherrrrrr deaaaad fuuuu-nerrraaaal Weeeeednesdaaaay." Obviously, a wireless telegraph, in the opinion of the local population, has its advantages, and is "more progressive."

Children's fiction as well did not escape Mrożek's attention as a possible vehicle for the grotesque. *Escape to the South* (*Ucieczka na*

Sławomir Mrożek (1930–)

południe, 1961)—illustrated by the author—relates the utterly non-sensical adventures of two young boys and their friend, a huge ape. It abounds in satire or outright farce; for instance, in a Godforsaken province the boys come across a poster tacked to a wall: "GODOT HAS ARRIVED. Citizens of the town! Polish agriculturists! You have waited a long time but not in vain! The moment has come when Godot has arrived! He is here! No later than tomorrow at 7 P.M. everybody will be able to see him in his only appearance, at the Peasant Militiamen Coop. UNFORGETTABLE IMPRESSIONS!" Since it is doubtful whether young readers will connect this with Samuel Beckett's *Waiting for Godot*, most likely the book is not for children at all.

With his first play, *The Police (Policja)*, produced in Warsaw in 1958, Mrożek's reputation in the theater grew in Poland and abroad, where his plays have been performed both on the stage and on television. *The Police* is a satirical fable on the self-perpetuating activity of the state security apparatus, which has to invent crimes in order to subsist and is thrown into despair when only one political offender is left.

After this play, Mrożek moved from rather traditional plot construction toward the technique of the "theater of the absurd," centering upon two or three people who are thrown into an existential "situation." The best examples of this phase of his work are one-act plays like *Out at Sea (Na pełnym morzu*, 1960) and *Striptease* (1961). In the first, three shipwrecked men, elegantly dressed and known, respectively, as The Fat One, The Medium One, The Small One, debate while stitting on their raft, over which of them should be eaten. Ideological harangues and democratic majority vote disguise the inevitable: The Small One must, of course, be the victim. In the second play, two middle-aged men with brief cases, who have been quietly "proceeding in order to succeed," are caught up by an unknown force and imprisoned in a room (literally, "thrown into a situation"). One of them is a proponent of internal freedom, which in the face of necessity can only be saved by inaction: if freedom is the possibility of choice, when we choose we reduce our possibilities. The other is devoured by the need for protest, for doing something no matter how absurd just to manifest his will. Yet when a Voice, and later an enormous Hand, orders them to undress step by step, both are forced to comply, and in the end both are executed.

After several plays experimenting with a few characters in a "situation," Mrożek wrote a complex, rich tragicomedy, *Tango* (produced in 1965), which is at once a portrayal of a society, a psychological drama, and a parable. Three generations of a family occupy the stage. Arthur, a student, is exasperated by the way his elders live, by their complete moral license and their very progressive belief in the relativity of all values. He punishes his grandmother for drinking vodka and playing cards by ordering her to stretch out on a specially prepared bier, yet he cannot cope with the complete mess—his mother living with a proletarian hanger-on, Edek; his father interested only in the most extreme avant-garde art; the uncle fawning over "modernity" (though a reactionary at heart). Arthur's successive attempts to impose a "form" upon his family result only in failure. A Hamlet struggling to cure corruption in Elsinore, at first he tries this through a return to tradition; he convinces his girl (Ophelia?) that they should ask for a parental blessing, should be duly married—much to her bewilderment, as they sleep together anyway; and he dresses everybody in Victorian clothes found in the attic. When these measures prove to be futile, he embarks upon an ideological campaign as a means of straightening morals, and, finally, having come to the conclusion that the only valid ideology is discipline for discipline's sake, he institutes a rule of terror. The boorish proletarian, Edek, proves to be stronger, however; he kills Arthur and takes power. The play ends in a tango danced by Edek and the reactionary uncle, who had been allied with Arthur but now meekly submits to Edek, though not without moral protests. Thus, without recourse to realistic techniques, Mrożek explores the disintegration of traditional values, presents a capsule history of Polish intelligentsia attitudes over several decades, and translates into an allegory the various solutions proposed in our century: the return to tradition, the search for ideology, fascism, and proletarian revolution. Unfortunately, a brief summary of the contents does not do justice to the play's theatrical appeal when properly staged. It was greeted by critics as the best play of the two postwar decades, and some of them even compared it to Wyspiański's *The Wedding*. Be that as it may, Mrożek was undoubtedly influenced by Witold Gombrowicz's work, particularly by *The Marriage Ceremony* (*Ślub*), which, however, had not been staged in Poland.

The Essay and Intermediary Genres

While many essays and studies in various fields have to be excluded for lack of space, some of them, because of their form, belong to creative writing rather than to scholarly contributions. For example, no novelist or diarist succeeded in analyzing everyday life in Nazi-occupied Poland (mostly from an economic angle) as well as Kazimierz Wyka, historian of literature and literary critic, whose name has already appeared several times in these pages. Wyka's *Life As If* (*Życie na niby*, written during the war and immediate postwar periods, but published in 1957), in a casual, ironic style hiding his

Kazimierz Wyka (1910–1975)

seriousness of purpose, draws an image of an improbable economic system thriving on the illegality of all its endeavors. Had the Nazi-imposed regulations been observed by the people of Poland, especially the inhabitants of towns, they would have starved to death. Instead, countless tricks for cheating the occupiers were devised, all of which amounted not to a marginal black market as in other occupied countries but to a whole system-within-a-system. The elaboration of such a setup was facilitated, in a way, by Nazi officials, with their propensity for theft and bribery. As a result, the market was flooded not only with staples but also with luxuries, adding to an eerie reality in which death from a bullet or in a concentration camp could engulf a passerby at every street corner.

Jan Kott   A native of Warsaw, Jan Kott studied law and French literature
(1914–) there, starting his literary career with poetry and essays on French surrealism. During the war he lived for a while in Lwów (under the Soviet rule), then after 1941 in Warsaw, where he joined the Communist underground and edited a clandestine periodical. As one of the editors of *The Forge*, beginning in 1945, he became known as a Marxist essayist, won a doctorate in Romance literatures, and specialized in the history of drama. A university professor since 1949 (first in Wrocław, then in Warsaw), he dedicated several studies to eighteenth-century Polish and French writers. His fascination with Enlightenment rationalism, distinguishable in all those connected with *The Forge*, is reflected in his very style. He learned much from the ironic, down-to-earth brilliancy of the French encyclopedists, but even more from the most eminent translator of French literature, the French-oriented essayist Tadeusz Boy-Żeleński, who distrusted the lofty constructions of intellectuals and searched for determinants of ideas in primitive desires and impulses: sex and money.

What Boy-Żeleński found in a liberal, anticlerical ideology, Kott found in Marxism, with its stress upon the material factors of human existence. Hard-working and prolific as an essayist, a translator from French, an editor of Old Polish writings, he was acutely sensitive to changes of mood in his intellectual and political milieu. His essays on Shakespeare, which, after being translated into several languages, caused a great stir abroad and influenced theater directors in England, grew out of his critical articles on the theater. *Shakespeare Our Contemporary* (*Szkice o Szekspirze*, 1964) is not, as might be assumed, the product of a detached investigator spending the greater part of his time in his study. Kott reacted to Shakespeare on the stage like the rest of Polish audiences in 1956, the year of the "Polish October," and during its aftermath. The Elizabethan poet proved to be much more in tune with the era of political murders, unscrupulous struggles for power, tyranny, and mutual spying than any writer of the twentieth century. Historical experience enabled everybody to identify himself with Hamlet, who now, contrary to psychological interpretations, was just a brave young man forced to play the fool in order to deceive a dangerous master and his plainclothesmen. Thus, Shakespeare was integrated into the traditional Polish concept of the theater as a public forum where problems of the community are debated by means of an artistic transposition. Since the existential frame of mind in Poland was nourished by the experience of people who felt the precariousness of the individual tossed around by the capricious forces of History, King Lear was played as Everyman, similar to the characters in "absurd" plays. Kott formulated all this more cogently than any of his Polish colleagues, and to the scholarly objections raised by some Western professors he might oppose a valid argument: his Shakespeare has an immediacy that all Western theater directors, if not all Western professors, might well envy.

As a young Marxist philosopher, Kołakowski taught in 1952–1954 at a Polish Workers' Party (Communist) school in Warsaw, the Institute for the Training of Scientific Workers, then at Warsaw University as a lecturer, and since 1959 has been a professor of the history of modern philosophy. Very orthodox and rigid in his early writings, in 1955 he joined the editorial staff of *Po prostu* ("Straight Talk"), a rebellious weekly of young Communist intellectuals. The paper was to become a major force preparing the "Polish October" of 1956 and was closed down by the authorities in 1957 as too radical in its demands for democratic changes within the socialist system of economy. In those years Kołakowski won the acclaim of the young generation as the sharpest mind among the so-called "revisionists," and several of his philosophical essays were translated into Western languages, often to his distaste, for he criticized the official doctrine from a Marxist point of view and had no wish to add fuel to the non-Marxist or anti-Marxist opposition. As a disciplined Party member he abstained, when ordered to do so, from publishing anything directly bearing on current issues of Marxist philosophy. In 1966 he was, however, excluded from the Party because of a university lecture commemorating the tenth anniversary of the "Polish October" in which he attacked the Party hierarchy for not fulfilling its promises to the population. Even more recently he was deprived of his chair at Warsaw University.

Leszek Kołakowski (1927–)

Kołakowski is a good example of the return to the mores of the Enlightenment, when a philosopher did not withdraw into an ivory tower but waged war on the creeds of his contemporaries and when the terms philosophy and literature were nearly interchangeable. His Voltairian irony exploits various literary genres, which serve only as vehicles for his ideas. In his scholarly books and papers, his style is dry, heavy, and, one is tempted to say, deliberately abstruse, as if he wished to bar access to his deeper thought. He wrote a book on Spinoza, edited Spinoza's letters, and his years of research on that epoch culminated in a huge volume of 650 pages, *Religious Consciousness and Church Structure, Studies on Nondenominational Christianity of the Seventeenth Century* (*Świadomość religijna i więź kościelna*, 1965). This is an investigation, unique in its thoroughness, of mystical currents in Holland and in France, with an awesome array of footnotes. The author's conclusions may be stated as follows: Religious movements, as they gather strength, are confronted at a given moment with a choice; they can either organize themselves as churches, impose orthodoxy upon their members, and betray their initial, genuine impetus or try to preserve their original purity, but then the price is disintegration and disappearance.

In striking contrast to Kołakowski's scholarly works, his theatrical plays and stories display his gifts as a jester in a casual colloquial language. In a play, *Hotel Eden*, for instance, we are present at the arrival of a guest who is greeted at the gate of the establishment by crowds of white-uniformed policemen. He is Adam Number X Thousand. The number is high because the gentle old director of the hotel has failed in his experiments with other guests, Adam's predecessors, owing to a malicious and powerful tempter on the premises, the Vice-Director of Hotel Eden. This time, too, the experiment fails. Adam meets Eve, but they are bored by the carefree life under constant supervision; only after Eve yields to the temptation of the Vice-Director who offers her a key to a forbidden room, and they have been expelled, waking up in a small hotel of a big city, are they happy. Moral: freedom without the possibility of choice is no freedom at all; man has to assume his condition and always choose at his risk and peril, even if the penalty is death.

The Bible furnished the themes for Kołakowski's paradoxical fables or parables in *The Heavenly Key, or Edifying Tales from Biblical History Collected for Instruction and Warning* (*Klucz niebieski albo opowieści budujące z historii świętej zebrane ku pouczeniu i przestrodze*, 1964). The title, a parody of the pious tracts of the Polish Baroque era, suggests the author's intent: jokingly he twists famous passages from the Bible into exercises in philosophical and moral ambiguity. To give but one example, in "Balaam, or The Problem of Objective Guilt," Balaam beats his she-ass, who refuses to move because she has been stopped by an angel that is invisible to Balaam. The angel materializes and scolds the man for beating an innocent beast. But Balaam protests that he did not see the angel. No matter, he is an "objective sinner": he has sinned by not seeing the invisible angel; he has sinned by beating an innocent beast; he has sinned by desiring to proceed against the will of God, who sent the angel; and he has sinned by quarreling with the angel. Now he is ordered to continue with his journey; so why was he stopped? That is an arrogant question coming from a sinner who does not profit from an opportunity to earn merit by stopping at an invisible obstacle. "Instruction and warning" in Kołakowski's tales are thus equated with pointing out the lack of any ready-made codes of behavior which would be valid for all circumstances. For this kind of outlook, his adversaries in Poland have been labeling him a crossbreed of Marxism and existentialism.

Outlandish fragments, such as parodies of sermons, supposed stenographic notes from the pronouncements of demons, perverse speeches put into the mouths of historic figures, go into the making of his *Conversations with the Devil* (*Rozmowy z diabłem*, 1965), where he plays with various forms. The chapter entitled "The Dialectical Observations of Arthur Schopenhauer, Metaphysician, Burgher from Danzig," for instance, is written in verse.

Respected because of his courage and integrity, Kołakowski seems to incarnate the rebellious spirit of the Polish rationalistic, anticlerical (in both the religious and the political sense) intelligentsia whose traditions go back to the Enlightenment and further, to the Protestant thinkers of the "Golden Age." In Kołakowski's case, the defense of free thought against the powers that be takes the shape of "humanistic socialism," of which he has been the main proponent in Poland.

Stanisław Jerzy Lec or "Baron Letz," as he was called by his friends (real name: de Tusch-Letz), was born in Lwów into a rich Viennese-Galician Jewish family with an aristocratic title. Brought up in Vienna and Lwów, he preserved throughout his life a warm feeling for German language and poetry. While a student at Lwów University, where he studied Polish literature and obtained a diploma in law, he started to publish lyrical and satirical poetry, politically committing himself to the extreme Left. During the war, he lived in Lwów; in 1941–1943 he was a prisoner in a Nazi extermination camp. He succeeded in escaping, however, and joined the Communist resistance movement in Warsaw. A soldier of the Communist People's Army, he distinguished himself as editor of the Army's periodicals and in guerrilla action. Decorated for bravery after the liberation, an officer in the army of People's Poland with the rank of major, he worked in Vienna as a member of the Polish Political Mission from 1946 to 1950. The pressures of the Stalinist era proved too much for him, and he broke with the government in 1950 to migrate to Israel. Being a Polish poet, he felt completely alien there; after two years he returned to Poland and settled in Warsaw.

Stanisław Jerzy Lec (1909–1966)

Lec's biography is indispensable for the appreciation of the peculiarity of his writings. His was an experience which rarely befalls a man: a Nazi death camp, which he survived by a series of miraculous narrow escapes; guerrilla warfare; the Stalinist system; prewar and postwar Vienna and Israel. One might say that he was well-initiated into the twentieth century. All this is traceable in his poetry, which, however, has never been similar to that of any Vanguard school. His preference ran to very short occasional verse, whether for a ferocious satirical attack or a lyrical note. His conciseness and furious, cold irony are such that his *fraszki* (a genre introduced to Polish literature by Jan Kochanowski and one for which Lec entertained a strong predilection) are already anthology pieces. Justly or unjustly, however, his poems were overshadowed by his aphorisms in prose, which he began to write in 1956, and which he also called *fraszki* ("trifles"). A libertarian of skeptical wisdom, Lec found himself in his element only after the totalitarian idols had crumbled in Poland. The first collection of his *Unkempt Thoughts* (*Myśli nieuczesane*) appeared in 1957; others followed. They made the public laugh, but at the same time, everybody was aware of their explosive content: that they were telling more about conclusions to be drawn from the experience of our century than pages and pages of other authors.

He called me a "rotten liberal." I slapped his face. He saw his mistake and apologized.

*

Evil, too, only wants to make us happy.

*

They tortured him. They were searching his brain for their own thoughts.

*

It is a terrible thing to swim against the current in a dirty river.

*

Some think they are descended from apes who sat on the tree of knowledge.
                                  (Translated by Maria Kuncewicz)

Only the dead can be resurrected. It's more difficult with the living.

*

Stupidity is the mother of crime. But the fathers are frequently geniuses.

*

Do I have no soul as punishment for not believing in the soul?

*

The constitution of a country should not violate the constitutions of its citizens.

*

I know why Jews are considered wealthy—they pay for everything.

*

"What do you do," asked a friend, "when you find, in your own bed, your wife's lover with another woman?"

*

Don't tell your dreams. What if the Freudists come to power?

*

Mankind deserves sacrifice—but not of mankind.

*

To God what is God's, to Caesar what is Caesar's. To humans—what?

*

It is unhealthy to live. He who lives, dies.

*

I wanted to tell the world just one word. Unable to do it, I became a writer.

*

Is it progress if a cannibal uses a knife and fork?

*

Are naked women intelligent?

*

"I'd like the world to be the Grand Guignol."
"You are a sadist."
"Oh, no. There they were only pretending."

*

When you jump for joy, beware that no one moves the ground from beneath your feet.

*

Many tried to create the philosopher's stone by petrifying thoughts.

*

I had a dream about reality. It was such a relief to wake up.

(Translated by Jacek Galazka)

Perhaps, after all, Lec should be regarded as a poet in his *Unkempt Thoughts*, which is but a distillate of his biting verse. On the other hand, the astringency of his aphorisms often makes one think of the cruel Warsaw street jokes, of Viennese witticisms, and of Jewish humor; did he not write:

You ask me, O beautiful lady, how long my thoughts mature. Six thousand years, my dear.

Centering his philosophy upon the defense of man oppressed by products of his own hands and brain, he represents the best in Polish literature of the decade 1956–1966. *Unkempt Thoughts* (which appeared weekly in periodicals at first) cannot be isolated from the libertarian mood of the reading public, nor from the ironic explorations of young poets, of S. Mrożek, and of essayists such as Kołakowski.

Émigré Literature

As a result of the 1939 invasion, Polish literature, for the second time in its history, found itself divided in two: one center was in Poland; the other in exile. Even though some writers returned home after the end of the hostilities, this division has persisted, and important *émigré* periodicals or publishing houses founded during the war, or immediately afterward, continued their activity throughout the two postwar decades. The approximately thirty-year span of *émigré* literature cannot be interpreted as the outgrowth of a neat political cleavage. The picture is much more complex. The writers who landed in Western Europe or America brought with them various shades of political opinion, which did not necessarily correspond to the crude classification into "right thinking" and "wrong thinking" applied after 1945 in both East and West in consequence of the cold war. Although access to Poland was barred, until 1956, for Polish books published abroad, after that date several of them were favorably reviewed in literary periodicals or reissued in new editions. Some authors, who had settled abroad permanently, would send their manuscripts to publishing houses in Warsaw. Postwar Poland witnessed departures as well as home-comings; these were motivated sometimes by political, sometimes by purely personal, reasons. New talents appeared among the young generation who were brought up as citizens of England or France but preserved an attachment to their ancestral tongue.

The contribution made by a few among the exiles to Polish letters is impressive, and it is an open question as to whether or not it outweighs the bulk of literary production in Poland. We lack perspective for such an answer. That many judgments will be revised is certain. Writers living abroad were uprooted but were not exposed to pressures from the authorities or from a narrow, oversophisticated milieu whose coffeehouse gossip and fads all too often favored a sham avant-gardism. Whatever is outstanding in the literature of the exiles has been created by isolated individuals struggling against financial odds and cut off from their potential readers. The majority of what might be called the reading public among the *émigrés*, "the intelligentsia" presented a not very high intellectual level, and their conservative taste turned to the familiar, the imitative, and thus, the second-rate. Nor did the "old emigration," whose several millions were of peasant descent and established mostly in the United States and France, offer encouragement: either they were parochial, locked within their ghettos, or they were culturally disassociated, having been absorbed into the "melting pot."

Prewar Poland's leading literary weekly, *Literary News* (*Wiadomości literackie*), continued its existence in London under the title of *News* and under the same editor, Mieczysław Grydzewski, who had managed to escape at the moment of the Nazi onslaught. Thanks to a feat of rare, singlehanded editorial skill and endurance, the periodical prospered, though it underwent a transformation along lines similar to the transformation observable among many *émigrés:* once a liberal organ (Grydzewski had also been editor of *Skamander*), it became conservative not only in its political outlook, but also in its choice of literary material.

A much more dynamic publication appeared in Paris. The monthly *Kultura* was also the accomplishment of one man's tenacity, and has been published without interruption since 1947. Its editor, Jerzy Giedroyć, had fought during the war as a soldier of the Carpathian Brigade in the battle of Tobruk; later, when he arrived in Rome as an officer of the Allied forces, he founded a publishing house there: The Literary Institute, which he soon moved to Paris. His ambitions were primarily political, and *Kultura* exerted considerable influence in Poland during the years 1956–1966. It was quite widely read there and even found contributors among Warsaw and Kraków authors. *Kultura*'s durable merit lies in the policy of opening its pages to high-quality literary texts; and The Literary Institute has been recognized as one of the most adventurous Polish postwar publishing houses.

Among other *émigré* publishers special notice is due to Poets' and Painters' Press in London, a small but efficient enterprise run by a couple of poets and printers, Czesław and Krystyna Bednarczyk, and dedicated mostly to editions of poetry.

Several authors who were, or still are, active in exile have already been discussed. The "Skamander" poets Julian Tuwim and Antoni Słonimski returned to Poland in 1946 and 1951, respectively, while Jan Lechoń and Kazimierz Wierzyński stayed on in the United States. For data on the novelist and playwright Witold Gombrowicz, on the essayist Jerzy Stempowski, and on the author of a saga about the Carpathian Mountains, Stanisław Vincenz, we must also refer the reader to the chapter on literature between 1918 and 1939 (see Chapter X, pp. 432–439). Gombrowicz, whose major position in modern (not only Polish) literature is indisputable, was slighted during his many years of exile in Argentina by the *émigré* press (with the exception of *Kultura*) as a megalomaniac, even a madman. Laudatory articles on him in the domestic Polish press after 1956 and praise from French, German, and Swedish critics, after his books had been translated and his plays produced in several countries, came to many people as a shock. The attitude of censorship in Poland toward his work has been typically capricious and inconsistent. Some of his books were reissued, others forbidden, while critical essays analyzed also those writings of his which were inaccessible to the public.

The novels of Teodor Parnicki, resident of Mexico, were dealt with in the section on prose in postwar Poland (see above, in this chapter, pp. 504–507). Parnicki, whose publisher abroad was, like Gombrowicz's, The Literary Institute, reached his true audience only in 1959, when his books were allowed to be published in Warsaw.

Sarcasm and irony were common fare in Poland, but the best work of pure humor was written and published in exile. This is the novel *Tourists from Crow's-Nests* (*Turyści z bocianich gniazd*, 1953) by Czesław Straszewicz (1911–1963). He was valued before the war as a promising prose writer, but his novel *Pity* (*Litość*, 1939), with its background of the Spanish Civil War, had put him on the "wanted list" of the Gestapo. By the time Poland was occupied, however, Straszewicz was already far away; the outbreak of the war caught him in Latin America, where he had gone to gather material for a novel on Polish immigrant life. He embarked immediately for Europe, but the Polish campaign was soon over, so he served in the Polish army in France and in England. Afterward, he lived mostly in Montevideo, Uruguay, where he wrote his novel. It is composed of two loosely connected tales whose action is placed, respectively, in a Latin American port called Punta Chata and on the Baltic coast in Poland. In the first, he created an unforgettable figure of a Polish wanderer, a simple sailor, Kostek, tough, clever, but, in truth, a sentimental young man. He displays a most refined sense of honor, not quite befitting his social status, as he is supported in Punta Chata by an Indian street-girl. But Kostek is able to feel culturally superior to his surroundings because wherever he goes he takes The Book ("this is my Constitution") — a Polish cookbook. In the second tale, the adventures of some sailors take the action to an office of the Security Police in a Polish port. Not so much a satire on totalitarian absurdity as an occasion for gentle laughter, this tale exemplifies Straszewicz's "milk of human kindness" approach to his characters. For instance, a high-ranking Security Police officer, who, in all of his habits, is a petty squire of the seventeenth century, knows Sienkiewicz's Trilogy practically by heart, and at night, in bed with his wife, he examines her no less thorough knowledge of its characters and their sayings.

Some personalities among the *émigré* writers were anathema in Poland to nearly everybody, and the horror with which their names were pronounced will be amusing or incomprehensible to future generations. Such was the fate of Józef Mackiewicz (1902–   ). The staunch antinationalism of this native of Lithuania, who remained faithful to the tradition of coexistence between nationalities and religions, offended the patriotic Poles; his total rejection of Communism in any form led to his being made into an "un-person" in Poland. Before the war and during the war, he resided in Wilno, where he worked as a journalist and published a book on the most distant Byelorussian provinces entitled *The Revolt of the Marshes* (*Bunt rojstów*, 1938). Mackiewicz may be defined as a "liberal conservative" in the nineteenth-century sense. His preference for the old-fashioned extended to his literary models. He is the most "Russian" of Polish authors because of his sympathy for Russia's civilization and her great novelists. His *Road to Nowhere* (*Droga do nikąd*, 1955) is a powerful, traditionally realistic novel on a most untraditional subject: life in Lithuania in 1940–1941 as it was being converted into a republic of the Soviet Union. *The Careerist* (*Karierowicz*, 1956) is a psychological study set against the background of small Lithuanian towns and villages during World War I. Mackiewicz's racy and brutal prose is at its best in what seems to be the specialty of all natives of Lithuania: descriptions of nature. His gloomy philosophy links him to the literary current of naturalism.

The ebb of the Polish element from the territory once designated as the Grand Duchy of Lithuania was not confined to the post-World War II exodus, as the biography of Florian Czarnyszewicz (1895–1964) shows. Born in a petty-gentry village on the banks of the Berezina in Byelorussia, he migrated to Poland after World War I when his native region became a part of the Soviet Byelorussian Republic. Feeling ill at ease there, he migrated further, in the 1920s, to Argentina. A manual worker, and a self-taught writer, he produced a huge novel, *The Inhabitants of Berezina Country* (*Nadberezyńcy*, 1942), which is a naïve, heroic epic of the civil war in this province in the years 1917–1920. For a Polish reader, the authenticity of the spoken language preserved in Czarnyszewicz's style, untouched by any modern sophistication, is completely captivating. For a sociologist or anthropologist, it is a gold mine, with its faithful portrayal of the mentality and way of life of the petty-gentry farmer, which seems not to have changed one iota since Mickiewicz depicted it in *Pan Tadeusz*. Similar human types are present in his *Fates of Foster Sons* (*Losy pasierbów*, 1958) as Polish immigrants to Argentina.

Fiction in Polish published abroad embraces at least a hundred titles, even if one limits oneself only to the better works. Therefore, but few of the most striking authors may be listed. Gustaw Herling-Grudziński (1919–   ) studied Polish literature in Warsaw before the war and belonged to the "new wave" of young literary critics who made a name for themselves shortly before 1939. During the war he was deported to a labor camp in the north of Russia. After his release he enlisted in the Polish army organized by the London government-in-exile and, with it, left for Iran and Iraq; then, as a soldier, he took part in the Allied invasion of Italy. After the war he lived in England for a short time, but returned to Italy, where he settled in Naples. His *World Apart* (*Inny świat*, 1953) stands out by virtue of its literary qualities among innumerable reports, memoirs, and testimonies written by ex-prisoners on labor camps of the Stalinist era, and is possibly among the best books on that theme written in any language. On the borders of the novel form, narrated in the first person, it is humane, intelligent, and well-balanced in its juxtaposition of horror and beauty (Northern nature in summer; a Russian woman convict identifying herself with the suffering characters of Dostoevsky). Compassion for his Russian fellow prisoners and respect for Russian literature also characterize Herling-Grudziński's essays, which he contributed to the Italian literary press and to *Kultura*. He also developed a short-story form of his own, and, had he published in Poland, his few stories (he is not prolific) would have earned him an exceptionally high position; he may be called a renovator of the cold, detached, "Stendhalian" style. The remote past, or even the present of Italy, his new home, provides the setting for his stories, which have been translated into several languages. In English they appeared as *The Island* (1967).

Young experimenters in Poland have a counterpart in Leo Lipski (1917–   ), a resident of Tel Aviv. He parallels them in his penchant for the grotesque and the macabre. With such techniques, he artistically transforms his experiences in the Soviet Union during the war and in Israel. His slim collection of stories, *Day and Night* (*Dzień i noc*, 1957), and a fantastic tale, *Pete* (*Piotruś*, 1960), secured him quite a high rank among Polish *émigré* writers.

The idol of Poland's young generation in 1956, author of brutal short stories, Marek Hłasko (1934–1969), went abroad in 1958 and stayed there, owing to his strained relations with the authorities. For a couple of years he earned his living in Israel (where he had only a temporary visa, not being a Jew) as a truck driver, a manual worker, and, he likes to stress in his autobiography, as a pimp. Israel is the setting for his short, violent novels *All Were Turned Away* and *Dirty Deeds* (*Wszyscy byli odwróceni; Brudne czyny*, 1964).

For another prose writer, residence in West Germany was a destiny reluctantly accepted. Tadeusz Nowakowski (1918–   ) spent five years in a Nazi concentration camp, then two years in a displaced persons' camp before he made his name as a journalist and an author of malicious, scornful stories as well as of a novel on Polish displaced persons in Germany, *All Souls' Camp* (*Obóz Wszystkich Świętych*, 1957). Much can be said for and against these authors, and a final judgment of their true stature would be premature.

Latin America provided material for the stories of Andrzej Bobkowski (1913–1961), who lived in Guatemala. His fiction, however, is somewhat sentimental and inferior to his day-by-day diary account of life in France during the war: *Sketched with a Quill* (*Szkice piórkiem*, two volumes, 1957). Every *émigré* literature abounds in memoirs and reminiscences, and Polish *émigré* literature is no exception, but Bobkowski's diary is unique: Nazi-occupied France is seen and judged by a perspicacious foreigner who is both enamored with the country and repulsed by the undignified behavior of its people. A curious book, it is an open avowal of the ambivalence (love-hate) Poles feel toward "the West."

Émigré literature has suffered from the lack of incisive literary criticism, and the activity of Konstanty Jeleński (1920) therefore acquires an exceptional character. A man of Italian-French education, a soldier of the Allied Forces landing in Europe during the last war, he settled in Paris where he became associated with refined literary-artistic circles. Writing with equal ease in French and in Polish, he was ideally suited for his role as an intermediary between French and Polish literatures. Attentive to everything of value which was published in Poland, he was instrumental in bringing several young Polish writers, primarily poets, to the attention of the French reading public.

Anthologie de la poésie polonaise (1965), edited by him, is a rare achievement. Translations from Polish poetry since the Middle Ages to our day were done by a team of poets among whom we find the most renowned names of French letters, and some versions may be considered as masterpieces of that difficult craft. Jeleński was also one of the first critics to grasp the significance of Witold Gombrowicz's writings. Without his articles and his admiring help, Gombrowicz's books would probably not have won such staunch defenders among the French literati. Jeleński's intellectual curiosity and receptiveness are not limited to literature; he is also an art critic.

It has been said that poetry cannot exist in separation from the native soil and from the everyday speech of the people; whether this contention is true or not, it should be qualified by the many examples of poets in the past, for instance, those of the Polish Great Emigration. During the war, poetry found a tremendous response among soldiers, and their favorite was probably the Communist (then anti-Stalinist) Władysław Broniewski. Later on, public taste outside of Poland remained frozen in its attachment to the easy lyrical flow of "Skamander" verse, and poets who catered to this preference merely produced a repetition of clichés; in Poland such poetry was regarded as antique. Thus, the poets who had started in the thirties and who were part of the Second Vanguard could not count on much esteem abroad.

Marian Czuchnowski (1909–   ) had been highly valued in avant-garde circles for his first volumes, with their dense and sensuous metaphors: *The Morning of Bitterness* (*Poranek goryczy*, 1930) and *Women and Horses* (*Kobiety i konie*, 1931). A permanent rebel by temperament, he evolved into a writer of the extreme Left, was arrested in Poland several times, and produced two revolutionary novels. In 1939–1941, he was a prisoner of labor camps in the north of Russia; released, he reached the Middle East and finally settled in London. His two postwar novels, strongly autobiographical, bear the imprint of his Russian experience. He remained true to his passion for exploring the situation of the underdog, and his most interesting postwar poems stem from his life as a factory worker in England. His verse is deliber-

ately crude, without meter or rhyme, and is marked by disenchantment. With its stream of conversations, factual data, obscene jokes, it
is the most "materialistic" in modern Polish poetry, as it reduces the
proletarian existence to its bare essentials: work and sex.

The best translator of Ukrainian and Russian poets (Blok, Akhmatova, Mandelstam, Pasternak, Tsvetaeva, Josif Brodsky) resides not
in Poland, but, paradoxically, in Spain. Józef Łobodowski (1909–
) was much talked about before the war not only because of his
"catastrophist" poems full of historical pathos but because of his political shifts: enthusiastic espousal of Communism followed by disillusionment. His poetry, owing to his feeling for the Ukraine, might be related
to the tradition of the Romantic "Ukrainian School." Awarded a prize by
the Polish Academy of Literature in 1937, he escaped to France in 1939,
where he edited an *émigré* paper; after the fall of France he was arrested while crossing the Pyrenees and detained for a year and a half
in a Spanish prison. Afterward, various circumstances inclined him to
stay in Madrid. Though irritatingly verbose in his long poems and
novels, he is neat and precise in his translations from Spanish and from
Slavic languages.

Jerzy Pietrkiewicz (1916–   ), from a peasant family in northern Poland, was connected before the war with the peasant "authenti-
cists." After his arrival in England during the war, his poetry acquired
greater intellectual complexity, which resulted in an estrangement
from the public. He obtained a doctorate from the University of London, where he has since been teaching Polish literature. He also wrote
successful novels in English. He has exerted influence upon the young
generation of *émigrés* as teacher, scholar, and translator of poetry
from English into Polish and from Polish into English.

Marian Pankowski (1919–   ) was able to draw nourishment
from French culture. A student at the outbreak of the war, he joined
the Resistance, was imprisoned by the Nazis, and went through several
concentration camps in Germany. His first volume of poems appeared
in 1946 in Brussels, where he settled permanently, and where, since
1950, he has been teaching at the university. His astonishing linguistic
sensitivity that endows words with the qualities of objects to be
touched, tasted, and smelled has permitted him to become a fine bilingual poet and an excellent translator of Polish poetry into French. The
same quality is visible in his experimental narratives in prose. His jest-
ing "novel" on the wanderings of a young Pole, *Matuga Marches On*
(*Matuga idzie*, 1958), published in a small number of copies, has been
ignored by *émigré* reviewers as a presumably pornographic and cynical exploit in buffoonery. Its stylized boorishness debunks the Polish
propensity for false sublimity and testifies to the author's plebeian re-

sentment; it is a journey through the "heart of darkness": concentration camps and the slum areas of Western European cities.

The two posthumously published volumes of poetry by Tadeusz Sułkowski (1907–1960) revealed an authentic philosophical poet. From the serenity of his chiseled, rhymed, and metrical verse, which is a pious praise of the world's beauty, one would never suspect that behind them stood a deeply unhappy man. Few poems of his appeared in print before the war. He fought as an officer in the 1939 campaign, spent five years in a prisoner-of-war camp in Germany, and afterward moved to Italy, then to London, where he led a solitary, miserable existence, earning his living from odd jobs. His *Golden House* (*Dom złoty*, 1961) and *Shield* (*Tarcza*, 1961) are a triumph of self-discipline.

The conflict between certain writers and the majority of *émigré* readers cannot be reduced merely to a matter of taste. It was the extension of prewar conflict between the intellectuals and the "intelligentsia," that peculiar social layer of white-collar workers not met with in either Western Europe or America. The split into liberals and Rightists within that layer tended to be forgotten in exile, which in effect meant a regression into the most traditional nationalistic attitudes. Because social changes in Poland carried her intellectuals and literature in the opposite direction, *émigré* readers were especially antagonistic to those writers who migrated only after a period of activity (varying in length from writer to writer) in People's Poland. Different mentalities engendered different sensibilities: the poetry of Czesław Miłosz, for example, was alien to *émigré* readers, and the problems that preoccupied him, repellent. Miłosz left Poland in 1951, lived for almost ten years in Paris as a free-lance writer, and in 1960 went to the United States, where he has been teaching Polish literature at the University of California in Berkeley. He has always considered himself primarily a poet, although he wrote several books in prose, some of which were translated into many languages. *The Captive Mind* (*Zniewolony umysł*, 1953) is an analysis of the mental acrobatics Eastern European intellectuals had to perform in order to give assent to Stalinist dogmas. It preceded similar denouncements in Poland by a few years, but was attacked in the *émigré* press as tainted with Hegelianism and Marxism. *The Valley of Issa* (*Dolina Issy*, 1955) is a novel close to the very core of Miłosz's poetry. It has been called "pagan" because of its childish amazement with the world; but this story of childhood in Lithuania, with its simple images of nature, is somewhat deceptive, as underneath lurks a Manichean vision. *Native Realm* (*Rodzinna Europa*, 1959) is written as the autobiography of an Eastern European, conducting him through his native Lithuania, Russia, Poland, and France. An appraisal of Miłosz's evolution as a poet and translator of poetry does not belong here for obvious reasons. In Poland, he was a strictly forbidden author from 1951 to 1956, extolled during the years 1956–1958, and again forbidden in the period 1958–1966; despite these fluctuations, his intimate ties with the Polish writers' community have not been destroyed.

The petrified attitudes of the *émigrés* provoked a rebellion among the young generation, who remembered prewar Poland only vaguely or not at all. Young poets in London, who were bilingual but chose to write in Polish (they had gone through English schools and were studying at English universities), contributed at first to a little student magazine in 1955 called *Merkuriusz*, named like the first Polish newspaper of 1661; later, from 1959 to 1964, they edited another little magazine, *Kontynenty* ("Continents"), and for a while were known as the "Kontynenty" group. They soon went their separate ways, however, and each has had a career of his own. Initially, they were motivated by a radical opposition to the Polish community in London, both in a political and in a literary sense. In their poetry they rejected "Skamander" poetics, and followed in the steps of the First and Second Vanguards; thus, their technique closely resembled that of their contemporaries in Poland. Preference given to any one of their number would be out of place at this time, because the development of a writer may be fast or slow. A few examples of biographies will have to suffice.

Bogdan Czaykowski (1932–   ) spent his childhood in Poland, the Soviet Union, and India, studied at the universities of Dublin and London, and migrated to Canada, where he has been teaching Polish language and literature. He best expressed the predicament of the poet in exile in his poem "Revolt in Verse" ("Bunt wierszem"):

> I was born there.
> I did not choose the place.
> Why was I not born simply in the grass.
> Grass grows everywhere.
> Only deserts would not accept me.
> Or I could have been born in a skein of the wind
> When the air is breathing.
> But I was born there.
> They chained me when I was a baby
> And they put me into the world with my little chains.
> I am here. I was born there.
> Had I at least been born at sea.
>
> You, magnetic iron
> Which turn me constantly toward the pole,
> You are heavy; without you I am so light

That I lose the perception of my weight.
So I bear those little chains
And I toss them as a lion tosses his mane.
People from over there shout:
Come back.
They call me: chip, chip, chip.
Millet and weeds are poured in vain.
Dog, into the kennel!
I am a poet (one has to have a name).
The language is my chain.
Words are my collar.
I was born there.
Why was I not simply born in the grass.

Urodziłem się tam
Nie wybierałem miejsca.
Chętnie bym się urodził po prostu w trawie.
Trawy rosną wszędzie.
Nie chciałyby mnie tylko pustynie.
Lub mogłem się przecież urodzić
W kłębuszku wiatru,
Gdy oddychają powietrza.
Ale urodziłem się tam.
Przykuli mnie gdy jeszcze byłem dzieckiem.
A później z łańcuszkami puścili w świat.
Jestem tutaj. Urodziłem się tam.
Gdybym choć się urodził na morzu.
Żelazo namagnesowane
Co wciąż mię na biegun kierujesz,
Ciężkie jesteś; bez ciebie mi tak lekko,
Że tracę wagę siebie.
Więc noszę te łańcuszki
I potrząsam nimi jak lew grzywą.
A ludzie stamtąd krzyczą:
Wróć.
Wołają: cip, cip, cip.
Proso z kąkolem na wiatr.
Pies do budy.
Ja jestem poeta (trzeba się nazwać).
Język moim łańcuchem.
Słowa obrożą moją.
Urodziłem się tam.
(Chętnie bym się urodził po prostu w trawie.)

The title for the anthology of the group's poetry, *Fish on the Sand* (*Ryby na piasku*, 1965), was borrowed from another poem of Czaykowski's. As for the other members of the group, Adam Czerniawski (1934–   ), poet, translator, author of critical essays and prose narratives, studied English literature at London University, then worked as a clerk in that city. Jerzy S. Sito (1934–   ) grew up in Persia and India, studied engineering in London, worked there successfully in his profession, then returned to Poland in 1959. His poetry translations especially from Marlowe and Shakespeare, are possibly a new departure in the long history of that art in Polish literature. Jan Darowski (1926–   ), a native of Silesia, was drafted into the *Wehrmacht*, but in Normandy he passed over to the American side, then joined the Polish forces. He has been working in London as a printer. Zygmunt Ławrynowicz (1925–   ), from Lithuania where he finished high school, was deported to Germany, studied economy and political science in Dublin, and is employed in London as a bank official. Bolesław Taborski (1927–   ) fought in the Warsaw Uprising, was a prisoner of war in Germany, and studied English drama in London, where he has been active as a theater critic, translator, and publicist. Florian Śmieja (1925–   ) during the war was a deportee in Germany; later, in Ireland and England, he specialized in Spanish literature; he is a translator of Old Spanish poetry into Polish and a university professor. The youngest of the group, Andrzej Busza (1938–   ), lived in the Middle East as a child, studied in England, then migrated to Canada, where he has been a professor of English literature.

These somewhat fantastic biographies seem to be a fitting finale for a book unfortunately much concerned with the hazards of history.

Epilogue

THE LATE 1960s

A basic difficulty for an investigator of Polish literature is the necessity of responding to its continually fluctuating political milieu. For that reason, certain dates in the political life of the country are used to mark the division of literary history into separate chapters.

The period of the so-called "our little stabilization" came to its end in March 1968. In appearance, student riots in that month could present some vague analogy with student riots in Western countries, especially in Paris. In fact, completely different causes were operating and there was in Poland much more activity on the part of police than on the part of the presumed rebels. The unrest among the young, provoked by an order of the authorities to suspend theatrical performances of Mickiewicz's *Forefathers' Eve* (an anti-Tzarist, i.e. anti-Russian, play) testified to a general malaise and was exploited by one faction in the Party in its struggle for power. Anti-Semitism was introduced in the guise of a purported Zionist plot behind the students' movement. The brutality of the police was a traumatic experience for the young generation and determined their subsequent evolution toward an open defiance. In summer 1968, Wiesław Gomułka, the first secretary of the Party, sent Polish troops to participate, together with the Russians, in the invasion of Czechoslovakia. Two years later, in December 1970, his attempt to raise the prices of basic foodstuffs led to workers' riots in Gdánsk and other cities on the Baltic coast; the use of tanks and machine guns against workers by police resulted in hundreds of dead and wounded and Gomułka was forced by the Party to step down, to be succeeded as first secretary by Edward Gierek.

In the wake of the anti-Zionist campaign and the invasion of Czechoslovakia, many intellectuals left Poland, either because they were personally attacked or because they found the political climate unbearable. Thus a new wave of emigration was added to that of 1939, contributing to the importance of émigré publications and institutions. A well-known philosopher, Leszek Kołakowski (see p. 517), moved to England where he was to work for several years on his monumental *Main Currents of Marxism* (*Główne nurty marksizmu*, 1976–1978, 3 vols.), the most thorough critical survey of Marxist philosophy ever attempted. Playwright Sławomir Mrożek (see p. 513), following publication of his open letter of protest against the invasion of Czechoslovakia, has lived in Italy and France; among his recent plays, *Vatzlav* and *Emigrés* (*Emigranci*) are the most significant, and have been performed in many translations. One of a few Polish writers exploring the themes of Jewish life in Poland and of the Holocaust, poet and novelist Henryk Grynberg (born 1937) settled in America; he published two volumes of his poems in Polish and four novels: *Jewish War* (*Żydowska wojna*, 1965), *Victory* (*Zwycięstwo*, 1969), *Ideological Life* (*Życie ideologiczne*, 1975), and *Personal Life* (*Życie osobiste*, 1979). The first was published while he was still in Poland, the last three when he was already abroad. Critic Jan Kott (see p. 516) became a professor in the United States.

In Poland, the whimsicalities of censorship favored writers who stayed away from politics and engaged in various kinds of artistic experimentation. It was a time of "linguistic poetry" that decomposed and composed anew words and sentences. Hardly comprehensible little volumes of poetry were issued by State publishing houses as a part of a general policy to placate the grumbling young. Nevertheless, probably the most durable achievements of that period belong to a few poets. Miron Białoszewski (see p. 479) developed, out of a magma of the language beaten to pulp, his peculiar style on the borderline of poetry and prose, reflecting the everyday life of the Warsaw streets. He surprised readers by his realistic report on a subject until then usually treated in a heroic manner: *Memoir of the Warsaw Uprising* (*Pamiętnik z Powstania Warszawskiego*, 1970). His language proved to be ideally adapted to his goal—to reconstruct from memory the tragic uprising of 1944 as lived through by civilians.

In her mature phase, Wisława Szymborska (see p. 485) grew to the stature of a philosophical poet, her conciseness matched only by Zbigniew Herbert (see p. 470). In spite of all the differences that separate them, they have something in common: a stoical attitude toward existence under a mask of self-irony. Such a return, after so many centuries, of stoicism as a philosophy makes one wonder.

An intensive experimentation also marked the theater. Through both the art of directing and the repertoire, Poland participated in a trend animating the theater in many countries, an animation sometimes embraced by the common name of the Second Reform, a reference to the First Reform occurring at the beginning of the century. The plays of Stanisław Ignacy Witkiewicz (see p. 414) provided exciting material for directors; Tadeusz Różewicz (see p. 462) moved from poetry to plays written in the new vein—for instance in *An Interrupted Act* (*Akt przerywany*, 1966), or in *An Old Woman as a Brooding Hen* (*Stara kobieta wysiaduje*, 1968). One of the originators of theatrical innovations, Tadeusz Kantor (born 1915) saw his persistence crowned by an international success when he produced *A Dead Class* (*Umarła klasa*, 1975). The "poor theater" of Jerzy Grotowski (born 1933) had a strong impact in several countries. Grotowski founded his Laboratory Theater in 1960 and worked steadily with his little group of actors for several years. His activity culminated in *Apocalypsis cum figuris*, 1968. The same year the International Festival of the Young Theater took place in Wrocław, Poland, at which plays from many countries were performed.

Writers coming from the former eastern provinces of Poland represented both various social backgrounds and various literary genres. Among them, Stanisław Lem from Lwów (see p. 501) achieved renown with his science fiction and then moved to another genre, essays— *Philosophy of Chance* (*Filozofia przypadku*, 1968), and *Fantasy and Futurology* (*Fantastyka i futurologia*, 1970), the latter a history of science fiction in two volumes. Tadeusz Konwicki (see p. 499) reached adolescence near the city of Wilno. His subsequent literary evolution is indicative of general changes in the mood of the country. In 1970 he was to write two novels of a violent political grotesquerie, *The Polish Complex* (*Kompleks polski*, 1979) and *A Little Apocalypse* (*Mała apokalipsa*, 1979). Brought up in Lwów, Julian Stryjkowski (born 1905), author of a novel on a small Galician Jewish town—*Voices in Darkness* (*Głosy w ciemności*, 1956)—placed the action of his *The Inn* (*Austeria*, 1966), in a similar Galician town in the summer of 1914 at the moment of the outbreak of World War I.

Melchior Wańkowicz (1892–1979) was a prolific inventor of tales based on the traditions of the Polish-Lithuanian gentry, who continued his fictionalized reminiscences after his return to Poland from abroad. He had early attempted to reconstruct the battle of Monte Cassino, basing his narrative upon testimonies of its participants, in *Battle of Monte Cassino* (*Bitwa o Monte Cassino*, 1945–1947, 3 vols.), published in Rome.

Censorship forced some authors to look for means of publishing abroad. They discovered the important role played by the émigré Literary Institute in France and its monthly *Kultura*. An author living in

Poland started to publish his novels on the Warsaw political establishment through the Literary Institute, under the pseudonym Tomasz Staliński: *Seen from Above* (*Widziane z góry*, 1967) and *Shadows in a Cave* (*Cienie w pieczarze*, 1971; written in 1969). Later he revealed his name—he was the popular liberal-Catholic columnist Stefan Kisielewski (see p. 490). Jerzy Andrzejewski (see p. 490) also became one of the authors of the Literary Institute when it issued his novel *An Appeal* (*Apelacja*, 1968), rejected by publishing houses in Poland for political reasons. Other writers followed suit and thus the distinction between Polish literature produced in exile and Polish literature produced in Poland gradually was losing its rigidity.

Among works of fiction published abroad, probably the most interesting was an "old-fashioned" novel by Józef Mackiewicz (see p. 534), *Don't Talk Out Loud* (*Nie trzeba głośno mówić*, 1969), a sort of sequel to his *A Road to Nowhere* (*Droga do nikąd*), whose action ends in 1941. During the Nazi occupation of Lithuania and Poland, 1941–1944, a maze of underground networks combat each other, working for London or Moscow. His descriptions have the power of an eyewitness report. For many Poles, Mackiewicz is a controversial figure because of his hostility to national shibboleths and his anti-Communist internationalism, but his passionate convictions give his prose a directness rarely met with in contemporary fiction. The advantages of writing without fear of censorship are visible here, as no similar vast panorama has appeared in print in Poland. Another prose writer who explores the time of war is Włodzimierz Odojewski (born 1930), whose huge panoramic novel *Snow Will Cover It Up, Will Bury It* (*Zasypie wszystko, zawieje*), unable to pass censorship, had to wait several years until it was published by the Literary Institute in 1973.

With the death of Witold Gombrowicz (see p. 432) in 1969 and the publication by the Literary Institute of his collected works, Gombrowicz's writings became recognized as classics of Polish literature. The staging in 1970 in Paris of his last play, *Operetta* (written in 1966), was a triumph. Characteristically, his books have been available in Poland only in copies smuggled from the West, even though his plays were performed in Poland and innumerable papers have been written on his work by Polish literary scholars.

The rich literary production since 1939 of Poles in exile at last found its émigré chroniclers. A basis for future research in that field is *Polish Literature Abroad, 1940–1960* (*Literatura polska na obczyźnie 1940–1960*, London, 1965, 2 vols.), edited by Tymon Terlecki. The first attempt at a general view came in the next decade: *Essays on Émigré Literature* (*Szkice o literaturze emigracyjnej*, Paris, 1978), by Maria Danilewicz-Zielińska.

THE 1970S

The 1970s were a very political decade, bearing the imprint of the events on the Baltic coast in December, 1970. The new secretary of the Party, Gierek, contrary to his predecessor who was wary about foreign loans, embarked upon a program of borrowing from the West in the hope of modernizing industry and increasing exports. For many reasons, including the world energy crisis and a heavy load imposed upon Poland by its participation in the Soviet armament program, the plan failed and the apparent boom that was due to foreign credits changed into a disaster. The inability of Party officials to oppose Soviet economic demands growing since 1975 (and which in many cases amounted to syphoning eastward borrowed Western capital) tipped the balance. An attempt to raise prices in 1976 provoked workers' riots in the city of Radom. Beatings of workers by the police and their subsequent trials on trumped-up charges incited young intellectuals to create K.O.R., Komitet Obrony Robotników (Committee for the Defense of Workers). With that event, an alliance between the intellectuals and the workers became a fact. In spite of constant harassment by the police, confinements, and searches, the new movement successfully proceeded to arouse public opinion through the clandestine periodicals and lectures of a "flying university." An independent publishing house, Nowa, though its initiators and directors were constantly tracked down by the police, gradually improved its technique and issued more and more books. At the end of the decade the causes of the incidental failures and even of the general unworkability of the system entered the realm of common knowledge. The visit of Pope John Paul II to his country in June 1979 gave to the people a sense of their unity and strength. They experienced being together at spontaneous mass rallies as a catharsis and a restoration of moral values. In July 1980 strikes over rising prices broke out in several cities. On August 16, in the Gdańsk shipyards on strike, the Interfactory Committee was created under the leadership of Lech Wałęsa. The independent union Solidarność ("Solidarity") was born, an event without precedent in Communist countries. Solidarity incarnated the social and national aspirations of the enormous majority of the Polish nation. Massive grass roots participation in it surpassed in scope the "Czech spring" of 1968. It brought to mind the historic Four Years Diet (1788–1792) with its élan and desire for a renewal. Soon the membership of Solidarity reached 10 million. The government, under pressure, recognized the new union and signed an agreement with it. During the sixteen months that followed, the government's bad faith radicalized locals of the union and produced sporadic strikes in various cities. Under the threat of a direct intervention by Moscow, the Party, weakened and divided, continuously rejected Solidarity's proposals for reform, as they would amount to sharing power and responsibility. At the same time the government made secret preparations with a view to repressive action. General Jaruzelski, made the first secretary of the Party in the summer of 1981, introduced martial law on December 13, 1981, crushed the workers' resistance with ZOMO (motorized police trained especially for that purpose), and arrested thousands of Solidarity activists, including Lech Wałęsa. Public opinion reacted to the proclaimed "state of war" with anger and dismay. Worsening economic conditions, fear of Soviet intervention, and finally the military coup prompted thousands of Poles to migrate to the West or to remain there, thus swelling the ranks of the diaspora.

The state of literature in the 1970s was largely determined by a number of writers critical of the system, who as a punishment were barred from access to State owned periodicals, publishing houses, and television. As a consequence, the Catholic press earned more importance and prestige. It attracted intellectuals who until then had been writing for Marxist publications. Traditionally, there had existed in Poland a rift between the Catholic Church and the intellectuals, going back to the intellectuals' free-masonic connections, perhaps even to their Protestant sympathies in the sixteenth century. Now a new alliance between them and the Church was in the making. In this respect, importance should be attached to *The Church, the Left, a Dialogue* (*Kościół, lewica, dialog*) by Adam Michnik, one of the leaders of the Committee for the Defense of Workers. Written in Poland and published by the Literary Institute in France in 1977, it elucidates the reasons for a rapprochement with the Church as an institution protecting the freedom and dignity of man.

With the appearance of clandestine and semi-clandestine periodicals, some of them of a high intellectual caliber, like *Record* (*Zapis*) and *Res Publica*, the weight shifted from the official literary life to those free expressions of the public opinion. Also Nowa and other independent publishing houses provided an outlet for black-listed writers and began to reprint forbidden émigré authors as well as to introduce taboo names such as that of George Orwell.

An evolution occurred, though, in the allowed publications as well. Books were appearing which analyzed the political situation under a cloak of historical studies, a device practiced previously by writers such as Jacek Bocheński (born 1926) whose *Divine Julius* (*Boski Juliusz*, 1961), a novel on Julius Caesar, and *Naso the Poet* (*Nazo poeta*, 1969), on Ovidius Naso, should be interpreted that way. The same form was practiced by Mieczysław Jastrun (see p. 408) in his volume of essays *Freedom of Choice* (*Wolność wyboru*, 1969), on Polish attitudes after the Third Partition of the country. Even more outspoken was Andrzej

Kijowski (born 1928) in his *A November Evening* (*Listopadowy wieczór*, 1972) on the era of the 1830 uprising. In *A Diabolic Pledge* (*Cyrograf*, 1971) Ludwik Flaszen (born 1930) took to task the era of Stalinism. Surprisingly, the most-discussed books of the period were literary essays and poetry: a volume of essays by the young poet and scholar Stanisław Barańczak (born 1946), *The Mistrustful and the Presumptuous* (*Nieufni i zadufani*, 1971); a volume of essays by Julian Kornhauser (born 1946) and Adam Zagajewski (born 1945), *The Undescribed World* (*Świat nieprzedstawiony*, 1974); and a new volume of Zbigniew Herbert's poems, *Mister Cogito* (*Pan Cogito*, 1974).

Poetry was undergoing a complete change of mood and style. The new generation, mistrustful both of official slogans and of experimentation for its own sake, used a linguistic approach to analyze and deride the language of propaganda. That was true of Stanisław Barańczak's poetry but also of the new poetry group Teraz ("Now") in Kraków. Its members, mostly disillusioned young Marxists (Stanisław Stabro, Julian Kornhauser, Adam Zagajewski, Wit Jaworski, Jerzy Piątkowski, Ryszard Krynicki), made a stir among contemporaries with their poetry and their rather naive manifestos in which they asked for a realistic portrayal of life in Poland, as if censorship did not exist. At the end of the decade, poetry was thoroughly politicized and satyrical in its presentation of reality through a twist given to the language. It was paralleled by some novels, like Janusz Anderman's (born 1949) *The Telephone Game* (*Zabawa w głuchy telefon*, 1977), and *Temporizing* (*Gra na zwłokę*, 1979); or Jan Komolka's (born 1947) *Escape to Heaven* (*Ucieczka do nieba*, 1980).

The victory of Solidarity had far-reaching consequences for literature: censorship practically disappeared and the three literatures—the officially allowed, the clandestine, and the émigré—were perceived and discussed as one body. The visit of the author of this book to Poland in June 1981 acquired a symbolic meaning, as it stressed the unity of Polish literature wherever it is created. During the short-lived period of freedom, an assessment of Polish authors living and publishing abroad assigned to some of them an eminent place in Polish letters. Gustaw Herling-Grudziński (see p. 525) won many admirers in Poland with his *A Diary Written at Night* (*Dziennik pisany nocą*, 1971–1980). It competed with the *Diary* (*Dziennik*) of Gombrowicz, now considered by many readers and critics as the most important work of that writer. In their turn, volumes of *Months* (*Miesiące*, 1981) by Kazimierz Brandys (see p. 499), who is now in opposition, employed a similar method of notes and reflections, though in this case they are day-to-day reactions to political realities. In the success of *My Age* (*Mój wiek*, London, 1977; translation forthcoming from the University of California Press) the posthumously published memoirs of Aleksander Wat (see p. 426), one may see a confirmation of the public's search for the truth about our century in non-fictional writings.

The 13th of December, 1981, will undoubtedly remain a sad date in the history of Poland, reminiscent of other dates of defeats in the nation's struggle for independence since the eighteenth century. In the future, as has happened so often in the past, Polish literature will probably witness an unresolved conflict between writers' commitment to the common cause of resistance and personal aspirations to express themselves as individuals.

On Polish Versification

Nothing definite can be said about the oldest rules of Polish verse, even though many literary products of the fifteenth century testify to their existence. The most typical form is what may be called an "imperfectly syllabic" verse, namely, lines of 8 syllables interspersed with lines of 6, 7, 9, 10 syllables. By analogy with some folk songs, it has been surmised that the principle was that of phrase intonation: the end of a line marked the end of a phrase. How verse was read, what was the role of the accent is, however, unknown. The accent in Polish falls upon the penultimate syllable of every word, so only one-syllable words are (but not always) oxytonic, i.e., pronounced with a stress and thus capable of being used as masculine rhymes. Yet there was a time when the accent was not stabilized; stabilization occurred but gradually. Rhymes found in the fifteenth century, grouped most often as *aa bb cc*, are also "imperfect" by later standards, and if an equivalence has to be established between, for instance, *darował* and *dał*, between *czas* and *obraz*, the question arises as to whether in performance the oxytonic endings would lose their accent, or whether the nonoxytonic endings would acquire one. Or, perhaps, the rhyming of stressed and unstressed syllables was simply accepted. Among the influences shaping the early Polish verse Czech poetry should be mentioned on the one hand and church music on the other. A medieval Easter hymn is still sung today with the stress upon the last syllables:

> Wesoły nam dzień dziś na-*stał*,
> Którego z nas każdy żą-*dał*,
> Tego dnia Chrystus zmartwych-*wstał*.
> Allelu-*ja*, Allelu-*ja*.

A translation from a Latin religious song, done around 1400, opens the history of Polish versification "systems." Three such successive systems made their appearance. The first was syllabic. Medieval Latin did not care for a quantitative verse; it used a count of syllables, and rhymes. The borrowing in question introduced into Polish poetry its most popular line: 13 syllables divided by a caesura (7 + 6). Here is the beginning of the Latin original:

Pa-tris sa-pi-en-ti-a, Ve-ri-tas di-vi-na,
Chris-tus Je-sus cap-tus est ho-ra ma-tu-ti-na.

The syllabic verse with a caesura entered into competition with older patterns and won the battle, but not before the middle of the sixteenth century was its position consolidated. A hesitancy is still noticeable in Mikołaj Rej, while in Jan Kochanowski's poetry "syllabism" is firmly established. The latter develops a great variety of models which will be used by poets of subsequent centuries. The rhymes correspond to the normal accentuation of spoken Polish.

The second system is called "syllabotonic." Accented and unaccented syllables gather themselves into units somewhat similar to quantitative "feet," thence their names: trochaic, dactylic, iambic, etc. The Polish language, because of its stable accent upon the penultimate, tends by nature to the trochee and the amphibrach; other "feet," however, are also used, with some unavoidable deviations at the beginning and the end of the line. Nothing would be more wrong than to look for a moment when the reign of the syllabic system ends and that of the "syllabotonic" system begins. "Syllabism" has remained till today a basis of Polish verse. Within that framework experimentation with "feet" was going on, particularly visible in the Renaissance period in Jan Kochanowski's poetry, then in "bourgeois lyrics" which were composed to dance tunes, later on in the classical verse of Ignacy Krasicki. As to the great poets of Romanticism, they handled both purely syllabic and "syllabotonic" verse, going as far as Mickiewicz, who applied once (in *Konrad Wallenrod*) a Polish equivalent of Greek hexameter. One can risk a thesis that "feet" serve Polish verse well only as long as they are woven into a syllabic pattern and not too obtrusively. The language does not favor a regular "beat" which, when attempted, creates monotony. The minor poets of the second half of the nineteenth century, with their preference for the "syllabotonic" line, were guilty of that abuse.

Neither can the third system, called "tonic," be clearly separated from the two previously listed. It is founded upon the number of accents in a line, not upon the count of syllables. The trouble is that the same poem can be sometimes read aloud in two ways—either with a stress upon "feet" or upon accentuated groups of words. The "tonic" system was an obvious preference of the nineteenth-century Juliusz Słowacki in his translations from Calderón and in some of his dramas in verse. Some poets at the turn of that century leaned toward it; Stanisław Wyspiański's dramas and Jan Kasprowicz's poetry are examples of its potentialities.

Coexistence of the three systems has contributed to the richness of forms in Polish poetry. What scholars term the fourth system denotes a search for rhythm not stemming from repetition either of counted syllables or of accents. That system was introduced by avant-garde schools in the beginning of our century and has been embraced by the majority of poets, particularly since World War II. As it modulates the phrase in a peculiar way in each case, adapting it to the temperament of the poet, it cannot be reduced to a formula. It has its antecedents in the past, for instance, in the period of the Baroque, when sometimes the long phrase was shaped in imitation of a biblical *verset*, and in some "free verse" of Romanticism.

Selected Bibliography

GENERAL SURVEYS AND ANTHOLOGIES

Badecki, Karol Józef, ed. *Polska liryka mieszczańska. Pieśni, tańce, padwany (Polish Bourgeois Lyrics. Songs, Dances and Pavans)*. Lwów: Towarzystwo Naukowe, Zabytki Piśmiennictwa Polskiego, 1936, 489 pp.

Borowy, Wacław, ed. *Od Kochanowskiego do Staffa. Antologia liryki polskiej (From Kochanowski to Staff. An Anthology of Polish Lyrics)*. Warsaw: Państwowy Instytut Wydawniczy, 1958, 426 pp.

Brückner, Aleksander. *Dzieje kultury polskiej (History of Polish Civilization)*. Warsaw, Kraków: Książka i Wiedza, F. Pieczątkowski, 1946–1958, four vols.

————. *Geschichte der polnischen Literatur*. 2nd ed. Leipzig: C. F. Amelung, 1909. Die Literaturen des Ostens in Einzeldarstellungen, I, 628 pp.

Budzyk, Kazimierz, and other eds. *Bibliographia literatury polskiej, "Nowy Korbut" (A Bibliography of Polish Literature, "The New Korbut")*. Warsaw: Państwowy Instytut Wydawniczy, 1963, five vols. plus vol. no. 12.

Coleman, Marion Moore, comp. *Polish Literature in English Translations: A Bibliography*. Cheshire, Conn.: Cherry Hill Books, 1963, 180 pp.

Davies, Norman. *God's Playground: A History of Poland*. New York: Columbia University Press, 1982, two vols., 605 + 725 pp.

Dłuska, Maria. *Studia z historii i teorii wersyfikacji polskiej (Studies in the History and Theory of Polish Versification)*. Kraków: Vol. 1, Polska Akademia Umiejętności, 1948, Prace Komisji Językowej, no. 33; Vol. 2, *Ibid.*, 1950, no. 35.

Dedecius, Karl, ed. and trans. *Polnische Poesie des 20 jahrhunderts*. Munich: Hanser Verlag, 1964, 236 pp.

————, comp. and trans. *Polnische Pointen*. 2nd ed. Munich: Hanser Verlag, 1962, 154 pp.

————, ed. *Polnische Prosa des 20 jahrhunderts*. Munich: Hanser Verlag, 1966, 600 pp.

Dyboski, Roman. *Periods of Polish Literary History*. The Ilchester lectures for the year 1923. London: Humphrey Milford, Oxford University Press, 1923, 163 pp.

Gerould, Daniel, ed. *Twentieth-Century Polish Avant-Garde Drama: Plays, Scenarios, Critical Documents.* Daniel and Eleanor Gerould, trans. Introduction by Daniel Gerould. Ithaca: Cornell University Press, 1977, 287 pp.

Gillon, Adam, and Krzyżanowski, Ludwik, eds. *Introduction to Modern Polish Literature. An Anthology of Fiction and Poetry.* New York: Twayne, 1964, 480 pp.

Gömöri, G. *Polish and Hungarian Poetry, 1945–1956.* Oxford: Clarendon Press, 1966, 266 pp.

Grydzewski, Mieczysław, ed. *Wiersze polskie wybrane (Selected Polish Poems)* 2nd ed. London: Orbis, 1948, 351 pp.

Holton, Milne, and Vangelisti, Paul, eds. *The New Polish Poetry.* Pittsburg: University of Pittsburg Press, 1978, 117 pp.

Jakubowski, Jan Zygmunt, ed. *Polska krytyka literacka, 1800–1918 (Polish Literary Criticism, 1800–1918).* Warsaw: Państwowe Wydawnictwo Naukowe, 1959, four vols.

————, ed. *Polska krytyka literacka, 1919–1939 (Polish Literary Criticism, 1919–1939).* Warsaw: Państwowe Wydawnictwo Naukowe, 1966, 655 pp.

Jeleński, Constantin, ed. *Anthologie de la poésie polonaise.* Paris: Éditions du Seuil, 1965, 453 pp.; Lausanne: L'Age d' Homme, 1981.

Korbut, Gabriel. *Literatura polska od początków do wojny światowej (Polish Literature From Its Beginnings to the World War).* Warsaw: Skład główny w Kasie imienia Mianowskiego, 1929–1931, four vols.

Korzeniewska, Ewa, and other eds. *Słownik współczesnych pisarzy polskich (A Dictionary of Modern Polish Writers).* Warsaw: Państwowe Wydawnictwo Naukowe, 1963, four vols.

Kridl, Manfred. *A Survey of Polish Literature and Culture.* Olga Scherer-Virski, trans. The Hague: Mouton & Co., 1956, 513 pp.

Krzyżanowski, Julian. *Historia literatury polskiej. Alegoryzm-Preromantyzm (A History of Polish Literature. Allegorism-Preromanticism).* 3rd ed. Warsaw: Państwowy Instytut Wydawniczy, 1966, 670 pp., illus.

————. *A History of Polish Literature.* Doris Ronowicz, trans. Warsaw: Polish Scientific Publishers, 1978, 807 pp.

Kuncewicz, Maria, ed. *The Modern Polish Mind. An Anthology of Stories and Essays.* Boston: Little, Brown and Co., 1962, 440 pp. Also in paperback.

Kutrzeba, Stanisław. *Historia ustroju Polski w zarysie (A History of Political Institutions in Poland in Survey).* Lwów: Gebethner i Wolff, B. Połoniecki, 1905–1917, four vols.

Lednicki, Wacław. *Life and Culture of Poland as Reflected in Polish Literature.* New York: Roy Publishers, 1944, XI, 328 pp.

Levine, Madeline G. *Contemporary Polish Poetry, 1925–1975.* Boston: Twayne Publishers, 1981, 195 pp.

Marcel, Simone. *Histoire de la littérature polonaise: Des Origines au début du XIX siècle.* Paris: La Colombe, 1957.

Matuszewski, Ryszard, and Pollak, Seweryn, eds. *Poezja polska 1914–1939 (Polish Poetry 1914–1939).* An anthology. Warsaw: Czytelnik, 1962, 898 pp.

Mayewski, Paweł, ed. *The Broken Mirror, A Collection of writings from contemporary Poland.* New York: Random House, 1958, 209 pp.

Miłosz, Czesław, ed. *Postwar Polish Poetry: An Anthology.* Garden City, New York: Doubleday, 1965, 149 pp. Expanded edition, Berkeley and Los Angeles: University of California Press, 1983, 175 pp.

Ordon, Edmond, ed. *Ten Contemporary Polish Stories.* Various trans. Introduction by Olga Scherer-Virski. Detroit: Wayne State University Press, 1958, 252 pp. Rpt. Westport, Conn.: Greenwood Press, 1974, 252 pp.

Pankowski, Marian, ed. and trans. *Anthologie de la poésie polonaise du quinzième au vingtième siècle.* Brussels: André de Rache, 1961, 140 pp.

Peterkiewicz [Pietrkiewicz], Jerzy, and Singer, Burns, eds. and trans. *Five Centuries of Polish Poetry, 1450–1950: An Anthology with Introduction and Notes.* London: Secker and Warburg, 1950, 154 pp. Rpts. London, New York: Oxford University Press, 1970, 137 pp.; Westport, Conn.: Greenwood Press, 1979, 137 pp.

Rutkowski, Jan. *Historia gospodarcza Polski do 1864 (Economic History of Poland to 1864).* Introduction by Witold Kula. Warsaw: Książka i Wiedza, 1953, 568 pp.

Scherer-Virski, Olga. *The Modern Polish Short Story.* The Hague: Mouton, 1955, 254 pp.

Segel, Harold B. *Polish Romantic Drama.* Ithaca, New York: Cornell University Press, 1977, 320 pp. Contains translations of *Forefathers' Eve, Part III*, by Adam Mickiewicz; *The Un-Divine Comedy*, by Zygmunt Krasiński; and *Fantazy*, by Juliusz Słowacki.

Taborski, Bolesław. "Polish Plays in English Translation: a bibliography," *The Polish Review,* IX, 3 (Summer 1964), pp. 63–101.

———. "Polish Plays in English Translation: a bibliography," addenda and corrigenda, *The Polish Review,* XII, 1 (Winter 1967), pp. 59–82.

Terlecki, Tymon, ed. *Literatura polska na obczyźnie 1940–1960 (Polish Literature Abroad 1940–1960).* London: B. Świderski, 1964–1965, two vols.

Tyrmand, Leopold, ed. *Explorations in Freedom: Prose, Narrative and Poetry from Kultura.* New York: Free Press, 1970, 442 pp.

———. *Kultura Essays.* New York: Free Press, 1970, 344 pp.

Williams, George Huntston, ed. *The Polish Brethren: Documentation of the History and Thought of Unitarianism in the Polish-Lithuanian Commonwealth and in the Diaspora, 1601–1685.* Harvard Theological Studies. Missoula, Montana: Scholars Press, 1980, two vols.

Wieniewska, Celina, ed. *Polish Writing Today.* Baltimore: Penguin Books, 1967, 206 pp.

Zhivov, M., and Stakheev, B., eds. *Polskaia Poeziia (Polish Poetry).* Moscow: Goslitizdat, 1963, two vols., 553 pp. (sixteenth to nineteenth centuries) plus 502 pp. (nineteenth to twentieth centuries).

THE MIDDLE AGES

Bogurodzica. Jerzy Woronczak, ed. Wrocław: Zakład Ossolineum, 1962. Polska Akademia Nauk: Instytut Badań Literackich. Biblioteka Pisarzów Polskich, ser. A, no. 1, 416 pp., facsim.

Długosz, Jan. *Roczniki czyli Kroniki sławnego Królestwa Polskiego (Annals or Chronicles of the Glorious Kingdom of Poland)*. Jan Dąbrowski, ed. Stanisław Gawęda, trans. Warsaw: Państwowe Wydawnictwo Naukowe, 1961, two vols. in one.
Jasienica, Paweł. *Polska Piastów (Poland of the Piasts)*. Wrocław: Zakład Ossolineum, 1960, 390 pp., illus.
————. *Trzej kronikarze (Three Chroniclers)*. Warsaw: Państwowy Instytut Wydawniczy, 1964.
Labuda, Gerard. *Studia nad początkami państwa polskiego (Studies on the Origin of the Polish State)*. Poznań: Księg. Akad., 1946. Biblioteka Historyczna Poznańskiego Towarzystwa Przyjaciół Nauk, I, 351 pp.
Łowmiański, Henryk. *Początki Polski; z dziejów Słowian w I tysiącleciu n.e. (The Beginnings of Poland: From the History of the Slavs in the First Millennium of Our Era)*. Warsaw: Państwowe Wydawnictwo Naukowe, 1963–1967, 3 vols.
Wojciechowski, Tadeusz. *Szkice historyczne jedenastego wieku (Historical Sketches of the Eleventh Century)*. Introduction by Aleksander Gieysztor. 3rd ed. Warsaw: Państwowy Instytut Wydawniczy, 1951, 391 pp.

THE SIXTEENTH–EIGHTEENTH CENTURIES

Borowy, Wacław. *O poezji polskiej w w. XVIII (On Polish Poetry in the Eighteenth Century)*. Kraków: Polska Akademia Umiejętności, 1948, 398 pp.
Bystroń, Jan Stanisław. *Dzieje obyczajów w dawnej Polsce (History of Morals and Manners in Old Poland)*, Wiek XVI–XVIII. Ed. changed and corrected. Warsaw: Państwowy Instytut Wydawniczy, 1960, two vols.
Dürr-Durski, Jan. *Arianie polscy w świetle własnej poezji. Zarys ideologii i wybór wierszy (The Polish Socinians in the Light of Their Own Poetry. Initiation to the Ideas and a Selection of Poems)*. Warsaw: Państw. Zakł. Wydawn. Szk., 1948, Biblioteka Polonistyczna, 319 pp.
Fabre, Jean. *Stanislas-Auguste Poniatowski et L'Europe des Lumières. Étude de cosmopolitisme*. Paris: Publication de la Faculté des lettres de L'Université de Strasbourg, 1952, 116, 746 pp.
Kochanowski, Jan. *Chants, traduits du polonais avec une introduction et un commentaire par Jacques Langlade*. Paris: Société d'édition "Les Belles Lettres," 1932, 147 pp.
————. *Dziela polskie (Polish Works)*. Julian Krzyżanowski, ed. 5th ed. Warsaw: Państwowy Instytut Wydawniczy, 1967, two vols.
————. *Izbrannye proizvedeniia*. S. S. Sovetov, ed. Leningrad: Izdatelstvo Akademii Nauk SSSR, 1960, 370 pp.
————. *Poems*. Dorothea Prall Radin, Marjorie Beatrice Peacock, and other trans. Berkeley: University of California Press, 1928, 156 pp.
————. *Poems*. Dorothea Prall Radin, trans. New York: AMS Press, 1978, 156 pp. Langlade, Jacques. *Jean Kochanowski: L'Homme, le penseur, le poète lyrique*. Paris: Les Belles Lettres, 1932, 415 pp.
Kot, Stanisław. *Socinianism in Poland: The Social and Political Ideas of the Polish Antitrinitarians in the Sixteenth and Seventeenth Centuries*. Boston: Star King Press, 1957, 226 pp.
Kott, Jan, ed. *Poezja polskiego Oświecenia: Antologia (Polish Poetry of the

Enlightenment: An Anthology). 2nd ed. Warsaw: Czytelnik, Z prac Instytut Badań Literackich, Polska Akademia Nauk, 1956, 499 pp.

Krasicki, Ignacy. *Pisma wybrane (Selected Works)*. Tadeusz Mikulski, ed. Warsaw: Państwowy Instytut Wydawniczy, 1954, four vols. Polska Akademia Nauk, Instytut Badań Literackich.

    Cazin, Paul. *Le Prince-évêque de Varmie, Ignace Krasicki, 1735–1801*. Paris: Bibliothèque polonaise, Centre d'études polonaises de Paris, 1940, 316 pp.

Krasiński, Valerian. *The Rise and Decline of the Reformation in Poland*. London: 1838–1840, two vols.

Krzyżanowski, Julian. *Proza polska wczesnego Renesansu (Polish Prose of the Early Renaissance, 1510–1550)*. Warsaw: Państwowy Instytut Wydawniczy, 1954, 553 pp., 11 pl.

Lewański, Julian, ed. *Dramaty staropolskie (Old Polish Dramas)*. Warsaw: Państwowy Instytut Wydawniczy, 1959–1963, six vols., illus.

Łoziński, Władysław. *Życie polskie w dawnych wiekach (Polish Life of Past Centuries)*. 12th ed. Kraków: Wydawnictwo Literackie, 1958, 272 pp.

Mikulski, Tadeusz. *Ze studiów nad Oświeceniem: Zagadnienia i fakty (Studies on the Enlightenment. Problems and Facts)*. Warsaw: Państwowy Instytut Wydawniczy, 1956, PAN, Instytut Badań Literackich, 553 pp., fifteen pl.

Modrzewski, Andrzej Frycz. *Opera omnia (Complete Works)*. Kazimierz Kumaniecki, ed. Warsaw: Państwowy Instytut Wydawniczy, 1953–1960, Academia scientiarum polona, five vols.

    Kot, Stanisław. *Andrzej Frycz Modrzewski: Studium z dziejów kultury polskiej w. XVI (Andrzej Frycz Modrzewski: A Study on the History of Polish Culture in the Sixteenth Century)*. Kraków: Krakowska Spółka Wydawnicza, 1923, 320 pp.

Niemcewicz, Julian Ursyn. *Under Their Vine and Fig Tree: Travels Through America in 1797–1799, 1805, with Some Further Account of Life in New Jersey*. Metchie J. E. Budka, ed. and trans. Newark, N. J.: New Jersey Historical Society, 1965, 398 pp.

Pasek, Jan Chryzostom. *Pamiętniki (Memoirs)*. Roman Pollak, ed. Warsaw: Państwowy Instytut Wydawniczy, 1963, 485 pp., illus.

————. *Les Memoirs de Jean-Chrysostome Pasek, gentilhomme polonais, 1656–1688*. Paul Cazin, trans. Paris: Les Belles Lettres, Collection de la littérature polonaise, 1929, 350 pp.

————. *Memoirs of the Polish Baroque*. Catherine S. Leach, ed. and trans. Berkeley, Calif.: University of California Press, 1976, 327 pp.

Ptaśnik, Jan. *Miasta i mieszczaństwo w dawnej Polsce (Cities and the Bourgeoisie in Old Poland)*. Introduction by Stanisław Arnold. 2nd ed. Warsaw: Państwowy Instytut Wydawniczy, 1949, 438 pp.

Sarbiewski, Maciej Kazimierz. *O poezji doskonałej czyli Wergiliusz i Homer (On Perfect Poetry or Virgil and Homer)*. Stanisław Skimina, ed. Marian Plezia, trans. Wrocław: Zakł. Ossol., PAN, Instytut Badań Literackich, Biblioteka Pisarzów Polskich, 1954, Ser. B, no. 4, 523 pp., ten pl.

Skarga, Piotr. *Pisma wszystkie (Complete Works)*. Stanisław Franciszek

Michalski-Iwieński, ed. Warsaw: Ultima Thule, 1923–1930, five vols.

Berga, Auguste. *Un Prédicateur de la cour de Pologne sous Sigismond III, Pierre Skarga: Étude sur la Pologne du XVI siècle et le Protestantisme polonais.* Paris: Société française d'imprimeries et de librairies, 1916, 376 pp.
————, ed. and trans. *Les Sermons politiques, sermons de Diète, 1597, du prédicateur du roi de Pologne Sigismond III.* Paris: Société française d'imprimeries et de librairies, 1916, 188 pp.

Smoleński, Władysław. *Przewrót umysłowy w Polsce wieku XVIII: Studia historyczne (The Intellectual Revolution in Poland in the Eighteenth Century: Historical Essays).* Introduction by Władysław Bieńkowski. 3rd ed. Warsaw: Państwowy Instytut Wydawniczy, 1949, 382 pp.

Sokołowska, Jadwiga, ed. *Poeci Renesansu (Poets of the Renaissance).* Anthology. Warsaw: Państwowy Instytut Wydawniczy, 1959, 522 pp.

Sokołowska, Jadwiga, and Żukowska, Kazimiera, eds. *Poeci polskiego Baroku (Poets of the Polish Baroque).* Anthology. Warsaw: Państwowy Instytut Wydawniczy, 1965, two vols.

Studia nad arianizmem (Research on Socinianism). Ludwik Chmaj, ed. Warsaw: Państwowe Wydawnictwo Naukowe, PAN, Instytut Socjologii i Filozofii, 1959, 563 pp.

Trembecki, Stanisław. *Wiersze wybrane (Selected Poems).* Juliusz W. Gomulicki, ed. Warsaw: Państwowy Instytut Wydawniczy, 1965, 201 pp.

Backvis, Claude. *Un Grand Poète polonais du XVIIIe siècle, Stanislas Trembecki: L'Étrange Carrière de sa vie et sa grandeur.* Paris: Bibliothèque polonaise, Centre d'études polonaises de Paris, 1937, 281 pp.

Wilbur, E. M. *A History of Unitarianism.* Cambridge: Harvard University Press, 1945–1952, two vols.

NINETEENTH-CENTURY ROMANTICISM, POSITIVISM

Askenazy, Szymon. *Napoleon a Polska (Napoleon and Poland).* Warsaw: Tow. Wydawn., 1918–1919, three vols.

Erlich, Victor. *The Double Image. Concepts of the Poet in Slavic Literatures.* Baltimore: The Johns Hopkins Press, 1964, 160 pp.

Fredro, Aleksander. *The Major Comedies of Alexander Fredro.* Harold B. Segel, trans. Princeton, N. J.: Princeton University Press, 1969, 405 pp.
————. *Pisma wszystkie (Complete Works).* Stanisław Pigoń and Kazimierz Wyka, eds. Warsaw: Państwowy Instytut Wydawniczy, 1955–1957, ten vols.

Głowacki, Aleksander. See Bolesław Prus.

Handelsman, Marceli. *Napoléon et la Pologne, 1806–1807. D'après les documents des archives nationales et des archives du Ministère des affaires étrangères.* Paris: F. Alcan, 1909, 280 pp.

Hertz, Paweł, ed. *Zbiór poetów polskich XIX w. (A Collection of Polish*

Poets of the Nineteenth Century). Warsaw: Państwowy Instytut Wydawniczy, 1959, five vols.

Krasiński, Zygmunt. *Iridion.* George Rapall Noyes, ed. Florence Noyes, trans. London: Oxford University Press, H. Milford, 1927, 281 pp. Rpt. Westport, Conn.: Greenwood, 1975, 281 pp.

————. *Pisma (Works).* Jan Czubek, ed. Jubilee ed. Kraków: Gebethner, 1912, eight vols.

————. *The Undivine Comedy.* Harriette E. Kennedy and Zofia Umińska, trans. London: G. G. Harrap; Warsaw: Książn. Polska, 1924, 111 pp. Rpt. Westport, Conn.: Greenwood, 1976, pp. 111.

————. *Die ungöttliche Komödie.* Franz Theodor Csokor, trans. Hamburg-Vienna: Zsolnay, 1959, 144 pp.

Günther, Władysław, ed. *Krasiński żywy: Książka zbiorowa wydana staraniem Związku Pisarzy Polskich na Obczyźnie (Krasiński Alive: A Symposium Published by the Association of Polish Writers Abroad).* London: B. Świderski, 1959, 314 pp.

Lednicki, Wacław, ed. *Zygmunt Krasiński, Romantic Universalist: An International Tribute.* New York: Polish Institute of Arts and Sciences in America, 1964, 228 pp.

Kukiel, Marian. *Dzieje Polski porozbiorowe 1795–1921 (A History of Poland after the Partitions).* 2nd ed. London: B. Świderski, 1963, 743 pp.

Lednicki, Wacław. *Bits of Table Talk on Pushkin, Mickiewicz, Goethe, Turgenev and Sienkiewicz.* The Hague: M. Nijhoff, International Scholars' Forum, 1956, 263 pp.

————. *Russia, Poland, and the West: Essays in Literary and Cultural History.* New York: Roy Publishers, 1954, 419 pp.

Limanowski, Bolesław. *Historia demokracji polskiej w epoce porozbiorowej (History of Polish Democracy after the Partitions).* 4th ed. Warsaw: Książka i Wiedza, 1957, two vols.

Mickiewicz, Adam. *Adam Mickiewicz, 1798–1855: Selected Poems.* Clark Mills, ed. New York: Noonday Press, 1956, 124 pp.

————. *Cours de littérature slave, professé au Collège de France.* Paris, 1860, five vols. *Pisma Adama Mickiewicza, Wydanie zupełne*: vols. 7–11.

————. *Dzieła (Works).* Julian Krzyżanowski, ed. Warsaw: Czytelnik, 1955, sixteen vols., illus.

————. *Forefathers.* Count Potocki of Montauk, trans. London: Polish Cultural Foundation, 1968, 288 pp.

————. *Konrad Wallenrod & Other Writings.* George R. Noyes, ed. Jewell Parish, trans. Westport, Conn.: Greenwood, 1975, 209 pp.

————. *Pan Tadeusz, or The Last Foray in Lithuania: A Story of Life among Polish Gentlefolk in the Years 1811 and 1812.* George Rapall Noyes, trans. London and Toronto: J. M. Dent; New York: E. P. Dutton, Everyman's Library, 1930, 354 pp.

————. *Pan Tadeusz, or the Last Foray in Lithuania.* Watson Kirkconnell, trans. Harold B. Segel, annotator. New York: Polish Institute of Arts and Sciences in America, 1962, 388 pp. Rpt. 1981, 388 pp.

————. *Pan Tadeusz, or the Last Foray in Lithuania.* Kenneth Mackenzie, trans. London: Polish Cultural Foundation, 1964; London: J. M. Dent, 1966; New York: Dutton, Everyman's Library, 1966, 291 pp., illus.

—————. *Pan Tadeusz oder die letzte Fehde im Litauen.* Herman Budden-sieg, trans. Munich: Fink Verlag, 1963, 386 pp., illus.

—————. *Pan Tadeusz.* Paul Cazin, trans. Paris: F. Alcan, 1934, 398 pp., illus.

—————. *Pan Tadeusz oder der letzte Einritt in Litauen.* Walter Panitz, trans. Reinbek: Rowohlt Verlag, 1956, 602 pp., illus.

—————. *Poems.* George Rapall Noyes, ed. Various trans. New York: Herald Square Press, 1944, 486 pp.

—————. *Selected Poems.* Clark Mills, ed. W. H. Auden and others, trans. New York: Voyages Press, 1957, 84 pp.

—————. *Sobranie Sochinenii.* D. D. Blagoi and others, eds.; M. Rylskii, chief ed. Moscow: Gos. Izd-vo Khudozhestvennoi Literatury, 1948–1954, five vols., illus.

—————. *La Tribune des Peuples.* Paris: E. Flammarion, 1907, 413 pp.

Adam Mickiewicz: Księga w stulecie zgonu. The centenary volume. London: Pol. Tow. Nauk, 1958, 539 pp.

Adam Mickiewicz, 1798–1855: In Commemoration of the Centenary of His Death. Paris: UNESCO, 1955, 277 pp.

Bugelski, B. R., ed. *Mickiewicz and the West: A Symposium.* Buffalo, N.Y.: The University of Buffalo, 1956, 75 pp.

Davie, Donald. *The Forests of Lithuania: A Poem.* Hessle, Yorkshire: Marvel Press, 1959, 62 pp.

Kridl, Manfred, ed. *Adam Mickiewicz, Poet of Poland: A Symposium.* New York: Columbia University Press, Columbia Slavic Studies, 1951, 286 pp.

Lednicki, Wacław, ed. *Adam Mickiewicz in World Literature: A Symposium.* Berkeley: University of California Press, 1956, 626 pp.

—————. *Pushkin's "Bronze Horseman": The Story of a Masterpiece.* With an appendix including, in English, Mickiewicz's "Digression," Pushkin's "Bronze Horseman," and other poems. Berkeley: University of California Press, 1955, 163 pp.

Levkovich, I. L., and other eds. *Adam Mickiewicz v russkoi pechati 1825–1955.* Moscow: Akademiia Nauk, 1957, 599 pp.

Scheps, Samuel. *Adam Mickiewicz, ses affinités juives.* Paris: Les Éditions Nagel, 1964, 103 pp.

Welsh, David. *Adam Mickiewicz.* New York: Twayne, World Authors Series, 1966, 168 pp.

Weintraub, Wiktor. *Literature as Prophecy: Scholarship and Martinist Poetics in Mickiewicz's Parisian Lectures.* The Hague: Mouton, 1959, 78 pp.

—————. *The Poetry of Adam Mickiewicz.* The Hague: Mouton, Slavistic Printings and Reprintings, No. 2, 1954, 302 pp.

Norwid, Cyprian. *Dzieła zebrane (Collected Works).* Juliusz W. Gomulicki, ed. Warsaw: Państwowy Instytut Wydawniczy, 1966, two vols. Vol. I Poems, 995 pp.; vol. II Commentary, 1087 pp.

—————. *Letters.* Jerzy Pietrkiewicz, trans. *Twelve Poems.* Christine Brooke-Rose, trans. Rome: Estratto, Botthege Oscure, No. 22, 1958, pp. 178–199.

—————. *Le Stigmate.* Paul Cazin, trans. Paris: La Nouvelle Revue Française, Collection Polonaise, VI, 1932, 222 pp.

Folejewski, Zbigniew. "C. K. Norwid's Prose and the Poetics of the Short Story," in *American Contributions to the Fifth International*

Congress of Slavists, Vol. II: *Literary Contributions*. The Hague: Mouton, 1963, pp. 115–128.

Kliger, George, and Albrecht, Robert C. "A Polish Poet on John Brown," *The Polish Review*, VIII, 3 (Summer 1963), pp. 80–85.

Potocki, Jan. *The Saragossa Manuscript: A Collection of Weird Tales*. Roger Caillois, ed. Elisabeth Abbott, trans. New York: Orion Press, 1960, 233 pp.

——. *New Decameron*. Elisabeth Abbott, trans. New York: Orion Press, Grossman, 1966, 433 pp.

Prus, Bolesław. (Głowacki, Aleksander, *pseud*.) *L'Avant-poste*. Maria Rakowska, trans. 8th ed. Paris: Gallimard, 1930. Collection polonaise, 1, 301 pp.

——. *The Doll*. David Welsh, trans. New York: Twayne, 1972; New York: Hippocrene, 1972, 702 pp.

——. *The Pharao and the Priest: An Historical Novel of Ancient Egypt*. Jeremiah Curtin, trans. London: S. Low, Maraton, 1910, 696 pp.

——. *Der Pharao*. Alfred Loepfe, trans. Freiburg und Olten: Walter, 1956, 651 pp.

——. *Pharao*. Kurt Harrer, trans. 8th ed. Berlin: Aufbau-Verlag, 1959, 723 pp.

——. *Die Puppe*. Kurt Harrer, trans. 2nd ed. Berlin: Aufbau-Verlag, 1954, 874 pp.

——. *La Poupée*. Simone Deligne, Wenceslas Godlewski, Michel Marcq, trans. Paris: Del Duca, 1963, Collection UNESCO d'oeuvres représentatives, two vols.

——. *Sochineniia*. Moscow: Gosudarstvennoe Izdatelstvo Khudozhestvennoi Literatury, 1955, five vols.

Sienkiewicz, Henryk. *The Deluge: An Historical Novel of Poland, Sweden and Russia* (A Sequel to *With Fire and Sword*). Jeremiah Curtin, trans. Boston: Little, Brown, 1928, two vols. Rpt. St. Clair Shore, Mich.: Scholarly Press, 1970; New York: AMS Press, 1971.

——. *Dzieła* (*Works*). Julian Krzyżanowski, ed. Warsaw: Państwowy Instytut Wydawniczy, 1948–1955, 60 vols.

——. *Hania*. Jeremiah Curtin, trans. Plainview, N. Y.: Books for Libraries, 1973, 551 pp.

——. *Pan Michael: An Historical Novel of Poland, the Ukraine, and Turkey* (A Sequel to *With Fire and Sword* and *The Deluge*). Jeremiah Curtin, trans. London: J. M. Dent, 1901, 527 pp. Rpt. Westport, Conn.: Greenwood, 1968.

——. *Portrait of America: Letters*. Charles Morley, ed. and trans. New York: Columbia University Press, 1959, 300 pp. illus.

——. *Quo Vadis?* C. J. Jogarth, trans. London: J. M. Dent, 1960; New York: E. P. Dutton, Everyman's Library 970, 1960, 448 pp.

——. *Quo Vadis?* Jeremiah Curtin, trans. New York: Airmont, 1969, 541 pp.

——. *Selected Tales*. Miami: American Institute of Polish Culture, 1975. A collection of short stories.

——. *Tales*. Monica Mary Gardner, ed. London: J. M. Dent, 1946; New York: E. P. Dutton, Everyman's Library 871, 1946, 332 pp.

——. *The Teutonic Knights. An Historical Novel*. Edinburgh: A. Tyszkiewicz, 1943, 728 pp.

——. *Western Septet: Seven Stories of the American West*. Marion

Moore Coleman, ed. and trans. Cheshire, Conn.: Cherry Hill, 1963, 161 pp.

———. *With Fire and Sword: An Historical Novel of Poland and Russia.* Jeremiah Curtin, trans. Boston: Little, Brown, 1898, 779 pp.

Kosko, Maria. *Un "Best-Seller" 1900.* Paris: Librairie Jose Corti, 1960, 185 pp.

Lednicki, Wacław. *Henryk Sienkiewicz: A Retrospective Synthesis.* The Hague: Mouton, Slavistic Printings and Reprintings, 1960, 81 pp.

Słowacki, Juliusz. *Dzieła wszystkie (Complete Works).* Juliusz Kleiner, ed. Wrocław: Zakład Ossolineum, 1952–1960, fourteen vols.

———. *Anhelli.* Dorothea Prall Radin, trans. George Rapall Noyes, ed. London: Allen & Unwin, Select Library of Polish Authors, 1930, 118 pp.

———. *La Genèse par l'esprit.* S. Dunin Karwicki, trans. Varsovie: J. Mortkowicz, 1926, fifty-five pls.

———. *Izbrannye sochineniia.* M. Rylskii, ed. Moscow: Gosudarstvennoe Izdatelstvo Khudozhestvennoi Literatury, 1960, two vols.

Bourilly, Jean. *La Jeunesse de Jules Słowacki (1809–1833): La Vie et les oeuvres.* Paris: A. G. Nizet, 1960, 502 pp.

Folkierski, Władysław, Giergielewicz, Mieczysław, and Stroński, Stanisław, eds. *Juliusz Słowacki, 1809–1849.* The Century Volume. London: The Polish Research Centre, 1951, 448 pp.

"Jules Słowacki (1809–1849)," *Revue des Sciences Humaines,* Fasc. 102, April–June 1961.

Kridl, Manfred. *The Lyric Poems of Juliusz Słowacki.* The Hague: Mouton, Contributions to the History of Slavic Literature and Culture, 1958, 77 pp.

Żabicki, Zbigniew, comp. Lewicka Jadwiga, ed. *Polish Short Stories.* Warsaw: Polonia Publishing House, 1958, 323 pp.

"YOUNG POLAND"

Brzozowski, Stanisław. *Dębina. Sam wśród ludzi (Oakwood. Alone Among Men).* Kraków: Wydawnictwo Literackie, 1957, 484 pp.

———. *Idee: wstęp do filozofii dojrzałości dziejowej (Ideas: Introduction to the Philosophy of Historical Maturity).* Lwów: B. Połoniecki, 1910, 503 pp.

———. *Legenda Młodej Polski: Studia o strukturze duszy kulturalnej (The Legend of Young Poland: Studies on the Structure of a Cultural Phase).* Lwów: B. Połoniecki, 2nd ed. 1910, 594 pp.

Miłosz, Czesław. "A Controversial Polish Writer: Stanisław Brzozowski," in *California Slavic Studies,* Vol. II, pp. 53–95. Berkeley: University of California Press, 1963.

Irzykowski, Karol. *Pałuba: Sny Marii Dunin (The Hag: Dreams of Maria Dunin).* Warsaw: Czytelnik, 1957, 425 pp.

Leśmian, Bolesław. *Poezje (Poems).* Warsaw: Państwowy Instytut Wydawniczy, 1965, 566 pp.

Przybyszewski, Stanisław. *Homo Sapiens.* Thomas Seltzer, trans. New York: AMS Press, 1970, 400 pp.

Herman, Maxime. *Un Sataniste polonais, Stanislas Przybyszewski: De 1868 à 1900.* Paris: Les Belles Lettres, 1939, 462 pp.

Reymont, Władysław. *The Peasants. A Tale of Our Own Times.* Michael H. Dziewicki, trans. New York: A. A. Knopf, 1942, four vols.

Wyka, Kazimierz. *Modernizm polski* (*Polish Modernism*). Kraków: Wydawnictwo Literackie, 1959, 338 pp.

Wyspiański, Stanisław. *Dzieła zebrane* (*Collected Works*). Leon Płoszewski, ed. Kraków: Wydawnictwo Literackie, 1958–1960, thirteen vols.

Backvis, Claude. *Le Dramaturge Stanislas Wyspianski.* Paris: Presses Universitaires de France, Université Libre de Bruxelles, Travaux de la Faculté de Philosophie et Lettres, 1952, 387 pp.

Żeromski, Stefan. *Ashes.* Helen Stankiewicz Zand, trans. New York: A. A. Knopf, 1928, two vols.

————. *Utwory wybrane* (*Selected Works*). 4th ed. Warsaw: Czytelnik, 1964, five vols.

FROM 1918 UNTIL TODAY

Andrzejewski, Jerzy. *The Appeal, A Novel.* Celina Wieniewska, trans. Preface by Jan Kott. Indianapolis: Bobbs-Merrill Co.; London: Weidenfeld and Nicolson, 1971, 118 pp.

————. *Ashes and Diamonds.* D. F. Welsh, trans. London: Weidenfeld and Nicolson, 1962, 238 pp. Rpt. New York: Penguin Books, 1980, 238 pp.

————. *The Gates of Paradise.* James Kirkup, trans. London: Weidenfeld and Nicolson, 1963, 157 pp. Rpt. London: Panther, 1967, 125 pp.

————. *He Cometh Leaping upon the Mountains.* Celina Wieniewska, trans. London: Weidenfeld and Nicolson, 1965, 190 pp. Rpt. London: Panther, 1968, 187 pp.

————. *The Inquisitors.* Konrad Syrop, trans. New York: A. A. Knopf, 1960, 158 pp. Rpt. Westport, Conn.: Greenwood Press, 1976, 158 pp.

————. *A Sitter for a Satyr.* Celina Wieniewska, trans. New York: Dutton, 1965, 190 pp.

Białoszewski, Miron. *A Memoir of the Warsaw Uprising.* Madeline Levine, ed. and trans. Ann Arbor, Michigan: Ardis, 1977, 234 pp.

————. *The Revolution of Things: Selected Poems.* Andrzej Busza and Bogdan Czaykowski, trans. and introd. Washington: Charioteer Press, 1974, 36 pp.

Bocheński, Jacek. *Göttlicher Julius. Aufzeichnungen eines Antiquars.* Walter Tiel, trans. Munich: Ehrenwirth, 1962, 256 pp.

Borowski, Tadeusz. *Le Monde de Pierre.* Erik Veaux, trans. Paris: Calmann-Lévy, 1964, 322 pp.

————. *Die Steinerne Welt.* Vera Cerny, trans. Munich: Piper Verlag, 1963, 280 pp.

————. *This Way for the Gas, Ladies and Gentlemen and Other Stories.* Barbara Vedder, ed. and trans. New York: The Viking Press, 1967, 160 pp. Rpt. Introduction by Jan Kott, New York: Penguin Books, 1976, 180 pp.

Brandys, Kazimierz. *A Question of Reality.* Isabel Burzun, trans. from the French. New York: C. Scribner's Sons, 1980, 180 pp.; London: Blond & Briggs Ltd., 1981, 180 pp.
————. *Sons and Comrades.* D. J. Welsh, trans. New York: Grove Press, 1961, 127 pp. paperback.
Breza, Tadeusz. *Das eherne Tor; römische Aufzeichnungen.* Peter Lachmann, trans. Berlin: Luchterhand, 196–, 610 pp.
Brycht, Andrew. *Zoom: A Novel.* Kevin Windle, trans. Toronto: Simon & Pierre, 1978, 154 pp.
Buczkowski, Leopold. *Black Torrent.* David Welsh, trans. Cambridge, Mass.: M.I.T. Press, 1969, 200 pp.
Burzyński, Tadeusz, and Osiński, Zbigniew. *Grotowski's Laboratory.* Bolesław Taborski, trans. Warsaw: Interpress, 1979, 147 pp.
Dąbrowska, Maria. *Nachte und Tage.* Leo Lasinski, trans. Berlin: Rutten and Loewing, 1955–1958, 3 vols.; Karlsruhe: Stahlberg, 749 pp.
————. *Pisma wybrane (Selected Works).* Warsaw: Czytelnik, 1956, three vols.
————. *A Village Wedding, and Other Stories.* Warsaw: Polonia, 1957, 215 pp.

Folejewski, Zbigniew. *Maria Dąbrowska.* New York: Twayne, World Authors Series, 1967, 123 pp.

Dygat, Stanisław. *Cloak of Illusion.* David Welsh, trans. Cambridge, Mass.: M.I.T. Press, 1969, 172 pp.
Gałczyński, Konstanty Idelfons. *Wybór poezji (Selected Poems).* Wrocław: Ossolineum, Biblioteka Narodowa, Seria 1, no. 189, 1967, 421 pp.
Gombrowicz, Witold. *Berliner Notizen.* Walter Tiel, trans. Pfullingen: Neske, 1965, 131 pp.
————. *Cosmos.* George Sédir, trans. Paris: Denoël, "Les Lettres Nouvelles," 1966, 188 pp.
————. *Cosmos.* Eric Mosbacher, the English version from the French and German trans. London: MacGibbon & Kee; New York: Grove Press, 1967, 166 pp.
————. *Ferdydurke.* Eric Mosbacher, trans. London: MacGibbon & Kee; New York: Harcourt, Brace & World, 1961, 272 pp. 2nd ed., New York: Grove Press, 1967, 272 pp.
————. *A Kind of Testament.* Dominique de Roux, ed. Alastair Hamilton, trans. Philadelphia, Penn.: Temple University Press; London: Calder & Boyars, 1973, 158 pp.; London: M. Boyars Merrimack Book Service, 1981, 158 pp.
————. *Indizien.* Walter Tiel, trans. Pfullingen: Neske, 1965, 186 pp.
————. *The Marriage.* Louis Iribarne, trans. New York: Grove Press, 1969, 158 pp.; London: Calder & Boyars, 1970, 153 pp.
————. *Operetta.* Louis Iribarne, trans. London: Calder & Boyars, 1971, 108 pp.
————. *Pornografia.* Alastair Hamilton, trans. London: Calder & Boyars, 1966, 160 pp.; New York: Grove Press, 1967, 191 pp.
————. *Possessed or the Secret of Myslotch.* J. A. Underwood and M. Boyars, trans. London: Merrimack Book Service, 1981, 221 pp.
————. *Princess Ivona.* Krystyna Griffith-Jones and Catherine Robins, trans. London: Calder & Boyars, 1969, 70 pp.
————. *Ivona Princess of Burgundia.* Krystyna Griffith-Jones and Catherine Robins, trans. New York: Grove Press, 1969, 83 pp.

————. *Yvonne. Die Trauung. 2 Dramen.* Heinrich Kunstman and Walter Tiel, trans. Frankfurt: S. Fischer, 1964, 194 pp.

————. *Yvonne, princesse de Bourgogne, et Le Marriage (Théâtre).* Paris: Julliard, "Les Lettres Nouvelles," 1965.

————. *Das Tagebuch des Witold Gombrowicz.* Walter Tiel, trans. Pfullingen: Neske, 1961, 402 pp.

————. *Three Novels: Ferdydurke, Pornografia, and Cosmos.* New York: Grove Press, 1978, 272, 191, 166 pp.

————. *Trans-Atlantic.* Walter Tiel, trans. Pfullingen: Neske, 1964, 158 pp.

Kurczaba, Alex. *Gombrowicz and Frisch. Aspects of the Literary Diary.* Bonn: Bouvier Verlag, 1980, 197 pp.

Grotowski, Jerzy. *Towards a Poor Theatre.* Eugenio Barba, ed. Preface by Peter Brook. Touchstone Books, 1970, 218 pp.; Eyre Spottiswood: Eyre Methuen Drama Books, 1976, 218 pp.

Grynberg, Henryk. *Child of the Shadows, Including the Grave.* London: Vallentine, Mitchell, 1969, 127 pp.

Hagenau, Gerda, ed. *Polen Erzählt.* Frankfurt am Main-Hamburg: Fischer Bucherei, 1961, 188 pp., paperback.

Harasymowicz, Jerzy. *Genealogy of Instruments.* Catherine Leach and Seymour Mayne, trans. Ottawa: Valley Editions, 1974.

————. *Planting Beeches.* Victor Contoski, trans. New York: New Rivers Press, 1974.

Herbert, Zbigniew. *Gedichte aus zehn jahren 1956–1966.* Karl Dedecius, trans. Frankfurt am Main: Suhrkamp Verlag, 1967, 194 pp.

————. *Selected Poems.* Czesław Miłosz and Peter Dale Scott, trans. London: Penguin Books, Penguin Modern European Poets, 1968, 139 pp.

————. *Selected Poems.* John and Bogdana Carpenter, trans. and introd. London: Oxford University Press, 1977, 82 pp.

Herling, Gustaw. *The Island, Three Tales.* Ronald Strom, trans. Cleveland and New York: The World Publishing Co., 1967, 151 pp.

————. *A World Apart.* Joseph Marek, trans. New York: Roy Publishers, 1951, 262 pp., illus.

Hłasko, Marek. *The Eighth Day of the Week.* Norbert Guterman, trans. New York: Dutton, 1958, 129 pp.; London: Allen & Unwin, 1959, 127 pp. Rpt. Westport, Conn.: Greenwood Press, 1975, 128 pp.

————. *The Graveyard.* Norbert Guterman, trans. New York: Dutton, 1959, 126 pp. Rpt. Westport, Conn.: Greenwood Press, 1975, 126 pp.

————. *Next Stop—Paradise.* Norbert Guterman, trans. New York: Dutton, 1960, 250 pp.

————. *Next Stop—Paradise and The Graveyard: Two Novels.* Norbert Guterman, trans. London: Heinemann, 1961, 311 pp.

Hostowiec, Paweł (Stempowski, Jerzy, *pseud.*). *Eseje dla Kassandry (Essays for Cassandra).* Paris: Instytut Literacki, 1961, 310 pp.

Iwaszkiewicz, Jarosław. *Der Höhenflug.* Kurt Harrer, trans. Frankfurt am Main: Suhrkamp Verlag, 1964, 109 pp.

————. *Der Kongress in Florenz: Die Mädchen vom Wilkohof. 2 Erzahlungen.* Kurt Harrer, trans. Leipzig: Ph. Reclam, 1959, 213 pp.

————. *Die Liebenden von Marona.* Klaus Dietrich Staemmler, trans. Munich: Lanfen/Müller, 1962, 336 pp.

————. *Mère Jeanne des Anges. Roman.* George Lisowski, trans. Paris: R. Laffont, 1959, 207 pp.

Jordan, Zbigniew A. *Philosophy and Ideology: The Development of Philosophy and Marxism-Leninism in Poland Since the Second World War.* Dordrecht, Holland: D. Reidel Publishing Co., 1963, 600 pp.

Kołakowski, Leszek. *The Devil and Scripture.* London: Oxford University Press, 1973, 150 pp.

————. *Main Currents of Marxism.* London: Oxford University Press, 1978, two vols.

Konwicki, Tadeusz. *The Anthropos-Spectre-Beast.* George and Audry Korwin-Rodziszewski, trans. New York: S. Phillips, 1977, 201 pp.

————. *A Dreambook for Our Time.* David Welsh, trans. Cambridge, Mass.: M.I.T. Press, 1969, 282 pp.; with an introduction by Leszek Kołakowski, New York: Penguin Books, 1976, 282 pp.

————. *Modernes Traumbuch: Roman.* Peter Lachmann, trans. Munich: Biederstein, 1964, 364 pp.

————. *The Polish Complex.* Richard Lourie, trans. New York: Farrar, Straus, Giroux, 1982, 211 pp.

Korczak, Janusz. *Ghetto Diary.* New York: Holocaust Library, 1978, 191 pp.

Kott, Jan. *The Eating of the Gods: An Interpretation of Greek Tragedy.* Bolesław Taborski and Edward J. Czerwiński, trans. New York: Vintage Books, 1974, 334 pp.

————. *Shakespeare Our Contemporary.* Bolesław Taborski, trans. New York: Doubleday, 1964, 241 pp.

Krzyżanowski, Julian. *A History of Polish Literature.* Doris Ronowicz, trans. Warsaw: PWN-Polish Scientific Publishers, 1978, 807 pp.

Kuncewiczowa, Maria S. *The Conspiracy of the Absent: A Novel.* Maurice Michael and Harry Stevens, trans. New York: Roy, 195–, 349 pp.; London: Hutchinson, 1950, 349 pp.

————. *The Forester: A Novel.* H. C. Stevens, trans. New York: Roy, 1954, 207 pp.; London: Hutchinson, 1954, 207 pp.

————. *The Keys: A Journey through Europe at War.* London, New York: Hutchinson International Authors, 1945[?], 176 pp.

————. *The Olive Grove.* New York: Walker, 1963, 240 pp.

————. *The Stranger: A Novel.* New York: L. B. Fischer, 1945, 224 pp.; B. W. A. Massey, trans. London: Hutchinson International Authors, 1947, 172 pp.

Lec, Stanisław J. *Unkempt Thoughts.* Jacek Galazka, trans. Introduction by Clifton Fadiman. New York: St. Martin's Press, 1962, 160 pp.

————. *More Unkempt Thoughts.* Jacek Galazka, trans. New York: Funk and Wagnalls, 1968, 1969, 60 pp.

Lem, Stanisław. *The Chain of Chance.* Louis Iribarne, trans. New York: Harcourt Brace Jovanovich, A Helen and Kurt Wolff Book, 1975, 179 pp.; London: Secker and Warburg, 1978, 119 pp.

————. *The Cosmic Carnival of Stanisław Lem: An Anthology of Entertaining Stories by the Modern Master of Science Fiction.* Michael Kandel, ed. and comp. New York: Continuum, 1981, 271 pp.

————. *The Cyberiad: Fables for the Cybernetic Age.* Michael Kandel, trans. New York: Seabury Press; London: Secker and Warburg, 1975, 295 pp.

————. *The Futurological Congress (from the Memoirs of Ijon Tichy).* Michael Kandel, trans. London: Secker and Warburg, 1975, 149 pp.; New York: Avon Books, 1976, 142 pp.

————. *The Investigation.* Adele Milch, trans. New York: Seabury Press, 1974, 216 pp.; New York: Avon Books, 1976, 189 pp.

————. *The Invincible.* Wendayne Ackerman, trans. (From the German.) New York: Seabury Press, 1973, 183 pp.; New York: Ace Books, 1975, 223 pp.; New York: Penguin Books, 1976, 187 pp.

————. *Memoirs Found in a Bathtub.* Michael Kandel and Christine Rose, trans. New York: Seabury Press, 1973, 188 pp.; New York: Avon Books, 1976, 192 pp.

————. *Mortal Engines.* Michael Kandel, trans. and introduction. New York: Seabury Press, 1977, 239 pp.

————. *More Tales of Pirx the Pilot.* Louis Iribarne, trans. New York, London: Harcourt Brace Jovanovich, A Helen and Kurt Wolff Book, 1982, 216 pp.

————. *A Perfect Vacuum.* Michael Kandel, trans. Mount Kisco, N. Y.: Futura Publications, 1978, 275 pp.; New York: Harcourt Brace Jovanovich, 1979, 229 pp.; London: Secker and Warburg, 1979, 229 pp.

————. *Return from the Stars.* Barbara Marszal and Frank Simpson, trans. New York: Harcourt Brace Jovanovich, 1980, 247 pp.

————. *Solaris.* Joanna Kilmartin and Steve Cox, trans. (From the French.) New York: Walker, 1970, 216 pp.; London: Faber and Faber, 1971, 216 pp.

————. *The Star Diaries.* Michael Kandel, trans. New York: Seabury Press, 1976, 275 pp.; London: Secker and Warburg, 1976, 275 pp.; New York: Avon Books, 1977, 321 pp.

————. *Tales of Pirx the Pilot.* Helen Wolff, ed. Louis Iribarne, trans. New York: Harcourt Brace Jovanovich, 1979, 206 pp.

Mackiewicz, Józef. *Road to Nowhere.* Lew Sapieha, trans. London: Collins and Harvill Press, 1963, 381 pp.

Miłosz, Czesław. *Une autre Europe.* Georges Sédir, trans. Paris: Gallimard, "Connaissance de Soi," 1964, 302 pp.

————. *Bells in Winter (Poems).* The author and Lillian Vallee, trans. New York: Ecco Press, 1978; London: Carcanet Press, 1980, 71 pp.

————. *The Captive Mind.* Jane Zielonko, trans. New York: A. A. Knopf, 1953, 251 pp.; paperback, Vintage Books, 1955; New York: Random House, 1981, 215 pp.

————. *Emperor of the Earth: Modes of Eccentric Vision (Essays).* Berkeley: University of California Press, 1977, 253 pp.

————. *Gedichte.* Karl Dedecius, trans. Frankfurt: Suhrkamp Verlag, 1982.

————. *The Issa Valley,* Louis Iribarne, trans. London: Sidgwick and Jackson; New York: Farrar, Straus & Giroux, 1981, 288 pp.

————. *Lied vom Weltende. Gedichte.* Karl Dedecius, trans. Cologne: Kiepenheuer and Witsch, 1966, 73 pp.

————. *Native Realm: A Search for Self-Definition.* Catherine S. Leach, trans. New York: Doubleday and Co., 1968; Berkeley: University of California Press, 1981, 300 pp.; London: Carcanet Press, 1981, 300 pp.; London: Sidgwick and Jackson, 1981, 300 pp.

————. *La Prise du pouvoir.* Jeanne Hersch, trans. Paris: Gallimard, "Du Monde Entier," 1953, 288 pp.

————. *The Seizure of Power.* Celina Wieniewska, trans. New York: Criterion Books, 1955; New York: Farrar, Straus & Giroux, 1982, 245 pp.

————. *Selected Poems.* New York: Ecco Press, 1981, 129 pp.

—————. *Sur les bords de l'Issa*. Jeanne Hersch, trans. Paris: Gallimard, "Du Monde Entier," 1956, 330 pp.

—————. *Tal der Issa. Roman*. Maryla Reifenberg, trans. Cologne-Berlin: Kiepenheuer and Witsch, 1957, 273 pp.

—————. *The Usurpers [The Seizure of Power]*. Celina Wieniewska, trans. London: Faber and Faber, 1955, 222 pp.

—————. *Utwory poetyckie (Poems)*. Ann Arbor, Mich.: Michigan Slavic Publications, 1977, 401 pp.

—————. *Visions from San Francisco Bay*. Richard Lourie, trans. New York: Farrar, Straus & Giroux, 1982, 226 pp.

—————. *West und Östliches Gelände*. Maryla Reifenberg, trans. Cologne-Berlin: Kiepenheuer and Witsch, n.d., 340 pp.

—————. *Wiersze (Poems)*. London: Oficyna Poetów i Malarzy, 1967, 340 pp.

Mrożek, Sławomir. *The Elephant*. Konrad Syrop, trans. New York: Grove Press, Evergreen Black Cat Book (paperback), 1965, 176 pp.; Westport, Conn.: Greenwood, 1975, 176 pp.

—————. *Six Plays*. Nicholas Bethell, trans. New York: Grove Press, 1967; London: Cape, 1968, 190 pp., paperback.

—————. *Striptease, Repeat Performance, and Three Prophets: Three Plays*. New York: Grove Press, 1972, 166 pp.

—————. *Tango: A Play in Three Acts*. Ralph Manheim and Teresa Dzieduszycka, trans. New York: Grove Press, 1968, 107 pp.

—————. *The Ugupu Bird*. Konrad Syrop, trans. London: Macdonald, 1968, 170 pp.

—————. *Vatzlav: A Play in 77 Scenes*. Ralph Manheim, trans. New York: Grove Press, 1970, 107 pp.; London: Cape, 1972, 107 pp.

Różewicz, Tadeusz. *The Card Index, and Other Plays*. Adam Czerniawski, trans. London: Calder & Boyars, 1969, 140 pp.

—————. *Faces of Anxiety: Poems*. Adam Czerniawski, trans. Chicago: Swallow Press, 1969, 63 pp.; London: Rapp and Whiting, 1969, 64 pp.

—————. *Formen der Unruhe*. Karl Dedecius, ed. and trans. Munich: Hanser Verlag, 1965, 112 pp.

—————. *Selected Poems*. Adam Czerniawski, trans. and introd. Harmondsworth, Baltimore: Penguin, 1976, 140 pp.

—————. *"The Survivor" and Other Poems*. Magnus J. Krynski and Robert A. Maguire, trans. and introd. Princeton, N. J.: Princeton University Press, 1976, 160 pp.

—————. *Unease*. Victor Contoski, trans. St. Paul, Minn.: New Rivers Press; Kensington, California: Small Press Distribution, 1980, 156 pp.

—————. *The Witnesses and Other Plays*. Adam Czerniawski, trans. London: Calder & Boyars, 1970, 136 pp.

Rudnicki, Adolf. *Ascent to Heaven*. H. C. Stevens, trans. London: Dobson, 1951, 203 pp.

—————. *The Dead and the Living Sea and Other Stories*. Jadwiga Zwolska, trans. Wrocław: Polonia, 1957, 419 pp.

Schulz, Bruno. *The Street of Crocodiles*. Celina Wieniewska, trans. New York: Walker, 1963, 159 pp. Rpt. Penguin Books, London, 1977, 160 pp.

—————. *Die Zimtläden und alle anderen Erzälungen*. Josef Hahn, trans. Munich: Hanser Verlag, 1965, 352 pp.

Straszewicz, Czesław. *Turyści z bocianich gniazd* (*Tourists from Crow's Nests*). Paris: Instytut Literacki, 1953, 254 pp.

Stryjkowski, Julian. *The Inn*. Celina Wieniewska, trans. New York: Harcourt Brace Jovanovich, 1971, 1972; London: Barrie and Jenkins, 1972, 205 pp.

Szymborska, Wisława. *Sounds, Feelings, Thoughts: Seventy Poems*. Magnus J. Krynski and Robert A. Maguire, trans. and introd. Princeton, N. J.: Princeton University Press, 1981, 215 pp.

Tuwim, Julian. *The Dancing Socrates and Other Poems*. Adam Gillon, trans. New York: Twayne, 1971.

————. *Wiersze wybrane* (*Selected Poems*). Wrocław: Ossolineum, Biblioteka Narodowa, Ser. 1, no. 184, 311 pp.

Vincenz, Stanisław de. *On the High Uplands; sagas, songs, tales, and legends of the Carpathians*. H. C. Stevens, trans. New York: Roy, 1955, 344 pp., illus.

Wańkowicz, Melchior. *Three Generations*. Krystyna Cekalska, trans. Toronto: Canadian-Polish Research Institute in Canada, 1973, 418 pp.

Wat, Aleksander. *Mediterranean Poems*. Czesław Miłosz, ed. and trans. Ann Arbor: Ardis, 1977, 58 pp.

Wierzyński, Kazimierz. *Selected Poems*. Clark Mills and Ludwik Krzyżanowski, eds. New York: Voyages Press, 1969, 45 pp.

Wirth, Andrzej, ed. *Modernes Polnisches Theater*. Neuwied and Berlin: Herman Luchterhand, 1967, two vols.

Witkiewicz, Stanisław Ignacy. *Beelzebub Sonata: Plays, Essays, Documents*. Daniel Gerould and Jadwiga Kosicka, eds. and trans. New York: Performing Arts Journal Publications, 1980, 183 pp.

————. *Dramaty* (*Dramas*). Warsaw: Państwowy Instytut Wydawniczy, 1962, two vols.

————. *Insatiability: A Novel in Two Parts*. Louis Iribarne, trans., introd., and comm. Urbana: University of Illinois Press, 1977, 447 pp.

————. *The Madman and the Nun and Other Plays*. Daniel C. Gerould and C. S. Durer, trans. Seattle: University of Washington Press, 1968, 303 pp.

————. *Nienasycenie; powieść* (*Insatiability; A Novel*). New ed. Warsaw: Państwowy Instytut Wydawniczy, 1957, two vols.

————. *Pożegnanie jesieni; powieść* (*Farewell to Autumn; A Novel*). Warsaw: F. Hocsick, 1927, 450 pp. Rpt. Lausanne: L'Age d'Homme, 1979, 473 pp.

————. *Tropical Madness: Four Plays*. Daniel and Eleanor Gerould, trans. New York: Winter House, 1972, 259 pp.

————. *Unersättlichkeit, Roman*. Walter Tiel, trans. Munich: R. Piper, 1966, 595 pp.

Gerould, Daniel. *Witkacy. Stanisław Ignacy Witkiewicz as an Imaginative Writer*. Seattle, Wash.: University of Washington Press, 1981, 362 pp.

Grabowski, Zbigniew A. "S. I. Witkiewicz: A Polish Prophet of Doom," *The Polish Review*, XII, 1 (Winter 1967), pp. 39–49.

Miłosz, Czesław. "Stanisław Ignacy Witkiewicz, a Polish Writer for Today," *Tri-Quarterly*, IX (Spring 1967), pp. 143–154.

Wittlin, Józef. *Salt of the Earth*. Pauline De Chary, trans. London: Methuen and Co., 1940, 271 pp.; Harrisburg, Penn.: Stackpole Books, 1970.

Wojtyła, Karol. *Collected Poems*. Jerzy Peterkiewicz, trans. and introd. London: Hutchinson, 1982, 191 pp.

Index